AF182754

The Ohio State Constitution

The Oxford Commentaries on the State Constitutions of the United States
Lawrence Friedman, Series Editor

Lawrence Friedman, Professor of Law at New England Law | Boston, serves as General Editor for this series, which in its entirety will cover the constitutions of each of the 50 states and Puerto Rico. Each volume of The Oxford Commentaries on the State Constitutions of the United States contains a historical overview of the state's constitutional development, plus a section-by-section analysis of the state's current constitution. In addition, each volume contains the text of the state's constitution, a bibliographic essay, a table of cases, and an index. This series provides essential reference tools for academics and students investigating state constitutional development and constitutional law, as well as lawyers and judges seeking a guide to understanding the particular provisions of a state's constitution.

The Ohio State Constitution

Second Edition

Steven H. Steinglass
and Gino J. Scarselli

Foreword by Honorable Maureen O'Connor (Second Edition)

Foreword by Honorable Thomas J. Moyer (First Edition)

THE OXFORD COMMENTARIES ON THE STATE
CONSTITUTIONS OF THE UNITED STATES
Lawrence Friedman, Series Editor

OXFORD
UNIVERSITY PRESS

OXFORD
UNIVERSITY PRESS

Oxford University Press is a department of the University of Oxford. It furthers the University's objective of excellence in research, scholarship, and education by publishing worldwide. Oxford is a registered trade mark of Oxford University Press in the UK and certain other countries.

Published in the United States of America by Oxford University Press
198 Madison Avenue, New York, NY 10016, United States of America.

© Oxford University Press 2022

All rights reserved. No part of this publication may be reproduced, stored in a retrieval system, or transmitted, in any form or by any means, without the prior permission in writing of Oxford University Press, or as expressly permitted by law, by license, or under terms agreed with the appropriate reproduction rights organization. Inquiries concerning reproduction outside the scope of the above should be sent to the Rights Department, Oxford University Press, at the address above.

You must not circulate this work in any other form
and you must impose this same condition on any acquirer.

CIP data is on file at the Library of Congress
ISBN 978–0–19–761972–8

DOI: 10.1093/oso/9780197619728.001.0001

Note to Readers
This publication is designed to provide accurate and authoritative information in regard to the subject matter covered. It is based upon sources believed to be accurate and reliable and is intended to be current as of the time it was written. It is sold with the understanding that the publisher is not engaged in rendering legal, accounting, or other professional services. If legal advice or other expert assistance is required, the services of a competent professional person should be sought. Also, to confirm that the information has not been affected or changed by recent developments, traditional legal research techniques should be used, including checking primary sources where appropriate.

(Based on the Declaration of Principles jointly adopted by a Committee of the American Bar Association and a Committee of Publishers and Associations.)

You may order this or any other Oxford University Press publication by visiting the Oxford University Press website at www.oup.com.

CONTENTS

Series Foreword by Lawrence Friedman *xix*
Foreword by Chief Justice Maureen O'Connor (Second Edition) *xxiii*
Foreword by Chief Justice Thomas J. Moyer (First Edition) *xxv*
Preface (Second Edition) *xxvii*
Preface and Acknowledgments *xxix*

PART ONE ■ The History of the Ohio Constitution

Introduction **3**

The Ohio Territory and the Northwest Ordinance: The Prelude to Statehood 5
Early Ohio 5
The Northwest Ordinance 9
Governance under Arthur St. Clair and the Push for Statehood 12
Statehood and Ohio's First Constitution 15
The Constitutional Convention of 1802 16
The Status of African Americans 18
Approval and Statehood 19
The Ohio Constitution of 1802 20
Ohio's Experience under the Constitution of 1802 24
Judicial Review: A Major Constitutional Crisis 26
Ohio's Second Constitution 30
The Campaign to Replace the Constitution of 1802 30
Campaign on the Constitutional Call 31
The Constitutional Convention of 1850–51 32
Elections, Suffrage, and the Status of African Americans 34
The Liquor Question 37
Other Reforms 38
Approval by the Electorate 38
The Ohio Constitution of 1851 39
The 1873–74 Constitutional Convention 44
From 1874 to the 1912 Constitutional Convention 47
The 1912 Constitutional Convention: Constitutional Revision in the Progressive Era 51
The Progressive Movement and the Call for a Convention 51
The Constitutional Convention of 1912 53
Initiative and Referendum 54

Home Rule 55
The Courts 56
Women's Suffrage 59
Short-Ballot Movement 59
The Campaign 60
Election Day 60
Rejected Amendments 61
The Defeat of Women's Suffrage 61
The Legacy of the 1912 Convention 62
Constitutional Change from 1912 to the End of the Twentieth Century 62
Constitutional Amendments—The Balance of the First Half of the Twentieth Century 62
Prohibition 66
Women's Suffrage 67
Tax-Related and Other Amendments 68
Rejected Amendments 68
Constitutional Amendments—The Second Half of the Twentieth Century 69
The 1950s and 1960s 70
Public Debt 70
Governmental Organization 71
Apportionment 71
Modern Courts Amendment 72
Miscellaneous Proposals 72
The 1970s and the Ohio Constitutional Revision Commission 72
The 1980s 74
The 1990s 75
The Court in the Twentieth Century—From 1912 to the End of the Twentieth Century 76
Change in Direction 78
Tort Reform 79
Education 80
New Judicial Federalism 80
The Ohio Constitution in the Twenty-First Century 82
Continued Piecemeal Constitutional Revision 83
General Assembly—Proposed Amendments 83
Initiated Amendments 84
The Role of the Initiative 85
The Ohio Constitutional Modernization Commission 86
Judicial Selection Redux 89
History of Judicial Selection in Ohio 89
Refocus on Judicial Election Reform 90
Stare Decisis and the Ohio Constitution 93
New Judicial Federalism in the Twenty-First Century 95

PART TWO ■ The Ohio Constitution and Commentary

Preamble **103**

Article I: Bill of Rights **105**

Methodological Issues—Sequencing and Weighing 107
State Constitutional Interpretation 110
Presumption of Constitutionality 112
Section 1. Inalienable rights 113
Section 2. Right to alter, reform, or abolish government; equal protection and benefit; repeal of special privileges 115
Inherent Political Power 115
Equal Protection and Benefit 116
Alter, Reform, or Abolish Government 123
Special Privileges or Immunities 124
Section 3. Right to assemble and petition 125
Section 4. Bearing arms; standing armies; military power 127
Section 5. Trials by jury 128
Criminal Cases 129
Civil Cases 130
Waivers 130
Re-Examination of Jury Findings 131
Jury Unanimity 131
Section 6. Slavery and involuntary servitude 132
Section 7. Rights of conscience; education; the necessity of religion and knowledge 133
Establishment Claims 134
Freedom of Conscience 134
Religious Tests 135
Bible Reading 136
Section 8. Writ of habeas corpus 136
Section 9. Bail and cruel and unusual punishment 137
Right to Bail 138
Excessive Fines and Cruel and Unusual Punishment 139
Death Penalty 139
Juvenile Sentences 141
Evolving National Consensus 142
Punitive Damages 143
Section 10. Trial for crimes; witnesses 143
Right to a Grand Jury Indictment/Notice of Accusation 144
Right to Counsel 145
Right to Appear and Confront Witnesses 146

Right to Compulsory Process 149
Right to a Speedy Public Trial 149
Privilege against Self-Incrimination 151
Double Jeopardy 154
Section 10a. Rights of victims of crime 158
2017 Amendment 159
Section 11. Freedom of speech; of the press; of libels 162
Defamation 163
Section 12. Transportation or forfeiture for crime 164
Section 13. Quartering troops 165
Section 14. Search and seizure 166
Section 15. No imprisonment for debt 169
Section 16. Open courts; right to a remedy; due course of law; sovereign immunity 170
Open Courts 171
Right to a Remedy 172
Due Course of Law 174
Procedural Due Process 177
Reputational Interests 178
Substantive Due Process 179
Juvenile Rights and Due Course of Law 181
Justice Administered without Delay 182
Sovereign Immunity 183
Section 17. No heredity privileges 184
Section 18. Suspension of laws 184
Section 19. Eminent domain 185
Section 19a. Damage for wrongful death 186
Section 19b. Protection of private property rights in ground water, lakes and other watercourses 187
Section 20. Powers reserved to the people 188
Section 21. Preservation of the freedom to choose health care 189

Article II: Legislative **191**

Section 1. Legislative power vested in General Assembly; initiative and referendum reserved to people 192
Separation of Powers 193
Delegation of Legislative Authority to Administrative Agencies 194
Initiative and Referendum 196
Section 1a. Initiative to amend constitution 196
Section 1b. Initiative to enact laws 198
Effective Dates and Conflicting Amendments and Statutes 201
Section 1c. Referendum to challenge laws enacted by General Assembly 201

Section 1d. Emergency and other laws not subject to referendum 204
Section 1e. Limitations of use of constitutional and statutory initiative 206
Limitations on the Statutory Initiative 208
Limitation on the Constitutional Initiative 208
Procedural and Substantive Issues 209
Section 1f. Initiative and referendum in municipalities 211
Administrative Actions 211
Pre-Election Substantive Judicial Review of Ballot Measures 212
Gatekeepers 212
Legislative Action 214
Scope of Review 214
Judicial Review of Board of Elections Decisions 215
One Proposal Limitations 215
Section 1g. Petition requirements; submission; ballot language; by Ohio ballot board; Ohio Supreme Court 216
Signatures 218
Self-Executing Provisions and Facilitating Legislation 220
One Amendment, Separate Vote Requirement 221
Majority Vote Requirement 222
Pre-Election Substantive Judicial Review 223
Supreme Court Review 223
Section 2. Election and terms of legislators 224
Section 3. Residence requirements for state legislators 226
Section 4. Dual office and conflict of interest prohibited 226
Section 5. Who shall not hold office 227
Section 6. Powers of each house 228
Section 7. Organization of the House of Representatives and Senate 229
Section 8. Regular and special session of General Assembly 230
Special Sessions 230
Section 9. House and Senate journals 231
Section 10. Rights of members to protest 231
Section 11. Filling vacancies in House or Senate 232
Section 12. Privilege of members from arrest, and of free speech 233
Section 13. When session to be public 234
Section 14. Power of adjournment 234
Section 15. How bills shall be passed 235
One-Subject Rule 237
Amending a Law and Signatures 239
Section 16. Bills to be signed by governor; veto 240
Line-Item Veto 241
Current Practice 241
Section 17. Repealed—Signing of bills 242
Section 18. Repealed—Style of laws 242

Section 19. Repealed—Exclusion from office 242
Section 20. Term of office, and compensation of officers 242
Section 21. Contested elections 243
Section 22. Appropriations 243
Section 23. Impeachments; how instituted and conducted 244
Section 24. Officers liable to impeachment; consequences 245
Section 25. Repealed—When session shall commence 245
Section 26. General laws to have uniform operation 246
Uniformity Rule 246
Legislative Submission 247
Section 27. Election and appointment of officers; filling vacancies 248
Section 28. Retroactive laws; obligation of contracts 249
Retroactivity Clause 249
Obligation of Contracts 251
Section 29. No extra compensation 252
Section 30. New counties 252
Section 31. Compensation of members and officers of the General Assembly 253
Section 32. Divorces and judicial power 253
Section 33. Mechanics' and contractors' liens 254
Section 34. Welfare of employees 256
Section 34 As a Limitation on Legislative Power 258
Section 34a. Minimum wage 259
Municipal Minimum Wages 261
Section 35. Workers' Compensation 262
Section 36. Conservation of natural resources 265
Section 37. Eight-hour day on public work 266
Section 38. Removal of officials 267
Section 39. Regulating expert testimony in criminal trials 268
Section 40. Registering and warranting land titles 268
Section 41. Prison labor 269
Section 42. Continuity of government operations in emergencies caused by enemy attack 270

Article III: Executive **271**

Section 1. Executive department 272
Section 1a. Joint vote for governor and lieutenant governor 273
Section 1b. Duties of lieutenant governor 273
Section 2. Terms of office 274
Section 3. Election returns 275
Section 4. Repealed— Presentation of Election Returns 276
Section 5. Executive power vested in governor 276

Section 6. Governor may require written information 276
Section 7. Governor's annual message and recommendations 277
Section 8. Governor may convene special session of General Assembly with limited purposes 277
Section 9. When the governor may adjourn the General Assembly 278
Section 10. Commander-in-chief of militia 278
Section 11. Governor may grant reprieves, commutations and pardons 279
Section 12. Seal of the state 280
Section 13. How grants and commissions issued 281
Section 14. Who is ineligible to serve as governor 281
Section 15. Succession in case of vacancy in office of governor 282
Section 16. Repealed—Duties of lieutenant governor 283
Section 17. Who shall act if a vacancy occurs in offices of both governor and lieutenant governor 283
Section 17a. Filling a vacancy in the office of the lieutenant governor 284
Section 18. Governor to fill vacancies in elected state offices 284
Section 19. Compensation of key state officers; change during term prohibited 285
Section 20. Annual reports of executive officers 285
Section 21. Appointments subject to advice and consent of Senate 285
Section 22. Supreme court to determine disability of governor or governor-elect and resolve succession questions 287

Article IV: Judicial **289**

Modern Courts Amendment 290
Jurisdiction and Justiciability 290
Standing 291
Public-Rights Actions 292
Advisory Opinions and Certified Questions 293
Ripeness 294
Mootness 295
Political Question Doctrine 296
State Remedies 296
Section 1. Judicial power vested in courts 297
Judicial Review 297
Statutory Courts 298
Section 2. Supreme Court 298
Original Jurisdiction 301
Modern Courts Amendment 301
Death Penalty Appeals 302
Section 3. Court of appeals 302
Death Penalty Appeals 302
Intracircuit Conflicts 304

Section 4. Common pleas court 305
Justiciable Matters 306
Section 5. Other powers of Supreme Court 307
Superintendence over Ohio Courts 308
Rule-Making 308
Disqualification of Judges 309
Section 6. Election of judges; compensation 309
Sections 7–12. Repealed 311
Section 13. Vacancy in office of judge 312
Section 14. Repealed—Compensation and holding other offices 312
Section 15. Changing number of judges; establishing other courts 312
Section 16. Repealed—Clerk of courts 313
Section 17. Judges removable 313
Section 18. Powers and jurisdiction 313
Section 19. Courts of conciliation 314
Section 20. Style of process, prosecution, and indictment 314
Section 22. Supreme court commission 315
Section 23. Judges in less populous counties; service on more than one court 316

Article V: Elective Franchise **317**

Section 1. Who may vote 317
Northwest Ordinance 318
1802 Constitution 318
1851 Constitution 319
Post-1851 Amendments 320
Non-partisan Judicial Ballot 321
Voter Registration and Purges 321
The 1977 Voter Registration Controversy 322
Section 2. By ballot 323
Voting Machines 324
Secret Ballot 324
Section 2a. Names of candidates on ballot 324
Section 3. Repealed—Privilege from arrest 326
Section 4. Exclusion from franchise 326
Section 5. Repealed—Residence of members of military 326
Section 6. Voting by idiots or insane persons 327
Section 7. Primary elections 327
Section 8. Term Limits for U.S. Senators and Representatives 328
Section 9. Eligibility of term-limited officeholders 329

Article VI: Education 331

Section 1. Funds for religious and educational purposes 332
Ministerial Lands 333
Section 2. School funds 334
A "Thorough and Efficient System of Common Schools" 335
DeRolph Litigation 336
Ohio Constitutional Modernization Commission 339
Support for Religious Schools 339
School Segregation 340
Section 3. Public school system, boards of education 341
State Control of the Public Schools 342
Local Boards of Education 344
Rural School Districts 346
Section 4. State board of education 346
1851 Constitutional Convention 346
1912 Constitutional Convention 347
Post-1912 History 347
Legislative Developments 348
Section 5. Loans for higher education 348
Section 6. Tuition credit program 349

Article VII: Public Institutions 353

Section 1. Insane, blind, and deaf and dumb 353
Section 2. Directors of penitentiary, trustees of benevolent and other state institutions; how appointed 355
Section 3. Vacancies, how filled 356

Article VIII: Public Debt and Public Works 357

Constitutional Changes in Ohio 358
Ban on Internal Improvements 360
Initiative Petitions and State Debt 360
Ohio Constitutional Revision Commission 361
Ohio Constitutional Modernization Commission 361
Section 1. Public debt; limitations 362
Revenue Bonds 363
Avoiding the Debt Limitation 364
Section 2. State may incur debt for defense or to retire outstanding debts 364
Section 2a. Repealed—World War I compensation 365
Section 2b. World War II compensation 366
Section 2c. Construction of state highway system 370
Section 2d. Korean Conflict compensation 371

Section 2e. Funds for public building construction 374
Section 2f. Bonds for public school classrooms, universities, recreation and conservation and state buildings 376
Section 2g. Bonds and other obligations for highway construction 379
Section 2h. Bonds for buildings for the state and for state-supported institutions of higher education, and for recreation and natural resources conservation 380
Section 2i. Capital improvement bonds 381
Section 2j. Vietnam Conflict compensation 385
Section 2k. Bonds for local government public infrastructure capital improvements 389
Section 2l. Bonds for capital improvements for state and local parks, for land and water recreation facilities, and for preservation of natural resources 391
Section 2m. Bonds for public infrastructure capital improvement 394
Section 2n. Bonds for facilities for common schools and state-supported and state-assisted institutions of higher education 397
Section 2o. Bonds for environmental conservation and revitalization 399
Section 2p. Bonds for capital improvements to public infrastructure and for research and development 402
Section 2q. Bonds for environmental revitalization and conservation 408
Section 2r. Persian Gulf, Afghanistan, and Iraq Conflict compensation 411
Section 2s. Issuance of bonds for public infrastructure capital improvements 417
Section 3. The state to create no other debt 420
Section 4. Credit of state; the state shall not become joint owner or stockholder 420
JobsOhio 422
Section 5. No assumption of debt by the state 422
Section 6. Counties, cities, towns, or townships, not authorized to become stockholders; regulation of insurance 423
Section 7. Sinking fund 424
Section 8. The commissioners of the sinking fund 424
Section 9. Biennial report of sinking fund commissioners 425
Section 10. Application of sinking fund 425
Section 11. Semiannual report of sinking fund commissioners 426
Section 12. Repealed—Superintendent of public works 426
Section 13. Economic development 426
The 1974 Amendment 428
Court Decisions 428
Section 14. Bonds for housing programs 429

Section 15. Bonds for development of coal technology 430
Section 16. Bonds and other assistance for housing programs 431
Section 17. Limitations on obligations state may issue 432

Article IX: Militia **435**

Section 1. Who shall perform military duty 435
Section 2. Repealed—Election of certain officers 436
Section 3. Officers to be appointed by the governor 436
Section 4. Power of governor to call forth militia 437
Section 5. Public Arms 437

Article X: County and Township Organizations **439**

Section 1. Organization and government of counties; county home rule; submission 440
Section 2. Township officers; election; power 441
Section 3. County charters; approval by voters 441
Section 4. County charter commission; duties; election 444
Section 5. Repealed 446
Section 6. Repealed 446
Section 7. Repealed 446

Article XI: Apportionment **447**

Background 448
Section 1. Ohio redistricting commission 451
Prior Provisions for Apportioning Seats 454
Section 2. Number of representatives per district 455
Section 3. Ratio of representation; requirements for general assembly house districts; splitting of counties, municipal corporations, and townships 455
Prior Population Ranges 459
Section 4. Composition and numbering of senate districts 460
Population in Senate Districts 461
Section 5. Change in boundaries of senate districts 462
Section 6. Nonpartisan, proportional, and compact assembly districts 462
Section 7. Creation of district boundaries based on decennial census 464
Section 8. Proceedings when Ohio redistricting commission fails to timely adopt final general assembly district plan 464
Section 9. Supreme court jurisdiction; proceedings upon determination of invalidity by court order 466

Section 10. Severability 469
Sections 11–15. Repealed 469

Article XII: Finance and Taxation 471

Section 1. Poll tax 471
Section 2. Limitation on tax rate; exemption 473
One Percent Limitation 474
Real Property Classifications and Exemptions 474
Tax Exemptions 476
Section 2a. Authority to classify real estate for taxation, two classes; procedures 476
Section 3. Imposition of taxes 477
Section 4. Revenue 479
Section 5. Levying of taxes 479
Section 5a. Use of motor vehicle license and fuel taxes restricted 480
Section 6. Debt for internal improvement 481
Section 7. Repealed—Inheritance tax 482
Section 8. Repealed—Income tax 482
Section 9. Apportionment of income, estate, and inheritance taxes 482
Section 10. Repealed—Excise and franchise taxes 483
Section 11. Sinking fund 483
Section 12. Repealed—Excise tax on sales or purchase of food prohibited 484
Section 13. Wholesale taxes on foods 484

Article XIII: Corporations 487

Section 1. Special acts conferring corporate powers prohibited 487
Section 2. Corporations, how formed 488
Section 3. Dues from corporations; how secured; inspection of private banks 490
Section 4. Corporate property subject to taxation 491
Section 5. Rights of way; full compensation; jury trial 491
Section 6. Organization of cities; limitations of power 492
Section 7. Association with banking powers 493

Article XIV: Ohio Livestock Care Standards Board 495

Jurisprudence 495
Ohio Livestock Care Standards Board 496

Article XV: Miscellaneous 499

Section 1. Seat of Government 499
Section 2. Repealed—Public printing 500

Section 3. Receipts and expenditures 500
Section 4. Officers to be qualified electors 500
Section 5. Repealed—Duelists ineligible for office 501
Section 6. Lotteries, charitable bingo, casino gaming 501
The 1850–51 Constitutional Convention 507
The Interregnum 508
The Ohio Lottery 509
Charitable Bingo 509
Casino Gaming 510
2009 Casino Gaming Amendment 511
Challenges to Video Lottery Terminals and Casino Gaming 512
What Exactly Is a Lottery? 512
Sports Gambling 512
Has the Ohio Constitution Already Approved Sports Gambling? 513
Section 7. Oath of officers 514
Section 8. Repealed—Bureau of statistics 514
Section 9. Repealed—Intoxicating Liquor 514
Section 9a. Repealed—Intoxicating Liquor 515
Section 10. Civil service 515
Section 11. Marriage 515

Article XVI: Amendments **517**

Section 1. How constitution to be amended; Supreme Court jurisdiction 518
Ballot Board 519
Ohio Supreme Court Jurisdiction 520
Pre-Election Substantive Judicial Review 521
One Amendment, Separate Vote Requirement 521
Effective Date of Amendments 522
Section 2. Convention 523
How Would a Convention Work? 524
Section 3. Question of constitutional convention to be submitted periodically 525

Article XVII: Elections **527**

Section 1. Time for holding 527
Section 2. Terms of officers, vacancies 528
Section 3. Repealed—Present incumbents 529

Article XVIII: Municipal Corporations **531**

Section 1. Classification of cities and villages 533
Section 2. General and additional laws 533

Section 3. Municipal powers of local self-government 534
The Conflict Approach 535
Statewide Concern Doctrine 537
Conflict and Implied Preemption 538
1912 Debates and Preemption 539
Other Limitations on Municipalities 541
Employee Rights 541
New Causes of Action 542
Section 4. Acquisition of public utility; contract for service; condemnation 542
Section 5. Referendum on acquiring or operating municipal utility 544
Section 6. Sale of surplus product of municipal utility 544
Section 7. Home rule; municipal charter 545
Section 8. Submission and adoption of proposed charter; referendum 546
Section 9. Amendment of charter; referendum 547
Section 10. Appropriation in excess of public use 548
Section 11. Assessments for cost of appropriating property 549
Section 12. Bonds for public utilities 550
Section 13. Taxation, debts, reports and accounts 550
Section 14. Municipal elections 551

Article XIX: Congressional Redistricting **553**

Section 1. Adoption of congressional district plan 555
Section 2. Requirements for a congressional district plan 561
Section 3. Jurisdiction; legal challenges; procedures upon invalidation of congressional district plan 565

Schedules to the Ohio Constitution 567
Appendix A: Table of Votes on Holding Constitutional Conventions under the 1802 and 1851 Constitutions 579
Appendix B: Table of Proposed Constitutional Amendments and Votes 581
Bibliographical Essay and Selected Bibliography 601
About the Authors 625
Table of Cases 627
Index 647

■ SERIES FOREWORD

It is difficult today to escape the focus in American political discourse on the U.S. Constitution and the Supreme Court's interpretations of it. But it is worth remembering that the U.S. Constitution did not emerge fully formed from the head of James Madison in 1787. Before the United States, there were the states—and state constitutions. As noted by G. Alan Tarr, the first Series Editor of the *Oxford Commentaries on the State Constitutions of the United States,* in his Series Foreword, the original state constitutions reflected a variety of approaches to democratic self-rule, experiments in governance that inspired audiences both across the Atlantic and closer to home.

Indeed, despite the misgivings about the state of the states entertained by some of the delegates gathered at the constitutional convention, they found in the existing state constitutions much to admire, from the Virginia Constitution's Declaration of Rights to the bicameral legislative scheme embraced by John Adams' Massachusetts Constitution of 1780. Which is not to slight the audacity of the U.S. Constitution, with its grant of limited powers of national scope to the federal government and preservation of state rule in virtually all other aspects of the lives of citizens. The framers, as Supreme Court Justice Anthony Kennedy observed in *U.S. Term Limits v. Thornton* (1995), had in effect "split the atom of sovereignty."

And the U.S. Constitution, as interpreted by Chief Justice John Marshall's Supreme Court, provided the young republic the national governmental structure it needed to thrive. The outcome of the Civil War validated the preeminence of the federal government in our constitutional scheme and the subsequent ratification of the Fourteenth Amendment anticipated the U.S. Constitution's eclipse of its state counterparts. For the Fourteenth Amendment's commitments to due process and equal protection in the face of state action became, in the middle decades of the twentieth century, the vessels by which the judiciary federalized the protection of individual rights and liberties as against the states.

The Supreme Court's extension of the Fourteenth Amendment's reach followed a period of change in the nature of state constitutions themselves, as popular movements succeeded in revising state charters to allow for varying opportunities for direct democratic law-making. One result was an increase in state constitutional provisions that resembled more closely legislative enactments than the core, foundational principles typically associated with constitutions. And so, as the decades passed, the utility of state constitutions as constitutions increasingly suffered by comparison to the U.S. Constitution—if not in terms of authority, for these documents still controlled the organization of state governments and served as the primary means by which those governments regulated their citizens, at least in terms of respect.

Just as changes to the federal judiciary's approach to the Fourteenth Amendment ushered in a new era of restrictions on the police power of states, with *Brown v. Board of Education* (1954), perhaps the most famous example, lawyerly and judicial interest in state constitutions was awakened when, in the 1970s, the U.S. Supreme Court signaled the beginning of its retreat from federal rights enforcement, a development playing out to this day. From this retreat was born the phenomenon called the "new judicial federalism," as individual rights advocates began to look to the protections contained in state constitutions as the basis for challenging state action. In state constitutions, moreover, lay what Alan Tarr referred to as "an unsuspected richness"—not just provisions that parallel those in the Bill of Rights, but constitutional guarantees regarding such matters as privacy and equality that have no federal counterpart. And rather than the exclusively negative orientation of federal constitutional protections, which forbid state action exceeding certain limits, state constitutions contain positive protections which appear to demand such action in respect to a range of interests, from the adequacy of educational standards to environmental protection.

And so, notwithstanding the predominance of the U.S. Constitution in American public discourse, state constitutions continue to play a vital and important role in the daily lives of citizens. The federal judicial retreat from rights-enforcement through the Fourteenth Amendment has led not just to the revitalization of state constitutional individual rights protections, but to fewer federal constitutional restraints on the ability of state governments to be the laboratories of American democracy to which Supreme Court Justice Louis Brandeis famously referred in *New State Ice Co. v. Liebmann* (1932). And the content of state constitutions continues to be a source of energetic debate among citizens, whether through efforts to codify in the state's charter a symbolic resistance to federal encroachment or to constitutionalize, through the initiative process, policy positions that legislatures would otherwise reject.

Operating in the shadow cast by the U.S. Constitution, state constitutions and the state court decisions interpreting them remain critical sources of governmental authority and restraint. It has been the goal of the *Oxford Commentaries on the State Constitutions of the United States* to illuminate these constitutions for a wide audience—to explain the unique history of each state constitution and explore, in an accessible way, what the various provisions of the American state constitutions in their great variety mean and how they have been interpreted and applied over time. Each book in the series—many now in their second or third editions—provides, in addition to a history of and commentaries on the provisions of each state's constitution, a bibliography of materials related to the constitution as well as a table of notable cases and a topical index. The series aims, in short, to present to lawyers, scholars, and students the most relevant and comprehensive guides to all the other U.S. Constitutions.

Lawrence Friedman
Series Editor

FOREWORD TO SECOND EDITION

It is my honor to write the foreword to this second edition of *The Ohio State Constitution,* not only because Steven Steinglass and Gino Scarselli have done yeoman's work in giving a comprehensive view of our constitution, but also because they have examined its strengths and weaknesses, historically and as it currently exists.

As the foundation upon which all laws of this state rest, the constitution is, and should remain, the subject of ongoing examination and improvement.

The first edition of this work was published in 2004 as an outgrowth of many decades of the authors' teaching, scholarly writing, and legal practice. The book not only sets forth the governing relationship of the executive, legislative, and judicial branches, thereby being an important resource for understanding how our state government operates, it is also a valuable addition to the narrative of the role of the courts through the growth of Ohio. Now more than fifteen years later, in this second edition, the authors have updated the book in significant ways giving it the same attention to detail and insight that made the first edition such a valuable resource. There are appropriate and important discussions of the new judicial federalism and the role of state constitutions in the courts that are enhanced by reference to the scholarly offerings of Chief Judge Jeffrey S. Sutton of the U.S. Court of Appeals for the Sixth Circuit and Justice Goodwin Liu of the California Supreme Court.

The book authoritatively details the evolution of the constitutions of Ohio. The inclusion of original material from the constitutional conventions and other original sources details the issues, proposals, and compromises at play and lays out the values, prejudices, interests, and motives of those responsible for the final products.

At this time, the summer of 2020, when the re-examination of social justice and America's troubled legacy relating to race, gender, and national origin is front and center in the nation's dialogue, the authors trace Ohio's response to those issues from pre-1803 forward. Ohio's governing instruments as well as the original source material demonstrate that our state failed to chart a path that would distinguish it as a leader in equality and equal justice.

The book is a good guide for anyone interested in understanding how our constitution has evolved since its drafting and how it continues to evolve. It can help lawmakers, legal scholars and practitioners, elected officials, and all who serve or are interested in serving in our government to develop a shared understanding of our state constitution's origins and of the protections and guarantees that permeate every aspect of our lives.

Maureen O'Connor, Chief Justice
The Supreme Court of Ohio

■ FOREWORD TO FIRST EDITION

The setting for this work begins some 200 years ago, when Ohio was the resting place for sunsets. This was the western horizon of a new nation still discovering the richness of its resources and the limits of its experiment in self-determination.

This was a time of hope and dreams, as the first European settlers moved westward across the Ohio River, bringing with them a strong faith that a civilized society works best if its authority is vested in popular sovereignty. The belief that citizens could change government and regulate their own progress motivated their western expansion.

As John Adams said, "among all the rights given man, the most important is the right to self governance."

All successive generations are thankful that our forefathers rejected Thomas Jefferson's admonition that the exercise of popular sovereignty might require the bloodshed of patriots and tyrants. Only once has America shed blood to bring about change in government.

Change occurs at a regular pace, but in a far less dramatic way than Jefferson suggested. The overturning of the ordinary happens hundreds of times each year in the passing of laws and ordinances. It occurs through a legislator's proposal and a governor's budget request. Change is evident in a citizen referendum and a constitutional amendment.

This book provides witness that popular sovereignty can rebalance the balance of power, provide citizens direct access to the legislative process, and be the civic embodiment of our morals and beliefs. The context of our laws provided by the authors breathes life into laws that may seem dispassionate.

The authors provide the narrative that the law is where a society organizes its shared experiences and forms its common values. The constitutions, statutes, and court dockets serve as a civic diary for our struggles over such issues as education, civil rights, and economic expansion. These issues are an important part of any social narrative.

This book will provide an understanding of our constitutional history. It is a comprehensive, convenient, and accessible resource. Any reader interested in the history of Ohio law, and the history of its development, will be grateful to the authors who have charted our history and offered a compass for our future.

Chief Justice Thomas J. Moyer

■ PREFACE TO SECOND EDITION

The second edition of this book reflects the substantial developments concerning the Ohio Constitution since the publication of the first edition in 2004. During this period, Ohio voters approved sixteen amendments to address such important and often controversial issues as casino gaming, same-sex marriage, healthcare, the minimum wage, the initiative and referendum, victims' rights, and reapportionment and redistricting.

During this period, the Ohio Supreme Court continued to play its role as the ultimate arbiter of the meaning of the Ohio Constitution, and the second edition covers more than a hundred new decisions by the court. This includes important cases involving the initiative and the referendum, home rule, and the use of the Ohio Constitution as a source of protection for individual rights. The court also frequently addressed separation of powers issues, including the single subject limitation on the work of the General Assembly and the use of the standing doctrine to avoid reaching the merits of state constitutional issues.

In addition, during this period the state attempted to replicate its successful experience of the 1970s with commission-based constitutional revision, and one of the authors (Dean Steinglass) served as Senior Policy Advisor to the Ohio Constitutional Modernization Commission (OCMC). The research and analysis that Dean Steinglass undertook for the commission and the commission's deliberations have provided us with new insights into the meaning and role of the Ohio Constitution, and this edition reflects these insights.

The second edition of this book does not simply chronicle new developments. Rather, it expands many earlier treatments of the Ohio Constitution and provides additional background to further explain its evolution. This includes paying more attention to the early uses of judicial review and to the origins and development of the new judicial federalism, expanding consideration of interpretative issues that arise when courts address rights-conferring state constitutional provisions, and providing greater coverage of issues barely covered in the first edition such as those involving gambling and the state and local initiative.

Finally, special thanks are extended to those colleagues who took the time to review many portions of this manuscript and suggest ways for it to be improved. Their help was invaluable, and we are sure that they helped us improve this edition and avoid many errors. Dean Steinglass also wants to thank the many students from his courses on the Ohio Constitution, whose insights helped educate him; his research assistants for the second edition, Elizabeth Carter and Christine Mika; the superb staff of the Cleveland-Marshall College of Law

Library; and the members of the OCMC, whose quest for information sent him on many new research paths. And we are deeply grateful for the support of our families during the preparation of this second edition, especially Dianne Steinglass and Angela Finn.

Steven H. Steinglass
Gino J. Scarselli

■ PREFACE AND ACKNOWLEDGMENTS

In 2003, Ohio celebrated its bicentennial, but most Ohioans are still unaware of the text or history of the state's constitution. This book seeks to fill this gap by providing a section-by-section commentary on the Ohio Constitution and by reviewing the constitutional history of the state. We hope that this book will serve not only as a guide to the text and the interpretation of the current Ohio Constitution, the state's second, but that it will also contribute to a greater interest in the state's constitutional history.

We have many people to thank over the course of this project, beginning with the students in Dean (then Professor) Steinglass' seminar on State Constitutional Law. Throughout this project we have benefited from the excellent law library at Cleveland State University's Cleveland-Marshall College of Law, and we extend special thanks to Law Library Director Michael J. Slinger and the law library staff, especially Leslie Pardo, Jessica Mathewson, Tom Hurray, and Marie Rehmar. We are also indebted to the law students who over the years have assisted in the research and review of this book. Special thanks go to Anthony Baucco, who spent a summer reviewing and helping to revise the commentary to each section of the constitution; to Tom Fourmas, who played an important role in the beginning of this project; and to many other law students who provided assistance over the years, including David Baloga, Jamie Callender, Scott Dean, and Kate Ryan. This book and the series of which it is a part would not have been written without the support and patience of Oxford University Press and the series editor, Lawrence Friedman. Finally, we are deeply grateful for the support of our friends and families, especially Dianne and Amanda Steinglass, Art and Gus Caliguire, and Mia Jackson.

PART ONE

The History of the Ohio Constitution

■ INTRODUCTION

In more than two centuries of statehood, Ohio, the seventeenth state admitted to the union and the first state carved out of the Northwest Territory, has had only two constitutions. The current constitution, the Ohio Constitution of 1851, which replaced the 1802 Constitution, is the sixth oldest in the country and the second oldest outside New England.[1] The state's constitutional history has its roots in the 1787 decision of the Confederation Congress,[2] acting under the Articles of Confederation, to enact the Ordinance of 1787, better known as the Northwest Ordinance,[3] which organized the western lands and set in motion

[1] The 1850–51 Ohio Constitutional Convention convened on May 6, 1850, and adjourned on March 10, 1851. The voters approved the constitution on June 17, 1851, and it became effective on September 1, 1851. The only state constitution outside New England that is older than the Ohio Constitution of 1851 is the Wisconsin Constitution of 1846. The Indiana Constitution of 1851 was adopted the same year as the Ohio Constitution, but it did not become effective until November 1, 1851, two months after the Ohio Constitution became effective. *See* William F. Swindler, ed., *Sources and Documents of United States Constitutions,* 7 vols. (New York: Oceana Publications Inc., 1978).

[2] The Confederation Congress (formally the United States in Congress Assembled) was the governing body of the United States from March 1, 1781, to March 4, 1789, when the U.S. Constitution became effective. The First and Second Continental Congresses preceded the Confederation Congress.

[3] Ordinance of 1787, *reprinted in* 1 U.S.C.A. at LVII–LIX (2012) (hereinafter Northwest Ordinance). In 1789, the first U.S. Congress re-enacted the Northwest Ordinance in virtually the same form. *See* Act of Aug. 7, 1789, ch. 8, 1 Stat. 50.

The Ohio State Constitution. Steven H. Steinglass and Gino J. Scarselli, Oxford University Press. © Oxford University Press 2022. DOI: 10.1093/oso/9780197619728.003.0001

a process that resulted in the creation of Ohio and four other new states from the Northwest Territory.

Despite having had only two constitutions, Ohio has had four constitutional conventions. The first, the Constitutional Convention of 1802, produced Ohio's first constitution and guided the territory into statehood with a government dominated by the legislative branch and a constitution resistant to amendment. The second, the Constitutional Convention of 1850–51, altered the balance of power among the branches of government by limiting legislative power and created a constitution that was easier to amend. The third convention, which took place in 1873–74, proposed a constitution that would have significantly restructured state government and given the governor the power to veto legislation, but the voters rejected it. The fourth, and last convention, the Constitutional Convention of 1912, avoided the fate of the proposed 1874 constitution and produced major constitutional change by presenting the electorate with forty-two independent amendments, thirty-four of which the voters adopted.

Ohio's constitutional history has always been closely tied to the economic, social, and political changes taking place nationally and within the state, and the three successful constitutional conventions followed popular democratic movements. The first convention produced a constitution that was not only the culmination of the movement for statehood but also the result of the successful effort, both nationally and in the Ohio Territory, by Thomas Jefferson and the Republicans to wrest political power from the Federalists. The 1802 Constitution represented a rejection of the Federalist belief in a strong centralized government and established a Jeffersonian model of government in which the legislature was the dominant branch of state government.[4]

Increasing dissatisfaction with state governments created a revisionist fervor that swept the country in the mid-1800s. Spurred in large part by the ideals of Jacksonian democracy, which emphasized popular control over government and a distrust of corporations and financial institutions, fourteen states, including Ohio, held constitutional conventions between 1842 and 1853, resulting in the approval of new constitutions in eleven states.[5] The particular grievances leading to the Ohio Constitutional Convention of 1850–51 included the legislature's financial irresponsibility in the construction of the state transportation system, its control over the judiciary and other state officers, and problems in the administration of the judicial system.

The Constitutional Convention of 1912 grew out of the Progressive movement that dominated American politics in the late nineteenth and early twentieth centuries. This last convention set the stage for the ad hoc or piecemeal

---

[4] Randolph C. Downes, "Ohio's First Constitution," 25 *Northwest Ohio Quarterly* 12 (1953) (hereinafter Downes, "Ohio's First Constitution").

[5] Howard McDonald, "A Study in Constitution Making–Ohio: 1802–1874" (Ph.D. dissertation, University of Michigan, 1916), 59 (hereinafter McDonald, "A Study in Constitution Making").

approach to constitutional revision that has characterized constitutional change in Ohio ever since.

Ohio currently operates under the 1851 Ohio Constitution, which the voters have amended 170 times. After the adoption of the constitution in 1851, the number of articles has grown from sixteen to nineteen, and the number of sections has increased from 169 to more than 225. The Ohio Constitution, which jumped to 59,858 words when the revised Article XI and the new Article XIX became effective on January 1, 2021, is almost eight times longer than the U.S. Constitution, and it is the nation's ninth longest state constitution.[6]

■ THE OHIO TERRITORY AND THE NORTHWEST ORDINANCE: THE PRELUDE TO STATEHOOD

Early Ohio

The State of Ohio has its origin in the experiences of the people who settled in the area west of Pennsylvania and north of the Ohio River in what was sometimes known as the "Ohio Territory" or "Ohio Country." Their experiences were shaped in a land that for much of its early history was in a state of nearly constant conflict as a result of competing claims from Indian tribes and from Great Britain and France, Europe's two most powerful nations.

The first inhabitants of what would become Ohio were Native Americans, but little is known of the Ohio tribes before 1600. The Erie inhabited the southern shore of Lake Erie in the early 1600s, but the Iroquois decimated them in the 1650s in the Beaver Wars.[7] The Iroquois had little interest in the Ohio lands other than as a hunting ground for beaver and did not establish any major settlements. Ohio thus remained largely uninhabited from the late 1650s until the early 1700s when the Miami emigrated southward and settled in the western part of Ohio. Around the same time, the Shawnee, Wyandot, and later the Delaware moved into the region from the east and north to escape the Iroquois and the western migration of white settlers.[8]

The French were the first Europeans to set foot in what would become Ohio. France based its claim on the purported discovery of Ohio by La Salle in

---

[6] *See* "General Information on State Constitutions," in *Book of the States* (The Council of State Governments, 2021), Table 1.3. *See also* Robert Hern, "A Statistical Approach to Ohio's Constitutional History . . . And a Calculation of Its Future," in *Book of the States* (The Council of State Governments, 2012) (hereinafter Hern, "A Statistical Approach to Ohio's Constitutional History").

[7] William A. Hunter, "History of the Ohio Valley," in William C. Sturtevant, ed., *Handbook of North American Indians*, vol. 15 Northeast (Washington: Smithsonian Institution, 1978), 588; R. Douglas Hurt, *The Ohio Frontier, Crucible of the Old Northwest, 1720–1830* (Bloomington: Indiana University Press, 1996), 7–9 (hereinafter Hurt, *The Ohio Frontier*).

[8] *See* Eugene H. Roseboom and Francis P. Weisenburger, *A History of Ohio* (Columbus: Ohio Historical Society, 1991), 13–16.

1669–70,[9] but by the mid-1700s, French, British, and colonial traders could be found throughout Ohio. In an attempt to re-establish alliances with tribes sympathetic to the British, the French-Canadian Céloron de Blainville in 1749 led an expedition from the Great Lakes to the Ohio River and reclaimed the Ohio Country in the name of Louis XV, King of France.[10]

By mid-century, Great Britain realized the growing importance of the area, and the colony of Virginia in 1748 established the original Ohio Company to secure lands along the Ohio River for settlement.[11] Recognizing the growing threat from the British, the French armed friendly tribes and with their help drove out the tribes aligned with the British. With the defeat of "La Demoiselle," the chief of a rebel group of Miami who had negotiated a treaty with the British, the French effectively gained control of the Ohio River valley.[12]

The escalating rivalry over the Ohio Territory finally led to the outbreak of the French and Indian Wars in 1754. After almost a decade of fighting, France surrendered most of its North American territories to Britain in the 1763 Treaty of Paris. In the same year, the British issued a proclamation limiting white colonial settlement west of the Allegheny Mountains to protect their interest in the fur trade and to avoid provoking another war with the Indians.[13] The 1763 Royal Proclamation was largely unenforceable, but it nonetheless outraged the colonists, especially land speculators and veterans of the French and Indian Wars to whom the British had promised land as bounty for fighting the French. The resulting resentment toward Britain's administration and control of the western territories was among the grievances against the British identified in the Declaration of Independence.

The defeat of the British in the Revolutionary War gave the United States clear title to what became Ohio, but the area was still subject to the land claims of Indian tribes and of certain states. During the Revolutionary War, the Confederation Congress had tried to persuade the colonies that claimed western lands through "sea-to-sea" clauses in their original charters (Connecticut, Massachusetts, and Virginia) or through their relationship with the Iroquois Confederacy (New York) to cede their lands to the United States.[14] The Confederation Congress viewed the western lands as a source of income for the

---

[9] Ibid., 18–19.

[10] James K. Richard, "Icon of Empire," *Timeline* (Columbus: Ohio Historical Society, April–May 1988), 18.

[11] Beverley W. Bond Jr., *The Foundations of Ohio*, in Carl Wittke, ed., *The History of the State of Ohio*, vol. 1 (Columbus: Ohio State Archaeological and Historical Society, 1941), 104 (hereinafter Bond, *Foundations of Ohio*).

[12] Hurt, *The Ohio Frontier*, 34–39.

[13] Bond, *Foundations of Ohio*, 174–75.

[14] Jack N. Rakove, "Ambiguous Achievement: The Northwest Ordinance," in Frederick D. Williams, ed., *The Northwest Ordinance: Essays on Its Formulation, Provisions, and Legacy* (East Lansing: Michigan State University Press, 1988), 8–9.

new government and as a means of paying the debt incurred during the war, but the states did not begin to surrender their claims until they faced bankruptcy in late 1779.[15] Eventually, all the states relinquished their claims, but Virginia and Connecticut, both of which had claims to the western territories north of the Ohio River, did so with reservations.

In January 1781, Virginia offered to cede its western lands under the condition that it be permitted to reserve a tract of land to compensate Revolutionary War veterans. The Confederation Congress eventually accepted this offer in 1784, and Virginia reserved four million acres, known as the Virginia Military District, between the Little Miami and Scioto Rivers.[16] Following Virginia, Connecticut ceded its western claims to the national government but, unlike Virginia, retained jurisdiction over its reserved lands. Indeed, Connecticut retained jurisdiction over its 3.8 million acres on the southern shore of Lake Erie until 1800, when it surrendered jurisdiction to the United States.[17] Settled mostly by New Englanders with strong Congregationalist roots, these lands, known as the Western Reserve, would develop an identity distinct from the rest of the state.[18]

With the elimination of most of Virginia's claims, the Confederation Congress began planning for the settlement of the northwest. The Land Ordinance of 1785 authorized the survey and sale of land in southeastern Ohio. Two years later, Congress enacted the Northwest Ordinance, which established a territorial government and a process for the admission of Ohio and eventually four other states into the union.

Instrumental in these developments was the Ohio Company of Associates, popularly known as the Ohio Company. Organized in 1786, this new Ohio Company was supported largely by New England veterans who had certificates for land from Congress for their services during the Revolutionary War. The moving force behind these developments was Manasseh Cutler, a New England Congregationalist minister, who was one of the founders of the Ohio Company, the leading advocate for the adoption of the Northwest Ordinance, and an organizer of the initial settlement of Ohio.[19]

In 1788, a small group of New Englanders established the first permanent, legal settlement in Ohio at Marietta on the Ohio River.[20] White settlement had actually begun in the Ohio Territory in the early eighteenth century when

---

[15] Ibid., 10.

[16] Bond, *Foundations of Ohio*, 252–53.

[17] Ibid., 252–53, 454–55; John D. Barnhart, *Valley of Democracy: The Frontier versus the Plantation in the Ohio Valley, 1775–1818* (Bloomington: Indiana University Press, 1953), 122–23 (hereinafter Barnhart, *Valley of Democracy*).

[18] *See generally* Bond, *Foundations of Ohio*, 371.

[19] *See generally* David McCullough, *The Pioneers: The Heroic Story of the Settlers Who Brought the American Ideal West* (New York: Simon & Schuster, 2019) (hereinafter McCullough, *The Pioneers*).

[20] Bond, *Foundations of Ohio*, 281–83.

many Scotch-Irish immigrants, who had first settled in New England, fled to the Quaker colony of Pennsylvania to seek religious freedom from Puritan persecution. The Scotch-Irish migration increased steadily and settlements began to appear in the western parts of Pennsylvania and Virginia. By the 1780s many western frontiersmen of Scotch-Irish ancestry had moved illegally into what is now Ohio.[21]

The Scotch-Irish from Pennsylvania and Virginia came with strong beliefs in individual freedom and economic independence and were extremely influential in Ohio's early development.[22] The Virginians, who settled mostly in southern Ohio, were chiefly responsible for the push for statehood and for Ohio's first constitution. The presence of Scotch-Irish squatters, however, created an obstacle for the orderly sale of Ohio lands. In 1785, the Confederation Congress ordered the army under the direction of Lt. Col. Josiah Harman to remove the squatters in preparation for legitimate settlement. Harman's expedition failed miserably, and the squatters remained until another war with the Indians forced them out.[23]

As the migration of white settlers increased, relations with the Indian nations worsened. During the revolution, most Ohio tribes had allied themselves with the British in the hope that this alliance would prevent colonial expansion in the Ohio Territory.[24]

After the war, Indian resentment toward the Americans, and to some extent the British, continued. The Ohio Indians believed that the British in the Treaty of Paris, which ended the Revolutionary War in 1783, had abandoned their pledge to respect Indian lands north of the Ohio River. And the provisions of the 1768 Treaty of Fort Stanwix between the British and the Iroquois, which had fixed the Ohio River as the boundary between the Colony of Virginia and Indian lands,[25] were ignored by the Continental Congress, which sought to pave the way for white settlement in what would become Ohio.[26]

Finally, in 1784 and 1785, the United States negotiated its own series of treaties in which a number of tribes surrendered their lands north of the Ohio River. This included a second Treaty of Fort Stanwix in 1784 with the Six Nations,[27] and the Treaty of Fort McIntosh in 1785 with the "the Sachems and

---

[21] Robert E. Chaddock, *Ohio before* 1850: *A Study of the Early Influence of Pennsylvania and Southern Populations in Ohio* (New York: Longmans, Green, 1908), 31–34 (hereinafter Chaddock, *Ohio before* 1850).

[22] Ibid., 33.

[23] *See* Hurt, *The Ohio Frontier*, 146–48.

[24] Ibid., 76.

[25] For a discussion of the 1768 Treaty, *see* Peter Marshall, "Sir William Johnson and the Treaty of Fort Stanwix, 1768," 1 *Journal of American Studies* 149 (1967).

[26] *See generally* Reginald Horsman, "American Indian Policy in the Old Northwest, 1783–1812," 18 *The William and Mary Quarterly* 35 (1961).

[27] The Six Nations, which was known as the Iroquois Confederation, was made up of the following tribes: Mohawk, Oneida, Onondaga, Cayuga, Seneca, and Tuscarora.

Warriors of the Wiandot, Delaware, Chippawa and Ottawa Nations" in which the tribes acknowledged being "under the protection of the United States and of no other sovereign whatsoever."[28]

Despite the treaties, relations with the Indians soured when the two most powerful tribes, the Miami and the Shawnee, refused to surrender their lands.[29] By 1791, the U.S. government and the Ohio Indians were on the brink of war. In the spring of that year, Congress appropriated money for the establishment of a western army to deal with the Indians. President George Washington appointed the Federalist governor of the Northwest Territory, Arthur St. Clair, to command this army, and in the fall of 1791, St. Clair launched a major, but spectacularly unsuccessful, military offensive against the Miami. St. Clair's army suffered the worst defeat ever of an American force by Indians at the Battle of the Wabash,[30] leading Washington to remove St. Clair and to give Major General "Mad" Anthony Wayne, the hero of the Battle of Stony Point, command of the western army.

On August 20, 1794, Wayne defeated the Indians at the Battle of Fallen Timbers (outside present-day Toledo). The defeat at Fallen Timbers forced the Indians to agree in 1795 to the Treaty of Greenville in which the Ohio tribes relinquished most of their claims. Although the conflict with the tribes did not end immediately, the Treaty largely took the Indians out of the path of white settlement of the Ohio Territory.[31]

The Northwest Ordinance

Ohio's constitutional history begins with the Northwest Ordinance, which can be viewed as Ohio's first "constitution." It not only established a government for the Northwest Territory—a prerequisite for the orderly settlement of the west—but also set the terms for the admission of Ohio and four other states into the union. The Ordinance, which Ohio's first historian Caleb Atwater wrote "was justly considered the Magna Carta of Ohio, and of all of the states northwest of the Ohio river,"[32] also guaranteed the inhabitants of the territory certain fundamental rights that would later become part of the Ohio Constitution.

---

[28] Treaty of Fort Stanwix with the Six Nations (1784); Treaty of Fort McIntosh (1785), Art. II. *See* Charles J. Kappler, ed., *Indian Affairs: Laws and Treaties*, vol. II (Treaties) (Washington: Government Printing Office, 1904).

[29] Hurt, *The Ohio Frontier*, 96.

[30] Ibid., 118 (estimating 623 soldiers killed and 258 wounded).

[31] Thomas H. Smith, ed., *An Ohio Reader: 1750 to the Civil War* (Grand Rapids: William B. Eerdmans Publishing Company, 1975), 69.

[32] Peter S. Onuf, "The Importance of the Northwest Ordinance," in *Liberty's Legacy: Our Celebration of the Northwest Ordinance and the United States Constitution* (Columbus: Ohio Historical Society, 1987), 14 (quoting Caleb Atwater).

The Northwest Ordinance provided a three-stage process for the creation of new states as the population of the territory increased. The idea of tying statehood to population had first appeared in Jefferson's Ordinance of 1784, the Confederation Congress' earlier attempt to establish the terms of statehood for the western territories, including territories south of the Ohio River.[33] Unlike the 1784 Ordinance, however, the Northwest Ordinance established a strong central government that was initially undemocratic. The 1784 Ordinance "though inoperative" was legally in force until 1787 and would have allowed the settlers of the territories to create their own government by adopting the constitution and laws of any one of the original states. But many members of Congress had doubts about the character and loyalty of the frontier settlers and believed that a strong central government was needed to attract the kind of settlers who would be better able to form republican governments.[34]

The Northwest Ordinance also differed from the Ordinance of 1784 by authorizing the creation of fewer states. On the recommendation of James Monroe, the Northwest Ordinance set an upper limit of five states that could be carved from the Northwest Territory rather than the ten that Jefferson had envisioned. Monroe believed that, if too many states were formed, some would never achieve a population sufficient for statehood and those that would be formed would have little in common with their eastern counterparts. He also believed that the creation of too many states in the Northwest Territory would work against the political interests of the federal government and the eastern states.[35]

The Northwest Ordinance gave the Confederation Congress supreme authority over the area during the first stage of development. In this initial stage, Congress would appoint a governor to function as chief executive with control over the militia, Indian affairs, and the appointment of magistrates and civil officers in the counties and townships. Congress would also appoint a secretary and provide the territory with a judicial system consisting of three judges who would exercise common law jurisdiction. Under the scrutiny of Congress, the three judges and the governor would have the authority to adopt criminal and civil laws for the territory.[36]

The next stage of development would occur once the population reached 5,000 "free male inhabitants, of full age."[37] At that point, the territory could elect representatives to a General Assembly consisting of the governor, an elected House of Representatives, and a five-member legislative council appointed

---

[33] Peter S. Onuf, *Statehood and Union: A History of the Northwest Ordinance* (Bloomington: Indiana University Press, 1987), 46–49 (hereinafter Onuf, *Statehood and Union).*

[34] Ibid., 49–50.

[35] Jay A. Barrett, *Evolution of the Ordinance of 1787* (New York: Arno Press, 1971), 34.

[36] Northwest Ordinance, §§ 3–8.

[37] Ibid., § 9.

by the Congress from a list of residents nominated by the territorial House of Representatives. All bills passed by a majority in the House of Representatives and in the legislative council would go to the governor for his assent at which point the governor would have the authority to exercise a veto.[38]

The Northwest Ordinance also contained "articles of compact, between the original States and the people and States in the said Territory, and forever remain unalterable, unless by common consent. . . . ."[39] The compact provided that a "state" would be ready for admission to the union when it reached a population of 60,000 "free inhabitants" and promised admission into the union "on an equal footing with the original states" and delineated the boundaries of three to five new states.[40] Any state that reached the population threshold could form a government and draft a permanent constitution, provided that "the constitution and government so to be formed, shall be republican, and in conformity to the principles contained in these articles."[41] The Ordinance also allowed admission to the union by an act of Congress (an enabling act) with fewer than the requisite 60,000 "free inhabitants."[42]

Eventually Ohio and all the states in the Northwest Territory other than Michigan entered the union through enabling acts,[43] which required the submission of state constitutions as one of the conditions of admission. Ohio was the first state for which Congress passed an enabling act to guide the admission process.[44]

In addition to providing a structure for the government of the Northwest Territory and the promise of statehood, the Northwest Ordinance contained a declaration of specific, fundamental rights. The Northwest Ordinance was, in fact, the first *national* document to include such a declaration or Bill of Rights. The Articles of Confederation, under which the Ordinance was enacted, contained no Bill of Rights, and the adoption of the first ten amendments to the U.S. Constitution did not occur until 1791. Among the rights guaranteed by the Northwest Ordinance in its Articles of Compact were the rights to religious freedom, habeas corpus, trial by jury, judicial proceedings according to the course of the common law, and reasonable bail (except in capital cases). The Ordinance also prohibited excessive fines, cruel and unusual punishment, and laws that impaired the obligation of contracts. Finally, it included a clause encouraging schools and the means of education, a provision promising respect

---

[38] Ibid., §§ 9–13.

[39] Ibid., § 14.

[40] Ibid., Articles of Compact, Art. V.

[41] Ibid.

[42] Ibid.

[43] *See* Susan P. Fino, *The Michigan State Constitution* (New York: Oxford University Press, 2011), 8.

[44] *See* Eric Biber, "The Price of Admission: Causes, Effects, and Patters of Conditions Imposed on States Entering the Union," 46 *Am. J. Legal Hist.* 119 (2004).

and fair treatment toward the Indians (which was generally ignored), and a prohibition against slavery and involuntary servitude.

The Northwest Ordinance provided that the prohibition against slavery as well as other individual rights contained in the Ordinance's Articles of Compact were intended to "forever remain unalterable."[45] This effort to bind the states, however, became the subject of an intense legal and political debate concerning the continuing legal effect of the Northwest Ordinance's prohibition against slavery. Ultimately, both the U.S. and Ohio Supreme Courts held that state constitutions superseded the Ordinance,[46] but the fundamental rights protected by the Northwest Ordinance, including the prohibition against slavery, became part of the 1802 Constitution and remain part of the current Ohio Constitution.

Governance under Arthur St. Clair and the Push for Statehood

With the adoption of the Northwest Ordinance, the Confederation Congress appointed Arthur St. Clair as territorial governor. No single person has likely had as great an influence on Ohio's constitutional history as St. Clair. Ironically, in reaction to St. Clair's turbulent rule as territorial governor, Ohio vested nearly all its governmental power in the legislature and created one of the weakest executive branches of any state.

Born in Scotland in the 1730s and indentured to a medical doctor, St. Clair purchased his freedom with an inheritance from his mother's death in the 1750s. He then received an ensign's commission in the British Army and came to the American colonies to begin a distinguished military career, though he later fought against Britain in the Revolutionary War. Initially commissioned as a colonel in the Continental Army, he worked his way to the rank of major general and became an advisor and close friend to George Washington. When the war ended, St. Clair entered political life as a Pennsylvania delegate to the Confederation Congress. In 1787, before becoming Northwest Territorial governor, he was elected president of the Confederation Congress, the most powerful position under the Articles of Confederation. Despite his devastating defeat at the hands of the Indians in 1791, he continued as territorial governor until Thomas Jefferson fired him in 1802 after St. Clair's speech at the 1802 Constitutional Convention.[47]

St. Clair was an ardent Federalist, and his tenure as governor was marked by an intense rivalry with the Jeffersonian Republicans (also called "Democrats" at that time). As governor, St. Clair was required "to represent the interests of the national government and exercise jurisdiction over some of the most fervent

---

[45] Northwest Ordinance, § 14.

[46] *Strader v. Graham* (1850); *State ex rel. Donahey v. Edmonson* (1913).

[47] William Henry Smith, ed., *The St. Clair Papers*, vol. I (Cincinnati: Robert Clarke, 1882), 2–4 (hereinafter Smith, *St. Clair Papers*).

believers in the primacy of local sovereignty and democracy in the nation."[48] The early settlers of the Northwest Territory were strongly individualistic and resistant to national authority. Not surprisingly, they were difficult to govern and despised St. Clair's autocratic rule. St. Clair, on his part, had described the settlers as "a multitude of indigent and ignorant people . . . ill qualified to form a constitution and government for themselves."[49]

The political rivalry between the Republicans and St. Clair reached new levels of acrimony soon after the election of the first territorial legislature in 1799. The political infighting between the governor and the mostly Republican legislature came to a head when the legislature began passing bills creating new counties, a power that St. Clair claimed was vested in him. Faced with these and other objectionable bills, St. Clair exercised his veto and struck down eleven bills passed during the first legislative session, including six that created new counties.[50] As a result, the territorial legislature and the settlers increasingly split along national party lines. New Englanders, for the most part, tended to side with the Federalist St. Clair, while the majority of settlers, mostly from Pennsylvania and southern states, tended to side with the Republicans.[51]

St. Clair's opposition to statehood increased his unpopularity among Republicans. By 1800, Republicans began setting their sights on statehood, but St. Clair, like most Federalists, felt the territory was not ready to become a state because it had not properly evolved through the process established by the Northwest Ordinance. The territory lacked political stability and did not yet meet the 60,000 population threshold for admission into the union. To delay statehood (and prevent the admission into the union of a Republican state), St. Clair proposed dividing the Northwest Territory into three districts rather than the two authorized under the Northwest Ordinance. St. Clair's plan called for the subdivision of the Northwest Territory into an eastern division with the Federalist-controlled Marietta as the capital, a central division with Cincinnati as its capital, and a western division with Vincennes in the Indiana Territory as its capital.[52]

For Federalists the plan had the advantage of splitting the strong Republican center of Ohio in half. Congress, however, rejected St. Clair's proposal and on May 7, 1800, divided the Northwest Territory into two districts, creating the

---

[48] J. Martin West, "Arthur St. Clair," *Timeline* (Columbus: Ohio Historical Society, April–May 1988), 53.

[49] Smith, *St. Clair Papers*, vol. II, 482 (quoted in Randolph C. Downes, *Frontier Ohio, 1788–1803* (Columbus: Ohio Historical Society, 1935), 189 (hereinafter Downes, *Frontier Ohio*)).

[50] *See* Thomas R. Swisher, ed., *Ohio Constitution Handbook* (Cleveland: Banks-Baldwin Law Publishing Co., 1990), xi (hereinafter Swisher, *Ohio Constitution Handbook*); Salmon P. Chase, ed., "A Preliminary Sketch of the History of Ohio," in *The Statutes of Ohio and the Northwestern Territory*, vol. I (Cincinnati: F.S. Benton, 1833) (hereinafter Chase, "A Preliminary Sketch"), 28–30.

[51] *See* Chaddock, *Ohio before 1850*, 56.

[52] Ibid., 57; Downes, "Ohio's First Constitution," 14.

Indiana Territory and establishing Chillicothe as the seat of the eastern division.[53] In 1801, St. Clair again proposed dividing the Northwest Territory into three districts, but this time, with the support of leading Cincinnati Republicans who wanted the capital moved from Chillicothe, he was able to push his plan through the second territorial legislature and resubmit it to Congress.[54] Although Congress again rejected St. Clair's proposed division, this time by a vote of eighty-one to five,[55] his plan nonetheless infuriated the Chillicothe Republicans. The tension between the governor and Chillicothe Republicans became so great that St. Clair narrowly escaped a mob when he visited the city in December 1801.[56] Ironically, rather than delay statehood, St. Clair's plan had the effect of accelerating it. Chillicothe became the center of the statehood movement, and a group of staunch Republicans known as the "Chillicothe faction" and led by Nathaniel Massie, Edward Tiffin, and Thomas Worthington, turned its attention to the nation's capital to lobby for statehood.

Worthington, Tiffin's brother-in-law and a native of Virginia who served in the territorial legislature, traveled to Washington to lobby Congress and the new Jefferson administration for early admission. Since the territory lacked 60,000 free inhabitants, Worthington sought a congressional act authorizing statehood. At the same time, the Chillicothe faction organized a committee to inundate Congress with petitions to demonstrate the strong public support for statehood. In Washington, Worthington was overwhelmed by the support of the Jeffersonians, who had just defeated the Federalists in the contested election of 1800. In a letter to Massie on January 14, 1802, Worthington wrote, "so far I can determine [I] have reason to believe we shall obtain our utmost wishes. . . ."[57]

The Jefferson administration welcomed the admission of Ohio since it gave the Republicans an opportunity to obtain two more senators, one more member of the U.S. House of Representatives, and three more electoral college votes.[58] Beyond the political advantages in bringing Ohio into the union, Jefferson had always disliked the form of territorial government established by the Northwest Ordinance. In a letter dated January 23, 1800, he wrote, "Surely such a government as the first form prescribed for the territories is a despotic oligarchy without one rational object."[59]

Worthington eventually met with President Jefferson and William B. Giles, a leader in the House of Representatives from Virginia. Giles, who strongly

---

[53] "An Act to Divide the Territory of the United States Northwest of The Ohio into Two Separate Governments," 6 *Cong. Ch. 41, 2 Stat.* 58 (May 7, 1800).

[54] *See* Downes, *Frontier Ohio*, 197–200.

[55] Bond, *Foundations of Ohio*, 470.

[56] Chaddock, *Ohio before 1850*, 58–59.

[57] Downes, *Frontier Ohio*, 213.

[58] McDonald, "A Study in Constitution Making," 7–8.

[59] Chaddock, *Ohio before 1850*, 61.

supported statehood, established a committee to collect petitions from Ohio citizens and to prepare a report on statehood for Congress. On March 4, 1802, the committee released its report calling for an enabling act to organize Ohio as a state.[60] In opposition, Federalists attacked the report on Republican principles. They argued that the enabling act would usurp the popular rights of the citizens of the territory since neither the territorial legislature nor the people through a referendum were given an opportunity to vote on statehood.[61] Moreover, the opponents of statehood maintained that the Articles of Compact of the Northwest Ordinance gave Congress no power to require a constitutional convention as a precondition of admission into the union.[62] Despite Federalist opposition, the bill had no trouble passing, and on April 30, 1802, President Jefferson signed it into law.[63]

The Enabling Act fixed the boundary of Ohio along the lines of the Northwest Ordinance and called for the election of thirty-five delegates to a constitutional convention in Chillicothe on the first Monday of November 1802. The act eliminated all property qualifications for voting and set the terms for the election of delegates. It also reserved a section of each township for the support of schools and offered the new state the salt springs in the Scioto and Muskingum valleys and a percentage of the proceeds from the sale of lands owned by Congress for public roads in exchange for a promise not to tax lands sold by Congress for five years.[64]

■ STATEHOOD AND OHIO'S FIRST CONSTITUTION

Predictably, the campaign for delegates to Ohio's first constitutional convention focused on the issue of statehood. With a majority of the territory favoring statehood, the Federalists were in a difficult position, having opposed the Enabling Act. Federalists (and some Cincinnati Republicans) continued to argue against the legality of the Enabling Act and for their earlier division plan (St. Clair's plan), which they contended would only temporarily delay statehood, if at all.[65] A number of Federalists also accused Republicans of wanting to introduce slavery—a charge vigorously denied by Massie, Worthington, and other Republican leaders.[66]

---

[60] Annals of Congress, 7 Cong. 1 Sess., 1097–100 (House of Representatives).

[61] Chaddock, *Ohio before 1850*, 59; *see also* Downes, *Frontier Ohio*, 216.

[62] *See* Annals of Congress, 7 Cong. 1 Sess. 1103, 1112–13 (House of Representatives).

[63] Act of Apr. 30, 1802, Ch. 40, 2 Stat. 173 (amended 1803).

[64] Ibid.; *see also* Caleb Atwater, *History of the State of Ohio, Natural and Civil* (Cincinnati: Glezen & Shepard, 1838), 170 (discussing the "inducements" offered to the people of the territory) (hereinafter Atwater, *History of the State of Ohio*).

[65] Barnhart, *Valley of Democracy*, 151; Downes, *Ohio Frontier*, 232–39.

[66] *See generally* Barbara A. Terzian, "Effusions of Folly and Fanaticism: Race, Gender and Constitution-Making in Ohio, 1802–1923" (Ph.D. dissertation, The Ohio State University, 1999), 59–70 (hereinafter Terzian, "Effusions of Folly").

In contrast to the Federalists, the Republicans had all the advantages. They had proven their commitment to statehood and ran a well-organized campaign creating numerous Republican societies throughout Ohio to galvanize support. Republicans were also aided by a change in the election law that allowed voters to cast their ballots in townships throughout each county as well as in the county seat, making it easier for backwoodsmen, mostly Republican, to vote. And, not surprisingly, the election resulted in a landslide victory for Republicans, who won at least twenty-six of the thirty-five seats to the constitutional convention.[67]

The Constitutional Convention of 1802

The thirty-five delegates who convened in Chillicothe on November 1, 1802, represented a diverse array of professionals, including lawyers, clergymen, physicians, merchants, farmers, and speculators, with lawyers predominating. Five delegates to the convention ultimately became Ohio governors: Edward Tiffin, Thomas Kirker, Samuel Huntington, Thomas Worthington, and Jeremiah Morrow.[68] The dominant Chillicothe faction included Massie, Worthington, Tiffin, and Michael Baldwin, a young lawyer originally from Connecticut. In addition to one delegate from Hamilton County, Federalists sent delegates from Washington County, which included the New England strongholds of Marietta and Zanesville, and Jefferson County with its county seat of Steubenville. Well-known Federalists included General Rufus Putnam, Benjamin Ines Gilman, Ephraim Cutler, and John Mclntire. An interesting aspect of the makeup of the delegates was their age, leading Caleb Atwater to remark that "[t]he framers . . . [though] well qualified . . . were generally . . . young men, who had been little engaged in legislation . . . [and] could not . . . take a very wide survey of human societies."[69] Over half of the delegates were under forty, including all of the leaders of the Chillicothe faction, and a number were in their twenties. Worthington was only twenty-nine years old, and Baldwin was three years younger.[70]

Most of the delegates were from Virginia (10), Pennsylvania (7), and Maryland (5).[71] Massie and Worthington were both born in Virginia. Tiffin, who emigrated from England in his teens, married and lived in Virginia before moving to Ohio. Several delegates had at various times lived in Kentucky, and only a handful were from New England.[72]

---

[67] Ibid., 74 (citing a letter from Thomas Worthington to President Jefferson).

[68] Governor James E. Campbell, speech reproduced in Charles B. Galbreath, *History of Ohio*, vol. 1 (Chicago: American Historical Society, 1925), 274 (hereinafter Galbreath, *History of Ohio*).

[69] Atwater, *History of the State of Ohio*, 171.

[70] Barbara A. Terzian, "Ohio's Constitutions: An Historical Perspective," 51 *Clev. St. L. Rev.* 357 (2004): 360–61 (hereinafter Terzian, "Ohio's Constitutions").

[71] Ibid., 361.

[72] *See* Barnhart, *Valley of Democracy*, 153–54.

The convention, firmly under the control of the Jeffersonians, elected Tiffin, who would become Ohio's first governor, as president and Thomas Scott, also of Chillicothe, as secretary. Arthur St. Clair, who was still territorial governor, was treated as an outsider, and Republicans thwarted his efforts to have a role at the convention. A motion was made on the third day of the convention to allow St. Clair to address the delegates. Worthington, who had previously submitted charges against St. Clair in an effort to have him dismissed as territorial governor, voted against the motion, but Massie voted in favor of allowing St. Clair to speak. No friend of the governor, Massie believed that, if allowed to speak, St. Clair would accomplish what Worthington and Massie could not—his removal from office. "Give him enough rope and he will hang himself."[73] Massie was right. Permitted to address the convention by a vote of nineteen to fourteen, St. Clair launched into a diatribe against Congress and the conditions imposed by the Enabling Act. He defiantly declared that the Enabling Act of 1802, passed by a Republican Congress, was null and void and that "[f]or all internal affairs we have a complete legislature of our own, and in them are no more bound by an act of Congress than we would be bound by edict of the first consul of France."[74] St. Clair's speech, which President Jefferson characterized as "an intemperance and indecorum of language toward the Legislature of the United States," convinced the president to remove him as governor, ending St. Clair's political career.

After St. Clair's address, the delegates, as required by the Enabling Act, voted on a resolution asking whether "it is expedient, at this time, to form a constitution and State government." St. Clair obviously did not dissuade the delegates, who approved the resolution by a vote of thirty-two to one. Ephraim Cutler, a staunch Federalist from Washington County and the son of Manasseh Cutler, the principal organizer of the Ohio Company, cast the only dissenting vote.[75]

Only seven of the delegates were Federalists. The remaining twenty-eight delegates were Jeffersonian, and even though only once voted on a recorded vote as a single block, "control of the convention was not in doubt."[76] Unfortunately, the journal of the convention does not transcribe the debates so there is no official record of the positions or arguments of individual delegates or even the delegates responsible for particular motions. For the most part, the journal recorded only the composition of committees, motions made on the floor of the convention, and the yeas and nays on particular votes.

---

[73] William T. Utter, *The Frontier State 1803–1825*, in Carl Wittke, ed., *The History of the State of Ohio*, vol. II (Columbus: Ohio State Archaeological and Historical Society, 1942), 12 (hereinafter Utter, *The Frontier State*) (quoting David Mead Massie, *Nathaniel Massie: A Pioneer of Ohio; A Sketch of His Life and Selections from His Correspondence* (Cincinnati: Robert Clark, 1896), 222–23).

[74] Smith, *St. Clair Papers*, vol. II, 594 (also published in Smith, *An Ohio Reader: 1750 to the Civil War*, 63).

[75] Barnhart, *Valley of Democracy*, 155.

[76] Ibid., 152, 155.

The Status of African Americans

Some of the most contested issues at the convention involved the status of African Americans. The delegates never voted on a proposal to introduce slavery—at least not on the floor of the convention. There were, however, two votes on the slavery section recorded in the convention's journal, but they involved votes on involuntary servitude and indentures.[77] Ephraim Cutler claimed in his memoirs (published by his daughter Julia Perkins Cutler almost four decades after his death) that the committee on the Bill of Rights narrowly defeated a motion by Republicans to permit a limited form of slavery,[78] but a number of historians have questioned the Cutler account.[79] In any case, the convention adopted a morally forceful, but probably legally ineffective, provision that perpetually barred the introduction of slavery. "[N]o alteration of this constitution shall ever take place, so as to introduce slavery or involuntary servitude into this state."[80]

Although there seems to have been no serious support for a proslavery amendment at the convention,[81] opposition to slavery did not translate into support for African American rights. On November 22, 1802, the committee of the whole submitted a draft that limited suffrage to white male residents who paid or were charged a state or county tax. The convention defeated a motion to omit the word "white" from that section by a vote of nineteen to fourteen.[82] After an unsuccessful motion that would have eliminated the tax requirement on voting, a motion to enfranchise "all male negroes and mulattoes now residing in this territory . . . if they shall within ___ months make a record of their citizenship" passed by a vote of nineteen to fifteen.[83]

This victory for African American suffrage, however, was short-lived, and on November 26, 1802, four days after extending the franchise to African

---

[77] *See Journal of the [1802] Convention*, published in *Ohio Archaeological and Historical Publications*, vol. 5 (1897), 110–11 (hereinafter *1802 Journal*).

[78] Julia Perkins Cutler, *Life and Times of Ephraim Cutler* (Cincinnati: Robert Clark, 1890) (reprinted New York: Arno Press, 1971), 74–76 (hereinafter Cutler, *Life of Ephraim Cutler*).

[79] *See, e.g.*, Terzian, "Ohio's Constitutions," 365 n. 49 ("Cutler's version is suspect."); *see also* Terzian, Effusions of Folly, 95–98; William Gilmore, *Life of Edward Tiffin* (Chillicothe: Homey & Son, 1897) (hereinafter Gilmore, *Life of Edward Tiffin*), 72–77; Helen M. Thurston, "The 1802 Constitutional Convention and Status of the Negro," 81 *Ohio Hist.* 15 (1972): 24. *But see* McCullough, *The Pioneers* (accepting Ephraim Cutler's recollection of his role in opposing slavery at the 1802 Constitutional Convention). Notwithstanding questions about the accuracy of Cutler's account of what occurred in committee, he is credited with having drafted the substance of the section banning slavery and involuntary servitude and having strongly supported African American rights. *See* Terzian, "Effusions of Folly," 98.

[80] 1802 Const., Art. VII, sec. 5.

[81] *See* Terzian, "Ohio's Constitutions," 365–66.

[82] *1802 Journal*, 113.

[83] Ibid., 114 (blank in *Journal*). The delegates, however, defeated a motion that would have extended the franchise to the descendants of African American voters by a single vote.

Americans, the convention reconsidered the issue and voted seventeen to seventeen on a motion to strike the language extending suffrage. The tie required Edward Tiffin, the president of the convention, to cast the deciding vote, and he joined his fellow Virginia Republicans in opposing suffrage.[84] Though he had freed his own slaves, Tiffin believed that "the immediate neighborhood of two slave-holding States made it impolitic to offer such an inducement for the influx of an undesirable class to the new State."[85]

Ironically, the decision by the convention to deny African Americans the right to vote was actually a vote to disenfranchise blacks. There had not been any racial limitation on voting for delegates to the convention, and there is evidence that at least one African American voted in the election for delegates.[86]

Following the initial votes on African American suffrage, the delegates voted nineteen to sixteen to approve an anticivil rights amendment that denied "negroes and mulattos" the right to hold office, to serve in the military, and to testify in any court against a white person.[87] Tiffin voted with the majority to deny African Americans these specific rights—the only time he voted other than to break a tie. And later that day, the convention reconsidered its earlier vote and defeated the anticivil rights amendment by a single vote. All of this led one commentator to conclude that "Ohio's new constitution established a Republican paradise for white men."[88] In effect, the convention decided to let the legislature determine the rights of African Americans. Less than two years later, the legislature would begin passing laws limiting African American rights and making clear that African Americans were not welcome in Ohio.[89]

Approval and Statehood

The convention adjourned on November 29, 1802, less than a month after the delegates had convened. Before adjourning, the delegates voted to accept, with slight modification, the proposals from Congress concerning the lands set aside for schools, the salt mines, and the sale of public lands. The delegates also adopted a schedule that provided for the transition from territorial law and set

---

[84] Ibid., 122. *See also* Terzian, "Ohio's Constitutions," 368.

[85] Terzian, "Ohio's Constitutions," 368 (quoting Gilmore, *Life of Edward Tiffin*, 76).

[86] Ibid., 359 n. 15.

[87] *1802 Journal*, 115–16. *See also* Terzian, "Ohio's Constitutions," 367–68.

[88] Terzian, "Ohio's Constitutions," 368.

[89] *See* Terzian, "Effusions of Folly," 113–18. *See also* Paul Finkelman, "Race, Slavery and Law in Antebellum Ohio," in Michael Les Benedict and John F. Winkler, eds., *The History of Ohio Law* (Athens: Ohio University Press, 2004), 748 (hereinafter *The History of Ohio Law*) (describing Ohio's complex policies on the treatment of African Americans during the antebellum period as ranging from racism to ambivalence but concluding that by the middle of the century Ohio and many of its political leaders had become leaders in the effort to increase racial fairness).

elections for the first Tuesday in January 1803.[90] Consistent with the practice of the time, the delegates defeated a proposal to submit the new constitution to the people for approval on a vote of twenty-seven to seven.[91] The Jeffersonian Republicans ironically argued against a popular verdict on the constitution on the ground that avoiding a referendum on the adoption of the constitution would "save labor and strife and prevent an unnecessary loss of time."[92]

Following the convention, Worthington traveled to Washington to meet with President Jefferson and members of Congress, and he delivered to the President and Congress a copy of the constitution and the convention's conditional acceptance of the proposals contained in the Enabling Act.[93] Congress acknowledged Ohio as a state in an act on February 19, 1803, but it never took formal action to admit Ohio into the union.[94] Consequently, there are a number of competing views as to when Ohio first became a state, and five different dates have been proposed, including April 30, 1802, the date on which Congress passed the Enabling Act permitting Ohio to pursue statehood; November 29, 1802, the date on which the convention adjourned; February 19, 1803, the date on which Congress passed an act extending federal laws to the "State" of Ohio; March 1, 1803, the date on which the General Assembly first met; and March 3, 1802, the date on which Congress consented to a final modification of the Enabling Act.[95] In 1902, the Ohio General Assembly officially recognized the birth of the state on March 1, 1803,[96] and in 1953, Congress formally recognized Ohio as the seventeenth state of the union.[97]

The Ohio Constitution of 1802

The Ohio Constitution of 1802 consisted of a preamble and eight articles. Article I (Legislative Power), the most prominent article, established the supremacy

[90] Schedule, 1802 Ohio Constitution.

[91] *1802 Journal*, 97–98. Prior to 1802, only two states—Massachusetts and New Hampshire—submitted their constitutions to the people for ratification. *See* McDonald, "A Study in Constitution Making," 51–52. *See also* Emilius O. Randall and Daniel J. Ryan, *History of Ohio, the Rise and Progress of an American State*, vol. III (New York: Century History Company, 1912), 125 (hereinafter Randall and Ryan, *History of Ohio*).

[92] McDonald, "A Study in Constitution Making," 49–50 (quoting Jacob Burnet, *Notes on the Early Settlement of the North-Western Territory* (Cincinnati: Derby, Bradley & Co., 1847), 354). Burnet considered the refusal to have a referendum to be "a bad precedent" and he observed that it "requires a large share of charity to adopt" the Republican's justification. Burnet at 354.

[93] *See* Alfred Byron Sears, *Thomas Worthington: Father of Ohio Statehood* (Columbus: The Ohio State University Press, 1958), 107–8.

[94] Act of Feb. 19, 1803, Ch. 7, 2 Stat. 201.

[95] *See* Utter, *The Frontier State*, 31.

[96] Ibid.

[97] Pub. L. No. 83–204, 67 Stat. 407 (1953).

of the legislature. Articles II (Executive) and III (Judiciary) defined the other branches of government. Other Articles provided for Electors and Elections (Art. IV), Militia Officers (Art. V), Civil Officers (Art. VI), Miscellaneous Provisions (Art. VII), and the Bill of Rights (Art. VIII).

Consistent with the Jeffersonian views of a majority of the delegates, the convention vested most of the political power of the state in a bicameral legislature. The General Assembly, which consisted of a Senate and a House of Representatives, was given the power to make law without interference from the executive branch. A bill would become law if passed by both houses of the General Assembly and signed by the president of the Senate and the speaker of the House (Art. I, sec. 17). The General Assembly had the power to appoint most civil officers, including the secretary of state (Art. II, sec. 16), the state treasurer and the state auditor (Art. VI, sec. 2), and all judges except justices of the peace (Art. III, sec. 8). The General Assembly also had broad power to apportion seats in the legislature (Art. I, secs. 2 and 6), to fix the number of senators (Art. I, sec. 6), and to create new counties (Art. VII, sec. 3). Since the General Assembly's power was plenary, unlike Congress, which has only powers that are specifically enumerated, the Ohio legislature could pass any act not specifically prohibited by the constitution (see Commentary, Article II, sec. 1).

The executive and judicial branches were clearly subordinate to the legislature. The executive power of the state was vested in the governor, who was elected to a two-year term and could serve at most six years in an eight-year period (Art. II, sec. 3). As a result of St. Clair's rule and Jefferson's distrust of a strong executive, the constitution severely restricted the governor's power. The governor was commander-in-chief of the militia (Art. II, sec. 10) and had the power to grant reprieves and pardons, except in cases of impeachment (Art. II, sec. 5), but the governor lacked veto power and had no power of appointment other than to fill certain vacancies while the General Assembly was in recess (Art. II, sec. 8) and to appoint the adjutant general of the state militia (Art. V, sec. 6).

Historian Caleb Atwater succinctly described the subordinate role of the governor.

> Owing to their ill will towards Governor St. Clair, the members of the convention, made our governor a mere cypher. He can pardon criminals, appoint the adjutant general, sign commissions, and fill temporary vacancies, but he has no voice in making the laws, no veto power, nor has he the power to interfere in appointing any of our officers.[98]

In fact, the 1802 Ohio Constitution was the only constitution adopted by a state between 1801 and 1830 that did not grant the governor power to veto legislation.[99] And the Whig Governor Tom Corwin once succinctly but irreverently

---

[98] Atwater, *History of the State of Ohio*, 172–73.

[99] G. Alan Tarr, "The Ohio Constitution of 1802: An Introduction" (February 2000) (Rutgers website).

observed that the powers of Ohio governors "are confined to the appointment of notaries and pardoning of democrats."[100]

The judiciary consisted of a Supreme Court, courts of common pleas, and justices of the peace. The legislature appointed all judges (other than justices of the peace) for seven-year terms "if so long they behave well" (Art. III, sec. 8), while voters of the respective townships elected justices of the peace, who were not subject to a good behavior requirement, to three-year terms (Art. III, sec. 11). The Supreme Court, which originally consisted of three justices, had both original and appellate jurisdiction and was obligated to hold court annually in every county of the state (Art. III, secs. 2 and 10). Common pleas courts had jurisdiction over all criminal, common law, and matters of equity, as well as probate and testamentary matters (Art. III, sec. 5).

The article on electors and elections limited the right to vote to white males above the age of twenty-one years (Art. IV, sec. 1), but it dropped the reference to "citizens" that had been used to define electors in both the Northwest Ordinance and the Enabling Act, thus seeming to expand the vote to noncitizens.[101] The article also continued the liberalization of voting qualifications begun by the Enabling Act by not including a freehold requirement (which was common in earlier state constitutions).[102] In its place, the article limited the vote to those "who have paid or are charged with a State or county tax," but it offset this limitation by extending the vote to persons "compelled to labor on the roads of their respective townships or counties" (see Art. IV sec. 5), an expansion of voting that may have led future U.S. Supreme Court Chief Justice Salmon P. Chase to describe Ohio as having "universal suffrage."[103] Finally, the inclusion of racial restrictions in state constitutions was unusual, and Ohio was the only northern state and the third state in the union (Delaware and South Carolina were the first two) to include a racial restriction on voting in its constitution.[104]

Both the structure of the new government and the inclusion of a Bill of Rights were designed to protect individual liberty. By limiting the power of the governor and establishing a system of legislative supremacy, the drafters sought to prevent abuse of governmental power. The constitution reflected a kind of popular democracy in which the legislature restrained executive power and the people restrained the legislature through frequent elections with representatives standing for election annually and senators biennially (Art. I, secs. 3 and 5). In addition to these structural protections, the Bill of Rights (Art. VII) included virtually all

---

[100] Galbreath, *History of Ohio*, vol. 1, 272 (quoting Governor James E. Campbell).

[101] *But see* Commentary, Art. V, sec. 1.

[102] *See* Alexander Keyssar, *The Right to Vote: The Contested History of Democracy in the United States* (Philadelphia: Basic Books, 2009 rev. ed.), 4–5.

[103] Chase, "A Preliminary Sketch," vol. 1, 34.

[104] *See* Delaware Const. of 1792, Art. IV, sec. 1; South Carolina Const. of 1778, Art. XIII.

of the protections that had been contained in the federal Bill of Rights and in the Northwest Ordinance.

The Ohio Bill of Rights, however, also included rights that were not taken from either the federal Bill of Rights or the Northwest Ordinance. For example, section 23 of the Ohio Bill of Rights prohibited poll taxes, calling them "grievous and oppressive." Section 7 gave every person redress in the courts "by due course of law, and right and justice administered, without denial or delay." Section 6 guaranteed free and open printing presses and, in contrast to the common law, allowed truth to be offered as a defense in prosecutions for libeling public officials. Also, section 25 prevented the passage of any law barring poor citizens from participating in schools, colleges, or universities receiving public funds. In total, the Ohio Bill of Rights included twenty-eight sections, which constituted a more detailed enumeration of rights and greater protection from government abuse than provided in the first ten amendments to the U.S. Constitution.

Given that the delegates drafted the 1802 Constitution in less than a month, it is not surprising that they borrowed many provisions from other sources. The relatively new U.S. Constitution of 1787, however, was not an important influence on the Ohio Constitution. Instead, as with most state constitutions at the start of the nineteenth century, the Ohio Constitution was structured along the lines of the Articles of Confederation, which vested most power in the legislature. The Ohio Constitution lacked an explicit separation of powers requirement as well as many of the checks and balances found in the U.S. Constitution; thus, with respect to the distribution of powers, Ohio state government was described by Howard McDonald in his study of nineteenth-century constitution-making in Ohio "as more in harmony with the real English Constitution than with the one described by Montesquieu."[105]

Republicans at the convention had apparently expected the Ohio Constitution to be based on the Virginia Constitution, but Virginia had not revised its constitution since 1776 and was seen as "somewhat out of fashion both as to form and content."[106] Judge Willing Byrd of Hamilton County, the Republican delegate chiefly responsible for choosing a model, instead looked to the more recent 1796 Tennessee Constitution.[107] And delegates borrowed 78 of the 106 sections in the Ohio Constitution from the constitutions of Tennessee (50), Pennsylvania (19), and Kentucky (9), and only four of its sections "show the direct influence of New England constitutions. . . ."[108]

Article I on Legislative Powers shared sixteen of twenty-eight sections with Tennessee, including sections providing for two-year terms for senators and a two-thirds quorum requirement in each house and a section allowing bills to

[105] *See* McDonald, "A Study in Constitution Making," 28.

[106] Ibid., 27.

[107] *See* ibid., 27; *see also* Cutler, *Life of Ephraim Cutler*, 69.

[108] *See* Barnhart, *Valley of Democracy*, 158.

originate in either house. Also, ten of sixteen sections of Article II on Executive Powers were borrowed from Tennessee, including the decision to deny the governor the veto power. All seven sections of Article V, which dealt with the militia, were based on the militia sections of the Tennessee Constitution, and ten of the twenty-eight sections in Article VIII, the Bill of Rights, were derived from the Tennessee Declaration of Rights.[109]

More than half of the twelve sections in Article III, which dealt with the Judiciary, were taken from the Pennsylvania and Kentucky documents, although this article contained almost five original sections.[110]

In addition, twenty-five of the twenty-eight sections of Article VIII, the Bill of Rights, came from other state constitutions, with fifteen coming from either the Tennessee or Pennsylvania Constitutions.[111]

Despite the similarities between the Ohio Constitution and the constitutions of Tennessee, Pennsylvania, and Kentucky, there were also important differences. For example, unlike the Pennsylvania and Kentucky Constitutions, the Ohio Constitution did not give the governor the veto power or very much of the appointment power. In addition, the Ohio governor and state senators served for terms of two years, less than the terms provided for those offices under the Pennsylvania and Kentucky Constitutions.[112] Unlike Tennessee, Ohio representatives were elected annually not biennially, and unlike Tennessee, where the governor, legislators, and voters were required to own freehold estates, there was no requirement that property be owned by Ohio legislators, the governor, or the electors (though suffrage was limited to those who owned property or were compelled to work on the roads).[113]

Reviewing the 1802 Constitution, one modern commentator noted the ironies and observed that "[a] generation earlier, radicals could not conceive of so strong a governor; a generation later, they would not allow one so weak."[114]

■ OHIO'S EXPERIENCE UNDER THE CONSTITUTION OF 1802

The Constitution of 1802 contained a number of major weaknesses that ultimately led to its complete revision in 1851. The most notable flaws concerned the supremacy of the General Assembly, the inefficiency of the judicial system, and the difficulty of amending the constitution. Without the possibility of a

---

[109] *See* ibid., 157–58.

[110] *See* ibid. (chart).

[111] Ibid.

[112] Ibid., 158.

[113] Ibid., 158–59.

[114] George Phillip Parkinson Jr., "Antebellum State Constitution-Making: Retention, Circumvention, Revision" (Ph.D. dissertation, University of Wisconsin, 1972), 146 (hereinafter Parkinson, "Antebellum State Constitution-Making").

gubernatorial veto, there was no check on legislative action. In addition, most of the General Assembly's time was spent on special legislation for corporations and municipalities. In fact, the General Assembly was accused of creating needless legislation to prolong legislative sessions and thus increase the compensation of members, who were paid on a daily basis.[115] The General Assembly also had the power to create new counties and appoint judges and other county officers, thus maintaining a widespread system of political patronage. Finally, there were few constitutional constraints on drawing legislative districts. As a result of this system of legislative supremacy, there were many abuses, including the all-too-common practices of logrolling and gerrymandering.[116]

The General Assembly's complete control over fiscal matters also led to unrestricted spending and to the creation of an enormous debt during the era of internal improvements from 1825, when the construction of the Ohio canals began, through the 1840s. During this period, the General Assembly authorized financing backed by the full faith and credit of the state for the construction of the state's transportation system. At one point, the annual state debt approached nearly twenty million.[117] As a result, the General Assembly turned to new forms of taxation and began taxing personal property as well as real property, thereby angering taxpayers. The public's outrage was further inflamed by special legislation that accompanied internal improvements, especially after the Panic of 1837. The General Assembly had given banks and canal, turnpike, and railroad companies special tax breaks and other benefits and had allowed banks to be chartered with little or no capital or hard currency, thus facilitating the failure of most Ohio banks when the financial crisis hit in 1837. In addition, under the Loan Act of 1837, also known as the "Plunder Law," the General Assembly was authorized to subsidize private transportation companies and even began to enter into risky ventures with them. Many of these companies went bankrupt, requiring taxpayers to make up the losses.[118]

The judicial system also began to show signs of strain soon after statehood. As early as 1815, Governor Thomas Worthington in his annual message to the General Assembly recommended revising the constitution to correct problems associated with the judiciary.[119] The principal problem that Governor Worthington identified concerned the inability of the courts to meet the needs of a growing population, and in his 1817 message he urged the necessity of a new convention.[120] The Ohio Supreme Court operated not only as an

---

[115] Chaddock, *Ohio before 1850*, 71.

[116] *See* Randolph C. Downes, "Ohio's Second Constitution," 25 *Northwest Ohio Quarterly* 71 (1953): 74 (hereinafter Downes, "Ohio's Second Constitution").

[117] For a short summary of this period, *see* Swisher, *Ohio Constitution Handbook*, xix–xxi.

[118] Ibid.

[119] McDonald, "A Study in Constitution Making," 62.

[120] Ibid., 63.

appellate court but also as a court of original jurisdiction. Moreover, the 1802 Constitution required the justices to ride circuit and hold court in each county annually (see Art. III, secs. 2 and 10). Ohio had only nine counties in 1802, but by 1835 there were seventy-five counties, more than eight times as many, and the circuit-riding requirement proved to be expensive and ultimately unworkable.[121] By 1850, when the second constitutional convention convened, the number of counties had increased to eighty-seven, one short of today's eighty-eight. And the Ohio Supreme Court could not handle the caseload resulting from the rapid growth of the state's population. Ohio had gone from a frontier state with 42,159 inhabitants in 1800, two years before statehood, to one of the largest states in the union by mid-century. In 1820, the state had approximately 581,000 inhabitants. By 1830, the population approached almost 938,000, and by 1850 there were nearly two million people living in Ohio.[122]

Judicial Review: A Major Constitutional Crisis

The 1802 Constitution, like the U.S. Constitution, did not include a provision expressly giving the judiciary the power to hold acts of the legislature unconstitutional. In 1803, the U.S. Supreme Court in *Marbury v. Madison* had recognized the doctrine of judicial review under the federal constitution but without using the phrase "judicial review." Even before *Marbury*, a number of state courts had implicitly or explicitly embraced the power of judicial review,[123] but Ohio (with its constitutional commitment to legislative supremacy and with a weak and dependent judiciary) seemed an unlikely place for judicial review to take root. Nonetheless, soon after statehood, a crisis of constitutional magnitude erupted over the power of the courts to hold statutes unconstitutional.[124]

The controversy involved an 1805 Act that gave justices of the peace jurisdiction in civil cases involving less than fifty dollars. In 1806, Judge Calvin Pease of the common pleas court for the Third Circuit (Jefferson and Belmont counties) declared the act void and in conflict with the right to a jury trial under Article VIII, section 8 of the Ohio Constitution. In 1807, the act was again challenged, and this time the case reached the Ohio Supreme Court. In *Rutherford*

---

[121] Commenting on the burdens of circuit-riding, in 1835 Justice John C. Wright of the Ohio Supreme Court wrote that the supreme court "now hold(s) Court in seventy-two counties each year, requiring twenty-two hundred and fifty miles travel! The number of cases on their trial docket, in 1834, was fourteen hundred and fifty-nine!" (quoted in Swisher, *Ohio Constitution Handbook*, xvii).

[122] *See* "Population of States and Counties of the United States: 1790–1990," U.S. Bureau of the Census, Department of Commerce, March 1996.

[123] *See* William E. Nelson, "Commentary: Changing Conceptions of Judicial Review: The Evolution of Constitutional Theory in the States, 1790–1860," 120 *U. Pa. L. Rev.* 1166 (1972): 1167–69.

[124] *See generally* Donald F. Melhorn Jr., *Lest We Be Marshall'd: Judicial Powers and Politics in Ohio, 1806–1812* (Akron: University of Akron Press, 2003) (hereinafter Melhorn, *Lest We Be Marshall'd*).

v. M'Fadden (1807),[125] Ohio Supreme Court Chief Justice Samuel Huntington and Supreme Court Justice George Tod in separate opinions ruled that the act was unconstitutional. In his opinion, Chief Justice Huntington declared that the judiciary "must [be] in compliance with their duty, compare the legislative act with the Constitution, and if they find such act contrary to the Constitution, or prohibited by it . . . [I]t is the duty of the court to declare it no law."[126] Relying on the Ohio Constitution as the basis for the decision, he acknowledged *Marbury* without expressly citing the case.

> I have considered this case as depending upon the construction of our own constitution and laws, without quoting the authority of other decisions, though well aware, that . . . I am supported by the judgment of the supreme court of the U.S. and of every court of the individual states, which has had the question before them, all of whom have decided that the courts of law possess the power of enquiring into the constitutionality of legislative acts.[127]

Justice Tod in his concurring opinion agreed that the act was unconstitutional. He explained that the principle "in our constitution [that courts may 'declare what the law was and is'] is founded in the wisest policy, as it raises an insuperable barrier against encroachments of the one branch on the rights and powers of another."[128]

The court's decision was not well received by the General Assembly, which passed a resolution on January 4, 1808, stating "[t]hat the judges of the state are not authorized by Constitution to set aside an act of the Legislature by declaring the same unconstitutional and void."[129] Soon after the gubernatorial election of 1808 in which Chief Justice Huntington, a Republican, became Ohio's third governor (and thus avoided impeachment), the House of Representatives approved articles of impeachment against Justice Tod and Judge Pease for "their exercise of the power of judicial nullification."[130] The Senate tried the judges in separate proceedings, but they both escaped conviction by votes of fifteen to nine, one vote short of the two-thirds majority required for conviction.[131]

Politically, the struggle over what became known as judicial review (but was generally referred to in nineteenth-century Ohio as the judicial veto or judicial nullification) split the Republican Party and helped elect Justice Huntington

---

[125] *Rutherford v. M'Fadden*, 71, 1807 (printed in Ervin H. Pollack, ed., *Ohio Unreported Judicial Decisions Prior to 1823* (1952), 102–3) (hereinafter Pollack, *Unreported Judicial Decisions*). *Rutherford*, Ohio's most important unpublished decision, is discussed at length in *State ex rel. Maurer v. Sheward* (1994).

[126] Ibid., 73.

[127] Ibid., 82–83.

[128] Ibid., 92.

[129] Randall and Ryan, *History of Ohio*, vol. V, 118.

[130] *See* Utter, *The Frontier State*, 45–51.

[131] *See* Pollack, *Unreported Judicial Decisions*, 102–3.

as governor over his Republican rival Thomas Worthington, who opposed judicial review.[132] The anticourt Republicans, however, continued to control the General Assembly after the impeachments, and notwithstanding the *M'Fadden* decision, the General Assembly extended the jurisdiction of justices of the peace in civil cases from fifty dollars to seventy dollars.[133] Finally, in 1810, the General Assembly passed the "sweeping resolution," which declared that all judicial offices carrying seven-year terms would be vacant even if the incumbent had taken office through an interim appointment to fill a vacancy. This resolution had the effect of "sweeping" from office judges who were then replaced by the General Assembly with judges more sympathetic to the majority of Republicans.[134] Nonetheless, "the practical defeat of the exponents of judicial review . . . was short-lived and merely had a delaying effect upon the application of the rule of judicial supremacy in the state courts."[135] And by 1815 the General Assembly appointed Judge Pease to the Supreme Court and Justice Tod to the position of presiding judge for the Third Circuit, thus vindicating both of them.[136]

During the second quarter of the nineteenth century—from 1825 to the adoption of the new constitution in 1851—the doctrine of judicial review became well established though rarely used.[137] In fact, in 1851, in one of his final opinions, Ohio Supreme Court Justice Peter Hitchcock, who served on the court for twenty-eight years between 1819 and 1851 (and was a delegate at the 1850–51 Convention), made the following observation about the power of the courts to declare laws unconstitutional:

> [T]his power seems now very generally conceded to the Courts; and I cannot well see how it could be otherwise. The constitution is the paramount law of the State. This instrument the Judges of the Court, as well as the other officers of the government, are sworn to maintain and defend. In it the powers of the several branches of the government are well defined. If the General Assembly, in the exercise of its legislative power, transcend the limits prescribed for it, such enactment is not a law, and no Court can, consistently with the oath imposed upon its members, enforce it as law.[138]

---

[132] William T. Utter, "Judicial Review in Early Ohio," XIV *Mississippi Valley Historical Review* 3 (1927): 13.

[133] *See* Pollack, *Unreported Judicial Decisions*, 102–3.

[134] *See* Utter, "Judicial Review in Early Ohio," 22–23.

[135] *See* Pollack, *Unreported Judicial Decisions*, 104.

[136] Ibid., 105.

[137] *See* J. H. Hixson, "The Judicial Veto in Ohio" (Master's thesis, Ohio State University, 1922), 23–24 (finding only seven reported decisions of the Ohio Supreme Court invalidating state laws in the first fifty years of statehood). *See also* Melhorn, *Lest We Be Marshall'd*, 182–83.

[138] *Griffith v. Commissioners of Crawford County* (1851) (Hitchcock, C. J., dissenting) (discussed in Melhorn, *Lest We Be Marshall'd*, 182–83).

And one year later, in 1852, in *Cincinnati, Wilmington & Zanesville RR Co. v. Clinton County Commissioners*, the court held that "[i]t is the right and duty of the judicial tribunals to determine, whether a legislative act drawn in question in a suit pending before them, is opposed to the constitution of the United States, or of this State, and if so found, to treat it as a nullity" (syllabus).

In explaining this decision, Justice Rufus P. Ranney, who served on the Ohio Supreme Court under both the 1802 and 1851 Constitutions, stated as follows:

> How any doubt could ever have been entertained upon this subject, is matter of no little astonishment; and yet the history of our own State shows, that the power was, at one time, not only doubted, but positively denied; and judges, for a fearless discharge of this duty, were subjected to impeachment by the house of representatives.
>
> * * *
>
> To adjudicate upon, and protect these rights and interests [of individual citizens], constitute the whole business of the judicial department. Each judge before he is permitted to enter upon so important a duty is required to bind his conscience by a solemn oath to support these constitutions. After all this, when he is clearly convinced, their provisions have been violated, and the rights of the individual secured by them, have been invaded by a legislative enactment, he has but one of two courses to pursue–either to regard his oath, vindicate the fundamental law, and protect the rights of the individual citizen, or to give effect to an act of usurped authority. In such case, it cannot be doubtful where the path of duty leads. The latter alternative can only be followed, when we are to nullify all constitutional guaranties, and proclaim the legislative body, like the British Parliament, omnipotent.[139]

And in 1854, in *Miller v. State*, the court reiterated its commitment to judicial review when it made the following observation:

> A statute may, upon its face, be repugnant to the constitution, and therefore void, no matter how regular may have been the steps by which it was enacted. And although the power was at one time very seriously denied, yet it is no longer to be doubted that the courts are bound to treat such a statute as a mere nullity.[140]

Notwithstanding these statements in support of judicial review, the court's reluctance to exercise judicial review during the first half of the century would change in the second half of the nineteenth century and in the years leading to the 1912 Constitutional Convention.

---

[139] *Cincinnati, Wilmington & Zanesville RR Co. v. Clinton County Commissioners* (1852), 81–82.

[140] *Miller v. State* (1854).

■ OHIO'S SECOND CONSTITUTION

The Campaign to Replace the Constitution of 1802

A major weakness of the 1802 Constitution was the difficulty of amending the document; as Randolph C. Downes, one of Ohio's foremost historians, stated, "it was practically unamendable."[141]

The 1802 Constitution provided that the voters had "at all times a complete power to alter, reform or abolish their government, whenever they may deem necessary" (Art. VIII, sec. 1). But short of revolution or what has been called a "circumvention convention,"[142] the only provision on structured constitutional change was the section permitting the General Assembly to propose a convention to the voters by vote of two-thirds of the members in each house of the General Assembly. The voters would then have to approve the proposal to hold a constitutional convention by a majority of those voting for members of the state House of Representatives (1802 Const., Art. VII, sec. 5).

Despite the flaws with the 1802 Constitution, there was little interest in calling a constitutional convention following the defeat of the convention call in 1819 by a vote of 29,315 to 6,987, see Appendix A, an action one modern commentator characterized as reflecting continued satisfaction with the constitution.[143]

The movement to revise the constitution picked up support following the Panic of 1837, which was popularly blamed on the General Assembly's banking and fiscal policies. One of the first calls for a convention came from Ohio historian Caleb Atwater. In his influential work, *History of the State of Ohio*, published in 1838, Atwater (who had served in the General Assembly) noted that the principal weakness of the 1802 Constitution was the extreme power it had given to the legislature and recommended specific changes to constrain legislative power.[144]

Besides the legislature's disastrous economic policies and the continuing problems with the judiciary, the public's disgust with gerrymandering contributed to the support for a call for a constitutional convention. During the 1840s, the Whigs and Jacksonian Democrats, the two major parties, were evenly split, and the party in power spent much of the legislative session engineering the next election.[145]

Popular support for a convention gained momentum in 1843, when Ohio Governor Wilson Shannon publicly called for a convention. Nonetheless, in the following year a resolution calling for a constitutional convention failed to

---

[141] Downes, "Ohio's Second Constitution," 71.

[142] *See* Parkinson, "Antebellum State Constitution-Making," 144.

[143] Ibid., 145.

[144] Atwater, *History of the State of Ohio*, 172–74; *see also* McDonald, "A Study in Constitution Making," 68–69.

[145] *See* Downes, "Ohio's Second Constitution," 75–76.

receive the required two-thirds vote of each house, as did subsequent resolutions in 1846 and 1847,[146] but support for a convention continued to grow.

During the 1840s, "[c]onstitutional reform quickly became the leading topic of state politics."[147] And the division over calling a convention split along party lines. The Democrats supported a convention, and the Democratic press "derided the 1802 constitution [and] reiterated standard tenets of [Jefferson's] generational revision theory."[148] The more conservative Whigs, on the other hand, opposed a convention call, and their press derided the Democrats as radicals.[149]

Ultimately, it took not only the financial and political crises that began in the late 1830s, but also the threat of a circumvention convention and a reapportionment fight in Hamilton County in the 1840s to break the political stalemate.[150]

By 1849 the political situation had changed, and with the support of Whig Governor William Bebb and the Free Soil Party, a new political party committed to the abolition of slavery, the General Assembly on March 23, 1849, approved almost unanimously a resolution to put the question of holding a constitutional convention on the fall ballot.[151]

Campaign on the Constitutional Call

The issues before the voters on the convention call had been framed, at least in part, by the work of the controversial Samuel Medary. Best known in the 1860s for his activities as a Peace Democrat, as a fierce opponent of President Lincoln's conduct of the Civil War, as the publisher of the controversial antiwar newspaper, *Crisis,* and for his indictment in 1864 for conspiracy against the federal government,[152] early in his career Medary had been deeply engaged in Ohio politics. A Jacksonian Democrat, he served single terms in both the Ohio Senate and the Ohio House in the 1830s, and in 1838 he became editor of the *Ohio Statesman,* the key Democratic newspaper.

Medary was a zealous supporter of constitutional revision for Ohio. After the vote to put a constitutional call on the ballot, he announced his plan to publish twenty-six weekly pamphlets, suitable for binding, titled *The New Constitution.*[153] True to this commitment, he published weekly pamphlets devoted to

[146] McDonald, "A Study in Constitution Making," 70.

[147] Parkinson, "Antebellum State Constitution-Making," 152.

[148] Ibid., 151.

[149] Ibid., 158–59.

[150] *See* ibid., 153–62.

[151] *See* McDonald, "A Study in Constitution Making," 71.

[152] *See* Reed W. Smith, *Samuel Medary & the Crisis: Testing the Limits of Press Freedom* (Columbus: The Ohio State University Press, 1995), 1–3.

[153] Samuel Medary, *Prospectus of the New Constitution,* 1 *New Const.* 1 (1849).

constitutional revision from May 5, 1849, to November 17, 1849.[154] Strongly criticizing the Ohio Constitution and the abuses of the General Assembly and freely sharing stories about constitutional revision in other states, Medary sought to reassure Ohioans who feared the changes that a new constitution might introduce. His "emphasis was a response to Whig fears of untried, drastic Democratic ideas. He sought to show that the revision of the Ohio Constitution would not necessarily bring chaos and an end to 'law and order.'"[155]

In fact, newspapers on each side of the issue had tried to influence the electorate before the October general election.[156] On the Democratic side, the *Ohio Statesman* was the most vocal supporter of a constitutional convention. Its special weekly paper supported a new constitution and promoted such reforms as universal, white manhood suffrage, judicial reform, the election of all government officials, and limitations on state debt.[157] On the other side, the leading Whig paper, the *Ohio State Journal*, urged the voters to defeat the call for a convention.[158]

The campaign culminated on October 9, 1849, in an overwhelming victory of 145,698 to 51,161 in support of a constitutional convention. See Appendix A. In February 1850, the General Assembly passed an act calling for the election of delegates in April and set the date for convening the convention for the first Monday in May 1850.[159]

The movement for constitutional change in Ohio was part of the "orgy of nineteenth century constitution-making" that swept the country.[160] Many of the states that held conventions to revise their constitutions had economic and structural problems similar to those in Ohio, and the people often blamed their legislatures for the problems that had result from internal improvements and bank failures.[161]

The Constitutional Convention of 1850–51

Ohio's second constitutional convention convened in Columbus on May 6, 1850. In contrast to the first convention, which consisted of 35 delegates, the second convention had 108 delegates, 64 Democrats, 41 Whigs, and 3 Free-Soilers.[162] The convention elected William Medill of Fairfield County as

---

154 Samuel Medary, *The End of the Volume—To the Friends of Constitutional Reform,* 1 *New Const.* 401 (1849).

155 Parkinson, "Antebellum State Constitution-Making," 156–57.

156 Ibid., 71–72.

157 Ibid., 72–73.

158 Ibid., 72.

159 Laws of Ohio, vol. 48, p. 19 (February 11, 1850).

160 G. Alan Tarr, *Understanding State Constitutions* (Princeton: Princeton University Press, 1998), 97.

161 *See generally* ibid., 111–13.

162 *See* Isaac Franklin Patterson, *The Constitutions of Ohio: Amendments and Proposed Amendments* (Cleveland: Arthur H. Clark, 1912), 109 (hereinafter Patterson, *The Constitutions of Ohio*). Patterson

president and W. H. Gill of Guernsey County as secretary. Also in contrast to the first convention, the second convention took much longer to complete its work, 163 days compared to less than a month. Owing to a cholera epidemic, the convention adjourned on July 9, 1850, and reconvened in Cincinnati on December 2, 1850, where the rest of the official business took place until the document was completed in March 1851.[163]

Among the delegates to the 1850–51 Convention, forty-three were lawyers, thirty were farmers, and eight were physicians.[164] The remainder included businessmen, publishers, and members of the trades. Fifteen of the delegates were judges, and more than half had served in Congress or the General Assembly. The convention included a number of prominent men from both parties. On the Democratic side, some of the most notable included: William Medill, president of the convention, who served in the General Assembly, Congress, and as governor; Rufus P. Ranney, who the General Assembly appointed to the Ohio Supreme Court under the 1802 Constitution on March 17, 1851, one week after the 1850–51 Convention adjourned and three months before the new constitution became effective (and who was one of five justices elected to the court in 1851 under the new constitution);[165] William Groesbeck, a well-known lawyer who later defended President Andrew Johnson at his impeachment trial; and Charles Reemelin, a German-born merchant who was a member of the legislature and one of the most radical Democrats. On the Whig side, Peter Hitchcock served as state senator and as state Supreme Court justice for twenty-years years; Joseph Vance was Ohio's first Whig governor; and Henry Stanbery, who served as Ohio's first attorney general, as attorney general of the United States, and with William Grosbeck as counsel for President Andrew Johnson during the latter's impeachment trial.[166]

The convention also had its share of delegates who, in the words of historian C. B. Galbreath, "would probably not have recognized a state constitution had it come walking up the principal street of the capital city."[167] The delegates spent much of the early days of the convention on a "silly discussion" over the form of the oath to be taken by the delegates, a dispute over inviting clergy to offer a prayer, and a partisan debate over the hiring of a printer.[168]

---

lists sixty-eight Democrats, but this apparently includes four who were chosen to replace delegates who had resigned.

[163] *See* McDonald, "A Study in Constitution Making," 98; Patterson, *The Constitutions of Ohio*, 109.

[164] Randall and Ryan, *History of Ohio*, vol. IV, 112.

[165] For a legal and political biography of Justice Ranney, who played a major role at the convention on multiple issues, *see* David M. Gold, *The Jacksonian Conservatism of Rufus P. Ranney* (Athens: Ohio University Press, 2017).

[166] *See* McDonald, "A Study in Constitution Making," 75–84 discussing ("The Personnel of the Convention").

[167] C. B. Galbreath, *Constitutional Conventions of Ohio* (Columbus: Stoneman Press, 1911), 23–24.

[168] Ibid., 24–25; *see also* Patterson, *The Constitutions of Ohio*, 33.

Political differences between Whigs and Democrats surfaced early and led to increasingly partisan debates by the end of the convention. In general, the Whigs, who either opposed or at best half-heartedly supported the convention, favored moderate changes to the existing constitution.[169] The Democrats, who were the driving force behind the convention, supported broad reforms and ultimately a new constitution. Economic and financial issues were at the center of the dispute. Jacksonians dominated the Democratic Party, and they shared a general distrust of corporations, especially banks. They were willing to restrict the legislature's power over fiscal matters and special legislation that benefited corporations, but they also wanted to give the legislature an unqualified power to repeal special privileges and benefits granted to corporations. The more radical antibank Democrats, or "Locofocos," who controlled a majority of the party, also wanted to ban all banks and prohibit the circulation of paper money. The Whig Party, on the other hand, was aligned with powerful financial and business interests, and most Whigs defended the existing economic order. Whigs fought especially hard against the repeal of special benefits for corporations. They considered corporate charters to be inviolable contracts that could not be abridged by legislative action.[170]

The Democrats had a strong majority and had they been united as a party they could have forced whatever reforms they wanted through the convention. A number of conservative Democrats, however, joined Whigs to defeat the more radical economic proposals supported by a majority of their party.[171] Nonetheless, there was enough support among Democrats (and some Whigs) for Democrats to achieve most of their economic goals, including constitutional provisions restricting the power of the legislature to tax, to incur debt, and to pass special legislation. And one prominent historian has concluded that the prohibition on state debt was "a victory for doctrinaire opponents of the active state."[172]

Elections, Suffrage, and the Status of African Americans

The views of former president Andrew Jackson also influenced the debate on elections and suffrage. The Jacksonian principle of popular democracy[173] led to a general agreement on the need to provide for the election of judges and other

[169] McDonald, "A Study in Constitution Making," 81.

[170] *See generally* Eugene H. Roseboom, "The Civil War Era: 1850–1873," in Carl Wittke, ed., *The History of the State of Ohio*, vol. IV (Columbus: Ohio State Archaeological and Historical Society, 1944), 124–34.

[171] McDonald, "A Study in Constitution Making," 81.

[172] Harry N. Scheiber, *Ohio Canal Era* (Athens: Ohio University Press, 1968), 298.

[173] *See generally* Arthur M. Schlesinger Jr., *The Age of Jackson* (Boston: Little, Brown, and Company, 1945).

government officials and to expand voting rights by eliminating the tax requirement on voting.

While the delegates supported universal manhood suffrage for white males, they bitterly debated the status of African Americans. Slavery was not at issue, but suffrage and equal rights for African Americans aroused some of the strongest emotions at the convention. Some delegates even objected to the receipt of petitions supporting African-American rights, especially petitions from African Americans themselves. William Sawyer of Auglaize County, the most outspoken opponent of African American rights, found such petitions "revolting" and refused to "permit even his fellow citizens to petition that negroes shall be entitled to all of the privileges and immunities of white men, without raising his voice against it."[174] Sawyer believed that blacks were an inferior race, that slavery had benefited blacks, and that the principle espoused in the Declaration of Independence that all men were created equal applied only to the Anglo-Saxon race.[175] He also predicted "bloodshed" and "persecution" if African Americans were permitted to vote.[176] Another delegate, Simeon Nash of Gallia County, argued that given the public sentiment the delegates risked having the constitution defeated by the voters if they proposed a constitutional amendment allowing African Americans to vote.[177] By a final vote of seventy-five to thirteen, the delegates rejected the proposal to remove the word "white" from the constitution with all of the votes in favor of African American suffrage coming from the Western Reserve.[178]

Sawyer's extreme views may not have been shared by a majority of delegates, but there is no question that there was strong anti-black sentiment at the convention and in many parts of the state. The convention received petitions not only opposing suffrage and equal rights for blacks but also supporting a ban on black immigration into Ohio and funds for the colonization of blacks to create, in effect, an "Ohio in Africa."[179] James Worthington, one of the delegates and the son of former governor Thomas Worthington, believed that "at the time of the Revolution there was less prejudice against the black race than there is at present" and in the future it was likely that "the longer the two races occupy the same soil, the greater will be their revulsion and the stronger the prejudice."[180]

Most of the opposition to African-American rights came from the southern counties along the Ohio River, although there were also strong anti-black

[174] *Report of the Debates and Proceedings of the Convention for the Revision of the Constitution of the State of Ohio, 1850–51*, vol. 1 (1851), 31, 56 (hereinafter *1850–51 Debates*).

[175] Ibid., vol. 1, 56–57.

[176] Ibid., vol. 2, 638; Frank U. Quillin, *The Color Line in Ohio: A History of Race Prejudice in a Typical Northern State* (New York: Negro Universities Press, 1913), 79.

[177] *1850–51 Debates*, vol. 2, 553; Quillin, *The Color Line in Ohio*, 80–81.

[178] 1850–51 *Debates*, vol. 2, 554, 556; Quillin, *The Color Line in Ohio*, 81.

[179] Terzian, "Ohio's Constitutions," 372–73.

[180] *1850–51 Debates*, vol. 2, 639.

feelings in the western part of the state.[181] In contrast, the greatest support for African-American rights came from the Western Reserve. Norton Townshend, S. J. Andrews, and Reuben Hitchcock, delegates from Lorain and Cuyahoga counties, respectively, advocated the removal of racial discrimination in voting by deleting the word "white" from the suffrage section. Townshend introduced the amendment to remove the word "white" and argued forcefully that to deny African Americans the right to vote was "unjust," "anti-democratic," and "impolitic."[182] And Hitchcock maintained that including the word "white" in the constitution violated the equality of men, "that great principle upon which our government is based," and was "hostile to everything that elevates and dignifies the name of man."[183]

The proposal to remove the word "white" from the section on voter qualifications failed by a vote of sixty-six to twelve.[184] Following this vote, James Taylor of Erie County moved to amend the section by allowing the General Assembly "to extend the right of suffrage to inhabitants of this State not hereby qualified as electors." Taylor's amendment was defeated sixty-eight to eleven.[185] Thus, the convention ensured not only that suffrage would continue to be limited to whites but that the General Assembly could do nothing about it. African Americans, however, would be counted for the purpose of apportionment.[186]

The delegates also rejected a motion to remove the word "white" from the article on the militia by a vote of sixty-six to twenty-two.[187] Thus, the state militia would continue to consist only of white males. A vote to insert the word "white" before "children" in the section requiring the General Assembly to "secure a thorough and efficient system of common schools, free to all children of the State" apparently passed but would have no effect since the delegates later voted to delete all language in the section after the phrase "common schools."[188] The delegates, however, rejected the amendments to ban immigration and to support the colonization of African Americans, although these amendments received more votes than the amendment for African-American suffrage. As

---

[181] *See* Terzian, "Effusions of Folly," 194–99.

[182] *1850–51 Debates*, vol. 2, 550–52; *see also* Terzian, "Ohio's Constitutions," 373; Terzian, "Effusions of Folly," 206–9.

[183] *1850–51 Debates*, vol. 2, 552.

[184] Terzian, "Effusions of Folly," 210. The final vote was seventy-five to thirteen; ten members were absent during the original vote, and later nine of them cast their vote against African-American suffrage. Ibid.

[185] *1850–51 Debates*, vol. 2, 555–56.

[186] In eliminating the language in Art. I, sec. 2, which had based apportionment for seats in the General Assembly on a population count of "white male inhabitants," the 1851 Constitution extended greater representation to those areas of the state where more African Americans lived but where there was greater prejudice against African American. *See* Quillin, *The Color Line in Ohio*, 82.

[187] *1850–51 Debates*, vol. 2, 350.

[188] *See* Quillin, *The Color Line in Ohio*, 83–84.

with suffrage, immigration and colonization generated heated debates.[189] The amendment to ban immigration met with so much opposition, including from opponents of African-American rights who pointed out that such a ban had been tried under the Black Laws for forty years and failed and would likely violate the U.S. Constitution, that it was withdrawn. In its place, proponents of the antiimmigration policy moved to add a section allowing the legislature to discourage the immigration of blacks "consistent with the Constitution of the United States." This motion failed by a vote of fifty-eight to thirty-nine.[190] Once it was recognized that there would be no ban on immigration, the amendment to finance the colonization of blacks lost supporters, and colonization failed by a vote of seventy-one to twenty-six.[191]

Compared to the debate on African-American suffrage, there was hardly any debate on women's suffrage at the convention, but the proposal for women's suffrage met the same fate. Notwithstanding an active women's suffrage movement outside the convention and the receipt of petitions signed by hundreds of women, the delegates overwhelming rejected an amendment to remove the word "male" by a vote of seventy-two to seven with the only favorable votes coming from the Western Reserve delegation.[192]

Clearly, the sentiment of the convention as a whole was not disposed toward racial or gender equality. Only white males were entitled to vote under the 1802 Constitution, and proposals to remove the words "white" and "male" from the constitution convention were rejected by the delegates. See Commentary, Article V, section 1. In addition, at the time of the 1850–51 Convention, Ohio schools were segregated by race, and a proposal was introduced to limit public education to white children. See Commentary, Article VI, section 2. Even more drastic proposals were offered, including amendments to restrict African-American immigration into Ohio, to "colonize" African Americans in Ohio, and to create a new state for them in Africa.[193] The delegates rejected these proposals,[194] but the vehemence with which they were debated suggests the extent of the opposition to granting African Americans equal rights.

The Liquor Question

Controversy concerning the licensing of liquor had been part of the constitutional debate in Ohio since the early nineteenth century. At common law the traffic in intoxicating liquors was a lawful business, *Baker v. Beckwith* (1876),

---

[189] *See* Terzian, "Effusions of Folly," 212–24.

[190] *1850–51 Debates*, vol. 2, 604.

[191] Ibid., vol. 2, 598, 605.

[192] *1850–51 Debates*, vol. 2, 555; *see also* Terzian, "Effusions of Folly," 210–12.

[193] *See 1850–51 Debates*, vol. 2, 597–604; *see also* Terzian, "Effusions of Folly," 212–22.

[194] *1850–51 Debates*, vol. 2, 604–5.

but by the middle of the nineteenth century, the temperance issue became part of the debate on the new constitution. To avoid the defeat of the new constitution by those opposed to the licensing of liquor, the delegates proposed that a separate amendment to prohibit the licensing of liquor be submitted to the voters along with the proposed 1851 Constitution.[195] Through what one commentator characterized as a "masterpiece of obfuscation," the schedule to the 1851 Constitution required a separate vote on the licensing of liquor with a "no license" vote being in favor of a constitutional prohibition on the granting of licenses.[196]

Other Reforms

In addition to rejecting suffrage for African Americans and women, the delegates rejected other reforms, including proposals to ban capital punishment and to prevent a home from being taken by creditors. Both these proposals, however, garnered more votes than either African-American or women's suffrage. The proposal to abolish capital punishment would have added the following section to the constitution: "Human life shall ever be held inviolate. The true object of punishment being, in addition to the security of society, to reform and not to exterminate mankind; human life shall never be taken as a punishment for crime, but the highest punishment inflicted for crime shall be imprisonment during life in the state penitentiary."[197] But the delegates tabled indefinitely this proposal, thus effectively defeating it, though it did receive a significant number of favorable votes.[198] The proposal guaranteeing the right to a home, introduced by J. McCormick of Adams County, provided that: "Each family is entitled to become and be possessed of a home, which shall be exempt from sale, for the payment of debts or discharge of liabilities arising from contract." McCormick's amendment failed by a vote of sixty to thirty-one.[199]

Approval by the Electorate

On March 10, 1851, the convention adjourned. Unlike the first convention, not all delegates supported the final document. The new constitution passed by a vote of seventy-nine to fourteen, with thirteen Whigs and one Free-Soiler voting against it.[200] Also, in contrast to the decision of the 1802 Convention and not

[195] The proposal, sec. 18 of the schedule to the 1851 Constitution, provided that "[n]o license to traffic in intoxicating liquors shall hereafter be granted in this state; but the general assembly may by law provide against evils resulting therefrom."

[196] Swisher, *Ohio Constitution Handbook*, xxvii.

[197] *1850–51 Debates*, vol. 2, 20.

[198] Ibid., vol. 2, 34.

[199] Ibid., vol. 2, 471, 475.

[200] Ibid., vol. 2, 870.

required to do so by the 1802 Constitution, the 1850–51 Convention decided to submit the new constitution to the people for approval.[201] The delegates also agreed to submit the question of whether the General Assembly could license the traffic in intoxicating liquor to the voters on a separate ballot. The liquor question was one of the most divisive at the convention. More than 20,000 Ohioans had signed petitions opposed to the traffic in liquor. The delegates opposed to trafficking in liquor, however, were divided between those who favored licensing so that it could be regulated and those who supported an outright ban and opposed licensing because they believed it made liquor, a social evil, respectable.[202]

On June 17, 1851, the Ohio electorate voted on whether to support the new constitution. As with the vote leading to the convention, the campaign and vote for ratification generally followed party lines. Democrats supported the constitution, while most Whigs and most of the Whig press opposed it. The voters approved the new constitution by a close vote of 125,564 to 109, 276.[203] The new constitution went into effect on September 1, 1851, and it remains the fundamental law of Ohio.

On a separate liquor licensing ballot a majority of the voters (113,237 to 104,255) voted "no," thereby (under the strange wording of the proposition) resulting in the approval by a narrow vote of an amendment providing that "[n]o license to traffic in intoxicating liquors shall hereafter be granted in this state; but the general assembly may by law provide against evils resulting therefrom." Thus, the voters prohibited the granting of licenses to traffic in intoxicating liquors.[204]

The Ohio Constitution of 1851

The 1850–51 Convention produced a document radically different form Ohio's first constitution. The 1851 Constitution contains almost 3,182 more words than the 8-article, 6,265-word 1802 Constitution, thus increasing the word count to 9,447 words[205] and the number of articles to 16.[206] The new articles

---

[201] After the approval of a convention by the electorate, the General Assembly as part of the legislation organizing the convention had adopted a statute requiring that the new constitution be submitted to the voters for their adoption or rejection, Laws of Ohio, vol. 48, p. 29, sec. 7 (February 22, 1850), a provision that was followed but that may not have been binding on the convention. *See* McDonald, "A Study in Constitution Making," 74.

[202] Ibid., 190–92.

[203] Patterson, *The Constitutions of Ohio*, 109.

[204] Schedule, 1851 Ohio Constitution.

[205] Relying on Patterson, *The Constitutions of Ohio*, 38, the first edition of this book reported that the number of words in the 1802 Constitution was 3,800 and the number in the 1851 Constitution was 6,700. Subsequent research, however, has revealed that the numbers were significantly higher. *See* Hern, "A Statistical Approach to Ohio's Constitutional History."

[206] Patterson, *The Constitutions of Ohio*, 38. The 1802 Constitution had eight articles. The 1851 Constitution dropped Art. VI on Civil Officers and added nine new articles. The current nineteen

dealt with education (Art. VI), public institutions (Art. VI), public debt and public works (Art. VIII), county and township organizations (Art. X), apportionment (Art. XI), finance and taxation (Art. XII), corporations (Art. XIII), jurisprudence (Art. XIV), and amendments (Art. XVI). The 1850–51 Convention also reordered the document by bringing the Bill of Rights, which was the final article in the 1802 Constitution, to the beginning of the new constitution.

The most sweeping changes to the 1802 Constitution involved the powers of the General Assembly. The 1802 Constitution reflected a view of the legislature as the embodiment of popular democracy and ideally as subject to as few restrictions as necessary to implement the public will. Over the course of five decades under the first constitution, however, the people began to see the legislature as the source of many, if not most, of the problems of government, and the new constitution reflected this general distrust of legislative power.

The 1851 Constitution curtailed legislative power in three principal ways. First, the new constitution took the appointment power away from the General Assembly. All key executive branch officers became elected officials, as did all judges.

Second, in a victory for Jacksonian Democrats, the 1851 Constitution contained a number of provisions limiting the power of the legislature to enact economic and special legislation. Article I, section 2 prohibited the General Assembly from granting special privileges and immunities that could not be altered or repealed. Article XIII, on corporations, contained a number of sections limiting the legislature's power to grant special powers and privileges to corporations. Section 1 of that article provided that the legislature "shall pass no special act conferring special corporate powers." Section 2 required corporations to be formed under the general laws, thereby effectively prohibiting the incorporation of private and municipal corporations by special acts. Section 3 imposed personal liability on stockholders, satisfying one of the main objectives of the Democratic agenda. Section 4 subjected corporations to the same taxation as individuals, and Section 6 prohibited the General Assembly from enacting laws "authorizing associations with banking powers" without a referendum. The article on finance and taxation, Article XII, required taxation by uniform rule, which meant that all property had to be assessed at its true value in money, and required the General Assembly to pass laws taxing banks.

Article VIII, on public debt and public works, addressed problems associated with the state debt. Article VIII limited the legislature's plenary power to incur debt and to finance internal improvement projects. Sections 1 through 3 of Article VIII set a maximum limit of $750,000 on the total amount of debt the state could carry annually from deficits or revenue failures except in times of emergency. Other provisions of Article VIII established a sinking fund to

articles include one article added in 1905 (Art. XVII, elections), one article added in 1912 (Art. XVIII, municipal corporations), and one article added in 2018 (Art. XIX, congressional redistricting).

pay off the existing state debt and prohibited the state from financing or entering into joint ventures with private corporations. Section 7 of Article XII contained perhaps the most drastic response to the debt resulting from internal improvements. It prohibited the General Assembly from incurring any debt for internal improvements.

Third, the 1851 Constitution limited the power of the legislature to apportion house and senate districts. Article XI, on apportionment, addressed the problems of gerrymandering by establishing a system of districting seats for the General Assembly based on county lines and a "population ratio" calculated by taking the state's population, as determined every ten years by the national census, and dividing by one hundred. The result was an apportionment formula that drastically limited the power of the majority party to draw legislative districts. Article XI, however, did not apply to U.S. congressional districts and thus gerrymandering at that level continued. The new constitution also dealt a serious blow to the system of political patronage by limiting the legislature's power to form new counties and thus create new offices. Article II, section 30 required new counties to contain at least 400 square miles and required the consent of the residents of existing counties before a new county could be formed.

In addition to these restrictions on legislative power, the new constitution required that compensation for legislators be fixed by law to eliminate the practice of prolonging legislative sessions to increase compensation. Finally, the new constitution established biennial sessions for both houses of the General Assembly to cut down on needless legislation that was often rushed through at the end of each legislative session.[207]

The 1851 Constitution also brought significant changes to the judicial branch. These changes addressed the inefficiency of the court system, especially at the Supreme Court level, and sought to make the judiciary independent of the legislature.

To alleviate the backlog of cases, the new constitution restructured the judiciary. It vested the judicial power of the state in a Supreme Court, district courts, courts of common pleas, probate courts, justices of the peace, and other inferior courts that the General Assembly could create. The new constitution established a five-judge Supreme Court with original jurisdiction limited to habeas corpus proceedings and special writs and with appellate jurisdiction "as may be provided by law" (Art. IV, sec. 2). In effect, this provision made the Supreme Court primarily a court of final review.

---

[207] The adoption of biennial sessions did not sit well with legislators. Beginning in 1855, the General Assembly adjourned for the entire second session, and in 1857 and 1859 proposed constitutional amendments to allow for annual sessions. Although the voters did not approve these amendments, the General Assembly continued its practice of adjourning after the first session until 1895. *See* Patterson, *The Constitutions of Ohio*, 22, 162, 169.

The new constitution also divided the state into nine common pleas districts and created, for the first time, intermediate appellate courts called "district courts." These intermediate appellate courts consisted of one Supreme Court judge and the judges of the courts of common pleas within the district, with a quorum consisting of any three judges. One district court was assigned to each of the nine common pleas districts and each exercised appellate jurisdiction over the decisions of the courts of common pleas. In addition, the constitution mandated the creation of a probate court for each county to hear probate matters that were previously heard in the common pleas courts.

The most important change in the judicial article removed judicial selection from the General Assembly by providing for the at-large election of Supreme Court justices. The decision to have judges elected rather than appointed followed the trend of most states that were revising their constitutions at that time.[208] The election of judges, however, did not come without debate. The opponents of an elective system argued that such a system would destroy any sense of merit and would lead to the election of "sons of the wealthy and well-born" who were politically connected.[209] Other delegates argued that Supreme Court justices should be elected by district rather than by the state at large. Their fear was that the justices would all be elected from the party that had control of the state, but ultimately, the proponents of statewide elections prevailed.[210]

Despite these changes, the constitution did not solve all the problems confronting the judiciary. While the popular election of judges insulated the judiciary from the legislature, it did not diminish the influence of political parties. The constitution allowed judges to be nominated by party caucuses or conventions and to run for election on party tickets.[211] The creation of intermediate appellate courts—the district courts—failed to stem the increasing docket of the Supreme Court or to lessen the court's burdens and became "only a halting place for cases on their way from the Common Pleas Court to the Supreme Court."[212] Moreover, the new constitution still required Supreme Court justices to ride circuit as district court judges since district courts were required to hold court in at least three places in their respective districts each year (1851 Const. Art. IV, sec. 5). The situation worsened to the point that the General Assembly in 1857 proposed a constitutional amendment that would have eliminated the requirement that Supreme Court justices sit as district court judges. When this amendment failed, the Supreme Court simply ignored the

208 *See* Francis R. Aumann, "The Selection, Tenure, Retirement and Compensation of Judges in Ohio," 5 *U. Cin. L. Rev.* 408 (1931): 410 n. 5.

209 *1850–51 Debates*, vol. 2, 353; *see* Frederick Woodbridge, "A History of Separation of Powers in Ohio: A Study in Administrative Law," 13 *U. Cin. L. Rev.* 191 (1939): 223–24.

210 *1850–51 Debates*, vol. 1, 585.

211 Aumann, "The Selection of Judges," 411–12.

212 Patterson, *The Constitutions of Ohio*, 25.

constitutional provision, upholding, without discussion, the constitutionality of a district court without a Supreme Court justice. *King v. Safford* (1869).[213]

The 1851 Constitution added the offices of lieutenant governor, auditor, treasurer, and attorney general to the executive branch, which under the first constitution consisted only of the governor and the secretary of state, but the executive branch remained the weakest of the three branches. There was some debate over giving the governor veto power, including a proposal that would have allowed the legislature to override a veto by a simple majority vote, but this was more of an attempt to prevent "hasty and ill-considered legislation" rather than to make the executive a coequal branch of government.[214] The attitude against a powerful executive in 1851 had changed only slightly since 1802. One delegate remarked that even a qualified veto would jeopardize the adoption of the new constitution. In the end, the opponents of an executive veto prevailed, and the office of the governor remained basically the same.[215]

The Bill of Rights generated little debate at the 1850–51 Convention. Most of the provisions were adopted by the convention with little or no change from the committee report. One exception was the second part of Article I, section 2, concerning the power of the legislature to amend or repeal special privileges and immunities. The debate on that provision, which implicated corporate charters, lasted more than a month. See Commentary, Article I, section 2.

Overall, the new constitution reorganized the Bill of Rights and reworded many of its provisions but made only a few substantive changes. Imprisonment for debt was restricted to cases involving fraud, and juries were required to determine compensation in cases where property was taken for public use. In addition, the 1851 Constitution replaced the prohibition against discriminating against the poor in education (1802 Const., Art. VIII, sec. 25), see Commentary, Article VI, with a new article on education requiring the state to establish "a thorough and efficient system of common schools" (Art. VI, sec. 2).

Article XVI of the new constitution addressed the ways to amend the constitution. The 1802 Constitution could only be amended through a constitutional convention recommended by two-thirds of the members of the General Assembly and approved by a majority of all electors voting at the election. The new constitution retained the ability to use a constitutional convention to "revise, amend, or change" the constitution, but it included three significant changes in the process of proposing and approving constitutional amendments.

First, the new constitution required that the question of whether to hold a constitutional convention be submitted to the voters every twenty years. Second, the new constitution gave the General Assembly the power to propose

---

[213] *See* Warren Cunningham, "The Judiciary in Ohio," 20 *U. Cin. L. Rev.* 239 (1951): 246.

[214] *1850–51 Debates*, vol. 2, 292–93; *see also* ibid., vol. 1, 310–11; McDonald, "A Study in Constitution Making," 133–34.

[215] *1850–51 Debates*, vol. 2, 292–93.

constitutional amendments through a three-fifths vote. Third, unlike the policies under the 1802 Constitution, amendments to the 1851 Constitution and proposed new constitutions had to be approved by the electorate. The new constitution, however, provided that amendments proposed by a constitutional convention would take effect if approved by a majority of those voting on the particular amendment. But amendments proposed by the General Assembly would become effective only if approved by a majority of those voting at the election rather than a simple majority of those voting on the proposition itself. This supermajority requirement for amendments proposed by the General Assembly became a serious limitation on constitutional revision and, along with the flawed judicial article, led to the call for a third constitutional convention in 1871.

■ THE 1873–74 CONSTITUTIONAL CONVENTION

Various interests converged in 1871 for the twenty-year vote on the question of holding a convention.[216] Both the liquor industry and the temperance movement wanted to revisit the liquor question. Corporate interests favored an end to unlimited shareholder liability, and railroad companies sought special privileges. Opponents of corporate power wanted stricter regulations on corporations and railroads. The women's suffrage movement lobbied to have the elective franchise opened, and the legal profession (with public support) pushed for changes to the judicial article.[217]

The liquor issue had not been resolved by the 1851 Constitution's prohibition on the granting of licenses to traffic in intoxicating liquors. The adopted provision did not constitute either a prohibition on liquor or liquor trafficking, but it did give the General Assembly broad regulatory power. Thus, in *Miller v. State* (1854), the Ohio Supreme Court upheld a statute making criminal the sale of intoxicating liquors to be drunk at the place where sold, the sale to minors, and the sale to persons intoxicated, and making the places where intoxicating liquor is sold in violation of the act a common nuisance to be shut up and abated. Declining to reach the issue of whether the legislature can wholly prohibit traffic in intoxicating liquors, the court made clear that both section 9 and the police power independently supported the power to regulate intoxicating liquors.

The need to revise the judicial system was probably the chief reason for calling a convention. By this time, "the supreme court was four years in arrears with its work and that with all diligence on the part of the judges the law's delays were destined to become more vexatious and expensive."[218] Besides the general recognition that the judicial article had to be revised, both the Democratic and Republican parties agreed that a convention was needed because of the

216 *See* Galbreath, *Constitutional Conventions of Ohio*, 32–34.

217 Ibid.

218 Galbreath, *Constitutional Conventions of Ohio*, 34.

continued difficulty in amending the constitution. The voters had not approved any of the seven amendments proposed by the General Assembly between 1851 and 1871, although six of the seven received a majority vote of those voting on the particular amendment. See Appendix B. Thus, these six amendments would have been approved but for the requirement that proposed amendments had to be approved by a majority of those voting at the election. With the support of both parties, the voters on October 10, 1871, approved the call for a convention by a vote of 267,618 to 104,231.

One hundred and five delegates convened in Columbus on May 13, 1873, and continuing in Cincinnati, the convention adjourned one year later on May 15, 1874. The delegates initially elected Morrison Waite as president, but President Ulysses S. Grant appointed him Chief Justice of the United States. The convention then elected Rufus King to the position.[219]

Republicans dominated the convention, as they had Ohio politics since the Civil War, but there was little sign of partisan politics. More than either of the first two conventions, the 1873–74 Convention was dominated by lawyers and labeled a "lawyers' convention."[220] In keeping with the label, the convention produced a record much longer than even the 1850–51 Convention. The proceedings and debates cover more than 4,800 pages, and the proposed constitution contained more than 15,000 words, almost 60 percent more than the 9,447-word 1851 Constitution.[221]

The proposed constitution addressed the two major areas of concern, the judiciary and the amendment process. The most innovative proposed amendment to the judicial article was a section that would have established a commission of Supreme Court justices whose terms expired in 1874 to assist the Supreme Court in deciding cases.[222] Regarding the process of amending the constitution, the convention proposed an amendment that would have required a three-fifths vote of the General Assembly to call a constitutional convention rather than the two-thirds vote necessary under the 1851 Constitution. Most important, the convention also proposed eliminating the supermajority requirement and replacing it with a simple majority vote to adopt proposed amendments. The delegates, however, proposed dispensing with the mandatory vote every twenty years on whether to call a convention.

The convention also proposed to give the governor veto power, which could be overridden by a three-fifths vote of both houses; to require a separate vote

---

[219] Patterson, *The Constitutions of Ohio*, 36. The proposed Constitution of 1874 is reprinted in Patterson, *The Constitutions of Ohio*, 182–236.

[220] Patterson, *The Constitutions of Ohio*, 176.

[221] Ibid., 38.

[222] Proposed 1874 Ohio Constitution, Art. IV, sec. 4. The proposed provision would have also allowed the General Assembly to authorize the governor to appoint other such commissions if requested by the supreme court. Proposed 1874 Const., Art. IV, sec. 4; *see* Patterson, *The Constitutions of Ohio*, 199.

recording the yeas and nays on any appropriation item if requested by a legislator; and to prohibit anyone interested in a state contract from becoming a member of the General Assembly. To lessen powerful corporate interests, the convention proposed to allow the General Assembly to "prevent unjust enrichment" by corporations, to prohibit railroads from imposing excessive fees, and to pass regulations providing for the health and safety of miners. The convention decided to allow cumulative voting in elections for corporate directors, and to allow cumulative voting in the two largest counties—at that time Hamilton and Cuyahoga counties.[223] On race and gender issues, the convention proposed removing the word "white" from the voter qualification section to make it consistent with the recently ratified Fifteenth Amendment to the U.S. Constitution, which guaranteed African Americans the right to vote, and from the section on the militia (Art. IX, sec. 1), but the proposal to remove the word "male" and thus grant women the right to vote failed to attract the votes of a majority of the delegates, as required by the convention rules.[224] And as a small consolation, the convention proposed that women be permitted to hold any school office other than state commissioner of public schools.[225]

The proposed constitution was much more detailed than the 1851 Constitution and contained a number of popular reforms, but it also included enough divisive provisions that "[a] great number of interests were displeased with one part or another of it, and it needed no prophet to foretell its defeat at the hands of the electors."[226]

Following the approach used in 1851 to separate the vote on the proposed constitution from the vote on the liquor issue, the convention had sought to improve the electoral prospects for the new constitution by having separate votes on controversial proposals: (1) to assure minority party representation on the supreme and circuit courts; (2) to allow the General Assembly to provide aid to railroads; and (3) to permit the granting of licenses to traffic in liquor.[227] Nonetheless, the presence of these provisions dealt a fatal blow to the entire document. Interest groups that opposed these proposals urged their defeat as well as the defeat of the proposed constitution. For example, prohibitionists voted "in mass" not only against the proposal to allow liquor licensing but also against the entire constitution "for fear that was the only way to defeat licens[ing]."[228]

Finally, the convention took so long to complete its work that whatever interest the press and public had in a new constitution faded.[229] Owing to a lack of

223 Proposed 1874 Const., Art. XIV, sec. 12; Patterson, *The Constitutions of Ohio*, 223.

224 Terzian, "Ohio's Constitutions," 380–81.

225 Proposed 1874 Const., Art. VI, sec. 3; Patterson, *The Constitutions of Ohio*, 206.

226 Patterson, *The Constitutions of Ohio*, 37.

227 *See* ibid., 232–36. *See also* Appendix B.

228 Patterson, *The Constitutions of Ohio*, 347–48 (quoting *The Ohio State Journal*, August 20, 1874).

229 Swisher, *Ohio Constitution Handbook*, xxviii.

interest, confusion, and misinformation, the voters rejected the proposed 1874 Constitution by a vote of 250,169 to 102,885, almost an exact reversal of the vote in favor of the constitutional call.[230]

FROM 1874 TO THE 1912 CONSTITUTIONAL CONVENTION

After the rejection of the proposed 1874 Constitution, Ohio would not have another constitutional convention for nearly forty years. In 1891, under the mandatory twenty-year vote, the voters rejected a proposal to hold a convention by a vote of 161,722 to 99,789.[231] And in 1897, the Ohio Supreme Court rejected an attempt by the General Assembly to enact a law allowing the electorate to vote on holding a constitutional convention because the General Assembly could not make or amend laws by joint resolution. See *State ex rel. Attorney General v. Kinney* (1897). Concerns about the tax system had motivated the convention's proponents, who surely thought the voters were on their side after an 1891 proposed amendment on taxation received almost 80 percent of the votes on the issue (but was rejected under the supermajority requirement). See Commentary, Article XVI, section 2.

During this almost forty-year period between constitutional conventions, many of the issues that had been addressed at the 1873–74 Constitutional Convention came before the voters as separate proposals, but they approved only eleven amendments while rejecting nineteen (though thirteen of these failed because of the supermajority requirement).

Taxes were the subject of a number of amendments proposed during this period. The 1851 Constitution established a uniform tax structure that required both real and personal property to be assessed alike according to their true value in money. The uniform rule sought to make the tax system more equitable by treating real and personal property the same, but valuation problems, the willingness of people to conceal their property, and the lack of serious enforcement produced some absurd results. For example, Hamilton County, which includes Cincinnati, with a population of over 460,000, recorded fewer money deposits in 1910 than Darke County, with a population of less than 43,000.[232]

Notwithstanding concerns about the equity of the tax system, the voters rejected six amendments to Article XII permitting the General Assembly to

[230] Patterson, *The Constitutions of Ohio*, 176.

[231] Appendix A. The proposal to hold a convention received less than one-eighth of the 803,328 total votes cast (*see* Patterson, "The Constitutions of Ohio," 269) and thus fell far short of the requisite "majority of all the electors voting at said election" required under Art. XVI, sec. 2.

[232] Lloyd Sponholtz, "Progressivism in Microcosm: An Analysis of the Political Forces at Work in the Ohio Constitutional Convention of 1912," (Ph.D. dissertation, University of Pittsburgh, 1969) (hereinafter "Progressivism in Microcosm"), 85–86.

adopt nonuniform classification.[233] Five of the six rejected amendments received more positive than negative votes, but failed under the supermajority requirement. The only tax amendment that the voters approved during this period was a 1905 amendment exempting state, local, and school bonds from taxation, but this was approved under the voting procedures permitted by the Longworth Act.

Taxation was not the only subject of multiple proposals. Problems of inefficiency and overcrowded dockets had long plagued the Ohio court system, and the General Assembly proposed four amendments concerning the courts in the ten years following the 1873–74 Convention, including proposals (approved by the voters) to create a Supreme Court commission to help deal with the court's backlog (1875), see Commentary, Article IV, section 22, and to replace the district courts (1883).

The most significant amendment adopted during this period changed the balance of power among the branches of government by giving the governor a veto power that included the power to line-item veto provisions in appropriation bills. Legislative supremacy had been somewhat tempered by the 1851 Constitution, but the effort at the convention to give the governor veto power was not successful. The 1874 proposed constitution included an amendment that would have given the governor veto power, but it failed with the rest of the constitution. Finally, with the support of both the Democratic and Republican parties, the voters in 1903, a hundred years after statehood, approved a constitutional amendment giving the governor the power to veto some acts of the General Assembly.

Among the other proposals that the voters approved were three amendments in 1885 changing the election day to the first Tuesday after the first Monday in November to conform to the federal election day; an amendment in 1885 concerning the terms of township officers; amendments in 1903 giving each county at least one representative in the Ohio House of Representatives and a provision affecting stockholder liability; and an amendment in 1905 concerning the terms of state and local elected officials and the filling of vacancies. See Appendix B.

In addition to five proposed amendments on tax classifications and two on the courts, the voters rejected two amendments involving liquor, three involving election dates, two involving apportionment, one involving the classification of cities, one involving biennial elections for various state and local officials, one involving biennial sessions of the General Assembly, one involving the override of vetoes, and one that would have imposed a special tax on dogs allowing them to be confiscated and killed if the tax was not paid.[234]

---

[233] *But see* Patterson, *The Constitutions of Ohio*,23 (counting seven rejected tax classification amendments).

[234] Ibid., 237–95 (full text of proposed amendments between 1875 and 1908).

Notwithstanding the adoption of some important amendments, the 1851 Constitution remained difficult to amend because of the supermajority requirement. Of the thirty-seven amendments that the General Assembly submitted to the voters between 1851 and the 1912 Constitutional Conventions (excluding the three proposed amendments submitted to the voters with the proposed 1874 Constitution and for which the supermajority requirement was inapplicable), the voters approved only eleven. Of the twenty-six that failed, nineteen received a majority of votes but not a majority of votes cast in the election and thus failed as a result of the supermajority requirement. See Appendix B.

The introduction of the Australian ballot in 1891 compounded the problem, as political parties supporting constitutional amendments were no longer able to have the "yes" part of the party ticket count as support for the amendment, and the great majority of voters voting straight party tickets failed to vote on proposed amendments.[235]

In 1902, the General Assembly adopted the Longworth Act,[236] which allowed political parties to place issues on the ballot in such a way that a straight party vote counted as a vote for the proposed party-endorsed amendment.[237] The Ohio Supreme Court approved this voting procedure, *State ex rel. Sheets v. Laylin* (1903), and in 1903 and 1905 the voters approved five of the eight amendments presented to them under the Longworth Act, including the amendment giving the governor veto power.[238] There were concerns, however, that the Longworth Act gave too much power to the General Assembly. And in 1908 the General Assembly repealed the act in advance of the 1908 vote on still another taxation amendment, leading to its rejection by the voters.[239] Thus, apart from this short period, the voters added only six amendments to the 1851 Constitution prior to 1912, but the pace of constitutional change in Ohio was about to accelerate rapidly.

Some of the impetus for a constitutional convention came from decisions of the Ohio Supreme Court. During the second half of the nineteenth century, the court generally did not interfere with legislative efforts to adopt moral standards in such areas as alcohol, taverns, gambling, and Sunday closing laws,[240] and it had rendered important decisions interpreting the Ohio Constitution in the area of

---

235 Ibid., 24.

236 95 Ohio Laws 352 (May 2, 1902).

237 *See* Galbreath, *Constitutional Conventions of Ohio*, 46–47. *See also* John Kulewicz, "Reinventing the Governor: A History of Executive Power under Ohio Law," in *The History of Ohio Law*, 139, 169 n. 250.

238 *See* Walter F. Dodd, *The Revision and Amendment of State Constitutions* (New York: Da Capo Press, 1970), 194–97.

239 Patterson, *The Constitutions of Ohio*, 25.

240 *See* Michael Les Benedict, "Civil Liberty in Ohio," in *The History of Ohio Law*, 675, 691–94 (hereinafter Benedict, "Civil Liberty in Ohio").

race.[241] But in the latter part of the nineteenth century and the first decade of the twentieth century the court began to exercise its power of judicial review aggressively. And during this period, the court struck down many legislative enactments, including a number that involved the health, safety, and economic security of Ohio's working people:[242]

> In 1895, the court held unconstitutional an act imposing a direct inheritance tax because it exempted estates not exceeding $20,000 in value and taxed larger estates at a higher rate, *State ex rel. Schwartz v. Ferris* (1895).
>
> In 1896 the court invalidated legislation that allowed subcontractors and laborers who did not contract with property owners to place mechanic's liens on the owners' property, *Palmer v. Tingle* (1896).
>
> In 1897, the court held unconstitutional the Torrens system of land registration, which was designed to simplify the transfer of real estate, *State ex rel. Attorney General v. Guilbert* (1897).
>
> In 1898, the court struck down an act that regulated the sanitary construction of house drainage and plumbing because it required some but not all plumbers to obtain a license, *State v. Gardner* (1898).
>
> In 1900, the court struck down an act that increased the compensation of miners by requiring the weighing of coal before screening, *In re Preston* (1900).
>
> In 1901, the court struck down an act providing pensions for schoolteachers because it took property from one citizen for the benefit of another, *Hibbard v. State* (1901).
>
> In 1902, the court held unconstitutional the eight-hour workday on public works, *City of Cleveland v. Clements Bros. Construction Co.* (1902).
>
> In 1902, the court struck down an act designed to protect life and property against injury or damage, resulting from the operation of steam engines and boilers by incompetent engineers, *Harmon v. State* (1902).
>
> In 1902, the court held unconstitutional city charters because they constituted local legislation, *State of Ohio ex rel. Knisely v. Jones* (1902).
>
> In 1906, the court invalidated an act to provide up to $25 quarterly in relief for the worthy blind on the ground that law required the expenditure of public funds

241 *See, e.g., Anderson v. Millikin* (1859) (holding unconstitutional statute that excluded mixed-race men from voting and prevented a man who was one-eighth black and seven-eighths white from voting); *Monroe v. Collins* (1868) (holding unconstitutional a statute that forbid voting by anyone "having a distinct and visible admixture of African blood"). *See also* Jonathan L. Entin, "An Ohio Dilemma: Race, Equal Protection, and the Unfulfilled Promise of a State Bill of Rights," 51 *Clev. St. L. Rev.* 395 (2004): 404–10 (hereinafter Entin, "An Ohio Dilemma").

242 Following a nonpartisan strategy and working with both Republicans and Democrats, the labor movement had great success in the General Assembly from the mid-1880s to the early 1990s. But the Ohio Supreme Court, relying on the right to contract and the inappropriate use of classifications, struck down many labor-inspired state statutes. *See generally* Michael Pierce, "Organized Labor and the Law," *The History of Ohio Law*, 883, 889–91. *See also* Commentary, Art. I, sec. 2.

raised by taxation for a private purpose, *Auditor of Lucas County v. State ex rel. Boyles* (1906).

In 1909, the court held that the use of voting machines violated the requirement of Article V, Section 2 that "[a]ll elections shall be by ballot," *State ex rel. Karlinger v. Board of Deputy State Supervisors of Elections* (1909).

Finally, the court's 1912 decision upholding Ohio's optional workers' compensation statute by a narrow four to two margin, *State ex rel. Yaple v. Creamer* (1912), on the eve of the convention raised concerns on the part of reformers who supported a compulsory program. The fact that the New York Court of Appeals in 1911 had invalidated that state's compulsory program on state constitutional grounds, *Ives v. South Buffalo Railway Co.* (1911), underscored the need to assure the existence of legislative power, as did an opinion of the Attorney General that called into question the authority of municipalities to insure public buildings and the authority of the state to regulate stated.[243]

■ THE 1912 CONSTITUTIONAL CONVENTION: CONSTITUTIONAL REVISION IN THE PROGRESSIVE ERA

The Progressive Movement and the Call for a Convention

The decades following Reconstruction marked the beginning of the transformation from agrarian to modern society. The expansion of the railroads, technological innovation, rapid industrialization, and a wave of southern and eastern European immigration brought great economic and social change to the country, but along with the creation of enormous wealth, these years also saw the emergence of what seemed to be a permanent underclass, urban slums, and the worst depression the country had yet experienced. In the late nineteenth and early twentieth centuries, the inequalities of the "Gilded Age" gave rise to the Progressive movement made up of diverse groups of social and political reformers. Progressives included political reformers, labor unions, prohibitionists, woman suffragists, and a host of other groups, and (though not unified by a specific social agenda or political party) they shared a common distrust of laissez-faire capitalism, unrestrained monopolies, and the corrupt political machines of the era.[244]

Progressives were at the forefront of drives to revise state constitutions between 1900 and 1920 when thirteen states held constitutional conventions. In Ohio, the call for a constitutional convention was led by the Direct Legislation

[243] *See* Sponholtz, "Progressivism in Microcosm," 116–20.

[244] *See* John Whiteclay Chambers II, *The Tyranny of Change: America in the Progressive Era, 1900–1917* (New York: St. Martin's Press, 1980), 113; Arthur S. Link and Richard L. McCormick, *Progressivism* (Arlington Heights: Harlan Davidson, 1983), 3–4.

League, a group of urban Progressives headed by Herbert S. Bigelow, a Congregational minister from Cincinnati and a protégé of Cleveland mayor Tom L. Johnson, one of the state's first great Progressive leaders. The Direct Legislation League's principal goal was to give citizens a more direct voice in government. Specifically, the League campaigned for the adoption of an initiative and referendum amendment that would allow citizens to sidestep the legislature (and thus powerful business interests) and directly petition the voters to enact new laws and to amend the constitution. Women could not vote, but women suffragist groups also supported the convention as a means of obtaining the right to vote.[245]

The call for a convention also drew support from conservative groups, the largest of which was the Ohio State Board of Commerce ("OSBC"). The OSBC opposed initiative and referendum, as well as most of the other Progressive reforms, but it nonetheless supported the call for a convention to overhaul Ohio's tax system by repealing the constitution's uniform tax rule. The OSBC favored a classification system that would tax different property at different rates with the goal of reducing taxes on businesses and investments.[246] See Commentary, Article XII, section 2. Finally, the liquor interests wanted the convention to approve an amendment that would permit the licensing of saloons.

A vote on whether to have a constitutional convention would normally have been held in 1911 under the mandatory twenty-year rule, but public support for a convention was so great that on March 9, 1910, the Ohio General Assembly passed a bill allowing the voters to decide whether to have a convention at the upcoming election. And both the Democratic and Republican parties agreed that every straight party ticket vote would be counted as a vote for a convention.[247]

The 1851 Constitution contained scant details about the operation of a convention other than specifying that the number of delegates would be the same as the number of members in the House of Representatives (which at the time was 119).[248] In 1911, however, the General Assembly accepted the proposal of William Green, president of the Senate and future president of the American

[245] Hoyt Landon Warner, *Progressivism in Ohio, 1897–1917* (Columbus: Ohio State University Press, 1964), 295 (hereinafter Warner, *Progressivism in Ohio*).

[246] Ibid.

[247] *See* Robert E. Cushman, "Voting Organic Laws: The Action of the Ohio Electorate in the Revision of the State Constitution in 1912," 28 *Political Science Quarterly* 208 (June 1913).

[248] Prior to the 1967 amendment that established the size of the House of Representatives at ninety-nine, the number of representatives was based on a complex, fluctuating formula. *See* David M. Gold, *Democracy in Session: A History of the Ohio General Assembly* (Ohio University Press: 2009), 423–25 (hereinafter Gold, *Democracy in Session*); *see also* Ohio Const., Art. XI, sec. 2 (as amended in 1967). At the time of the 1912 Convention, there were 119 members in the House of Representatives. *See* Lloyd Sponholtz, "The 1912 Constitutional Convention in Ohio: The Call-Up and Nonpartisan Selection of Delegates," 79 *Ohio Hist.* 209 (1970): 212.

Federation of Labor, that the delegates be elected on a nonpartisan basis.[249] This decision to circumvent the political parties, according to the Cleveland Federation of Labor, "gives workers the opportunity to unite on good men... who will guard the interest of the workers in making a new Constitution."[250] In addition to requiring a nonpartisan ballot, the act provided for the nomination of delegates only by petition.[251]

With the support of the two major political parties, the vote for a convention passed by a ten-to-one margin, 693,263 to 67,718. Commenting on this vote, Hoyt Landon Warner, the leading authority on Progressivism in Ohio, noted that "[n]ever before in the sixty-year span has this date fallen at such a psychologically favorable time. There was a pent-up demand among various groups for such reforms as municipal home rule, legal protection of workers, improvements in court procedures, and woman suffrage."[252] Nonetheless, "the most insistent pleas for a constitutional convention came from three well-organized groups [the Direct Legislation League, the Ohio State Board of Commerce, and the liquor industry] dedicated to their own particular reform."[253]

The Constitutional Convention of 1912

The convention, dominated by Progressives, assembled in Columbus on January 8, 1912, with 119 delegates, including 62 Democrats, 52 Republicans, 3 Independents, and 2 Socialists.[254] The first few weeks were taken up mostly by speeches from notable Progressive leaders, including former president Theodore Roosevelt, his future Bull Moose running mate Governor Hiram Johnson of California, and three-time presidential candidate William Jennings Bryan. Sitting president William Howard Taft attended and gave a brief welcoming speech, but the delegates (amid some heated debate) refused to invite Socialist

[249] *See* S.B. 15, 79th Gen. Assemb., Reg. Sess. sec. 15 (Ohio 1911), 102 Ohio Laws 298, 302; *see also* Michael Pierce, "Organized Labor and the Law in Ohio," in *The History of Ohio Law*, 883, 897.

[250] *See* ibid., 897 (alteration in original) (quoting Cleveland Federation of Labor, *Labor Day Year Book and Souvenir Program of the Ohio State Federation of Labor* 26 (1912)); *see also* ibid., 896–99 (discussing the important role labor played in securing and supporting the convention).

[251] Ohio S.B. 15 sec. 6, 102 Ohio Laws 299. The act also permitted, but did not require, delegates to file statements on whether they favored the separate submission to the voters of a question on the licensing of liquor. *See* ibid., sec. 11, 102 Ohio Laws 301.

[252] Warner, *Progressivism in Ohio*, 295.

[253] Ibid.

[254] The election was nonpartisan, and the delegates did not have to declare their party affiliation. As a result, there is no authoritative tally as to the party affiliations of the delegates, but the tally above comes from Sponholtz, "Progressivism in Microcosm," 37 nn. 62–63. *But see* Galbreath, "Constitutional Conventions of Ohio," 59–60 (chart breaking down 119 delegates as follows: 63 Democrats, 49 Republicans, 2 Socialists, 4 Independents, and 1 Independent Republican).

leader Eugene V. Debs, who was to become a formidable fourth party candidate for president later in 1912.[255]

Despite the nonpartisan election, controversy along political lines emerged over the selection of the convention's president with most Democrats supporting Herbert S. Bigelow. Although Bigelow was the front-runner and eventually won the position, it took eleven ballots to elect him president.[256] Apart from the election of Bigelow, party politics seems to have played at best a minor role at the convention. And "[t]he real division [according to Bigelow] was between conservatives and progressives, between 'those,' in the words of Macaulay, 'who cling to the past, distrusting change; and those who instinctively challenge precedent.'"[257]

Early in the convention, the delegates recognized that proposals for controversial amendments could result in the rejection of the entire constitution, as many believed had happened in 1874. To avoid this risk, the delegates agreed not to present a new constitution to the voters or to submit the proposals together for an all-or-nothing vote. Instead, the delegates adopted a variant of the piecemeal approach first suggested in 1838 by Caleb Atwater, who had urged that amendments be submitted article by article,[258] and recommended that each constitutional amendment be submitted to the voters as a separate issue. In the end, the convention proposed forty-two amendments to the voters, who adopted thirty-four of them.

Initiative and Referendum

The Direct Legislation League prevailed on its core issue, the initiative and referendum. Since Progressives dominated the convention, there was little doubt that the delegates would adopt an initiative and referendum amendment in some form. The amendment that was proposed (and which the voters approved) provided for a direct initiative to amend the constitution (Art. II, sec. 1a), for an indirect initiative to enact new laws (which required statutory proposals to be first presented to the General Assembly) (Art. II, sec. 1b), and for a referendum to challenge statutes enacted by the General Assembly (Art. II, sec. 1c).

The proposed initiative and referendum amendment did not please the most radical Progressives because it did not provide for a direct initiative to enact laws and had higher percentages of required signatures than they had wanted.

---

[255] *Proceedings and Debates of the Constitutional Convention of the State of Ohio: Convened January 9, 1912* (Columbus: F.J. Heer Printing, 1912), 230, 865–67 (hereinafter *1912 Debates*).

[256] "Elect Bigelow by Hard Fight in Convention," 9 *Cleveland Press* 1 (January 1912).

[257] *See* Landon Warner, "Ohio's Constitutional Convention of 1912," 61 *Ohio St. Arch. Hist. Q.* 11 (1952): 18 (quoting remarks of Herbert S. Bigelow published in James K Mercer, ed., *Ohio Legislative History*, vol. I (Columbus: Edward T. Miller Co., 1909–1913), 410).

[258] Atwater, *History of the State of Ohio*, 175.

Moreover, laws providing for tax levies, appropriations for the expenses of the state government and state institutions, and emergency measures were not subject to the referendum (Art. II, sec. 1d). In addition, Article II, Section 1e barred the use of the statutory initiative to pass laws classifying property at different rates for tax purposes or to adopt a "single tax on land."[259] On the other hand, laws enacted by the statutory initiative could not be vetoed by the governor, and the initiative and referendum could be used to enact or challenge municipal laws. Most important to the Progressives, the electors could bypass the legislature and directly amend the constitution. Overall, most Progressives, including Bigelow, were pleased with the amendment.[260]

With the approval of the initiative and referendum by the voters, there were then three ways to propose amendments to the constitution: by initiative petition, by proposals from the General Assembly, and by constitutional convention. The voters also approved an amendment that made it easier to amend the constitution by allowing the electorate to approve a constitutional amendment proposed by the General Assembly with a simple majority vote of those voting on the amendment rather than a majority of those voting in the election.[261]

Despite the convention's support for the initiative and the referendum, a number of other proposals about the processes of government failed to obtain the support of the delegates. The most ardent Progressives sought to limit the role of political parties in the electoral process, but the delegates defeated proposals calling for nonpartisan election of state legislators and county judges and for an open primary. They also rejected proposals to permit the use of the initiative to call a constitutional convention, to prohibit legislators from serving as delegates at future conventions, and to permit the General Assembly by a two-thirds vote to ask the voters to approve the appointment of a fifteen-person commission to recommend changes in the constitution.[262]

Home Rule

For Progressives, second in importance to securing the initiative and referendum was the adoption of a municipal home rule amendment that would give municipalities powers independent of the General Assembly. Municipal home

---

[259] Opponents of the initiative supported this limitation in the hope that its approval would burden the initiative and referendum proposal with the politically charged issues of the single tax and the controversial policies of Economist Henry George. But the Progressives did not swallow this poison pill and supported the restrictions on the statutory initiative. *See New Constitution for Ohio—An Explanation of the Work of Ohio's Fourth Constitutional Convention by the President, Hon. Herbert S. Bigelow* (July 5, 1912), 14–15.

[260] Warner, "Ohio's Constitutional Convention of 1912," 22.

[261] Warner, *Progressivism in Ohio*, 323. The delegates supported the proposal to eliminate the supermajority requirement by a vote of 105–1, *1912 Debates*, 1913.

[262] *1912 Debates*, 1368, 1911. *See also* Sponholtz, "Progressivism in Microcosm," 185.

rule was of particular importance to urban Progressives, including Toledo's mayor Samuel Milton Jones, Cleveland's late (and legendary) Mayor Tom L. Johnson, and Johnson's protégé Newton D. Baker.

Their quest for increased control over local affairs had been thwarted by the state's embrace of Dillon's Rule, under which municipalities were limited to exercising those powers granted to them by the General Assembly. See Commentary, Article XVIII. And, ironically, the ability of the state to exercise control was undercut in 1902 when the Ohio Supreme Court struck down as prohibited special legislation the system of classification of cities in which each of the state's twelve major cities was in a classification and grade of its own. *State of Ohio ex rel. Knisely v. Jones* (1902). Representatives of the cities believed that local governmental reform and a reduction in corruption required that cities be given greater freedom to manage their own affairs.

The proposed home rule amendment had three goals: to allow cities to choose different types of municipal governments, to reverse Dillon's Rule, and to allow cities to control and operate public utilities.[263] The proposal drew strong opposition from the public utility lobby, which feared that municipal ownership would result in unfair competition, and from delegates who thought that the grant of control over local matters could be used by cities to regulate liquor.[264] But the voter's subsequent approval of Article XVIII significantly expanded the power of municipalities to control their own affairs. See generally Commentary, Article XVIII.

The Courts

The proposals that generated the most interest to the legal profession concerned the judiciary. The convention proposed and the voters approved three amendments that made a number of important changes in the structure and operation of the courts to address the problem of overcrowded dockets and to limit the ability of the Ohio Supreme Court to hold acts of the legislature unconstitutional.

At the time of the convention, the Ohio courts included justices of the peace, common pleas courts, circuit courts, and the Ohio Supreme Court, which had six justices with the position of chief justice rotating among the six.[265]

Overcrowded dockets and long delays in resolving litigation could be attributed as much, if not more, to the structure of the judiciary as to the increase in the state population. The most glaring problems were at the circuit

---

[263] *See* Harvey Walker, "Municipal Government in Ohio before 1912," 9 *Ohio St. L. J.* 1 (1948): 13–14; *1912 Debates,* 1433.

[264] Warner, "Ohio's Constitutional Convention of 1912," 24; Walker, "Municipal Government in Ohio before 1912," 14–15.

[265] Sponholtz, "Progressivism in Microcosm," 190.

court and the Supreme Court. Circuit courts did not function solely as appellate courts but also held trials de novo. Thus, litigants who lost at the trial court could relitigate their entire case in the circuit courts. The Ohio Supreme Court functioned as an ordinary appellate court, but, as one delegate noted, the circuit courts were considered a "sieve through which everybody goes to the supreme court."[266] By the time of the convention, the Ohio Supreme Court's docket was so overcrowded that it was said to take between two and five years to have the court decide a case.[267]

To improve the efficiency of the courts, the voters approved a proposed amendment that replaced the circuit courts with courts of appeals that had only limited authority to hold trials de novo. The amendment also limited the Supreme Court's appellate jurisdiction by allowing appeals as of right only in cases arising under the federal or state constitution, felony cases, and cases originating in the courts of appeals. A provision, however, allowed for discretionary review "in cases of public or great general interest." The Supreme Court itself was transformed by an increase in the number of justices from six to seven and the creation of an elected, not a rotating, position of chief justice. Other amendments designed to improve the efficiency of the lower courts included an amendment requiring the assignment of a common pleas judge to each county with the legislature being able to add additional judges and a provision that replaced the constitutional requirement for justices of the peace with one permitting the legislature to create such judicial offices.

The most controversial issue regarding the judiciary concerned the number of votes needed for the Supreme Court to strike down a law as unconstitutional. Judge Hiram Peck of Hamilton County introduced a proposal that would have required a unanimous vote to declare an act unconstitutional.[268] Peck's proposal, which had the support of William Jennings Bryan, was aimed at the Ohio Supreme Court, which had a reputation for striking down legislation that protected workers' rights.[269]

Opinions of the members of the judiciary committee on the Peck proposal ranged from requiring unanimity to a simple majority vote.[270] Eventually, the delegates reached a compromise, and the convention proposed and the voters approved the amendment requiring the concurrence of all but one Supreme Court justice to reverse an appellate court judgment upholding a law as constitutional. If the appellate court found the law unconstitutional, however, only a

[266] *1912 Debates,* 1026 (quoted in Jonathan L. Entin, "Judicial Supermajorities and the Validity of Statutes: How *Mapp* Became a Fourth Amendment Landmark Instead of a First Amendment Footnote," 52 *Case W. Res. L. Rev.* 441 (2001): 445 n. 28) (hereinafter Entin, "Judicial Supermajorities").

[267] *1912 Debates,* 1025–26.

[268] Ibid., 143–44 (Proposal No. 184); *see also* Entin, "Judicial Supermajorities," 445.

[269] Ibid., 443–45.

[270] Warner, *Progressivism in Ohio,* 328–29.

simple majority of supreme court justices was needed to uphold the decision. Ironically, the approved amendment effectively acknowledged the power of the courts to declare laws unconstitutional.[271]

The Peck proposal was an alternative to a proposal made by former president Theodore Roosevelt to permit the recall of unpopular judicial decisions. In his February 21, 1912, speech to the convention, he outlined his proposal for the recall of judicial decisions.[272] At the time, he was challenging his successor, President William Howard Taft, for the Republican nomination, but Progressives who strongly supported the initiative and the referendum were split on the issue of the recall of judicial decisions. The delegates, however, did support an amendment to permit the recall or removal of public officials (in addition to impeachment), a proposal that was controversial because many saw it as an attack on the independence of judges.[273]

The voters also approved a number of amendments that altered the rights of litigants, including amendments that provided for three-fourths jury verdicts in civil cases, that prohibited limits on damages in wrongful death actions, that allowed the legislature to pass laws regulating the size and vote of grand juries and the use of expert witness testimony in criminal trials, that permitted prosecutors to comment on a defendant's exercise of the privilege against self-incrimination in criminal cases, and that permitted both the state and the defendant to take depositions in criminal cases. See Appendix B.

Finally, the voters approved at least seven amendments that either directly overruled decisions of the Ohio Supreme Court or that removed potential judicial barriers to legislative action:

> Article II, Section 33—overruling *Palmer v. Tingle* (1896) to allow subcontractors and laborers who did not contract with property owners to place mechanic's liens on the owners' property;
>
> Article II, Section 34—overruling such cases as *Hibbard v. State* (1901) (striking down pensions for school teachers) and *Auditor of Lucas County v. State ex rel. Boyles* (1906) (providing for relief for the worthy blind) and removing constitutional uncertainty concerning legislation to provide for the comfort, health, safety, and general welfare of employees;
>
> Article II, Section 35—removing constitutional uncertainty concerning the enactment of a compulsory workers' compensation program;
>
> Article II, Section 37—overruling *City of Cleveland v. Clements Bros. Construction Co.* (1902) to establish the eight-hour work-day on public works;

---

[271] *See State ex rel. Turner v. U. S. Fid. & Guar. Co. of Baltimore, Md.* (1917) ("Of all the states of the Union the Constitution of ours alone has thus expressly granted this great power to its highest court, and we are reminded that it should be exercised with the greatest possible care and reserve.").

[272] *1912 Debates*, 378–87. *See also* George E. Mowry, *Theodore Roosevelt and the Progressive Movement* (Madison: University of Wisconsin Press, 1947), 212–18.

[273] Sponholtz, "Progressivism in Microcosm," 153.

Article II, Section 40—overruling *State ex rel. Attorney General v. Guilbert,* (1897) to permit the use of theTorrens system of land registration;

Article VIII, Section 6—removing constitutional uncertainty as to the authority of municipalities to insure public buildings and of the state to regulate insurance;

Article XVIII—overruling *State of Ohio ex rel. Knisely v. Jones* (1902) and proposing the municipal home rule amendment.

Women's Suffrage

The amendment concerning women's suffrage received a great deal of attention at the convention and nationally.

Three of the most influential women present at the convention were Myron B. Vorce, representing the Women's Suffrage Party of Cleveland; Elizabeth Hauser of the Ohio Equal Suffrage Association; and Dora Bachman, a Socialist attorney from Cincinnati. Their main goal from the beginning of the convention was to influence the committee on elective franchise. On January 18, 1912, Dora Bachman presented a proposed amendment concerning women's suffrage to the committee. The proposal was simple in that it eliminated the word "male" from the voter qualification section.[274]

Delegate W. B. Kilpatrick of Trumbull County was the most outspoken supporter of women's suffrage. Bigelow initially opposed women's suffrage but agreed to support it if it were offered as a separate amendment.[275] The convention approved the suffrage amendment by a vote of seventy-four to thirty-seven and agreed to submit it to the voters as a separate ballot by a vote of seventy-six to thirty-four, but soon afterward, the delegates agreed to submit all amendments separately.[276]

Short-Ballot Movement

An issue that animated Progressives throughout the country concerned the large number of state officials on the ballot. The short-ballot movement sought to limit this number and give the power of appointment to the governor. Former president Roosevelt supported the short ballot in his convention speech, and nationally, a broad array of notable public officials did as well, including the governor of New York (and future chief justice of the United States) Charles Evan Hughes, New Jersey governor (and future president) Woodrow Wilson, President William Howard Taft, and California governor Hiram W. Johnson.

Nonetheless, despite the lengthy debate, the issue did not get very far.[277] The proposal that the delegates debated was a watered-down version that only

---

[274] "Suffragets Plank Written By Woman," *Cleveland Press* 2 (January 18, 1912).

[275] Terzian, "Effusions of Folly," 271–72.

[276] Terzian, "Ohio's Constitutions," 390–91.

[277] *1912 Debates*, 956–74; 993–1014.

eliminated elections as the way to choose the secretary of state and the treasurer of state. The delegates had already proposed making the superintendent of public instruction an appointed position, see Commentary, Article VI, section 4, and the delegates tabled the short-ballot proposal at its second reading by a vote of fifty-seven to forty-seven.[278]

The Campaign

In total, the convention recommended forty-two amendments to the voters in a special election scheduled for Tuesday, September 3, 1912, the day after Labor Day, a date chosen with union voters in mind. Progressives led by Bigelow had begun organizing for the campaign in January while the convention was still in progress.[279] Labor leaders and Socialists supported the amendments as a whole, as did most of the press. Opposition to the amendments did not begin in earnest until late in the campaign.[280] With the defeat of its efforts to rid the constitution of the uniform taxation rule, the OSBC, which had been one of the primary groups calling for the convention, opposed passage of most amendments. The OSBC attacked the work of the delegates, especially in the rural press, and mounted a campaign under the slogan "When in doubt, vote no," to which a Progressive newspaper, the *Cleveland Plain Dealer*, responded, "When in doubt, vote yes."[281]

Election Day

On election day the voters approved thirty-four of the forty-two proposed constitutional amendments. See Appendix B. As provided in the schedule adopted by the delegates for the submission of amendments to the voters and Article XVI, section 3, the supermajority requirement for approving amendments did not apply to amendments proposed by a constitutional convention, and therefore proposed amendments only needed to receive more affirmative than negative votes to become part of the constitution, regardless of whether a particular amendment received a majority of votes cast in the election.[282]

In addition to the amendments already mentioned, the voters approved amendments that included a reduction in the vote required by the legislature to overturn a veto from two-thirds to three-fifths, the establishment of direct

---

[278] Ibid., 1692–96. The supporters of the short-ballot tried again in 1913, when the General Assembly proposed two amendments to reduce the number of state and local elected officials, but after a spirited public debate the voters rejected both amendments by 2:1 margins. *See* Appendix B.

[279] Warner, Progressivism in Ohio, 339.

[280] Ibid.

[281] Ibid., 340.

[282] Ibid., 342; *see also* Appendix B for the popular vote on all proposed amendments.

elections for most public officials, the licensing of liquor, civil service reform, and the establishment of a superintendent of public instruction as an officer of the executive department to replace the state commissioner of common schools.

Rejected Amendments

The voters rejected eight amendments, including amendments to permit debt for intercounty roads in excess of the constitutional limit, to allow the regulation of outdoor advertisements, to limit the use of injunctions in labor disputes, to ban capital punishment, and to permit the use of voting machines. The voters also rejected an amendment to delete the word "white" from the voter qualification section of the constitution and two women's rights amendments, one to give women the right to vote and the other to allow women to be appointed as notary publics and to offices of institutions or departments that were concerned with the interests of women or children.[283]

The Defeat of Women's Suffrage

The proposed women's suffrage amendment attracted the largest number of total votes, but despite the efforts of women's rights advocates, the proposal lost by the largest margin, a vote of 336,875 to 249,420. Appendix B. Had it been approved, Ohio would have become the first state east of the Mississippi to give women the right to vote.[284]

The major reason given for the failure of women's suffrage was the fear that giving women the right to vote would add momentum to the temperance movement, which women overwhelmingly supported. Percy Andreae, leader of the antiprohibition forces in Ohio, claimed that "woman suffrage owes its defeat to the Anti-Saloon League, which made of it a wet and dry issue and thus alienated from it the sympathy of the large liberal forces of the state, which stand sternly opposed to prohibition, no matter what guise it may masquerade in."[285] Another reason the suffrage vote failed may have been that the women's movement aligned itself with the third-party presidential candidate Theodore Roosevelt. The *New York Herald*, in an article on the women's suffrage amendment in Ohio, wrote that "the support of the Progressive candidate proved to be the blight, instead of life and vigor." And the *New York World* stated that "if the suffragists permit themselves to be bass-drummed into a third-party camp they will make two enemies for every friend they gain."[286]

---

[283] *See 1912 Debates*, 2111.

[284] Terzian, "Effusions of Folly," 274.

[285] Cushman, "Voting Organic Laws," 223.

[286] "Ohio's Rebuilt Constitution," *Literary Digest*, 405 (discussing possible reasons for the defeat of women's suffrage, and quoting *New York Herald* and *New York World*).

The Legacy of the 1912 Convention

The adoption of thirty-four amendments in 1912 fundamentally altered the constitutional landscape in Ohio, but the election itself was in some respects disappointing. Voter turnout was relatively low, with about half as many votes cast as in the 1908 election for governor. Geographically, there was little consensus across the state. The urban parts of Ohio overwhelmingly voted in favor of all the amendments except women's suffrage and voting machines. Of the thirty-four amendments that the voters approved, nineteen would have failed if not for the urban vote.[287] In contrast, rural areas overwhelmingly opposed most of the amendments on the ballot. There was also a division among the northern and southern regions of the state with the north more favorable toward the amendments, as a whole, compared to the south. This was likely the result of large labor movements in the northern industrial cities that saw the constitutional amendments as favorable to their cause.[288]

Despite the victory of the Progressive movement, there was a general dissatisfaction among the people of the state. Many felt that the Progressives forced the constitutional convention and the amendment process on them and that there was too much of a rush to bring about change. Some commentators believed that not enough time was given for the electorate to study the amendments and that this may have contributed to voter confusion and low voter turnout.[289]

The convention of 1912 was the last constitutional convention in Ohio. Voters rejected the call for constitutional conventions in 1932, 1952, 1972, 1992, and 2012, when the issue was on the ballot under the mandatory twenty-year rule. Appendix A. But the 1912 convention did not mark the end of constitutional change. The piecemeal approach to constitutional change reflected in the decision to present separate amendments to the electorate became the model for constitutional change in Ohio.

■ CONSTITUTIONAL CHANGE FROM 1912 TO THE END OF THE TWENTIETH CENTURY

Constitutional Amendments—The Balance of the First Half of the Twentieth Century

The 1912 Constitutional Convention is an important dividing line in Ohio constitutional history. From the adoption of Ohio's second constitution in 1851 to the 1912 Convention, the voters amended the Ohio Constitution only eleven

[287] Cushman, "Voting Organic Laws," 220.

[288] Warner, *Progressivism in Ohio*, 341–42.

[289] *See* C. L. Martzoloff, "Ohio: Changes in the Constitution," 6 *Am. Pol. Sci. Rev.* 573 (November 1912).

times, with the most significant amendment being the 1903 provision giving the governor the veto power. In 1912 alone, however, the voters approved thirty-four of the forty-two amendments proposed by the convention, more than three times as many amendments as they had approved in the sixty years since the adoption of the 1851 Constitution. The 1912 Constitutional Convention also made the process of amending the constitution less difficult, and in the 107 years from 1913 through 2021 the voters approved 125 of 225 proposed amendments. Before 1912, amendments could be proposed by the General Assembly or by a constitutional convention, but approval of amendments proposed by the General Assembly required a majority of the voters who voted at the election. The 1912 Convention recommended and the voters approved the use of the initiative as another method for proposing constitutional amendments. But even more important in terms of its impact on constitutional revision, the voters approved a change in the votes needed to adopt an amendment proposed by the General Assembly from a majority of those voting in the election to a majority of votes on the specific amendment. From 1851 to 1912 under this supermajority requirement, the voters had approved only eleven of the thirty-seven amendments the General Assembly proposed. The supermajority requirement, however, did not apply to amendments proposed by constitutional conventions (Art. XVI, sec. 3), and in 1912, the convention recognized this, providing in the schedule approved by the voters that "[e]ach amendment on which the number of affirmative votes shall exceed the number of negative votes shall become a part of the constitution." See *Schedules to the Ohio Constitution*, 1912; see also Tables I.1 and I.2.

The post-1912 increase in the number of approved amendments is largely explained by the repeal of the supermajority requirement and not by the adoption of the initiative. In fact, during this 110-year period, the voters approved 106 of 154, or 68.8 percent, of the amendments proposed by the General Assembly but only nineteen of seventy-one, or 26.8 percent, of the amendments proposed by initiative petition. See Table I.2.

TABLE I.1 Amendments to the 1851 Constitution 1852–2021

	Proposed	Approved	Percent Approved	Amendments Approved by Year
1852 to 1911	40[*]	11	27.5	.2
1912	42	34	81.0	34.0
1913 to 2021	225	125	55.4	1.2
Total	307	170	55.5	1.02

[*]This includes the three proposed amendments submitted separately to the voters in 1874 and rejected by them along with the proposed constitution of 1874.

TABLE I.2 Amendments Proposed and Approved by Decade by General Assembly and Initiative 1913–2021

Decade	GA Proposed	GA Approved	GA Rejected	Initiative Proposed	Initiative Approved	Initiative Rejected	Total Proposed	Total Approved	Total Rejected
1913–1919	7	2	5	14	4	10	21	6	15
1920s	11	4	7	5	0	5	16	4	12
1930s	5	3	2	8	3	5	13	6	7
1940s	7	6	1	2	2	0	9	8	1
1950s	23	18	5	1	0	1	24	18	6
1960s	22	16	6	1	0	1	23	16	7
1970s	42	28	14	11	1	10	53	29	24
1980s	11	6	5	7	0	7	18	6	12
1990s	11	10	1	6	4	2	17	14	3
2000s	8	7	1	11	3	8	19	10	9
2010s	7	6	1	5	2	3	12	8	4
Total	154	106	48	71	19	52	225	125	100
		(68.8 percent)			(26.8 percent)				

TABLE I.3 Amendments Proposed and Adopted by Decade 1912–2021

	Proposed	Approved	Approval Percent
1913–1919	21	6	28.6
1920s	16	4	25
1930s	13	6	46.2
1040s	9	8	88.9
1950s	24	18	75
1960s	23	16	69.6
1970s	53	29	54.7
1980	18	6	33.3
1990s	17	14	82.4
2000s	19	10	52.6
2100s	12	8	66.7
Total	225	125	55.4

In the years immediately following the 1912 Convention, there was great interest in using initiative petitions to propose constitutional amendments, but the voters' interest in constitutional revision in general and in the initiative in particular waned.

During the balance of the second decade of the century, the initiative petition was used to propose fourteen amendments, the highest number in any decade, but the voters approved only four of them (while approving two of the seven amendments proposed by the General Assembly). This initial experience with the initiative may have diminished its allure, and in the next three decades—the period from 1920 to 1950—the voters approved only five of the fifteen amendments proposed by initiative petition (while approving thirteen of the twenty-three proposed by the General Assembly). See Table I.3. Indeed, in 1926, Newton D. Baker, an icon of the Progressive movement, a close associate and protégé of former Cleveland mayor Tom L. Johnson, a former mayor of Cleveland, and an active supporter of the Progressive agenda, expressed his disappointment that the initiative and referendum had "been tried and found of less value in practice than they promised in theory."[290]

In the years subsequent to the 1912 Convention, a number of issues that the delegates had addressed continued to be important parts of the state's constitutional agenda, especially issues involving intoxicating liquor and women's suffrage.

[290] Newton D. Baker, "Where Are the Pre-War Radicals?" 8 *Survey* 556 (1926).

Prohibition

The 1874 defeat of the proposal to permit the granting of licenses to traffic in liquor did little to end the controversies concerning liquor, and the General Assembly attempted to regulate liquor in other ways. For example, in 1882, the General Assembly enacted a statute that required every person engaged in the traffic of intoxicating liquor to pay a specified sum of money annually and execute a bond, and in 1883 it adopted another statute that provided for a lien on real estate occupied by a tenant who is a dealer in liquors. But the Ohio Supreme Court considered these measures licenses and struck them down. *State v. Hipp* (1882); *State v. Sinks* (1884). Meanwhile in 1883, the General Assembly proposed two amendments on liquor, one of which would have permitted the General Assembly to regulate and tax intoxicating liquor and the other of which would have prohibited the licensing and manufacture of intoxicating liquors. The voters rejected the first amendment by almost a 3:1 margin, and the second amendment (which received almost 100,000 more positive than negative votes) was rejected because it failed to receive the requisite majority of all votes cast in the election.[291]

Nor did the 1912 approval of the amendment permitting the licensing of liquor end the controversies. In the decade after the convention, there were nine proposed constitutional amendments (all via initiative petition) addressing directly or indirectly liquor issues.

In 1914, the voters approved for the first time an amendment proposed by initiative petition. The amendment, advanced by the brewing industry, denied the General Assembly the power to adopt laws that prohibited municipalities from approving the sale of intoxicating liquor and further barred the passing laws "prohibiting the sale, furnishing or giving away of intoxicating liquors throughout the state at large." Article XV, section 9a (repealed in 1918). And in 1915 and 1917, the voters rejected amendments proposed by initiative petition to prohibit the manufacture and sale of alcohol beverages. See Appendix B.

Despite these losses by the prohibitionists, the momentum began to turn in their direction. In 1915, the voters had also rejected a proposed "Stability Amendment" that would have created a six-year bar on using the initiative petition to propose an amendment that had been defeated twice. The Stability Amendment, which was advanced by the brewing industry, sought to block the repeated efforts to adopt prohibition in Ohio.[292]

Meanwhile, in 1918, prohibitionists led by the Anti-Saloon League, which had been founded in Oberlin in 1893 and had grown into a national organization, convinced Congress to propose the Eighteenth Amendment to ban the sale,

---

[291] Patterson, *The Constitutions of Ohio*, 249–50.

[292] *See* Steven H. Steinglass, "Constitutional Revision: Ohio Style," 77 *Ohio St. L. J.* 281 (2016): 315 n. 248 (hereinafter Steinglass, "Constitutional Revision").

manufacture, and transportation of intoxicating liquor. The liquor industry in Ohio tried to prevent ratification of the Eighteenth Amendment by supporting an initiative petition for an amendment to the Ohio Constitution to subject state ratification to a referendum. Ohio voters approved this amendment in 1918, but the U.S. Supreme Court held it unconstitutional in violation of Article V of the U.S. Constitution, which the Court interpreted as placing ratification solely in the hands of state legislatures or state conventions. *Hawke v. Smith* (1920).[293]

Nationally, prohibition became effective on January 17, 1920, but in Ohio it had become effective in 1918 as a result of voter approval of an amendment proposed by initiative petition to prohibit the sale and manufacture of liquor. See Appendix B. And prohibition remained in Ohio until 1933, when the Twenty-first Amendment to the U.S. Constitution ended national prohibition, and Ohio voters approved a constitutional amendment to repeal statewide prohibition by more than a 2:1 margin. See Appendix B.

Women's Suffrage

In the years immediately after the 1912 rejection of the proposed amendment on women's suffrage, Ohio voters again addressed constitutional amendments concerning the rights of women and women's suffrage. In 1913, the voters approved a General Assembly–proposed amendment giving women the right to serve on boards or commissions that dealt with issues affecting women and children, but in 1914, the voters again rejected an amendment (proposed by initiative petition) to give women the right to vote. Unlike the prohibition on the manufacture and sale of liquor issue, which was initially accomplished through an amendment to the Ohio Constitution, the extension of the right to vote to women was the direct result of an amendment of the U.S. Constitution. Thus, it was not until 1920 with the ratification of the Nineteenth Amendment to the U.S. Constitution that women in Ohio achieved the right to vote.

With women joining African American men as eligible to vote by federal mandate, Ohio voters in 1923 finally removed the phrase "white male" from the Ohio Constitution (Art. V, sec. 1). This revision, however, was only symbolic because the Fifteenth and Nineteenth Amendments to the U.S. Constitution had already prohibited voter disqualification on account of race and gender.[294] Thus, it took fifty-three years from the ratification of the Fifteenth Amendment in 1870

---

[293] The state amendment would have also subjected the state legislature's approval of the Nineteenth Amendment's extension of the vote to women to a referendum, but the decision in *Hawke* resulted in a state referendum on the Nineteenth Amendment never taking place. *See* Terzian, "Effusions of Folly," 278–79.

[294] *See* Cleveland Plain Dealer, "Voters Will Pass on 3 Amendments" (October 31, 1923) (describing this amendment as being "without significance" and bringing Ohio up to date by repealing a meaningless provision that the voters failed to repeal in 1912).

for Ohio to bring its constitution into harmony with the federal constitution. It would take nearly forty more years before race and gender limitations were completely deleted from the Ohio Constitution. The voters finally removed the word "white" from Article IX, section 1 listing the qualifications for militia service in 1953, five years after President Harry Truman's executive order desegregating the military, and they did not remove "male" from the same section until 1961.

Tax-Related and Other Amendments

Other notable amendments during the years from 1913 to 1950 included a number of tax-related amendments. In 1918, the General Assembly and an initiative proposed two irreconcilable amendments involving the taxation of property, and the voters approved both of them. The Ohio Supreme Court, however, held that the amendment proposed by the General Assembly would take effect over the conflicting amendment proposed by initiative petition since, pursuant to Article II, section 1b, the former received a larger number of affirmative votes. *State ex rel. Greenland v. Fulton* (1919).

In 1921, the voters began a tradition that has continued unabated and approved an amendment to Article VIII to permit the issuance of bonds for bonuses for veterans of World War I notwithstanding the $750,000 limitation on state debt. In 1923, the voters expanded the powers of the Industrial Commission over worker's compensation, and in 1929, the voters approved an amendment that imposed a 1.5 percent limit on unvoted ad valorem property taxes. But in 1933, in the midst of the Depression, in the first two successful uses of the initiative petition to approve an amendment in fifteen years, the voters not only lowered the unvoted ad valorem property taxes to 1 percent but also approved an amendment proposed by initiative petition to extend home rule to counties. And in 1936, the voters again used the initiative petition to propose an amendment advanced by the governor for political reasons (and which the voters ultimately approved) to prohibit excise taxes (i.e., sales taxes) on food consumed off the premises.

Finally, in 1949, the voters adopted an amendment proposed by initiative petition to require office-type ballots where candidate names were listed under each elected office rather than by party affiliation, thus barring straight party ticket voting. See Article V, section 2a.

Rejected Amendments

During the balance of the first half of the twentieth century, the voters rejected a number of noteworthy proposed amendments.

In 1921, in keeping with Ohio's tradition against poll taxes, the voters overwhelmingly rejected an amendment proposed by the General Assembly to permit the levying of a poll tax; in 1926, they rejected an amendment proposed by initiative petition to effectively scrap the use of the primary; in 1938, they rejected an amendment proposed by initiative petition to replace the election of Supreme Court and other appellate judges with an appointed system; and in 1939, they rejected two amendments proposed by initiative petition (and advanced by Herbert S. Bigelow, the president of the 1912 Constitutional Convention) to reduce the signature requirements for placing statutory and constitutional initiatives on the ballot and to create a program of old age pensions.[295]

Constitutional Amendments—The Second Half of the Twentieth Century

Since 1912, the voters have approved amendments to nearly every article of the Ohio Constitution, with the articles dealing with the three branches of government (Art. II, III, and IV), public debt and public works (Art. VIII), and finance and taxation (Art. XII) having been amended the most (Table I.4). Together, these five articles account for approximately two-thirds of the changes made to the Ohio Constitution since 1912.

The second half of the twentieth century marks another dividing line in the post-1912 history of constitutional revision in Ohio. During this period, the increase in the number of amendments proposed and approved by the voters continued. In the pre-1912 period, the voters approved only eleven of twenty-six or 42.3 percent of the proposed amendments, but in the thirty-year period from the 1912 Convention to 1950, the voters approved twenty-four of fifty-nine or 40.7 percent of the proposed amendments. And in the second half of the century, the voters approved 83 of 135 or 61.5 percent of the proposed amendments.

The comparison between the amendments proposed by the General Assembly and by initiative petition may be even more significant. In the thirty-eight-year period after the 1912 Convention, the voters approved fifteen of thirty amendments proposed by the General Assembly but only nine of twenty-nine proposed by initiative petition. On the other hand, in the last half of the century, voter approval of amendments proposed by the General Assembly increased significantly to 78 of 109 or 71.6 percent while voter approval of amendments proposed by initiative petition fell to only five of twenty-six or 19.2 percent, thus illustrating the expanding role that the General Assembly was playing in constitutional revision and the more modest role played by the initiative.

Finally, the pace of constitutional change since 1912 has fluctuated with the most amendments adopted in the 1950s, 1960s, and 1970s when the voters approved sixty-three out of a hundred proposed amendments. See Table I.4, *infra*. The approval of more amendments in the 1970s than in any other decade

[295] *See* Steinglass, "Constitutional Revision," 315 n. 249.

TABLE I.4 Number of Approved Amendments by Article 1913 to 2021[*]

I	Bill of Rights	3	XI	Apportionment	2
II	Legislative	17	XII	Finance and Taxation	14
III	Executive	9	XIII	Corporations	1
IV	Judicial	16	XIV	[Jurisprudence] Ohio Livestock Care Standards Board	2
V	Elective Franchise	10	XV	Miscellaneous	11
VI	Education	4	XVI	Amendments	1
VII	Public Institutions	1	XVII	Elections	5
VIII	Public Debt and Public Works	27	XVIII	Municipal Corporations	2
IX	Militia	2	XIX	Redistricting	1
X	County and Townships	3			

[*]In some cases the number of approved amendments noted in this table is less than the total number of approved amendments since some amendments affect more than one article.

was, in large part, the result of the work of the Ohio Constitutional Revision Commission (OCRC).[296]

The 1950s and 1960s

In the 1950s, the voters approved eighteen of twenty-three amendments proposed by the General Assembly, and in the 1960s they approved sixteen of twenty-two proposed by the General Assembly. During this two decade period, only two amendments were proposed by initiative petition, and the voters rejected both of them—a 1958 proposal to adopt a "right-to-work amendment" that would have prohibited closed-shop union contracts, and a 1962 proposal to limit the state's power with respect to Sunday closing laws.

During these decades the most significant constitutional amendments involved issues of public debt, governmental reorganization, apportionment, and the judicial system.

Public Debt. Article VIII, which concerns the state's public debt and public works, is the longest article in the constitution and the article that the voters have amended most often. The 1851 Constitution imposed a $750,000 limitation on the amount of general obligation debt that the state could incur. See Commentary, Article V, sections 1, 2, and 3. Prior to 1950, the voters had

[296] Ohio Constitutional Revision Commission, *Recommendations for Amendments to the Ohio Constitution: Final Report* (1977), 16 (hereinafter OCRC, *Final Report*).

approved only two amendments that avoided this limitation and provided compensation to World War I and World War II veterans. But in this two-decade period, the voters approved eight amendments to this article to permit debt financing for a wide array of educational, highway, industrial developmental, parks and recreation projects as well as to provide compensation for Korean Conflict veterans. But in 1967 the voters overwhelmingly rejected an amendment advanced by Governor James A. Rhodes to create the Ohio Bond Commission and eliminate the need to submit amendments proposing state debt to the voters.[297] See Commentary, Article VIII.

Governmental Organization. During the 1950s and 1960s, the voters approved multiple amendments proposed by the General Assembly concerning the organization of state government. This included a 1954 amendment that extended the two-year term of office of the governor, the lieutenant governor, the secretary of state, the treasurer of state, and the attorney general to four years[298] and limited the governor to two successive terms (a limitation subsequently applied to other state officers); a 1956 amendment that provided four-year terms for state senators; a 1953 amendment that created a state board of education with responsibility for appointing the superintendent of public instruction, an official who had been appointed by the governor; and a 1961 amendment that authorized the General Assembly to require the advice and consent of the state Senate for gubernatorial appointments after the Ohio Supreme Court had struck down a statute that had given the Senate this power. See Commentary, Article III, section 21.

Apportionment. During this period, the voters addressed the issue of apportioning seats in the General Assembly. Ohio's apportionment scheme was based on county lines and created a "rural bloc" that favored voters in rural counties over voters in metropolitan counties.[299] But the U.S. Supreme Court held in 1964 that the Equal Protection Clause of the Fourteenth Amendment to the U.S. Constitution required that state legislatures be apportioned according to population. *Reynolds v. Sims* (1964).

As a result, in 1967 the General Assembly proposed and the voters approved a constitutional amendment replacing the county-based apportionment scheme with one based on population (though retaining a preference for the drawing of districts based on county lines). See Commentary, Article XI. These provisions of Article XI remain in effect until after the 2020 census at

[297] *See* Tom Diemer, Lee Leonard, and Richard G. Zimmerman, *James A. Rhodes: Ohio Colossus* (Kent: Kent State University Press, 2014), 49–51 (hereinafter Diemer, *Ohio Colossus*); *see also* Richard G. Zimmerman, "Rhodes's First Eight Years: 1963-1971," in Alexander P. Lamis and Brian Usher, eds., *Ohio Politics* (Kent: Kent State University Press, 2007) (revised and updated), 98–99 (hereinafter Lamis, *Ohio Politics*).

[298] The auditor already had a four-year term under the 1851 Constitution (Art. III, sec. 2).

[299] Swisher, *Ohio Constitution Handbook*, xxxvi, 427.

which time the new Ohio Redistricting Commission will govern both apportionment of the General Assembly and congressional redistricting (which had not previously been addressed in the Ohio Constitution). See Commentary, Articles XI and XIX.

Modern Courts Amendment. In 1968, the voters approved the Modern Courts Amendment, the first major revision of the judiciary article since the 1912 Convention. This amendment reorganized the structure and the administration of the courts to address the problems of overcrowded dockets and court backlogs that had plagued Ohio since the early days of statehood.[300]

The Modern Courts Amendment placed superintendence of the courts under the direction of the Ohio Supreme Court. The amendment gave the full court responsibility for the adoption of administrative rules for the courts, and it gave the chief justice special responsibility for court administration,[301] including the power to assign common pleas and court of appeals judges to other districts.

The amendment also gave the Ohio Supreme Court explicit authority to adopt rules governing the practice and procedures in the Ohio courts. Finally, it repealed the controversial provision, first adopted in 1912, requiring the concurrence of all but one Supreme Court justice for the court to hold unconstitutional a statute that a court of appeals had upheld.

Miscellaneous Proposals. During this period, the voters also approved a number of amendments to repeal obsolete provisions, including a provision dealing with the eligibility of women to hold office as well as the entirety of Article XIV on "Jurisprudence," which had created a commission in 1851 to draft the code of civil procedure that the General Assembly subsequently adopted in 1853.[302]

Amendments proposed by the General Assembly that the voters rejected during these decades included a proposal in 1954 to establish four-year terms for both representatives and senators, a proposal in 1958 to permit county voters to form metropolitan federations, a proposal in 1969 to lower the voting age from twenty-one to nineteen, and a proposal in 1968 to create a homestead tax exemption.

The 1970s and the Ohio Constitutional Revision Commission

The 1970s represent the high-water mark of constitutional revision in the latter half of the twentieth century, with the voters approving twenty-nine

---

300 *See generally* William W. Milligan and James E. Pohlman, "The 1968 Modern Courts Amendment to the Ohio Constitution," 29 *Ohio St. L. J.* 811 (1968) (hereinafter Milligan and Pohlman, "Modern Courts Amendment").

301 Ibid., 822.

302 Harvey Walker, ed., *An Analysis and Appraisal of the Ohio Constitution 1851–1951* (Cincinnati: Stephen J. Wilder Foundation, 1951), 51.

amendments, more than in any other decade since the 1912 Constitutional Convention. During this decade, the voters approved twenty-eight of the forty-two amendments proposed by the General Assembly but only one of the eleven proposed by initiative petition.

The increase in constitutional revision during the 1970s is largely attributable to the work of the OCRC. Established in 1969 by the General Assembly in preparation for the mandatory twenty-year vote in 1972 on whether to hold a constitutional convention, the commission was a thirty-two--person bipartisan body composed of twelve legislators, divided evenly by party and chamber, and twenty public members. The enabling legislation charged the commission with undertaking a review of the constitution for the purpose of recommending (by a two-thirds vote) constitutional amendments to the General Assembly.[303]

Constitutional conventions had fallen out of favor nationally, and Ohio voters rejected the call for a constitutional convention in 1972 by an overwhelming vote. But constitutional revision commissions had become popular, and the Ohio commission succeeded in having many of its recommendations incorporated into amendments that the General Assembly proposed and the voters approved.[304] In total, the commission made sixty-three discrete recommendations, and the General Assembly incorporated twenty-eight of them into the sixty amendments that the voters approved. Fourteen other recommendations were incorporated into the four amendments that the voters rejected, and the remaining twenty-one recommendations (for a variety of reasons) were never included in amendments proposed by the General Assembly.[305]

Some of the more important amendments that had their origins in the recommendations of the commission involved the reorganization of the legislative article, the joint election of the governor and lieutenant governor, gubernatorial succession, the creation of the Ohio Ballot Board, the lowering of the voting age to eighteen (to conform to the Twenty-Sixth Amendment to the U.S. Constitution), the reduction in the durational voting residency requirements to thirty days (to conform to the U.S. Supreme Court decision in *Dunn v. Blumstein* (1972)), as well as various amendments involving county charters, prison labor, the tax system, the permissible purposes for issuing industrial development bonds, and the repeal of obsolete constitutional provisions.

---

303 *See* Steinglass, "Constitutional Revision," 315 n. 249.

304 *See* OCRC, *Final Report*, 20–21. By the time the commission's Final Report was completed in May 1977, the voters had approved thirteen amendments originating from commission recommendations. Subsequently, the voters approved three more amendments that originated from the commission; one that gave the General Assembly more control over regulating prison labor; one that modified the provisions for adopting or amending county charters; and one that expanded the duties of the Ohio Ballot Board.

305 *See generally* Steinglass, "Constitutional Revision," 334–45.

Despite these successes, the voters rejected commission-inspired amendments to eliminate the $750,000 debt limit and change the process for incurring general obligation debt, to repeal the 1851 provision permitting the General Assembly to appoint "courts of conciliation," to eliminate the 1875 provision creating a supreme court commission to assist the court in disposing of cases, and to repeal the provision barring voting by convicted embezzlers.

Important amendments adopted during the 1970s that did not have their origins in the work of the commission included a 1973 amendment establishing a state lottery, a 1975 amendment authorizing charitable bingo, and a 1975 amendment to simplify the ballot and require delegates to national party conventions to be elected by the voters. The voters also approved non-commission amendments to increase the homestead exemption for senior citizens and disabled residents, and to issue bonds to provide bonuses to Vietnam veterans.

On the other hand, during this decade the voters rejected ten of the eleven amendments proposed by initiative. The rejected amendments included proposals addressing utility rate-making, nuclear power plant safety, debt infrastructure, procedures for the initiative, the state income tax, and the use of leg traps and other devices causing prolonged suffering to animals. The voters in 1975 also rejected four proposals by Governor James A. Rhodes (advanced to the ballot by initiative petition) that would have authorized state and local debt for infrastructure and economic development.[306]

The one amendment proposed by initiative petition and approved by the voters was the controversial 1977 amendment to adopt the state's first mandatory statewide voter registration requirement, under which persons could only vote if registered for thirty days prior to an election. See Commentary, Article V, section 1. This amendment also required the purging of the voting rolls of registered voters who had not voted in a four-year period, a federal challenge to which was rejected by the U.S. Supreme Court in 2018.[307]

The 1980s

During the 1980s, the voters approved six of the eleven amendments proposed by the General Assembly and none of the seven proposed by initiative petition. Three of the six approved amendments were the addition of new sections to Article VIII to permit the issuance of bonds to finance low-cost housing (1982), coal research (1985), and local governments projects to improve water, sewer, and waste facilities (1987). During this decade, the voters also approved an amendment creating an exemption from the "uniform rule" and permitting

---

[306] *See* Appendix B; *see also* Plain Dealer, "Governor Rhodes' Package Is Itemized," sec. 1, 34 (November 2, 1975) (reviewing the four amendments advanced by Governor Rhodes).

[307] *See Husted v. A. Philip Randolph Institute*, 138 S.Ct. 1833 (2018).

reductions in the assessed value of residential and agricultural property (1980), an amendment requiring all proceeds from the state lottery to be used for education (1987), and an amendment concerning filling vacancies in the office of lieutenant governor (1989).

The five amendments proposed by the General Assembly but rejected by the voters included four proposals to amend Article VIII to issue bonds for the public financing and operation of electric utilities through nonprofit corporations (1980); for highway improvements (1980); for private, low-cost housing (1980); and for high-speed rail (1982). Governor Rhodes advanced these proposals as alternatives to raising taxes, but the proposed amendments lacked the bipartisan support that historically characterized successful efforts to incur debt for public improvements.[308] Finally, the voters rejected by a 52.4 percent to 47.6 percent vote a proposal to amend Article X, section 4, and Article XVIII, section 8, to change the method for delivering proposed municipal or county charter amendments to the voters by leaving the means for publicizing the proposals to the General Assembly (1980).

The seven unsuccessful amendments proposed by initiative petition during the 1980s included: two proposals in 1981 to authorize private companies to sell workers' compensation insurance and to change apportionment methods for both General Assembly and congressional districts; a proposal in 1982 to elect members of the Public Utilities Commission and to finance publicly their campaigns; three proposals in 1983 to raise the drinking age to twenty-one, to repeal all taxes passed since 1982, and to require a three-fifths majority of the General Assembly to levy new taxes; and a proposal in 1987 to establish a merit system under which the governor would initially appoint supreme court and court of appeals judges.

The 1990s

The pace of constitutional change increased in the 1990s, when the voters approved fourteen of seventeen amendments, including ten of the eleven proposed by the General Assembly and four of the six submitted by initiative petition.

Five of the amendments proposed by the General Assembly and approved by the voters concerned taxes or state debt, including a proposal to extend the homestead exemption for surviving spouses (1990), and four proposals to issue bonds for low-cost housing (1990), the improvement of parks and the conservation of natural resources (1993), public works and highways (1995), and public school facilities (1999). The 1999 approval of bonds for public schools followed the rejection of that amendment in 1998 and included a formula for limiting

308 *See* Diemer, *Ohio Colossus*, 86–88 (describing politicization of bond issues); Richard G. Zimmerman, "Rhodes's Second Eight Years, 1975–1983" in Lamis, ed., *Ohio Politics*, 129–32.

debt service payments. And the voters approved a 1994 amendment to Article VI, section 6, to protect the viability of prepaid tuition programs and prevent federal taxation of program income.

In the 1990s, the voters also approved four amendments that reflected the mood of the public in support of victims of crime and against criminal defendants. In 1994, the voters approved an amendment to afford victims of criminal offenses "fairness, dignity, and respect in the criminal justice system" and an amendment eliminating the role of Ohio's Courts of Appeals in death penalty cases. In 1997, they approved the second amendment to the Bill of Rights since 1851, an amendment making bail more difficult. Finally, in 1995 the voters approved an amendment limiting the governor's power to commute sentences, an amendment that was in direct response to the commutation of seven death sentences in early 1991 by out-going governor Richard F. Celeste and upheld by the Ohio Supreme Court. See *State ex rel. Maurer v. Sheward* (1994).

Reflecting the national movement to hold elected officials more accountable to the public, Ohio voters approved three separate amendments, all proposed by initiative petition, imposing term limits on members of the U.S. Congress, the Ohio General Assembly, and key executive branch officers (other than the governor, whose term was already term-limited). Subsequently, the U.S. Supreme Court held unconstitutional state-imposed term limits for U.S. senators and members of the House of Representatives, *U.S. Term Limits, Inc. v. Thornton* (1995), and the Ohio limitation on federal legislators never went into effect. Nonetheless, the provisions of the Ohio Constitution expanding term limits for state officeholders and imposing them on members of the General Assembly, though still controversial, went into effect and remain the law in Ohio.

In this decade, the voters also approved a 1994 amendment proposed by initiative petition to bar the application of a sales tax on soft drinks, but they rejected amendments proposed by initiative petition to permit casino gambling in 1990 and riverboat casino gambling in 1996. Finally, in 1992, the voters rejected the mandatory twenty-year question on holding a constitutional convention by another overwhelming vote. See Appendix A.

■ THE COURT IN THE TWENTIETH CENTURY—FROM 1912 TO THE END OF THE TWENTIETH CENTURY

For most of Ohio's history, constitutional revision primarily involved the political process, with the General Assembly and the electorate playing the pivotal roles. The judiciary, though often the subject of constitutional attention because of persistent backlogs and, at least at the 1912 Constitutional Convention, because of its perceived abuse of its power of judicial review, was an important but not the principal player on the constitutional stage.

The Ohio Supreme Court had approved judicial review in 1807, but it exercised this power modestly in the first half of the nineteenth century. In the second half of the century, however, the court picked up the pace and decided important cases involving the Ohio Constitution, including cases involving bible reading in the schools,[309] liquor,[310] voter registration,[311] and the requirements for a convention call.[312]

Despite such decisions, the court's role in construing the Ohio Constitution was relatively modest until the latter part of the nineteenth and first decade of the twentieth century, when it began making the decisions that earned it the enmity of the cities, the unions, and the supporters of the Progressive movement. Relying on such doctrines as the right to contract, the fundamental nature of property rights, and a judicially enforceable expectation that the General Assembly act reasonably, the court routinely second-guessed the General Assembly and struck down laws designed to regulate business, to protect workers, and to provide for the social welfare. Ultimately, the court—undoubtedly chastened by the antijudiciary sentiments expressed at the 1912 Convention and the amendments approved that year—changed its course, and until the 1980s was generally deferential to the legislature.

The more limited role played by the Ohio Supreme Court in exercising judicial review during the period from the 1912 Convention to 1968 was also influenced, in part, by the limitation that the supermajority requirement placed on the court.[313] By requiring "the concurrence of all but one of the judges" to declare a law unconstitutional when the court of appeals had rejected such a challenge, the constitution made it more difficult for the court to exercise judicial review. And the requirement resulted in a number of decisions in which the constitutionality of statutes was upheld by votes of two to five. The voters removed this provision, which the U.S. Supreme Court had upheld, *Ohio ex rel. Bryant v. Akron Metropolitan Park District* (1930), when they approved the Modern Courts Amendment in 1968.

The Ohio Supreme Court, however, did not completely ignore the Ohio Constitution, and between 1912 and 1980, the court played its traditional role of construing the Ohio Constitution to resolve controversies between the branches of state government and between state and local government. This included important decisions addressing the meaning of the constitutional provisions adopted in 1912, especially in the area of municipal home rule and the initiative,

309 *See Cincinnati Board of Education v. Minor* (1872).

310 *See, e.g., State v. Sinks* (1884); *State v. Hipp* (1882); *State v. Miller* (1854).

311 *See Daggett v. Hudson* (1885).

312 *See State ex rel. Attorney General v. Kinney* (1897).

313 *See* Entin, "Judicial Supermajorities," 452–53 ("To the extent that the supermajority requirement was intended to remind the supreme court that the people wanted the judiciary to show greater deference to the legislature, the message came through loud and clear.").

as well as decisions concerning the carrying of concealed weapons, the appointment power, gubernatorial term limits, state taxation, county charters, and state debt.[314]

During this period, however, the court was generally not sympathetic to the use of the Ohio Constitution to protect individual rights. For example, in 1923, it rejected a state constitutional challenge to the school funding formula, *Miller v. Korns* (1923); in 1933, it rejected a challenge to racial segregation at the university level without considering the possibility that the Ohio Constitution might be relevant, *State ex rel. Weaver v. Board of Trustees* (1933); and in 1936, it reiterated its rejection of the reasoning of the U.S. Supreme Court's position that that unconstitutionally seized evidence is inadmissible in federal criminal proceedings without considering whether evidence seized in violation of the Ohio Constitution should be subject to a state exclusionary rule.[315] But in 1941, the court expressed its intention to continue to apply the right to contract doctrine to limit governmental regulation, which in this case involved the sale and installation of plumbing fixtures, *Direct Plumbing Supply Co. v. Dayton* (1941).[316]

Change in Direction

In the late 1970s and early 1980s under the leadership of Chief Justice Frank D. Celebrezze Jr., one of Ohio's most controversial chief justices,[317] the court began to take a more active approach to Ohio law, especially in such areas as tort and insurance law, workers' rights, municipal sovereign immunity, and charitable immunity. But despite the unseemly and even embarrassing conflicts within the court and between the chief justice and the organized bar and the media, the most important legacy of the Celebrezze court may well have been its willingness to break with tradition and embrace a more activist approach to the law. And this "shift won the approval of the labor movement and other liberal groups

---

[314] *See, e.g., Fitzgerald v. City of Cleveland* (1913) (home rule); *State v. Nieto* (1920) (concealed carry); *State ex rel. Howland v. Krause* (1936) (county charters); *State ex rel. Burns v. DiSalle* (1961) (advice and consent); *State ex rel. Saxbe v. Brand* (1964) (state debt); *Denison University v. Board of Tax Appeals* (1965) (state tax exemptions); *State ex rel. Rhodes v. Brown* (1973) (gubernatorial term limits).

[315] *See State v. Lindway* (1936) (refusing to apply an exclusionary rule to evidence seized in violation of the state constitution); *see also State v. Mapp* (1960) (holding that evidence obtained by an unlawful search and seizure is admissible in a criminal prosecution notwithstanding the application of the Fourth Amendment to the states), *rev'd, Mapp v. Ohio* (U.S. 1961).

[316] During the 1950s and 1960s, the court resisted the trend of federal decisions and rejected challenges to state policies in such areas as movie censorship, the regulation of political speech, and the rights of the criminally accused. *See* Benedict, "Civil Liberty in Ohio," 715–20.

[317] *See* G. Alan Tarr and Mary Cornelia Porter, "Ohio: Partisan Justice," in *State Supreme Courts in State and Nation* (New Haven: Yale University Press, 1988), 124–83.

but displeased insurance companies, other business groups, and the medical community."[318]

Chief Justice Celebrezze's valedictory may have been his concurring opinion in *State ex rel. The Repository v. Unger* (1986), a case involving the open courts provision of Article I, section 16. Issued in the last week of December 1986 (after the voters rejected his re-election bid), the chief justice's long concurring opinion relied on *Direct Plumbing* and state court decisions by Oregon Supreme Court Justice Hans A. Linde and Massachusetts Supreme Judicial Court Associate Justice Oliver Wendell Holmes Jr., to support his conclusion about the importance of independently relying on the Ohio Constitution.

During this period, the court also began to view the Ohio Constitution as a source of protection for individual rights, and this process accelerated in the 1990s when the court rendered major constitutional decisions in the areas of tort reform and school funding, issues that continued to fester in the twenty-first century.

The late twentieth-century history of the Ohio Supreme Court (even after the 1986 electoral defeat of Chief Justice Celebrezze), however, was marked by sharp ideological, political, and even personal splits on the court as well as by an unusually vitriolic struggle between the court and the General Assembly over the constitutionality of legislative limits on the power of the judiciary and over the duty of the General Assembly to act affirmatively to meet its constitutional obligations. The former is best seen in decisions protecting the interests of personal injury plaintiffs in the face of tort reform legislation and the latter by the controversy over the role of the court in addressing the adequacy of public funding for education.[319]

Tort Reform

In the last two decades of the twentieth century, as the General Assembly began enacting probusiness legislation often in response to judicial changes in tort law, the Ohio Supreme Court, relying on the Ohio Constitution, began to show a greater willingness to strike down measures that directly or indirectly limited the rights of workers and tort victims. During this period, the court invalidated legislation that would have imposed strict time limits on suits brought by medical malpractice claimants, *Hardy v. VerMeulen* (1987); *Mominee v. Scherbarth* (1986) as well as legislation that would have limited the ability of employees to sue their employers for intentional torts, *Van Fossen v. Babcock & Wilcox Co.* (1988).

The conflict between the Ohio Supreme Court and the General Assembly over tort reform continued into the 1990s with the court striking down a cap on

[318] Lawrence Baum, "Judicial Election & Appointment at the State Level," 77 *Ky. L. J.* 645 (1988–1989): 653.

[319] Jonathan L. Entin, "Judicial Selection and Political Culture," 30 *Cap. U. L Rev.* 523 (2002): 526–38 (hereinafter Entin, "Judicial Selection").

medical malpractice damage awards. *See Morris v. Savoy* (1991). This struggle, which a leading commentator described as a "war" between the court and the legislature,[320] appeared to culminate in the 1999 decision in *State ex rel. Ohio Academy of Trial Lawyers v. Sheward* (1999), in which the court, in the course of striking down omnibus tort reform legislation on the basis of the one-subject rule of Article II, section 15(C), reaffirmed the primacy of its role in interpreting the Ohio Constitution. Stating that interpretation of the state and federal constitutions is a role "exclusive to the judicial branch," the *Sheward* court further noted that "[t]he power and duty of the judiciary to determine the constitutionality and, therefore, the validity of the acts of the other branches of government have been firmly established as an essential feature of the Ohio system of separation of powers."

And relying on several state constitutional grounds, including the right to a jury trial, the right to a remedy, separation of powers, and the one-subject rule, the *Sheward* court rejected the legislative re-enactment of a number of statutory provisions that the court had previously held unconstitutional. But the next chapter in this story would not be written until the twenty-first century.

Education

The dispute between the court and the General Assembly over education has been even more contentious than the dispute over tort reform and even included a threatened use of the judicial recall.[321] Beginning with its landmark 1997 decision in *DeRolph v. State* (1997) and culminating in its December 2002 ruling in the same case, the court held that Ohio's system of public education relied too heavily on property taxes in violation of the constitutional duty imposed by Article VI, section 2 on the General Assembly to provide "a thorough and efficient system of common schools throughout the state." Despite an intervening constitutional amendment in 1999 (approved by the voters) to authorize the borrowing of funds for school facilities, the court ultimately reinstated its earlier holding and "direct[ed] the General Assembly to enact a school-funding scheme that is thorough and efficient." *DeRolph IV* (2002). Ultimately, however, the court chose to not exercise continuing jurisdiction over the case and prevented the lower courts from doing so. See Commentary, Article VI, section 2.

New Judicial Federalism

In contrast to its aggressive approach to tort reform and educational financing, the Ohio Supreme Court was initially reluctant to follow U.S. Supreme Court

---

320 Stephen J. Werber, "Ohio Tort Reform in 1998: The War Continues," 45 *Clev. St. L. Rev.* 539 (1997).

321 *See Cincinnati Post*, "Lawmaker Seeks to Oust 3 Justices" (January 17, 2003). *See also* David Mayer, "Legislature Should Oust 4 Justices," *Columbus Dispatch* (June 6, 2001).

Justice William J. Brennan Jr.'s 1977 exhortation to look to state constitutions as independent sources for the protection of individual rights.[322] The court's reluctance caught the eye of commentators. And in 1984, two political scientists sharply criticized the court for its failure to construe independently the rights-protecting provisions of the state constitution.[323]

The court acknowledged this critique in *Arnold v. City of Cleveland* (1993),[324] in which it announced its willingness to treat the Ohio constitution as "a document of independent force."[325] Describing the right to bear arms under Article I, section 4, of the Ohio Constitution, as a fundamental right,[326] the court issued what one scholar characterized as its "Declaration of Ohio State Constitutional Independence."[327] In doing so, the court described federal law as a floor below which state court judgments (actually the court referred to state court decisions) could not fall.

> In joining the growing trend in other states, we believe that the Ohio Constitution is a document of independent force. In the areas of individual rights and civil liberties, the United States Constitution, where applicable to the states, provides a floor below which state court decisions may not fall. As long as state courts provide at least as much protection as the United States Supreme Court has provided in its interpretation of the federal Bill of Rights, state courts are unrestricted in according greater civil liberties and protections to individuals and groups.[328]

In the early 1990s, the Ohio Supreme Court appeared to be on the brink of embracing what is often referred to as the "new judicial federalism." Most notably, in the area of search and seizure, it gave Article I, section 14, an independent

---

[322] William J. Brennan Jr., "State Constitutions and the Protection of Individual Rights," 90 *Harv. L. Rev.* 489 (1977).

[323] *See* Mary Cornelia Porter and G. Alan Tarr, "The New Judicial Federalism and the Ohio Supreme Court: Anatomy of a Failure," 45 *Ohio St. L. J.* 143 (1984); *see also* Kevin Francis O'Neill, "The Road Not Taken: State Constitutions as an Alternative Source of Protection for Reproductive Rights," 11 *N. Y. L. Sch. J. Hum. Rts.* 1 (1993): 35–38.

[324] *Arnold v. City of Cleveland*, 67 Ohio St. 3d 35, 42 n.8, 616 N.E.2d 163, 168 n.8 (1993) ("When presented with opportunities to do so, this court has not, on most occasions, used the Ohio Constitution as an independent source of constitutional rights.").

[325] Ibid. For discussions of the New Judicial Federalism in Ohio, see Marianna Brown Bettman, "Ohio Joins the New Judicial Federalism Movement: A Little To-ing and a Little Fro-ing," 51 *Clev. St. L. Rev.* 491 (2004); Richard B. Saphire, "Ohio Constitutional Interpretation," 51 *Clev. St. L. Rev.* 437 (2004); Robert F. Williams, "The New Judicial Federalism in Ohio: The First Decade," 51 *Clev. St. L. Rev.* 415 (2004) (hereinafter, Williams, "The New Judicial Federalism in Ohio").

[326] Despite treating the right to bear arms as fundamental, the *Arnold* court upheld a municipal ban on the possession and sale of assault weapons. *See* Commentary, Art. I, sec. 4.

[327] Williams, "The New Judicial Federalism in Ohio," 419.

[328] *Arnold*, 67 Ohio St. 3d at 42, 616 N.E.2d at 169.

meaning even though the state provision was the mirror image of the Fourth Amendment to the U.S. Constitution. See *State v. Storch* (1993); *State v. Brown* (1992).

But the court subsequently drew back, declared the protections provided by the state and federal search and seizure provisions to be coextensive, and stated that the court would "harmonize our interpretation of Section 14, Article I of the Ohio Constitution with the Fourth Amendment, unless there are persuasive reasons to find otherwise." *State v. Robinette* (1997). The court then reversed a number of rulings that had given the Ohio Constitution an independent construction, including the 1992 *Brown* decision.[329]

And when the court identified the Ohio Constitution as a basis for its decisions, it often did so in opinions that combined discussion of the state and federal provisions and that lacked the clarity necessary to insulate its judgments from U.S. Supreme Court review. As a result, under the adequate and independent state ground doctrine (as reinvigorated by the U.S. Supreme Court's 1983 decision in *Michigan v. Long*), the Court treated a number of Ohio decisions that appeared to rely on the Ohio Constitution as not having done so with a plain statement; thus, the Court concluded that the decisions were based on federal law and subject to its review.[330]

The full impact of the *Arnold* decision, however, would have to await the twenty-first century, when the volume of state constitutional claims began to increase and the Ohio Supreme Court had new opportunities to develop its state constitutional jurisprudence.

■ THE OHIO CONSTITUTION IN THE TWENTY-FIRST CENTURY

There are five areas in which there have been significant developments concerning the Ohio Constitution in the twenty-first century. First, the ad hoc or piecemeal process of constitutional revision has continued with the voters approving eighteen amendments and with the General Assembly continuing to play the major role in proposing amendments. Second, the General Assembly attempted to replicate the experience of the 1970s with commission-based constitutional revision by creating the Ohio Constitutional Modernization

[329] *See* Williams, "The New Judicial Federalism in Ohio," 420–25 (identifying the stages of the new judicial federalism, describing Ohio as a "latecomer," and noting the "backlash" in response to the expansion of rights for criminal defendants). *See also* Commentary, Art. I, sec. 14.

[330] *See, e.g., Ohio v. Reiner* (U.S. 2001) (per curiam) (stating that the "decision at issue fairly appears . . . to be interwoven with the federal law and that no adequate and independent state ground is clear from the face of the opinion") (internal quotations omitted); *Ohio v. Robinette* (U.S. 1996) ("Although the opinion below mentions Art. I, § 14, of the Ohio Constitution in passing . . ., the opinion clearly relies on federal law nevertheless."); *Ohio v. Johnson* (U.S. 1984) ("A review of the court's syllabus indicates that the court did not articulate an independent state-law ground for the decision.").

Commission (OCMC). Third, there was continued interest in reforming the process for selecting judges. Fourth, the Ohio Supreme Court addressed the issue of stare decisis as a court with an ever-changing membership has had to determine which precedents to follow and which to discard. And fifth, the court has been responding to the increase in efforts to use the Ohio Constitution as a source of protection for individual rights as it addresses the challenge of developing an independent, robust and principled Ohio constitutional jurisprudence.

Continued Piecemeal Constitutional Revision

In the first two decades of the twenty-first century, Ohio voters approved eighteen of thirty-one amendments, which included thirteen of the fifteen amendments proposed by the General Assembly but only five of the sixteen proposed by initiative. This difference in the approval rate is consistent with historic patterns in which the voters have been far more likely to approve amendments proposed by the General Assembly than those proposed by initiative petition. But during this period there have been some changes in the nature of the amendments being proposed by initiative.

General Assembly—Proposed Amendments

In the first two decades of the century, the General Assembly proposed six amendments to Article VIII to authorize the issuance of bonds for conservation and economic development, and the voters approved five of them. The approved amendments included two to borrow funds for environmental conservation (2000 and 2008), two to support Governor Bob Taft's Third Frontier program for research and development in support of Ohio industry, commerce, and business (2005 and 2010), and one for capital improvements (2014). The rejected amendment was the governor's initial 2003 Third Frontier proposal. *See generally* Article VIII, sections 2o, 2p, 2q, and 2s, and Commentaries.

The eight other amendments proposed by the General Assembly and approved by the voters covered a broad range of issues and included: earlier filing deadlines for initiatives (2008), the reaffirmation of property owners' right to ground water to smooth the way for Ohio's approval of the Great Lakes-St. Lawrence River Basin Sustainable Water Resources Agreement (2008), the creation of the Ohio Livestock Care Standards Board (2009), the issuance of bonds for war bonuses for veterans of the Persian Gulf, Afghanistan and Iraq conflicts (2009), the relocation of the Columbus/Franklin County casino (2010), the restriction on the use of the initiative to create monopolies (2015), the apportionment of the General Assembly (2015), and congressional redistricting (2018).

The one rejected (and not re-submitted) amendment proposed by the General Assembly in 2011 sought to revise Article IV to raise the judicial retirement age and to eliminate obsolete provisions authorizing supreme court commissions and courts of conciliation. *See* Commentaries, Article IV, sections 6, 19, and 22.

Initiated Amendments

Amendments proposed in this century by initiative petition did not fare nearly as well at the polls as those proposed by the General Assembly, but the approval of five of the sixteen amendments (or 31.3 percent) proposed by initiative petition was slightly higher than the historic average of 26.8 percent. *See* Table I.2.

The five approved amendments proposed by initiative petition included high-visibility amendments to bar same-sex marriage (2004), to require annual increases in the minimum wage (2006), to authorize casino gambling in four locations (2009), to nullify the individual mandate in the federal Affordable Care Act (2011), and to expand the rights of crime victims (2017).

These amendments continued a trend that began in the 1990s, when the voters approved initiative petitions with populist flairs. This pattern has been characterized by well-funded campaigns, some of which were undertaken for political reasons. Supporters of the ban on same-sex marriage in 2004 and the increase in the minimum wage in 2006 (regardless of their commitment to those measures) used the proposals to gin up the turnout of voters who, it was hoped, would be sympathetic to the supporters' candidates in presidential and gubernatorial elections. The 2009 casino gambling proposal, which was advanced for business reasons and which has been seen by many as the poster-child for the shortcomings of the constitutional initiative, and the 2017 proposal to expand the rights of victims in criminal cases, were advanced by well-funded out-of-state interests, and the 2011 anti-Obamacare freedom to choose healthcare proposal was part of a national effort to organize around and politicize the issue of health care reform.

Voter participation on these post-2000 initiatives was high—ranging from 93 to 98 percent of those going to the polls—and the only proposed amendments that received favorable votes from less than 60 percent of the voters were the minimum wage proposal (56.7 percent) and the casino gambling proposal (54 percent).[331]

The eleven rejected amendments included five advanced by good government groups to alter electoral policies through changes in state reapportionment and congressional redistricting (2005 and 2012), two seeking constitutional authorization for gambling (2006 and 2008), one seeking the legalization of the recreational use of marijuana (2015), two seeking sentencing reforms for drug-related crimes (2002 and 2018), and one involving smoking (2006).

---

[331] *See* Table of Initiated Constitutional Amendments Approved by Ohio Voters, Ohio Constitution—Law and History (CM Law Website).

There were also a substantial number of proposed initiated amendments that, for a variety of reasons, have not yet made it to the ballot (after having received permission to begin collecting signatures). These included multiple marijuana and gambling proposals as well as initiatives to bar puppy mills, to expand the availability of kidney dialysis, to support green energy programs (with a generous payment to out-of-state program administrators), to protect state sovereignty, to provide consumer protection for short-term loans, to extend the constitutional rights of initiative and referendum to the people of counties and townships, to protect the right of community self-government, to convert the current chamber-specific legislative term limits to lifetime term limits, to adopt ethics reforms, to regulate bottle bills, to repeal the ban on same-sex marriage, to protect voter rights, to recognize the personhood of fetuses (in order to bar abortions and force a re-examination of *Roe v. Wade* (1973)), to increase the minimum wage, and to guarantee the freedom to join or not join labor organizations (thus making Ohio a right to work state).[332] The quantity and the range of these proposals illustrate the fact that the initiative process is very much a part of the political process in Ohio.

The Role of the Initiative

There is no single explanation for the current interest in Ohio in the constitutional initiative, especially in light of its modest success rate. In the 110 years since its adoption in 1912, the voters rejected 68.8 percent of all proposed constitutional initiatives that reached the ballot. *See* Table I.2, *supra*.

It is expensive in Ohio to collect the requisite number of signatures from a minimum of forty-four counties and to wage a serious campaign in support of a ballot issue, but those costs do not come close to the costs in California and other states where the constitutional initiative has flourished (for better or worse) for many years.[333] In 2009, for example, the proponents of the successful casino gaming initiative spent $48.7 million in support of their proposal while the opponents spent $12.2 million. Nonetheless, money does not tell the whole story. And in the two most recent hotly contested Ohio initiative campaigns—the 2015 marijuana legalization proposal and the 2018 proposal to reduce penalties for drug-related offenses—the amendments' proponents spent $21.2 and $31.7 million respectively, approximately nine times more than the opponents on each issue, only to see the voters defeat their proposals by substantial margins.[334]

---

[332] *See* List of Petitions Submitted to the Attorney General's Office (Attorney General Website).

[333] *See generally* David S. Broder, *Democracy Derailed: Initiative Campaigns and the Power of Money* (New York: Harcourt Inc., 2000).

[334] *See* FollowtheMoney.org—Election Overview (National Institute on Money in Politics) (website).

Efforts to use the constitutional initiative have come from groups across the political spectrum, and those who seek to make political points or to advance their special interest will likely continue to use the constitutional initiative even if they lack the funds or the ability to wage credible campaigns. And despite its secondary role in constitutional revision, the initiative has opened up the political process by serving as a means for opening up political debate through the proposal of amendments that, for a variety of reasons, the General Assembly would not propose.

The constitutional initiative clearly has detractors, but it also has strong supporters. And initiative reform is a lightning rod for political controversy, as the OCMC learned in 2017.[335]

The Ohio Constitutional Modernization Commission

In 2011, one year before the scheduled vote on the 20-year mandatory convention call, the General Assembly created a thirty-two-member OCMC.[336] Modeled after the 1970s OCRC, the General Assembly gave the OCMC an identical charge to study the Ohio Constitution and, by a two-thirds vote, to make recommendations to the General Assembly for constitutional amendments.[337] As in the 1970s, the General Assembly gave the OCMC a ten-year term to complete its work, but in 2017 it killed the commission four years in advance of its scheduled sunset.

The challenge facing the OCMC was substantial. With nearly 57,000 words and more than 220 sections at the time the General Assembly created the commission, the Ohio Constitution was the nation's tenth longest state constitution. And beyond the issue of length, it was full of obsolete, unconstitutional, statutory-like, and dysfunctional provisions; and it lacked the clarity and transparency one should want in a state's fundamental charter.

Slow to get off the ground and not fully staffed until mid-2014, the commission in its three-year working life approved reports and recommendations to repeal or amend twenty-one sections of the constitution. This included proposals to repeal two obsolete sections in Article IV involving the judiciary (courts of conciliation and supreme court commissions); two obsolete sections in Article VII involving the directors of the state penitentiary; nine obsolete sections in Article VIII involving bonds that had been paid off; and five obsolete sections also in Article VIII and involving the no-longer operating sinking fund commission. It also proposed the adoption of two technical provisions

---

[335] *See* Ohio Constitutional Modernization Commission, Minutes (June 8, 2017) (tabling initiative reform recommendation in response to strong expression of opposition).

[336] Am. H.B. 188, 129th Gen. Assembly (2011).

[337] For an in-depth review of the Ohio Constitutional Modernization Commission from its inception through 2015, *see* Steinglass, "Constitutional Revision," 345–54.

involving state debt and one proposed replacement of the offensive phrase "the insane, blind, deaf and dumb" in the current provision authorizing services for the handicapped. See Commentary, Article VII, section 1.

Had the General Assembly presented these proposals to the voters and had the voters approved them, the Ohio Constitution would have been shortened by more than 20 percent.

The premature sunset of the commission left the constitution full of provisions on which the commission did not recommend changes. These include:

- Committee-approved proposals to strengthen the statutory initiative, to revise term limits for state legislators, to reform grand jury proceedings, to replace the offensive phrase "idiot, or insane person" from those who are denied the right to vote, and to remove inappropriate gender-specific language from thirty-eight sections;
- Unconstitutional provisions establishing a right to refuse to participate in federal healthcare programs, barring same sex marriage, placing term limits on members of the U.S. Congress, and permitting prosecutors to comment on the invocation of the privilege against self-incrimination;
- Obsolete provisions authorizing preferential votes for U.S. senators (supplanted by the Seventeenth Amendment to the U.S. Constitution), and requiring popular votes before granting banks new powers such as the power to issue currency;
- Detailed provisions better suited for statutes, such as those on casino gambling, the minimum wage, and the Ohio Livestock Care Standards Board; and
- Highly visible topics such as the one-subject limitation on state legislative logrolling, election of local school boards, selection of the state board of education, judicial selection, and home rule.

The demise of the commission also resulted in the following articles receiving little or no review: Article III (executive); Article X (county and township organizations); Article XII (finance and taxation); Article XIII (corporations); Article XVI (amendments); and Article XVIII (municipal corporations).

The major success of the commission was the fact that its work product was used in 2015 by the General Assembly to recommend two amendments that the voters approved: a complete revision of Article XI on apportionment; and the adoption of a limitation on the ability to use the constitutional initiative to create monopolies, to determine state taxes, and to confer special interests. See Commentary, Article II, section 1e. And the 2018 approval of a new Article XIX, which placed congressional redistricting in the Ohio Constitution for the first time, can be directly traced to the work of the commission.

The commission left behind a substantial record, and its proceedings and reports are available to future policymakers and members of the public who wish to address issues involving the Ohio Constitution. Nonetheless, those who are considering state constitutional revision may look at the experience of the commission and ask why it was not more successful.

Although resembling the 1970s Commission in most respects, the 2011 legislation that created the OCMC rejected the singular strength of the earlier commission—its strong commitment to public (i.e., nonlegislative) leadership. Richard C. Carter, a respected businessman from Fostoria, Ohio, served as the chair for almost the entire life of the 1970s Commission. The statutory language that created the Commission in 2011, however, only permitted current legislators to serve as cochairs.

The implications of legislative control of the commission were huge. It included control of the appointment of the public members, control of hiring staff, control of outreach, control of the budget, and control of meeting agendas. And most importantly, legislative control effectively prevented any of the twenty public members from playing a strong leadership role.

In addition to strong public leadership in the early 1970s, that period lacked the partisanship that the OCMC faced, and the legislative members of the 1970s Commission were committed to constitutional revision.

Under the best circumstances, state constitutional revision is not easy. Professor Robert F. Williams of Rutgers Law School, one of the nation's foremost state constitutional law scholars, has quoted a 1983 observation by Georgia governor George D. Busbee on the difficulty of state constitutional revision and on the importance of leadership:

> Constitutional revision is not for the faint of heart. It is not a Sunday drive in the mountains. It is an incredibly difficult, sometimes tedious, sometimes exhilarating, always challenging undertaking requiring the cooperation of the leadership of all three branches of state government, of counties, municipalities, and local school boards, of the business community and the labor community, of public-interest groups and private-interest groups, of people inside the government and people outside the government—in short, it requires the cooperation of just about everybody.[338]

Governor Busbee's comments help explain how the effort to modernize the Ohio Constitution through the use of a commission in the 2010s was undercut by an excess of legislative control, by a lack of effective leadership, by the absence of legislative commitment to constitutional revision, and by a corrosive partisan political climate.

---

[338] Robert F. Williams, *The Law of American State Constitutions* (New York: Oxford University Press, 2011), 379.

Judicial Selection Redux

The Ohio Supreme Court's expanded role in controversial issues involving the Ohio Constitution, including tort reform and educational funding, its interpretations of Ohio law in areas such as employment, insurance, personal injury, and workers' compensation law, and its conflicts with the General Assembly contributed to a politicization of the judicial selection process similar to that which existed in the mid-1980s. And in the early years of the century this was accompanied by an increase in the involvement of special interest groups in judicial elections, including groups representing the interests of attorneys, doctors, business, and labor, and in a significant increase in the amount of money spent on judicial campaigns.

These developments led some to question again whether Ohio's commitment to an elected judiciary is consistent with the goal of having an independent and impartial judiciary.

History of Judicial Selection in Ohio

Under the 1802 Constitution, Ohio had an "elected" judiciary, but the General Assembly did the electing. This changed under the 1851 Constitution, which transferred responsibility for selecting judges to the voters.

The 1851 Constitution, however, did not address the nature of judicial elections, and political parties nominated judges through party conventions.[339] But in 1911, at the height of the Progressive movement, the General Assembly enacted the Nonpartisan Judiciary Act under which judges were elected at general elections on a "separate and independent ballot" without party designations.[340]

The 1911 Act did not alter the way in which the political parties nominated candidates for judgeships. But in 1912 the voters approved an amendment proposed by the convention to require the use of direct primaries to nominate candidates for state and most local elective offices, including judges (Art. V, sec. 7). And, as with the 1911 law, the 1912 amendment did not require judicial primaries to be nonpartisan.[341]

The changes in 1911 and 1912 "abolished the formal nominating power of party conventions, established partisan primaries to nominate judges (and other elective officials), and provided for nonpartisan election of judges."[342] This left

[339] Prior to 1912, the prevailing method for nominating judges in Ohio was by political party conventions though there was a rarely used petition process that permitted independent candidates to reach the ballot. *See* Aumann, "The Selection of Judges," 411 n.8.

[340] Ibid., 412. *See also* O.R.C. sec. 3505.04 (version through 2021).

[341] Kathleen L. Barber, "Ohio Judicial Elections—Nonpartisan Premises with Partisan Results," 32 *Ohio St. L. J.* 762 (1971).

[342] *See* Michael E. Solimine and Richard B. Saphire, "The Selection of Judges in Ohio," in *The History of Ohio Law* 237.

Ohio in the odd position of being the only state with a partisan judicial election primary followed by a general election with a nonpartisan judicial ballot. But in 2021, the General Assembly eliminated the nonpartisan general election ballot for Ohio Supreme Court and Court of Appeals elections that had been adopted by the General Assembly in 1911.[343]

The most significant result of the 1911 and 1912 changes was the sharp drop-off in the percentage of voters who cast votes for judges in general elections.[344] The separate judicial ballot prevented straight party ticket voting, and the nonpartisan judicial ballot denied the voters the party labels that the political scientists view as the primary cues for voters in judicial elections.[345] Though nominally nonpartisan, general election races for the Ohio Supreme Court (but generally not races for lower courts) have been "ferociously competitive,"[346] but this is not surprising. As one contemporary commentator observed, "[I]f legal doctrine is politically salient, those who care about the law will seek to influence the composition of the judiciary."[347]

Twentieth century efforts to address judicial selection have not been successful, and the voters rejected proposed initiated amendments to replace the election of supreme court and other appellate judges with a mixed-appointed/judicial retention system (what became known as the Missouri Plan) in 1938 and 1987, both times by almost 2:1 margins. See Appendix B. And in 1967, the Ohio House of Representatives stripped the Missouri plan provisions from the comprehensive joint resolution that the voters approved in 1968 as the Modern Courts Amendment.[348]

Refocus on Judicial Election Reform

Efforts in support of judicial selection reform began again early in this century. One of the two sharply contested supreme court races in 2000 had been

---

[343] *See Judicial Selection in the States: Appellate and General Election Courts* (American Judicature Society, 2013). See also S.B. 80 (134th GA) (2021).

[344] In the general elections from 1908 to 1920, there was a sharp decline in the number of voters who cast ballots for the statewide judicial candidates. In 1908 and 1910 there was virtually no drop-off with only 1.6 percent and 3.1 percent, respectively, of those voting for governor not voting in the highest turnout Supreme Court race. But from 1912 to 1920, the corresponding drop from the gubernatorial election voter participation to the highest turnout Supreme Court justice race was between 24.8 percent and 30.7 percent. *See* Ohio Election Statistics (Ohio Secretary of State).

[345] Lawrence Baum, "Judicial Elections and Judicial Independence: The Voter's Perspective," 64 *Ohio St. L. J.* 13 (2003): 24–28. Some who decried Ohio's hybrid system argued that the absence of party labels violated the First Amendment. *But see Ohio Council 8 American Federation of State, County & Municipal Employees v. Husted*, 814 F.3d 329 (6th Cir. 2016) (upholding the policy of precluding judicial candidates from listing their political parties on the general-election ballot, concluding that, at most, it is only a minimal burden on First Amendment rights).

[346] Michael Solimine, "The False Promise of Judicial Elections in Ohio," 30 *Cap. U. L. Rev.* 559, 561 (2002).

[347] Entin, "Judicial Selection," 525.

[348] Milligan and Pohlman, "Modern Courts Amendment," 812–13.

characterized by a bare-knuckle campaign and the expenditure of $1.9 million for one seat and $1.4 million for the general election and primary for a second seat[349]—–a level of spending not seen since the record $2.7 million spent in the hotly contested 1986 race for chief justice.[350] And this was followed in 2002 and 2004 by elections marked by $6.2 and $6.3 million respectively in total candidate spending for the contested seats on the court.[351] Moreover, during this period independent committees began raising large sums, and (although not permitted to coordinate their activities with candidates) their fund-raising prowess made them a force in judicial elections.

In January 2004, an ad hoc organization convened by the League of Women Voters of Ohio, the Ohio State Bar Association, Ohio Supreme Court Chief Justice Thomas J. Moyer, and two university-based public policy institutes issued a report recommending that steps be taken to strengthen the independence and impartiality of the state judiciary. Recognizing the unlikelihood that Ohio voters would support changes in the method of selecting judges, the organizations focused instead on ways to improve Ohio's system of electing judges. The recommendations included the lengthening of judicial terms, an increase in the "years of practice" judicial qualification, mandatory pre-election judicial training, and increases in judicial salaries, all of which could be accomplished legislatively.[352]

The organization did not recommend requiring disclosure of the financiers of third-party "issue ads" because of the pendency of *McConnell v. Federal Election Commission* (2003), in which the U.S. Supreme Court ultimately upheld the disclosure provisions of the federal Bipartisan Campaign Finance Act.[353] The Supreme Court, however, subsequently overruled *McConnell* in *Citizens United v. Federal Election Commission* (2010), thus effectively removing disclosure as a strategy for judicial *election* reform.

Despite the interest in judicial election reform, the U.S. Supreme Court had set the stage for even more robust and more expensive judicial campaigns. In *Republican Party of Minnesota v. White* (2002), relying on the First Amendment, the Court struck down ethical rules that limited the speech of judicial candidates. Despite concerns raised by Justice Sandra Day O'Connor in a concurring opinion about the impact of judicial elections on the independence of the state judiciary,

[349] *See* Kara Baker, "Is Justice for Sale in Ohio? An Examination of Ohio Judicial Elections and Suggestions for Reform Focusing on the 2000 Race for the Ohio Supreme Court," 35 *Akron L. Rev.* 159 (2001).

[350] *See* Lawrence Baum, "Judicial Election & Appointment at the State Level," 77 *Ky. L. J.* 645 (1988–1989).

[351] *See* FollowtheMoney.org—Election Overview (National Institute on Money in Politics) (website).

[352] *See* Progress Report, Judicial Impartiality: The Next Steps (January 2004).

[353] Ibid., 7.

the Court effectively took the position that jurisdictions that wish to continue to elect their judges will have to tolerate more contentious judicial elections.

The application of the First Amendment to judicial races makes it even more difficult to impose effective spending and fundraising limitations. And some expected *White* to lead to even more robust and expensive judicial elections and ironically to a more widely perceived need to alter the electoral approach to judicial selection. In Ohio, however, the level of candidate spending has gone down to an average of $2.7 million per election in total candidate spending in the seven biennial elections for seats on the Ohio Supreme Court between 2006 and 2018.[354] And while the First Amendment has removed some of the constraints on judicial electioneering[355] and there are still concerns about the role of money in judicial elections and in the effectiveness of recusal policies,[356] there is no indication of growing support for changing the role of elections in selecting judges.

Nonetheless, in response to a range of concerns about the operation of judicial elections, including concerns about the large number of voters who leave judicial ballots blank, another Ohio chief justice took the lead in proposing judicial election reform. In 2013, Chief Justice Maureen O'Connor issued a working proposal designed to improve the quality of judicial elections.[357] Her proposal sought to expand voter knowledge of the judicial candidates, to increase the qualifications for serving as judges, and to move judicial elections to the top of the ballot in odd-number years. The latter item, which would have required a constitutional amendment, sought to address the drop-off in voter participation in judicial races, which are now held in even-numbered years—those years in which there is high voter turnout because of either gubernatorial or presidential elections on the ballot. These proposals, however, did not lead to any serious effort in the General Assembly to address the issues raised by the chief justice.

The history of judicial selection in Ohio strongly suggests that there is a great deal of public sentiment in favor of the current system of electing judges, and those who propose to revisit this issue will likely continue to face an uphill battle. And despite efforts to limit the role of money in judicial election and create more transparency, third parties will likely continue to spend heavily to support judicial candidates whom they believe will be sympathetic to their interests.

---

354 *See* FollowtheMoney.org—Election Overview (National Institute on Money in Politics) (website).

355 For example, during the 2004 campaign for a seat on the Ohio Supreme Court, a federal district court judge enjoined the court's Disciplinary Counsel from investigating whether a judicial candidate who had expressed opinions on disputed legal and political issues violated the Ohio Code of Judicial Conduct (*O'Neill v. Coughlan*, 2004).

356 *See The Politics of Judicial Elections* (Brennan Center for Justice, 2019); *see also* Catherine Turcer and Mia Lewis, *Can Money Buy Justice: Contributions to Ohio Supreme Court Candidates 2018* (Common Cause of Ohio, 2018)(discussing spending on judicial races and the need for stronger recusal policies).

357 Maureen O'Connor, *A Proposal for Strengthening Judicial Elections* (Ohio Courts, May 2013).

Stare Decisis and the Ohio Constitution

Efforts to alter the judicial selection process continued in this century against the backdrop of controversial judicial decisions and contentious judicial races, and in 2003 the Ohio Supreme Court reviewed its approach to its earlier decisions under the doctrine of stare decisis.

In *Westfield Insurance Co. v. Galatis* (2003), the court overruled its four-year old decision in *Scott-Pontzer v. Liberty Mutual Fire Insurance Co.* (1999), in which it had provided uninsured motorist coverage to an off-duty employee driving a spouse's car. *Scott-Pontzer* was very controversial, and the court in *Westfield* addressed when it would overrule earlier decisions. And in its 4–3 decision written by (future Chief) Justice Maureen O'Connor, the *Westfield* court declined to follow its precedent, describing its approach to stare decisis as follows:

> A prior decision of the Supreme Court may be overruled where (1) the decision was wrongly decided at that time, or changes in circumstances no longer justify continued adherence to the decision, (2) the decision defies practical workability, and (3) abandoning the precedent would not create an undue hardship for those who have relied upon it.
>
> Ibid. (syllabus).

Concurring in the majority opinion in *Westfield*, Chief Justice Thomas J. Moyer, who had dissented in *Scott-Pontzer*, also voted to overrule the earlier decision. Recognizing that stare decisis embodies "a fundamental element of American jurisprudence—consistency and predictability" (quoting *Gallimore v. Children's Hospital Medical Center* (1993)), the Chief Justice noted that the *Westfield* tripartite standard honored stare decisis by preventing arbitrary and discriminatory enforcement of the law while relieving courts of the obligation to follow precedents with "petrifying rigidity" (quoting *Clark v. Southview Hospital & Family Health Center* (1994)).

Agreeing that *Scott-Pontzer* was wrongly decided, the chief justice expressed support for overruling it rather than minimizing its impact "by creating a patchwork of exceptions . . . and limitations" to the earlier decision. *Westfield*. Nonetheless, he put the bench, the bar, the public, and the General Assembly on notice that changes in composition of the court will not necessarily result in a wholesale overruling of precedents:

> We serve the bench and the bar by adopting a cogent, clear standard by which to test claims that our precedents should not be followed. There can be little doubt that *Scott-Pontzer* should be limited under this standard. Our decision today does not mark a change in my belief in the importance of the predictability and consistency produced by stare decisis. No one should assume that our decision heralds a new era in which prior cases of this court will be routinely or arbitrarily overruled.

> Our decision, rather, is a narrow response to a decision widely recognized as an error of law, which, if left uncorrected, would have continued to produce consequences that even the majority in *Scott-Pontzer* could not have foreseen.

Westfield involved insurance and contract law, and the court subsequently made clear that the *Westfield* approach to stare decisis is not applicable in other settings, such as the interpretation of evidentiary rules where issues of reliance are not involved, see *State v. Silverman* (2009), and—more importantly—state constitutional interpretation.

Traditionally, the doctrine of stare decisis is strongest in statutory or common law cases because of the relative ease with which a legislature can overrule a judicial decision. But in cases involving constitutional interpretation, courts apply a weaker form of stare decisis given the difficulty of amending constitutions. And the Ohio Supreme Court has followed this less deferential approach to constitutional precedent notwithstanding the ease of amending the Ohio Constitution (as compared to the difficulty of amending the U.S. Constitution). For example, in *City of Rocky River v. State Employment Relations Board* (1989), the court had stated that "[s]tare decisis is not inflexibly applicable to constitutional interpretation." And in 2011, in *State v. Bodyke*, the court reaffirmed the *Rocky River* approach and stated that "[s]tare decisis remains a controlling doctrine in cases presenting questions on the law of contracts, property, and torts, but it is not controlling in cases presenting a constitutional question."

The court has also refused to apply stare decisis in constitutional cases "merely because" a statute "is similar to previous enactments" that the court had held unconstitutional. For example, in its 2007 re-examination of its major tort reform precedents, the court described its less deferential approach to stare decisis as follows: "To be covered by the blanket of stare decisis, the legislation must be phrased in language that is substantially the same as that which we have previously invalidated." *Arbino v. Johnson & Johnson* (2007).

Given this recognition of the less deferential approach to stare decisis in cases involving constitutional issues, the doctrine should not present a significant obstacle to the court if it decides to more aggressively review its past constitutional decisions in the course of interpreting the Ohio Constitution.

Nonetheless, it is unclear whether the court will be overruling or distinguishing precedents to which it is no longer committed. Despite the admonition of Chief Justice Moyer, the court has often been split on whether to overrule or to distinguish precedents. In some cases, the court has overruled earlier cases to provide clearer guidance to the bench, the bar, and the public.[358] But in other cases, court has written narrowly and distinguished older cases,[359] thus leaving

---

[358] *See, e.g., Ruther v. Kaiser* (2012) (overruling *Hardy v. VerMeulen* (1987) which had imposed strict time limits on suits brought by medical malpractice claimants).

[359] *See Arbino v. Johnson & Johnson*, 2007 (distinguishing *Sorrell v. Thevenir* (1994) and holding that a statutory cap on damages does not deny an injured party a right to trial by jury).

stakeholders the challenging task of navigating the path forward. And with five members of the court in their first term as we approach the 2022 judicial elections, the court's approach to stare decisis may have a significant impact on the development of Ohio constitutional law.

The breadth of the doctrine of stare decisis may also be particularly relevant in cases in which the court has treated provisions of the Ohio and U.S. Constitutions as coextensive. But decisions equating state and federal provisions without an independent analysis of the state provisions are not consistent with the expectation in *Arnold v. City of Cleveland* (1993) that the court review provisions of the state constitution independently. Likewise, decisions that announce *ex cathedra* that state provisions provide greater rights than their federal counterparts without an independent analysis of the state provisions are not consistent with the *Arnold* expectation that the court review provisions of the state constitution independently. And the doctrine of stare decisis, which only has a limited impact in the area of constitutional law, should be even less of an inhibiting force when the court is reviewing state constitutional provisions that had not been subjected to an independent review.

New Judicial Federalism in the Twenty-First Century

During the first two decades of this century, the Ohio Supreme Court increasingly decided cases that sought to rely upon the Ohio Constitution as a source of protection for individual rights. And this has taken place against the backdrop of the 1993 *Arnold* decision in which the court announced its willingness to join the national movement to construe the state constitutions independently as the source of expanded protections for individual rights. But during this period, the practice of combining the analysis of state and federal provisions has continued, though somewhat abated, as the court has not fully absorbed the lesson of *Michigan v. Long* (1983).

The early years of the century were marked by the legacy of the contentious battle over tort reform and what appeared to be the denouement of the struggle over educational funding. See Commentary, Article V, section 2.

In 2003, the General Assembly enacted an omnibus tort reform statute that contained the extraordinary request that the Ohio Supreme Court reconsider some of its earlier decisions. Addressing the court directly in a series of uncodified "statements of findings and intent," the General Assembly "respectfully request[ed] the Ohio Supreme Court . . . [to] reconsider its holdings on damage caps . . . on the deductibility of collateral source benefits . . . [and] on statutes of repose" and identified the decisions it wanted reconsidered. Am. Sub. S.B. 80, 125th General Assembly. And in 2007, the court responded, ruling that S.B. 80 "does not violate the right to a trial by jury, the right to a remedy, the right to an open court, the right to due process of law, the right to equal protection of the laws, or the separation of powers, and is therefore constitutional on its face."

Arbino v. Johnson & Johnson (2007). *Arbino,* however, distinguished but did not overrule the court's tort reform precedents, and it expressly left open the possibility of as-applied challenges to facially valid provisions. Thus, the struggle over tort reform continues, albeit on a smaller scale.

With respect to educational funding, in 2003, after having concluded that the Ohio statutory scheme for funding the public schools violated the Ohio Constitution, the court refused to permit the lower Ohio courts to exercise continuing jurisdiction to enforce the earlier decision. *State ex rel. State v. Lewis* (2003). Thus, those who believe that the General Assembly still has not brought school funding, especially for operating expenses, into constitutional compliance have been left with the challenge of working with the General Assembly to fashion a legislative solution to state's putatively inadequate educational funding policies with only the threat of a new and likely very expensive court challenge or an initiated constitutional amendment as deterrents to legislative recalcitrance. See Commentary, Article VI, section 2.

During this century, the court continued to decide cases involving a broad range of state constitutional issues, including cases involving the initiative and referendum (Art. II, secs. 1a–1g), the Modern Courts Amendment (Art. IV), state apportionment (Article XI), state taxation (Article XII), and home rule (Art. XVIII, sec. 3). See Commentaries to specific articles and sections. This litigation has often required the court to address structural matters, including the separation of powers doctrine, the one-subject rule, standing and other door-closing doctrines. And substantively, these cases have included such high-visibility issues as abortion, apportionment, gambling, gun control, the taking of property, and the rights of criminal defendants.

In the area of individual rights and civil liberties the court repeatedly relied on *Arnold* to reiterate its position that the Ohio Constitution is an independent source of rights not contained in the federal constitution; and in a number of cases the court interpreted the Ohio Constitution to provide greater rights than those available under the U.S. Constitution.

For example, in 2000, in *Humphrey v. Lane,* the court relied on textual differences in state and federal provisions to reject the U.S. Supreme Court's free exercise jurisprudence and to hold that Article I, section 7, protects religious freedom from religiously neutral laws of general application. In 2002, in *State ex rel. Ohio AFL-CIO v. Ohio Bureau of Workers' Compensation,* the court initially stated that Article I, section 14, is "virtually identical to the Fourth Amendment." But it then relied on the "special considerations for Ohio's workers" to provide "additional and independent protection" against warrantless and suspicionless searches as a condition of receiving workers' compensation benefits. And in 2003, in *State v. Brown,* the court acknowledged its 1997 decision in *Robinette* requiring "harmonization," but it nonetheless held that Article I, Section 14 "provides greater protection than the Fourth Amendment to the U.S. Constitution against warrantless arrests for minor misdemeanors."

Finally, in 2006 in *City of Norwood v. Horney*, one of the court's most important decisions interpreting the Ohio Bill of Rights, Justice O'Connor, writing for a unanimous court, construed the taking/public use provision in Article I, Section 19, as not permitting the taking of private property solely for economic development.

In rejecting the U.S. Supreme Court's controversial 5–4 decision in *Kelo v. City of New London* (2005), interpreting the Taking Clause of the Fifth Amendment to permit takings for economic development, the *Norwood* court recognized *Kelo*; but (without even citing *Arnold*) the court spent most of its lengthy and scholarly opinion reviewing the history and role of property in Ohio and throughout the country, other provisions of the Ohio Constitution, the decisions of the Ohio Supreme Court and other state courts, the evolution of federal policies on eminent domain, and considerations of public policy.[360]

Norwood contains an elaborate identification of the many factors that the court will examine in determining the meaning of a state constitutional provision, even one with a federal counterpart. In *Norwood*, the court considered the Ohio provision treating the right to property as "inviolate" and noted the treatment of property in Article I, sec. 1 ("All men . . . have certain inalienable rights, among which are those of . . . acquiring, possessing, and protecting property."). But in no place did the court suggest that because of the similarity in the text of the state and federal taking provisions there would have to be a state-specific justification to support a departure from the federal interpretation. Instead, the court looked at the history of this provision and simply concluded that a better model for interpreting it was the analysis in a similar case by the Supreme Court of Michigan, the dissent in *Kelo* in the Supreme Court of Connecticut, and the dissent in the U.S. Supreme Court in *Kelo*. See also Commentary, Article I, section 19.

In addition to the provisions discussed above (Art. I, secs. 7, 14, and 19), the court in this century has sometimes defined the following provisions of the Bill of Rights more broadly than the corresponding provisions of the U.S. Constitution: the equal protection and benefit clause (sec. 2), the right to trial by jury (sec. 5), the ban on cruel and unusual punishment (sec. 9), the double jeopardy protection (sec. 10), the privilege against self-incrimination (sec. 10), the free speech clause in private figure defamation cases (sec. 11), and the due course of law provision (sec. 16).

But in many cases in which the court declined to give state provisions an independent meaning, it did not provide a careful explanation for its decisions. For example, in the area of search and seizure the court described its interest in "harmonizing" decisions construing the state and federal guarantees, but it has

[360] *See generally* Kathleen Trafford, "City of Norwood v. Horney—Much More Than Eminent Domain: A Forceful Affirmation of the Independent Authority of the Ohio Constitution and the Court's Power to Enforce It," 48 *Akron L. Rev.* 35 (2015).

also found independent meaning in the state counterpart without defining what it means by "harmonizing." In the area of equal protection, the court has pointed to the "functional equivalence" of the Ohio equal protection and benefit clause meaning and the Equal Protection Clause of the Fourteenth Amendment, but it has been willing to treat the state provision as having an independent without defining what it means by "functional equivalence." And in the area of due process/ due course of law, the court has equated the state and federal provisions, but it has also been willing to treat the state due course of law provision as having an independent meaning.[361]

As the commentary on Article I illustrates, the court has not always spoken with one voice on how to interpret the Ohio Constitution. All members of the court who have addressed the issue recognize that the Ohio Constitution is a source of independent rights, but members of the court have often disagreed sharply on how to construe provisions that are identical or at least similar to federal provisions. And these disagreements have been most pronounced in cases involving three of the most important provisions in the Bill of Rights—the equal protection and benefit clause, the prohibition against unreasonable searches and seizures, and the due course of law provision.

A major part of these disagreements concerns whether the court should follow the approach it announced in 1997, when it described the search and seizure provisions of the state and federal constitutions as coextensive and stated that the provisions should be harmonized "unless there are persuasive reasons to find otherwise." *State v. Robinette*.[362]

Under this approach, sometimes referred to pejoratively as "lock-stepping," courts presumptively follow analogous federal provisions and only interpret state provisions differently if the deviation is supported by state-specific factors such as text or history.[363] But in *City of Norwood v. Horney* (2006), the court made clear that it could interpret identical language differently when it concluded that its analysis of "public use" was sounder than the U.S. Supreme Court's construction of the same language in the analogous federal provision.[364]

Despite cases like *Norwood*, which dispensed with the need to find state-specific factors to construe state constitutional provisions, there is no question

---

[361] *See* Commentaries, Art. I, secs. 2, 14, and 16.

[362] *See also State v. Wogenstahl* (1996) (declining to find a state right to counsel at a line-up under sec. 10 simply noting that the "appellant has presented us with no compelling reasons why Ohio constitutional law should differ from the federal law on this issue").

[363] *See* Commentary, Art. I.

[364] *See also State v. Mole* (2016) (plurality) (treating equal protection and benefit provision of sec. 2 as barring imposition of strict criminal liability on police officers who engage in nonoccupation related sexual misconduct with minors); *State v. Bode* (2016) (treating due course of law provision of sec. 16 as forbidding the use of uncounseled juvenile dispositions to enhance the penalty for a subsequent offense); *State v. Brown* (2015) (treating unreasonable search and seizure provision of sec. 14 as barring extraterritorial traffic stops and arrests for minor misdemeanors).

that state-specific factors are important tools for construing state constitutions. For example, in *State v. Mole* (2016), the plurality stated, "we embrace the notion that we may, and should, consider Ohio's conditions and traditions in interpreting our own state's constitutional guarantees."

And as Justice Goodwin Liu of the California Supreme Court has observed, "state courts should look first to state-specific sources in deciding an issue of state constitutional law."[365] But he has also argued persuasively on federalism grounds that "[t]he legitimacy of state constitutionalism does not primarily depend on the development of a distinctive, state-centered jurisprudence." He further noted that, "when there is no state-specific text or history to guide the analysis, it is no embarrassment for a state court to disagree with federal precedent on the basis of constitutional reasoning that transcends state boundaries."[366] Indeed, our federal system assumes that there could be different interpretations of individual rights and liberties under the U.S. Constitution and various state constitutions.

But reliance on the constitutions of other states does not require that decisions of the U.S. Supreme Court be ignored. Indeed, the willingness to look to interpretations of federal provisions for guidance (without treating them as presumptively correct) is not surprising given the familiarity that most judges and lawyers have with federal rights-conferring provisions and the often well-developed jurisprudence interpreting provisions of the U.S. Constitution.[367]

Although the Ohio Supreme Court has found independent meaning in many provisions of the Ohio Constitution, it has not settled on a single or preferred approach to interpreting the Ohio Constitution. This has resulted in an ad hoc or pragmatic approach to the state constitution. And it has left unresolved important issues about the need for state-specific justifications to support deviations from federal interpretations as well as methodological issues such as sequencing (i.e., whether to address state or federal constitutional issues first), deference (i.e., how much weight to give U.S. Supreme Court interpretations of analogous rights-conferring provisions), and other unique issues of state constitutional interpretation.

But the uncertainty that flows from the court's pragmatic approach to the Ohio Constitution may not be all that bad. In playing its role as the ultimate

[365] Goodwin Liu, "State Constitutions and the Protection of Individual Rights: A Reappraisal," 92 *N.Y.U. L. Rev.* 1307, 1312 (2017) (hereinafter Liu, "State Constitutions").

[366] Ibid. *Accord State v. Mole, supra* ("We can and should borrow from well-reasoned and persuasive precedent from other states and the federal courts, but in so doing we cannot be compelled to parrot those interpretations."); Jeffrey S. Sutton, *51 Imperfect Solutions: States and the Making of American Constitutional Law* (New York: Oxford University Press, 2018), 174 ("There is no reason to think, as an interpretive matter, that constitutional guarantees of independent sovereigns, even guarantees with the same or similar words, must be construed in the same way.").

[367] Liu, "State Constitutions," 1315. *See also State ex rel. Heller v. Miller* (1980) (stating that "decisions of the United States Supreme Court can be utilized to give meaning to the guarantees of Article I of the Ohio Constitution").

arbiter of the meaning of the Ohio Constitution, the court is responsible for resolving disputes in a way that is fair to the parties and that works for those who rely on the state constitution. And the pragmatic role that the court is playing may be appropriate for an elected judiciary that is not only resolving disputes but is also seeking to develop an appropriate and independent approach to interpreting Ohio's most fundamental document.

PART TWO

The Ohio Constitution and Commentary

Preamble

We, the people of the State of Ohio, grateful to Almighty God for our freedom, to secure its blessings and promote our common welfare, do establish this Constitution.

The preamble to the current constitution has remained unchanged since its adoption as part of the 1851 Constitution. It is much shorter (28 words as compared to 165 words) than the preamble to the 1802 Constitution, which provided as follows:

> We, the people of the eastern division of the territory of the United States, northwest of the river Ohio, having the right of admission into the general government, as a member of the Union, consistent with the constitution of the United States, the ordinance of congress of one thousand seven hundred and eighty-seven, and of the law of congress, entitled "An act to enable the people of the eastern division of the territory of the United States, northwest of the river Ohio, to form a constitution and state government, and for the admission of such state into the Union, on an equal footing with the original states, and for other purposes;" in order to establish justice, promote the welfare and secure the blessings of liberty to ourselves and our posterity, do ordain and establish the following constitution or form of government; and do mutually agree with each other to form ourselves into a free and independent state, by the name of the State of Ohio.

The Ohio State Constitution. Steven H. Steinglass and Gino J. Scarselli, Oxford University Press. © Oxford University Press 2022. DOI: 10.1093/oso/9780197619728.003.0002

The earlier preamble expressly referred to the Northwest Ordinance and to the 1802 Enabling Act. It also quoted the phrase that appeared in both the Northwest Ordinance and the Enabling Act and pledged to the people of the eastern division of the Northwest Territory admission into the union "on an equal footing with the original states." In addition, the earlier preamble referred to the compact among the people of the territory to establish for themselves an independent state "in order to establish justice, promote the welfare and secure the blessings of liberty to ourselves and our posterity." Also, unlike the preambles to the current constitution and the constitutions of forty-five states, the preamble to the 1802 Constitution made no reference to a Supreme Being. See William F. Swindler, *Sources and Documents of United States Constitutions* (Dobbs Ferry, NY: Oceana, 1982).

During the 1850–51 Constitutional Convention the delegates rejected without a recorded vote a proposal to replace the reference in the preamble to "people" with "free white male citizens." See *Report of the Debates and Proceedings of the Convention for the Revision of the Constitution of the State Of Ohio 1850–51*, vol. 2 (Columbus: S. Medary, 1851), 326.

The Ohio Supreme Court has cited the preamble in a number of cases, see, for example, *Palmer v. Tingle* (1896), but none of its decisions have relied exclusively on the preamble as the basis for a ruling. See Commentary, Article I, section 1.

Article I

*Bill of Rights**

Apparently recognizing the importance of the provisions in the Bill of Rights, the delegates to the 1850–51 Constitutional Convention moved the Bill of Rights from the end of the 1802 Constitution (Art. VIII) to the first article of the new constitution. The record of the 1850–51 Constitutional Convention, however, provides little direct evidence of what the delegates had in mind when they did this.

Certain rights guaranteed in the Bill of Rights of both the 1802 and 1851 Ohio Constitutions were also in the Northwest Ordinance, including the right to habeas corpus, trial by jury, the precursor to due course of law, the right to reasonable bail (except in capital cases), the prohibitions against excessive fines and cruel and unusual punishment, the ban on slavery, and full compensation for takings. See Ordinance of 1787, Article II, section 14. But the 1802 Constitution borrowed most provisions of the Bill of Rights from other state constitutions, specifically the Tennessee, Kentucky, and Pennsylvania Constitutions. See The History of the Ohio Constitution, *supra*.

* Article headings of the Ohio Constitution, such as "Bill of Rights," were formally ratified by the voters, but the section headings were not. The section headings, which are displayed in bold and precede the constitutional text of each section, are generally taken from Constitution of the State of Ohio (J. Kenneth Blackwell, Secretary of State (undated), although when those headings are not sufficiently descriptive, alternatives are taken from other sources, including Baldwin's Ohio Revised Code Annotated Constitution of the State of Ohio, Table of Proposed Amendments to Ohio Constitution (West Group 2002).

The Ohio State Constitution. Steven H. Steinglass and Gino J. Scarselli, Oxford University Press. © Oxford University Press 2022. DOI: 10.1093/oso/9780197619728.003.0003

With the exception of the addition of the "equal protection and benefit" and the "special privileges or immunities" clauses in section 2, the guarantee of the right to be a witness without regard to religious beliefs in section 7, the prohibition on imprisonment for debt in section 17, and the adoption of a process for taking private property for public use in section 19, the 1850–51 Convention did not add any significant provisions to the Bill of Rights. It did, however, make the article more concise by combining some sections and moving others to different articles. In reducing the number of sections from twenty-eight to twenty, it also dropped a number of potentially important provisions for reasons that are not clear. See, for example, 1802 Constitution, Article VIII, section 10 ("That no person arrested or confined in jail shall be treated with unnecessary rigor. . . ."); 1802 Constitution, Article VIII, section 14 ("All penalties shall be proportioned to the nature of the offense."); 1802 Constitution, Article VIII, section 21 ("That no person . . . [other than those employed in the military] shall be subject to corporal punishment, under the military law."); and 1802 Constitution, Article VIII, section 25 ("That no law shall be passed to prevent the poor . . . from an equal participation in the schools, academies, colleges and universities within this State . . . .").

The proposed 1874 Constitution, which the voters rejected, contained only minor proposed changes in the Bill of Rights. But subsequently, the voters approved nine amendments to Article I––four as a result of proposals made by the 1912 Constitutional Convention, two in the 1990s as a result of proposals from the General Assembly, and three in the twenty-first century, two of which had been proposed by initiative petitions. See Appendix B.

Many provisions of Article I have counterparts in the federal Bill of Rights, in the Fourteenth Amendment to the U.S. Constitution, and in other parts of the U.S. Constitution. But the Ohio Bill of Rights also has provisions with no federal analogues, such as section 10a's guarantee of rights of crime victims, section 16's open courts and right-to-remedy provisions, section 19a's guarantee of full compensation in wrongful death actions, and section 21's provision on healthcare coverage.

A number of the provisions of Article I with parallel federal provisions are expressed in very different language, with provisions of the Ohio Bill of Rights often framed as affirmative rights, in contrast to the U.S. Constitution's rights-conferring provisions, which generally are limitations on the power of government. For example, the equal protection and benefit clause of Article I, section 2; the right to assemble in Article I, section 3; the provision that "[a]ll persons shall be bailable" in Article I, section 6; the free speech clause in Article I, section 11; and the due course of law provision in Article I, section 16 are affirmative rights. See also Commentaries on Article VI, section 2, and Article VII, section 1 (affirmatively requiring General Assembly to support common schools and institutions for the disabled).

The Ohio Supreme Court's 1993 decision in *Arnold v. City of Cleveland* (1993) (which interpreted Art. I, sec. 4) described the Ohio Constitution as "a document of independent force" and a source of protection of individual rights and civil liberties. This decision set the stage for an increase in cases involving the rights-conferring provision of the Ohio Bill of Rights.

The independent use of the state constitution, however, has its roots in the late nineteenth and early twentieth century, when the court applied the Ohio Constitution to thwart employee and social welfare legislation. That brand of activism may have slowed down, but it did not end with the limitations placed on the court as a result of the proposals of the 1912 Convention. And in 1941, in *Direct Plumbing Supply Co. v. City of Dayton*, the court reaffirmed its willingness to use the Ohio Constitution to protect the right to contract and private property from "unreasonable" government regulation.

Cases like *Direct Plumbing Supply* (and its antecedents) involved the protection of private property, the right to contract, the judicially enforceable requirement that government act reasonably, and what is now often referred to as substantive due process. On the other hand, *Arnold* represents the court's modern movement to interpreting the Ohio Constitution independently to protect individual rights and civil liberties. Nonetheless, the court's interest in protecting property has not abated, as illustrated by the unanimous decision in *City of Norwood v. Horney* (2006), in which the court construed the state constitution's taking provision independently and concluded that it was more protective of private property than its textually identical (in key parts) federal counterpart. See The History of the Ohio Constitution, *supra*, and Commentary, Article I, section 19.

The Ohio Supreme Court's decisions in *Arnold* and in the many cases relying upon it suggest that the new judicial federalism has begun to take root in Ohio. See Article I, sections 2, 4, 7, 9, 10, 11, 14, 16, and 19, and Commentaries thereon.

But the court has not always been consistent, and it has often stated that provisions of the state constitution should be considered as functionally equivalent or coextensive with their federal counterparts. This has happened most frequently in discussions of the equal protection guarantees, see Commentary, Article I, section 2, but the court has also equated state and federal provisions in its discussions of sections 10 (double jeopardy), 11 (free speech), 14 (search and seizure), and 16 (due course of law).

■ METHODOLOGICAL ISSUES—SEQUENCING AND WEIGHING

Two of the most important issues in state constitutional litigation involve methodology. These include the sequencing issue—whether to begin the analysis with the state or federal constitutions and when to end it—and the weighing issue—how much deference to give federal interpretations of analogous constitutional provisions.

Most state courts first look to U.S. Supreme Court interpretations of analogous provisions of the U.S. Constitution and defer to them when construing their state constitution. See generally Robert F. Williams, *The Law of American State Constitutions* (New York: Oxford University Press, 2011), 135–85 (hereinafter Williams, *The Law of American State Constitutions*). Under this approach, often referred to by critics as lock-stepping, state courts treat federal decisions construing analogous provisions as presumptively correct and only deviate from them when there are strong state-specific reasons for doing so.

In contrast to the lock-stepping approach, some state courts follow the primacy approach, initially and most notably developed by Oregon Supreme Court Justice Hans A. Linde, one of the most influential commentators on state constitutions, see Hans A. Linde, "First Things First: Rediscovering the States' Bills of Rights," 9 *U. Balt. L. Rev.* 379 (1980), and adopted by the Oregon Supreme Court in *Sterling v. Cupp* (Or. 1981) (Linde, J.). And this approach has been strongly endorsed by Jeffrey S. Sutton, Chief Judge of the U.S. Court of Appeals for the Sixth Circuit. See Jeffrey S. Sutton, *51 Imperfect Solutions: States and the Making of American Constitutional Law* (New York: Oxford University Press, 2018), 179–82 (hereinafter Sutton, *51 Imperfect Solutions*).

Under the primacy approach (which, according to Judge Sutton, has only been adopted in its pure form by Maine, New Hampshire and Oregon), state courts should first look to their own constitutions and construe them without regard to the meaning of an analogous federal provision. If the state constitution provides a rule of decision in favor of the rights-asserting party, the courts should end their analysis without reaching the federal claim. See Hans A. Linde, "Without Due Process: Unconstitutional Law in Oregon," 49 *Or. L. Rev.* 125 (1970): 133–34 ("While a defendant may have both a state and a federal constitutional claim to present, legally these are not cumulative but alternative . . . .") (hereinafter Linde, "Without Due Process"). But under this approach state courts are expected to first address "losing" or "weak" state constitutional claims even when cases can be more easily resolved on federal grounds.

In supporting the primacy approach, Judge Sutton has provided a powerful federalism-based argument for prioritizing state constitutional claims and addressing them first as well as a devastating critique of the lock-step approach. See Sutton, *51 Imperfect Solutions*, 174–82.

The proponents of the primacy approach, however, do not simply argue that it is supported by "constitutional avoidance" prudential considerations similar to those developed by Justice Louis D. Brandeis in *Tennessee Valley Authority v. Ashwander* (1936) (Brandeis, J., concurring). Rather, they take the position that the Fourteenth Amendment *requires* the primacy approach. As Justice Linde explained in *Sterling v. Cupp*:

> The proper sequence is to analyze the state's law, including its constitutional law, before reaching a federal constitutional claim. *This is required,* not for the sake either of parochialism or of style, but *because the state does not deny any right claimed under the federal Constitution when the claim before the court in fact is fully met by state law.*

Ibid. (emphasis added). See also Linde, "Without Due Process," 133–34.

But the U.S. Supreme Court more than a century ago rejected the argument that the Fourteenth Amendment is limited to actions authorized by state law, and it stated that the "reach of the Amendment is shown to be coextensive with any exercise by a state of power, in whatever form exerted." *Home Telephone & Telegraph Co. v. City of Los Angeles* (1913). And the strongest argument for rejecting the lock-stepping approach is not the doctrinal argument advanced by Justice Linde, but rather the pragmatic argument that its use inhibits the development of state constitutional law through the presumptive use of federal interpretations or an overreliance on them.

The expectation of the primacy method is that an analysis of cases with potential state and federal constitutional claims should begin with a review of the state provision. That approach may make sense in most cases for prudential reasons, but the adoption of a required primacy approach would bar state and federal courts from addressing "easy" federal issues before addressing difficult state issues. And it would prevent courts from following the common practice of relying on alternative grounds to support their judgments.

Moreover, as Professor Williams has pointed out, the lock-stepping approach does not merely involve state courts following U.S. Supreme Court interpretations of analogous provisions. Rather, under what he dubs "prospective lock-stepping," state courts follow federal interpretations of analogous provisions wherever those interpretations may lead. See Williams, *The Law of American State Constitutions*, 224–29. Thus, "prospective lock-stepping" represents an abdication of state sovereignty and inhibits the development of an independent state constitutional jurisprudence. See also *Stolz v. J & B Steel Erectors, Inc.* (2018) (Fischer, J., concurring) (characterizing the treatment of state constitutional provisions as the functional equivalent of federal provisions as an "upward delegation of the duty to interpret the Ohio Constitution [that] is improper under our federal system and unconstitutional under the Ohio Constitution").

Between the poles of lock-stepping and primacy are variants of these approaches, including what has been called the interstitial approach, in which state courts interpret their constitutions to fill gaps between federal protections, and the dual sovereignty approach, in which state courts address both the state and federal provisions. And still other state courts have adopted a "criteria" approach, in which the federal provision is presumptively applicable unless identified factors or criteria for deviations are met. What these approaches have in common, with the exception of the pure primacy approach, is a review of the federal counterpart, albeit at different points in the analysis. See generally Williams, *The Law of American State Constitutions*, 193–209 (discussing various forms of lock-stepping).

In addressing the Ohio Bill of Rights, the Ohio Supreme Court has not adopted a single or official interpretive approach. And, under what could be described as "modified lock-stepping," the court has often looked first to U.S.

Supreme Court interpretations of analogous federal constitutional provisions for guidance in interpreting the state constitution. But in applying this pragmatic or ad hoc approach, the court has also been willing to construe state provisions independently.

As the following commentary illustrates, members of the court have often strongly disagreed on how to construe provisions of the Ohio Constitution. And these disagreements have been most pronounced in cases involving three of the most important provisions in the Bill of Rights: the equal protection and benefit clause, the prohibition against unreasonable searches and seizures, and the due course of law provision. See Commentary, Article I, sections 2, 14, and 16.

■ STATE CONSTITUTIONAL INTERPRETATION

In addition to the methodological issues—sequencing and weighing—state courts must identify and apply the tools of state constitutional interpretation. To be sure, text, history, and precedent are always important, but there are also unique interpretive issues that arise, including the weight to give the extensive debates at the 1850–51 and 1912 Conventions, the persuasiveness of the official explanations of amendments presented to the voters, the application of rules of statutory construction to constitutional interpretation, the political and historical context (often described in contemporaneous newspaper articles) in which the voters considered proposed amendments, and the legal and political culture of the state.

In approaching the Ohio Constitution, the Ohio Supreme Court has often declined to look at constitutional provisions in isolation and has followed a more holistic approach in which it construes provisions *in pari materia*. See *Toledo Edison Co. v. Bryan* (2000) ("Where provisions of the Constitution address the same subject matter, they must be read *in pari materia* and harmonized if possible."); see also *Hill v. Higdon* (1855) ("It is our duty to give a construction to the constitution as will make it consistent with itself, and will harmonize and give effect to all its various provisions."). And the court has applied this approach to constitutional interpretation to cases involving the Bill of Rights. See, for example, *Steele v. Hamilton County Community Mental Health Bd.* (2000) (reading section 1 *in pari materia* with section 16 as the basis for the "fundamental right" to refuse medical treatment); *State ex rel. Heller v. Miller* (1980) (reading sec. 16 "in conjunction with Sections 1, 2 and 19"); *Hocking Val. Coal Co. v. Rosser* (1895) (relying on Art. I, secs. 1, 2, and 16, to strike down a state statute that required a $5.00 attorney fee award in wage claims because it "permits one party, or class of people, to invoke the action of our tribunals of justice at will, while the other party, or another class of citizens, does so at the peril of being mulct in an attorney fee, if an honest but unsuccessful defense should be interposed").

State constitutions, including Ohio's, are also characterized by their inclusion of both affirmative rights and self-executing provisions and in the relative ease of amendment should the voters believe the court got it wrong. And the political and legal heritage of Ohio with the backdrop of its Jeffersonian, Jacksonian, and Progressive Era influences provides an elected judiciary with the difficult task, as well as the opportunity, to identify state-specific values that can inform the interpretation of state constitutional provisions. Finally, the constitutions of other states (including their text, history, and interpretation) may have even greater relevance to Ohio than decisions of the U.S. Supreme Court interpreting the U.S. Constitution. See generally Robert F. Williams, "Interpreting State Constitutions as Unique Legal Documents," 27 *Okla. City U. L. Rev.* 189 (2002).

But the Ohio Supreme Court has often characterized rights-conferring provisions of the state and federal constitutions as coextensive or functionally equivalent with federal provisions, thus eliminating the need to review independently the state provisions. Such characterizations, however, seem particularly inappropriate when the provisions are not textually identical. And even when provisions are identical or virtually identical, equating them without an independent inquiry into the history and the meaning of the state provision also seems inappropriate.

In most cases, however, there will not be any *obvious* state-specific historical or other evidence to support or reject the conclusion that identically worded provisions should be equated. Nonetheless, in such cases the court should still reject any presumptions about provisions being coextensive or functionally equivalent. And it should follow the lead of *Norwood* and review the state provisions independently.

In reviewing decisions that had combined discussions of state and federal provisions, the court has sometimes been reluctant to abandon conclusions about rights-conferring state constitutional provisions simply because the U.S. Supreme Court has changed its interpretation of the federal provisions. See, for example, *Wampler v. Higgins* (2001) (allowing rights-protecting free speech ruling under Ohio Constitution to remain in place after a U.S. Supreme Court decision narrowed the federal guarantee); *State v. Gallagher* (1976) (on remand from U.S. Supreme Court) (clarifying its earlier decision, which had combined its discussion of the state and federal provisions, and holding that the state constitution was the basis of its decision to treat as inadmissible testimony about utterances made by an accused to his parole officer); *cf. Simmons–Harris v. Goff* (1999) (stating that the court will not "irreversibly tie ourselves" to an interpretation of the Ohio Constitution that is based on federal law and that "[w]e reserve the right to adopt a different constitutional standard pursuant to the Ohio Constitution, whether because the federal constitutional standard changes or for any other relevant reason."). But see *State v. Robinette* (1997) (reversing earlier judgment on state constitution after remand from the U.S. Supreme Court); *American Association of University Professors v. Central State University* (1999) (same).

Prior to *Arnold v. City of Cleveland* (1993), the court often combined discussions of state and federal provisions, a practice that inhibited the development of an independent state constitutional jurisprudence and that subjected the court's judgments to U.S. Supreme Court review under the expanded authority of *Michigan v. Long* (1983). See The History of the Ohio Constitution, *supra*. But in cases involving precedents that had combined their review of state and federal provisions, the court should, albeit belatedly, be willing to undertake an independent review of the state constitutional provisions as contemplated by the *Arnold* decision.

Although the Ohio Supreme Court has addressed some issues of state constitutional interpretation, it has only provided limited guidance on how these factors relate to one another and to the larger question of how to construe the Ohio Constitution. And given the weaker commitment to stare decisis in cases involving the state constitution, the court has broad leeway to revisit decisions that applied a lock-step approach to the interpretation of provisions of the Ohio Constitution or that equated state and federal provisions without an independent analysis of the former. See The History of the Ohio Constitution, *supra* (discussing stare decisis).

■ PRESUMPTION OF CONSTITUTIONALITY

In interpreting the Ohio Constitution, the Ohio Supreme Court often (but not consistently) relies upon a presumption of constitutionality that places a heavy burden on those challenging the constitutionality of state statutes. See, for example, *Ohio Grocers Association v. Levin*, (2009) ("Laws are entitled to a strong presumption of constitutionality, and the party challenging the constitutionality of a law bears the burden of proving that the law is unconstitutional beyond a reasonable doubt.") (internal quotations omitted). See also *State ex rel. Dickman v. Defenbacher* (1955) (syllabus).

The presumption has been questioned, see *State ex rel. Weinberger v. Miller* (1912) (Davis, C. J., dissenting); *State ex rel. Attorney Gen. v. Cincinnati* (1870), and most recently this criticism has been embraced by Justice Paul Pfeifer, a former legislator, in his dissent in *Ohio Grocers Association*. At bottom, however, the presumption reflects a reluctance to exercise judicial review as well as an arguably appropriate deference to the political branches. But more difficult to understand is the heavy burden of "proving that the law is unconstitutional beyond a reasonable doubt." Ibid. Simply put, despite the presumption's pedigree, it is difficult to see how a standard of proof borrowed from the criminal law can be relevant to the issue of the constitutionality of a statute. *Accord Wilson v. Kasich* (2012) (Pfeifer, J., dissenting) ("Proof beyond a reasonable doubt is typically necessary only in criminal cases. Such a high burden of proof in the current constitutional matter turns this court into a rubber stamp, not the guardian of the constitution that it is designed to be."). But see *League of Women Voters of Ohio v. Ohio Redistricting Commission* (2022) (League I) (applying the beyond a reasonable doubt standard to a challenge to a state redistricting plan adopted by the Ohio Redistricting Commission, but stating that "[t]he presumption of constitutionality and the application of a high standard of proof do not prevent this court from 'say[ing] what the law is'") (quoting *Marbury v. Madison* (1803)).

Section 1
Inalienable rights.

All men are, by nature, free and independent, and have certain inalienable rights, among which are those of enjoying and defending life and liberty, acquiring, possessing, and protecting property, and seeking and obtaining happiness and safety.

Adopted as part of the 1851 Constitution and never amended, section 1 was based on the first part of Article VIII, section 1 of the 1802 Constitution, which in turn was based on language in a number of early constitutions and declarations of rights, including the Virginia (1776) and Massachusetts (1780) Declarations of Rights and the first section of Article IX of the 1790 Pennsylvania Constitution. Section 1 is also similar to the Declaration of Independence ("We hold these truths to be self-evident, that all men are created equal, that they are endowed by their Creator with certain unalienable Rights, that among these are Life, Liberty and the pursuit of Happiness"), but it has no direct textual parallel in the U.S. Constitution, even though the Fifth Amendment to the U.S. Constitution includes a reference to "life, liberty, or property" (as does the Fourteenth Amendments to the U.S. Constitution).

Section 1 is a statement of political philosophy—that individuals possess certain inalienable rights derived from natural law. The Ohio Supreme Court in *Palmer v. Tingle* (1896) recognized this in interpreting the term "liberty" in this section "to embrace the right of man to be free in the enjoyment of the faculties with which he has been endowed by his Creator, subject only to such restraints as are necessary for the common welfare." The *Palmer* court also described the right to contract as one of the "inalienable rights" of man that has existed since "the earliest dawn of history" and further made clear that the power of the General Assembly to interfere with the right to contract is limited.

> Liberty to acquire property by contract can be restrained by the general assembly only so far as such restraint is for the common welfare and equal protection and benefit of the people, and such restraining statute must be of such a character that a court may see that it is for such general welfare, protection, and benefit. The judgment of the general assembly in such cases is not conclusive.
>
> Ibid. (syllabus).

See also *Hibbard v. State* (1901) (per curiam) (relying, in part, on the "inalienable right of enjoying liberty and acquiring property" as identified in *Palmer* in striking down an act that provided pensions for schoolteachers); *City of Cleveland v. Clements Bros. Construction Co.* (1902) (holding unconstitutional the eight-hour workday on public works as a violation of "sections 1 and 19 of article 1 of the constitution of Ohio, because it violates and abridges the right of parties to contract").

And the court went even further in *Auditor of Lucas County v. State ex rel. Boyles* (1906), when it relied on sections 1, 2, and 19 to invalidate an act that provided up to $25 quarterly in relief for the worthy blind on the ground that the expenditure of public funds for a private purpose violated an inherent limitation of the constitution. See ibid. ("[T]he power of the state to take the property of its citizens by a tax is not broader than the purpose for which the state is formed, and so is not wholly within the discretion of the Legislature, but, without express prohibition, is subject to the *inherent limitation* that it may be exercised only for a public purpose.") (emphasis added).

The approval by voters of Article II, section 33, in 1912 rejected the *result* in *Palmer* (which had held mechanics' liens to be unconstitutional), but the Ohio Supreme Court has not overruled *Palmer*. See Commentary, Article I, section 33.

Despite a decision in 1923 that relied solely on section 1 to strike down a law allowing the appointment of a guardian to handle the property of a physically disabled but mentally competent adult as "an unwarranted abridgement of . . . [the] right to acquire, possess, and protect property," *Schafer v. Haller* (1923), the court has rejected the use of section 1, standing alone, as a source of self-executing rights. For example, in *State v. Williams* (2000), a case involving a challenge by criminal defendants to Ohio's sex offender registration and notification law, the court rejected arguments that the law violated the rights of privacy, favorable reputation, acquisition of property, and ability to pursue an occupation, all of which, the defendants contended, were natural law rights protected under this section. One basis for the decision in *Williams* was the court's conclusion that section 1 was not an independent source of self-executing constitutional rights.

> Similar to the language of the Declaration of Independence and other state constitutions, the language in Section 1, Article I of the Ohio Constitution is not an independent source of self-executing protections. Rather, it is a statement of fundamental ideals upon which a limited government is created. But it requires other provisions of the Ohio Constitution or legislative definition to give it practical effect. This is so because its language lacks the completeness required to offer meaningful guidance for judicial enforcement.
>
> Ibid.

Although section 1 may not, standing alone, confer any rights, when read *in pari materia* with other provisions it can be a source of enforceable rights. For example, in *Steele v. Hamilton County Community Mental Health Bd.* (2000), a decision rendered after *Williams*, the Ohio Supreme Court stated that sections 1 and 16 were the source of the "fundamental right" to refuse medical treatment on the basis that "personal security, bodily integrity, and autonomy are cherished liberties." See also ibid. ("These liberties were not created by statute or case law. Rather, they are rights inherent in every individual.").

In 2018, a member of the court, relying on *Palmer*, interpreted this section as encompassing a right to pursue one's chosen profession free from arbitrary and unreasonable governmental restraints; he then argued that a court-adopted disciplinary rule was unconstitutional because it treated an out-of-state attorney who practiced law exclusively from an office in Ohio as engaged in the unauthorized practice of law. *In re Application of Jones* (2018) (DeWine, J., concurring in judgment only).

Section 2

Right to alter, reform, or abolish government; equal protection and benefit; repeal of special privileges.

All political power is inherent in the people. Government is instituted for their equal protection and benefit, and they have the right to alter, reform, or abolish the same, whenever they may deem it necessary; and no special privileges or immunities shall ever be granted, that may not be altered, revoked, or repealed by the General Assembly.

Adopted in 1851 and never amended, this section contains four distinct clauses: (1) an inherent political power clause; (2) an "equal protection and benefit" clause; (3) a right to "alter, reform, or abolish" government clause; and (4) a "special privileges or immunities" clause.

Inherent Political Power

The first sentence of this section, which provides that "[a]ll political power is inherent in the people," and the clause, which gives the people "the right to alter, reform, or abolish" the government, were derived from the second part of Article VIII, section 1 of the 1802 Constitution, which provided in its entirety as follows:

> That all men born equally free and independent, and have certain natural, inherent and unalienable rights; amongst which are the enjoying and defending life and liberty, acquiring, possessing and protecting property, and pursuing and obtaining happiness and safety; and every free republican government, being founded on their sole authority, and organized for the great purpose of protecting their rights and liberties, and securing their independence; to effect these ends, they have at

> all times a complete power to alter, reform or abolish their government, whenever they may deem it necessary.

The first sentence of 1802 section is nearly identical to Article IX, section 2 of the 1790 Pennsylvania Constitution and Article XI, section 1 of the 1796 Tennessee Constitution, and it reflects the Jeffersonian principle embodied in the Declaration of Independence that all political power is derived from the people.

Equal Protection and Benefit

The second sentence of section 2 contains an equal protection clause or, more precisely, an equal protection and benefit clause, which provides that "[g]overnment is instituted for [the people's] equal protection and benefit . . . ." This clause is patterned after section 3 of the 1776 Virginia Declaration of Rights and Article V of the 1776 Pennsylvania Constitution, both of which contained an aspirational provision providing that "government is, or ought to be, instituted for the common benefit, protection, and security of the people, nation or community."

The 1802 Ohio Constitution did not contain an equal protection and benefit clause, and the adoption of this clause along with the adoption of the "special privileges or immunities" clause later in this section were the most important changes made in the Bill of Rights in the 1851 Constitution. Unlike other parts of this section, the equal protection and benefit clause is an affirmative guarantee of equal protection and not simply a limitation on government or a statement of political philosophy. The clause also predates the Equal Protection Clause of the Fourteenth Amendment to the U.S. Constitution, which the states did not ratify until 1868.

The equal protection and benefit clause received little independent attention at the 1850–51 Constitutional Convention, but it was addressed during the lengthy and impassioned debate on the special privileges or immunities clause. Recognizing the relationship between the equal protection and benefit and special privileges clauses, future Ohio Supreme Court Justice Rufus P. Ranney of Trumbull County, the leader of the anticorporation Jacksonian Democrats and a fierce supporter of the right to repeal (special privileges), described the inconsistency that would exist if government refrained from extending special privileges or immunities to corporations:

> Whenever this provision is lived up to, and carried out in its true spirit, all special privileges will cease and die away as an accursed thing. You are willing to say that government is instituted for the equal protection and benefit of all, but when you are asked to say that same government shall have the power to repeal such laws as violate this provision, and confer special privileges upon some, that cannot be enjoyed by all, you refuse to do it.

> Beautiful consistency that! The benefits of government ought to be equal to all, but if a few get more than their share in the way or special benefits conferred by law, the people have no power to right the wrong—no power ever after to make it a government of equal benefits, but must permit those that have got the advantage, to enjoy it to the end of time. Such is your doctrine, and if it is true, the declaration that the government is instituted, for the equal protection and benefit of the people, is a falsehood, and should be stricken out.
>
> *Report of the Debates and Proceedings of the Convention for the Revision of the Constitution of the State of Ohio, 1850–51,* vol. 2 (1851), 478–79 (hereinafter *1850–51 Debates).*

Despite the limited discussion of the equal protection and benefit clause, equality was a topic of interest, and the delegates received a number of petitions urging them to support a provision that guaranteed equal rights "without regard to color or sex" or words to that effect. Not only did they fail to include language to guarantee equality to all Ohioans regardless of race or gender, many delegates strongly opposed even the mere introduction of these petitions. See Barbara A. Terzian, "Ohio's Constitutions: An Historical Perspective," 51 *Clev. St. L. Rev.* 357 (2004): 372–74 (hereinafter Terzian, "Ohio's Constitutions").

The Ohio Supreme Court did not address or even cite the equal protection and benefit clause in the first four and a half decades after its adoption, but in 1895 this changed abruptly. In May 1895 the court relied on the clause in *Hocking Val. Coal Co. v. Rosser* (1895) and held unconstitutional a state statute that awarded $5 in an attorney fee to a party who successfully advanced a wage claim. In the following month in *State ex rel. Schwartz v. Ferris* (1895), the court relied on the clause to invalidate a statute that created a graduated estate tax that distinguished rich and poor taxpayers.

Hocking Valley and *Schwartz* were followed by a torrent of cases relying on the equal protection and benefit clause, and in the late nineteenth and early twentieth centuries the Ohio Supreme Court relied on the clause to limit the ability of government to adopt economic or social welfare legislation that contained classifications that the court concluded were not reasonable. See, for example, *Palmer v. Tingle* (1896) (invalidating legislation that allowed subcontractors and laborers who did not contract with property owners to place mechanic's liens on the owners' property); *State v. Gardner* (1898) (invalidating statute that required licenses for individual plumbers but not for those working in firms that employed a licensed plumber because the Bill of Rights "prohibits the granting of privileges to one which are denied to others of the same class, and the imposition of restrictions or burdens upon certain citizens from which others of the same class are exempt"); *Hibbard v. State* (1901) (invalidating an act that provided pensions for schoolteachers because it took property from one citizen for the benefit of another); *Harmon v. State* (1902) (invalidating a statute that required a licensing examination for engineers who had not been operating steam engines and boilers for three continuous years).

These cases reflect an early approach to statutory classifications that required the rejection of classifications that favored one class and did not fully deal with the underlying problem. See Michael Les Benedict, "Civil Liberty in Ohio," in Michael Les Benedict and John F. Winkler, eds., *The History of Ohio Law*, vol. 2 (Athens: Ohio University Press, 2004), 675, 703–4 (hereinafter Benedict, "Civil Liberty in Ohio"); see also Howard Gillman, *The Constitution Besieged: The Rise and Fall of Lochner Era Police Powers Jurisprudence* (Durham: Duke University Press, 1993), 6–10.

The principle underlying equal protection, however, is that similarly situated persons must be treated the same or substantially the same under the law. And unlike the early Ohio decisions, much of modern federal equal protection law has developed in cases involving racial and gender discrimination. See John Marquez Lundin, "The Law of Equality before Equality Was Law," 49 *Syracuse L. Rev.* 1137 (1999): 1141. But there is no indication from the debates at the 1850–51 Convention that the equal protection and benefit clause or any other provision of the new constitution was understood to end or ameliorate racial or gender discrimination or to give African Americans or women the rights of state citizenship. Indeed, two decades after the convention adjourned, the Ohio Supreme Court upheld the classification of common school students by race under the U.S. Constitution without even citing the state equal protection and benefit clause. *State ex rel. Garnes v. McCann* (1872). And, in 1933, the court rejected a challenge to a policy of segregating college students by race, again without even considering the state provision. *State ex rel. Weaver v. Board of Trustees* (1933); see generally Jonathan L. Entin, "An Ohio Dilemma: Race, Equal Protection, and the Unfulfilled Promise of a State Bill of Rights," 51 *Clev. St. L. Rev.* 395 (2004).

Despite decisions that ignored the rights-conferring potential of the equal protection and benefit clause, the Ohio Supreme Court has recognized that equal protection is an evolving concept. And it has gone far beyond any possible original understanding of the clause to acknowledge that it bars racial and gender classifications as well as classifications based on illegitimacy and national origin. See *State v. Thompson* (2002).

In one of its earliest equal protection and benefit cases, however, the court sought to cabin the doctrine by pointing out that not "every little inconvenience" is actionable, and it held that the General Assembly is not barred from enacting laws that distinguish between individuals by prohibiting the names of candidates from appearing more than once on the ballot. *State ex rel. Bateman v. Bode* (1896); see also Commentary, Article V, section 2. Indeed, even in the late nineteenth and early twentieth centuries, the court, despite its probusiness bias, upheld most classifications that did not single out one class for special treatment. See Benedict, "Civil Liberty in Ohio," 704.

And in the last fifty years the court has generally upheld classifications if "reasonable grounds exist for making a distinction between those within and those without a designated class." *State v. Buckley* (1968) (rejecting equal protection challenge to aesthetic regulation of junk yards but not scrap yards). See also *McCrone v. Bank One Corp.* (2005) (treating the state and federal equal protection clauses as essentially the same, and applying the rational basis test to hold that the exclusion from workers' compensation coverage of psychological or psychiatric conditions that do not arise from a compensable physical injury or occupational disease does not violate equal protection).

Notwithstanding this deferential approach, the court has found an absence of reasonable grounds for legislative classifications and struck down on equal protection and benefit grounds legislation that imposed a two-year statute of limitations on personal injury actions brought against political subdivisions by minors but not by adults, *Adamsky v. Buckeye Local School District* (1995); that precluded suits against drivers and owners of motor vehicles by nonpaying guests but not by paying guests, *Primes v. Tyler* (1975); and that imposed enhanced penalties for private sexual batteries on minors by peace officers, *State v. Mole* (2016) (plurality).

Level of Scrutiny. The federal equal protection analysis includes a complex multitiered approach to legislative classifications with sliding scales of deference and a highly deferential rational basis review for claims not involving fundamental rights. The level of scrutiny applied to legislative classifications is one of the most important aspects of federal equal protection law, and the Ohio Supreme Court, though not required to do so, has generally followed the federal model. For example, in *State v. Thompson* (2002), the court applied strict scrutiny to a statute that prohibited solicitation of homosexual but not heterosexual activity. Treating the classification as a content-based restriction on speech, the court struck down the statute in the absence of a compelling state interest in the classification.

> When a discriminatory classification based on sex or illegitimacy is at issue, we employ heightened or intermediate scrutiny and require that the classification be substantially related to an important governmental objective. . . . And when classifications affect a fundamental constitutional right, or when they are based on race or national origin, we will conduct a strict-scrutiny inquiry. . . . This latter level of scrutiny demands that a discriminatory classification be narrowly tailored to serve a compelling state interest.
>
> Ibid.

The court, however, has sometimes deviated from the federal strict scrutiny/ fundamental rights approach under which classifications involving fundamental rights are only upheld if they are supported by a compelling state interest. For example, in *Cincinnati Board of Education v. Walter* (1979), a case challenging the financing of Ohio schools, the court rejected the use of the federal approach for identifying fundamental rights when the issue was the determination of the required level of scrutiny under the state constitution. And in *Arnold v. City of Cleveland* (1993), it held that the right to bear arms was a fundamental right under the Ohio Constitution but subjected the right only to rational review. See Commentary, Article I, section 4.

Functional Equivalence. The Ohio Supreme Court has often equated the state and federal equal protection provisions by describing them as "functionally equivalent." See, for example, *State v. Moore* (2016) ("Most recently, we have considered the two guarantees to be 'functionally equivalent' and employed the same analysis under both provisions."); *Eppley v. Tri-Valley Local Sch. Dist. Bd. of Educ.* (2009) ("We have held that the equal protection provisions of the Ohio and federal Constitutions are functionally equivalent and require the same analysis."); *State ex rel. Dayton Fraternal Order of Police Lodge No. 44 v. State Employment Relations Board* (1986) (describing the state equal protection and benefit clause as the "functional equivalent" of the federal provision); *State ex rel. Heller v. Miller* (1980) ("The Ohio Constitution's guarantees in [Sections 1, 2, 16 and 19 of Article I] . . . are substantially equivalent to the United States Constitution's guarantees."); *cf. Kinney v. Kaiser Aluminum & Chemical Corp.* (1975) ("The limitations placed upon governmental action by the Equal Protection Clauses of the Ohio and United States constitutions are essentially identical."). But see *State v. Noling* (2016) (cryptically stating that "the Equal Protection Clause of the Ohio Constitution is coextensive with, or stronger than, that of the federal Constitution").

Despite statements that equate the provisions, the clauses are textually distinct; they have different origins and different histories; and they have been the subject of wildly diverging interpretations. The chance that their interpretive trajectories would intersect and that the Ohio provision would suddenly be tied to the federal provision does not seem plausible, and it represents a form of "prospective lock-stepping" that has been sharply criticized. See Williams, *The Law of American State Constitutions,* 205–9.

Notwithstanding the widespread use of the phrase "functional equivalence" or similar formulations to equate the state and federal equal protection guarantees, there are significant questions about the origins of the phrase and the approach that it contemplates.

Perhaps recognizing the questionable origins of the functional equivalence approach, the court in 1996 asserted that "[a]s early as 1895 . . . [it had] recognized the functional equivalence" of both clauses. *Austintown Board of Trustees v. Tracy* (1996). But a close reading of *State ex rel. Schwartz v. Ferris* (1895), the 1895 case on which the *Austintown* court relied, makes clear that the court in *Schwartz* had only stated that the Equal Protection Clause of the Fourteenth amendment is "*not broader* than the second section of our bill of rights, and that, therefore, a statute upon this subject, authorized by our bill of rights, would not be in conflict with this section of the constitution of the United States." Ibid. (emphasis added). Thus, the 1895 decision in *Schwartz* treated the federal provision as a floor and relied exclusively on the state provision to invalidate a statute that distinguished rich and poor taxpayers under the state's graduated estate tax.

In 1999, after a remand from the U.S. Supreme Court, the Ohio Supreme Court declared that the equal protection guarantee under the Ohio Constitution is "to be construed and analyzed *identically*" to its federal counterpart under the Fourteenth Amendment. *American Association of University Professors v. Central State University* (emphasis added). The court also applied this equivalency in its 2007 tort reform decision holding that the statutory limitation on noneconomic damages did not violate the equal protection and benefit provision, *Arbino v. Johnson & Johnson* (2007), and in subsequent decisions in which it stated that the Ohio provision is "essentially the same" as the federal Equal Protection Clause, see *Ohio Apartment Assn. v. Levin* (2010), and that the state and federal equal protection clauses "are functionally equivalent and require the same analysis." *State v. Williams* (2010).

In these decisions the court did not review the significance of the provision's language and history. Nor did it explain how evolving federal equal protection standards can, in effect, be given responsibility for defining the meaning of the Ohio provision, or how deference to federal interpretations can be reconciled with the proper role of the Ohio Supreme Court and the judicial oath of office to support the Ohio Constitution. And perhaps even more importantly, the court has not explained what it means when it states that the provisions are functionally equivalent.

Even though equating the equal protection clauses may lack textual, historical, and even logical support, it may be too late to put the genie back in the bottle; and the court may be reluctant to revisit the many cases in which it described the state and federal equal protection provisions as either "functionally equivalent" or "coextensive." But "functionally equivalent" or "coextensive" treatment is not the same as *identical* treatment, and the court has room to recognize that both equal protection clauses seek to promote equal treatment by the government with the details of the protections varying significantly.

The Experience of Other States. Most state constitutions contain equality provisions, but only fifteen contain "equal protection of the law" clauses. Most state courts follow the federal model in construing their equality provision regardless of the text, see Williams, *The Law of American State Constitutions*, 209–24, but unlike federal equal protection law, which is encumbered by the need to develop standards applicable in all fifty states, see *San Antonio v. Rodriguez* (1973), states are not similarly burdened when applying their own equality provisions. See Sutton, *51 Imperfect Solutions*, 35–41

The Ohio Supreme Court looks to decisions of other states for insights in interpreting the state constitution. But only four other states––Kansas, Idaho, South Dakota, and Utah––have "equal protection and benefit" clauses, and these clauses are in constitutions that were adopted after the 1851 Ohio Constitution.

Thus, none of the other states provides a model for Ohio's equal protection and benefit clause, and decisions from these states do not shed direct light on the meaning of the Ohio provision.

But despite the absence of a direct antecedent, the experience of other states in construing "equal protection and benefit" and other equality provisions may provide insights into a proper interpretation of the Ohio clause. See generally Jeffrey M. Shaman, *Equality and Liberty in the Golden Age of State Constitutional Law* (New York: Oxford University Press, 2008), 41; Williams, *The Law of American State Constitutions,* 209–24; Jennifer Friesen, *State Constitutional Law: Litigating Individual Rights, Claims, and Defenses* (New York: Lexis Law Pub., 4th ed., 2006 & 2015 Supp.), Ch. 3.

State v. Mole. The different approaches to construing the equal protection and benefit clause and to the larger question of interpreting the Ohio Constitution are illustrated by *State v. Mole* (2016) (plurality). In *Mole,* the court relied on the equal protection and benefit clause to strike down a state statute that imposed enhanced penalties for a private sexual battery by a peace officer on a minor more than two years younger than the perpetrator.

In her plurality opinion, Chief Justice O'Connor acknowledged that "in the wake of *Arnold,* we have often, but inconsistently, heeded the hortatory call to the new federalism . . . ." She then observed that the state equal protection guarantee can provide greater protections than its federal counterpart and addressed the court's approach to construing the Ohio Constitution.

> We once again reaffirm that this court, the ultimate arbiter of the meaning of the Ohio Constitution, can and will interpret our Constitution to afford greater rights to our citizens when we believe that such an interpretation is both prudent and not inconsistent with the intent of the framers. We also reaffirm that we are not confined by the federal courts' interpretations of similar provisions in the federal Constitution any more than we are confined by other states' high courts' interpretations of similar provisions in their states' constitutions.
>
> Ibid.

And to further support the approach that she had described, she pointed to the observation of Judge Sutton, who stated:

> There is no reason to think, as an interpretive matter, that constitutional guarantees of independent sovereigns, even guarantees with the same or similar words, must be construed the same. Still less is there reason to think that a highly generalized guarantee, such as prohibition on "unreasonable" searches, would have just one meaning for a range of differently situated sovereigns.
>
> Ibid. (quoting Jeffrey S. Sutton, "What Does—and Does Not—Ail State Constitutional Law," 59 *U. Kan. L. Rev.* 687 (2011)).

Two dissenting justices, however, challenged this approach. One criticized the plurality opinion because its "interpretation of Ohio's Equal Protection Clause is not based on its text or history but on the lead opinion's sense of judicial necessity. However, our constitutional interpretation should be guided *exclusively* by the language and history of the clause at issue." *State v. Mole* (Kennedy, J., dissenting) (emphasis added).

And another dissenting justice, acknowledging the independent role of the Ohio Constitution in protecting individual rights, nonetheless emphasized the need to identify state-specific factors to justify deviations from federal interpretations.

> [T]he lead opinion has declared without any textual analysis or support that a right secured by the Ohio Constitution affords broader protection to its citizens than the federal Constitution . . . . . I wholeheartedly agree that the Ohio Constitution may provide greater protection of individual rights than the federal Constitution and that federal opinions do not control our independent analyses in interpreting the Ohio Constitution . . . . But that is exactly what is missing from the lead opinion: an independent analysis of the equal-protection guarantee in Article I, Section 2 of the Ohio Constitution premised on its language, history or early understandings. Absent that analysis, the lead opinion has not presented any compelling reasons why Ohio constitutional law should differ from the federal law. (internal quotations omitted).
>
> Ibid. (French, J., dissenting).

In the wake of this sharp disagreement, a different member of the court urged a reexamination of the "functional equivalence" issue. "[T]he unique language and historical background of this state's Equal Protection Clause, Article I, section 2 of the Ohio Constitution, should be carefully analyzed. . . . [and] this court should reexamine our precedent holding that the Ohio Equal Protection Clause is actually the 'functional equivalent' of the Equal Protection Clause of the Fourteenth Amendment to the United States Constitution." *Stolz v. J & B Steel Erectors, Inc.* (2018) (Fischer, J., concurring).

In *Matter of Adoption of Y.E.F.* (2020), the Ohio Supreme Court held that "[i]ndigent parents are entitled to counsel in adoption proceedings in probate court as a matter of equal protection of the law under the Equal Protection Clauses of the Fourteenth Amendment to the United States Constitution and Article I, Section 2, of the Ohio Constitution." In so ruling, the court concluded that a state statute that required the appointment of counsel for some parents faced with the loss of parental rights was "unconstitutionally underinclusive as applied to indigent parents facing the loss of their parental rights in probate court."

Alter, Reform, or Abolish Government

The third clause in this section, which gives the people the right to "alter, reform, or abolish" government, is (like sec. 1 and the first clause of sec. 2 of this article) a statement of political principle derived from the Declaration of Independence. Even though this clause provided support to those who suggested in the 1840s that a circumvention convention was needed to revise the first Ohio Constitution, see The History of the Ohio Constitution, *supra* ***25–27, as a practical matter the people's right to reform or abolish government is accomplished through the electoral process and through amendment to the constitution as provided in Articles II and XVI.

Special Privileges or Immunities

In contrast to the limited discussion of the equal protection and benefit clause, the debate at the 1850–51 Convention over the "special privileges or immunities" clause was lengthy and intense. See *1850–51 Debates*, vol. 2, 476–83; 485–550; 556–59.

The debate on this provision, which did not have a counterpart in the 1802 Constitutions, centered on a fundamental disagreement between Democrats and Whigs over the General Assembly's power to repeal grants of special privileges and immunities. It was common practice in the first half of the nineteenth century for the General Assembly to form corporations through special acts and in the process to include special privileges and immunities in corporate charters, including, for example, exemptions from future taxation and monopolies on tolls for road and canal companies. See generally Justin Long, "State Constitutional Prohibitions on Special Laws," 60 *Clev. St. L. Rev.* 719 (2012).

In Article II, section 26, the 1851 Constitution effectively barred special legislation by requiring that "[a]ll laws, of a general nature, shall have a uniform operation throughout the state" and section 2 provided that "no special privileges or immunities shall ever be granted, that may not be altered, revoked, or repealed by the General Assembly."

In 1819, the U.S. Supreme Court had held that corporate charters were contracts that could not be abridged by later legislative enactment without violating the federal contracts clause in Article I, section 10 of the U.S. Constitution. *Trustees of Dartmouth College v. Woodward* (1819); see generally Stephen A. Siegel, "Understanding the Nineteenth Century Contract Clause: The Role of the Property-Privilege Distinction and 'Takings' Clause Jurisprudence," 60 *S. Cal. L. Rev.* 1 (1986).

In response to *Dartmouth College*, the General Assembly began adding express reservations to corporate charters, which allowed the amendment or repeal of special privileges and immunities. But many Democrats at the 1850–51 Convention wanted to give the General Assembly an unqualified right to alter or repeal all special privileges and immunities. Led by convention delegate and future Ohio Supreme Court Justice Ranney, the leading opponent of corporate special privilege, most, if not all, of the supporters of an unqualified right of repeal were Jacksonian Democrats, who opposed in principle all grants of special privileges and immunities. See generally David M. Gold, *The Jacksonian Conservatism of Rufus P. Ranney* (Athens: Ohio University Press, 2017), 30–34.

Whigs, on the other hand, believed that corporate charters were inviolable and opposed a constitutional provision that would permit their repeal. Whigs ultimately prevailed with the support of a number of conservative Democrats, and the language finally approved gave the General Assembly the power to alter or repeal special privileges and immunities that were incorporated into future charters, but it prohibited the General Assembly from altering or revoking special privileges and immunities that had been previously granted without an express reservation. See Howard McDonald, "A Study in Constitution Making–Ohio: 1802–1874" (Ph.D. dissertation, University of Michigan, 1916), 128–31 (hereinafter McDonald, "A Study in Constitution Making"). And the inclusion of a ban on retroactive legislation further strengthened the hand of those who wanted to protect corporate charters from the General Assembly. See Commentary, Article II, section 28.

For a number of years, the Ohio Supreme Court rejected the U.S. Supreme Court's decision that corporate charters were contracts and thus constitutionally protected under the federal contracts clause; and even after the adoption of the 1851 Constitution, the court went as far as to describe the *Dartmouth College* doctrine as a "gross absurdity." *Milan and Richland Plank Rd. Co. v. Husted* (1854). But not long thereafter, the court relented and accepted the supremacy of federal law. See *Matheny v. Golden* (1856) ("The decision of the Supreme Court of the United States on the construction of the constitution or laws of the United States, are binding on the state courts.").

Although the history of this clause is intimately tied to issues concerning corporate charters, the Ohio Supreme Court has read the clause *in pari materia* with the equal protection and benefit clause of the same section to give additional meaning to the latter. See, for example, *Primes v. Tyler* (1975) (holding that the Ohio guest statute "denies equal protection and benefit of the law to the people of this state by its grant of a special privilege and immunity to negligent drivers who injure nonpaying passengers").

Section 3

Right to assemble and petition.

The people have the right to assemble together, in a peaceable manner, to consult for their common good; to instruct their representatives; and to petition the General Assembly for the redress of grievances.

Adopted in 1851 and never amended, this section is almost identical to its predecessor, Article VIII, section 19 of the 1802 Constitution, which contained virtually the same language as Article XVI of the 1776 Pennsylvania Declaration of Rights, except for the inclusion of the phrase "in a peaceable manner." This limiting phrase can be traced to language in the declarations of rights in a number of state constitutions, including those of Maryland, Massachusetts, and Tennessee See Maryland Declaration of Rights, Article XI (1776); Massachusetts Declaration of Rights, Article XIX (1780); Tennessee Declaration of Rights, Article XI (1796).

The rights to assemble and to petition date to medieval England, and at the time of the ratification of the Articles of Confederation in 1781, seven of the original thirteen states included either a right to petition or to assemble or both in their state constitutions. See Norman B. Smith, "'Shall Make No Law Abridging . . .': An Analysis of the Neglected, but Nearly Absolute, Right of Petition," 54 *U. Cin. L. Rev.* 1153 (1986).

Section 3 also has a federal counterpart in the First Amendment to the U.S. Constitution, which provides that "Congress shall make no law... abridging... the right of the people peaceably to assemble, and to petition the government for a redress of grievances." The First Amendment, however, phrases the assemble and petition clauses as limitations on the power of the government rather than as affirmative statements of the rights of the people. And the First Amendment, unlike this section, does not guarantee a right to instruct representatives, but some of the early state constitutions do. See, for example, North Carolina Declaration of Rights Article XVIII (1776); Massachusetts Declaration of Rights Article XIX (1780). The instruction provision remains part of this section, but there are no Ohio Supreme Court cases interpreting it.

The right to assemble and the right to petition are distinct rights under the Ohio and U.S. Constitutions. The right to assemble includes not only the right to assemble for the purpose of petitioning the government but also the right to assemble or congregate for any lawful purpose. *Richmond Newspapers, Inc. v. Virginia* (1980); *City of Toledo v. Sims* (1960).

Because courts analyze most cases involving protests, demonstrations, and other forms of assembly as free speech or freedom of association cases, there are relatively few right to assemble cases under either this section or the First Amendment. In the few cases in which the Ohio courts have interpreted the right to assemble, they have generally treated it the same as the corresponding right under the First Amendment. For example, in *City of Cleveland v. Anderson* (1968), an Ohio appellate court held that a city ordinance that made mere presence at a noisy or disorderly assembly a crime violated the right to assemble under this section and the First Amendment.

In *City of Cincinnati v. Coates* (1971), the U.S. Supreme Court overturned a decision of the Ohio Supreme Court that had rejected a state and federal challenge to a city ordinance making it unlawful for "three or more persons to assemble, except at public meeting of citizens, on any of the sidewalks, ... and there conduct themselves in a manner annoying to persons passing by . . . . ." Besides finding the ordinance unconstitutionally vague, the U.S. Supreme Court, relying only on the First Amendment, held that the right to assemble cannot be abridged simply because some people might find the exercise of the right "annoying."

There are no Ohio Supreme Court cases interpreting the petition clause, but an Ohio appellate court has recognized a tort of malicious interference with the right to petition government for a redress of grievances. In a case involving allegations by a landowner that members of the city planning board maliciously misrepresented facts to the planning board and city council (which resulted in the denial of the landowner's request for a zoning change), the court held that the right to petition the government for redress may be violated by false statements made knowingly and maliciously by public officials for the purpose of inducing a public body to act adversely to the petitioner. *Singer v. City of Fairborn* (1991). The court, however, rejected the claim "that a mere omission may give rise to liability, since that would have an unduly chilling effect upon the speaker's exercise of his rights to free speech."

Section 4

Bearing arms; standing armies; military power.

The people have the right to bear arms for their defense and security; but standing armies, in time of peace, are dangerous to liberty, and shall not be kept up; and the military shall be in strict subordination to the civil power.

Adopted in 1851 and never amended, this section is similar to Article VIII, section 20 of the 1802 Constitution, which had provided that "the people have a right to bear arms for the defense of themselves and the State; and as standing armies in time of peace are dangerous to liberty, they shall not be kept up: and that the military shall be kept under strict subordination to the civil power."

The final two clauses of this section, which prohibit standing armies in time of peace and require the military to be kept in strict subordination to civil power, were not in the Second Amendment to the U.S. Constitution; and their presence in the 1802 and 1851 Ohio Constitutions underscores the relationship of the "right to bear arms" provision to the collective security provided by the militia. See Patrick J. Charles, *The Second Amendment: The Intent and Its Interpretation by the States and the Supreme Court* (Jefferson NC: McFarland Publishing, 2009), 167–69.

The 1851 Constitution changed the language of this section by replacing the phrase "for the defense of themselves and the State" with "for their defense and security." Although the language differs from the 1802 provision, there is no evidence that the delegates sought to enlarge the protective scope of the provision. Ibid., 161.

Before the U.S. Supreme Court construed the Second Amendment to contain an individual right to own a gun for self-protection and applied that right to the states, see *District of Columbia v. Heller* (2008); *McDonald v. City of Chicago* (2010), the Ohio Supreme Court construed this section as one of the provisions of the Ohio Bill of Rights that affords greater protection than its federal counterpart. See *Arnold v. City of Cleveland* (1993).

Equating the constitutional "right to bear arms" with the personal right to possess and carry firearms, the *Arnold* court ruled that this section "secures to every person a fundamental *individual* right to bear arms for 'their defense and security . . . .'" (emphasis in original). Nonetheless, the court held that the right is not absolute and that it reasonably may be restricted in the interests of the health, safety, morals, or general welfare of the public. Thus, the court declined to apply strict scrutiny to limitations on the right to bear arms and upheld a law that banned the possession and sale of assault weapons.

The constitutionality of prohibitions on the carrying of concealed weapons under this section has arisen a number of times. In 1859, the state adopted its first law barring the carrying of concealed weapons, which provided that "whoever shall carry a weapon or weapons, concealed on or about his person, such as a pistol, bowie-knife, dirk, or any other dangerous weapon, shall be deemed guilty of a misdemeanor." *An Act to prohibit the carrying or wearing of Concealed Weapons*, section 1 (Ohio 1859).

In 1920, the Ohio Supreme Court addressed the constitutionality of this statute (which had not been changed in significant ways) and held that it was a reasonable exercise of the police power, stating that the prohibition against "carrying concealed arms even in one's home, is not in contravention of Const. art. 1, §4, securing the right to bear arms." *State v. Nieto* (1920).

And in 2003, the court reaffirmed the *Nieto* decision and, applying the reasonableness test embraced by *Arnold*, upheld the constitutionality of a law barring the carrying of concealed weapon, stating that "there is no constitutional right to bear concealed weapons." *Klein v. Leis* (2003). The General Assembly, however, responded by enacting a concealed carry law that authorized county sheriffs to issue licenses to carry concealed handguns in limited circumstances. See O.R.C. section 293.125.

Many of the Ohio Supreme Court's recent decisions involving the right to bear arms have been in cases addressing the power of municipalities to exercise their home rule power to limit the right to carry or possess arms. See Commentary, Article XVIII, section 3.

Section 5
Trials by jury.

The right of trial by jury shall be inviolate, except that, in civil cases, laws may be passed to authorize the rendering of a verdict by the concurrence of not less than three-fourths of the jury.

Adopted in 1851, the first clause of this section comes directly from Article VIII, section 8, of the 1802 Constitution, which also provided that the right shall be "inviolate."

Historians have discredited the view that the Magna Carta is the source of the right to trial by jury, but they have located the origins of the right in early Anglo-Saxon England. See Jefferson Edward Howeth, "*Holland v. Illinois*: The Supreme Court Narrows the Scope of Protection against Discriminatory Jury Selection Procedures," 48 *Wash. & Lee L. Rev.* 579 (1991): 587–88.

Nonetheless, the Ohio Supreme Court traces the right to a jury trial to the Magna Carta, *Butler v. Jordan* (2001), and the Northwest Ordinance specifically provided that the inhabitants of the territory "shall always be entitled to the benefits . . . of the trial by jury." Ordinance of 1787, section 14, Article II. But the right to a jury trial in the Ohio courts is only guaranteed to the extent that the right existed at common law in 1802, when Ohio adopted its first constitution. *Belding v. State ex rel. Heifner* (1929). This historical test is similar to the approach taken by the U.S. Supreme Court, which construes the mandate in the Seventh Amendment to the U.S. Constitution that "the right to trial by jury shall be preserved" as only guaranteeing a right to a jury trial in civil cases in federal court if the right existed at common law in 1791, when the Seventh Amendment was ratified. *Dimick v. Schiedt* (1935). Unlike most of the interests protected by the federal Bill of Rights, the U.S. Supreme Court has not applied the Seventh Amendment to the states. *Minneapolis & St. L.R. Co. v. Bombolis* (1916).

The 1802 Constitution had given the jury a role in determining not only the facts but also the law. See 1802 Constitution, Article VIII, section 6 ("[I]n all indictments for libels the jury shall have the right to determine the law and the facts as in other cases."). The 1851 Constitution dropped this cryptic provision, which had been in the section dealing with indictments for libel and not in the section dealing with the right to jury trial (sec. 8), but it appeared to address the role of the jury more generally. See John F. Winkler, "The Legal Literature of Ohio," in Michael Les Benedict and John F. Winkler, eds., *The History of Ohio Law*, vol. 2 (Athens: Ohio University Press, 2004), 501, 508.

Criminal Cases

In criminal cases, Ohio's guarantee of the right to a jury trial under this section (and under sec. 10 of this article) is broader than the federal right under the Sixth Amendment to the U.S. Constitution. Under the Sixth Amendment, the right is generally not available for crimes that carry a potential sentence of six months or less, *Blanton v. City of North Las Vegas* (1989), but, consistent with the common law rule in 1802, the right to a jury trial under the Ohio Constitution is available if a crime carries the potential for any incarceration. See *State v. Keich* (1956) (Phillips, J., concurring) (rejecting defendants' claim for a jury trial for operating a business on a Sunday since imprisonment is not a part of the penalty for a first offense). Nor is there a right to a jury trial under this section for minor offenses that impose only fines, since it was well established at common law that such cases could be heard without a jury. *Inwood v. State* (1884). But Ohio has extended the right to a jury trial in criminal cases by statute, and defendants in criminal cases have the right to a jury trial in all cases except minor misdemeanors and those in which the maximum penalty does not include either the possibility of imprisonment or a fine in excess of $1,000. See O.R.C. section 2945.17.

Civil Cases

At common law, the right to trial by jury in Ohio applied only in cases where a person risked losing his life, liberty, or private property. *Mason v. State ex rel. McCoy* (1898). For example, a party contesting a will does not have a right to a jury trial, since in 1802 there was no right to a jury trial in will contests. *State ex rel. Kear v. Lucas County Court of Common Pleas* (1981). Neither does an attorney in a fee dispute with another attorney have a right to a jury trial over the mandatory arbitration procedure required under the disciplinary rules, since the courts administered "virtually all aspects of the practice of law" in 1802. *Shimko v. Lobe* (2004). The right to a jury trial, however, is available in intentional tort and negligence actions, since juries decided such cases in 1802. *Kneisley v. Lattim-Stevens Co.* (1988).

In *Sorrell v. Thevenir* (1994), the Ohio Supreme Court held that the mandatory deduction of collateral benefits from tort damage awards violated the right to jury trial, but in *Arbino v. Johnson & Johnson* (2007), the court distinguished *Sorrell* and held that a statutory cap on damages does not deny an injured party a right to trial by jury. See ibid. ("So long as the fact-finding process is not intruded upon and the resulting findings of fact are not ignored or replaced by another body's findings, awards may be altered *as a matter of law*.").

Nonetheless, a statute permitting a jury to determine eligibility for punitive damages, but which gave the court responsibility for determining the amount of punitive damages violates the right to trial by jury under this section. *Zoppo v. Homestead Insurance Co.* (1994).

In *McClain v. State* (2022), the court will be addressing the availability of a jury trial in a statutory wrongful imprisonment action brought in the Court of Common Pleas.

Waivers

Though constitutionally guaranteed under this section, the right to trial by jury in the Ohio courts can be waived in both criminal and civil cases. See generally *Cassidy v. Glossip* (1967).

In civil cases in the Ohio courts, a party who has a right to a jury trial must demand one in writing under Rule 38(B) of the Ohio Rules of Civil Procedure.

Likewise, in the federal courts a party who has the right to trial by jury under the Seventh Amendment to the U.S. Constitution must demand one in writing under Rule 38(B) of the Federal Rules of Civil Procedure. Thus, both plaintiffs and defendants may demand a trial by jury in civil cases, and a jury trial will be waived if none of the parties makes a timely request for one.

In criminal cases in the Ohio courts, on the other hand, a defendant is presumed to demand a jury trial unless the defendant "knowingly, intelligently and voluntarily" waives the right and the waiver is in writing. *Cassidy v. Glossip, supra*. But a defendant charged with a "petty" or non-serious offense (i.e., one that carries a sentence of six months or less) must demand a jury trial in writing to avoid waiving the right (Ohio Rules of Criminal Procedure Rule 23(A)).

In criminal cases in the federal courts, a one-party waiver is not available because a defendant does not have a federal constitutional right to have a case tried to the court. *Singer v. United States* (1965). But under rules promulgated by the Ohio Supreme Court under the Modern Courts Amendment, the right to a jury trial belongs to defendants in state court criminal cases, and defendants may waive their right to trial by jury and be tried before a judge without regard to the preference of the prosecutor. See generally Judicial Impact Statement on H.B. 265 (129th GA) (Judicial Conference) (2011) (proposing change in Ohio approach).

Re-Examination of Jury Findings

The Seventh Amendment to the U.S. Constitution, in addition to preserving the right to trial by jury in civil cases in federal courts, provides that "no fact tried by a jury, shall be otherwise re-examined . . . [other] than according to the rules of the common law." The Ohio right to trial provision does not include a "re-examination" clause, but a member of the Ohio Supreme Court, relying in part on the debates at the 1850–51 Convention, has observed that "a primary purpose of the trial by jury was to safeguard the rights of individual citizens . . . from judicial bias and judicial reexamination of jury-determined facts." *Arbino, supra* (Cupp, J., concurring).

Jury Unanimity

The second part of this section allows nonunanimous jury verdicts in civil cases in the Ohio courts by permitting juries to render verdicts with a three-fourths vote.

The 1912 Constitutional Convention proposed and the voters approved this deviation from the unanimity rule previously applied in the Ohio courts under this section and historically applied in federal courts under the Seventh Amendment, see *American Publishing Co. v. Fisher* (1897), in part to prevent an obstinate juror from causing a mistrial by withholding a vote and to discourage compromise verdicts. See *Proceedings and Debates of the Constitutional Convention of the State of Ohio: Convened January 9, 1912* (Columbus: F. J. Heer Printing Co., 1912), 168–72 (hereinafter *1912 Debates*). Thus, in this significant way Ohio's right to a jury trial in civil cases differs from the policies followed in federal courts under the Seventh Amendment. For a history of the nonunanimity provision, see generally Edward H. Siddens, "Smaller Juries and Non-Unanimity: Analysis and Proposed Revisions of the Ohio Jury System," 43 *U. Cin. L. Rev.* 583 (1974).

Section 6

Slavery and involuntary servitude.

There shall be no slavery in this state; nor involuntary servitude, unless for the punishment of crime.

Adopted in 1851 and never amended, this section borrowed its language from the first sentence of Article VIII, section 2, of the 1802 Ohio Constitution and from Article VI of the Northwest Ordinance, which provided that "[t]here shall be neither slavery nor involuntary servitude in the said territory, otherwise than in the punishment of crimes, whereof the party shall have been duly convicted . . . ."

Both the Northwest Ordinance and the 1802 Constitution, however, included other provisions related to slavery. The Northwest Ordinance allowed the return of fugitive slaves, and the 1802 Constitution permitted males aged twenty-one or older and females aged eighteen or older "to serve any person as a servant" if the choice was made while "in a state of perfect freedom, and on condition of a bona fide consideration received, or to be received, for their service . . . ." 1802 Constitution, Article VIII, section 2.

The 1802 Constitution also included a clause allowing "negroes" and "mulattos" to be indentured as apprentices: "Nor shall any indenture of any negro or mulatto, hereafter made and executed out of the state, or if made in the state, where the term of service exceeds one year, be of the least validity, except those given in the case of apprenticeships." Ibid. According to one commentator, this last clause was inserted to prevent indentures from being used to avoid the prohibition against slavery. See Terzian, "Ohio's Constitutions," 366.

In 1856, in a case involving a slave who had traveled from Kentucky to Ohio with the permission of his master, the Ohio Supreme Court ruled that a slave who entered Ohio was immediately emancipated. *Anderson v. Poindexter* (1856). Stating that "there has never been a period during our state government, when a slave could for one single moment, by the consent and act of its owner, be placed and continued in bondage here," the court held that principles of comity and respect for another state's laws did not abrogate the constitution and laws of Ohio prohibiting slavery. The status of fugitive slaves, however, was another matter. Notwithstanding this section, the federal 1850 Fugitive Slave Act required states to return slaves who had escaped into the state, and the Ohio Supreme Court recognized the supremacy of federal law. See *Ex parte Bushnell* (1859).

Not surprisingly, there have been very few modern cases on this section, but one reported case concerned the practice of a municipal court judge of forcing indigent defendants to work for the county to pay for appointed counsel. The Ohio Supreme Court held that this requirement "constitutes involuntary servitude for a debt, not punishment for a crime" in violation of the prohibition against involuntary servitude under this section and the Thirteenth Amendment to the U.S. Constitution. *State ex rel. Carriger v. City of Galion* (1990).

Section 7

Rights of conscience; education; the necessity of religion and knowledge.

All men have a natural and indefeasible right to worship Almighty God according to the dictates of their own conscience. No person shall be compelled to attend, erect, or support any place of worship, or maintain any form of worship, against his consent; and no preference shall be give, by law, to any religious society; nor shall any interference with the rights of conscience be permitted. No religious test shall be required, as a qualification for office, nor shall any person be incompetent to be a witness on account of his religious belief; but nothing herein shall be construed to dispense with oaths and affirmations. Religion, morality, and knowledge, however, being essential to good government, it shall be the duty of the General Assembly to pass suitable laws, to protect every religious denomination in the peaceable enjoyment of its own mode of public worship, and to encourage schools and the means of instruction.

Adopted in 1851 and never amended, this section is nearly identical to Article VIII, section 3 of the 1802 Constitution. The first two sentences of this section, which guarantee freedom of worship and prohibit the support of religion and interference with the rights of conscience, are similar to Article XI, section 3 of the 1796 Tennessee Constitution and Article IX, section 3 of the 1790 Pennsylvania Constitution. The Northwest Ordinance also guaranteed the right to religious freedom. "No person, demeaning himself in a peaceable and orderly manner, shall ever be molested on account of his mode of worship or religious sentiments, in the said territory." Finally, much of the final sentence of this section also has its origins in the Northwest Ordinance.

The first sentence of this section is phrased affirmatively and provides that "[a]ll men have a natural and indefeasible right to worship Almighty God according to the dictates of their own conscience." The second sentence, which contains prohibitions against compelled support for religion, against religious preferences, and against interference with the rights of conscience, has federal counterparts in the Establishment and Free Exercise Clauses of the First Amendment to the U.S. Constitution ("Congress shall make no law respecting an establishment of religion, or prohibiting the free exercise thereof.").

Establishment Claims

The language in Ohio's "establishment" and "free exercise" clauses differs significantly from the language in the First Amendment to the U.S. Constitution, and the Ohio Supreme Court has stated that the religion clauses of the Ohio Constitution are not "coextensive" with those in the First Amendment. *Simmons-Harris v. Goff* (1999). Nonetheless, the court has adopted the federal test in establishment cases.

Simmons-Harris was a challenge to the 1995 Ohio Pilot Project Scholarship Program, which provided school vouchers to some students in Cleveland, and the Ohio Supreme Court adopted the U.S. Supreme Court's three-part establishment clause test from *Lemon v. Kurtzman* (1971). Under *Lemon*, a law survives constitutional scrutiny only if (1) it has a secular purpose, (2) its primary effect neither advances nor inhibits religion, and (3) it does not excessively entangle the government with religion.

Stating that it was not bound to adopt the *Lemon* test, the Ohio Supreme Court relied on *Lemon* in rejecting a challenge under this section to the voucher program because the "elements of the *Lemon* test are a logical and reasonable method by which to determine whether a statutory scheme establishes religion." Nonetheless, the court expressly reserved the "right to adopt a different constitutional standard pursuant to the Ohio Constitution, whether because the federal constitutional standard changes or for any other relevant reason." Thus, the fact that the U.S. Supreme Court subsequently discredited *Lemon*, see *American Legion v. American Humanist Association* (2019), does not mean that the Ohio Supreme Court will follow suit and modify its analysis in cases raising state establishment claims.

Despite its conclusion that the voucher program did not violate the state or federal establishment clauses, the court struck down the statute in its entirety because the law creating the program violated the "one-subject rule" of Article II, section 15(D). Subsequently, the General Assembly re-enacted the voucher program, and the U.S. Supreme Court held under a "refined" *Lemon* test, see *Zelman v. Simmons-Harris* (2002) (O'Connor, J., concurring), that the program, which in substance was the same as the 1995 program, did not violate the federal Establishment Clause. See also Commentary, Article VI, section 2.

Freedom of Conscience

The freedom of conscience clause in this section provides greater protection for the free exercise of religion than is provided by the Free Exercise Clause of the First Amendment. Before 1990, there was little, if any, distinction between the state and federal provisions, and courts reviewed laws that allegedly infringed the right of religious freedom under strict scrutiny: to be upheld, the law had to be the least restrictive means of furthering a compelling state interest. In *Employment Division, Oregon Department of Human Resources v. Smith* (1990), however, the U.S. Supreme Court in a sharply divided 5–4 decision abandoned the strict scrutiny test and held that laws of general application that did not target religion did not violate the federal Free Exercise Clause irrespective of the effect of the law on religious practice. Nonetheless, in *Humphrey v. Lane* (2000), a case involving a Native American prison guard's challenge to a hair-length regulation, the Ohio Supreme Court expressly rejected *Smith* and held that strict scrutiny remains the appropriate test for religious freedom claims under the Ohio Constitution.

Relying on the text of the state constitutional provisions, the *Humphrey* court held that Ohio's prohibition against "any interference with the rights of conscience" was broader than the First Amendment's prohibition against laws that prohibit the free exercise of religion and that the Ohio provision barred state laws that had only an indirect or tangential effect on the free exercise of religion.

> The Ohio Constitution allows no law that even *interferes* with the rights of conscience. The federal Constitution concerns itself with laws that *prohibit* the free exercise of religion. By its nature the federal Constitution seems to target laws that specifically address the exercise of religion, *i.e.*, not those laws that tangentially affect religion. Ohio's ban on any interference makes even those tangential effects potentially unconstitutional.
>
> Ibid. (emphasis in original).

Accordingly, under this section, generally applicable laws that interfere with the exercise of religious beliefs, *even if religiously neutral*, are unconstitutional unless the state can show that the law is the least restrictive means of furthering a compelling state interest. But see *Humphrey v. Lane, supra* (Cook, J., dissenting) ("I see the majority's compelling-state interest standard as 'open[ing] the prospect of constitutionally required religious exemptions from civic obligations of almost every conceivable kind.' ") (quoting *Smith*).

Religious Tests

The third sentence in this section contains two clauses. The first prohibits religious tests for public office. The second forbids the exclusion of witnesses on account of their religious beliefs, but it does not dispense with the requirement of oaths or affirmations. In an early case, the Ohio Supreme Court held that a person must have some belief in a supreme being in order to take an oath, *Clinton v. State* (1877), but that case has been largely ignored. Indeed, Rule 603 of the Ohio Rules of Evidence, adopted by the Ohio Supreme Court, requires an oath or affirmation to testify, but the oath or affirmation need only be "administered in a form calculated to awaken [the witness's] conscience." The staff notes to Rule 603 specifically state that "[t]he rule is designed to afford flexibility in dealing with children, persons with mental defects, atheists, members of religions not willing to swear an oath to God."

Bible Reading

The last sentence of section 7, derived in part from the Northwest Ordinance, see Ordinance of 1787, section 14, Article 3, provides that "[r]eligion, morality, and knowledge" are "essential to good government" and requires the General Assembly "to protect every religious denomination in the peaceable enjoyment of its own mode of public worship, and to encourage schools and the means of instruction."

This provision was the subject of the 1872 case involving Bible reading and religious instruction in the Cincinnati public schools. The Cincinnati Bible reading case was the first serious challenge to nonsectarianism and "the most significant Bible reading case of the nineteenth century." Steven K. Green, *The Second Disestablishment* (Oxford NY: Oxford University Press, 2010), 275–76.

In *Cincinnati Board of Education v. Minor* (1872), the Ohio Supreme Court upheld a school board policy that prohibited the reading of the Bible in the Cincinnati public schools. The board had issued its policy after complaints from Catholic parents over the use of the Protestant King James Bible. A lower court had found that the board's ruling violated this provision of the Ohio Constitution, but the Ohio Supreme Court reversed and rejected the argument that this provision mandated teaching not simply religion but the Christian religion. Concluding that this section neither required nor prohibited bible reading, the court ruled that the school board was free to ban school-mandated bible reading. See generally Linda Przybyszewsk, "Scarlet Fever, Stanley Matthews, and the Cincinnati Bible War," 42 *Journal of Supreme Court History* 256 (2017).

Section 8

Writ of habeas corpus.

The privilege of the writ of habeas corpus shall not be suspended, unless, in cases of rebellion or invasion, the public safety require it.

Adopted in 1851 and never amended, this section was originally part of the provision on bail in Article VIII, section 12 of the 1802 Constitution. It is almost identical to Article 1, section 9 of the U.S. Constitution, which provides that "[t]he privilege of the writ of habeas corpus shall not be suspended, unless when in cases of rebellion or invasion the public safety requires it." Along with trial by jury and the right to bail, the writ of habeas corpus was one of fundamental protections from government contained in the Northwest Ordinance. The roots of the "Great Writ," as it is also called, can be traced to the beginning of the common law, and the U.S. Supreme Court described it as "the most celebrated writ in the English law." *Fay v. Noia* (1963).

The writ of habeas corpus is a petition filed with a court to seek the release of a person who has been wrongfully imprisoned or has had his or her liberty otherwise unlawfully restrained where "there is no adequate remedy in the ordinary course of law." *Pegan v. Crawmer* (1996). The writ is not a substitute for direct appeal or for a motion for postconviction relief, *Brown v. Rogers* (1995), and the writ of habeas corpus in Ohio is generally not the appropriate procedure for raising constitutional errors at trial, for challenging the constitutionality of a law, *Shie v. Leonard* (1998), or for determining whether a defendant was innocent of the crime, *Cook v. Maxwell* (1965).

A writ of habeas corpus is the appropriate remedy, however, where a court lacks jurisdiction over a defendant. For example, the Ohio Supreme Court held that a writ of habeas corpus is the proper remedy where a justice of the peace lacked statutory authority to enter judgment against a criminal defendant and sentence him to jail, *In re Locket* (1952), and where a juvenile is unlawfully transferred to a common pleas court to be tried as an adult, *Johnson v. Timmerman-Cooper* (2001). A writ of habeas corpus is also appropriate where a pretrial detainee raised a claim of excessive bail and there was no other adequate remedy at law. *State ex rel. Pirman v. Money* (1994).

Although habeas corpus is generally used in criminal cases, the Ohio Supreme Court has found the writ to be a proper remedy in civil cases challenging involuntary commitment to a mental institution, *In re Fisher* (1974), and in child custody cases, *Pegan, supra.*

Section 9

Bail and cruel and unusual punishment.

All persons shall be bailable by sufficient sureties, except for a person who is charged with a capital offense where the proof is evident or the presumption great, and except for a person who is charged with a felony where the proof is evident or the presumption great and where the person poses a substantial risk of serious physical harm to any person or to the community. Where a person is charged with any offense for which the person may be incarcerated, the court may determine at any time the type, amount, and conditions of bail. Excessive bail shall not be required; nor excessive fines imposed; nor cruel and unusual punishments inflicted.

The General Assembly shall fix by law standards to determine whether a person who is charged with a felony where the proof is evident or the presumption great poses a substantial risk of serious physical harm to any person or to the community. Procedures for establishing the amount and conditions of bail shall be established pursuant to Article IV, Section 5(B) of the Constitution of the state of Ohio.

Adopted in 1851 and amended in 1997, the first sentence of this section includes language from two sections of the 1802 Ohio Constitution.

The right to bail had originally been part of the habeas corpus provision in Article VIII, section 12 of the 1802 Constitution; and the prohibition against excessive bail and the infliction of cruel and unusual punishment were originally in Article VIII, section 13 of the 1802 Constitution. The right to bail (except in capital cases) and the prohibition against cruel and unusual punishment were guaranteed by the Northwest Ordinance and are also found in the Eighth Amendment to the U.S. Constitution, which provides that "[e]xcessive bail shall not be required, nor excessive fines imposed, nor cruel and unusual punishment inflicted."

The 1802 Constitution had also placed constraints on the power of the state to inflict punishments on persons arrested or convicted. See, for example, Article I, section 10 ("That no person arrested or confined in jail shall be treated with unnecessary rigor . . . ."); section 14 ("All penalties shall be proportioned to the nature of the offense."); section 21 ("That no person . . . [other than those employed in the military] shall be subject to corporal punishment, under the military law."). But the 1851 Constitution dropped these provisions.

Right to Bail

Unlike the bail provision of the Eighth Amendment to the U.S. Constitution, which only prohibits excessive bail, the 1851 version of this section contains both an identically worded provision prohibiting excessive bail as well as an affirmative statement that "[a]ll persons shall be bailable" except where the defendant was charged with a capital offense. *State v. Bevacqua* (1946).

The 1997 amendment to this section added language to this section that limited the right to bail in noncapital felony cases by providing that a defendant charged with a felony has no right to bail "where the proof is evident or the presumption great" that the defendant committed the crime and "poses a substantial risk of serious physical harm to any person or to the community." The amendment expressly authorized the Ohio Supreme Court, acting under its rule-making power under Article IV, section 5(B), to establish the amount and conditions of bail. Under rules adopted by the court, a court determining the amount of bail must weigh a number of factors, including the nature of the offense; the weight of the evidence; and the defendant's history of flight, character, and ties to the community (Ohio Crim. Rule 46).

In 2005, the Ohio Supreme Court, relying on the text of this section, its history, and the purpose of the 1997 amendment, held that a cash-only bail bond is unconstitutional. *Smith v. Leis* (2005). In 2014, the court held that this section is violated when a court requires that 10 percent of the bail be paid in cash and prohibits a defendant from posting a surety bond for the full amount. *State ex rel. Sylvester v. Neal* (2014).

In *DuBose v. McGuffey* (2022), the court held that the "sole purpose of bail is to ensure a person's attendance in court" and that in reviewing a trial court's setting of bail an appellate court should apply a de novo, rather than an abuse an of discretion, standard. The court further held that the safety concerns of a victim's family were not proper considerations with respect to the *financial* conditions of bail and that a bail of $1.5 million was constitutionally excessive. Finally, the court noted that this section required the General Assembly to adopt a statute governing the denial of bail in cases where there is a "substantial risk of serious physical harm to any person or to the community" and that it delegated to the court the power to adopt "[p]rocedures for establishing the amount and conditions of bail." In response to *DuBose,* a proposal has been made to amend this section by removing the delegation of rule-making to the court and by providing that in setting the amount of bail courts "shall consider public safety, a person's criminal record, the likelihood a person will return to court, and the seriousness of a person's offense." *See* H.J.R. 2 (134th GA) (2022).

Excessive Fines and Cruel and Unusual Punishment

This section also prohibits excessive fines and cruel and unusual punishment. These provisions mirror the prohibitions contained in the Eighth Amendment, and the U.S. Supreme Court has applied both the Eighth Amendment's Cruel and Unusual Punishment Clause, *Robinson v. California* (1962) and its Excessive Fines Clause, *Timbs v. Indiana* (2019), to the states, but it has not decided whether the Excessive Fines Clause applies to civil in rem forfeitures. Ibid.

In determining whether a fine or punishment violates these prohibitions, the Ohio Supreme Court requires judges to look to whether the penalty is so disproportionate to the crime as to "shock the sense of justice of the community." *State v. Chaffin* (1972). In applying this standard, the court held that a sentence of twenty to forty years for selling cannabis did not violate the state or federal prohibitions against cruel and unusual punishment, but in a subsequent case the court declined to decide whether a delay of more than five years between the imposition of a ten-day sentence for driving under the influence and the execution of the sentence because of jail overcrowding was cruel and unusual punishment under the state or federal constitutions. *State v. Zucal* (1998).

And, in *State v. Hairston* (2008), the court held that an aggregate 134-year prison term did not constitute cruel and unusual punishment in violation of either the Eighth Amendment to the U.S. Constitution or this section of the Ohio Constitution; noting that "[w]here none of the individual sentences imposed on an offender are grossly disproportionate to their respective offenses, an aggregate prison term resulting from consecutive imposition of those sentences does not constitute cruel and unusual punishment."

Death Penalty

Capital punishment existed in Ohio before statehood, and execution by public hanging was the sole method of carrying out the death penalty until 1897.

Originally public executions took place in each county, but in 1844 the state eliminated public executions, and in 1885 the state moved all executions to the Ohio Penitentiary in Columbus. From 1897 to 1993, the state used the electric chair, but it then gave those being executed the option of choosing the electric chair or a lethal injection. Finally, since 2001, lethal injections have been the sole method of carrying out executions. See Capital Punishment in Ohio (Ohio Dept. Rehab. and Corr.) (website); see also Albert Post, "The Anti-Gallows Movement in Ohio," 54 *Ohio History* 105 (1945).

At the 1850–51 Convention, the delegates debated an effort to amend the constitution to abolish capital punishment. The proposed amendment provided that:

> Human life shall ever be held inviolate. The true object of punishment being, in addition to the security of society, to reform and not to exterminate mankind; human life shall never be taken as a punishment for crime; but the highest punishment inflicted for crime shall be imprisonment during life in the State Penitentiary.
>
> *1850–51 Debates*, vol. 2, 20.

But despite a fierce debate that included religious, moral, and historical arguments, the delegates postponed indefinitely their consideration of the proposal. Ibid., 20–23.

Abolitionists were more successful in 1912, and the 1912 Constitutional Convention proposed an amendment that would have banned the use of the death penalty by adding the following language to this section: "nor shall life be taken as a punishment for a crime." *1912 Debates*, 1823–24. The voters, however, rejected this proposed amendment by a vote of 303,246 to 258,706.

The Ohio Supreme Court has consistently rejected challenges under this section to Ohio's death penalty. In *State v. Jenkins* (1984), the court upheld the state's 1981 reinstatement of the death penalty after U.S. Supreme Court's 1972 decision in *Furman v. Georgia* (1972), striking down the death penalty nationally. In *Jenkins* the court held that "Ohio's statutory framework for imposition of capital punishment . . . does not violate the Eighth and Fourteenth Amendments to the United States Constitution or, any provision of the Ohio Constitution." The court has also held that execution by electrocution does not violate the state and federal constitutions. *State v. Coleman* (1989). And finally, the court has rejected the argument that Ohio's capital sentencing scheme, including electrocution and lethal injections, violates the state and federal constitutions. See *State v. Carter* (2000), and cases cited.

In 2001, in *State v. Scott*, the court also rejected the claim that this section prohibits the state from executing persons with biologically based severe mental illnesses such as schizophrenia. In so ruling, the court noted that it was not aware of any authority that supported the claim that the prohibitions against cruel and unusual punishment of the Eighth Amendment and the Ohio Constitution precluded the execution of mentally ill persons who understand their crimes and the capital punishment that they face.

But a member of the *Scott* court filed a sharp dissent. Relying on *Arnold v. City of Cleveland* (1993) and the power of the court to give the state constitution an independent meaning, the dissent argued that the court should consider Ohio values as a basis for supporting a bar on the execution of the seriously mental ill.

> When the Supreme Court of the United States sets constitutional standards, it does so for the entire country and therefore considers the ethos of the entire country. Our Constitution is not the product of the deeply conservative South or of the liberal Northeast. The Ohio Constitution is the product of Ohio, an enlightened, progressive state. When Ohioans consider the countries that still practice slavery, we call them uncivilized; when Ohioans consider the countries that do not permit women to vote, we call them repressive; when Ohioans consider the countries that commit state-sponsored torture, we call them barbaric. This court has a chance to take a step toward being a more civilized and humane society. This court could declare that in the interests of protecting human dignity, Section 9, Article I of the Ohio Constitution prohibits the execution of a convict with a severe mental illness. I believe that the "evolving standards of decency that mark the progress of" Ohio call for such a judicial declaration."
>
> *State v. Scott* (2001) (Pfeifer, J., dissenting).

The Ohio Supreme Court has acknowledged the special importance in capital cases of the right of allocution, which it has described as a defendant's last opportunity to plead his case or express remorse, noting that the denial of allocution can undermine the "constitutional reliability" of a death sentence. *State v. Roberts* (2013).

Juvenile Sentences

In 2012, in *In re C.P.*, the Ohio Supreme Court recognized that the Ohio Constitution "contains its own prohibition against cruel and unusual punishment" and held for the first time that this section "provides protection independent of the protection provided by the Eighth Amendment." The case involved a statute that imposed automatic, lifelong registration and notification requirements on juvenile sex offenders tried within the juvenile system. In holding that the statute violated the state constitutional prohibition against cruel and unusual punishment the court focused on the rehabilitative goals of the juvenile justice system and concluded that the statute "shock[s] the sense of justice of the community" and thus violates Ohio's prohibition against cruel and unusual punishments.

In *Miller v. Alabama* (2012), the U.S. Supreme Court held that state sentencing schemes that *mandated* life without the possibility of parole for juvenile offenders convicted of murder were unconstitutional under the Eighth Amendment, but the court did not completely bar such life sentences and left many questions unanswered. See generally Mark Denniston and Christoffer Binning, "The Role of State Constitutionalism in Determining Juvenile Life Sentences," 17 *Geo. J. L. & Pub. Policy* 599 (2019). State courts have taken a variety of approaches to these issues under their constitutions, but the Ohio Supreme Court has not addressed whether this section requires that all children have the right to a meaningful opportunity for release regardless of the crimes they committed. See *State v. Long* (2014) (relying on the Eighth Amendment in concluding that trial courts are required specifically to consider a defendant's status as a juvenile offender as a mitigating factor before imposing a sentence of life imprisonment without possibility of parole, but expressly declining to reach the Ohio constitutional issue because of the defendant's failure to raise it).

In *State v. Patrick* (2020), the Ohio Supreme Court, without independently construing the state constitution, held that a trial court must separately consider the youth of a juvenile offender as a mitigating factor before imposing a life sentence, even if the sentence includes eligibility for parole.

Evolving National Consensus

The U.S. Supreme Court has held that an evolving national consensus bars the execution of the mentally retarded and bars the imposition of sentences of life without the possibility of parole sentences on juveniles. See, for example, *Roper v. Simmons* (2005) (barring the execution of an adult for a crime committed at the age of seventeen, and noting that "we have established the propriety and affirmed the necessity of referring to the evolving standards of decency that mark the progress of a maturing society to determine which punishments are so disproportionate as to be cruel and unusual") (internal quotations omitted); *Atkins v. Virginia* (2002) (relying on evolving standards of decency and barring the execution of mentally retarded criminals).

The court has not addressed whether a similar national consensus supports a bar on the execution of the seriously mentally ill, but in 2011 a member of the Ohio Supreme Court noted that such a consensus was forming and urged the General Assembly to address the issue. See *State v. Lang* (2011) (Stratton, J., concurring) (noting that a national consensus was forming "to stop executing persons with severe mental illness" and stating that "[i]f executing persons with mental retardation/developmental disabilities or executing juveniles offends 'evolving standards of decency,' *Roper*, . . . then I simply cannot comprehend why these same standards of decency have not yet evolved to also prohibit execution of persons with severe mental illness at the time of their crime").

Even if the U.S. Supreme Court does not bar the execution of the seriously mentally ill, the Ohio Supreme Court's willingness to undertake an independent analysis of state cruel and unusual punishment claims, see *In re C.P., supra*, suggests that some independent state cruel and unusual punishment claims will be available. But *cf. State v. Broom* (2016) (reviewing the state prohibition against cruel and unusual punishment independently and concluding that it would not "shock the public's conscience to allow the state to carry out . . . [an] execution" after an earlier failed attempt).

Punitive Damages

The Excessive Fines Clause of the Eighth Amendment to the U.S. Constitution has not been construed to limit awards of punitive damages in civil cases between private parties, *Browning-Ferris Industries of Vermont, Inc. v. Kelco Disposal, Inc.* (1989), but the Due Process Clause of the Fourteenth Amendment bars grossly excessive awards of punitive damages, *State Farm Mutual Automobile Insurance Co. v. Campbell* (2003).

The Ohio Supreme Court has not addressed whether excessive awards of punitive damages violate either the excessive fines clause of this section or the due course of law guarantee of Article I, section 16. But the court has used its common law power to hold that the failure of a trial court to find a punitive damages award of $49 million excessive was an abuse of discretion, and it reduced the award to $30 million. *Dardinger v. Anthem Blue Cross & Blue Shield* (2002).

Section 10

Trial for crimes; witnesses.

Except in cases of impeachment, cases arising in the army and navy, or in the militia when in actual service in time of war or public danger, and cases involving offenses for which the penalty provided is less than imprisonment in the penitentiary, no person shall be held to answer for a capital, or otherwise infamous, crime, unless on presentment or indictment of a grand jury; and the number of persons necessary to constitute such grand jury and the number thereof necessary to concur in finding such indictment shall be determined by law. In any trial, in any court, the party accused shall be allowed to appear and defend in person and with counsel; to demand the nature and cause of the accusation against him, and to have a copy thereof; to meet the witnesses face to face, and to have compulsory process to procure the attendance of witnesses in his behalf, and a speedy public trial by an impartial jury of the county in which the offense is alleged to have been committed; but provision may be made by law for the taking of the deposition by the accused or by the state, to be used for or against the accused, of any witness whose attendance can not be had at the trial, always securing to the accused means and the opportunity to be present in person and with counsel at the taking of such deposition, and to examine the witness face to face as fully and in the same manner as if in court. No person shall be compelled, in any criminal case, to be a witness against himself; but his failure to testify may be considered by the court and jury and may be the subject of comment by counsel. No person shall be twice put in jeopardy for the same offense.

Adopted in 1851 and amended in 1912, this section is derived from sections 10 and 11 of Article VIII of the 1802 Constitution. Many, though not all, of its provisions protecting the rights of defendants in criminal cases first appeared in the Northwest Ordinance and were also in the Fifth and Sixth Amendments to the U.S. Constitution. The protections in the 1802 precursors to this section were virtually the same as the provisions in the Tennessee Constitution of 1796.

In addition to combining the above sections of the 1802 Constitution, this section of the 1851 Constitution added the first sentence, guaranteeing a right to a grand jury, using language that was largely borrowed from the Fifth and Sixth Amendments. As a result, most of the protections guaranteed to criminal defendants under this section mirror those afforded criminal defendants in federal court under the U.S. Constitution.

Well into the twentieth century, the Fifth and Sixth Amendments (and indeed the entire federal Bill of Rights) did not apply to the states. Thus, the Ohio Constitution was the principal source of constitutionally based procedural safeguards available to state criminal defendants (other than the Due Process of Law provision in the Fourteenth Amendment).

In 1912, the convention proposed and the voters approved amendments to this section to limit the privilege against self-incrimination, to authorize the General Assembly to provide for the taking of depositions of witnesses who could not attend a trial, and to permit the General Assembly to determine the number of persons on grand juries.

Right to a Grand Jury Indictment/Notice of Accusation

The grand jury clause provides that "no person shall be held to answer for a capital, or otherwise infamous, crime, unless on presentment or indictment of a grand jury" and the section further provides that "the party accused shall be allowed . . . to demand the nature and cause of the accusation against him, and to have a copy thereof."

Prior to the adoption of the 1802 Constitution, grand juries were used in Ohio under the common law, and they were one of the most significant protections against malicious or untoward prosecutions. *State ex rel. Doerfler v. Price* (1920). Neither the Northwest Ordinance nor the 1802 Constitution required indictment by grand jury, but the 1851 Constitution included such a requirement without addressing the size of the grand jury.

At common law, a grand jury consisted of at least twelve members, but in 1912 the Constitutional Convention recommended and the voters approved an amendment to permit the General Assembly to determine "the number of persons necessary to constitute such grand jury and the number thereof necessary to concur in finding such indictment." Under Ohio criminal rules, the number of grand jurors is nine with as many as five alternative jurors, and the rules require the concurrence of at least seven jurors for the issuance of an indictment. See Ohio Criminal Rule 6(A) and 6(F). See also *State v. Brown* (1988) (holding that court rules on the size of the grand jury and the voting requirement supersede otherwise applicable state statutes). A prosecutor, however, may dispense with a grand jury and proceed with an information if the prospective defendant in a criminal case waives prosecution by indictment. *Wells v. Maxwell* (1963).

Most states make some use of grand juries to initiate criminal prosecutions, and the Fifth Amendment to the U.S. Constitution requires their use in federal but not state prosecutions. *Branzburg v. Hayes* (1972). But the right to a grand jury is the only right under the Fifth and Sixth Amendments that the U.S. Supreme Court has not applied to the states.

Unlike petit or trial juries, grand juries do not determine the guilt or innocence of the accused. Their main role is to determine whether there is sufficient evidence to indict the accused and proceed with trial. See Oh. Jur.3d Jury, section 4.

Under this section, "the party accused shall be allowed . . . to demand the nature and cause of the accusation against him, and to have a copy thereof." This requirement, which is almost identical to a provision in the Sixth Amendment, is satisfied by an indictment from a grand jury or by a presentation (if the accused waives the right to a grand jury indictment). The indictment must include every essential element of the offense, but it can be amended as long as the defendant has not been misled or prejudiced. *State v. O'Brien* (1987).

Under Ohio law, grand jurors and prosecuting attorneys are required to keep grand jury proceedings secret, but the same obligation does not extend to witnesses. See generally Lewis R. Katz, John Martin, and Jay Macke, *Baldwin's Ohio Practice Criminal Law*, section 39:22, (3d ed., Thomson Reuters, 2021) (hereinafter *Ohio Criminal Practice*). And defendants are generally not entitled to evidence introduced during grand jury proceedings other than their own testimony and the testimony of alleged co-conspirators. *State v. Greer* (1981).

In addition to screening evidence presented by prosecutors, grand juries have the power to investigate crimes. See *Ohio Criminal Practice*, section 39:2.

Right to Counsel

The right to counsel clause provides that "[i]n any trial, in any court, the party accused shall be allowed to appear and defend in person and with counsel . . . ." This right to counsel applies without regard to whether the accused can afford an attorney, and Ohio statutes have required the provision of counsel to indigent defendants as early as 1816. *Conlan v Haskins* (1964).

In the landmark case of *Gideon v. Wainwright* (1963), the U.S. Supreme Court held that the Sixth Amendment requires states to provide counsel to indigent defendants in felony prosecutions. The Court subsequently extended *Gideon* to misdemeanor cases where the defendant receives a jail term, *Argersinger v. Hamlin* (1972), and eventually to cases involving suspended sentences that could result in imprisonment, *Alabama v. Shelton* (2002).

In *State v. Wellman* (1974), a decision not addressing the state constitution, the Ohio Supreme Court applied the *Argersinger* standard and held that "absent a knowing and intelligent waiver, no person may be imprisoned for any offense, whether classified as petty, misdemeanor, or felony, unless he was represented by counsel at his trial." See also *Ohio Criminal Practice*, section 75:3.

The U.S. Supreme Court's 2002 decision in *Shelton* brought it into line with Ohio, which since 1973 had provided that a defendant has a right to counsel in all cases (including both felonies and misdemeanors) involving charges that carry a statutory penalty of more than six months even if imprisonment will not be imposed. See Ohio Criminal Rule 44(A) (July 1, 1973) ("Where a defendant charged with a serious offense is unable to obtain counsel, counsel shall be assigned to represent him at every stage of the proceedings from his initial appearance before a court through appeal as of right, unless the defendant, after being fully advised of his right to assigned counsel, knowingly, intelligently, and voluntarily waives his right to counsel."). See also *Ohio Criminal Practice*, section 75:3.

Both this provision of the Ohio Constitution and the Sixth Amendment guarantee defendants a right to counsel in criminal proceedings in which they face the possibility of incarceration. And under both constitutions, the right to counsel attaches once criminal proceedings have been initiated, in other words, once a defendant has been indicted or otherwise formally charged with a crime. *State v. Stricklen* (1980).

By statute, however, the right to counsel in Ohio is broader than the state or federal constitutional right, and a prospective defendant is entitled to counsel upon arrest, detention, or any form of custody. See O.R.C. sections 2935.14 and 2935.20; see also *Ohio Criminal Practice*, section 75:5 ("In Ohio . . . there is a statutory right to counsel upon being taken into custody . . . which goes beyond the constitutional right, and requires that a suspect be given effective communication with retained counsel.").

Finally, the Ohio Supreme Court has held that the right to appointed counsel does not mean that an indigent defendant must be given a lawyer of his or her choice. *Thurston v. Maxwell* (1965).

Right to Appear and Confront Witnesses

The clause guaranteeing that accused parties have the right to appear and confront witnesses provides as follows: "the party accused shall be allowed to appear and defend in person and with counsel; to demand the nature and cause of the accusation against him, and to have a copy thereof; to meet the witnesses face to face, and to have compulsory process to procure the attendance of witnesses in his behalf. . . ."

In 1902, the Ohio Supreme Court strictly construed the face-to-face requirement of the state confrontation clause to only permit a limited exception to the requirement.

> In the trial of a criminal case, evidence of the testimony delivered in a previous trial of the same case by a witness not dead, but beyond the jurisdiction of the court, or limits of the state, is not admissible unless it appear [sic] to the satisfaction of the trial court, that the witness is absent through the connivance, or by the procurement of the accused.
>
> *State v. Wing* (1902).

In 1912, however, the voters approved an amendment proposed by the constitutional convention to add the following language to this section to more broadly permit the admissibility of depositions of witnesses who were not available at trial.

> [P]rovision may be made by law for the taking of the deposition by the accused or by the state, to be used for or against the accused, of any witness whose attendance can not be had at the trial, always securing to the accused means and the opportunity to be present in person and with counsel at the taking of such deposition, and to examine the witness face to face as fully and in the same manner as if in court.

Under this section and the Sixth Amendment to the U.S. Constitution, a defendant has a right to confront witnesses at trial. The purpose of the confrontation clauses is to allow for the cross-examination of witnesses, *State v. Self* (1990), and the U.S. Supreme Court has held that out-of-court witness statements that are testimonial are barred under the Sixth Amendment's confrontation clause unless the witnesses are unavailable and the defendants had prior opportunity to cross-examine them without regard to whether the trial court deems such statements reliable. *Crawford v. Washington* (2004) (overruling the interpretation of the Confrontation Clause in *Ohio v. Roberts* (1980), and holding that, "[w]here testimonial statements are at issue, the only indicium of reliability sufficient to satisfy constitutional demands is the one the Constitution actually prescribes: confrontation").

The language of the state confrontation clause differs from its federal counterpart. The state clause is more detailed and specifically provides that the defendant has a right to "meet the witnesses face to face," but the Sixth Amendment provides only that the "accused shall enjoy the right . . . to be confronted with witnesses against him."

Nonetheless, the Ohio Supreme Court ignored the textual difference in 1980 when it upheld a state statute that permitted the admissibility at trial of prior recorded testimony taken at a preliminary hearing upon a showing that, despite a good faith effort to secure the presence of the witness at trial, the witness was unavailable, and that the prior recorded testimony of the witness bears an "adequate indicia of reliability." *State v. Madison* (1980) (applying O.R.C. section 2945.49). But see *State v. Madison, supra* (Paul W. Brown, J., dissenting) ("The language in the Ohio Constitution must be read to give a defendant greater rights to confrontation and cross-examination than that given under the federal constitution.").

And, in 1990, the court held that the state provision "provides no greater right of confrontation than the Sixth Amendment" and held that the use of a child sexual abuse victim's videotaped deposition at trial in place of live testimony did not violate the state right of confrontation. *State v. Self, supra.*

Subsequently, however, relying on the textual differences between the two provisions (including the deposition alternative in the provision), the Ohio

Supreme Court recognized that the state confrontation clause requires the state to establish the unavailability of a child declarant before the child's extrajudicial statements can be admitted into evidence, thus seeming to construe the state provision as being more protective of defendants' rights than the Sixth Amendment. *State v. Storch* (1993). In any case, the right to confront witnesses face-to-face does not mean that witnesses must always testify at trial in the presence of the accused. And the court has interpreted this section, which specifically allows for the taking of testimony by deposition of a witness, to only require live testimony "where reasonably possible." Ibid.

Finally, in *State v. Arnold* (2010), following the U.S. Supreme Court's decision in *Crawford v. Washington, supra,* which strengthened the federal provision, the Ohio Supreme Court restated its earlier position that the state constitutional protection "provides no greater right of confrontation than the Sixth Amendment." Ibid. (quoting *State v. Self* (1990)). And it held that statements made by a child victim at a child advocacy center that served primarily an investigative purpose were testimonial and as such their admission violated the defendant's confrontation rights. *State v. Arnold, supra.*

Many confrontation clause cases involve the testimony of young children, particularly where the defendant is accused of sexual abuse. See generally Myrna S. Raeder, "Navigating between Scylla and Charybdis: Ohio's Efforts to Protect Children without Eviscerating the Rights of Criminal Defendants—Evidentiary Considerations and the Rebirth of Confrontation Clause Analysis in Child Abuse Cases," 25 *U Tol. L. Rev.* 43 (1994). In such cases, the U.S. Supreme Court has permitted the testimony of young children from behind a one-way screen, see *Coy v. Iowa* (1988), and by closed-circuit television, see *Maryland v. Craig* (1990), and the Ohio Supreme Court has allowed the testimony of young children by videotape deposition, *State v. Self, supra.* Although the presumption under this section is that a child will testify at trial, the court requires that a determination be made at a pretrial hearing of the psychological effect of live testimony on the child and the reliability of the child's statements. *Storch, supra.*

The right to appear at trial is also guaranteed by both this provision of the Ohio Constitution and by the federal due process protection. And the Ohio Supreme Court has concluded that absent a waiver or extraordinary circumstances, a defendant has the right to appear at every stage of the trial. See *State v. Williams* (1983). Nonetheless, the defendant's absence at a particular stage will not overturn a conviction unless the defendant is denied a fair trial. For example, in *Williams* the court ruled that despite a clear violation of the defendant's right to appear at a voir dire proceeding at which prospective jurors are examined, the defendant's absence did not result in the denial of a fair trial and therefore did not support the reversal of the subsequent conviction.

A criminal defendant also has the right to be present at every stage of criminal proceeding, including the imposition of sentence. See *State v. Welch* (1978). See also Commentary, Article I, section 9 (right of allocution in capital cases).

In 1925, the Ohio Supreme Court, after reviewing in depth the proceedings at the 1850–51 Constitutional Convention, rejected the state's argument that the right to appear at trial and confront witnesses only applied in capital cases. *Decker v. State* (1925).

Right to Compulsory Process

The compulsory process clause provides that an accused party has the right to "compulsory process to procure the attendance of witnesses in his behalf. . . ."

The rights to compulsory process under the Sixth Amendment to the U.S. Constitution and under this section are not unlimited. The testimony of the witness must be both material and favorable to the defendant. *U.S. v. Valenzuela-Bernal* (1982); *State v. Brown* (1992).

And the Ohio Supreme Court has held that the compulsory process clause cannot be used to force the attendance of a witness who is intent on asserting his or her privilege against self-incrimination merely to have the witness assert the privilege in front of the jury. *State v. Kirk* (1995).

In cases involving confidential informants, the defendant's right to force the informant to testify at trial must be balanced against the state's interest in keeping the informant's identity secret. A defendant who seeks to discover the identity of an informant has the burden of showing that the informant's testimony would at least be helpful or beneficial to the defense. *State v. Brown, supra.* Where the defendant already knows the identity of the informant, the burden is on the state to show that the testimony would not be helpful. Generally, the proper procedure in such cases is for the court to hold an *in camera* or private examination of the potential witness. Ibid.

Right to a Speedy Public Trial

The Speedy Public Trial Clause provides that an accused party has the right to "a speedy public trial by an impartial jury of the county in which the offense is alleged to have been committed . . . ." The right to a speedy public trial is also guaranteed by the Sixth Amendment to the U.S. Constitution, and the U.S. Supreme Court has described this right as designed to avoid lengthy incarcerations and restrictions on liberty before trial and to "shorten the disruption of life caused by arrest and the presence of unresolved criminal charges." *U.S. v. MacDonald* (1982).

In 1906, the Ohio Supreme Court held that a criminal defendant does not waive the state constitutional right to a public speedy trial by silence. See *State v. Hensley* (1906) ("The right cannot be waived by silence any more than can the right to be tried by jury where the accusation is a felony and the plea is not guilty."). Rather, the court requires a contemporaneous objection under the criminal rules to preserve the erroneous failure to state on the record the underlying agreement on which a negotiated plea of guilty is offered in a felony case. See *State v. Bethel* (2006).

The right to a speedy trial attaches automatically once a person is indicted or arrested for a crime. The U.S. Supreme Court, however, has not specified a fixed amount of time within which a defendant must be brought to trial, and it has held that states are free to establish reasonable time limits. *Barker v. Wingo* (1972). A number of states, including Ohio, have speedy trial statutes with specific time limits. And the Ohio Supreme Court has stated that, "for purposes of bringing an accused to trial, the statutory speedy trial provisions of R.C. 2945.71 et seq. and the constitutional guarantees found in the United States and Ohio Constitutions are coextensive." *State v. O'Brien* (1987).

Although a criminal defendant's right to a speedy trial is generally governed by the Ohio statute, there are instances in which the statute is not applicable. See, for example, *State v. Kelley* (1991) ("[A] guilty plea waives a defendant's right to challenge his conviction on *statutory* speedy trial grounds" (emphasis added)); see also *Ohio Criminal Practice,* section 39:22 ("The constitutional right has not lost its importance, however, since it applies in cases not reached by the statutory right."). In such cases, Ohio courts follow the U.S. Supreme Court's analysis in *Barker v. Wingo, supra,* to determine whether there has been a speedy trial violation under the Sixth Amendment and this section.

Under *Barker,* courts consider four factors in determining whether a defendant's constitutional right to a speedy trial has been violated: (1) the length of the delay in bringing the defendant to trial, (2) the reason for the delay, (3) whether the defendant asserted his right to a speedy trial, and (4) whether the defendant has suffered prejudice because of the delay. A defendant can waive the statutory and constitutional rights to a speedy trial, but the waiver must either be in writing or made on the record in open court. *State v. King* (1994).

"The constitutional guarantees of a speedy trial are applicable to unjustifiable delays in commencing prosecution, as well as to unjustifiable delays after indictment." *State v. Meeker* (1971) (syllabus). And the Ohio Supreme Court has held that a statute of limitations for commencing prosecution is irrelevant to a speedy trial claim, and the court has ruled that a thirteen-month delay in indicting defendant on felony drug charges after alleged offenses and more critically ten months after filing of criminal complaint violated the federal right to a speedy trial, which the court noted is similar to the state provision. *State v. Selvage* (1997).

This speedy trial provision of this section also requires that criminal trials be public and held in front of "an impartial jury of the county in which the offense is alleged to have been committed . . . ." Relying on this section as well as on the open courts provision of Article I, section 16, the Ohio Supreme Court has held that a trial held within a prison violates the right to a public trial. *State v. Lane* (1979). But the use of an anonymous jury according to a local court rule designed to protect the privacy of jurors does not necessarily violate the defendant's right to a public trial before an impartial jury. *State v. Hill* (2001). The right to trial by an impartial jury is also not violated by having the same jury at the guilt and sentencing phases, *State v. Zuern* (1987), or by extensive pretrial publicity unless the publicity leads to an unfair trial, *State v. White* (1998).

Notwithstanding the constitutional requirement of a trial before jurors "of the county in which the offense is alleged to have been committed[,]" a trial court may move the trial to a different county if the court concludes that the defendant's right to a fair and impartial jury is at risk. *State v. Lundgren* (1995). Moreover, the decision to change venue or keep the trial in the same county is within the trial court's discretion and will only be reversed when there has been a clear abuse of discretion. Ibid.

Privilege against Self-Incrimination

The Privilege Against Self-Incrimination Clause provides that "[n]o person shall be compelled, in any criminal case, to be a witness against himself . . ." This language is similar to section 11 of the 1802 Ohio Constitution, which provided that "in all criminal prosecutions the accused . . . shall not be compelled to give evidence against himself."

The Northwest Ordinance did not contain a privilege against self-incrimination, but eight of the original thirteen states included the privilege in their constitutions. See Leonard Levy, *Origins of the Fifth Amendment* (New York: Oxford University Press, 1968), 408–9 (hereinafter Levy, *Origins of the Fifth Amendment*); see also R. Carter Pittman, "The Colonial and Constitutional History of the Privilege against Self-Incrimination in America," 21 *Va. L. Rev.* 763 (1935).

The language in the 1802 Constitution defining the privilege is virtually identical to the language in both the Tennessee Constitution (1796) and the Fifth Amendment to the U.S. Constitution, which provides that "[n]o person . . . shall be compelled in any criminal case to be a witness against himself . . . ."

By its terms, the privilege appears to apply only to defendants in criminal cases, but the leading Fifth Amendment scholar, Leonard Levy, has concluded that this apparent textual limitation "was the result of poor drafting." Levy, *Origins of the Fifth Amendment*, 407. In any case, this limitation has not precluded the application of the Fifth Amendment privilege in noncriminal cases. As the U.S. Supreme Court stated in *Lefkowitz v. Turley* (1973):

> The Amendment not only protects the individual against being involuntarily called as a witness against himself in a criminal prosecution but also privileges him not to answer official questions put to him in any other proceeding, civil or criminal, formal or informal, where the answers might incriminate him in future criminal proceedings.

An Ohio state appellate court has observed that the Ohio privilege is "virtually identical" to the privilege under the Fifth Amendment in an opinion that relied on both the state and federal constitutions. *State v. Evans* (2001). In explaining the provisions, the court stated that the provisions have "been interpreted to extend well beyond the confines of the courtroom" and that they extend "to a person's privilege 'not to answer official questions put to him in any other proceeding, civil or criminal, formal or informal, where the answers might incriminate him in future criminal proceedings.'" Ibid. (quoting *Lefkowitz v. Turley*).

Without addressing the state privilege, the Ohio Supreme Court has applied decisions of the U.S. Supreme Court to hold that a person is privileged not only from testifying but also from producing personal records and other evidence that reveals his or her communications even if the same evidence can be obtained from third parties. Thus, a person cannot be forced to produce tax returns, although the same returns can be subpoenaed from his or her accountant. *City of Cincinnati v. Bawtenheimer* (1992). In limiting the Fifth Amendment privilege to evidence involving communications, the court has held that a person may be forced to submit to field sobriety tests, *City of Piqua v. Hinger* (1968), and to give handwriting samples, *State v. Heston* (1972).

To invoke the privilege against self-incrimination, a person must reasonably believe that testifying could lead to criminal liability. The mere assertion of the privilege is not sufficient, and courts must decide whether there is a reasonable risk that the person asserting the privilege could be exposed to criminal liability. *Ohio v. Reiner* (2001). Under federal law, once a person asserts the privilege the state may offer immunity and compel the person to testify. *Kastigar v. United States* (1972).

The Fifth Amendment privilege against self-incrimination is coextensive with a grant of immunity precluding the *use* of compelled testimony ("use immunity") and any derivative evidence ("derivative use immunity") against the witness. Ibid. Put somewhat differently, "the Fifth Amendment does not require 'transactional immunity'; it is sufficient if use and derivative use immunity is offered." *Ohio Criminal Practice*, section 70:5.

By statute, however, Ohio courts may only grant "transactional immunity," a broader form of immunity than use or derivative immunity and one that protects a witness not only from the use of compelled and derivative evidence but also from prosecution for *any* criminal activity about which the witness testifies. *State ex rel. Koren v. Grogan* (1994). The Ohio immunity statute, which is found in O.R.C. section 2945.44, thus extends rights beyond those contained in the Fifth Amendment. See *Ohio v. Reiner* (2001).

In *Miranda v. Arizona* (1966), the U.S. Supreme Court construed the privilege against self-incrimination as requiring the police to advise persons of their right to "remain silent" when they are subject to "custodial interrogations." A person is subject to "custodial interrogations" or in "custody" under *Miranda* if he or she is either formally arrested or has his or her freedom of movement similarly restrained. *California v. Beheler* (1983). Since conversations between suspects and undercover police officers lack the kind of pressure that is typical in custodial interrogations, undercover officers are not required to give *Miranda* warnings before questioning suspects. *Illinois v. Perkins* (1990). Similarly, the U.S. Supreme Court has held that the Fifth Amendment does not require probation officers to give *Miranda* warnings when speaking with probationers unless the probationers are in police custody. *Minnesota v. Murphy* (1984).

The Ohio Supreme Court, however, has taken a different approach to the privilege. In *State v. Gallagher* (1976), after a remand by the U.S. Supreme Court "to explicate whether or not its [earlier] judgment relies on federal law," *Ohio v. Gallagher* (1976), the court held that the Ohio Constitution was the basis of its earlier decision to treat as inadmissible testimony as to utterances made by an accused to his parole officer. The state court in *Gallagher* expressed the view that the result would be the same under the state and federal provisions, but it looked to factors unique to Ohio in construing the state provision. And, in 1987, the court looked at the totality of circumstances and the need for trust to hold that the Ohio privilege requires *Miranda* warnings in some cases in which a probationer in custody is being questioned. *State v. Roberts* (1987); see generally *Ohio Criminal Practice*, 25:5.

Although the Ohio Supreme Court typically follows the lead of the U.S. Supreme Court in construing the privilege, it has construed the privilege to provide greater protection of physical evidence than is provided under the Fifth Amendment. See *State v. Farris* (2006) ("To hold that the physical evidence seized as a result of unwarned statements is inadmissible, we would have to hold that Section 10, Article I of the Ohio Constitution provides greater protection to criminal defendants than the Fifth Amendment to the United States Constitution. We so find here.").

Under this provision of the Ohio Constitution, a defendant's "failure to testify may be considered by the court and jury and may be the subject of comment by counsel." This language was proposed by the 1912 Constitutional Convention (and approved by the voters) to redress what many delegates saw as a defect in the criminal justice system that unfairly favored criminal defendants. Before 1912 prosecutors could not comment on a defendant's refusal to take the stand, and many delegates believed that this allowed guilty defendants to go free simply by refusing to testify.

As a result of this amendment, Ohio prosecutors were permitted to comment on the failure of defendants to testify. In 1965, however, the U.S. Supreme Court held that commenting on a defendant's refusal to testify was "a remnant of the inquisitorial system of criminal justice . . . which the Fifth Amendment outlaws." *Griffin v. California* (1965). And the following year, the Ohio Supreme Court recognized that this provision of the Ohio Constitution violated federal constitutional standards. *State v. Lynn* (1966).

In 1976, the Ohio Constitutional Revision Commission (OCRC) recommended the repeal of the language in this section permitting consideration by courts and comments by prosecutors on failures to testify, see OCRC, *Recommendations for Amendments to the Ohio Constitution: Final Report, Index to Proceedings and Research* (1977), 460–61, but the General Assembly did not act on this recommendation.

Double Jeopardy

The Double Jeopardy Clause provides that "[n]o person shall be twice put in jeopardy for the same offense." This prohibition prevents the state from repeated attempts to convict or punish a person for the same offense.

The 1802 Constitution included a prohibition against double jeopardy, and the 1851 Constitution included a nearly identical provision.

The prohibition against double jeopardy dates back at least to the twelfth-century controversy in England between Thomas Becket and Henry II over civil and ecclesiastical courts, but the prohibition did not become well established in England until the seventeenth century. See Alfredo Garcia, "The Fifth Amendment: A Comprehensive and Historical Approach," 29 *U. Tol. L. Rev.* 209 (1998).

A prohibition of double jeopardy was in the 1641 Massachusetts Body of Liberties, but it was not included in the Northwest Ordinance. And only one state, New Hampshire, had such a provision in its constitution before the ratification of the Fifth Amendment. See ibid.

Probably influenced by the inclusion of double jeopardy clauses in the Fifth Amendment, the second Pennsylvania Constitution (1790), the Tennessee Constitution (1796), and the second Kentucky Constitution (1799), the 1802 Ohio Constitution contained a double jeopardy clause.

A delegate to the 1912 Convention proposed an amendment that would have allowed a defendant to be retried after acquittal if a legal error was made at trial, but the proposal never made it out of committee. *1912 Debates*, 1594, 1600–1601.

Textually, the prohibitions against double jeopardy in this section and in the Fifth Amendment are substantially the same. The Ohio Supreme Court has generally relied on U.S. Supreme Court decisions in construing the Ohio provision, and it has observed that the double jeopardy clauses of both constitutions prohibit "(1) a second prosecution for the same offense after acquittal, (2) a second prosecution for the same offense after conviction, and (3) multiple punishments for the same offense." *State v. Gustafson* (1996).

Although the general principle that double jeopardy protects against successive prosecutions and multiple punishments for the same offense is easy to state, the Ohio Supreme Court has described the law in this area as "a veritable labyrinth." *State v. Moss* (1982).

Double jeopardy "applies only to being placed in jeopardy more than once for the same offense and not two separate offenses arising out of the same transaction, facts, circumstances or situation," *State v. Ferguson* (1964); thus, one of the major difficulties is determining what constitutes "the same offense." The prevailing test was stated by the U.S. Supreme Court in *Blockburger v. United States* (1932): "[W]here the same act or transaction constitutes a violation of two distinct statutory provisions, the test to be applied to determine whether there are two offenses or only one is whether each provision requires proof of a fact which the other does not." See also *Ohio Criminal Practice*, section 73:2.

Applying the *Blockburger* test, the Ohio Supreme Court has held that a defendant cannot be convicted for both robbery and grand theft since grand theft requires proof of the same elements as robbery. *State v. Harris* (1979). Likewise, it has held that an indictment for ethnic intimidation violates both double jeopardy clauses, where the defendants had previously been convicted of aggravated menacing and the charges arose from the same incident. *State v. Mutter* (2017).

The Ohio Supreme Court follows the *Blockburger* test in cases involving successive *prosecutions, Harris, supra*; *State v. Tolbert* (1991), and it has recognized that the double jeopardy safeguard also bars multiple *punishments* for the same crime.

To provide guidance in cases involving the possibility of multiple punishments for the same crime, Ohio enacted an allied offense statute to codify the prohibition and determine when two crimes are the same. See *In re A.G.* (2016) ("R.C. 2941.25 codifies the protections established by the Ohio Constitution."). Adopted in 1973 and never amended, this statute has been subject to many "shifting judicial interpretations." *Ohio Criminal Practice*, section 73:10.

Under the state statute there may only be a single conviction for conduct that constitutes "allied offenses of similar import." But a defendant charged with multiple offenses may be convicted of all the offenses if any one of the following is true: (1) the conduct constitutes offenses of dissimilar import, (2) the conduct shows that the offenses were committed separately, or (3) the conduct shows that the offenses were committed with separate animus. See *State v. Ruff* (2015).

In *State v. Ruff* (2015), the Ohio Supreme Court summarized the law and concluded that the determination of whether two offenses are allied offenses of similar import must be based on a case-specific review of the conduct of the defendant and not on an abstract bright-line rule.

> Rather than compare the elements of two offenses to determine whether they are allied offenses of similar import, the analysis must focus on the defendant's conduct to determine whether one or more convictions may result, because an offense may be committed in a variety of ways and the offenses committed may have different import. No bright-line rule can govern every situation.
>
> Ibid.

At common law, the protection against double jeopardy became effective only after the defendant's acquittal or conviction, but the U.S. Supreme Court has noted that since the early nineteenth century it has been clear that jeopardy can also attach before a trial ends. *Crist v. Bretz* (1978). When jeopardy attaches depends on "the nature of the proceedings." *State v. Gustafson, supra.* In jury trials, jeopardy attaches when the jury is sworn in, but in bench trials, the right attaches when the judge begins to hear evidence. Ibid. Nonetheless, the state is not necessarily barred from reprosecuting a defendant when the first trial ends in a mistrial or dismissal. See *State v. Lovejoy* (1997). See also *Ohio Criminal Practice*, sections 74:4–74:13.

The state may sometimes also reprosecute a defendant whose conviction has been reversed on appeal. The U.S. Supreme Court has ruled that under federal law, if the reversal is based on an error that occurred at trial, a retrial is appropriate. *Lockhart v. Nelson* (1988). On the other hand, if the reversal is based upon an insufficiency of the evidence, a retrial violates double jeopardy. *Burks v. United States* (1978).

In determining whether to permit the retrial of a case that has been reversed because of a trial error, the U.S. Supreme Court applies an "all evidence" standard under which retrial is permitted if all the evidence admitted by the trial court is sufficient to support a guilty verdict. *Lockhart, supra.* In 1997, however, the Ohio Supreme Court, though rejecting a double jeopardy defense, adopted a "remaining evidence" standard under which only admissible evidence could be considered in a retrial. *State v. Lovejoy* (1997).

But in 2009, the court stated that it applies the two double jeopardy clauses "co-extensively." *State v. Brewer* (2009). It then ruled that the erroneous taking of judicial notice of an element of an offense was trial error but that a reviewing court could consider the fact (of which judicial notice had been taken) in finding that the evidence was sufficient to sustain the conviction; thus, double jeopardy did not bar retrial.

Recognizing the conflict between federal law and *Lovejoy,* Chief Justice Thomas J. Moyer dissented and urged the *Brewer* court to construe the Ohio double jeopardy clause as conferring more rights than its federal counterpart.

> [P]ursuant to *Lovejoy,* Ohio's Double Jeopardy Clause would offer greater protection from multiple prosecutions than the federal clause by narrowing the circumstances under which a defendant may be retried when the state fails to prove its case during the first go-around. Although we have historically found Ohio's Double Jeopardy Clause to be coextensive with its federal counterpart, Ohio's clause is not limited by the federal clause.
>
> *State v. Brewer* (2009) (Moyer, C. J., dissenting).

In 2013, notwithstanding *Brewer,* in *State v. Kareski,* the court applied the more rights-protective Ohio "remaining evidence" rule and reasoned that when a trial judge improperly takes judicial notice of a fact after the prosecution fails to prove that element, an appellate court cannot consider this evidence in determining whether sufficient evidence existed. It then concluded that double jeopardy bars retrial when the appellate court finds that judicial notice was improper, and (without the judicially noticed evidence) the evidence would be insufficient to support the conviction.

A concurring justice in *Kareski* would have overruled *Brewer* to hold that the Ohio double jeopardy provision requires the appellate court to consider only properly admitted evidence in making the sufficiency of evidence determination. (Lanzinger, J., concurring). A dissenting justice, on the other hand, would have followed the federal rule and permitted the appellate court to consider all the evidence presented at trial, whether properly admitted or not, in making the sufficiency of evidence determination. (French, J., dissenting).

Despite *Kareski* and its approval of a more rights-conferring interpretation of the state double jeopardy provision, the Ohio Supreme Court stated in 2017 that "[t]he protections afforded by the Ohio and U.S. Constitutions' Double Jeopardy Clauses are coextensive." *State v. Mutter* (2017). And the court reiterated that position in a number of subsequent cases in which the criminal defendant did not raise the state law claim and the court, perhaps significantly, called attention to that failure. See *State v. Soto* (2019) ("Because neither party has presented a contrary argument, we have no opportunity to revisit that determination today."); *City of Girard v. Giordano* (2018) (same); *Clark v. Adult Parole Authority* (2017) (same).

In *State v. Anderson* (2016) (plurality opinion), the court concluded that double jeopardy is not offended when the state seeks to retry a defendant after a series of properly declared mistrials. In so ruling, the plurality followed "the lead of the United States Supreme Court and conclude[d] that when a defendant challenges his or her retrial, the Double Jeopardy Clause controls over the more general Due Process Clause." But see *State v. Anderson*, *supra* (Lanzinger, J., concurring in judgment) ("I do not agree with the plurality that the Due Course of Law Clause of the Ohio Constitution provides no protection to defendants who are incarcerated for unfair and excessive lengths of time without having been convicted of a crime.").

The Ohio Supreme Court has held that the double jeopardy clause of the Ohio Constitution does not bar the state from carrying out an execution after failing to execute that same person once before. *State v. Broom* (2016). The court has also held that juveniles are entitled to the same constitutional double jeopardy protections as adults. *In re A.G.* (2016) ("We . . . acknowledge that both the federal and Ohio Constitutions protect juveniles subject to delinquency proceedings from double jeopardy in the same fashion as they do adults.").

Finally, under the "dual sovereign doctrine," a person is subject to prosecution for the same conduct by both federal and state authorities; thus, a conviction or acquittal of a defendant in a federal prosecution is not a bar to subsequent criminal proceedings by the state and vice versa. *State v. Fletcher* (1971); see also

Gamble v. United States (2019). Likewise, the dual sovereignty doctrine applies to successive prosecutions by different states. *Heath v. Alabama* (1985); *State v. Brown* (1981).

Section 10a

Rights of victims of crime.

(A) To secure for victims justice and due process throughout the criminal and juvenile justice systems, a victim shall have the following rights, which shall be protected in a manner no less vigorous than the rights afforded to the accused:

(1) to be treated with fairness and respect for the victim's safety, dignity and privacy;

(2) upon request, to reasonable and timely notice of all public proceedings involving the criminal offense or delinquent act against the victim, and to be present at all such proceedings;

(3) to be heard in any public proceeding involving release, plea, sentencing, disposition, or parole, or in any public proceeding in which a right of the victim is implicated;

(4) to reasonable protection from the accused or any person acting on behalf of the accused;

(5) upon request, to reasonable notice of any release or escape of the accused;

(6) except as authorized by section 10 of Article I of this constitution, to refuse an interview, deposition, or other discovery request made by the accused or any person acting on behalf of the accused;

(7) to full and timely restitution from the person who committed the criminal offense or delinquent act against the victim;

(8) to proceedings free from unreasonable delay and a prompt conclusion of the case;

(9) upon request, to confer with the attorney for the government; and

(10) to be informed, in writing, of all rights enumerated in this section.

(B) The victim, the attorney for the government upon request of the victim, or the victim's other lawful representative, in any proceeding involving the criminal offense or delinquent act against the victim or in which the victim's rights are implicated, may assert the rights enumerated in this section and any other right afforded to the victim by law. If the relief sought is denied, the victim or the victim's lawful representative may petition the court of appeals for the applicable district, which shall promptly consider and decide the petition.

(C) This section does not create any cause of action for damages or compensation against the state, any political subdivision of the state, any officer, employee, or agent of the state or of any political subdivision, or any officer of the court.

(D) As used in this section, "victim" means a person against whom the criminal offense or delinquent act is committed or who is directly and proximately harmed by the commission of the offense or act. The term "victim" does not include the accused or a person whom the court finds would not act in the best interests of a deceased, incompetent, minor, or incapacitated victim.

(E) All provisions of this section shall be self-executing and severable, and shall supersede all conflicting state laws.

(F) This section shall take effect ninety days after the election at which it was approved.

Adopted in 1994 and replaced in 2017, this section provides support for victims of crime. The earlier amendment, which was proposed by the General Assembly, provided that victims of criminal offenses "shall be accorded fairness, dignity, and respect in the criminal justice process, and . . . shall be accorded rights to reasonable and appropriate notice, information, access, and protection and to a meaningful role in the criminal justice process." The earlier provision had required the General Assembly to define these rights.

Prior to the adoption of the 1994 amendment, Ohio law did not permit the admission of victim-impact statements at the sentencing phase of criminal trials, but the earlier version of section 10a, along with the state's Victim Rights Act (which was adopted in 1994), extended to victims of crime and their families certain rights, including the right to notice of criminal proceedings and the right to make an oral or written statement to the court regarding the effect of the crime on their lives. *State v. White* (1999).

The impetus behind these developments was the victim rights movement and the decision of the U.S. Supreme Court in *Payne v. Tennessee* (1991), in which the court reconsidered its previous rejection of victim-impact evidence and permitted the introduction of such evidence at criminal trials, albeit on a limited basis. Indeed, as of 2009, thirty-two states had adopted victims' rights amendments to their state constitutions, and almost all the other states had statutes that extended similar rights to victims. See Paul G. Cassell, "In Defense of Victim Impact Statements," 6 *Ohio St. J. Crim. L.* 611 (2009).

In construing the earlier version of section 10a, the Ohio Supreme Court recognized the existence of limitations on the use of victim impact statements, especially in capital cases in which sentencing is primarily the responsibility of the jury. For example, in *State v. Lang* (2011), the court recognized that it had held in *White* "that testimony about the impact on *victims of noncapital crimes* in a capital-murder case was improper." Nonetheless, the *Lang* court held that it was not an abuse of discretion for a trial court to admit limited (i.e., not overly emotional) testimony of the impact of the crime on the victims of a capital crime.

2017 Amendment

In 2017, the voters approved by almost a 5:1 margin an amendment proposed by initiative petition to replace section 10a with a provision to strengthen the rights of victims of crimes and their families. The new version, which was proposed as part of a nationwide campaign to enact so-called Marsy's Laws in memory of a crime victim, enumerated in greater detail than its predecessor an enhanced set of victims' rights. And it provided that these rights "shall be protected in a manner no less vigorous than the rights afforded to the accused." The new version also rejected the dependence on the General Assembly (which was a feature of the earlier version) by providing that the new provision is self-executing.

The new provision provides a more detailed enumeration of rights of victims and their representatives, including the right to receive notice of public proceedings involving the criminal offense, the right to be present at all such proceedings, and the right to be heard in any public proceeding involving release, plea, sentencing, disposition, or parole. Article I, sections 10a(2) and 10a(3).

Consistent with the replaced provision, the new provision limits its reach by providing expressly that it "does not create any cause of action for damages or compensation against the state, any political subdivision of the state, any officer, employee, or agent of the state or of any political subdivision, or any officer of the court."

The current and prior versions of this section address their relationship to other provisions of the U.S. and Ohio Constitutions in different ways. The prior version stated that "[t]his section does not confer upon any person a right to appeal or modify any decision in a criminal proceeding, [and] does not abridge any other right guaranteed by the Constitution of the United States or this constitution." The current version drops this language and provides only that "except as authorized by section 10 of Article I of this constitution, [victims have the right] to refuse an interview, deposition, or other discovery request made by the accused or any person acting on behalf of the accused . . . ."

The impact of these changes is not clear. It is unlikely that a criminal defendant will be able to rely on this section to appeal or seek a modification of any decision in a criminal proceeding, so the deletion of the reference to appeals by criminal defendants does not appear to be significant.

On the other hand, the right of a victim to refuse a discovery request may conflict with the rights of criminal defendants. There is little question that the rights of victims under this section can be limited by the U.S. Bill of Rights and the Fourteenth Amendment, so the deletion of the reference to the U.S. Constitution does not appear to have any impact.

With respect to the Ohio Constitution, the new provision recognizes that victims' rights under this section are limited by the rights of criminal defendants under Article I, section 10. But the new provision does not recognize that other provisions of the Ohio Constitution also protect the rights of criminal defendants. The proponents of the 2017 amendment had argued that the proposed amendment would have no impact on the rights of defendants, but the opponents argued that the proposed amendment gave victims the right to refuse to turn over potential evidence and that it was in conflict with essential guarantees in the Bill of Rights, including double jeopardy, confrontation, and speedy trial. See Ohio Secretary of State, 2017 Issues Report (website).

Issues under this section will likely arise when victims' right to notification and participation may delay cases where prompt bail hearings are necessary to avoid unnecessary pretrial incarceration or where the right to be present at all proceedings interferes with the ability of the judge to exclude victims from phases of trials at which they are planning to testify as fact witnesses. Because there is no analogous federal constitutional provision, courts construing this provision will likely consider the recent experiences in other states in which courts are grappling with the same issues.

The new provision protects not only the rights of victims but also the rights of the lawful representatives of victims. Accordingly, the provision supports the use of victim-impact statements by family members at the sentencing phase of criminal cases, including capital cases. But see *City of Centerville v. Knab* (2020) (holding that municipal corporations are not "victims" under this section).

The earlier provision only applied to the "criminal justice system," but the new provision also extends to the juvenile justice system, seeking "[t]o secure for victims justice and due process throughout the criminal and juvenile justice systems . . . ."

Victim-impact statements, as the phrase suggests, involve victims testifying at the sentencing stage of criminal trials on the impact of the crime on them. But neither prior Ohio law nor this section permits victims (or their lawful representatives) to testify as to their preferences for the sentences to be imposed on convicted defendants.

Unlike the earlier version, the new provision permits victims (and their representatives) who are denied relief to "petition the court of appeals for the applicable district, which shall promptly consider and decide the petition." But the amendment does not provide guidance on the nature of such proceedings, and the Ohio Supreme Court has held that a writ of prohibition is not the correct mechanism for crime victims to obtain judicial review of trial court discovery orders affecting rights under this section. See *State ex rel. Thomas McGinty* (2020).

In *State ex rel. Suwalski v. Peeler* (2021), the court held that under this section a writ of prohibition was the appropriate way for a victim of domestic violence to challenge the decision of a common pleas court to restore the gun possession rights of a man who had been convicted of misdemeanor domestic violence and was prohibited by federal law from possessing firearms.

The new provision, unlike the earlier one, contains a severability provision, which provides a way to preserve the core of the amendment if some of its provisions conflict with constitutional provisions that protect the rights of the criminally accused.

Section 11

Freedom of speech; of the press; of libels.

Every citizen may freely speak, write, and publish his sentiments on all subjects, being responsible for the abuse of the right; and no law shall be passed to restrain or abridge the liberty of speech, or of the press. In all criminal prosecutions for libel, the truth may be given in evidence to the jury, and if it shall appear to the jury, that the matter charged as libelous is true, and was published with good motives, and for justifiable ends, the party shall be acquitted.

Adopted in 1851 and never amended, this section is virtually identical to the speech and press clauses of the Connecticut, New York, and California Constitutions, see Connecticut Constitution, Article I, sections 5–7 (1818); New York Constitution, Article VII, section 8 (1821); California Constitution, Article I, section 9 (1849); but it differs significantly from its Ohio predecessor, Article VIII, section 6 of the 1802 Constitution. The earlier Ohio provision, which had its roots in the 1790 Pennsylvania Constitution, contained an opening clause guaranteeing the freedom of the printing press: "That the printing presses shall be open and free to every citizen who wishes to examine the proceedings of any branch of government, or the conduct of any public officer, and no law shall ever restrain the right thereof." The 1802 version also limited the defense of truth in criminal prosecutions for libel to cases involving public officials and to cases in which the truth concerned matters "proper for public information." Finally, the 1802 version provided that the jury is responsible for determining the law and facts in libel prosecutions.

The first two sentences of this section encompass the rights of free speech and free press found in the speech and press clauses of the First Amendment ("Congress shall make no law . . . abridging the freedom of speech, or of the press"). Unlike the First Amendment, however, this section casts the rights of free speech and press as affirmative rights of the people. In 1992, the Ohio Supreme Court held that the state ethnic intimidation statute (which provided for a separate criminal offense when a specified predicate offense is committed "by reason of the race, color, religion, or national origin of another person or group of persons") created a "thought crime" in violation of both this section and the First Amendment. *State v. Wyant* (1992). In so holding, the court noted that the Ohio Constitution "is even more specific" than the First Amendment in that "it guarantees to every citizen freedom to 'speak, write, and publish his sentiments on all subjects.' It follows that a citizen of Ohio is free to have 'sentiments on all subjects.'" Ibid.

But in 1994, after the U.S. Supreme Court upheld the constitutionality of a Wisconsin statute that increased the maximum sentence if a defendant intentionally selects the victim because of his or her protected status, see *Wisconsin v. Mitchell* (1993), the Ohio Supreme Court reversed its earlier decision without even addressing the independent force of the Ohio Constitution. See *State v. Wyant* (1994) (on remand).

Despite the textual differences in the state and federal free speech guarantees, the court in 1994 expressly held that "the free speech guarantees accorded by the Ohio Constitution are no broader than the First Amendment." *Eastwood Mall, Inc. v. Slanco* (1994). The U.S. Supreme Court had previously held that there is no First Amendment right of free speech over the objections of a private property owner, but the court permitted states to provide greater protections for speech on private property under their state constitutions. See *Pruneyard Shopping Center v. Robbins* (1980). The Ohio Supreme Court in *Slanco* rejected this invitation, and it held that the free speech guarantees of this section did not protect speech at a privately owned shopping center, notwithstanding the rulings of other state courts (including the California and New Jersey Supreme Courts) that had protected speech on private property under identical state constitutional provisions. *Robins v. Pruneyard Shopping Center* (1979); *State v. Schmidt* (1980).

One of the results of the court's approach to free speech has been the tendency to ignore the state constitution and decide cases entirely on First Amendment grounds. For example, in *City of Seven Hills v. Aryan Nations* (1996), the court held that an injunction prohibiting the simultaneous picketing of an alleged Nazi war criminal's residence by groups with opposing viewpoints violated the First Amendment without even mentioning the right of free speech under the Ohio Constitution.

The Ohio Supreme Court, however, has relied on this section (along with the open courts provision of Art. I, sec. 16) to hold that a common pleas judge acted unconstitutionally by preventing the media from reporting on a manslaughter trial until a jury was empaneled in a separate criminal case. *State ex rel. Toledo Blade Co. v. Henry County Court of Common Pleas* (2010).

Defamation

Despite its statement in *Slanco* that free speech rights under this section are no broader than under the First Amendment, the Ohio Supreme Court has interpreted this section as placing limits on defamation actions that not required by the First Amendment. In *New York Times Co. v. Sullivan* (1964) and its progeny, the U.S. Supreme Court held that the First Amendment requires public officials to prove by clear and convincing evidence that the defendant either knew that the statement being made was false or made the statement with "reckless disregard for the truth."

Although the Ohio Supreme Court generally follows the U.S. Supreme Court's First Amendment jurisprudence in public figure defamation cases, it has developed its own approach in private figure defamation cases.

In private figure defamation cases involving matters of public concern, the U.S. Supreme Court has held that the First Amendment requires private figure plaintiffs to prove by clear and convincing evidence that the defendant acted with some degree of fault (i.e., with at least negligence). See *Gertz v. Robert Welch, Inc.* (1974). The Ohio Supreme Court, however, has held that the free speech guarantee of this section requires the same standard of proof without regard to whether the matter is of public or purely private concern. In other words, under the Ohio Constitution, all private figure plaintiffs must prove that the defendant acted at least negligently and proof of negligence must be made by clear and convincing evidence. *Lansdowne v. Beacon Journal Publishing Co.* (1987).

In addition, the Ohio Supreme Court has held that media defendants are entitled to a "separate and independent" protection for statements of opinion, see *Vail v. The Plain Dealer Publishing Co.* (1995), and that this protection also extends to nonmedia defendants, see *Wampler v. Higgins* (2001). In contrast, the U.S. Supreme Court has held that there is no separate and additional protection for opinions under the First Amendment. *Milkovich v. Lorain Journal Co.* (1990).

The last sentence of this section concerning criminal prosecutions for libel has no counterpart in the First Amendment. As noted earlier, the 1802 version of this section limited the introduction of truth as a defense in libel actions to cases involving government officials. Although criminal prosecutions for defaming government officials seem unthinkable today, they were not unheard of at the time of the 1802 Constitution. In fact, by allowing truth as a defense the 1802 version of this section tempered the common law crime of seditious libel, which prohibited the introduction of truth as a defense. See generally Thomas R. Swisher, ed., *Ohio Constitution Handbook* (Cleveland: Banks-Baldwin Publishing Co., 1990), 109 (hereinafter Swisher, *Ohio Constitution Handbook*).

With the adoption of this section in 1851, truth, at least if offered for "good motives," could have been offered in evidence in criminal prosecutions charging defendants with defaming private individuals. Criminal prosecutions for libel are permissible under this section; but they are a relic of the past, and the General Assembly repealed Ohio's last criminal libel statute in 1974. See former O.R.C. section 2901.37.

Section 12

Transportation or forfeiture for crime.

No person shall be transported out of the State, for any offense committed within the same; and no conviction shall work corruption of blood, or forfeiture of estate.

Adopted in 1851 and never amended, this section is a combination of provisions found in Article VIII, sections 16 and 17, of the 1802 Constitution. The first clause of this section prohibited the common practice in England and in the colonies before the Revolutionary War of exiling criminals. See Swisher, *Ohio Constitution Handbook*, 127. Notwithstanding the prohibition on exiling criminals, an Ohio trial court in 1855 held that the governor may grant a pardon contingent on the prisoner's agreement not to return to the state for five years, *Ex parte Lockhart* (1855), and in 1982 a federal district court construed this provision as not precluding a condition of parole that effectively barred a parolee from returning to the state for approximately forty years, *Carchedi v. Rhodes* (1982).

The second clause, "no conviction shall work corruption of blood, or forfeiture of estate," addressed another English practice: that of preventing a felon from inheriting, retaining, or passing his estate to his heirs. A similar provision abolishing corruption of blood and forfeiture in cases of treason except during the life of the defendant is in the U. S. Constitution. See U.S. Constitution, Article III, section 3, clause 2. In an early case, the Ohio Supreme Court explained the meaning of the clause and why it was included in the 1802 Constitution:

> We know that in England, the conviction of many offenses, works "corruption of blood and forfeiture of estate." And this operates in many, if not in all cases, from the time of the commission of the offense. The forfeiture is to the king. The blood is also corrupted. The attainted person can not inherit lands from his ancestor, neither can he transmit an inheritance to his heirs. In truth, the punishment of the offense is not confined to the individual offender, but is extended to his wife, his children, and his heirs, by depriving them of his estate, and thereby, in some instances, of the means of subsistence. It was against a state of things like this, that the convention intended to provide and they have, therefore, put it beyond the power of the legislature to enact "that any conviction shall work a corruption of blood or forfeiture of estate."
>
> *McMillan's Lessee v. Robbins* (1831).

The Ohio Supreme Court has interpreted this section to prevent forfeiture as a punishment for a crime, except to abate a nuisance. *Miller v. State* (1854). The court, however, has held that the sale and confiscation of personal property used in conjunction with illegal drug activity are not "forfeitures" under this section but "a remedy designed to prevent the continuation of unlawful acts rather than a punishment for unlawful activity." *State ex rel. Miller v. Anthony* (1995). A statute that prohibited a person convicted of murder from inheriting from the murder victim does not violate this provision. *In re Estate of Fiore v. DiPrima* (1984).

Section 13
Quartering troops.

No soldier shall, in time of peace, be quartered in any house, without the consent of the owner; nor, in time of war, except in the manner prescribed by law.

Adopted in 1851 and never amended, this section is derived almost verbatim from Article VIII, section 22 of the 1802 Constitution and is identical to the Third Amendment to the U.S. Constitution. This section and the Third Amendment prohibit the English practice of quartering troops in private homes. Since the prohibition against quartering soldiers is so well established, there are few cases involving the Third Amendment and no Ohio cases interpreting this section.

Section 14
Search and seizure.

The right of the people to be secure in their persons, houses, papers, and possessions, against unreasonable searches and seizures shall not be violated; and no warrant shall issue, but upon probable cause, supported by oath or affirmation, particularly describing the place to be searched, and the person and things to be seized.

Adopted in 1851 and never amended, this section is derived from Article VIII, section 5, of the 1802 Ohio Constitution and is almost identical to the Fourth Amendment to the U.S. Constitution. This section and the Fourth Amendment forbid "unreasonable searches and seizures" and require all warrants to be supported by probable cause "particularly describing the place to be searched, and the person and things to be seized." (The Fourth Amendment refers to "persons or things.") These protections were aimed directly at the English "writs of assistance," which were general warrants that gave officials of the Crown unlimited authority to search and seize without probable cause. Extremely unpopular in colonial America, these writs were one of the major grievances that led to the Revolutionary War. See Timothy Lynch, "In Defense of the Exclusionary Rule," 23 *Harv. J.L. & Pub. Policy* 711 (2000): 721–22.

Protections from "unreasonable searches and seizures" were contained not only in the Fourth Amendment but in the influential Tennessee, Kentucky, and Pennsylvania Constitutions. They were not, however, in many of the other eighteenth-century state constitutions, which often barred general warrants without imposing the reasonableness and other requirements of this section. See generally Nelson B. Lasson, *The History and Development of the Fourth Amendment to the United States Constitution* (New York: De Capo Press, 1970), 79–82.

In the latter part of the twentieth century, Ohio Supreme Court decisions addressing the relationship between this section and the Fourth Amendment were characterized by a lack of consistency.

For example, in 1981, in *State v. Geraldo,* the court reasoned that the Ohio provision "with respect to the warrantless monitoring of a consenting informant's telephone conversation is coextensive with that of the Fourth Amendment to the United States Constitution." It then concluded that the "failure to prove a violation of the Fourth Amendment dictates the conclusion that . . . rights under Section 14, Article I, of the Ohio Constitution have not been violated either." But in 1984, the court held that evidence obtained through an unlawful search and seizure was inadmissible in a probation revocation proceeding. *State v. Burkholder* (1984). Twelve years later, in *State ex rel. Wright v. Ohio Adult Parole Authority* (1996), the court overruled *Burkholder*. Stating that this section "has been interpreted to protect the same interests and in a manner consistent with the Fourth Amendment[,]" *Wright* held that "evidence obtained through an unreasonable or unlawful search and seizure is generally admissible in probation and/or parole revocation proceedings." In so ruling, the court criticized *Burkholder* for having "mechanically applied the exclusionary rule and ignored the balancing test adopted by the Supreme Court of the United States." Ibid. See generally Marianna Brown Bettman, "Ohio Joins the New Judicial Federalism Movement: A Little To-Ing and a Little Fro-Ing, 51 *Clev. St. L. Rev.* 491 (2004): 497–500.

In 1992, prior to *Wright*, the court had found more protection from warrantless searches under this section than under the Fourth Amendment. In *State v. Brown* (1992) (hereinafter "*Brown 1992*"), for example, the court rejected the U.S. Supreme Court's decision in *New York v. Belton* (1981), which had held that the warrantless search of the passenger compartment of an automobile and all interior containers following a custodial arrest did not violate the Fourth Amendment. In *Brown 1992*, the Ohio court explicitly stated that "[i]f *Belton* does stand for the proposition that a police officer may conduct a detailed search of an automobile *solely* because he has arrested one of its occupants, *on any charge*, we decline to adopt its rule." The following year, commenting on *Brown 1992*, the court stated that "[w]e found the right to be free from unreasonable search and seizure guaranteed by the Ohio Constitution to be greater than that guaranteed by the Fourth Amendment, even though the words of the two provisions are very similar." *State v. Storch* (1993). The *Brown 1992* decision and its approach to this section, however, were short-lived.

In *State v. Robinette* (1997) (on remand), a year after the *Wright* decision, the court expressed the view that the U.S. Constitution was the "primary mechanism to safeguard an individual's rights." It then observed that "where the provisions are similar and no persuasive reason for a differing interpretation is presented, this court has determined that protections afforded by Ohio's Constitution are coextensive with those provided by the United States Constitution." And further, it stated that it was "disinclined to impose greater restrictions in the absence of explicit state constitutional guarantees protecting against invasions of privacy that clearly transcend the Fourth Amendment." Finally, it held that Ohio courts "should harmonize our interpretation of Section 14, Article I of the Ohio Constitution with the Fourth Amendment, unless there are persuasive reasons to find otherwise." See also *State v. Orr* (2001) (stating that "we have interpreted the two provisions as affording the same protection" and holding that a driver's license checkpoint is not an unconstitutional seizure under either provision).

Subsequently, in *State v. Murrell* (2002), the court expressly overruled *Brown 1992* and permitted the search of the passenger compartment of an automobile as a contemporaneous incident of a lawful custodial arrest. Applying *Robinette*, the *Murrell* court announced that there were no "persuasive reasons to depart from the principle that section 14, Article I and the Fourth Amendment should be harmonized whenever possible."

Although the "harmonization" requirement permitted departures from U.S. Supreme Court interpretations of the Fourth Amendment when there are "persuasive reasons" to do so, *Murrell* required the Ohio courts to harmonize the state and federal provisions "wherever possible." *Murrell* thus appeared to raise the bar and narrow the circumstances in which section 14 could be an independent source of rights. *Murrell*, however, may have marked the high point of deference to the U.S. Supreme Court's Fourth Amendment jurisprudence.

Despite *Robinette*, the Ohio Supreme Court had often not "harmonized" these provisions or treated them as "coextensive." For instance, in 1914 the U.S. Supreme Court adopted the exclusionary rule, which prohibited the introduction of evidence obtained in violation of the Fourth Amendment. *Weeks v. United States* (1914). *Weeks*, however, only applied to prosecutions in federal court, and until 1961, when the U.S. Supreme Court made the exclusionary rule binding on state courts, see *Mapp v. Ohio* (1961), the Ohio Supreme Court explicitly rejected the *Weeks* approach and permitted the introduction of evidence obtained in violation of this section. See *State v. Lindway* (1936).

And since the decision in *Robinette*, the court has been willing to depart from the interpretation of the Fourth Amendment but without fully explaining the basis for these departures.

For example, in *State v. Brown* (2003) (hereinafter "*Brown 2003*"), the Ohio Supreme Court held that "Section 14, Article I of the Ohio Constitution provides greater protection than the Fourth Amendment to the United States Constitution against warrantless arrests for minor misdemeanors." (syllabus). The court then explicitly rejected the U.S. Supreme Court's decision in *Atwater v. Lago Vista* (2001), in which the court had held that the arrest of a person for a minor misdemeanor punishable only by a fine did not violate the Fourth Amendment. Recognizing the "independent force" of the Ohio Constitution and relying on its own precedent, the *Brown 2003* court cryptically held that the balancing test "provides ample reason for holding that section 14, Article I of the Ohio Constitution provides greater protection than the Fourth Amendment to the United States Constitution against warrantless arrests for minor misdemeanors." Thus, the arrest of a person for a minor misdemeanor does not violate the Fourth Amendment but does violate section 14, and Ohio courts must suppress evidence seized in a search incident to such arrests.

And in *State v. Brown* (2015), the court held that an extraterritorial search, which was not authorized by Ohio statutes, violated this section even though the search did not violate the U.S. Constitution. But see ibid. (French, J., dissenting) ("In light of the nearly identical text of Article I, Section 14 of the Ohio Constitution and the Fourth Amendment to the United States Constitution, coupled with the Ohio framers' reliance on the preexisting Fourth Amendment in drafting Ohio's constitutional search-and-seizure provision, I discern no compelling basis for affording Article I, Section 14 of the Ohio Constitution broader reach than the Fourth Amendment.").

The U.S. Supreme Court has created a good faith exception to the Fourth Amendment's exclusionary rule, see *United States v. Leon* (1984), but at least one-third of the states have declined to adopt such an exception under their constitutions. See Sutton, *51 Imperfect Solutions*, 64.

The Ohio Supreme Court has followed the lead of the U.S. Supreme Court and applied the good faith exception to cases in which defendants challenged searches and seizures under the Fourth Amendment. *See State v. Wilmoth* (1986); see also *State v. Johnson* (2014) (holding that an officer who attached a GPS tracking device to a defendant's vehicle had a good faith, objectively reasonable belief that a warrant was not needed, and evidence obtained was not subject to the exclusionary rule of the Fourth Amendment). But the court has not addressed whether evidence that is admissible under the good faith exception to the Fourth Amendment may sometimes be excluded from state proceedings based on the prohibition against unreasonable searches and seizures in the Ohio Constitution.

Finally, the court has held that the exclusionary rule was not an appropriate remedy under the state constitution for a violation of statutory knock-and-announce rule in the execution of a valid search warrant. *State v. Bembry* (2017). Distinguishing other cases in which it had deviated from federal law, the court noted that this case, unlike the others, involved a valid warrant. And the court elected to follow *Robinette* and "harmonize" its interpretation of the state and federal provisions.

In *State v. Jordan* (2021), the court held that a police officer is not required under either the U.S. or the Ohio Constitution to secure an arrest warrant every time it is practicable to obtain one, and it noted that "we [have] never found greater protection regarding *felony* arrests under the Ohio Constitution than that provided by the United States Constitution . . . " (emphasis in original).

Section 15

No imprisonment for debt.

No person shall be imprisoned for debt in any civil action, on mesne or final process, unless in cases of fraud.

Adopted in 1851 and never amended, this section forbids any person from being imprisoned for a debt in civil cases except in cases of fraud. This section offers more protection to debtors than its predecessor, Article VIII, section 15 of the 1802 Constitution, which, other than in cases where there was a strong presumption of fraud, only prohibited keeping debtors in jail after they had delivered their entire estate to their creditors. This section was aimed at the English practice of jailing debtors both after final verdicts and under the "mesne process," where a debtor could be jailed before trial on a creditor's sworn statement that the debt had not been paid or the debtor was about to abscond or conceal property. See Andrew J. Duncan, "From Dismemberment to Discharge: The Origins of Modern American Bankruptcy Law," 100 *Com. L. J.* 191 (1995).

A "debt" under this section includes any money obligation arising from an express or implied contract. *Second Nat. Bank v. Becker* (1900). The Ohio Supreme Court treats court costs as the result of an implied contract between litigants and the court, and the court has interpreted this section as barring imprisonment for failing to pay court costs. *Strattman v. Studt* (1969). The court does not consider the obligation to pay alimony, *State ex rel. Cook v. Cook* (1902), and child support, *Cramer v. Petrie* (1994), to be debts under this section, and thus courts may use their contempt power to imprison persons who fail to make required alimony and child support payments. On the other hand, although the state income tax creates a debt within the meaning of this section, in the absence of willful failure, refusal, or fraud an individual cannot be imprisoned for failing to pay the tax. *City of Cincinnati v. DeGolyer* (1971).

Section 16

Open courts; right to a remedy; due course of law; sovereign immunity.

All courts shall be open, and every person, for an injury done him in his land, goods, person, or reputation, shall have remedy by due course of law, and shall have justice administered without delay. Suits may be brought against the state, in such courts and in such manner, as may be provided by law.

Adopted in 1851 and amended in 1912, the first sentence of this section, except for minor changes, is identical to its predecessor, Article VIII, section 7 of the 1802 Constitution, which, in turn, was almost a verbatim copy of the first sentence of Article XI, section XVII, of the 1796 Tennessee Constitution and Article IX, section 11, of the 1790 Pennsylvania Constitution (with the primary difference being Ohio's replacement of "every man" with "every person"). Although the first sentence is often treated as a single provision guaranteeing injured persons access to the courts, it actually contains four distinct components: an open courts provision, a remedy provision, a due course of law provision, and a delay of justice provision.

In 1912, the convention proposed and the voters approved the second sentence of this section, which allows the General Assembly to enact laws to abrogate state sovereign immunity.

Open Courts

The open courts provision in this section provides that "[a]ll courts shall be open" and thus guarantees the public a right of access to courts and judicial proceedings. The right of the public to attend trials has been part of the English system of justice since at least the twelfth century. See Jack B. Harrison, "How Open Is Open? The Development of the Public Access Doctrine under State Open Court Provisions," 60 *U. Cin. L. Rev.* 1307 (1992): 1308–11.

In the colonies, open courts provisions were in some of the earliest American documents, including the 1676 Fundamental Laws of West New Jersey, which provided "[t]hat in all publick courts of justice for tryals of causes, civil or criminal, any person or persons, inhabitants of the said Province may freely come into, and attend the said courts, and hear and be present, at all or any such tryals as shall be there had or passed, that justice may not be done in a corner nor in any covert manner," and the 1682 Frame of Government of the Colony of Pennsylvania, which included a provision containing the same language—"all courts shall be open"—that is used in this section. See Bernard Schwartz, *The Bill of Rights: A Documentary History* (New York: Chelsea House Publishers, 1971), 129, 140; see also Harrison, "How Open Is Open?" 1311–12. Twenty-four states in addition to Ohio have open courts provisions in their state constitutions, see Harrison, "How Open Is Open?" 1307, but there is no analogous provision in the federal Bill of Rights.

In one of the most detailed examinations of the open courts provision, an Ohio appellate court held that it guaranteed the public a right of access to criminal trials independent of the defendant's right to a public trial. *E.W. Scripps Co. v. Fulton* (1955). The *Scripps* court overturned a trial court order that had barred the press and the public from the courtroom during cross-examination of the prosecution's witness so defense counsel "would be better able to compel the witness to tell the truth." In holding that the public had a right to be present (notwithstanding the defendant's waiver of his right to a public trial), the court emphasized the public's interest in the administration of justice—an interest that, according to the court, is as important as the defendant's individual right to a public trial.

In 1979, the Ohio Supreme Court, relying on the open courts provision and on Article I, section 10, held that a criminal trial held within a prison violates the right to a public trial. *State v. Lane* (1979).

Although the U.S. Constitution contains no provision expressly providing a right of public access to the courts, the U.S. Supreme Court in 1980 recognized a right of public access implicit in the First Amendment. *Richmond Newspapers,*

Inc. v. Virginia (1980). Subsequently, the Ohio Supreme Court adopted a First Amendment analysis in interpreting the Ohio provision and expressly held that the open courts provision confers no greater right of access than the Free Speech and Press Clauses of the First Amendment and section 11 of this Article. *In re T.R.* (1990).

Under both constitutions, the right of public access creates a presumption in favor of open court proceedings. But the presumption "may be overcome by an overriding interest based on findings that closure is essential to preserve higher values and is narrowly tailored to serve that interest." Ibid. (quoting U.S. Supreme Court decision in *Press-Enterprise Co. v. Superior Ct.* (1984) (*Press-Enterprise I*)).

Following the lead of the U.S. Supreme Court, the Ohio Supreme Court has held that the right of public access applies only "to court proceedings that have historically been open to the public and in which public access plays a significantly positive role." *In re T.R., supra* (syllabus). Thus, there is no presumption of openness in proceedings that have been historically closed to the public, such as grand jury and juvenile court proceedings. But both the U.S. and Ohio Supreme Courts have recognized a constitutional right of access to criminal pretrial hearings, to criminal trials, and to the transcripts of proceedings that are constitutionally open to the public. See *State ex rel. The Repository v. Unger* (1986); *Press-Enterprise Co. v. Superior Court* (1986) (*Press-Enterprise II*).

In *State ex rel. Toledo Blade Co. v. Henry County Court of Common Pleas* (2010), the Ohio Supreme Court held that a common pleas judge who prevented the media from reporting on a manslaughter trial until a jury was empaneled in a separate criminal case violated not only the open courts provision of this section but also the free speech provisions of Article I, section 11. See Commentary, Article I, section 11.

The Ohio Supreme Court has also held that the open courts provision contains a right of public access to court records concerning requests by minors for abortions but only as long as the records were redacted to protect the identity of the minors. *State ex rel. The Cincinnati Post v. Second District Court of Appeals* (1992).

Right to a Remedy

In language identical to the 1802 Constitution, the right-to-remedy provision in this section guarantees that "every person, for an injury done him in his lands, goods, person or reputation, shall have remedy by the due course of law . . . ."

The remedy provisions of state constitutions have been traced to Article 40 of the Magna Carta, which provided that "[t]o no one will We sell, to no one will We deny or delay, right or justice." *Davidson v. Rogers* (1978) (Linde, J., concurring). See also John H. Bauman, "Remedy Provisions in State Constitutions and the Proper Role of the State Courts," 26 *Wake Forest L. Rev.* 237 (1991): 241–44 (hereinafter Bauman, "Remedy Provisions in State Constitutions").

Remedy provisions first appeared in the colonies in section 12 of the 1776 Delaware Declaration of Rights, see *Smothers v. Gresham Transfer, Inc.* (2001), and in Article XVII of the 1776 Maryland Declarations of Rights, but efforts by North Carolina and other states to incorporate a remedy provision in the federal Bill of Rights failed. See David Schuman, "Oregon's Remedy Guarantee: Article I, Section 10 of the Oregon Constitution," 65 *Or. L. Rev.* 35 (1986): 39–40. Thus, as with the open courts provision, the remedy provision has no federal counterpart, although at least thirty-five states have some form of remedy provision in their state constitutions. See Bauman, "Remedy Provisions in State Constitutions," 237, 284–88.

The Ohio Supreme Court has construed the right-to-remedy provision as barring the General Assembly from enacting an unreasonable statute of limitations, *Lafferty v. Shinn* (1882); from adopting legislation that changed the presumption and burden of proof on malice in defamation cases, *Byers v. Meridian Printing Co.* (1911); from denying a remedy to an unborn viable child, *Williams v. Marion Rapid Transit, Inc.* (1949); and from adopting a guest statute that denied a remedy to some but not all persons injured in automobile accidents, *Primes v. Tyler* (1975).

In 1987, the court applied the right-to-remedy provision to strike down a statute that barred medical malpractice actions more than four years after the act or omission constituting malpractice even if victims did not or could not reasonably discover their injuries within that time. *Hardy v. VerMuelen* (1987); see also *Brennaman v. R.M.I. Co.* (1994) (invalidating statutes that barred negligence actions against contractors more than ten years after the completion of a project even if damage did not yet occur); *Burgess v. Eli Lilly & Co.* (1993) (striking down statute that barred claims related to diethylstilbestrol ("DES") exposure two years after a woman was informed or had reason to know that her injuries could *possibly* be related to DES exposure rather than actually caused by DES).

And, in 1999 in *State ex rel. Ohio Academy of Trial Lawyers v. Sheward* (1999), the court adhered to its earlier right-to-remedy rulings in holding unconstitutional the 1995 Omnibus Tort Reform Act that it had held violated not only principles of separation of powers but also the one-subject rule.

Subsequently, however, the court changed direction, explicitly overruled *Hardy*, made clear that the right-to-remedy provision only applied to vested rights, and held that "[t]he [relevant] medical-malpractice statute of repose . . . does not extinguish a vested right and thus does not violate the Ohio Constitution, Article I, Section 16." *Ruther v. Kaiser* (2012). And in 2016, the court took *Ruther* one step further and ruled "that Ohio's medical-malpractice statute of repose . . . is constitutional even to the extent that it prohibits bringing suit on a cause of action that has vested." In so ruling, the court stated that there were significant public-policy considerations that support granting repose to defendants and that "the General Assembly has determined that four years is a reasonable length of time to bring a medical-malpractice claim." *Antoon v. Cleveland Clinic Foundation* (2016).

Because the court has held that the right-to-remedy provision only applies where the injured person has a clear, preexisting right to a claim, there is no violation of this provision when a claim is otherwise barred by sovereign immunity. *Fabrey v. McDonald Village Police Department* (1994).

Due Course of Law

The due course of law language in this section is the source of Ohio's guarantee of what is generally referred to as procedural and substantive due process. This language is identical to Article VIII, section 7 of the 1802 Constitution and provides that "every person, for an injury done him in his land, goods, person or reputation, shall have remedy by due course of law . . . ."

The concept of due process dates back to the Magna Carta. But unlike state right-to-remedy provisions (with roots in chapter 40 of the Magna Carta), due process has its origins in chapter 39, which provided that "[n]o free man shall be seized or imprisoned, or stripped of his rights or possessions, . . . except by the lawful judgement of his equals or by the law of the land." And the Northwest Ordinance provided that "[n]o man shall be deprived of his liberty or property, but by the judgment of his peers, or the law of the land" and that "inhabitants of the said territory shall always be entitled to . . . judicial proceedings according to the course of the common law." Ordinance of 1787, section 14, Article II.

Almost all eighteenth-century state constitutions contained "due course of law" or "law of the land" provisions (and sometimes both), but none used the phrase "due process of law." Indeed, the first use of "due process of law" in an American Constitution was in 1791 in the Fifth Amendment to the U.S. Constitution, which provided: "nor [shall any person] be deprived of life, liberty, or property, without due process of law." See A. E. Dick Howard, *Commentaries on the Constitution of Virginia* (Charlottesville: University Press of Virginia 1974), vol. 1, 122–23. And "due process of law" did not appear in any state constitution until the 1821 New York Constitution. Ibid.

Although it is easy to understand why the delegates to the 1802 Constitutional Convention did not adopt a "due process of law" clause, it is more difficult to determine why they also rejected a "law of the land" clause. Unfortunately, aside from the issue of slavery, there is no direct and little indirect evidence to explain the decisions that the delegates made in 1802 concerning the Ohio Bill of Rights. See McDonald, "A Study in Constitution Making," 3.

Part of the explanation as to why the delegates used "due course of law" may be that the three states on which the delegates relied most heavily as models for the Bill of Rights—Tennessee, Kentucky, and Pennsylvania—had "due course of law" provisions. To be sure, these states also had "law of the land" provisions (in addition to provisions that that protected the rights of criminal defendants).

Still, the Ohio delegates may have selected "due course of law" because they already had adopted a very detailed set of protections for criminal defendants and may have concluded that a "law of the land" provision was not necessary.

The decision to reject a "law of the land" provision may have also been influenced by the history of the Fifth Amendment, which rejected a "law of the land" provision in favor of a "due process of law" provision. See generally Ryan C. Williams, "The One and Only Substantive Due Process Clause," 120 *Yale L.J.* 408 (2010): 445–46 (hereinafter Williams, "The One and Only Substantive Due Process Clause"). The federal rejection of "law of the land," however, still does not fully explain why Ohio used "due course of law" rather than due process of law. And the best explanation for its selection may be that a "law of the land" provision was not necessary, that "due course of law" was a well-established and familiar provision, and that "due process of law" was not.

The search for a definitive explanation of the origin and purpose of "due course of law" risks overlooking the key fact that the drafters of the Ohio "due course of law" provision (like the drafters of other early state constitutions) sought to limit the power of the state. And as noted by Howard Jay Graham, "this guarantee of judicial redress . . . was a powerful factor in encouraging strong use of the due process-due course-law of the land concept as a weapon against legislative excesses." Howard Jay Graham, "Procedure to Substance–Extra-Judicial Rise of Due Process, 1830–1860," 40 *Cal. L. Rev.* 483 (1952–53): 495.

Former Oregon Supreme Court Justice Hans A. Linde, however, has argued that state constitutional provisions that provide a right to a "remedy by due course of law" should not be construed as "due process" clauses, noting that their origin and language predate the ratification of the Fifth Amendment. See Hans A. Linde, "Without Due Process: Unconstitutional Law in Oregon," 49 *Or. L. Rev.* 125 (1970): 136–38 (hereinafter Linde, "Without Due Process"). Relying on both text and history (including the 1802 Ohio Constitution and the 1851 Indiana Constitution), Justice Linde has noted with emphasis that Oregon "*has no due process clause.*" Thus, those seeking due process protections in Oregon must look to other parts of that state's constitution or to the Fourteenth Amendment. Ibid., 135.

The Ohio Supreme Court, however, has not seen it this way, and it has characterized "due course of law" as a due process clause since at least 1887. *Adler v. Whitbeck* (1887) ("'Due course' and 'due process of law' is one and the same thing."); see also *Salt Creek Valley Turnpike Co. v. Parks* (1893) (treating the clauses as equivalent, but construing sections 5 and 16 *in pari materia* to hold unconstitutional a statute that authorized probate courts to declare a toll road abandoned without the intervention of a jury and a right to appeal).

Decisions of the Ohio Supreme Court in the two decades leading up to the 1912 Convention often prioritized the protection of property and the right to contract and assigned the courts responsibility for determining the reasonableness (and thus the constitutionality) of legislation. See generally Commentary,

Article I, sections 1 and 2. These decisions, though typically not relying on this section, have much in common with U.S. Supreme Court decisions in the so-called *Lochner* era. And these decisions contributed to the calling of the 1912 Constitutional Convention. See The History of the Ohio Constitution, *supra*. But despite approval by the voters of at least seven amendments to overrule the results in these and other decisions, the underlying doctrines remained in place. And the Ohio Supreme Court, though chastened, continued to protect private property and the right to contract from what it saw as unreasonable legislation.

For example, in 1941, in *Direct Plumbing Supply, Co. v. City of Dayton*, the court, though equating the state and federal due process provisions, relied solely on the state provision to strike down a city ordinance that unreasonably regulated the sale and purchase of plumbing fixtures. See also *City of Cincinnati v. Correll* (1943) ("We are of opinion that this ordinance [limiting the operating hours of barber shops] bears no real and substantial relation to the health, safety, morals or general welfare of the public, that it is not a valid exercise of the police power, that the ordinance is arbitrary, discriminatory and unreasonable and upon reason and authority must be condemned.").

Direct Plumbing, which in many ways was a lament that the U.S. Supreme Court had been watering down the federal protections for private property, remained largely ignored by the Ohio Supreme Court for almost four decades. And during this period the court cited it only rarely and never to support a decision that found a violation of the state constitution. But see *State ex rel. Heller v. Miller* (1980) (relying on *Direct Plumbing* and the due process and equal protection protections of both the state and federal constitutions to recognize the right of indigent parents to appointed counsel in cases involving the permanent involuntary termination of their parental rights).

Beginning in the 1980s, however, the court resurrected the *Direct Plumbing* approach and relied on the substantive protections of due course of law to reject efforts by the General Assembly to change tort law, particularly in cases alleging medical malpractice.

In *Mominee v. Scherbarth* (1986), the court struck down a statute of limitations that required minors to bring action within one year from the date the cause of action accrued, or four years from the date the alleged medical malpractice occurred, whichever came first, despite the age of injured child. In so ruling the court held that the statute "is unconstitutional as applied to minors under the due course of law provisions of the Ohio Constitution." (syllabus).

In *Morris v. Savoy* (1991), the court held that a statute that set a $200,000 cap on general damages that may be awarded for medical malpractice was in violation of the due course of law provision "because it does not bear a real and substantial relation to public health or welfare and further because it is unreasonable and arbitrary."

And in *Sorrell v. Thevenir* (1994), the court held that the mandatory deduction of collateral benefits from a plaintiff's final award of compensatory damages in tort actions violated several provisions of the state constitution, including the due course of law provision. In so ruling, the court equated the federal and state due process/due course of law provisions but rested its holding only on the state provision.

But in *Arbino v. Johnson & Johnson* (2007), the court distinguished but did not overrule its tort reform precedents in the course of holding that the statutory limitation on noneconomic damages for all but the most serious injuries and the statutory limitations on punitive damages did not violate due course of law. In so ruling the court, equated the state and federal provisions. See ibid. ("We have recognized this provision as the equivalent of the 'due process of law' protections in the United States Constitution."); see also *In re B.C.* (2014) ("We have found that the due-process rights provided by the Fourteenth Amendment and those provided by Article I, Section 16 of the Ohio Constitution are coextensive.").

Simply equating the state and federal provisions, however, does not shed light on the meaning of due course of law, and such an approach is inconsistent with the obligation to undertake an independent review of state constitutional provisions.

Procedural Due Process

The Ohio Supreme Court has recognized that due course of law, like the Due Process Clause of the Fourteenth Amendment, contains both procedural and substantive protections.

In the criminal area, the detailed set of procedural safeguards in the state Bill of Rights for the protection of criminal defendants has reduced the availability of this section. See *State v. Anderson* (2016) (plurality opinion) (stating that "when a defendant challenges his or her retrial, the Double Jeopardy Clause controls over the more general Due Process Clause").

In the civil area, on the other hand, procedural due process has had a direct impact in assuring the fairness of procedures that the government must follow before it deprives a person of life, liberty, or property. And the Ohio Supreme Court, relying on cases construing both state and federal provisions, has held that "[b]oth the Fourteenth Amendment to the United States Constitution and Section 16, Article I of the Ohio Constitution . . . guarantee a reasonable opportunity to be heard after a reasonable notice of such hearing." *Ohio Valley Radiology Associates Inc. v. Ohio Valley Hospital Association* (1986).

Since the 1970s, the U.S. Supreme Court has developed a strict, text-based approach to limit the reach of procedural due process in the civil arena. First, the clause is only applicable when "life, liberty, or property" is at stake. See *Board of Regents v. Roth* (1972). Second, there must be a "deprivation," which depends, in part, on the state of mind of the putative rights violator. See *Daniels v. Williams*

(1986); *Parratt v. Taylor* (1981). And finally, if there is a "deprivation" of a protected "property" (or other interest), the court undertakes a balancing approach to determine how much process is due. See *Mathews v. Eldridge* (1976).

Unlike the Due Process Clause of the Fourteenth Amendment, which is a limitation on government, the Ohio provision is framed affirmatively and is not dependent on the presence of a "life, liberty, or property" interest or on a "deprivation." But the Ohio Supreme Court has ignored the textual differences between the state and federal provisions and has followed the federal approach to procedural due process. See, for example, *State v. Hochhausler* (1996). Nonetheless, the court could analyze the state provision independently and engage in its own version of *Mathews* balancing to determine how much process is due.

Prior to its decisions in *Arnold* and *Norwood*, the Ohio Supreme Court often decided cases by combining its discussions of the state and federal provisions instead of analyzing them separately.

For example, in 1980, in a case decided before *Michigan v. Long* (1983), the court relied on the due process (as well as the equal protection) clauses of both the state and federal constitutions to recognize a right of indigent parents to appointed counsel in cases involving the permanent involuntary termination of their parental rights. *State ex rel. Heller v. Miller* (1980). The U.S. Supreme Court subsequently removed one of the four pillars that supported *Heller* and held that there was no across-the-board federal due process right to appointed counsel in parental rights termination cases, see *Lassiter v. Department of Social Services* (1981), but the Ohio Supreme Court has continued to rely upon its state constitutional holdings in *Heller*. See *State ex rel. Howard v. Ferreri* (1994) (quoting *Heller's* statement that: "[i]n actions instituted by the state to force the permanent, involuntary termination of parental rights, the United States and Ohio Constitutions' guarantees of due process and equal protection of the law require that indigent parents be provided with counsel and a transcript at public expense for appeals as of right."). But *cf. Liming v. Damos* (2012) (concluding "that the Due Process Clauses of the Ohio and United States Constitutions do not require that an indigent parent has the right to appointed counsel at a purge hearing, when that parent was previously represented by counsel at the originating civil-contempt proceeding").

And it remains unclear whether the court will adhere to its earlier interpretation of the due course of law clause of the Ohio Constitution in *Heller*, whether it will change its interpretation of the state provision to reflect the change in the interpretation of the federal provision, or whether it will undertake an independent analysis of due course of law.

Reputational Interests

Unlike the Fourteenth Amendment, the state due course of law provision *expressly* protects reputational interests. The U.S. Supreme Court has relied on the text of the Due Process Clause to conclude that reputation, standing alone, is not a protected liberty interest. *Paul v. Davis* (1976). But the Ohio due course of law provision expressly refers to "land, goods, persons, or reputation." And this specific reference to reputation strongly supports an interpretation of due course of law as providing redress for injuries to reputation without another corresponding injury.

Nonetheless, in *State v. Williams* (2000), the court relied on *Paul v. Davis, supra,* in upholding the constitutionality of Ohio's sex offender notification and registration law without even addressing the text of the Ohio provision. Instead, the court stated that a "favorable reputation is not a protected liberty interest" and relied on its interpretation of Article I, section 1, as not, standing alone, providing protections to reputations. See Commentary, Article I, section 1.

Substantive Due Process

The doctrine of substantive due process seeks to prevent the state from arbitrarily depriving a person of life, liberty, or property without regard to the fairness of the applicable procedures. And "[b]y the time of the ratification of the Fourteenth Amendment in 1868, courts in at least twenty of the thirty-seven then-existing states had endorsed some version of substantive due process in connection with interpreting either due process, law-of-the-land, or similar provisions in their own constitutions or the Fifth Amendment Due Process Clause." Williams, "The One and Only Substantive Due Process Clause," 469.

The phrase "substantive due process" did not become part of the lexicon until the second half of the twentieth century, but earlier in the century the U.S. Supreme Court, during the *Lochner* era, repeatedly struck down economic and social legislation by relying on the right to contract and a judicially enforceable requirement that government act reasonably. See, for example, *Adkins v. Children's Hospital* (1923) (striking down minimum wage statute for women and children in the District of Columbia); *Adair v. United States* (1908) (striking down federal statute that banned contracts that prohibited workers from joining unions). This pattern ended in the 1930s when the court changed direction overruled *Adkins* and began deferring to the legislative branches in cases involving economic regulation. See *U.S. v. Carolene Products, Co.* (1938) (footnote four discussion recognizing change in court's focus).

Foreshadowing this change, the U.S. Supreme Court in the 1920s applied the First Amendment to the states, see *Gitlow v. New York* (1925), and began to interpret "liberty" in the Fourteenth Amendment more aggressively to place substantive restrictions on the power of the states to enact noneconomic legislation. See, for example, *Pierce v. Society of Sisters* (1925) (striking down state law prohibiting private schools); *Meyer v. Nebraska* (1923) (striking down state law prohibiting teaching of grade school children in any language than English).

In 1941 in *Direct Plumbing* the Ohio Supreme Court lamented what it saw as a retreat by the U.S. Supreme Court in its protection private property and the right to contract, and the Ohio court made clear that it would be willing to use the state constitution to fill the gap. And although it did not use the phrase "substantive due process," the decision in *Direct Plumbing,* which struck down a regulation of the sale of plumbing fixtures, represents an example of the application of a state-based substantive due process approach to governmental regulation.

Despite *Direct Plumbing,* the Ohio Supreme Court has generally followed the U.S. Supreme Court in determining when a law not involving a fundamental right satisfies due process. See, for example,, *Fabrey v. McDonald Village Police Dep't* (1994) ("Under the Ohio Constitution, an enactment comports with due process if it bears a real and substantial relation to the public health, safety, morals or general welfare of the public and if it is not unreasonable or arbitrary. . . . Federal due process is satisfied if there is a rational relationship between a statute and its purpose.") (internal quotations omitted). See also *State v. Thompkins* (1996) (holding that mandatory suspension of driver's license for individuals convicted of or pleading guilty to drug offenses whether or not motor vehicle was used in commission of crime did not violate state or federal due process clauses). On the other hand, when a law impinges upon a fundamental right, the U.S. Supreme Court applies strict scrutiny and finds the statute unconstitutional unless it promotes a compelling governmental interest.

Most recently, in *State v. Aalim* (2017) (*Aalim II*) (on reconsideration), the court equated the state and federal substantive due process protections in the course of holding that "the mandatory bindover of certain juveniles to adult court . . . does not violate the Due Course of Law Clause . . . of the Ohio Constitution and the analogous provisions of the Fourteenth Amendment . . . ."

In rejecting the availability of constitutionally required amenability hearings, the court, apparently seeking to narrow the substantive leg of due course of law, stated that "[t]he touchstones of the court's analysis of substantive-due-process claims are whether the asserted right is grounded in history and tradition and whether the right protects against government intrusion into private conduct[.]" Ibid. And the court further observed that the U.S. Supreme Court has "continually limited substantive-due-process to matters relating to marriage, family, procreation, and the right to bodily integrity") (internal quotation omitted). See also ibid. (DeWine, J., concurring) (describing the "tortured path" in which the court took a "procedural due-process standard and transform[ed] it into a substantive one; . . . . that [it then] . . . transplanted into the Ohio Constitution."). But see ibid. (O'Neill, J., dissenting) ("Liberty therefore demands special treatment for children regardless of the momentary whims of our organized society. . . . [and] '[n]either the Bill of Rights nor the specific practices of States at the time of the adoption of the Fourteenth Amendment marks the outer limits of the substantive sphere of liberty which the Fourteenth Amendment protects' " (quoting *Planned Parenthood of Southeastern Pennsylvania v. Casey* (1992)).

Juvenile Rights and Due Course of Law

The due course of law clause, once a key provision in the tort reform battles, has taken center stage in litigation involving the rights of juveniles. And decisions in this area have addressed such issues as the sentences imposed by juvenile courts, the use of juvenile adjudications to enhance sentences in "adult" courts, and the transfer of cases from juvenile to "adult" courts.

Juvenile proceedings are civil, but in 1967 the U.S. Supreme Court held that a juvenile's right to counsel in a delinquency proceeding is guaranteed by the Due Process Clause of the Fourteenth Amendment. See *In re Gault* (1967). Ohio also treats juvenile proceedings as civil, and neither the state nor federal constitutions has extended the right to a jury trial to all stages of juvenile adjudications. See *State v. D.H.* (2009) (holding that because of the central role of the juvenile judge in a juvenile's rehabilitative process, fundamental fairness did not require the same jury-trial rights for juveniles as required for adults).

In *In re C.P.* (2012), the court held that a statute that imposed "automatic, lifelong registration and notification requirements on juvenile sex offenders tried within the juvenile system, . . . violates . . . the Due Process Clause of the Fourteenth Amendment to the United States Constitution and the Ohio Constitution, Article I, Section 16." (syllabus). In so holding, the court focused on "the due process requirement of fundamental fairness" and on the special role that juvenile courts in Ohio play in protecting juveniles; it then concluded that the removal of the judge from the deliberative process was inconsistent with "the juvenile system's core emphasis on individual, corrective treatment and rehabilitation."

In *State v. Bode* (2015), the court held that "[a]n adjudication of delinquency may not be used . . . to enhance the penalty for a later offense when the adjudication carried the possibility of confinement, the adjudication was uncounseled, and there was no effective waiver of the right to counsel.") (syllabus). In so holding, the court recognized that the Ohio due process provision sometimes provides greater rights to juveniles than its Fourteenth Amendment counterpart; it then focused on the special role of the juvenile justice system and on the right to counsel under Ohio law.

In 2016, in *State v. Hand*, the court held that a state statute that required the use of juvenile determinations to enhance adult court sentences "violates the Due Process Clauses of Article I, Section 16 of the Ohio Constitution and the Fourteenth Amendment to the United States Constitution because it is fundamentally unfair to treat a juvenile adjudication as a previous conviction that enhances either the degree of or the sentence for a subsequent offense committed as an adult." (syllabus).

Although the *Hand* court did not rule that there is a constitutional right to a jury trial at all stages of juvenile proceedings, it made clear that juvenile adjudications absent the opportunity for a trial by jury cannot be held against an adult defendant without violating constitutional safeguards rooted in the Due Process Clause of Article I, section 16 of the Ohio Constitution. See Ibid. ("In order to continue holding that a jury trial is not required for juveniles, we must maintain the civil nature of juvenile adjudications. It is contradictory and fundamentally unfair to allow juvenile adjudications that result from these less formal proceedings to be characterized as criminal convictions that may later enhance adult punishment."). In so holding, the court again focused on fundamental fairness and on the special nature of the Ohio system of juvenile justice.

And later in 2016, the court first held that "[t]he mandatory transfer of juveniles to the general division of a common pleas court violates juveniles' right to due process as guaranteed by Article I, section 16 of the Ohio Constitution." In so ruling, the court focused on fundamental fairness and the role of the juvenile judge in meeting the rehabilitative goals of the juvenile justice system. *State v. Aalim* (2016) (*Aalim I*). But the next year, the court reconsidered the *Aalim* decision, equated the state and federal protections and held that "these provisions cannot have created a substantive right to a specific juvenile-court proceeding." *State v. Aalim* (2017) (*Aalim II*) (on reconsideration). *See supra* (discussing substantive due process).

None of the opinions in the cases addressing the due course of law rights of juveniles focused on the text of the state constitutional provision. But some members of the court have pointed to the absence of juvenile courts at the time of the adoption of the relevant constitutional provisions to support a narrow interpretation of the due course of law provision. See *Aalim II, supra.* Other members of the court, however, have concluded that the state provision has an independent meaning by relying on the state's commitment to the rehabilitative goals of the juvenile justice system.

Unless the court takes the view that the due course of law provision retains the meaning it had at the time of its adoption, it should permit this provision to evolve just as it has permitted the evolution of the state's equal protection and benefit provision. See Commentary, Article I, section 2.

Finally, even if state-specific factors such as the special rehabilitative role played by juvenile courts do not support an independent interpretation of the state due course of law provision, the court is still free to rely on its own interpretation of the provision; thus, it may reach decisions that it believes are correct without having to justify deviations from the prevailing interpretation of the federal counterpart. See The History of the Ohio Constitution, *supra.*

Justice Administered without Delay

The final provision in the first sentence of this section provides that every person "shall have justice administered without denial or delay." It was borrowed almost verbatim from Article VIII, section 7, of the 1802 Constitution, and it is similar, but not identical, to Article 40 of the Magna Carta.

This provision does not have a counterpart in the U.S. Constitution, and the Ohio Supreme Court has interpreted it to require a state prison warden to provide an inmate an opportunity for a timely meeting with prospective counsel. *Thomas v. Mills* (1927). See also *State ex rel. Spirko v. Judges of Court of Appeals* (1986) (holding that a defendant in a capital case must be afforded a complete, full, and abridged transcript of all proceedings in order to pursue an effective appeal).

Finally, the court has held that an unlimited number of reversals on the weight of the evidence is inconsistent with state constitutional principles of an inviolate right to a trial by jury and the administration of justice without delay. *Isaac v. Intercoast Sales Corp.* (1937).

Sovereign Immunity

The last sentence of this section provides that "[s]uits may be brought against the state, in such courts and in such manner, as may be provided by law." Adopted in 1912 and never amended, this provision was directed at the common law doctrine of sovereign immunity, which was a complete defense to all actions against the state. The doctrine of sovereign immunity, which had been well established in Ohio since the state joined the union, was derived from the maxim "the king can do no wrong." *Haas v. Hayslip* (1977 (Brown, J., dissenting)).

This provision apparently created some confusion among the delegates to the 1912 Constitutional Convention. A number of delegates believed that its adoption would automatically abolish sovereign immunity, see Stefan Schnopp, "Garrett v. Sandusky: Justice Pfeifer's Fight for Full and Fair Legal Redress: Does Sovereign Immunity Violate Ohio's 'Open Court Provision?" 27 *U. Tol. L. Rev.* 729 (1996): 743–44, but the Ohio Supreme Court has held that this provision is not self-executing and requires legislative action as a prerequisite to bringing an action against the state in its own courts. *Raudabaugh v. State* (1917). See also *Krause v. State* (1972) ("When the people of Ohio, in 1912, adopted Section 16 of Article I as part of the organic law of this state, they foreclosed to this or any other court the authority to examine the 'soundness' or 'justice' of the concept of governmental immunity.").

In 1975, the General Assembly abolished the state's sovereign immunity by enacting the Court of Claims Act. The act established a Court of Claims with exclusive jurisdiction over all actions brought against the state except "[t]o the extent that the state has previously consented to be sued." O.R.C. section 2743.02(A)(1). The state had previously permitted declaratory actions but not actions for injunctive relief or money damages. See *Friedman v. Johnson* (1985). Accordingly, the Court of Claims has exclusive jurisdiction over all actions against the state and its instrumentalities that contain claims for injunctive relief or damages, including actions against the state under Title VII of the federal

Civil Rights Act of 1964, as amended, barring employment discrimination. *Manning v. Ohio State Library Board* (1991).

The Court of Claims Act did not abolish the common law sovereign immunity of municipalities. *Haas, supra.* The Ohio Supreme Court, however, judicially abolished the immunity of municipalities and other political subdivisions in *Haverlack v. Portage Homes, Inc.* (1982), but in 1985 the General Assembly reintroduced the immunity subject to enumerated statutory exemptions in the Political Subdivision Tort Liability Act. See O.R.C. chapter 2744. But see *Garrett v. Sandusky* (1993) (Pfeiffer, J., concurring) (arguing that "[i]n light of the original intent of the delegates to the Constitutional Convention of 1912 and the plain reading of Section 16, Article I of the Ohio Constitution, the remaining vestiges of local governmental immunity should be abolished.").

Ohio's waiver of sovereign immunity in the Court of Claims Act did not waive the state's Eleventh Amendment immunity from suit in federal court on either state or federal claims. See generally *Pennhurst State School & Hospital v. Halderman* (1984).

Section 17

No heredity privileges.

No hereditary emoluments, honors, or privileges, shall ever be granted or conferred by this State.

Adopted in 1851 and never amended, this section prevents the state from granting "hereditary emoluments, honors, or privileges." This provision is virtually identical to Article VIII, section 24, of the 1802 Ohio Constitution. A similar provision in Article I, section 9, of the U.S. Constitution prohibits the United States from granting "any Title of Nobility" and further provides that "no Person holding any Office of Profit or Trust . . . shall without the Consent of the Congress, accept of any present, Emolument, Office, or Title, of any kind whatever, from any King, Prince or foreign State." In addition, Article I, section 10 of the U.S. Constitution (but not this section) provides that "[n]o state shall grant any Title of Nobility."

Section 18

Suspension of laws.

No power of suspending laws shall ever be exercised, except by the General Assembly.

Adopted in 1851 and never amended, this section is based on Article VIII, section 9, of the 1802 Ohio Constitution. It provides that only the General Assembly, and thus not the governor, has the power to suspend laws. The Ohio

Supreme Court has reviewed delegations of legislative authority under this section, see Commentary, Article II, section 26; and held that neither a statute that delegated authority to county and township officials to issue permits nor a statute that granted the Civil Service Commission authority to issue and enforce rules violated this section. *Fox v. Fox* (1873); *Green v. State Civil Service Commission* (1914). The court has also held that the adoption of amendments to a city charter under the proper exercise of a city's home rule power does not violate this section. *Hile v. City of Cleveland* (1923).

Section 19

Eminent domain.

Private property shall ever be held inviolate, but subservient to the public welfare. When taken in time of war or other public exigency, imperatively requiring its immediate seizure, or for the purpose of making or repairing roads, which shall be open to the public, without charge, a compensation shall be made to the owner, in money, and in all other cases, where private property shall be taken for public use, a compensation therefor shall first be made in money, or first secured by a deposit of money, and such compensation shall be assessed by a jury, without deduction for benefits to any property of the owner.

Adopted in 1851 and never amended, this section is derived from Article VIII, section 4 of the 1802 Ohio Constitution, which stated that "[p]rivate property ought and shall ever be held inviolate, but always subservient to the public welfare, provided a compensation in money be made to the owner." Article II of the Northwest Ordinance also contained a provision guaranteeing full compensation for the taking of private property. Similarly, the Takings Clause of the Fifth Amendment to the U.S. Constitution provides that private property shall not "be taken for public use, without just compensation." The Ohio provision, however, differs from the Fifth Amendment by specifying when and under what circumstances private property may be taken.

Section 19 reflects the philosophy that private property shall not be taken by the state except when necessary for the public welfare. As stated by the Ohio Supreme Court in 2001:

> No government could long continue to function if all property rights were unqualifiedly inviolate. But, on the other hand, the constitutional guaranty of the right of private property would be hollow if all legislation enacted in the name of the public welfare were *per se* valid. To be truly in the public welfare within the meaning of Section 19, and thus superior to private property rights, any legislation must be reasonable, not arbitrary, and must confer upon the public a benefit commensurate with its burdens upon private property.
>
> *Holeton v. Crouse Cartage Co.* (2001)
> (quoting *Direct Plumbing Supply Co. v. Dayton*, 1941).

In times of emergency and for work related to the construction or repair of roads, the state may acquire private property through eminent domain and then compensate the owner. In all other cases, the state must compensate the owner of private property before property is taken. In both situations, section 19 mandates that compensation will be determined by a jury and forbids the deduction of benefits gained by the property owner due to public improvements.

Section 19 applies to both real and personal property. *Lucas v. Carney* (1958). A "taking" for the purpose of this section occurs where a person's property is either physically taken or seized or where there is a "deprivation of an intangible interest" that interferes with a person's dominion, use, or disposition over his property. *State ex rel. OTR v. Columbus* (1996). In cases involving land use regulations, such as zoning laws, a taking occurs if the law or regulation fails to substantially advance legitimate state interests or denies the owner all economically viable use of the land. *State ex rel. Shemo v. City of Mayfield Heights* (2002).

In *City of Norwood v. Horney* (2006), one of the Ohio Supreme Court's most important cases interpreting the Ohio Bill of Rights, the court rejected the U.S. Supreme Court's interpretation of the "public use" limitation on takings in *Kelo v. City of New London* (2005), and it interpreted this section of the Ohio Constitution as more protective of property rights. The *Norwood* court required lower courts to apply heightened scrutiny when reviewing statutes that regulate eminent domain. Although permitting consideration of economic factors, the court held that the fact that an appropriation of property would provide an economic benefit to the government and the community, standing alone, does not satisfy the "public use" requirement of this section. The court further held that the void for vagueness doctrine applies to laws and ordinances regulating the use of eminent domain, and it concluded that the use in a city ordinance of "deteriorating area" as a standard for determining whether private property is subject to appropriation is inherently speculative and void for vagueness.

The Ohio Supreme Court has held that a state statute that bars the payment of interest on unclaimed funds held by the state is a taking of property in violation of this section. *Sogg v. Zurz* (2009).

Section 19a

Damage for wrongful death.

The amount of damages recoverable by civil action in the courts for death caused by the wrongful act, neglect, or default of another, shall not be limited by law.

Adopted in 1912 and never amended, this section sought to prohibit monetary caps on wrongful death claims. Causes of action for wrongful death were not available at common law, but in 1851 the General Assembly enacted legislation permitting wrongful death actions. The legislation, however, limited the amount of damages that could be recovered, see Swisher, *Ohio Constitution Handbook*, 207; and the delegates at the 1912 Convention disagreed with this limitation and proposed this provision, which the voters approved.

The Ohio Supreme Court has interpreted this section as prohibiting laws that place specific limitations on the amount of recovery, but the court has held that laws may be passed to limit the kind of damages that are recoverable in wrongful death action. *Kennedy v. Byers* (1923). For example, in *Kennedy* it held that a former version of Ohio's wrongful death statute, which limited recovery to pecuniary loss, did not violate this section. Current laws covering wrongful death actions are found in chapter 2125 of the Ohio Revised Code.

Section 19b

Protection of private property rights in ground water, lakes and other watercourses.

(A) The protection of the rights of Ohio's property owners, the protection of Ohio's natural resources, and the maintenance of the stability of Ohio's economy require the recognition and protection of property interests in ground water, lakes, and watercourses.

(B) The preservation of private property interests recognized under divisions (C) and (D) of this section shall be held inviolate, but subservient to the public welfare as provided in Section 19 of Article I of the Constitution.

(C) A property owner has a property interest in the reasonable use of the ground water underlying the property owner's land.

(D) An owner of riparian land has a property interest in the reasonable use of the water in a lake or watercourse located on or flowing through the owner's riparian land.

(E) Ground water underlying privately owned land and nonnavigable waters located on or flowing through privately owned land shall not be held in trust by any governmental body. The state, and a political subdivision to the extent authorized by state law, may provide for the regulation of such waters. An owner of land voluntarily may convey to a governmental body the owner's property interest held in the ground water underlying the land or nonnavigable waters located on or flowing through the land.

(F) Nothing in this section affects the application of the public trust doctrine as it applies to Lake Erie or the navigable waters of the state.

(G) Nothing in Section 1e of Article II, Section 36 of Article II, Article VIII, Section 1 of Article X, Section 3 of Article XVIII, or Section 7 of Article XVIII of the Constitution shall impair or limit the rights established in this section.

Proposed by the General Assembly in 2008 and approved by almost 72 percent of the voters, this amendment makes explicit that a private property owner has a right to make reasonable use of the groundwater that lies beneath the owner's land or on a bordering lake or other watercourse. The new amendment, however, makes clear that this right is subordinate to the public welfare.

The impetus behind this amendment was a concern that the proposed Great Lakes-St. Lawrence River Basin Sustainable Water Resources Agreement (popularly known as the Great Lakes Water Compact) would trample private property rights by designating groundwater as publicly owned. Opponents of the amendment argued that the amendment was not necessary, since "[t]he Supreme Court of Ohio [has] already determined that private property owners have rights to the ground water underlying their land and to the watercourse flowing on and through their land." And they further argued that the proposed amendment would give private property owners (who do not actually own the water beneath their land) the false sense of security that their land cannot be taken away at a later date. Amendment proponents responded by arguing that the amendment avoided future costly litigation on the rights of property owners. See 2008 Issues Report (Ohio Secretary of State) (website).

This amendment does not appear to have made any changes in preexisting law, and, in one of the first cases interpreting it, an Ohio appellate court held that it did not give property owners the right to pollute wetlands on their property with improperly treated sanitary sewage. *State ex rel. Cordray v. Helms* (2011).

Section 20

Powers reserved to the people.

This enumeration of rights shall not be construed to impair or deny others retained by the people; and all powers, not herein delegated, remain with the people.

Adopted in 1851 and never amended, this section is modeled on the Ninth and Tenth Amendments to the U.S. Constitution. It is also based on section 28 of Article VIII of the 1802 Constitution, which provided as follows: "To guard against the transgressions of the high powers, which we have delegated, we declare, that all powers, not hereby delegated, remain with the people."

Like Article I, section 2, this section expresses the fundamental precept of American political theory—that government is derived from the people—but this section has had little legal force.

The Ohio Supreme Court has not recognized specific rights under this section 20, and the court has held that this section imposes no restrictions on the powers delegated by other provisions of the constitution on legislative power. *State ex rel. Attoeney General v. Covington* (1876). But in a case that involved a challenge to a per capita tax on the owner of land on which dogs were kept, the court relied, in part, on section 20 and struck down this statute as an arbitrary and unreasonable exercise of the police power. *Mirick v. Gims* (1908). See also *Evans v. Mannix* (1914) (relying on *Mirick* and holding that a statute that imposed a tax against real estate when a tenant had illegally sold intoxicating liquors without knowledge, consent, or participation of the property owner was an arbitrary, unreasonable, and unconstitutional exercise of the police power).

Section 21

Preservation of the freedom to choose health care.

(A) No federal, state, or local law or rule shall compel, directly or indirectly, any person, employer, or health care provider to participate in a health care system.

(B) No federal, state, or local law or rule shall prohibit the purchase or sale of health care or health insurance.

(C) No federal, state, or local law or rule shall impose a penalty or fine for the sale or purchase of health care or health insurance.

(D) This section does not affect laws or rules in effect as of March 19, 2010; affect which services a health care provider or hospital is required to perform or provide; affect terms and conditions of government employment; or affect any laws calculated to deter fraud or punish wrongdoing in the health care industry.

(E) As used in this Section,

(1) "Compel" includes the levying of penalties or fines.

(2) "Health care system" means any public or private entity or program whose function or purpose includes the management of, processing of, enrollment of individuals for, or payment for, in full or in part, health care services, health care data, or health care information for its participants.

(3) "Penalty or fine" means any civil or criminal penalty or fine, tax, salary or wage withholding or surcharge or any named fee established by law or rule by a government established, created, or controlled agency that is used to punish or discourage the exercise of rights protected under this section.

Adopted in 2011, this amendment, which was proposed by initiative petition and approved by the voters by an almost 2:1 margin, provides that no person, employer, or health care provider be compelled to participate in a health care system. This provision targeted the federal Affordable Care Act, popularly known as Obamacare. The 2012 decision of the U.S. Supreme Court in *National Federation of Independent Business v. Sebelius*, rejecting a federal constitutional challenge to the act by a 5–4 vote, undercut the principal purpose of this provision.

State constitutions cannot override federal law, but it has been argued that the surviving parts of section 21(A) prevent the state from requiring that insurance cover certain medical conditions. The Ohio Supreme Court, however, has not addressed this issue.

The Ohio Supreme Court has recognized that the fundamental right to refuse medical treatment, based on the fact that "personal security, bodily integrity, and autonomy are cherished liberties." *Steele v. Hamilton Cty. Community Mental Health Bd.* (2000) (construing Art. I, sec. 1); *see* also Commentary, Article I, section 1. The court has not addressed whether this section bars the state from providing involuntary medical treatment, but a state appeals court has held that this amendment did not prohibit involuntary treatment at psychiatric hospitals of persons acquitted of crimes on the basis of insanity. *State v. Rohrer* (2015).

Article II

Legislative

Article II and the following two articles, on the executive and the judiciary, respectively, outline the structure and powers of the three branches of state government. The 1802 Ohio Constitution established a bicameral General Assembly, but in accordance with their strong beliefs in representative democracy, the Jeffersonian Republicans, who dominated Ohio's first constitutional convention, vested near-absolute power in the legislature. Under the 1802 Constitution, the General Assembly dominated the other two branches of government. It appointed by joint ballot the judges of the Supreme Court and the courts of common pleas. It also appointed by joint ballot all executive branch officers other than the governor and, in the absence of a gubernatorial veto, had complete control over legislation. As a prominent delegate to the 1850–51 Constitutional Convention noted, "the legislature swallowed up all the rest of the government." *Report of the Debates and Proceedings of the Convention for the Revision of the Constitution of the State Of Ohio 1850–51*, vol. 1 (Columbus: S. Medary, 1851), 175 (Mr. Reemelin) (hereinafter *1850–51 Debates*).

The framers of the 1851 Ohio Constitution limited the power of the General Assembly by placing restrictions on its power to make appropriations, by requiring that laws of general nature have uniform application, and by eliminating most of the General Assembly's appointment power. Besides the limitations imposed by this article, the 1851 Constitution restricted the General

The Ohio State Constitution. Steven H. Steinglass and Gino J. Scarselli, Oxford University Press. © Oxford University Press 2022. DOI: 10.1093/oso/9780197619728.003.0004

Assembly's powers to incur debt (Art. VIII), to tax (Art. XII), and to grant special privileges to corporations (Art. XIII). The 1851 Constitution also provided for the popular election of judges and executive branch officers, but it still made no provision for a gubernatorial veto. A 1903 amendment gave the governor the veto, and in 1912, following a convention dominated by Progressives, the voters approved an amendment that gave them the powers of initiative and referendum.

Most of the sections of Article II deal with the organization and membership of the General Assembly, although this article also contains provisions for the initiative and referendum and for the governor's veto power. Since 1912, Article II has been one of the most frequently amended articles of the constitution, and in 1973, following recommendations made by the Ohio Constitutional Revision Commission (OCRC), the General Assembly proposed a significant reorganization of this article, which the voters approved that same year. See OCRC, *Recommendations for Amendments to the Ohio Constitution: Final Report, Index to Proceedings and Research* (1977), 96–136 (hereinafter OCRC, *Final Report*).

In 2017, a committee of the Ohio Constitutional Modernization Commission (hereinafter OCMC) unanimously recommended a comprehensive revision of key provisions on the statutory and constitutional initiative, but the proposal proved controversial and the full commission tabled the proposal at its final meeting. See OCMC, *Constitutional Revision and Updating Committee, Report and Recommendation, Article II, Sections 1 through 1i, 15(G) and 17* (The Ohio Constitutional and Statutory Initiative) (May 11, 2017), and OCMC, Constitutional Revision and Updating Committee, Minutes (May 11, 2017). See also OCMC, Minutes (June 8, 2017).

Section 1

Legislative power vested in General Assembly; initiative and referendum reserved to people.

The legislative power of the state shall be vested in a General Assembly consisting of a Senate and House of Representatives but the people reserve to themselves the power to propose to the General Assembly laws and amendments to the constitution, and to adopt or reject the same at the polls on a referendum vote as hereinafter provided. They also reserve the power to adopt or reject any law, section of any law or any item in any law appropriating money passed by the General Assembly, except as hereinafter provided; and independent of the General Assembly to propose amendments to the constitution and to adopt or reject the same at the polls. The limitations expressed in the constitution, on the power of the General Assembly to enact laws, shall be deemed limitations on the power of the people to enact laws.

Adopted in 1851 and amended in 1912, 1918, and 1953, this section vests the legislative authority of the state in a bicameral General Assembly. The opening clause ("The legislative power of the state shall be vested in a General Assembly consisting of a Senate and House of Representatives . . . .") is derived from the

1802 Constitution. The remainder of the first sentence is the result of the 1912 amendments establishing the rights of initiative and referendum. See Article II, sections 1a–1g.

In 1918, the voters approved an amendment to this section proposed by initiative petition to permit the referendum to be used to review decisions of the General Assembly ratifying proposed amendments to the U.S. Constitution. The liquor industry supported the amendment in an effort to prevent ratification of the Eighteenth Amendment, but the U.S. Supreme Court held that the proposed amendment violated Article V of the U.S. Constitution, which assigned the power of ratification to state legislatures and state conventions. *Hawke v. Smith* (1920). And, in 1953, the General Assembly proposed and the voters approved an amendment that repealed this unconstitutional provision.

In adopting a constitution, the people of Ohio delegated all legislative power to the General Assembly subject only to other constitutional limitations. This grant of plenary legislative power differs fundamentally from the grant of legislative power to Congress under the U.S. Constitution. Unlike the federal constitution, which grants Congress only specific, enumerated powers, the Ohio Constitution "is primarily a limitation on the legislative power of the General Assembly." *State v. Warner* (1990). Thus, the General Assembly may enact any law not prohibited by the state or federal constitutions, and a law passed by the General Assembly is presumed constitutional unless it is incapable of a fair reconciliation with the constitution. *State ex rel. Jackman v. Cuyahoga County Court of Common Pleas* (1967).

■ SEPARATION OF POWERS

Ohio does not have a constitutional provision expressly providing for a separation of powers among the branches of government, see generally Curtis Rodebush, "Separation of Powers in Ohio: A Critical Analysis," 51 *Clev. St. L. Rev.* 505 (2004), and it is one of only ten states without such a provision. See John Devlin, "Toward a State Constitutional Analysis of Allocation of Powers: Legislators and Legislative Appointees Performing Administrative Functions," 66 *Temple L. Rev.* 1205 (1993). Nonetheless, the Ohio Supreme Court has held that the separation of powers "doctrine is implicitly embedded in the entire framework of those sections of the Ohio Constitution that define the substance and scope of powers granted to the three branches of government." *City of South Euclid v. Jemison* (1986). In this respect, the Ohio Constitution follows the federal model, in which the doctrine is implied from the powers granted to the legislative, executive, and judicial branches. See *Morrison v. Olson* (1988). In step with the federal model, Ohio has not required a strict, absolute division among the three branches of government. "It seems to be assumed that the separation of executive, legislative, and judicial powers is complete and distinct under the Constitution. Theoretically it is so; but in practice it is not so, and never was so." *Village of Fairview v. Giffee* (1905). According to the Ohio Supreme Court, "government would prove abortive if it . . . attempted to follow such a policy [of strict separation] to the letter." *Bogen v. Clemmer* (1932).

The Ohio Constitution recognizes that the powers of one branch can overlap with the powers of another. The constitution gives the governor power to veto legislation (Art. II, sec. 16) and to convene the General Assembly on extraordinary occasions (Art. III, sec. 8). The governor has general clemency power, but the General Assembly has that power in cases of treason (Art. III, sec. 11). The house has the sole power to impeach, but impeachment cases are tried before the Senate (Art. II, secs. 23 and 24). The Senate also has the power of advice and consent over certain executive branch offices (Art. III, sec. 21). The General Assembly may disapprove rules of practice and procedure promulgated by the Ohio Supreme Court (Art. IV, sec. 5(B)), and may remove judges by a two-thirds vote of both houses (Art. IV, sec. 17). And the General Assembly is barred from granting divorces or exercising any judicial powers (Art. II, sec. 32).

A government organized around the principle of separation of powers has a system of checks and balances, and the courts will act when one branch usurps the powers that properly belong to another or exerts undue influence over another branch. For example, in *Jemison, supra,* the Ohio Supreme Court found a separation of powers violation in a statute that granted the registrar of motor vehicles the power to review judicial decisions finding violations of the state financial responsibility law. By giving the executive branch the right to review suspensions of drivers' licenses, the statute permitted the executive to exercise appellate review over trial courts, thus usurping the power granted to appellate courts and violating the doctrine of separation of powers. Likewise, sections of the Ohio Adam Walsh Act, which authorized the attorney general to reclassify sex offenders who had already been classified by judges, violated the doctrine of separation of powers. *State v. Bodyke* (2010).

■ DELEGATION OF LEGISLATIVE AUTHORITY TO ADMINISTRATIVE AGENCIES

As a general principle, the General Assembly cannot delegate its legislative authority. Traditionally, the courts have drawn a distinction between the impermissible delegation of legislative authority, which involves a determination of what the law will be, and the permissible delegation of administrative authority, which involves the administration or execution of the law. *State ex rel. Meshel v. Keip* (1981). The Ohio Supreme Court, however, has recognized that this distinction is more or less a fiction. See *Redman v. Ohio Dept. of Industrial Relations* (1996) (quoting Davis, *Administrative Law Text* (3d ed., 1972, 37)) ("The early method of escape from the proposition that legislative power may not be delegated was by pretending that 'filling up the details' was not an exercise of legislative power."). Instead of categorizing delegation cases into those that involve legislative authority and those that involve administrative authority, the court has focused on whether a delegation results in "unbridled agency discretion." Ibid. The General Assembly may delegate its authority to administrative officers and agencies if their discretion is reasonably restricted. Under this flexible approach, the court has specifically held that the General Assembly does not unconstitutionally delegate its authority "if it establishes, through legislative policy and such standards as are practical, an intelligible principle to which the administrative officer or body must conform and further establishes a procedure whereby exercise of the discretion can be reviewed effectively." *Blue Cross of Northeast Ohio v. Ratchford* (1980) (syllabus).

The General Assembly has incorporated provisions of the federal Internal Revenue Code into the Ohio Tax Code, thus effectively delegating the task of defining aspects of Ohio tax law to the United States. A number of courts and commentators have questioned prospective delegations, see OCRC Proceedings, 1764–1769, *Income Tax: Adoption of federal tax provisions prospectively* (Research Study 14A) (October 4, 1972), but the Ohio Supreme Court has not addressed whether such a policy violates the Ohio nondelegation doctrine.

In 2013, the Ohio Supreme Court held that the delegation of authority by the General Assembly to the Ohio Controlling Board included the power to permit the state to participate in the expansion of the Medicaid program under the federal Affordable Care Act. *State ex rel. Cleveland Right to Life v. State of Ohio Controlling Board* (2013). The court further held that the intent of the General Assembly could not be based on a putative statutory limitation on the Controlling Board that was the subject of a line-item veto by the governor and that the vetoed provision did not represent a negation or limitation on the exercise of the delegated power.

In addressing the delegation of legislative power to administrative agencies, the Ohio Supreme Court has deferred to agency expertise, including their familiarity with the law that controls their activities. This approach, which in the federal system is often referred to as *Auer-Chevron* deference, has become the subject of great controversy in the federal courts, see, for example, Christopher J. Walker, "Attacking Auer and Chevron Deference: A Literature Review," 16 *Geo. J. L. & Pub. Policy* 103 (2018); and the suggestion has been made that the Ohio Supreme Court take a fresh look at the administrative-deference doctrine, see *State ex rel. McCann v. Delaware County Bd. of Elections* (2018) (DeWine, J., concurring in judgment).

On March 24, 2021, the General Assembly overrode a veto by Ohio Governor Mike DeWine and adopted legislation that authorized the General Assembly by concurrent resolution to cancel state health orders. This legislation, S.B. 22 (134th GA) (2021), the constitutionality of which was questioned on separation of powers grounds in the governor's veto message, sought to expand the power of the General Assembly at the expense of the power of the governor. But the grant of power to the General Assembly to "legislate" through concurrent resolutions (which cannot be vetoed) is likely in violation of the principle of separation of powers and beyond what can be accomplished through concurrent resolutions. *Cf. State ex rel. Attorney General v. Kinney* (1897) ("The statute law of the state can neither be repealed nor amended by a joint resolution of the general assembly.").

■ INITIATIVE AND REFERENDUM

Section 1 also reserves to the people the powers of initiative and referendum. The term "initiative and referendum" actually refers to two distinct processes. Initiative is the means by which the electors may propose laws and constitutional amendments; referendum is the means by which the electors may reject laws enacted by the General Assembly. In 1898, South Dakota became the first state to grant the powers of initiative and referendum, and from 1910 to 1915, Ohio and eleven other states adopted some version of initiative and referendum. See OCRC, *Final Report*, 344. Ohio voters approved the initiative and referendum in 1912 as a result of an amendment proposed by the 1912 Constitutional Convention. The powers of initiative and referendum are set forth in detail in sections 1a–1g of this article.

Section 1a

Initiative to amend constitution.

The first aforestated power reserved by the people is designated the initiative, and the signatures of ten per centum of the electors shall be required upon a petition to propose an amendment to the constitution. When a petition signed by the aforesaid required number of electors, shall have been filed with the secretary of state, and verified as herein provided, proposing an amendment to the constitution, the full text of which shall have been set forth in such petition, the secretary of state shall submit for the approval or rejection of the electors, the proposed amendment, in the manner hereinafter provided, at the next succeeding regular or general election in any year occurring subsequent to one hundred twenty-five days after the filing of such petition. The initiative petitions, above described, shall have printed across the top thereof: "Amendment to the Constitution Proposed by Initiative Petition to be Submitted Directly to the Electors."

Adopted in 1912 as part of the initiative and referendum amendment proposed by the 1912 Constitutional Convention, and amended in 2008, this section authorizes the use of the initiative to amend the constitution. For a proposed constitutional amendment to be placed on the ballot, a petition signed by 10 percent of the state's electors must be filed with the secretary of state. The 10 percent figure is determined by the total vote of those who voted for governor in the last gubernatorial election, and there is a geographic distribution requirement for signatures. See Commentary, Article II, section 1g. If the secretary of state determines that the petition has the requisite number of signatures, the secretary places the proposed amendment on the ballot at the next regular election, where it must be approved by a majority of those voting on the issue. This use of the initiative to amend the constitution is known as a "direct initiative," because a proposed amendment does not have to first be submitted to the General Assembly. And Ohio is one of sixteen states that allows amendments to the constitution through a direct constitutional initiative. See *Book of the States, "Constitutional Amendment Procedure: By Initiative, Constitutional Provisions,"* 2018, Table 1.4.

Before beginning to collect signatures, Ohio statutory law requires proponents of an amendment to submit an initial petition signed by 1000 registered voters with the full text of the proposed amendment and a summary of it to the attorney general, who has ten days to determine whether the summary is a "fair and truthful" statement of the proposed amendment. After the statement is certified as fair and truthful, the attorney general is required to forward the petition to the Ohio Ballot Board for a determination of whether the petition contains only one proposed amendment. Only then may the petitioners begin collecting signatures, which they must submit to the secretary of state.

If the attorney general rejects a petition because it is not "fair and truthful," petitioners who wish to continue the process must submit a new summary to the attorney general. If the petitioners satisfy the attorney general, the matter then goes to the Ballot Board for a determination of whether the petition contains only one proposed amendment. If it does, the petitioners must begin the process anew by preparing separate petitions with new summaries and by resubmitting them to the attorney general for "fair and truthful" determinations.

The percentage or number of signatures required for a petition varies among the states. Ohio, like most states that permit the use of the initiative to amend the constitution and to adopt statutes, requires more signatures for the constitutional initiative than for the statutory initiative. See OCRC, *Final Report,* 350.

Because the number of qualified signatures is based on voter turnout in the last gubernatorial election, the requisite number of signatures can fluctuate sharply based on voter turnout. For example, after the low-turnout 2014 gubernatorial election, the 10 percent requirement for proposed amendments was 305,591, but the high-turnout 2018 gubernatorial election increased the requirement by almost 50 percent to 442,958 signatures until 2023. See Governors Percentage Chart (2018) (Secretary of State website).

Unlike amendments proposed by the General Assembly, amendments and laws that are proposed by initiative and laws challenged by referendum may only be placed on the ballot in the "regular or general election," which is the fall election. And under this section, the petitions and signatures must be filed with the secretary of state at least 125 days prior to the fall election.

Section 1b

Initiative to enact laws.

When at any time, not less than ten days prior to the commencement of any session of the General Assembly, there shall have been filed with the secretary of state a petition signed by three per centum of the electors and verified as herein provided, proposing a law, the full text of which shall have been set forth in such petition, the secretary of state shall transmit the same to the General Assembly as soon as it convenes. If said proposed law shall be passed by the General Assembly, either as petitioned for or in an amended form, it shall be subject to the referendum. If it shall not be passed, or if it shall be passed in an amended form, or if no action shall be taken thereon within four months from the time it is received by the General Assembly, it shall be submitted by the secretary of state to the electors for their approval or rejection, if such submission shall be demanded by supplementary petition verified as herein provided and signed by not less than three per centum of the electors in addition to those signing the original petition, which supplementary petition must be signed and filed with the secretary of state within ninety days after the proposed law shall have been rejected by the General Assembly or after the expiration of such term of four months, if no action has been taken thereon, or after the law as passed by the General Assembly shall have been filed by the governor in the office of the secretary of state. The proposed law shall be submitted at the next regular or general election occurring subsequent to one hundred twenty-five days after the supplementary petition has been filed in the form demanded by such supplementary petition, which form shall be either as first petitioned for or with any amendment or amendments which may have been incorporated therein by either branch or by both branches, of the General Assembly. If a proposed law so submitted is approved by a majority of the electors voting thereon, it shall be the law and shall go into effect as herein provided in lieu of any amended form of said law which may have been passed by the General Assembly, and such amended law passed by the General Assembly shall not go into effect until and unless the law proposed by supplementary petition shall have been rejected by the electors. All such initiative petitions, last above described, shall have printed across the top thereof, in case of proposed laws: "Law Proposed by Initiative Petition First to be Submitted to the General Assembly." Ballots shall be so printed as to permit an affirmative or negative vote upon each measure submitted to the electors. Any proposed law or amendment to the constitution submitted to the electors as provided in 1a and 1b, if approved by a majority of the electors voting thereon, shall take effect thirty days after the election at which it was approved and shall be published by the secretary of state. If conflicting proposed laws or conflicting proposed amendments to the constitution shall be approved at the same election by a majority of the total number of votes cast for and against the same, the one receiving the highest number of affirmative votes shall be the law, or in the case of amendments to the constitution shall be the amendment to the constitution. No law proposed by initiative petition and approved by the electors shall be subject to the veto of the governor.

Adopted in 1912 as part of the initiative and referendum amendment proposed by the 1912 Constitutional Convention, and amended in 2008, this section deals with the use of the initiative to enact legislation. The Ohio initiative is known as an "indirect statutory initiative," or simply an "indirect initiative," since petitions to propose new laws must be submitted to the General Assembly before the voters have an opportunity to vote on them. *Pfeifer v. Graves* (1913).

Under this section, a petition proposing a new law must have the signatures of at least 3 percent of the electors based on the total vote cast for governor in the last gubernatorial election, and there is a geographic distribution requirement for these signatures and for signatures on a supplementary petition. See Article II, section 1g. As a result of the high-turnout 2018 gubernatorial election, the number of required initial signatures for an initiated statute will be 132,887 until 2023. See Governors Percentage Chart (2018) (Secretary of State website).

Before beginning to collect signatures, proponents of a statute are required by statutory law to submit to the attorney general an initial petition signed by 1,000 registered voters with the full text of the proposed statute and a summary of it. The attorney general has ten days to determine whether the summary is a "fair and truthful" statement of the proposed law. After the statement is certified as fair and truthful, the attorney general is required to forward the petition to the Ohio Ballot Board for a determination as to whether the petition contains only one proposed law. Only then may the petitioners begin collecting signatures, which they must submit to the secretary of state.

Upon determining that the petition has the requisite number of signatures, the secretary of state transmits it to the General Assembly, which may pass the proposed law and submit it to the governor for signature. If the General Assembly fails to pass the proposed law, passes it in an amended form, or fails to take any action within four months, the proposed law (with or without amendments) may be submitted directly to the voters at the next general election but only after the proponents file a supplementary petition with the secretary of state. The supplementary petition must be filed within ninety days after the General Assembly rejects the proposed law or after four months if the General Assembly takes no action on the proposal. And the supplementary petition must contain the signatures from an additional 3 percent of the votes in the last gubernatorial election.

Of the twenty-one states with a statutory initiative, Ohio is the only one that requires the collection of a substantial number of additional signatures on a supplementary petition as the exclusive way of placing a statutory initiative on the ballot. See OCMC, Constitutional Revision and Updating Committee, *Report and Recommendation*, Article II, sections 1 through 1i, 15(G), and 17 (The Ohio Constitutional and Statutory Initiative) (May 11, 2017), 9.

The governor may veto laws proposed by initiative petition and approved by the General Assembly, but the governor cannot veto laws proposed by initiative petition and approved by the voters. If the governor vetoes a law proposed by initiative and passed by the General Assembly, a supplementary petition cannot be used to put the law on the ballot. In such cases, the proponents of the law can urge the General Assembly to override the veto. Or they can repropose the law (by following the requirements of the statutory initiative) and urge the General Assembly to not pass it. This will open the way for the proponents to submit a supplementary petition and move the proposed statute to the voters.

Laws proposed by initiative and subsequently passed by the General Assembly (in original or amended form) and signed by the governor are subject to the referendum. But laws proposed by initiative and approved by the voters are not. See Commentary, Article II, section 1c.

Ten of the twenty-one states that have the statutory initiative have a "safe harbor" or "anti-tampering" provision that limits the power of the legislature to repeal or to amend a statute adopted by initiative. See National Conference of State Legislatures, *Initiative and Referendum in the 21st Century: Final Report and Recommendations of the NCSL I&R Task Force*, Table 2 (July 2002). Ohio, however, does not have such a provision. Accordingly, the General Assembly may repeal a statute adopted by initiative, but a statute repealing or amending an initiated statute is itself subject to the referendum.

Because of the supplementary signature requirement and the absence of a "safe harbor" provision, the Ohio statutory initiative has rarely been used. In fact, as of 2014, 86.1 percent of all initiatives placed on the ballot in Ohio were constitutional and not statutory initiatives. In the other thirteen states that have both a statutory and a direct constitutional initiative, the constitutional initiative was the initiative of choice in an average of 52.7 percent of all cases, which ranges from 25 to 68.8 percent of all cases. See Jennie Bowser, *Use of the Statutory Initiative vs. the Constitutional Initiative* (2014) (unpublished).

Under an amendment proposed by the General Assembly and approved by the voters in 2008, it will become harder to use the statutory initiative. Under this amendment, a law proposed by the statutory initiative must be submitted to the voters at the next regular or general election occurring subsequent to 125 days (the prior deadline was ninety days) after the filing of the supplementary petition, thus making it difficult to bring a proposed statute to the ballot in a single calendar year. See *Ohio Manufacturers' Association v. Ohioans for Drug Price Relief Act* (2016) (French, J., concurring) ("But neither the people nor the public officials elected to accommodate them can effectively exercise that constitutional power under deadlines and timelines that no longer make sense."). Indeed, since 1912, there have been only eleven statutory initiatives placed on the ballot after the failure of the General Assembly to adopt statutes proposed by the initiative; and the voters have only approved three of them (which were for old age pensions in 1933, colored oleomargarine in 1949, and smoke-free workplaces in 2006).

The disproportionate use of the constitutional as compared to the statutory initiative led a committee of the OCMC in 2017 to recommend the strengthening of the statutory initiative by eliminating the supplementary signature requirement and by adopting a "safe harbor" provision as part of a comprehensive effort to revise Ohio's statutory and constitutional initiatives. But the full commission never addressed the proposal. See Commentary, Article II (introduction).

■ EFFECTIVE DATES AND CONFLICTING AMENDMENTS AND STATUTES

Although primarily concerned with the statutory initiative, this section establishes the effective date for both initiated amendments and initiated statutes as well as the standard for resolving what happens when the voters approve conflicting amendments or statutes.

Unlike constitutional amendments proposed by the General Assembly, which take effect when approved by the voters, see Commentary, Article XVI, section 1, this section provides that both laws and constitutional amendments approved through the initiative take effect thirty days after the election at which the voters approved them. But an initiated amendment and an initiated statute may include a later effective date as long as the effective date is presented to the voters and approved by them. They cannot, however, adopt an earlier effective date. *Cf. State ex rel. Duffy v. Sweeney* (1949) ("The schedule cannot provide for an earlier effective date than that provided in the existing constitutional provisions.").

This section also addresses what happens when the voters approve conflicting amendments or conflicting laws by providing that "the one receiving the highest number of affirmative votes shall be the law, or in the case of amendments to the constitution shall be the amendment to the constitution." This provision has been applied only once, when, in 1918, the voters approved two proposed amendments to Article XII, section 2, concerning the taxation of real property. The Ohio Supreme Court resolved this conflict by holding that the amendment proposed by the General Assembly would take effect over the conflicting amendment proposed by initiative petition since, pursuant to this section, the former received a higher number of affirmative votes. See Appendix B; see also Commentary, Article XII, section 2.

Section 1c

Referendum to challenge laws enacted by General Assembly.

The second aforestated power reserved by the people is designated the referendum, and the signatures of six per centum of the electors shall be required upon a petition to order the submission to the electors of the state for their approval or rejection, of any law, section of any law or any item in any law appropriating money passed by the General Assembly. No law passed by the General Assembly shall go into effect until ninety days after it shall have been filed by the governor in the office of the secretary of state, except as herein provided. When a petition, signed by six per centum of the electors of the state and verified as herein provided, shall have been filed with the secretary of state within ninety days after any law shall have been filed by the governor in the office of the secretary of state, ordering that such law, section of such law or any item in such law appropriating money be submitted to the electors of the state for their approval or rejection, the secretary of state shall submit to the electors of the state for their approval or rejection such law, section or item, in the manner herein provided, at the next succeeding regular or general election in any year occurring subsequent to one hundred twenty-five days after the filing of such petition, and no such law, section or item shall go into effect until and unless approved by a majority of those voting upon the same. If, however, a referendum petition is filed against any such section or item, the remainder of the law shall not thereby be prevented or delayed from going into effect.

Adopted in 1912 as part of the initiative and referendum amendment proposed by the 1912 Constitutional Convention, and amended in 2008, this section reserves to the people the power to approve or reject laws enacted by the General Assembly. In contrast to the initiative, which allows the voters to enact legislation, "the referendum is a right reserved to the people to have any legislative enactment submitted for their approval or rejection, and thus it resembles the executive veto power." Richard A. Chesley, "The Current Use of Initiative and Referendum in Ohio and Other States," 53 *U. Cin. L. Rev.* 541 (1984) (hereinafter Chesley, "The Current Use of Initiative and Referendum").

In 1915, shortly after the adoption of the initiative and referendum, the Ohio Supreme Court described the amendment as "one of the most essential safeguards to representative government." *State ex rel. Nolan v. ClenDening* (1915). It further noted that

> [t]he potential virtue of the "I. & R." does not reside in the good statutes and good constitutional amendments initiated, nor in the bad statutes and bad proposed constitutional amendments that are killed. Rather, the greatest efficiency of the "I. and R." rests in the wholesome restraint imposed automatically upon the general assembly and the governor and the possibilities of that latent power when called into action by the voters.
>
> Ibid.

Under Ohio statutory law, the referendum process begins with those challenging a statute filing an initial petition signed by 1000 registered voters with the secretary of state and the attorney general. The petition must contain the full text of the law being challenged and a summary of it. The secretary of state is charged with verifying the signatures and the attorney general is charged with determining whether the summary is a "fair and truthful statement" of the law being challenged. See O.R.C. section 3519.01(B)(3). The attorney general, however, has no statutory authority to refuse to certify a referendum petition because of a belief that it is not within the scope of the referendum. *State ex rel. Barren v. Brown* (1977).

The Ohio Supreme Court has held that "a single referendum petition may not be filed attacking two or more separate and distinct laws passed by the General Assembly." *State ex rel. Patton v. Myers* (1933) (syllabus).

After the attorney general certifies the summary as "fair and truthful," the challengers may begin collecting signatures; and they must file petitions that are signed by 6 percent of the electors based on the total vote cast for governor in the last gubernatorial election and that meet the geographic distribution requirement. See Article II, section 1g and Commentary.

As a result of the high-turnout 2018 gubernatorial election, the number of required signatures for a referendum will be 221,479 until 2023.

If the petition is filed with the secretary of state with the requisite number of signatures within ninety days after the governor files the law with the secretary of state, the law is suspended until the voters approve it. See Article II, section 16, and Commentary.

In 2007, the Ohio Supreme Court added a judicial gloss to the ninety-day requirement by holding that the time period did not begin to run until the court rendered a decision that treated a disputed bill as having been duly enacted. *State ex rel. Ohio General Assembly v. Brunner* (2007). *But cf. State ex rel. Ohioans for Secure and Fair Elections v. LaRose* (2020) (Kennedy, J., concurring in judgment only) (stating that under "the plain and unambiguous language of Article II, Section 1a . . . an initiative petition to amend the Constitution must be filed 125 days before the next regular or general election in order to appear on that ballot").

The court, however, has not addressed the validity of the legislation (adopted in 1931) that effectively shortened the ninety-day period by requiring referendum petitions to be first filed with the attorney general for a "fair and truthful" determination, but an Ohio Court of Appeals has upheld this legislation. See *Schaller v. Rogers* (2008). But see *State ex rel. Tulley v. Brown* (1972 (Schneider, J., dissenting) (concluding that requiring submission to the attorney general denies petitioners the full ninety-day period).

In October 2019, opponents of Am. H.B. 6 (133rd GA) (2019), which permitted the addition of a monthly charge on all Ohio retail electric bills for seven years, attempted to use the referendum to challenge what they described as a "corporate bailout." The effort to obtain a "fair and truthful" determination consumed thirty-eight of the ninety-day period for collecting signatures, and the opponents filed an action in the U.S. District Court for the Southern District of Ohio alleging that the thirty-eight-day "blackout period" (during which they were not permitted to collect signatures but during which the ninety-day clock was running) violated their rights under the First Amendment to the U.S. Constitution. See *Ohioans against Corporate Bailouts v. LaRose* (2019).

Because the issues in the federal suit depended, at least in part, on the meaning of state law, the district court certified a series of questions to the Ohio Supreme Court, the most important of which asked whether the referendum proponents were entitled to a full ninety days to collect signatures. Ibid. The Ohio Supreme Court initially agreed to answer the certified questions, *Ohioans against Corporate Bailouts v. LaRose* (2019), but the court dismissed the certified question proceeding because of the voluntary dismissal of the federal case, *Ohioans against Corporate Bailouts v. LaRose* (2020).

The right of referendum applies to any law, section of a law, or item in a law appropriating money, except those specifically exempted in sections 1d and 1e. If only part of a law is challenged by referendum, the remaining parts take effect ninety days after the governor files the law with the secretary of state, except for laws providing for taxes, appropriations for current expenses, and emergencies, all of which go into effect immediately upon the governor's signature as provided by section 1d of this article. *State v. Lathrop* (1915). The ninety-day delay gives opponents of the legislation an opportunity to seek a referendum.

The referendum has only been used thirteen times since 1912, but in eleven of these cases the voters voted "no" thus rejecting a duly enacted statute. The two cases in which the voters voted "yes" and thus approved the enacted statute involved statewide prohibition in 1920 and restrictions on payday lending in 2008.

The most prominent recent rejection of a statute through the referendum came in 2011, when the voters rejected a statute designed to limit public sector collective bargaining. And the most spectacular failure to place a referendum on the ballot took place in 2019, when opponents of Am. H.B. 6 attempted to use the referendum to challenge a statute that permitted a monthly charge to be added to all Ohio retail electric bills. Recognizing the popularity of the anti-bailout position, supporters of the legislation mounted an expensive and successful multi-faceted campaign to discourage "bailout" opponents from signing petitions to place the referendum on the ballot.

By the terms of this section, the referendum is limited to laws approved by the General Assembly, and thus it is not applicable to laws proposed by initiative and approved by the voters.

Section 1d

Emergency and other laws not subject to referendum.

Laws providing for tax levies, appropriations for the current expenses of the state government and state institutions, and emergency laws necessary for the immediate preservation of the public peace, health or safety, shall go into immediate effect. Such emergency laws upon a yea and nay vote must receive the vote of two-thirds of all the members elected to each branch of the General Assembly, and the reasons for such necessity shall be set forth in one section of the law, which section shall be passed only upon a yea and nay vote, upon a separate roll call thereon. The laws mentioned in this section shall not be subject to the referendum.

Adopted in 1912 as part of the initiative and referendum amendment proposed by the 1912 Constitutional Convention and never amended, this section identifies three areas of legislation that are exempt from the referendum: tax levies, appropriations for current expenses of state government and state institutions, and emergency laws.

Many states that allow referenda have exemptions for certain kinds of legislation, but Ohio is the only state that explicitly excludes all tax levies. See Chesley, "The Current Use of Initiative and Referendum."

For legislation to be considered a tax levy, the law must be self-executing (i.e., must actually impose a tax) and must state the property subject to taxation, the time it is payable, and the rate of taxation. *State ex rel. Keller v. Forney* (1923).

Legislation that merely "relates to" or "concerns" tax levies is not exempt from referendum. Thus, "an act to revise and codify the laws relating to the levy of taxes, and the issue of bonds by taxing subdivisions, and to establish a budget system for local expenditure" is not a tax levy for the purpose of this section and can be challenged by referendum. And exceptions to the general rule of referendum "must be strictly construed." Ibid. Finally, the court has stated that "[t]he powers of initiative and referendum should be liberally construed to effectuate the rights reserved." *State ex rel. Hodges v. Taft* (1992).

In 2019, the Ohio Supreme Court had an opportunity to address the meaning of the bar on the use of the referendum to challenge "tax levies" in a case in which supporters of Am. H.B. 6 (133rd GA) (2019), which authorized a monthly charge on all Ohio retail electric bills, filed an original action in which they argued that the fees were actually "taxes" and thus were not subject to the referendum. The court, however, dismissed the action because of the "lack of a current controversy for which it has jurisdiction." *FirstEnergy Solutions Corp. v. Ohioans against Corporate Bailouts* (2019).

The inclusion of a section of a bill providing for appropriations of current expenses does not exempt the entire bill from the referendum but only the sections containing appropriations. *State ex rel. Ohio AFL-CIO v. Voinovich* (1994). In *State ex rel. Ohioans for Fair Districts v. Husted* (2011), the Ohio Supreme Court held that a statute that created new congressional districts is subject to referendum despite the inclusion of an appropriation in other sections of the statute. And in *State ex rel. LetOhioVote.org v. Hon. Jennifer Brunner* (2009), the court held that provisions in the state's 2010–11 budget bill authorizing installation of up to 17,500 video lottery terminals at horse racing tracks are subject to a referendum because they do not fall within any of the exceptions to the referendum even though the provisions are part of the state biennial budget bill.

The three cases cited in the above paragraph all involved whether the General Assembly or the secretary of state could prevent the referendum from being used to challenge specific pieces of enacted legislation involving, at least in part, appropriations, and in each case the court, exercising its original jurisdiction, rejected efforts to keep the referendum off the ballot.

The Ohio Supreme Court, however, has not addressed the related issue of whether the court may play a gatekeeper role to keep referenda not authorized by this section off the ballot in the same way it keeps off the ballot-proposed constitutional amendments that violate the "one amendment, separate vote requirement." See Commentary, Article II, section 1g.

In 2019, however, the court had an opportunity to address the gatekeeper issue, but it dismissed the original action in *FirstEnergy Solutions Corp. v. Ohioans against Corporate Bailouts* (2019), because of the "lack of a current controversy for which it has jurisdiction."

Though cryptic, the court's order seemed to treat the controversy as not being ripe until the challengers obtained the requisite number of signatures. And if the court may keep proposed referenda that are barred by this section off the ballot, there is a secondary question as to whether this power should be exercised before the opponents of the legislation are permitted to begin collecting signatures or after the secretary of state has concluded that they have submitted the requisite number of signatures.

To be considered an emergency measure, a law must explicitly state that it is being passed as such, and it must receive a two-thirds vote in each house. The determination of whether a law is an emergency is within the sole discretion of the legislature and is not subject to judicial review. See *State ex rel. Schorr v. Kennedy* (1937) ("[T]he people in their Constitution have made the General Assembly the exclusive arbiter of whether a proposed act is in truth an emergency measure upon a dual affirmative vote of at least two-thirds of the elected members, no court has the power or authority to interfere with the judgment so exercised.").

The Ohio Supreme Court has also applied the prohibition of judicial review to emergency measures enacted by municipalities. See *Youngstown v. Aiello* (1951); see also *State ex rel. Davis Invest. Co. v. Columbus* (1963).

Although tax levies, appropriations for current expenses, and emergency laws are specifically excluded from the referendum, Ohio electors can still challenge specific acts of legislation in these areas by proposing laws that effectively repeal them through the use of the statutory initiative. See OCRC, *Final Report,* 359.

In addition to the state limitations on the use of the referendum set forth in this section, federal law bars the use of the referendum to challenge the legislative ratification of proposed amendments to the U.S. Constitution. See Commentary, Article II, section 1 (introduction), and *Hawke v. Smith* (1920). But federal law does not bar the use of the referendum to give voters an opportunity to challenge congressional redistricting legislation. See *Davis v. Hildebrant* (1915).

Section 1e

Limitations of use of constitutional and statutory initiative.

(A) The powers defined herein as the "initiative" and "referendum" shall not be used to pass a law authorizing any classification of property for the purpose of levying different rates of taxation thereon or of authorizing the levy of any single tax on land or land values or land sites at a higher rate or by a different rule than is or may be applied to improvements thereon or to personal property.

(B)(1) Restraint of trade or commerce being injurious to this state and its citizens, the power of the initiative shall not be used to pass an amendment to this constitution that would grant or create a monopoly, oligopoly, or cartel, specify or determine a tax rate, or confer a commercial interest, commercial right, or commercial license to any person, nonpublic entity, or group of persons or nonpublic entities, or any combination thereof, however organized, that is not then available to other similarly situated persons or nonpublic entities.

(2) If a constitutional amendment proposed by initiative petition is certified to appear on the ballot and, in the opinion of the Ohio ballot board, the amendment would conflict with division (B)(1) of this section, the board shall prescribe two separate questions to appear on the ballot, as follows:

(a) The first question shall be as follows:

"Shall the petitioner, in violation of division (B)(1) of Section 1e of Article II of the Ohio Constitution, be authorized to initiate a constitutional amendment that grants or creates a monopoly, oligopoly, or cartel, specifies or determines a tax rate, or confers a commercial interest, commercial right, or commercial license that is not available to other similarly situated persons?"

(b) The second question shall describe the proposed constitutional amendment.

(c) If both questions are approved or affirmed by a majority of the electors voting on them, then the constitutional amendment shall take effect. If only one question is approved or affirmed by a majority of the electors voting on it, then the constitutional amendment shall not take effect.

(3) If, at the general election held on November 3, 2015, the electors approve a proposed constitutional amendment that conflicts with division (B)(1) of this section with regard to the creation of a monopoly, oligopoly, or cartel for the sale, distribution, or other use of any federal Schedule I controlled substance, then notwithstanding any severability provision to the contrary, that entire proposed constitutional amendment shall not take effect. If, at any subsequent election, the electors approve a proposed constitutional amendment that was proposed by an initiative petition, that conflicts with division (B)(1) of this section, and that was not subject to the procedure described in division (B)(2) of this section, then notwithstanding any severability provision to the contrary, that entire proposed constitutional amendment shall not take effect.

(C) The supreme court of Ohio shall have original, exclusive jurisdiction in any action that relates to this section.

Adopted in 1912 as part of the initiative and referendum amendment proposed by the constitutional convention and amended in 2015, this section initially only placed limitations on the use of the statutory initiative. But in 2015 the voters approved an amendment proposed by the General Assembly to place limitations on the use of the constitutional initiative.

■ LIMITATIONS ON THE STATUTORY INITIATIVE

The original provision, which is now subsection (A), prohibited the use of the statutory initiative to adopt laws that classify different kinds of property at different tax rates or that tax improvements and personal property according to different rules. During the 1912 Constitutional Convention, many delegates, especially those from rural areas, feared that urban voters and supporters of the "single tax" philosophy advanced by Henry George would use the initiative to shift the burden of taxation to rural areas by taxing land at a higher value. See Chesley, "The Current Use of Initiative and Referendum;" see also The History of the Ohio Constitution, *supra* and Commentary, Article XII, section 2.

Although this subsection bars the use of the initiative to adopt nonuniform tax laws, it does not preclude the use of the constitutional initiative to amend this limitation or to adopt constitutional amendments that classify property at nonuniform rates. *Thrailkill v. Smith* (1922). Nor does it prevent the use of the statutory initiative to propose otherwise-proscribed tax measures to the General Assembly. *State ex rel. Durell v. Celebrezze* (1979).

■ LIMITATION ON THE CONSTITUTIONAL INITIATIVE

In 2015, Ohio voters approved a constitutional amendment proposed by the General Assembly to make it more difficult to use the initiative to create monopolies, to determine tax rates, or to confer special benefits on favored groups. See generally Steven H. Steinglass, "Constitutional Revision: Ohio Style," 77 *Ohio St. L. J.* 281 (2016): 326–29 (hereinafter Steinglass, "Constitutional Revision").

This amendment, which added (B) and (C) to section 1e, was widely (and accurately) seen as part of an effort to undercut a proposed initiated amendment to permit the growth, cultivation, manufacture, distribution, and sale of marijuana products for both recreational and medical uses. The marijuana legalization amendment, described by its proponents as an investor-driven initiative, would have given commercial growing licenses to ten groups of investors. Many of its opponents characterized the proposal as an effort to embed a monopoly into the constitution, and the ballot explanation by the Ballot Board so characterized the proposal. See *State ex rel. ResponsibleOhio v. Ohio Ballot Bd.* (2015).

The voters overwhelmingly rejected the marijuana amendment but narrowly approved the antimonopoly amendment. See Appendix B. As a result, the Ohio Constitution now contains its first explicit limitation on the use of the constitutional initiative. But it is not an absolute bar to the proposed amendments that it targets, though it makes their approval less likely.

The antimonopoly provision identifies three categories of initiatives that it seeks to keep off the ballot: (a) amendments that "would grant or create a monopoly, oligopoly, or cartel"; (b) amendments that would "specify or determine a tax rate"; and (c) amendments that would "confer a commercial interest, commercial right, or commercial license . . . that is not then available to other similarly situated persons or nonpublic entities." Article II, section 1e(B)(1).

Under the complex procedures created by this amendment, the Ballot Board must determine whether a proposed amendment conflicts with the new standards. See Article II, section 1e(B)(2). Even if there is a conflict, the proposed amendment may still appear on the ballot, but it will be the second of two separate questions presented to the voters.

The first question will ask the voters:

> Shall the petitioner, in violation of division (B)(1) of Section 1e of Article II of the Ohio Constitution, be authorized to initiate a constitutional amendment that grants or creates a monopoly, oligopoly, or cartel, specifies or determines a tax rate, or confers a commercial interest, commercial right, or commercial license that is not available to other similarly situated persons?
>
> Article II, section 1e(B)(2)(a).

The second question describes the proposed constitutional amendment, and the voters can approve the proposed amendment only by responding affirmatively to both questions. Article II, section 1e(B)(2)(c). Thus, unlike the limitations on the initiative in some states, see, for example, *Wirzburger v. Galvin* (2005) (barring the use of the initiative to amend the Massachusetts constitutional provision that prohibits public financial support for private, religiously affiliated schools), the Ohio limitation creates an obstacle, indeed a high obstacle, so that voters may only approve an otherwise prohibited initiated amendment if they respond affirmatively to the question of whether they want to violate the limitation in this section.

Some states distinguish constitutional amendments from constitutional revisions and only permit the initiative to be used for the former. There is textual support in Ohio for such a classification, but this issue does not appear to have arisen in any Ohio litigation. See generally Steinglass, "Constitutional Revision," 323–25.

■ PROCEDURAL AND SUBSTANTIVE ISSUES

This new antimonopoly constitutional provision raises a number of procedural and substantive issues. The provision does not clearly state whether the Ballot Board must make the "monopoly/tax rate/special benefit" determination early in the process when it is addressing the "one amendment, separate vote requirement," or late in the process after signatures have been submitted and the board is determining what will go on the ballot. In its first review of a proposed amendment after the adoption of the new provision, the Ballot Board took the position that the determination will be made at the end of the process. See Steinglass, "Constitutional Revision," 328 n. 326.

Substantively, it is unclear precisely what is barred. The new provision does not define "monopoly, oligopoly, or cartel," but courts should be able to figure out their meaning. The limitation on initiatives that "specify or determine a tax rate" seems to be unmodified, but the official explanation issued by the Ballot Board described this provision as limiting the use of the initiative to "establish a preferential tax status," presumably based on the limiting language in the final clause of the provision. But it is unclear whether a strict application of the "last-antecedent" rule of construction only limits the "similarly situated" language to the final provisions concerning special benefits or whether it also relates back to the tax provision. What is clear, however, is that proposed initiated amendments that seek to confer special benefits to favored groups (or that seek to establish tax rates) will have to go through a difficult process and will undoubtedly be the subject of litigation.

In addition to framing the issues for the public debate on the proposed marijuana legalization amendment, the antimonopoly amendment expressly provided that it would trump the marijuana amendment had the voters approved both of them. Article II, section 1e(B)(3). But permitting an initiated amendment approved by a lower number of votes (and with a thirty-day delay in its effective date) to prevail over an amendment proposed by the General Assembly that received more votes is inconsistent with the constitutional provision on effective dates. See Article II, section 1b, and Commentary; see also Steinglass, "Constitutional Revision," 326 n. 313. This issue, however, did not have to be addressed by the courts, however, because the voters rejected the marijuana amendment.

Section 1e(C) also gives the Ohio Supreme Court original and exclusive jurisdiction over any actions that relate to this section, but it does not address whether the court may serve as a gatekeeper and provide pre-election judicial review (as it does on the "one amendment, separate vote requirement"), see Commentary, Article II, section 1g, to determine whether the requirements of this section have been met.

Finally, to limit the reach of the antimonopoly provision (and presumably to avoid a conflict with the operators of the four casinos authorized by the 2009 gaming amendment, see Commentary, Art. XV, sec. 6), the amendment to this section included a schedule that provided that the new requirements did not apply to provisions of the constitution in effect prior to the effective date of the antimonopoly provision. See Schedules to the Ohio Constitution.

Section 1f
Initiative and referendum in municipalities.

The initiative and referendum powers are hereby reserved to the people of each municipality on all questions which such municipalities may now or hereafter be authorized by law to control by legislative action; such powers shall be exercised in the manner now or hereafter provided by law.

Adopted in 1912 as part of the initiative and referendum amendment proposed by the 1912 Constitutional Convention and never amended, this section reserves the initiative and referendum to the people of each municipality. The amendment did not, however, extend the initiative and referendum to counties, but in 1933 the voters approved an amendment proposed by initiative petition to extend home rule, including the right of the initiative and referendum, to the people of each county that adopts a county charter. See Commentary, Article X, section 3.

The Ohio Supreme Court has contrasted the use of the initiative to enact legislation under section 1f, which is expressly reserved to the people of each municipality, with the right to adopt and amend a municipal charter under Article XVIII, sections 8 and 9. The more detailed provisions in Article XVIII describe the procedures that municipalities must follow in adopting and amending charters. And under section 9 a board of elections may only put proposed municipal charter amendments on the ballot if the city council passes an ordinance instructing the board to do so. *State ex rel. Maxcy v. Saferin* (2018); see Commentary, Article XVIII, section 9.

Municipal ordinances, even those adopted by initiative, may be repealed or revised by action of the city council (unless the charter provides to the contrary). But charter amendments adopted by the voters may only be repealed or revised by the voters. *State ex rel. Singer v. Cartledge* (1935).

■ ADMINISTRATIVE ACTIONS

The powers of initiative and referendum "reserved to the people of each municipality" are only available on questions that municipalities are "authorized by law to control by legislative action." Thus, actions by local governments that are administrative rather than legislative, such as a city council's approval of a site plan for the construction of low-income housing, cannot be challenged by either initiative or referendum. *Buckeye Community Hope Foundation v. City of Cuyahoga Falls* (1998). "The test for determining whether an action is legislative or administrative is whether the action taken is one enacting a law, ordinance or regulation, or one executing or administering a law, ordinance or regulation already in existence." *Donnelly v. Fairview Park* (1968).

■ PRE-ELECTION SUBSTANTIVE JUDICIAL REVIEW OF BALLOT MEASURES

The Ohio Supreme Court has rejected the availability of pre-election substantive *judicial* review of *statewide* ballot issues, see Commentary, Article II, section 1g, and it has applied the same constitutional principles to deny courts the power to exercise pre-election substantive judicial review of local ballot measures.

In 1921, in describing its hands-off approach to local initiatives, the court explained its rejection of pre-election substantive judicial review of local ballot measures.

> This court has no authority to pronounce a judgment or decree upon the question whether a proposed law or ordinance will be valid and constitutional if enacted by a legislative body or adopted by the electors. And where the mandatory provisions of the Constitution or statute prescribing the necessary preliminary steps to authorize the submission to the electors of an initiative statute or ordinance have been complied with, the submission will not be enjoined.
>
> *City of Cincinnati v. Hillenbrand* (1921) (syllabus).
> See also Commentary, Article XVIII, section 9.

■ GATEKEEPERS

Despite the absence of the power to exercise substantive pre-election judicial review of ballot measures, courts and election officials may keep issues that are not subject to the initiative and referendum off the ballot.

In 1998, the Ohio Supreme Court stated that "[e]lection officials serve as gatekeepers, to ensure that only those measures that actually constitute initiatives or referenda are placed on the ballot." *Buckeye Community Hope Foundation, supra* (internal quotation omitted). And in 2015, the court reaffirmed this position, stating that, "[b]ecause a referendum on an administrative matter is a legal nullity, boards of elections have not only the discretion but an affirmative duty to keep such items off the ballot." *State ex rel. Walker v. Husted* (2015). But the gatekeeper role does not extend to giving election officials "authority to determine whether a ballot measure falls within the scope of the constitutional power of referendum (or initiative) [and] does not permit election officials to sit as arbiters of the legality or constitutionality of a ballot measure's substantive terms." Ibid.

One day after the *Walker* decision, the court in *State ex rel. City of Youngstown v. Mahoning County Board of Elections* (2015) explained more fully the basis for its unwillingness to permit election officials to exercise pre-election substantive judicial review of ballot measures. Identifying the separation of powers problems that would arise if board of elections officials were permitted to serve as even the initial arbiters of the constitutionality of ballot measures, the court stated:

> The boards of elections, however, do *not* have authority to sit as arbiters of the legality or constitutionality of a ballot measure's substantive terms. An unconstitutional amendment may be a proper item for referendum or initiative. Such an amendment becomes void and unenforceable only when declared unconstitutional by a court of competent jurisdiction. Any other conclusion would authorize a board of elections to adjudicate a constitutional question and require this court to affirm its decision even if the court disagreed with the board's conclusion on the underlying constitutional question, so long as the board had not abused its discretion.
>
> Ibid.

Access to the ballot for local initiatives raises issues that are frequently litigated. For example, in April 2018, the court ruled that a county board of elections may not keep a proposed amendment to a municipal charter off the ballot because the board believed that the proposed amendment contained provisions that exceeded the city's legislative power. *State ex rel. Khumprakob v. Mahoning County Board of Elections* (2018). And, less than five months later, the court ruled that a board of elections has no authority to review the substance of a proposed charter amendment and no discretion to block the measure from the ballot based on such a review. *State ex rel. Maxcy v. Saferin* (2018). See also *State ex rel. Abernathy v. Lucas County Board of Elections* (2019) (plurality) ("[A] board of elections has no legal authority to review the substance of a proposed charter amendment [to create a Lake Erie Bill of Rights] and has no discretion to block the measure from the ballot based on an assessment of its suitability.").

Notwithstanding these decisions, the court has not been consistent on when issues may be kept off the ballot. In 2016, it ruled that a county board of elections may refuse to certify a proposed municipal ordinance for the ballot when the ordinance was beyond the scope of the municipality's home rule power, in this case an ordinance that created a fifth-degree felony that imposed no incarceration for the possession or use of marijuana and hashish. *State ex rel. Sensible Norwood v. Hamilton County Board of Elections* (2016). And in 2017, the court, relying on *Sensible Norwood*, held in *State ex rel. Flak v. Betras* that a county board of elections acted properly in keeping off the ballot an amendment to the city charter because it created a private cause of action, a power that the board concluded was beyond the scope of the city's home rule authority. But almost exactly one year later, the court rejected *Flak* and returned to its earlier position that county election officials had no authority to keep a proposed charter provision off the ballot based on its review of whether the proposal was valid under the city's home rule power. *Maxcy v. Saferin* (2018).

At best, what seems to emerge from these cases is a difficult-to-apply distinction that a county board of elections, acting as a gatekeeper, may keep off the ballot measures that are beyond the scope of the initiative but not measures that exceed the home rule power of the municipality. See *State ex rel. McGinn v. Walker* (2017) (Fischer, J., dissenting) (characterizing this distinction as an "unworkable standard" and "unnecessarily confusing").

■ LEGISLATIVE ACTION

In 2016, the General Assembly entered the fray and addressed the scope of the power of county boards of elections to keep proposed issues off the ballot. It did so by *requiring* election officials to provide pre-election substantive review of proposed municipal regulations and proposed county charters or charter amendments. 2016 Sub. H.B. 463. This legislation conflated the "beyond the scope" issue relating to the availability of the initiative with the issue of whether the municipality or the county had the home rule power to enact the underlying ordinance. It then defined "scope of authority" broadly to include both the procedural requirements for an initiative and the underlying substantive requirements of the proposal. See O.R.C. section 3501(M)(1)(a) and (b).

This legislation expressly gives election officials the power to exercise pre-election substantive review over proposed initiated ordinances. But, if applied literally, this delegation of power could result in nonjudicial officers sitting as arbiters of the meaning of state law, a power that arguably belongs only to the judiciary. This enactment will also give the executive branch the power to overturn decisions entrusted to the legislative branch, another potential separation of powers issue, while interfering with the constitutional status of the local initiative under Article II, section 1f.

Some members of the Ohio Supreme Court believe that this enactment is unconstitutional. See *State ex rel. Khumprakob v. Mahoning County Board of Elections* (2018) (Fischer, J., concurring); *State ex rel. Espen v. Wood County Board of Elections* (2017) (plurality) ("To the extent that R.C. 3501.38(M)(1)(a) authorizes and requires boards of elections to make substantive, preenactment legal evaluations, it violates the separation-of-powers doctrine and is unconstitutional."). But the court has not decided this issue.

■ SCOPE OF REVIEW

Courts typically review decisions of administrative bodies, including boards of elections, under a deferential abuse of discretion standard. But permitting election officials to review the constitutionality of proposed ballot measures and only reviewing their decisions under an abuse of discretion standard may impinge on the role of the courts and raise substantial separation of powers issues. See *State ex rel. Twitchell v. Saferin* (2018) (Fischer, J., dissenting) (encouraging the court to consider using a de novo standard of review when reviewing legal determinations made by a board of elections).

In 2019, the U.S. Court of Appeals for the Sixth reversed a federal district court ruling that had held that the absence of a state constitutional or statutory right to de novo judicial review of decisions by boards of elections to keep proposed municipal initiatives off the ballot unreasonably infringed on the First Amendment. *Schmitt v. Husted* (2019). In so ruling, the Sixth Circuit did not question the power of boards of elections to play gatekeeper roles, but the court equated mandamus review with de novo review and treated the availability of the former as providing all the postdeprivation judicial review required by the Due Process Clause of the Fourteenth Amendment.

■ JUDICIAL REVIEW OF BOARD OF ELECTIONS DECISIONS

The burden on those seeking to challenge board of elections decisions concerning municipal ballot issues is compounded by the limited availability of a judicial forum with the power to review such decisions. This can be contrasted with the review available when a county board of elections places or refuses to place a proposed county charter amendment on the ballot. See Commentary, Article X, section 3. In cases involving county charters, Ohio law creates two mutually exclusive statutory procedures for obtaining judicial review. See *State ex rel. Fleming v. Fox* (2019) (Fischer, J., concurring).

But when a municipal charter amendment or other local initiative is proposed, the municipal legislative body has sole statutory authority to determine whether the petition satisfies the requirements for submission to the voters. *State ex rel. Abernathy v. Lucas County Board of Elections* (2019) (plurality). In such cases, those affected by a decision to keep a measure off the ballot may only seek judicial review through an extraordinary writ from the Ohio Supreme Court or an appellate court.

The absence of a statutory procedure for judicial review of decisions concerning the placement of proposed municipal initiatives on the ballot places a burden on those seeking to challenge such decisions. And while the absence of an adequate remedy at law may support the availability of an extraordinary writ, the existence of a clear legal duty is a required element of such writs. Thus, in close cases review may be effectively unavailable. See *State ex rel. Sensible Norwood v. Hamilton County Bd. of Elections* (2016) ("Relators have failed to establish a clear legal right to their requested relief and a clear legal duty on the part of the board to provide it.").

■ ONE PROPOSAL LIMITATIONS

A state statute limiting initiative petitions to "one proposal of law or constitutional amendment," O. R.C. section 3519.01, applies to statewide ballot issues but not to initiatives to amend local charters. *State ex rel. Citizens Action for a*

Livable Montgomery v. Hamilton County Board of Elections (2007). Proposed amendments to county charters, however, must meet a "one subject" requirement, see Article X, section 4, but there is no analogous constitutional requirement for amendments to city charters. Nonetheless, state law provides that "[n]o ordinance, resolution, or bylaw shall contain more than one subject," O.R.C. section 731.19, and many city charters contain "one proposal" or "one subject" limitations. But the Ohio Supreme Court has not addressed the constitutionality of these limitations on local initiatives. *State ex rel. Beard v. Hardin* (2018).

Section 1g

Petition requirements; submission; ballot language; by Ohio ballot board; Ohio Supreme Court.

Any initiative, supplementary, or referendum petition may be presented in separate parts but each part shall contain a full and correct copy of the title, and text of the law, section or item thereof sought to be referred, or the proposed law or proposed amendment to the constitution. Each signer of any initiative, supplementary, or referendum petition must be an elector of the state and shall place on such petition after his name the date of signing and his place of residence. A signer residing outside of a municipality shall state the county and the rural route number, post office address, or township of his residence. A resident of a municipality shall state the street and number, if any, of his residence and the name of the municipality or the post office address. The names of all signers to such petitions shall be written in ink, each signer for himself. To each part of such petition shall be attached the statement of the circulator, as may be required by law, that he witnessed the affixing of every signature. The secretary of state shall determine the sufficiency of the signatures not later than one hundred five days before the election.

The Ohio supreme court shall have original, exclusive jurisdiction over all challenges made to petitions and signatures upon such petitions under this section. Any challenge to a petition or signature on a petition shall be filed not later than ninety-five days before the day of the election. The court shall hear and rule on any challenges made to petitions and signatures not later than eighty-five days before the election. If no ruling determining the petition or signatures to be insufficient is issued at least eighty-five days before the election, the petition and signatures upon such petitions shall be presumed to be in all respects sufficient.

If the petitions or signatures are determined to be insufficient, ten additional days shall be allowed for the filing of additional signatures to such petition. If additional signatures are filed, the secretary of state shall determine the sufficiency of those additional signatures not later than sixty-five days before the election. Any challenge to the additional signatures shall be filed not later than fifty-five days before the day of the election. The court shall hear and rule on any challenges made to the additional signatures not later than forty-five days before the election. If no ruling determining the additional signatures to be insufficient is issued at least forty-five days before the election, the petition and signatures shall be presumed to be in all respects sufficient.

No law or amendment to the constitution submitted to the electors by initiative and supplementary petition and receiving an affirmative majority of the votes cast thereon, shall be held unconstitutional or void on account of the insufficiency of the petitions by which such submission of the same was procured; nor shall the rejection of any law submitted by referendum petition be held invalid for such insufficiency. Upon all initiative, supplementary, and referendum petitions provided for in any of the sections of this article, it shall be necessary to file from each of one-half of the counties of the state, petitions bearing the signatures of not less than one-half of the designated percentage of the electors of such county. A true copy of all laws or proposed laws or proposed amendments to the constitution, together with an argument or explanation, or both, for, and also an argument or explanation, or both, against the same, shall be prepared. The person or persons who prepare the argument or explanation, or both, against any law, section, or item, submitted to the electors by referendum petition, may be named in such petition and the persons who prepare the argument or explanation, or both, for any proposed law or proposed amendment to the constitution may be named in the petition proposing the same. The person or persons who prepare the argument or explanation, or both, for the law, section, or item, submitted to the electors by referendum petition, or against any proposed law submitted by supplementary petition, shall be named by the General Assembly, if in session, and if not in session then by the governor. The law, or proposed law, or proposed amendment to the constitution, together with the arguments and explanations, not exceeding a total of three hundred words for each, and also the arguments and explanations, not exceeding a total of three hundred words against each, shall be published once a week for three consecutive weeks preceding the election, in at least one newspaper of general circulation in each county of the state, where a newspaper is published. The secretary of state shall cause to be placed upon the ballots, the ballot language for any such law, or proposed law, or proposed amendment to the constitution, to be submitted. The ballot language shall be prescribed by the Ohio ballot board in the same manner, and subject to the same terms and conditions, as apply to issues submitted by the General Assembly pursuant to Section 1 of Article XVI of this constitution. The ballot language shall be so prescribed and the secretary of state shall cause the ballots so to be printed as to permit an affirmative or negative vote upon each law, section of law, or item in a law appropriating money, or proposed law, or proposed amendment to the constitution. The style of all laws submitted by initiative and supplementary petition shall be: "Be it Enacted by the People of the State of Ohio," and of all constitutional amendments: "Be it Resolved by the People of the State of Ohio." The basis upon which the required number of petitioners in any case shall be determined shall be the total number of votes cast for the office of governor at the last preceding election therefor. The foregoing provisions of this section shall be self-executing, except as herein otherwise provided. Laws may be passed to facilitate their operation, but in no way limiting or restricting either such provisions or the powers herein reserved.

Adopted in 1912 as part of the initiative and referendum amendment proposed by the 1912 Constitutional Convention and amended in 1971, 1978, and 2008, this section contains the detailed procedural requirements for the initiative and referendum.

The 1971 amendment replaced the requirement that the secretary of state mail the proposed amendment or law and other information to each elector with the current requirement that the proposed amendment or law, together with explanations and arguments for and against the proposal, be published in at least one newspaper of general circulation in each county once a week for three consecutive weeks preceding the election.

The 1978 amendment gave the Ohio Ballot Board, which had been created in 1974, responsibility for prescribing ballot language for initiated amendments "in the same manner, and subject to the same terms and conditions, as apply to issues submitted by the General Assembly" under Article XVI, section 1. See Commentary, Article XVI, section 1. And the 2008 amendment established earlier filing deadlines for statewide ballot issues and expanded the original jurisdiction of the Ohio Supreme Court.

■ SIGNATURES

Petitions may be circulated in parts as long as each part contains a full and correct copy of the title and the text of the item for which signatures are sought. "Each signer of any initiative, supplementary, or referendum petition must be an elector of the state . . . ."—that is, a person meeting the qualifications entitling a person to vote. See Article V, section 1.

This section includes a geographic distribution requirement under which there must be signatures on "all initiative, supplementary, and referendum petitions" from not less than half of the "designated percentage" of the electors from each of forty-four counties (which is one-half of the counties in the state) based on the total number of votes cast for governor in each county in the last gubernatorial election.

The "designated percentage" refers to the percentage required for the particular petition (10 percent to propose a constitutional amendment, 6 percent to submit a law to referendum, 3 percent to propose a new law, and an additional 3 percent to move a proposed statute to the ballot). The requirement that petitions must contain a designated number of signatures from electors in at least one-half of the counties in the state stems from a fear that the initiative and referendum could be used to permit urban counties to control rural ones. See Chesley, "The Current Use of Initiative and Referendum."

In 1975, the OCRC recommended the repeal of the geographic distribution requirement because of concerns about its consistency with the "one man, one vote" principle. See OCRC, *Final Report*, 368–69. But the General Assembly did not include this proposal in the amendment that went to the voters in 1978.

Of the eighteen states that currently have either a direct or indirect constitutional initiative, Ohio is one of ten with a geographic distribution requirement, but it is one of only three with a distribution requirement tied to counties. See *Book of the States, "Constitutional Amendment Procedure: By Initiative, Constitutional Provisions,"* 2018, Table 1.4.

Sections 1a, 1b, 1c, and 1g require petition-signers to be "electors" and to include their place of residence on the petition, but these sections do not expressly provide that electors who sign petitions must also be *registered* voters. Ohio law, on the other hand, requires that those *signing* petitions be registered voters. See O.R.C. section 3503.06(B).

Ohio did not have mandatory statewide voter registration until 1978, and in 1912 (when the voters approved sec. 1g) state law required voter registration in less than one-fourth of Ohio counties. See Article V, section 1, and Commentary. Thus, it is difficult to reconcile the statutory requirement that petition-signers be registered voters (as contrasted to electors with the ability to register) with the text and history of section 1g, but proponents of the voter registration requirement will likely argue that the voter registration requirement should be upheld under this section as facilitating legislation. See *infra* (Self-Executing Provisions and Facilitating Legislation).

Section 1g requires that circulators attach a statement to the petition attesting to the fact that they "witnessed the affixing of every signature." But it does not, by its terms, require that persons circulating petitions be electors.

The U.S. Supreme Court has held that states may not require petition-circulators for proposed initiatives to be registered electors, *Buckley v. American Constitutional Law Foundation* (1999), and the Ohio Supreme Court has recognized that the statutory provision requiring circulators to be *registered* electors could not be enforced, *State ex rel. Oster v. Lorain County Board of Elections* (2001).

In 2008, the U.S. Court of Appeals for the Sixth Circuit held that the petition-circulator residency requirement (in cases involving access to the ballot by third-party presidential candidates) violated the First Amendment. *Nader v. Blackwell* (2008). And in 2015 a federal district court held that the First Amendment also barred the application of a petition-circulator residency requirement to petitions for initiated amendments. *Citizens in Charge, Inc. v. Husted* (2015).

Under state law, signatures must be valid when made. See O.R.C. 3501.38 ("The facts of qualification shall be determined as of the date when the petition is filed."), but nothing in this section requires petitions to be submitted within any definite time period. And in 1913 the attorney general so advised a prosecuting attorney who had been asked by the Ohio Woman's Suffrage Association whether signatures secured in 1913 would be valid in a petition filed in 1914. See 1913 OAG Opinion 1116 (January 10, 1913).

Ohio is one of only three states without a limitation on how long signatures remain valid, see National Conference of State Legislatures, *Initiative and Referendum in the 21st Century: Final Report and Recommendations of the NCSL I&R Task Force,* Table 11 (Circulation Periods) (July 2002), but the requirement that signatures must be valid when the petition is filed discourages long delays in the filing of old petitions that are likely to include stale signatures.

■ SELF-EXECUTING PROVISIONS AND FACILITATING LEGISLATION

Section 1g provides that "the foregoing provisions of this section shall be self-executing." A self-executing provision is one that contains "more than a mere framework, and specifically provides for carrying into immediate effect the enjoyment of the rights established therein without [further] legislative action." *In re Protest Filed by Citizens for the Merit Selection of Judges, Inc.* (1990).

The delegates to the 1912 Constitutional Convention drafted section 1g to include as many details as possible. Although the initiative and referendum sharply divided the delegates, both those who opposed the proposal and those who supported it did not want to leave the details to the General Assembly. The opponents sought to include as many restrictions as possible to limit the number of petitions and thus protect the legislative process. Those in favor thought the absence of detailed constitutional requirements would allow the General Assembly to enact laws that would severely curtail the use of the initiative and referendum. See OCRC, *Final Report,* 366.

Notwithstanding this disagreement, the delegates recognized the need for legislation to fill in details concerning the initiative and referendum, and section 1g permits the General Assembly to pass laws "to facilitate" the operation of the initiative and referendum "but in no way limiting or restricting either such provisions or the powers herein reserved."

The Ohio Supreme Court has provided only limited guidance on how to determine whether statutes go beyond "facilitating" the operation of the initiative and referendum and "limit" or "restrict" these powers. But in 2016, the court adopted the reasoning (but not necessarily the result) of the Tenth District Court of Appeals decision in *Schaller v. Rogers* (2008), and stated that "[a] statute facilitates the initiative process if the purpose of the requirement is 'not to restrict the power of the people to vote or to sign petitions, but to ensure the integrity of and confidence in the process.'" *State ex rel. Ethics First—You Decide Ohio Political Action Committee v. DeWine* (2016).

The appellate court in *Schaller* reviewed the statutes that had been adopted since 1929 under the authority of the facilitating provision. And in the case before it, the court upheld the oft-amended statute, which requires those using the referendum to submit a summary of the challenged law to the Attorney General. Until the attorney general (who has ten business days to act) determined that the summary was a "fair and truthful" statement of the challenged law, the opponents could not begin collecting signatures. In upholding this requirement, the *Schaller* court treated the "fair and truthful" requirement as facilitating the referendum even though it took time away from the ninety-day period for collecting signatures.

The statutory requirement for obtaining a "fair and truthful" determination also applies to constitutional and statutory initiatives, but the time constraints under the referendum (caused by the fact that a law subject to referendum does not go into effect if the requisite number of signatures are obtained within the ninety-day period) are not as impactful for constitutional and statutory initiatives. Thus, the Ohio Supreme Court could reject the application of the "fair and truthful" requirement to referendum petitions (or modify the time limit for them) but leave intact its application to constitutional and statutory initiatives.

■ ONE AMENDMENT, SEPARATE VOTE REQUIREMENT

This section does not contain an explicit one amendment, separate vote requirement like the one in Article XVI, section 1, which by its terms applies only to amendments proposed by the General Assembly. But in 1931 in *State ex rel. Hubbell v. Bettman*, the Ohio Supreme Court distinguished petition from ballot requirements and held that an initiative petition for a constitutional amendment "may propose several separate and distinct amendments . . . even though they do not all relate to the same subject matter" as long as "the individual voters may vote separately upon each separate proposal" (syllabus). *Hubbell* involved a petition that contained twenty-six proposed amendments of fifteen sections of the constitution. In 1978, the General Assembly proposed and the voters approved a cryptic amendment to this section that focused on the ballot language and sought to apply the requirements for amendments proposed by the General Assembly to the ballot language for amendments proposed by initiative petition.

> The ballot language shall be prescribed by the Ohio ballot board in the same manner, and subject to the same terms and conditions, as apply to issues submitted by the General Assembly pursuant to Section 1 of Article XVI of this constitution. The ballot language shall be so prescribed and the secretary of state shall cause the ballots so to be printed as to permit an affirmative or negative vote upon each . . . proposed amendment to the constitution.
>
> Article II, section 1g.

In 2006, the General Assembly enacted a statute that rejected the holding in *State ex rel. Hubbell v. Bettman* (1931) and provided that an initiative petition could contain only one proposed amendment. See O.R.C. section 3519.01(A); see also O.R.C. section 3505.062(A) (requiring the Ballot Board to review an initiative petition "to determine whether it contains only one proposed . . . constitutional amendment so as to enable the voters to vote on a proposal separately").

In 2010, in *State ex rel. Ohio Liberty Council v. Brunner* (2010), the Ohio Supreme Court had an opportunity to address whether the 1978 amendment made the one amendment, separate vote requirement applicable to amendments proposed by initiative petition. In holding that the Ballot Board had acted inappropriately in dividing a proposed initiated amendment concerning healthcare into two separate amendments, the court equated the constitutional and statutory requirements. "Because this [statutory] separate-petition requirement is comparable to the separate-vote requirement for legislatively initiated constitutional amendments under Section 1, Article XVI of the Ohio Constitution, our precedent construing the constitutional provision is instructive in construing the statutory requirement." Ibid.

In so ruling, it is unclear whether the court interpreted this section to apply the one amendment, separate vote requirement to initiative petitions, or whether it implicitly concluded that the application of the statutory one amendment, separate vote requirement to initiated amendments was valid facilitating legislation.

The court revisited this issue in *State ex rel. Ethics First—You Decide Ohio Political Action Committee v. DeWine* (2016), and it appeared to treat the application of the statutory one amendment, separate vote requirement to initiated constitutional amendments as valid facilitating legislation. In so ruling, however, the court distinguished the collection of signatures for multiple amendments on a single petition from the requirement that the voters be given the opportunity to vote on multiple amendments on separate ballots. Thus, *Ethics First* does not reject the constitutional basis of the court's decision in *State ex rel. Hubbell v. Bettman* (1931).

Finally, in *State ex rel. Ohioans for Secure and Fair Elections v. LaRose* (2020) (plurality) (per curiam), a case involving an initiative petition that had proposed several changes in voting requirements, the court had an opportunity to remove any confusion about the source of the one amendment, separate vote requirement. But its per curiam opinion disposed of the case without attracting a majority of the court, and the case illustrates the deep split on the court on these issues. See ibid. (Kennedy, J., concurring in judgment only) ("reject[ing] the conclusion reached in *Ohio Liberty Council* that each constitutional amendment proposed by the people is restricted to a single subject" and arguing that *Ohio Liberty Council* should be overruled).

On the merits, the court's disposition of *Secure and Fair Elections* relied upon the standards used under both Article XVI and the Ohio Revised Code and concluded that the proposed voting-related amendments to Article V, section 1, had a single subject, purpose, or object, and thus could be included in one petition for the collection of signatures and on a single ballot.

■ MAJORITY VOTE REQUIREMENT

To avoid the problem that existed under the 1851 Constitution when proposed amendments were only approved if they received a majority of all votes at the election, this section provides that voter approval of an amendment only requires a majority of those voting on the particular amendment. See The History of the Ohio Constitution, *supra*.

■ PRE-ELECTION SUBSTANTIVE JUDICIAL REVIEW

The Ohio Supreme Court has historically declined to provide pre-election *substantive* judicial review of proposed initiated statutes and proposed initiated constitutional amendments. For example, a year after the adoption of the initiative, the court in the landmark case of *Pfeifer v. Graves* (1913) stated in the syllabus that "This court has no authority to pronounce an opinion, a judgment, or a decree upon a mere moot question as to whether a proposed law will conflict with the Constitution, if it shall be enacted by the General Assembly, or be adopted by the people." The *Pfeifer* court further reasoned that such an intervention in the legislative process is outside and independent of the court's authority. See also *Weinland v. Fulton* (1918) ("In an action to enjoin the Secretary of State from submitting for the approval or rejection of the electors a constitutional amendment proposed by petition . . . a court cannot consider or determine whether such proposed amendment is in conflict with the Constitution of the United States.").

And in 1983, the court reaffirmed its unwillingness to provide pre-election substantive judicial review. "It is well-settled that this court will not consider, in an action to strike an issue from the ballot, a claim that the proposed amendment would be unconstitutional if approved, such claim being premature." *State ex rel. Cramer v. Brown* (1983).

Despite its unwillingness to provide pre-election substantive judicial review of proposed ballot measures, the court has served as a gatekeeper to assure that the *procedural* prerequisites of placing issues on the statewide ballot are met. For example, in 1972 the court enforced the one amendment, separate vote requirement to keep off the ballot amendments proposed by the General Assembly that violated this requirement. *State ex rel. Roahrig v. Brown* (1972). See also Article VI, section 2, and Commentary (discussing *Roahrig*).

And the court has also played a gatekeeper role for proposed constitutional conventions; in 1897, it refused to put on the ballot an amendment proposed by the General Assembly because the joint resolution that called for a convention included provisions that could only be adopted by statute. *State ex rel. Attorney General v. Kinney*. See Commentary, Article XVI, section 1.

■ SUPREME COURT REVIEW

The 1978 amendment provided the Ohio Supreme Court with original and exclusive jurisdiction "over all challenges made to petitions and signatures upon such petitions under this section." It also created a new cause of action to challenge (i.e., oppose) signatures and petitions. This new cause of action, however, does not extend to challenges to other decisions by the secretary of state or county boards of elections, such as decisions to *reject* petitions, but those challenges can still be brought in extraordinary writs under the court's original (but not exclusive) jurisdiction. *State ex rel. Jones v. Husted* (2016) (*Jones I*).

The grant of original and exclusive jurisdiction in this section applies to statewide ballot issues, including constitutional and statutory initiatives and referenda. *Ohio Manufacturers' Assn. v. Ohioans for Drug Price Relief Act* (2016). But by its terms it does not appear to apply to local initiatives.

Section 1g also contains an earlier (not later than ninety-five days before the election) and more detailed set of deadlines for hearing such cases than is in the grant of original and exclusive jurisdiction in Article XVI, section 1, in cases challenging the adoption or submission of constitutional amendments proposed by the General Assembly. See Commentary, Article XVI, section 1.

The Ohio Supreme Court has adopted a special set of rules to provide expeditious consideration of election cases that are filed within ninety days of elections. See S. Ct. Prac. R 12.08(A)(1) (Expedited Election Cases) (first adopted in 1994). But the court has sought to avoid manipulation of the rules by assuming the existence of prejudice for purposes of a laches defense when a delay in the filing of a petition brings the case within the ninety-day period. *State ex rel. Duclos v. Hamilton County Board of Elections* (2016).

Section 2

Election and terms of legislators.

Representatives shall be elected biennially by the electors of the respective House of Representatives districts; their term of office shall commence on the first day of January next thereafter and continue two years.

Senators shall be elected by the electors of the respective senate districts; their terms of office shall commence on the first day of January next after their election. All terms of senators which commence on the first day of January, 1969 shall be four years, and all terms which commence on the first day of January, 1971 shall be four years. Thereafter, except for the filling of vacancies for unexpired terms, senators shall be elected to and hold office for terms of four years.

No person shall hold the office of State Senator for a period longer than two successive terms of four years. No person shall hold the office of State Representative for a period longer than four successive terms of two years. Terms shall be considered successive unless separated by a period of four or more years. Only terms beginning on or after January 1, 1993 shall be considered in determining an individual's eligibility to hold office.

In determining the eligibility of an individual to hold office in accordance to this article, (A) time spent in an office in fulfillment of a term to which another person was first elected shall not be considered provided that a period of at least four years passed between the time, if any, in which the individual previously held that office, and the time the individual is elected or appointed to fulfill the unexpired term; and (B) a person who is elected to an office in a regularly scheduled general election and resigns prior to the completion of the term for which he or she was elected, shall be considered to have served the full term in that office.

Section 2 deals primarily with the length and number of terms for state representatives and senators. Originally, the 1802 Constitution set the terms of office for representatives at one year and senators at two years. With the adoption of the 1851 Constitution, section 2 extended the terms of both representatives and senators to two years.

Following the pattern set in the 1802 Constitution, see 1802 Constitution, Article I, section 3, the 1851 Constitution continued to provide that election day would be "the second Tuesday of October," see 1802 Constitution, Article II, section 1, but in 1885 the General Assembly proposed and the voters approved three separate amendments moving election day to the "first Tuesday after the first Monday in November." See Article, II, section 2. The amendment to this section moved the date of election for both senators and representatives. The other amendments approved in 1885 also established the November date for the election of state officers, Article III, section 1, and county officers, Article X, section 2.

In 1956, the General Assembly proposed and the voters approved the extension of senate terms to four years with the terms of house members remaining two years. And in 1967, the voters approved a technical amendment proposed by the General Assembly to eliminate some of the transitional language and make clear that one-half the senators shall stand for election every two years.

In 1992, the voters approved an amendment proposed by initiative petition to limit the terms of state senators to "two successive terms of four years" and the terms of state representatives to "four successive terms of two years." These are chamber-specific consecutive term limits not lifetime term limits, and Ohio legislators who are term-limited in one chamber may run for the other chamber. In addition, term-limited senators and representatives may run again for a term in their current chamber after a four-year hiatus. As a result of the adoption of this provision, forty-five members of the Ohio House and six members of the Ohio Senate were term-limited in 2000 and thus barred from running for the chamber in which they had been serving. The last paragraph of the section concerns the method for determining time in office.

Ohio is one of fifteen states that have legislative term limits embedded in their state constitutions. See National Conference of State Legislatures, *Term-Limited States.* In fourteen of these states, including Ohio, the constitutional initiative was used to adopt legislative term limits.

Section 3

Residence requirements for state legislators.

Senators and representatives shall have resided in their respective districts one year next preceding their election, unless they shall have been absent on the public business of the United States, or of this state.

Adopted in 1851 and amended in 1967, this section deals with the residency requirement for state legislators. It mandates that senators and representatives reside in the district they represent for one year preceding their election to office unless they were absent on public business with the state of Ohio or the United States. The original version of this section allowed legislators to meet the residency requirement if they lived outside their district but within the county in which their district was located. The 1967 amendment made residency by senators in their districts mandatory.

Section 4

Dual office and conflict of interest prohibited.

No member of the General Assembly shall, during the term for which he was elected, unless during such term he resigns therefrom, hold any public office under the United States, or this state, or a political subdivision thereof; but this provision does not extend to officers of a political party, notaries public, or officers of the militia or of the United States armed forces.

No member of the General Assembly shall, during the term for which he was elected, or for one year thereafter, be appointed to any public office under this state, which office was created or the compensation of which was increased, during the term for which he was elected.

Adopted as part of the Ohio Constitution in 1851 and amended in 1973, this section has two parts. The first prohibits members of the General Assembly from holding public offices other than those specifically named. The original version prohibited state legislators from holding offices under the authority of the United States or "any lucrative office" of this state, but it did not apply to township officers, justices of the peace, notaries, or officers of the militia. The 1973 amendment, which was recommended by the OCRC, see OCRC, *Final Report*, 97–102, proposed by the General Assembly and approved by the voters eliminated the ambiguous modifier "lucrative" and changed the offices exempted from the prohibition.

This prohibition against holding more than one public office is designed to prevent conflicts of interest. In determining whether an office is deemed public, the courts have held that the defining characteristic is the exercise of some portion of the state's sovereign power. *State ex rel. Meshel v. Keip* (1981). A person exercises sovereign power and is therefore considered a public officer where "specific statutory and independent duties are imposed upon . . . in relation to the exercise of the police powers of the state, if the [officer] is invested with independent power in the disposition of public property or with power to incur financial obligations upon the part of the county or state, [or] if [the person] is empowered to act in those multitudinous cases involving business or political dealings between individuals and the public, wherein the latter must necessarily act through an official agency." *State ex rel. Landis v. Board of County Commissioners* (1917). Clerical and ministerial duties are generally not considered an exercise of sovereign power. A county clerk whose duties are clerical does not hold a public office, ibid., nor do members of a state rail authority controlling board that has only limited authority by statute to manage the internal operations of the authority's budget and appropriation process. *Keip, supra.*

The second part of this section, which was added in 1973, was borrowed with slight modification from section 19 of this article (which was repealed in 1973). It forbids the appointment of members of the General Assembly to public offices that were either created or that had an increase in compensation during a member's term and the year thereafter. A similar prohibition was included in Article I, section 20, of the 1802 Constitution to prevent the General Assembly from using its broad appointment powers to create offices and increase salaries of existing offices as a "logrolling technique." See OCRC, *Final Report*, 39.

Under the 1802 Constitution, the General Assembly chose the secretary of state, treasurer, auditor, judges, chief military officers, and U.S. senators. The governor had no constitutional right of appointment (except when the General Assembly was in recess) and no veto power, so this provision prevented the General Assembly from using its powers to create offices and increase salaries as political favors. Given the prohibition from holding offices in the first part of this section and the significant restrictions on the General Assembly's powers of appointment, see Article II, section 27, this section has little impact today. The Seventeenth Amendment to the U.S. Constitution provided for the election of senators by popular vote; Article II, section 27 of the Ohio Constitution took from the General Assembly the power to make appointments; and amendments to Articles III and IV made the secretary of state, treasurer, auditor, and judges elected officers. See OCRC, *Final Report*, 38–40.

Section 5

Who shall not hold office.

No person hereafter convicted of an embezzlement of the public funds, shall hold any office in this state; nor shall any person, holding public money for disbursement, or otherwise, have a seat in the General Assembly, until he shall have accounted for, and paid such money into the treasury.

Adopted in 1851 and never amended, this section is based on Article I, section 28 and Article IV, section 4 of the 1802 Constitution. This section provides that no person convicted of embezzlement of public funds may hold public office in Ohio. In addition, no person holding public money for disbursement may serve in the General Assembly until he or she has accounted for such money. This section specifically forbids only convicted embezzlers of public funds from holding public office, but the General Assembly has expanded the prohibition to include any person who has used a public office to steal or embezzle government property. O.R.C. section 2921.41.

In 1971, the OCRC recommended the repeal of this provision, see OCRC, *Final Report,* 103–4, and in 1972 the General Assembly proposed an amendment to that effect. But the joint resolution contained two other unrelated proposed amendments, and the Ohio Supreme Court struck it from the ballot for violating the one amendment, separate vote requirement. *State ex rel. Roahrig v. Brown* (1972). In 1973, the General Assembly again recommended the repeal of this section, this time in a stand-alone ballot measure, but the voters rejected the proposal by more than a 3:2 margin. See Appendix B.

Section 6
Powers of each house.

Each house shall be the judge of the election, returns, and qualifications of its own members. A majority of all the members elected to each house shall be a quorum to do business; but, a less number may adjourn from day to day, and compel the attendance of absent members, in such manner, and under such penalties, as shall be prescribed by law.

Each house may punish its members for disorderly conduct and, with the concurrence of two-thirds of the members elected thereto, expel a member, but not the second time for the same cause. Each house has all powers necessary to provide for its safety and the undisturbed transaction of its business, and to obtain, through committees or otherwise, information affecting legislative action under consideration or in contemplation, or with reference to any alleged breach of its privileges or misconduct of its members, and to that end to enforce the attendance and testimony of witnesses, and the production of books and papers.

Adopted in 1851, the first part of this section is derived from Article I, section 8, of the 1802 Constitution and is similar in many respects to Article I, section 5, of the U.S. Constitution. The current section provides that each house of the General Assembly may judge the election, qualification, and returns of its members. All business must be performed with a quorum, which consists of a majority of members of the respective house, but the General Assembly may adopt rules that permit a lesser number to compel members to attend.

The balance of this section was originally in Article II, section 8, of the 1851 Constitution, but it was moved to this section as part of the 1973 reorganization of Article II. Under this provision, each house of the General Assembly may punish its members for disorderly conduct and, with a two-thirds vote, expel a member, but a member may not be expelled a second time for the same cause.

On June 16, 2021, the Ohio House of Representatives exercised its power under this section for the first time since 1857, and by a 75–21 vote expelled House Speaker Larry Householder, who had been indicted (but not convicted) for his role in an alleged $61 million bribery scheme linked to a billion-dollar bailout of two nuclear power plants.

In 1912, the voters approved a revision in the original version of section 8 to add the final provision giving each house the power "to obtain, through committees or otherwise, information affecting legislative action under consideration or in contemplation, or with reference to any alleged breach of its privileges or misconduct of its members, and to that end to enforce the attendance and testimony of witnesses, and the production of books and papers." This language was transferred to the new section 6 in 1973.

Section 7

Organization of the House of Representatives and Senate.

The mode of organizing each House of the General Assembly shall be prescribed by law.

Each house, except as otherwise provided in this constitution, shall choose its own officers. The presiding officer in the Senate shall be designated as president of the Senate and in the House of Representatives as speaker of the House of Representatives.

Each house shall determine its own rules of proceeding.

Adopted in 1851, and amended in the 1973 reorganization of this article, this section originally dealt only with the organization of the House of Representatives and provided that the "mode of organizing the house of representatives, at the commencement of each regular session, shall be prescribed by law." The 1973 amendment referred to both houses, identifying the presiding officers of each and further providing that each house shall determine its own rules of proceeding. Rules governing legislative procedures that are not part of the constitution are entirely within the control of the General Assembly, and violations of such rules are not subject to judicial review. *State ex rel. City Loan & Savings Co. of Wapakoneta v. Moore* (1931).

The second and third paragraphs borrow most of their language from Article II, section 8, of the 1851 Constitution.

Procedures for the organization of the House of Representatives and the Senate are contained in chapter 101 of the Ohio Revised Code. Section 101.02 covers the election of officers in the Senate, and section 101.13 covers the election of House officers. These statutes provide that after members-elect have taken the oath of office and a quorum is present, the members of each branch shall elect their respective officers. Chapter 101 also includes procedures for compelling the attendance of members, in section 101.24, and journal requirements, in section 101.61.

Section 8

Regular and special session of General Assembly.

Each General Assembly shall convene in first regular session on the first Monday of January in the odd-numbered year, or on the succeeding day if the first Monday of January is a legal holiday, and in second regular session on the same date of the following year. Either the governor, or the presiding officers of the General Assembly chosen by the members thereof, acting jointly, may convene the General Assembly in special session by a proclamation which may limit the purpose of the session. If the presiding officer of the Senate is not chosen by the members thereof, the President pro tempore of the Senate may act with the speaker of the House of Representatives in the calling of a special session.

Adopted in 1973 and never amended, this section defines the regular and special sessions of the General Assembly. The history of legislative sessions in Ohio is somewhat confusing. Under the 1802 Constitution, the General Assembly met annually, but the 1851 Constitution sought to reduce the power of the General Assembly by creating biennial sessions. In 1857 and 1859, however, the voters rejected proposed amendments that would have reinstated annual sessions of the General Assembly.

Notwithstanding the rejection of annual sessions by the voters, by 1857 the General Assembly was again meeting in annual sessions through a parliamentary device; they would "recess" at the end of the regular session and a second session would be held in "adjournment" during the second year. *State ex rel. Hodges v. Taft* (1992). This practice continued until the 1973 adoption of this section to conform the constitution to the prevailing practice. The new section created annual sessions of the General Assembly by convening the first regular session in odd-numbered years, and by providing for a second regular session in the following year.

■ SPECIAL SESSIONS

The second part of this section addresses how special sessions are convened. Before 1973, only the governor, in accordance with Article III, section 8, could call special sessions of the General Assembly. The 1973 amendment to this section allows either the governor or the presiding officers of both houses, acting jointly, to convene special sessions. Unlike special sessions convened by proclamation of the governor, the proclamation convening special sessions under this section need not limit the purpose of the session.

The delegation to the General Assembly of the power to convene special sessions came largely in response to a report of the Citizens Conference on State

Legislatures in the early 1970s. The report ranked Ohio forty out of the fifty states in the control the legislature had over its own activities and in its independence from the other branches of government. One of the reasons given in the report was the General Assembly's lack of power to call special sessions, and this change was among the recommendations of the OCRC approved by the voters. See OCRC, *Final Report*, 111.

As a result of the 1953 amendment, the holding of special sessions, sometimes pejoratively referred to as lame-duck sessions, is now a common practice.

Section 9

House and Senate journals.

Each house shall keep a correct journal of its proceedings, which shall be published. At the desire of any two members, the yeas and nays shall be entered upon the journal; and, on the passage of every bill, in either house, the vote shall be taken by yeas and nays, and entered upon the journal.

Adopted in 1851 and amended in 1973, this section is based on Article I, section 9, of the 1802 Constitution. The 1973 amendment simply removed the last clause from the 1851 version, which had provided that "no law shall be passed, in either house, without the concurrence of a majority of all the members elected thereto," and incorporated it, with slight modification, into section 15 of this article.

This section ensures that proper procedures are followed in enacting legislation. The clerks of each house are responsible for keeping daily records of the proceedings, which, under statute, must be read and corrected in their presence. O.R.C. section 101.54. Journal provisions similar to section 9 are in Article I, section 5, of the U.S. Constitution.

Legislative journals are conclusive evidence of the passage of a bill and control over the subsequent reporting of an act, *Ritzman v Campbell* (1915), and over parole evidence (i.e., contemporaneous oral evidence) that calls the passage of a law into question. *State ex rel. Herron v. Smith* (1886). A bill that is not recorded in the legislative journals as it is passed cannot be sustained as law. *Burke v. City of Cincinnati* (1900).

This section also calls for the entry of "yeas and nays" on the passage of any bill. This allows for the legislative records to reflect roll call votes on all bills that passed either house. In addition, any two members may require the legislative records to reflect the votes on bills that did not pass.

Section 10

Rights of members to protest.

Any member of either house shall have the right to protest against any act or resolution thereof; and such protest, and the reasons therefor, shall, without alteration, commitment, or delay, be entered upon the journal.

Adopted in 1851 and never amended, this section is based on Article I, section 10 of the 1802 Constitution, which guaranteed members the right to protest an act or resolution and have it immediately recorded without alteration in the legislative journal. Common in the early nineteenth century (but with no equivalent in the U.S. Constitution), this provision allowing members of the General Assembly to publicize their objections seems curiously outdated, and only a few states still have similar provisions in their constitutions. See OCRC, *Commission to Study the Legislature*, vol. 10, 1109–10 (October 15, 1971).

An "act" as used in this section refers to an act of the legislature as a whole and not an act of a particular committee or member. In a suit brought by a member of the Senate to order the printing of a proposed resolution, an Ohio appellate court held that a senate subcommittee's refusal to have the resolution printed was not an "act" under this section and therefore the member had no right of protest. *State ex rei. Carney v. Brown* (1967).

Section 11

Filling vacancies in House or Senate.

A vacancy in the Senate or in the House of Representatives for any cause, including the failure of a member-elect to qualify for office, shall be filled by election by the members of the Senate or the members of the House of Representatives, as the case may be, who are affiliated with the same political party as the person last elected by the electors to the seat which has become vacant. A vacancy occurring before or during the first twenty months of a Senatorial term shall be filled temporarily by election as provided in this section, for only that portion of the term which will expire on the thirty-first day of December following the next general election occurring in an even-numbered year after the vacancy occurs, at which election the seat shall be filled by the electors as provided by law for the remaining, unexpired portion of the term, the member-elect so chosen to take office on the first day in January next following such election. No person shall be elected to fill a vacancy in the Senate or House of Representatives, as the case may be, unless he meets the qualifications set forth in this constitution and the laws of this state for the seat in which the vacancy occurs. An election to fill a vacancy shall be accomplished, notwithstanding the provisions of section 27, Article II of this constitution, by the adoption of a resolution, while the Senate or the House of Representatives, as the case may be, is in session, with the taking of the yeas and nays of the members of the Senate or the House of Representatives, as the case may be, affiliated with the same political party as the person last elected to the seat in which the vacancy occurs. The adoption of such resolution shall require the affirmative vote of a majority of the members elected to the Senate or the House of Representatives, as the case may be, entitled to vote thereon. Such vote shall be spread upon the journal of the Senate or the House of Representatives, as the case may be, and certified to the secretary of state by the clerk thereof. The secretary of state shall, upon receipt of such certification, issue a certificate of election to the person so elected and upon presentation of such certificate to the Senate or the House of

Representatives, as the case may be, the person so elected shall take the oath of office and become a member of the Senate or the House of Representatives, as the case may be, for the term for which he was so elected.

Adopted as part of the 1851 Constitution and amended in 1961, 1968, and 1973, this section preserves "the political status quo" by providing that vacancies are to be filled by the members of the political party of the person whose seat has become vacant. See Thomas R. Swisher, ed., *Ohio Constitution Handbook* (Cleveland: Banks-Baldwin Publishing Co., 1990), 238 (hereinafter Swisher, *Ohio Constitution Handbook*). Under the 1802 Constitution, see 1802 Constitution, Article I, section 12, and the 1851 Constitution, see Article II, section 11, all vacancies were filled by election.

The 1961 amendment qualified the provision for filling temporarily vacancies in the Senate that occur before or during the first twenty months of a senatorial term. Such vacancies may be filled temporarily by "election" as provided in this section but only until the last day of December following the next general election occurring in an even-numbered year.

The 1968 amendment dropped the requirement that vacancies in the house be filled by election, thus permitting the balance of the vacant term to be filled by a replacement selected by the house.

The 1973 amendment, recommended by the OCRC, was solely corrective, substituting "election" for "appointment" and "elected" for "appointed" but making no substantive changes in the section. See OCRC, *Final Report*, 115–17.

Vacancies may result from death, expulsion, resignation, failure to qualify for office, or from a member accepting other employment or office incompatible with his or her membership in the General Assembly. A resignation takes effect on the date specified in a letter of resignation sent to the president of the Senate or the speaker of the House, depending on the member's house. If the General Assembly is not in session, the resignation takes effect on the date specified in a letter of resignation sent to the governor. O.R.C. section 101.25.

The election of a new member to a vacant seat requires the adoption of a resolution while the particular house is in session. A majority of the members of the incumbent's party from his or her respective house must approve the resolution. The vote must be certified with the secretary of state, who issues a certificate of election. To take office, the member-elect must meet all qualifications set forth in the constitution.

Section 12

Privilege of members from arrest, and of free speech.

Senators and representatives, during the session of the General Assembly, and in going to, and returning from the same, shall be privileged from arrest, in all cases, except treason, felony, or breach of the peace; and for any speech, or debate, in either house, they shall not be questioned elsewhere.

Adopted in 1851 and never amended, this section is based on Article I, section 13, of the 1802 Constitution and is analogous to Article I, section 6, of the U.S. Constitution. It prohibits the use of arrest to influence or disrupt the legislative process, and it guarantees the rights of free speech and debate that are vital to the legislative process. Under this section, senators and representatives enjoy an absolute privilege for statements made in session. *Costanzo v. Gaul* (1980). Statements made by legislators (including local legislators) outside a legislative session or a related meeting are only entitled to a qualified privilege against defamation—that is, the statements are protected unless they were made with knowledge that they were false or were made with reckless disregard of the truth. Ibid.

This section exempts "treason, felony, or breach of the peace" from the prohibition against arrest. The phrase has long been used in matters of parliamentary privilege. Prior to the American Revolution, it was used in England to exclude criminal offenses from the privilege against arrest because all criminal offenses were considered breaches of the peace. See *Williamson v. United States* (1908).

In adopting Article I, section 6 of the U.S. Constitution, the framers followed English precedent and continued to exempt criminal offenses from the privilege against arrest and to apply the privilege only to arrests in civil cases. Ibid. Thus, the privilege against arrest in the U.S. Constitution does not apply to criminal arrests. The Ohio Supreme Court has followed the U.S. Supreme Court and limited the privilege to civil arrests by holding that it does not apply to crimes and misdemeanors. *City of Akron v. Mingo* (1959).

Section 13
When session to be public.

The proceedings of both houses shall be public, except in cases which, in the opinion of two-thirds of those present, require secrecy.

Adopted in 1851 and never amended, this section is based on the first sentence of Article I, section 15, of the 1802 Ohio Constitution, which provided that "[t]he doors of each house, and of committees of the whole, shall be kept open, except in such cases as, in the opinion of the house, require secrecy." The current section provides that house and senate proceedings must be open to the public except where two-thirds of the membership of a house vote to keep the proceedings secret. The General Assembly has enacted a "sunshine" law that requires governmental meetings to be open to the public, unless specifically exempt. O.R.C. section 121.

Section 14
Power of adjournment.

Neither house shall, without the consent of the other, adjourn for more than five days, Sundays excluded; nor to any other place than that, in which the two houses are in session.

Adopted in 1851 and amended in 1973, this section is substantially the same as Article I, section 15, of the 1802 Constitution, which prohibited adjournment without the consent of the other house for more than two days (Sundays excluded). This section prevents the disruption of the legislative process by one house that could adjourn for an appreciable period of time. Provisions similar to this section are very common. If the two houses disagree on adjournment, the governor has the power to adjourn the General Assembly until a time the governor determines proper, but not beyond regular meetings. See Article III, section 9.

To get around the two-day limitation on adjournment by a single house, the General Assembly had developed the practice of holding "skeleton" sessions on Mondays. Noting that "a requirement that is being observed through the device of a technicality deserves reconsideration[,]" the OCRC recommended that the two-day period be changed to a five-day period. OCRC, *Final Report,* 118–19. In 1973, the General Assembly proposed and the voters approved an amendment to prohibit adjournment without consent of the other house for more than five days.

Section 15

How bills shall be passed.

(A) The General Assembly shall enact no law except by bill, and no bill shall be passed without the concurrence of a majority of the members elected to each house. Bills may originate in either house, but may be altered, amended, or rejected in the other.

(B) The style of the laws of this state shall be, "be it enacted by the General Assembly of the state of Ohio."

(C) Every bill shall be considered by each house on three different days, unless two-thirds of the members elected to the house in which it is pending suspend this requirement, and every individual consideration of a bill or action suspending the requirement shall be recorded in the journal of the respective house. No bill may be passed until the bill has been reproduced and distributed to members of the house in which it is pending and every amendment been made available upon a member's request.

(D) No bill shall contain more than one subject, which shall be clearly expressed in its title. No law shall be revived or amended unless the new act contains the entire act revived, or the section or sections amended, and the section or sections amended shall be repealed.

(E) Every bill which has passed both houses of the General Assembly shall be signed by the presiding officer of each house to certify that the procedural requirements for passage have been met and shall be presented forthwith to the governor for his approval.

(F) Every joint resolution which has been adopted in both houses of the General Assembly shall be signed by the presiding officer of each house to certify that the procedural requirements for adoption have been met and shall forthwith be filed with the secretary of state.

Amended in 1973 as part of a major reorganization of Article II that had its origin in the 1971 recommendations of the OCRC, this section is an amalgamation of pre-1973 versions of sections 9, 15, 16, 17, and 18. See OCRC, *Final Report*, 96–136.

Section 15(A) outlines the procedural requirements for enacting a bill into law. A bill may be introduced in either house and amended or rejected in the other. To be passed, a bill requires the concurrence of a majority of the members elected to both the House and the Senate (as opposed to a majority of a quorum). Although not constitutionally required, by tradition budget bills are introduced in the House of Representatives. See *A Guide for Ohio Legislators* 75 (Legislative Services Commission (2017)).

Section 15(B) requires that each law must begin with the enacting clause, "Be it enacted by the General Assembly of the State of Ohio." There is no clear authority as to whether this enacting clause is mandatory or merely directory.

Section 15(C) requires that each bill be considered three times by each house, although each house may suspend the operation of this requirement by a two-thirds vote. Originally adopted in 1851 as a three-*reading* requirement, the voters approved an amendment in 1973 to convert this into a three-*consideration* requirement. In recommending this change, the OCRC noted that the "original reasons for the three reading rule appear to have been the absence of printing and the inability of some members of state legislatures to read and therefore become informed about matters on which they were obliged to vote." See OCRC, *Final Report*, 123. The OCRC pointed out that these reasons no longer existed, but it nonetheless believed that "safeguards against hasty consideration of legislation" should be maintained and it "hesitated to recommend abandonment of a requirement calling for action upon three separate days." Ibid.

Although intended to ensure that legislation is considered without undue haste, the Ohio Supreme Court long considered this requirement (former sec. 16) directory, not mandatory, and refused to enforce it. Moreover, since there was no requirement to record each consideration of a bill in the daily legislative journals, the court presumed that the three-reading requirement had been satisfied: "[W]here the journals show that a bill was passed, and there is nothing in them to show that it was not read as the constitution requires, the presumption is that it was so read, and this presumption is not liable to be rebutted by proof." *Miller v. State* (1854).

With the adoption of this section in 1973, however, each consideration of a bill had to be recorded in the daily journals. Subsequently, the court held that the presumption in *Miller* was no longer warranted; as a result, if the legislative journals did not show that the bill was considered three times, its subsequent enactment was invalid. *Hoover v. Board of County Commissioners* (1985). A bill that was considered three times and later amended, however, did not have to be considered three more times if the amendment did not "vitally alter" the subject matter of the original bill—that is, if the original bill and the amended version still shared a "common purpose or relationship." *State ex rel. Ohio AFL-CIO v. Voinovich* (1994).

The court, however, has not been willing to go beneath the surface of the legislative process. See *Youngstown City School District Board of Education v. State of Ohio* (2020) ("[T]he three-consideration rule does not allow this court to consider the legislative proceedings leading to an amendment. . . . It is not our role to police how the amended language came into existence."); but see ibid. (Donnelly, J., dissenting) (reviewing in detail the process by which legislation permitting the takeover of local school boards was adopted, and concluding that "[t]oday's decision sets a new low for constitutional compliance with Article II, Section 15(C) of the Ohio Constitution"); (Stewart, J., dissenting) ("[T]he hasty and covert efforts to amend the bill before it was enacted are important to recognizing the constitutional violation."). On the other hand, some members of the court believe that the court should be even less aggressive in monitoring the legislative process. See ibid. (French. J., concurring) (arguing "that it is time to overrule our flawed test in *Hoover* . . . for determining whether a legislative enactment violates the three-consideration rule"); (Kennedy, J., concurring and concurring in part in judgment only) ("I disagree with the lead opinion's analysis regarding Article II, section 15(C), however, because in my view, that provision is directory only and not enforceable in the courts.").

Although the three-consideration requirement, standing alone, could be seen as unduly rigid, there is an escape hatch when speedy consideration of a proposed statute is essential. Under this section, a recorded vote of two-thirds of the members in the house where the bill is pending may suspend the requirement.

Finally, section 15(C) also provides that no bill may be passed "until the bill has been reproduced and distributed to members of the house in which it is pending and every amendment been made available upon a member's request."

■ ONE-SUBJECT RULE

The first sentence of section 15(D) prohibits a bill from containing more than one subject and further requires that the subject "shall be clearly expressed in its title." The one-subject rule is designed to prevent deceptive legislative tactics such as "logrolling" (i.e., the practice of joining unrelated items that could not pass on their own into a single bill to ensure their passage). See *State ex rel. Ohio Academy of Trial Lawyers v. Sheward* (1999).

The one-subject rule has evolved, from a direction to the General Assembly to a judicially enforceable limitation on the work of the General Assembly. In 1856, in its first case construing this provision of the 1851 Constitution the Ohio Supreme Court held that the one-subject rule was "directory only, and the supervision of its observance must be left to the general assembly." *Pim v. Nicholson* (1856) ("We are . . . of the opinion, that in general the only safeguard against the violation of these rules of the houses, is their regard for, and their oath to support the constitution of the state.").

Historically, the court has been reluctant to enforce the rule for fear that it would unduly burden the legislative process, see generally John J. Kulewicz, "The History of the One-Subject Rule of the Ohio Constitution," 45 *Clev. St. L. Rev.* 591 (1997), but *Pim* had left open whether "a manifestly gross and fraudulent violation of these rules might authorize the court to pronounce a law unconstitutional." And, in 1984, the court resurrected the *Pim* suggestion, noting that a legislative enactment will only be invalidated if there is a "manifestly gross and fraudulent violation of the one-subject rule." *State ex rel. Dix v. Celeste* (1984). Then, in 1985 in *Hoover v. Board of County Commissioners, Franklin County,* the court identified the standard to be applied in reviewing legislation under the one-subject rule.

> [E]very presumption in favor of the enactment's validity should be indulged. The mere fact that a bill embraces more than one topic is not fatal, as long as a common purpose or relationship exists between the topics. However, where there is a blatant disunity between topics and no rational reason for their combination can be discerned, it may be inferred that the bill is a result of log-rolling-the practice by which several matters are consolidated in a single bill for the purpose of obtaining passage for proposals which would never achieve a majority if voted on separately. This is the very practice which Section 15(D) was designed to prevent.

Applying *Dix* and *Hoover,* the court began to enforce the one-subject rule aggressively and regularly found enactments invalid because they contained more than one topic that did not share a "common purpose or relationship." See generally Stephanie Hoffer and Travis McDade, "Of Dignity and Logrolling: Ohio's One-Subject Rule and the Very Evils It Was Designed to Prevent," 51 *Clev. St. L. Rev.* 557 (2004).

In 1991, the court invalidated a liquor control law that was included in a bill concerning the state judicial system. *State ex rel. Hinkle v. Franklin County Board of Elections* (1991). In 1994, it invalidated an intentional tort and child labor reform in a bill dealing with workers' compensation. *State ex rel. Ohio AFL-CIO v. Voinovich* (1994). In 1999, it invalidated a school voucher program that was enacted as part of a general appropriations bill, *Simmons-Harris v. Goff* (1999), and omnibus legislation that combined a wide range of tort and civil litigation provisions addressing such topics as employment discrimination claims and class actions arising from the sale of securities. *Sheward, supra.*

In some of these cases, the court severed or excised the unrelated parts of the offending legislation after identifying its primary or core purpose and saved other portions, see *Hinkle; Ohio AFL-CIO;* but in rare cases the court rejected the offending legislation in its entirety, *Sheward, supra.*

And in this century the court continued to enforce the one-subject rule. For example, in 2004, it rejected a provision in a wide-ranging appropriations bill that excluded certain public employees from the collective bargaining process, finding a disunity in subject between the exclusion and the state budget. *State ex rel. Ohio Civil Service Employees Association v. State Emp. Relations Bd.* (2004). See also *In re Nowak* (2004).

But in *State ex rel. Ohio Civil Serv. Employees Association v. State* (2016), a case challenging the inclusion of prison privatization provisions in a budget bill, the court appears to have changed direction and become less willing to overturn state legislation based on the one-subject rule. Initially, the court reaffirmed that section 15(D) is a "mandatory" legal rule, even though the courts' "role in its enforcement remains limited" in order to "accord appropriate deference to the General Assembly's law-making function." Ibid.

Relying on the principles developed in *Dix* and *Hoover*, the court emphasized the importance of identifying the primary purpose of legislation and rejected both a whole-bill challenge to the biennial budget bill and a narrower challenge to the inclusion of the prison privatization provisions because all "provisions relate to the overall subject of state expenditures and revenues . . . balancing state expenditures against state revenues to ensure continued operation of state programs." Ibid.

The court has also addressed the standing requirements in one-subject rule cases, holding that "[a] party challenging multiple provisions in an enactment of the General Assembly as violating the Single Subject Clause of the Ohio Constitution must prove standing as to each provision the party seeks to have severed from the enactment by demonstrating it suffered or is threatened with direct and concrete injury in a manner or degree different from that suffered by the general public because of each provision." *Preterm-Cleveland, Inc. v. Kasich* (2018) (syllabus no. 2). See Commentary, Article IV.

■ AMENDING A LAW AND SIGNATURES

The second sentence of section 15(D) contains requirements relating to reviving, amending, or repealing laws. The section seeks to avoid confusion by requiring that the new act contain the entire act revived or sections amended, but the section does not prevent the continued operation of the doctrine of repeal by implication. See *State v. Sullivan* (2001) ("When a court strikes down a statute as unconstitutional, and the offending statute replaced an existing law that had been repealed in the same bill that enacted the offending statute, the repeal is also invalid unless it clearly appears that the General Assembly meant the repeal to have effect even if the offending statute had never been passed."). Thus, the use of amending and reviving clauses is mandatory; but the use of repealing clauses is only directory, which permits the continued operation of the long-recognized rule of repeal by implication. See *Lehman v. McBride* (1863).

Sections 15(E) and 15(F) require the signatures of the presiding officers of each house for bills passed by both houses and for joint resolutions (sec. (F)).

These sections ensure that the proper procedures are followed in enacting bills and joint resolutions. The duty to sign is mandatory and cannot be used to veto or thwart legislation. *Maloney v. Rhodes* (1976). A bill passed in accordance with the constitution and signed by the governor but which lacks the necessary signature or signatures of the presiding officers is invalid. Ibid.

Section 16

Bills to be signed by governor; veto.

If the governor approves an act, he shall sign it, it becomes law and he shall file it with the secretary of state.

If he does not approve it, he shall return it with his objections in writing, to the house in which it originated, which shall enter the objections at large upon its journal, and may then reconsider the vote on its passage. If three-fifths of the members elected to the house of origin vote to repass the bill, it shall be sent, with the objections of the governor, to the other house, which may also reconsider the vote on its passage. If three-fifths of the members elected to the second house vote to repass it, it becomes law notwithstanding the objections of the governor, and the presiding officer of the second house shall file it with the secretary of state. In no case shall a bill be repassed by a smaller vote than is required by the constitution on its original passage. In all cases of reconsideration the vote of each house shall be determined by yeas and nays, and the names of the members voting for and against the bill shall be entered upon the journal.

If a bill is not returned by the governor within ten days, Sundays excepted, after being presented to him, it becomes law in like manner as if he had signed it, unless the General Assembly by adjournment prevents its return; in which case, it becomes law unless, within ten days after such adjournment, it is filed by him, with his objections in writing, in the office of the secretary of state. The governor shall file with the secretary of state every bill not returned by him to the house of origin that becomes law without his signature.

The governor may disapprove any item or items in any bill making an appropriation of money and the item or items, so disapproved, shall be void, unless repassed in the manner prescribed by this section for the repassage of a bill.

Adopted in 1851 and amended in 1903, 1912, and 1973, this section gives the governor the power to veto legislation passed by the General Assembly. The 1802 Constitution conferred no veto power on the governor, and the delegates at the 1850–51 Constitutional Convention rejected by a vote of 50–41 a proposal to give the governor a veto that could be overridden by a simple majority of both houses. See *1850–51 Debates*, vol. 2, 292–93. The 1873–74 Constitutional Convention proposed giving the governor the veto power, but this proposal failed together with the entire proposed constitution. See John Kulewicz, "Reinventing the Governor: A History of Executive Power under Ohio Law," in Michael Les Benedict and John F. Winkler, eds., *The History of Ohio Law*, vol. 1 (Athens: Ohio University Press, 2004), 139, 159–62 (hereinafter *The History of Ohio Law*).

In 1903, a hundred years after Ohio joined the union, the General Assembly proposed and the voters approved giving the governor the veto power. Under this veto power, the governor could veto legislation, but the veto could be overridden by a two-thirds vote of both houses. Under this amendment, however, "[t]he votes for the repassage of said bill shall in each house respectively be no less than those given on the original passage." The 1903 amendment also gave the governor a broad line-item veto power applicable to both appropriation and non-appropriation sections of bills (subject to the same two-thirds override requirement). Thus, in an amendment that the voters approved overwhelmingly by operation of the Longworth Act, see The History of the Ohio Constitution, *supra,* Ohio governors went from having no veto power to one of the strongest in the nation.

In 1912, the constitutional convention proposed and the voters approved an amendment to reduce the two-thirds vote required for an override to three-fifths. The amended veto power also eliminated the requirement that the veto is not effective if the bill is repassed by a smaller vote than on its original passage by adopting a cryptic reference that the repassage vote may not be "smaller . . . than is required by the constitution on its original passage." Thus, a three-fifths vote is all that is required to override a veto without regard to the absolute number of favorable votes on the bill either initially or on the override.

■ LINE-ITEM VETO

The 1912 amendment to this section also revised the line-item veto under which the governor could disapprove of a specific item or items in a bill without vetoing the entire legislation. As a result, the line-item veto only applies to appropriation bills, and a bill is considered an "appropriations" bill for the purpose of this provision only if it *expressly* makes some appropriation of money. *State ex rel. Akron Education Association v. Essex* (1976). An "item" for the purpose of the line-item veto is any separate and distinct provision that differs from other provisions of an appropriations bill by either its subject matter, purpose, or amount of appropriation. *State ex rel. Brown v. Ferguson* (1972).

It would be a violation of the governor's constitutional power, and thus of the separation of powers doctrine, to rely on a vetoed item to limit the power of the Controlling Board. *State ex rel. Cleveland Right to Life v. State of Ohio Controlling Board* (2013).

■ CURRENT PRACTICE

This section provides that legislation approved by the governor must be signed and then filed with the secretary of state. If the governor does not approve the legislation, he or she must return it to the house of origination with written objections, where a three-fifths vote of both houses will override the veto. There is no deadline in this provision by which the General Assembly may act to override the veto.

This section also provides that a bill becomes law if the governor fails to return the bill to the General Assembly within ten days (Sundays excluded), unless the General Assembly has adjourned. If the General Assembly has adjourned, the governor has ten days after such adjournment to return the bill to the General Assembly with the governor's objections and thus veto it. The time period in which the governor may veto a bill runs from the date of adjournment sine die by the General Assembly and not from the date of presentment. *State ex rel. Ohio Gen. Assembly v. Brunner* (2006).

Section 17
Repealed—Signing of bills

Adopted in 1851 but repealed as part of the 1973 reorganization of this article, this section, which addressed the signing of bills and joint resolutions, has been incorporated into Article II, sections 15(E) and (F).

Section 18
Repealed—Style of laws

Adopted in 1851 but repealed as part of the 1973 reorganization of this article, this section, which referred to the style of laws, has been incorporated into Article II, section 15(B).

Section 19
Repealed—Exclusion from office

Adopted in 1851 but repealed as part of the 1973 reorganization of this article, this section, which prohibited legislators from holding offices that were either created or had their compensation increased during the legislator's term, has been incorporated into the second paragraph of Article II, section 4.

Section 20
Term of office, and compensation of officers.

The General Assembly, in cases not provided for in this constitution, shall fix the term of office and the compensation of all officers; but no change therein shall affect the salary of any officer during his existing term, unless the office be abolished.

Adopted in 1851 and never amended, this section requires the General Assembly to set the terms of office and the compensation of all officers whose terms or compensation are not covered elsewhere in the constitution. Article III, section 2, covers the terms of office of key executive branch officers, and Article IV, section 6, covers both the terms and compensation of judges.

This section applies to both appointed and elective offices. *State ex rel. McNamara v. Campbell* (1916). This section also prohibits the General Assembly from increasing the amount of compensation provided to officers during their terms in office, but the prohibition only applies during the statutory period to which the person is appointed or elected. Thus, the salary of an officer who holds over and begins a new statutory period can be increased without violating this provision. *State ex rel. Glander v. Ferguson* (1947).

Section 21
Contested elections.

The General Assembly shall determine, by law, before what authority, and in what manner the trial of contested elections shall be conducted.

Adopted in 1851 and never amended, this section provides that the General Assembly may enact laws to resolve contested elections. These procedures are codified in Ohio Revised Code sections 3515.08 to 3515.16.

Section 22
Appropriations.

No money shall be drawn from the treasury, except in pursuance of a specific appropriation, made by law; and no appropriation shall be made for a longer period than two years.

Adopted in 1851 and never amended, this section is based on Article I, section 21, of the 1802 Constitution and Article I, section 9, of the U.S. Constitution. It limits the power of the General Assembly by prohibiting appropriations for a period longer than two years. This provision also prohibits the General Assembly from entering into contracts that extend beyond its life or from leaving debts or liabilities outstanding beyond the two-year period. *State v. Medbery* (1857); see also *Sorrentino v. Ohio National Guard* (1990). Under this section, the General Assembly may not draw money from the state treasury except to make a "specific" appropriation, which is one that fairly and reasonably identifies the uses to which the money is spent. *State ex rel. Kauer v. Defenbacher* (1950).

Despite the limitations on the General Assembly imposed by this section, its requirements may be overridden by other sections of the constitution. And it has become a common practice since the adoption of Article VIII, section 2c in 1953 to make this provision inapplicable to selected bond-authorizing amendments. See Article VIII, sections 2c, 2g, 2i, 2k, 2l, 2m, 2n, 2o, 2p, 2q, 2s, and Commentaries thereon.

Section 23

Impeachments; how instituted and conducted.

The House of Representatives shall have the sole power of impeachment, but a majority of the members elected must concur therein. Impeachments shall be tried by the Senate; and the senators, when sitting for that purpose, shall be upon oath or affirmation to do justice according to law and evidence. No person shall be convicted, without the concurrence of two-thirds of the senators.

Adopted in 1851 and never amended, this section and the following section concerning impeachment are substantially the same as Article I, sections 23 and 24, of the 1802 Constitution, which were based on the Impeachment Clauses in Article I, sections 2 and 3, and Article II, section 3, of the U.S. Constitution. This section gives the Ohio House of Representatives the power to impeach public officials by a majority vote of its members. The Senate, acting as a court, tries the official and renders a conviction if two-thirds of the senators vote to convict. The U.S. Constitution, however, does not require a two-thirds vote of all senators but only "two-thirds of the Members present."

The most celebrated impeachment cases in Ohio history occurred in 1808 when the House impeached (but the Senate acquitted) Ohio Supreme Court Justice George Tod and Common Pleas Court Judge Calvin Pease. The reason for the impeachments was the decision in *Rutherford v. M'Fadden* (1807), in which the court held that the judiciary can find acts of the General Assembly unconstitutional. See The History of the Ohio Constitution, *supra*.

Besides removal by impeachment and conviction, the Ohio Revised Code provides statutory methods of removing public officials. See O.R.C. sections 3.04–3.10. Additionally, Article IV, section 17, provides for removal of judges by concurrent resolutions passed by two-thirds of the members elected to each house of the General Assembly. See Commentary, Article IV, section 17.

No state officials have been impeached in Ohio since the early 1800s, but efforts to impeach state officials, especially judges, were common in the first four decades of statehood, perhaps because the General Assembly (which was responsible for selecting judges) felt that it was entitled to review their performance and remove them when necessary. Between 1808 and 1839, impeachment proceedings were begun against seventeen Ohio judges, but the House of Representatives impeached only eight of them. The Senate acquitted six of the impeached judges and convicted two. See Julie Ann Hack, "'Misdemeanor[s]' Worthy of Judicial Impeachment in Early Ohio Constitutional History" (Spring 2009) (Ohio Constitution—Law and History) (Cleveland-Marshall Law Website).

In 2008, articles of impeachment were filed against Attorney General Mark Dann, but he resigned from office before any proceedings of substance on the resolution.

The impeachment of public officials by the General Assembly under Article II, sections 23 and 24, is the exercise of legislative power and it is considered a political question that is not subject to judicial review. See *In re Bostwick* (1932).

Section 24

Officers liable to impeachment; consequences.

The governor, judges, and all state officers, may be impeached for any misdemeanor in office; but judgment shall not extend further than removal from office, and disqualification to hold any office under the authority of this state. The party impeached, whether convicted or not, shall be liable to indictment, trial, and judgment, according to law.

Adopted in 1851 and never amended, this section provides that the governor, judges, and state officials may be impeached for committing a misdemeanor in office. The term "misdemeanor" undoubtedly means "misdeed" since it would otherwise "require the absurd conclusion that officers guilty of felonies are exempt from impeachment." Swisher, *Ohio Constitution Handbook*, 257. See also David F. Forte and Matthew Spalding, eds., *The Heritage Guide to the Constitution* (Washington D.C.: The Heritage Foundation, 2nd ed., 2014), 293–97 (discussing the federal impeachment provisions).

Similar to the analogous provision of the U.S. Constitution, see Article II, section 4, this section provides that "[t]he party impeached, whether convicted or not, shall be liable to indictment, trial, and judgment, according to law." And both constitutions provide that the judgment shall not extend further than "removal from office" and disqualification from holding office. The Disqualification Clause of the federal provision has been interpreted to require only a simple majority vote in the U.S. Senate on a separate vote to bar convicted officials from holding any federal office, but there is no language in the Ohio Constitution that addresses, even indirectly, the nature of the Senate vote required to disqualify a convicted official from holding state office. And one of the two convicted and disqualified Ohio judges was disqualified as part of the conviction vote while the other was apparently disqualified in a separate vote. See Julie Ann Hack, "'Misdemeanor[s]' Worthy of Judicial Impeachment in Early Ohio Constitutional History."

Section 25

Repealed—When session shall commence.

Adopted in 1851 but repealed in 1973, this section concerned the commencement of general sessions of the legislature, provisions that are now in section 8 of this article.

Section 26

General laws to have uniform operation.

All laws, of a general nature, shall have a uniform operation throughout the state; nor, shall any act, except such as relates to public schools, be passed, to take effect upon the approval of any other authority than the General Assembly, except, as otherwise provided in this constitution.

Adopted in 1851 and never amended, this section sought to change the General Assembly's approach to legislation, which typically involved the enactment of legislation to support one group or locality, most often a particular corporation or municipality.

Before 1851, most of the General Assembly's work involved the adoption of special legislation. See W. T. Mallison Jr., "General versus Special Statutes in Ohio," 11 *Ohio St. L. J.* 462 (1950); see also David M. Gold, *Democracy in Session: A History of the Ohio General Assembly* (Athens: Ohio University Press, 2009), 212–28 (hereinafter, Gold, *Democracy in Session*). As one delegate at the 1851 Convention remarked, "[I]t has been frequently said that three-fourths of the laws of Ohio are special and local in their nature; and I believe that an effort will be made to confine the Legislature to general regulations exclusively." *1850–51 Debates*, vol. 1, 285 (quoted in Mallison, *supra*, 466).

Notwithstanding the adoption of this section and Article XIII, sections 1 and 6, see Commentaries, the General Assembly continued to adopt special laws through the use of putative general laws that contained statutory classifications. In 1896, however, the Ohio Supreme Court rejected an improper classification involving highways. See *Hixson v. Burson* (1896) (holding unconstitutional an act relating to highways applicable "to any county having a population of not less than 35,190, and not to exceed 35,200"). And in 1902, the court struck a fatal blow to the use of municipal statutory classifications, which had placed each of the state's eleven largest cities in its own special class and grade. *State ex rel. Knisely v. Jones* (1902). See also Commentary, Article XVIII; Gold, *Democracy in Session*, 218–21 (discussing subterfuge by classification).

When read in isolation, this section does not expressly bar special laws, but when read *in pari materia* with Article XIII, section 1 ("The General Assembly shall pass no special act conferring corporate powers.") and Article XIII, section 6 ("The General Assembly shall provide for the organization of cities, and incorporated villages; by general laws"), it represents a clear constitutional preference for the use of general, not special, laws.

■ UNIFORMITY RULE

The uniformity rule of this section requires that "[a]ll laws, of a general nature, shall have a uniform operation throughout the state. . . ." This provision has certain similarities to the equal protection and benefit clause of Article I, section

2, in that both require that government classifications be rationally related to a legitimate governmental purpose. See Commentary, Article I, section 2.

But arbitrary classifications only violate the uniformity clause if they are created by a statute that is special or local, rather than general, in nature. *Austintown Township Board of Trustees v. Tracy* (1996). Thus, arbitrary classifications that favor or disadvantage similarly situated persons but are not the result of special or local legislation are properly analyzed under the equal protection and benefit clause and not under the uniformity clause, Ibid. See also Robert F. Williams, "Equality Guarantees in State Constitutional Law," 63 *Tex. L. Rev.* 1195 (1985).

To satisfy the uniformity clause, a statute must be both general in nature and operate uniformly throughout the state. *Desenco, Inc. v. City of Akron* (1999). A law is deemed to be of a general nature if "the subject does or may exist in, and affect the people of, every county, in the state." *Hixson v. Burson* (1896). The general nature requirement, therefore, focuses on the subject matter of the legislation. For example, "tax statutes have been viewed . . . to be of a general nature." *State ex rel. Zupancic v. Limbach* (1991). Likewise, collective bargaining statutes are of a general nature. *State ex rel. Dayton Fraternal Order of Police Lodge No. 44 v. State Employment Relations Board* (1986).

The requirement that the law operate uniformly throughout the state may be satisfied even if the law does not apply to all persons or all localities within the state as long as the law can potentially apply to all persons and localities. *Denseco, supra.* Thus, an act that classified taxing districts according to whether they had electric power plants with start-up costs over $1 billion operated uniformly. Despite the fact the act applied to only one district, there was nothing in the act that prevented its prospective application to other districts. *Zupancic, supra.* On the other hand, a statute that created a special taxing district for Lake Erie islands not connected to the mainland violated the uniformity requirement since it could not apply to other parts of the state. *Put-in-Bay Island Taxing District Authority v. Colonial, Inc.* (1992).

In the 2021 biennial budget bill, Am. Sub. H.B. 110 (134th GA) (2021), the General Assembly approved legislation to prohibit park districts in counties with populations of between 220,000 and 240,000 from using eminent domain to provide recreational trails until June 30, 2026. This legislation, which only applies in Lake and Mahoning Counties, is of questionable validity under the requirement that laws have a uniform operation throughout the state.

■ LEGISLATIVE SUBMISSION

The second clause of this section prohibits the General Assembly from allowing some other authority to approve a law before it goes into effect. *Strain v. Southerton* (1947). Adopted after a heated debate about the delegation of legislative power and the role of representative bodies, this requirement sought to prevent the practice of conditioning legislation on the approval by voters. See

1850–51 Debates, vol. 2, 217–21. This practice has been described as an optional referendum, and in modern times it has been used in some states to obtain approval of proposed bond issues. See John J. Dinan, *The American State Constitutional Tradition* (Lawrence: University Press of Kansas, 2006), 77–84.

This provision has some flexibility, however, and the General Assembly may sometimes condition the operation of a law on a future event. For example, a law that reduced the number of municipal court judges by directing that the next two vacancies remain unfilled did not violate this section. *State ex rel. Krieg v. Matia* (1941).

The exception for public schools was inserted in this provision to preserve the practice of giving local school districts the option of whether to be bound by certain state statutes. See *1850–51 Debates*, vol. 2, 832. Thus, the bar on legislation from becoming effective upon approval of another authority does not apply to legislation relating to public schools. *In re Proposed Annexation by Columbus City School Dist.* (1976).

In 1998 the General Assembly took the unprecedented step of relying on the public schools exception to submit a *statewide* proposal to the voters for an increase in state taxes (ultimately rejected by the voters) to provide additional school funding to comply with the *DeRolph* decision. See Commentary, Article VI, section 2. And in a decision based almost exclusively on a textual review of the exception (and dismissing the convention debate as only "imprecise speeches by individual drafters"), the Ohio Supreme Court held that the General Assembly's submission of this proposed statute to the voters was permissible. *State ex rel. Taft v. Franklin County Court of Common Pleas* (1998).

This provision may prevent the state from adopting a so-called trigger law that would ban or limit abortions if an outside event––the overruling of *Roe v Wade* (1973) by the U.S. Supreme Court––takes place. See S.B. 123 (134th G.A.) (providing that proposed abortion legislation becomes effective if the U.S. Supreme Court issues "an opinion that upholds, in whole or in part, a state's authority to prohibit abortion"). See also S.B. 123 (134th G.A.) (LSC Analysis) (2021) (noting potential constitutional infirmity of proposed abortion trigger legislation).

Section 27

Election and appointment of officers; filling vacancies.

The election and appointment of all officers, and the filling of all vacancies, not otherwise provided for by this constitution, or the constitution of the United States, shall be made in such manner as may be directed by law; but no appointing power shall be exercised by the General Assembly, except as prescribed in this constitution; and in these cases, the vote shall be taken "viva voce."

Adopted in 1851 and amended in 1953, the earlier version of this section included a provision concerning the election of U.S. senators by the General

Assembly. But the Seventeenth Amendment to the U.S. Constitution, which was ratified by the states in 1913, effectively abrogated this provision and gave the voters the right to elect U.S. senators. The earlier provision remained in the constitution until 1953, when the voters approved amendments proposed by the General Assembly to repeal various obsolete provisions.

Article V, section 7, provides that all nominations must be by direct primary or by petition, see Commentary, but that section does not address what to do when vacancies occur in nominations at a time when it is not practicable to select a new candidate either by direct primary or petition. This section fills the void by giving the General Assembly authority to provide proper elective processes in cases not otherwise addressed by the Ohio or the U.S. Constitution. *State ex rel. Gottlieb v. Sulligan* (1963).

Section 27 also requires the General Assembly to pass laws prescribing the manner by which public officers are appointed, but it specifically prohibits the General Assembly from exercising the appointment power, except as provided in the Ohio Constitution. This provision prohibits legislative patronage, as "it was generally believed that a practice had grown up, among members of the legislative bodies, to barter votes for offices in exchange for votes for laws." *State ex rel. Attorney General v. Kennon* (1857). Because of this distrust of legislative patronage, even when the General Assembly is permitted to exercise the power of appointment, this section requires that the vote must be "viva voce" (i.e., by "ayes and nays").

The prohibition against legislative appointments only applies to "public offices," which are offices that exercise some portion of the state's sovereign power. *State ex rel. Meshel v. Keip* (1981); see Commentary, Article II, section 4. This prohibition, however, does not prevent the General Assembly from creating commissions or committees to investigate and report their findings to the legislature as long as the General Assembly does not name specific individuals to serve on such bodies. *State ex rel. Herbert v. Ferguson* (1944).

Section 28

Retroactive laws; obligation of contracts.

The General Assembly shall have no power to pass retroactive laws, or laws impairing the obligation of contracts; but may, by general laws, authorize courts to carry into effect, upon such terms as shall be just and equitable, the manifest intention of parties, and officers, by curing omissions, defects, and errors, in instruments and proceedings, arising out of their want of conformity with the laws of this state.

■ RETROACTIVITY CLAUSE

Adopted in 1851 and never amended, this section prevents the General Assembly from enacting retroactive laws or laws impairing the obligation of contracts.

The retroactivity clause prohibits the General Assembly "from passing new laws that reach back and create new burdens, new duties, new obligations, or new liabilities not existing at the time." *Miller v. Hixson* (1901). The prohibition against retroactive laws is broader than the prohibition in Article I, section 10, of the U.S. Constitution against ex post facto laws. Ex post facto laws refer only to criminal laws, but the prohibition on retroactive laws in this section refers to both criminal and civil laws. The delegates to the 1851 Convention expressly rejected an amendment that would have substituted "ex post facto" for "retroactive" in this section. See *1850–51 Debates*, vol. 2, 832. The delegates also saw this provision as part of its effort to place limits on the power to repeal corporate charters. See Commentary, Article II, section 2.

Notwithstanding the retroactivity clause, this section does not forbid all retroactive laws, and the Ohio Supreme Court in *Bielat v. Bielat* (2000), made this clear.

> We emphasize the phrase "*unconstitutionally* retroactive" to confirm that retroactivity itself is not always forbidden by Ohio law. Though the language of Section 28 . . . provides that the General Assembly "shall have no power to pass retroactive laws," Ohio courts have long recognized that there is a crucial distinction between statutes that merely apply retroactively . . . and those that do so in a manner that offends our Constitution.

In determining whether a statute violates this section, courts must first determine whether the General Assembly intended the statute to apply retroactively. And the General Assembly presumes that laws are prospective. See O.R.C. section 1.48 ("A statute is presumed to be prospective in its operation unless expressly made retrospective."). But when this presumption is overcome, courts must determine whether the retroactive application of a statute affects substantive or remedial law. *Bielat, supra.*

The distinction between substantive and remedial law is not always clear. In *Bielat,* the court explained that to be "unconstitutionally retroactive" a law must impair a right that is "vested" or creates a "reasonable expectation of finality." And the prohibition does not apply to "remedial" laws that affect "the methods and procedure by which rights are recognized, protected and enforced, not . . . the rights themselves." Ibid. (quoting *Weil v. Taxicabs of Cincinnati, Inc.* (1942)). Nor does it apply to a remedial law that extends personal jurisdiction over nonresident defendants. *Kilbreath v. Rudy* (1968).

But statutes that create heightened intent standards for intentional torts affect substantive rights and cannot be applied retroactively. *Van Fossen v. Babcock & Wilcox Co.* (1989). And statutes of limitations, though generally considered remedial in nature, may not be applied retroactively when they "operate to destroy an accrued substantive right . . . ." *Gregory v. Flowers* (1972).

The application of registration requirements to sex offenders who committed crimes before the effective date of the act establishing the registration requirement violates the prohibition on retroactive laws. *State v. Williams* (2011). But a repeat offender statute that requires counting juvenile offenses as a prior offense can, notwithstanding the bar on retroactive legislation, apply to a juvenile offense that was committed prior to the enactment of the statute. *State v. Adkins* (2011). Nor is the prohibition on retroactive laws violated by a state statute that required nonlicensed public school staff to submit to a criminal background check and required school districts to terminate employees found to have past convictions for certain offenses. *Doe v. Ronan* (2010).

And in *State v. Hubbard* (2021), the Ohio Supreme Court held that Sierah's Law, O.R.C. sec. 2903.42 et seq., which created a violent offender database and required the posting of the names of violent offenders, applied to violent conduct that occurred prior to the effective date of the statute and did not violate the retroactivity clause. In so ruling, the court reasoned that Sierah's Law is remedial and neither punitive nor substantive; and it concluded that "[t]he duty to enroll as a violent offender is far less burdensome than the registration duties imposed by . . . the Adam Walsh Act."

The protection against retroactive laws applies to individuals and private corporations but not to political subdivisions such as school boards. *Toledo City Board of Education v. State Board of Education* (2016).

Notwithstanding the prohibition in the first clause of this section, the final clause permits the General Assembly to pass general laws that retroactively allow courts to cure deficiencies in instruments and proceedings to give effect to the intention of the parties. There is little case law construing this provision. It has, however, been held to be permissive and not mandatory. *Hout v. Hout* (1870), and it applies only to omissions, defects, and errors in the instruments or proceedings themselves *Goshorn v. Purcell* (1860).

■ OBLIGATION OF CONTRACTS

The prohibition against laws that "impair the obligation of contracts" was one of the rights protected under the Northwest Ordinance. It is also found in Article VIII, section 16 of the 1802 Ohio Constitution ("No ex post facto law nor any law impairing the validity of contracts, shall ever be made;"), and in Article I, section 10 of the U.S. Constitution. See generally Commentary, Article I, section 2 (special privileges and immunities).

Despite the seemingly unequivocal wording of both the state and federal provisions, the U.S. and Ohio Supreme Courts recognize that the prohibitions are not absolute and only prohibit substantial impairments and then only if the legislation is not "reasonable and necessary to serve an important public purpose." *U. S. Trust Co. of New York v. New Jersey* (1977); *City of Middletown v. Ferguson* (1986). The Ohio Supreme Court, however, appears to have moved closer to finding near-absolute prohibitions in this section, suggesting that subsequent legislation cannot alter the binding terms of a valid contract (*Aetna Life*

Insurance Co. v. Schilling (1993) ("The provisions of . . . [the statute in question], as applied to contracts entered into before the effective date of the statute, impair the obligation of contracts in violation of Section 28, Article II of the Ohio Constitution."); see also *Ross v. Farmers Insurance Group of Companies* (1998).

Section 29
No extra compensation.

No extra compensation shall be made to any officer, public agent, or contractor, after the service shall have been rendered, or the contract entered into; nor shall any money be paid, on any claim, the subject matter of which shall not have been provided for by preexisting law, unless such compensation, or claim, be allowed by two-thirds of the members elected to each branch of the General Assembly.

Adopted in 1851 and never amended, this section provides that no officer, public agent, or contractor shall be given extra compensation after his or her services have been rendered. In addition, the section mandates that no money can be expended on any claim not authorized by preexisting law unless authorized by two-thirds of both houses of the General Assembly. Thus, a resolution by one house of the General Assembly to increase the salary of its sergeant-at-arms without a vote of two-thirds of both houses violated this section. *State ex rel. Field v. Williams* (1877).

Section 30
New counties.

No new county shall contain less than four hundred square miles of territory, nor shall any county be reduced below that amount; and all laws creating new counties, changing county lines, or removing county seats, shall, before taking effect, be submitted to the electors of the several counties to be affected thereby, at the next general election after the passage thereof, and be adopted by a majority of all the electors voting at such election, in each of said counties; but any county now or hereafter containing one hundred thousand inhabitants, may be divided, whenever a majority of the voters residing in each of the proposed divisions, shall approve of the law passed for that purpose; but no town or city within the same shall be divided, nor shall either of the divisions contain less than twenty thousand inhabitants.

Adopted in 1851 and never amended, this section gave the voters a say in the creation of new counties. Previously, under the 1802 Constitution the General Assembly had the power to establish new counties.

Section 30 provides that no new county shall consist of less than 400 square miles. At the time of the approval of the 1851 Constitution, seven counties were less than 400 square miles with Lake County at 227 square miles being the smallest.

To establish new counties, the voters of the area affected must approve any law establishing a new county or adjusting a county's boundaries. In addition, this section provides that every county having more than 100,000 inhabitants may be divided into two counties if the electors living in each of the proposed divisions approve the division by a majority vote. But no city or town can be divided between two counties, and no new county can have a population of less than 20,000 inhabitants.

Even though the process of establishing new counties is in the hands of the voters, the conditions imposed by this section make it difficult to create new counties. Thus, it is not surprising that the state has not created any new counties under the authority of the 1851 Constitution.

Section 31

Compensation of members and officers of the General Assembly.

The members and officers of the General Assembly shall receive a fixed compensation, to be prescribed by law, and no other allowance or perquisites, either in the payment of postage or otherwise; and no change in their compensation shall take effect during their term of office.

Adopted in 1851 and never amended, this section provides that the members and officers of the General Assembly receive a fixed compensation and no other allowances while in office. The previous version under Article I, section 19, of the 1802 Constitution listed the amount of salaries for particular offices and permitted travel expenses of $2 for every twenty-five miles. The purpose of this section was to prevent legislators and other officers from enriching themselves while in office, particularly by charging personal expenses to the state treasury. *State ex rel. Harbage v. Ferguson* (1941); see also *1850–51 Debates*, vol. 2, 211–14. Although this section requires that the compensation of members and officers of the General Assembly remain fixed during their terms, yearly cost-of-living adjustments are provided for in the Revised Code. O.R.C. section 101.27. Moreover, notwithstanding the prohibition on allowances and perquisites, a specific "allowance" for travel expenses has been held to be part of a legislator's fixed compensation and therefore not a violation of this section. *Harbage, supra.*

Section 32

Divorces and judicial power.

The General Assembly shall grant no divorce, nor exercise any judicial power, not herein expressly conferred.

Adopted in 1851 and never amended, this section prohibits the General Assembly from granting divorces and exercising judicial power. It is one of a number of provisions of the constitution that establishes the principle of separation of powers among the branches of government. Although the term "judicial power" is not defined, the Ohio Supreme Court has construed it as the power to hear and determine controversies between parties by applying the law to the facts and rendering a final judgment. *Village of Fairview v. Giffee* (1905).

The prohibition on exercising judicial power means, at least in part, that the General Assembly "cannot annul, reverse, or modify a judgment of a court already rendered, nor require the courts to treat as valid laws those which are unconstitutional." *Bartlett v. State* (1905). Nor can the General Assembly limit the inherent powers of the courts, and thus it cannot deny a court the power to issue a stay pending appeal. *State v. Hochhausler* (1996); see also *Norwood v. Horney* (2006) ("[B]lanket proscription on stays or injunctions against the taking and using of appropriated property pending appellate review is an unconstitutional encroachment on the judiciary's constitutional and inherent authority in violation of the separation-of-powers doctrine.").

The General Assembly, however, may require judges to consider certain factors when making judicial determinations without contravening this section. For example, in *State v. Thompson* (2001), the court upheld a statute listing factors that a court must consider, such as the offender's prior criminal record and the age of the victim, in determining whether a person convicted of a sex offense should be classified as a "sexual predator" (i.e., a person who is likely to engage in a sexual offense in the future) and therefore subject to strict notification and registration requirements. Although the statute required judges to consider certain evidence, this section was not violated because the judge could still determine how much weight, if any, should be assigned to each factor. Ibid.

The 1851 Constitution included a prohibition against the General Assembly granting divorces in the wake of the decision of the Ohio Supreme Court in *Bingham v. Miller* (1848). In that case, the court had held that the General Assembly did not have the power to grant divorces despite the legislative practice of granting divorces, a practice that dated back to the beginning of statehood. See Isaac F. Patterson, *The Constitutions of Ohio: Amendments and Proposed Amendments* (Cleveland: Arthur H. Clark Co., 1912), 17.

Section 33

Mechanics' and contractors' liens.

Laws may be passed to secure to mechanics, artisans, laborers, subcontractors and material men, their just dues by direct lien upon the property, upon which they have bestowed labor or for which they have furnished material. No other provision of the constitution shall impair or limit this power.

Adopted in 1912 and never amended, this section sought to help laborers and subcontractors receive payment for materials and labor expended on a job. It provides that laws may be passed allowing laborers and others to place mechanic liens on property. Significantly, it also includes a supremacy clause, which provides that "[n]o other provision of the constitution shall impair or limit this power."

The delegates proposed this section as a response to the Ohio Supreme Court decision in *Palmer v. Tingle* (1896). At common law, only general contractors and laborers who contracted directly with property owners could place liens on the owners' property. Thus, subcontractors who did not get paid had no recourse against property owners. In 1894, the Ohio General Assembly adopted legislation that allowed subcontractors and laborers who did not contract with property owners to place liens on the owners' property, but the court in *Palmer* held that the statute violated property owners' freedom of contract.

The U.S. Circuit Court of Appeals for the Sixth Circuit rejected the *Palmer* court's interpretation of the state constitution and held that the state law did not deprive property owners of property without due process of law or unreasonably interfere with their liberty of contract under the Ohio Constitution. Subsequently, the U.S. Supreme Court affirmed the Circuit Court decision and (in what today seems like an unusual jurisdictional decision) upheld the independent exercise of judgment by a federal court, acting under its diversity jurisdiction, and agreed with its rejection of *Palmer*. *Great Southern Fire Proof Hotel Co. v. Jones* (1904).

Despite these federal decisions, the delegates at the 1912 Constitutional Convention sought to remove all doubt about the power of the General Assembly to enact mechanics' liens under the state constitution. That the focus of the amendment was the Ohio Supreme Court is made clear in the official explanation that the delegates adopted for this provision.

> This amendment is necessary to permit laws to be passed securing to laborers, mechanics and sub-contractors their wages for work done and to materialmen the amount justly due them for material furnished. It is the prevailing opinion that under decisions of the supreme court of this state the general assembly has not the power at present to pass a mechanics' lien law which will furnish adequate protection for the persons named above.
>
> *Proceedings and Debates of the Constitutional Convention of the State of Ohio: Convened January 9, 1912* (Columbus: F. J. Heer Printing, 1912), 2034 (hereinafter *1912 Debates*).

In 1931, the Ohio Supreme Court addressed the underlying issue and recognized that section 33 "removed all doubts of the validity" of the type of liens earlier found unconstitutional under the Ohio Constitution in *Palmer*. *Chapel State Theatre Co. v. Hooper* (1931). Nonetheless, the Ohio Supreme Court has not overruled *Palmer*, and it is occasionally cited favorably. See Commentary, Article I, section 1.

Section 34

Welfare of employees.

Laws may be passed fixing and regulating the hours of labor, establishing a minimum wage, and providing for the comfort, health, safety and general welfare of all employees; and no other provision of the constitution shall impair or limit this power.

Adopted in 1912 and never amended, this section provides express authority for a minimum wage and other employee welfare legislation, topics that were of particular concern to the delegates at the 1912 Constitutional Convention because of Ohio Supreme Court decisions invalidating employee and social welfare legislation. See The History of the Ohio Constitution, *supra*.

Given the plenary legislative power of the General Assembly, an express grant of legislative power was not needed for the General Assembly to adopt minimum wage legislation. See *Strain v. Southerton* (1947) ("Without constitutional authorization [provided in Article II, Section 34] the General Assembly of Ohio could have enacted a minimum wage law in the exercise of the police power . . . ."). But the argument was made that the power should be given expressly to avoid any questions about the authority of the General Assembly to enact minimum wage legislation. See *1912 Debates*, 1334 ("I want the power given expressly so there will not be any question. You all recognize the necessity." (Mr. Dwyer)). And in the heyday of the economic substantive due process and right to contract doctrines, the inclusion of a supremacy clause (which was identical to the one in Art. II, sec. 33) was a way to protect minimum wage and other employee welfare legislation from the courts.

The significance of this section flows from the method by which it insulates legislation from judicial invalidation. Through the inclusion of the supremacy clause, which provides that "no other provision of the constitution shall impair or limit this power," this section gave legislation enacted under its authority an enhanced status that literally protects such legislation from all challenges under the Ohio Constitution.

In 1933, without relying on the supremacy clause, the Ohio Supreme Court held that state legislation requiring the director of the department of industrial relations to establish minimum fair wage rates for women and minors did not violate either the federal or the state constitutions. *Strain v. Southerton* (1947).

The first portion of this section expressly refers to "establishing a minimum wage" and to "fixing and regulating the hours of labor," but it also applies to "the comfort, health, safety and general welfare of all employees . . . ."

The Ohio Supreme Court has broadly construed the vaguely worded "general welfare of all employees" language, thus permitting the supremacy clause to trump other constitutional provisions. For example, in 1989 the court refused to reach the merits of a home rule challenge to the compulsory arbitration provisions of the state's public employee collective bargaining act, which the court held was "indisputably concerned with the 'general welfare' of employees." *City of Rocky River v. State Employment Relations Board* (1989). And, in 2009 the court, again relying on the supremacy clause, upheld a state statute that limited the ability of political subdivisions to impose residency requirements on employees as conditions of employment. *City of Lima v. State* (2009). In both cases, the court found no need to even discuss whether the state statute was inconsistent with the home rule provision of the state constitution. See also *City of Cleveland v. State* (2019) (Kennedy, J., plurality opinion) ("We have described the language used in Section 34 as so clear and unequivocal that resort to secondary sources, such as the constitutional debates, is actually unnecessary. . . . [I]t is the duty of courts to enforce the provision as written.") (internal footnotes omitted).

The broad interpretation of when the supremacy clause of section 34 overrides otherwise applicable constitutional limitations has the potential of immunizing state statutes from a wide array of state constitutional provisions, including the home rule provision of Article XVIII, the rights-conferring provisions in Article I, and the various provisions in Article II regulating the legislative process. See *City of Rocky River v. State Employment Relations Board* (1989) (Wright, J., dissenting).

But in 2019, one member of the court, relying on "the structure, text, and context of our Constitution, along with the historical record," concluded that "the comfort, health, safety and general welfare of all employees" language should be limited to laws "regulating the workplace environment." *City of Cleveland v. State* (2019) (DeWine, J., concurring in judgment only); see also ibid. (O'Connor, C. J., dissenting, joined by Justices Donnelly and Stewart) (construing Art. II, sec. 34, as limited to "wages, hours, or workplace conditions and hazards"). Thus, a majority of the court appears to no longer support an uncabined construction of this section.

The court's literal approach to the supremacy clause has resulted in its not going behind the text to determine what the delegates to the 1912 Constitutional Convention were attempting to achieve by the inclusion of the supremacy clause in this section.

During the 1912 debates, the delegates combined the initial proposal authorizing minimum wage legislation with the supremacy clause language that was being proposed as part of the amendment to permit legislation authorizing the eight-hour day and override a case that had struck down that legislation. See Commentary Article II, section 37. And the debate makes clear that the delegates' concern was the judicial decisions of the courts. By combining elements of both proposals, the delegates sought to protect the minimum wage and other employee benefit legislation from the doctrines that the court had embraced to strike down numerous pieces of social legislation. See *1912 Debates*, 1343–44.

Given the unusual nature of the supremacy clause and its potential for subordinating large areas of the Ohio Constitution to the General Assembly, there are strong historical and policy arguments for construing the provision narrowly and limiting it so that it only insulates legislation from the economic substantive due process and right to contract doctrines.

Finally, the delegates made clear the judicial focus of this amendment in the official explanation that it adopted for the amendment.

> This amendment will permit the passage of humane laws in conformity with modern industrial development to improve the conditions of employment of men, women and children. In the absence of such a provision in our state constitution a number of such laws have heretofore been held void.
>
> *1912 Debates*, 2034.

Because few voters would likely review the lengthy debates of the convention, the delegates ordered the printing of a document that included a facsimile ballot, the text of each proposed amendment, and an explanation of the amendment. Newspapers throughout the state that agreed to publish the document were provided free copies, and each delegate was provided 1000 copies of the document in pamphlet form. See *1912 Debates*, 2056–57. Thus, many voters who voted on this amendment were advised that its focus was the courts.

■ SECTION 34 AS A LIMITATION ON LEGISLATIVE POWER

The best reading of section 34 is that it made clear (1) that the General Assembly had the power to enact minimum wage, hours of labor, and other employee benefit legislation regulating the workplace environment, and (2) that the courts are limited in their ability to strike down such legislation under the Ohio Constitution.

For a limited period, however, the Ohio Supreme Court treated this section as also a limitation on the power of the General Assembly. Ignoring the plenary power of the General Assembly to legislate, a plurality of the court (and a justice concurring in the judgment) concluded in 1991 that the General Assembly could not adopt a labor law that did not further the "comfort, health, safety and general welfare of all employees." *Brady v. Safety-Kleen Corp.* (1991). And relying on both sections 34 and 35, the court invalidated in toto legislation that attempted to "balance" employer and employee rights under the workers' compensation system by limiting the ability of employees to sue employers for intentional torts. Thus the court did not have to reach whether the supremacy clause of this section insulated the law from challenges under other provisions of the constitution.

In *Johnson v. BP Chems., Inc.* (1999), the court, relying on *Brady* and section 34, reiterated its position that any statute created to provide employers with immunity from liability for their intentional tortious conduct cannot withstand constitutional scrutiny. But in *Kaminski v. Metal & Wire Products Company* (2010), the court changed direction and made clear that section 34 was a broad *grant* of authority to the General Assembly and not a limitation on the power to enact legislation. Without overruling *Johnson,* the court held that the General Assembly did not exceed its authority under section 34 by requiring a more restrictive standard of proof for "intentional tort" lawsuits by injured workers against their employers than the common law standard of proof for such claims.

Section 34a
Minimum wage.

Except as provided in this section, every employer shall pay their employees a wage rate of not less than six dollars and eighty-five cents per hour beginning January 1, 2007. On the thirtieth day of each September, beginning in 2007, this state minimum wage rate shall be increased effective the first day of the following January by the rate of inflation for the twelve month period prior to that September according to the consumer price index or its successor index for all urban wage earners and clerical workers for all items as calculated by the federal government rounded to the nearest five cents. Employees under the age of sixteen and employees of businesses with annual gross receipts of two hundred fifty thousand dollars or less for the preceding calendar year shall be paid a wage rate of not less than that established under the federal Fair Labor Standards Act or its successor law. This gross revenue figure shall be increased each year beginning January 1, 2008 by the change in the consumer price index or its successor index in the same manner as the required annual adjustment in the minimum wage rate set forth above rounded to the nearest one thousand dollars. An employer may pay an employee less than, but not less than half, the minimum wage rate required by this section if the employer is able to demonstrate that the employee receives tips that combined with the wages paid by the employer are equal to or greater than the minimum wage rate for all hours worked. The provisions of this section shall not apply to employees of a solely family owned and operated business who are family members of an owner. The state may issue licenses to employers authorizing payment of a wage rate below that required by this section to individuals with mental or physical disabilities that may otherwise adversely affect their opportunity for employment.

As used in this section: "employer," "employee," "employ," "person" and "independent contractor" have the same meanings as under the federal Fair Labor Standards Act or its successor law, except that "employer" shall also include the state and every political subdivision and "employee" shall not include an individual employed in or about the property of the employer or individual's residence on a casual basis. Only the exemptions set forth in this section shall apply to this section.

An employer shall at the time of hire provide an employee the employer's name, address, telephone number, and other contact information and update such information when it changes. An employer shall maintain a record of the name, address, occupation, pay rate, hours worked for each day worked and each amount paid an employee for a period of not less than three years following the last date the employee was employed. Such information shall be provided without charge to an employee or person acting on behalf of an employee upon request. An employee, person acting on behalf of one or more employees and/or any other interested party may file a complaint with the state for a violation of any provision of this section or any law or regulation implementing its provisions. Such complaint shall be promptly investigated and resolved by the state. The employee's name shall be kept confidential unless disclosure is necessary to resolution of a complaint and the employee consents to disclosure. The state may on its own initiative investigate an employer's compliance with this section and any law or regulation implementing its provisions. The employer shall make available to the state any records related to such investigation and other information required for enforcement of this section or any law or regulation implementing its provisions. No employer shall discharge or in any other manner discriminate or retaliate against an employee for exercising any right under this section or any law or regulation implementing its provisions or against any person for providing assistance to an employee or information regarding the same.

An action for equitable and monetary relief may be brought against an employer by the attorney general and/or an employee or person acting on behalf of an employee or all similarly situated employees in any court of competent jurisdiction, including the common pleas court of an employee's county of residence, for any violation of this section or any law or regulation implementing its provisions within three years of the violation or of when the violation ceased if it was of a continuing nature, or within one year after notification to the employee of final disposition by the state of a complaint for the same violation, whichever is later. There shall be no exhaustion requirement, no procedural, pleading or burden of proof requirements beyond those that apply generally to civil suits in order to maintain such action and no liability for costs or attorney's fees on an employee except upon a finding that such action was frivolous in accordance with the same standards that apply generally in civil suits. Where an employer is found by the state or a court to have violated any provision of this section, the employer shall within thirty days of the finding pay the employee back wages, damages, and the employee's costs and reasonable attorney's fees. Damages shall be calculated as an additional two times the amount of the back wages and in the case of a violation of an anti-retaliation provision an amount set by the state or court sufficient to compensate the employee and deter future violations, but not less than one hundred fifty dollars for each day that the violation continued. Payment under this paragraph shall not be stayed pending any appeal.

This section shall be liberally construed in favor of its purposes. Laws may be passed to implement its provisions and create additional remedies, increase the minimum wage rate and extend the coverage of the section, but in no manner restricting any provision of the section or the power of municipalities under Article XVIII of this constitution with respect to the same.

If any part of this section is held invalid, the remainder of the section shall not be affected by such holding and shall continue in full force and effect.

Proposed by initiative petition in 2006 and approved by the voters, this detailed provision imposes an affirmative obligation on the state to raise the minimum wage annually to account for inflation. The General Assembly already had the power to adopt and increase the state minimum wage under its plenary power, and Article II, section 34, insulated the minimum wage from challenges under the Ohio Constitution.

The new section increased the state minimum wage to $6.85 per hour, effective January 1, 2007, and contained a detailed mandate for future increases. Advanced by unions and their supporters, this proposal was used to encourage greater voter turnout in the 2006 election in much the same way that the prohibition on same-sex marriage in Article XV, section 11, was used to gin up voter turnout in the 2004 presidential election.

Designed not only to assure future increases in the statewide minimum wage but also to broaden its coverage, this section declares that it "shall be liberally construed in favor of its purposes." Toward this end, the section gives the General Assembly power to implement its provisions and to "create additional remedies, increase the minimum wage rate and extend the coverage of the section . . . ."

The section appears to have been written to be self-executing, which would eliminate the need for the General Assembly to take steps to implement it. See *Castillo v. Morales, Inc.* (2014). The Ohio Supreme Court, however, has not decided whether the section is self-executing, but it has held that the definition of "employee" in this section incorporates the exclusions and exemptions of the federal Fair Labor Standards Act. *Haight v. Minchak* (2016).

This section also sought to limit the role of the General Assembly and the courts in enforcing the minimum wage by addressing a range of procedural and remedial issues, including the statute of limitations, damages, attorney's fees, and costs. It also barred the use of exhaustion requirements as well as special procedural, pleading and burden of proof requirements. Finally, this section permitted "an employee or person acting on behalf of an employee or all similarly situated employees in any court of competent jurisdiction," thus permitting traditional class actions rather than the opt-in collective action available under the Federal Labor Standards Act. See *Castillo v. Morales, Inc., supra* (permitting traditional class action). For a critical discussion of the implementation of this section, see Jason R. Bristol, Ashley A. Weaver, and Thomas A. Downie, "Intended and Unintended Consequences: The 2006 Fair Minimum Wage Amendment of the Ohio Constitution," 58 *Clev. St. L. Rev.* 367 (2010).

■ MUNICIPAL MINIMUM WAGES

The section also contemplates that municipalities might seek to legislate in this area, and it expressly bars the General Assembly from adopting laws "restricting any provision of the section or the power of municipalities under Article XVIII of this constitution with respect to" the available remedies, the minimum wage rate, and its coverage.

Despite these limitations on the power of the General Assembly, it has been argued that this section, along with Article II, section 34, bars municipalities from adopting a minimum wage that is higher than the state minimum wage. See Ohio OAG Opinion, No. 2016–21 (June 30, 2016).

The argument against a higher municipal minimum wage is buttressed by a 2016 statute, see O.R.C. section 4113.85, which provides that "[n]o political subdivision shall establish a minimum wage rate different from the wage rate required under this section." The statute contains findings that refer to the "General Assembly's exclusive authority under Section 34 of Article II, Ohio Constitution, to fix and regulate the hours of labor and provide for the comfort, health, safety, and general welfare of employees." The findings also attempt to counter any use of the home rule power by providing "that the regulation of the employment relationship between an employer and the employer's employees as it pertains to hours of labor and fringe benefits is a matter of statewide concern that requires uniform statewide regulation."

Despite these findings, there is nothing in section 34 that states or implies that the General Assembly has "exclusive authority" over wages. More importantly, the 2016 statute ignores the specific provision in section 34a that expressly recognizes the power of municipalities to increase the minimum wage; thus, the more detailed provision of section 34a should prevail in a conflict with legislation enacted under section 34, notwithstanding the general language of the supremacy clause of section 34.

Section 35
Workers' Compensation.

For the purpose of providing compensation to workmen and their dependents, for death, injuries or occupational disease, occasioned in the course of such workmen's employment, laws may be passed establishing a state fund to be created by compulsory contribution thereto by employers, and administered by the state, determining the terms and conditions upon which payment shall be made therefrom. Such compensation shall be in lieu of all other rights to compensation, or damages, for such death, injuries, or occupational disease, and any employer who pays the premium or compensation provided by law, passed in accordance herewith, shall not be liable to respond in damages at common law or by statute for such death, injuries or occupational disease. Laws may be passed establishing a board which may be empowered to classify all occupations, according to their degree of hazard, to fix rates of contribution to such fund according to such classification, and to collect, administer and distribute such fund, and to determine all rights of claimants thereto. Such board shall set aside as a separate fund such proportion of the contributions paid by employers as in its judgment may be necessary, not to exceed one per centum thereof in any year, and so as to equalize, insofar as possible, the burden thereof, to be expended by such board in such manner as may be provided by law for the investigation and prevention of industrial accidents and diseases. Such board shall have full power and authority to hear and determine whether or not an injury, disease or death resulted because of the failure of the employer

> to comply with any specific requirement for the protection of the lives, health or safety of employees, enacted by the General Assembly or in the form of an order adopted by such board, and its decision shall be final; and for the purpose of such investigations and inquiries it may appoint referees. When it is found, upon hearing, that an injury, disease or death resulted because of such failure by the employer, such amount as shall be found to be just, not greater than fifty nor less than fifteen per centum of the maximum award established by law, shall be added by the board, to the amount of the compensation that may be awarded on account of such injury, disease, or death, and paid in like manner as other awards; and, if such compensation is paid from the state fund, the premium of such employer shall be increased in such amount, covering such period of time as may be fixed, as will recoup the state fund in the amount of such additional award, notwithstanding any and all other provisions in this constitution.

Adopted in 1912 and amended in 1923, this section allows the General Assembly to establish a compulsory state fund to compensate workers who are injured or acquire a disease while employed. The delegates to the 1912 Constitutional Convention proposed this section to address the growing number of work-related injuries that were causing great economic burdens for disabled Ohio citizens.

Before adoption of this section, employees injured on the job had to seek compensation in court, but employers nearly always had an advantage. The employee had to prove that the employer was negligent and had to overcome a number of defenses that the employer could assert, particularly contributory negligence, assumption of risk, and the fellow servant rule. At common law, these defenses were complete bars to the employee's recovery. Thus, given the difficulty of seeking redress in the courts, few injured employees were able to receive compensation. See Mark A. Clayborn, "Ohio's 'Employment Intentional Tort': A Workers' Compensation Exception, or the Creation of an Entirely New Cause of Action?" 44 *Clev. St. L. Rev.* 381 (1996) (hereinafter Clayborn "Ohio's Employment Intentional Tort").

The year before the convention, the New York Court of Appeals had struck down that state's workers' compensation program, *Ives v. South Buffalo Railway Co.* (1911), and less than five weeks after the 1912 Convention began its work, the Ohio Supreme Court upheld the constitutionality of Ohio's first workers' compensation law by a 4–2 vote, *State ex rel. Yaple v. Creamer* (1912). The Ohio statute, however, was voluntary, and in upholding its constitutionality the court emphasized the voluntary nature of the act and strongly suggested that coercive legislation would contravene constitutional provisions. See *Taylor v. Academy Iron & Metal Co.* (1988).

Section 35 authorized the adoption of a *compulsory* workers' compensation program. And its companion employee rights provision, see Article II, section 34, protected the program from constitutional attack by providing "a broad grant of authority to the legislature to provide for the welfare of all working persons" (*City of Rocky River v. State Employment Relations Board*, 1989) and by "empower[ing] the General Assembly to regulate the employment relationship without running afoul of the now-obsolete judicial doctrine of 'economic substantive due process'" (*Brady v. Safety-Kleen Corp.*, 1991) (Brown, J., concurring). See generally *1912 Debates*, 1331, 1334–35.

The 1924 amendment to this section, proposed by the General Assembly and approved by the voters, allowed for the establishment of a board to administer the workers' compensation fund and to hear cases in which it is claimed that the employer failed to keep the workplace safe and disease-free. This amendment permitted an employee who was injured or contracted a disease because of the employer's failure to maintain a safe workplace to receive additional compensation (between 15 and 50 percent) and required the employer to pay a higher premium into the fund. Currently, legislation covering Ohio's workers' compensation is found in chapters 4121–27 of the Ohio Revised Code.

Ohio's workers' compensation system is administered exclusively by the state, see *In re Suburban Motor Freight, Inc.* (1993), and in 1981, the voters rejected by an 84 percent to 16 percent vote a proposal made by initiative petition to amend this section to allow private insurance companies to sell workers' compensation insurance.

The Ohio Supreme Court has stated that this section "represents a social bargain in which employers and employees exchange their respective common-law rights and duties for a more certain and uniform set of statutory benefits and obligations." *Holeton v. Crouse Cartage Co.* (2001).

Under this section, employers who pay a premium into the workers' compensation fund are not, as a general matter, liable for death, injury, or occupational diseases. In *Blankenship v, Cincinnati Milacron Chemicals, Inc.* (1982), however, the Ohio Supreme Court held that if an employer commits an intentional tort the employee can still bring a legal action notwithstanding the waiver of the right to sue. According to the court, intentional torts committed by an employer fall outside the employment context and therefore are not covered by workers' compensation laws.

The court in *Blankenship* did not define an intentional tort, but in *Jones v. VIP Development Co.* (1984), the court described an intentional tort as "an act committed with the intent to injure another, or committed with the belief that such injury is substantially certain to occur." The *Jones* court also held that the receipt of workers' compensation benefits did not preclude an employee from suing for an intentional tort and that workers' compensation benefits could not be used to set off an award for damages.

After *Jones* the Ohio Supreme Court modified the definition of an intentional tort in several decisions that struck down attempts by the General Assembly to limit the ability of employees to recover from their employers. See Clayborn, "Ohio's Employment Intentional Tort," 391–99. For example, in 1999, the court held that a law requiring an employee to show by clear and convincing evidence that the employer deliberately and intentionally caused the employee's injury was tantamount to requiring the employee to prove criminal assault (*Johnson v. BP Chems., Inc.* (1999)). And, relying on an interpretation of sec. 34 that it subsequently rejected, the *Johnson* court held that the clear and convincing standard was "clearly not a law that furthers the . . . comfort, health, safety and general welfare of all employees."

But in *Kaminski v. Metal & Wire Products Company* (2010), the court narrowed *Johnson* and held that section 35 (like sec. 34) is "is a *grant* of authority to the General Assembly, not a *restriction* of that body's authority to legislate." See Commentary, Article II, section 34.

The "notwithstanding" final clause of this section seeks to protect this provision from inroads that might be made by other provisions of the constitution, but it is not as powerful as the supremacy clause in section 34, which on its face protects employee welfare *legislation* from limitations imposed by other provisions in the constitution.

Provisions of the Ohio workers' compensation law have also been the subject of litigation under specific provisions of the Ohio Bill of Rights. See, for example, *Holeton v. Crouse Cartage Co.* (2001) (answering certified question and concluding that statute limiting workers' compensation recoveries by expanding the right of subrogation violates Art. I, secs. 2, 16, and 19); see also Commentary, Article I, sections 2, 16, and 19.

Section 36
Conservation of natural resources.

Laws may be passed to encourage forestry and agriculture, and to that end areas devoted exclusively to forestry may be exempted, in whole or in part, from taxation. Notwithstanding the provisions of section 2 of Article XII, laws may be passed to provide that land devoted exclusively to agricultural use be valued for real property tax purposes at the current value such land has for such agricultural use. Laws may also be passed to provide for the deferral or recoupment of any part of the difference in the dollar amount of real property tax levied in any year on land valued in accordance with its agricultural use and the dollar amount of real property tax which would have been levied upon such land had it been valued for such year in accordance with section 2 of Article XII. Laws may also be passed to provide for converting into forest reserves such lands or parts of lands as have been or may be forfeited to the state, and to authorize the acquiring of other lands for that purpose; also, to provide for the conservation of the natural resources of the state, including streams, lakes, submerged and swamp lands and the development and regulation of water power and the formation of drainage and conservation districts; and to provide for the regulation of methods of mining, weighing, measuring and marketing coal, oil, gas and all other minerals.

Adopted in 1912 and amended in 1973, this section allows laws to be enacted to encourage forestry through full or partial exemption of these lands from taxation. The Ohio Supreme Court has held that "[t]he language, 'Laws may also be passed . . . to provide for the conservation of the natural resources of the state, including streams, lakes,' etc., is so broad and comprehensive that any natural tract of land bearing a reasonable relation to these words is clearly comprehended within the terms of this constitutional amendment." *MacNab v. Board of Park Commissioners* (1923). In addition to upholding the power of the General Assembly to create park districts, the *MacNab* court made clear that this section was not a limitation on the broad power of the General Assembly.

In addition, this section allows laws to be passed to convert land forfeited to the state into forest reserves and to acquire land for natural resources. Laws may also be passed to regulate methods of mining coal, gas, oil, and other minerals. Legislation regarding this section can be found in Ohio Revised Code sections 5713.30–5713.37.

The 1973 amendment to this section, which was proposed by the General Assembly and approved by the voters, permits land devoted exclusively to agricultural use to be valued for real property tax purposes at the value such land has for agricultural use, and further provides that laws may be passed to recoup the difference of such taxation of the land had it been taxed under Article XII, section 2, which requires the uniform classification of real property. See Commentary, Article XII, section 2. This amendment was proposed to protect owners of agricultural land from the spike in the market value of their land.

Section 37
Eight-hour day on public work.

Except in cases of extraordinary emergency, not to exceed eight hours shall constitute a day's work, and not to exceed forty-eight hours a week's work, for workmen engaged on any public work carried on or aided by the state, or any political sub-division thereof, whether done by contract, or otherwise.

Adopted in 1912 and never amended, this section is a response to *City of Cleveland v. Clements Brothers Construction Co.* (1902), in which the Ohio Supreme Court held that the state's 1904 maximum hour law violated the right to contract. See *1912 Debates, 1939*; see also *City of Rocky River v. State Employment Rel. Bd.* (1989) (Wright, J., dissenting). This section limited work on public projects to eight hours per day with a maximum of forty-eight hours per week. The Ohio Supreme Court, however, has read this section to impose the work hour limitations only with respect to the construction of public improvements and not to their maintenance or operation. *State v. Peters* (1924). Other state laws concerning working hours, conditions, or wages may be enacted and given special protection under the plenary power of the General Assembly and its special authority under Article II, section 34. See Commentary on Article II, section 34.

Section 38

Removal of officials.

Laws shall be passed providing for the prompt removal from office, upon complaint and hearing, of all officers, including state officers, judges and members of the General Assembly, for any misconduct involving moral turpitude or for other cause provided by law; and this method of removal shall be in addition to impeachment or other method of removal authorized by the constitution.

Adopted in 1912 and never amended, this section provides a means for removing state and local public officers other than by impeachment or by the other methods authorized by the constitution. This section requires the General Assembly to enact legislation to facilitate the removal of government officials for "misconduct involving moral turpitude or for other cause provided by law." The removal of public officers, including judges, is governed by O.R.C. sections 3.07–3.10. The removal of judges is also governed by O.R.C. sections 2701.11–12, by Rule IIIA of the Supreme Court Rules for the Government of the Judiciary, and by Article IV, section 17 of the Ohio Constitution. Section 3.04 of the Ohio Revised Code also provides for the removal of officers appointed by the governor.

Under this section and its implementing legislation, officers, which include state and local officials, can be removed from office for misconduct if the officer "willfully and flagrantly exercises authority or power not authorized by law, refuses or willfully neglects to enforce the law or to perform any official duty imposed upon him by law, or is guilty of gross neglect of duty, gross immorality, drunkenness, misfeasance, malfeasance, or nonfeasance." O.R.C. section 3.07. This authority is not limited to misconduct relating to the office or arising out of official acts, and it includes gross immorality and misconduct involving moral turpitude that is in no way connected with official duties. *In re Bostwick* (1931). The section also permits the General Assembly to provide grounds for removal in addition to "misconduct involving moral turpitude."

Section 3.08 of the Revised Code outlines the procedures for the removal of officers, and it requires the submission of a written complaint setting forth the charge and signed by not less than 15 percent of the qualified electors of the state or political subdivision.

When the officer sought to be removed is the sheriff, county prosecuting attorney, or mayor, the governor may sign and file a complaint without the otherwise necessary signatures. The removal proceedings are filed in the court of common pleas and tried by a judge unless the officer requests a jury in writing. A hearing and complaint are necessary to determine the factual basis for discharge and to allow the officer to present a defense. These procedures are also required for removals under any legislation enacted under this section of the constitution, such as O.R.C. section 3.08. *State ex rel. Hughes, v. Brown* (1972).

This section requires that a statute that authorizes a board of county commissioners to remove a county treasurer must provide for a complaint and hearing before authorizing the removal. *State ex rel. Zeigler v. Zumbar* (2011).

Unlike the impeachment of public officials, the removal of public officials under this section is a function of judicial power and is subject to judicial review. *In re Bostwick* (1932).

This section provides an alternative to the other constitutional provisions for the impeachment and removal of state officers under Article. II, sections 23 and 24, and for the removal of judges under Article. IV, section 17. In fact, the last clause of section 38 specifically states that procedures adopted under this section are "in addition to impeachment and other methods of removal authorized by law." *State ex rel. Hoel v. Brown* (1922).

Section 39

Regulating expert testimony in criminal trials.

Laws may be passed for the regulation of the use of expert witnesses and expert testimony in criminal trials and proceedings.

Adopted in 1912 and never amended, this section reflected the belief of many delegates to the 1912 Constitutional Convention that medical expert testimony was not trustworthy. Speaking on the subject, one delegate said: "I say the ordinary medical expert is not worthy of belief, and I want to cross examine him with great care before I accept him as a witness at all. He is a special pleader seated on a witness box." *1912 Debates*, 1836. The specific reference to medical experts was eventually disregarded in committee, and the section that the convention sent to the voters (and that the voters approved) allowed for laws to be passed regulating all expert witness testimony at criminal trials and proceedings. Rules governing the use of expert testimony are found in Rules 701–705 of the Ohio Rules of Evidence.

Section 40

Registering and warranting land titles.

Laws may be passed providing for a system of registering, transferring, insuring and guaranteeing land titles by the state or by the counties thereof, and for settling and determining adverse or other claims to and interests in, lands the titles to which are so registered, insured or guaranteed, and for the creation and collection of guaranty funds by fees to be assessed against lands, the titles to which are registered; and judicial powers with right of appeal may by law be conferred upon county recorders or other officers in matters arising under the operation of such system.

Adopted in 1912 and never amended, this section allows the General Assembly to establish laws creating a system of land registration. In 1896, the

General Assembly enacted a Torrens law under which a state-created register of lands operated as conclusive evidence of ownership of property. The Torrens system differs from general recording laws under which evidence of title to land is recorded, see 1 *Oh. Jur.* 3d *Abstracts and Land Titles,* section 6 (2019), and the main purpose of the Torrens system is to make transfers of real property as efficient as transfers of personal property. See OCRC, *Final Report,* 95.

In 1897, however, the Ohio Supreme Court held the statute unconstitutional, in part, because it attempted to vest a county recorder with judicial power. *State ex rel. Attorney General v. Guilbert* (1897).

The approval by the votes of this section in 1912 effectively overruled *Guilbert,* and in 1913, the General Assembly adopted a new Torrens Act. See 1913 Ohio Laws 914.

Notwithstanding this section, most property in Ohio is not registered under the Torrens system but under the general recording laws. See 1 *Oh. Jur.* 3d *Abstracts and Land Titles,* section 8 (2019) ("Torrens registration is designed to provide a conclusive method of determining title, thereby doing away with secret liens and hidden equities."). But the General Assembly, acting under this section, has exercised the power to limit Torrens registration, and an Ohio appellate court has rejected the argument that county abolition of land registration violates this section or represents a taking of property without just compensation. *Weyandt v. Davis* (1996). See also 1 *Oh. Jur.* 3d *Abstracts and Land Titles,* section 6 (2019).

Section 41
Prison labor.

Laws may be passed providing for and regulating the occupation and employment of prisoners sentenced to the several penal institutions and reformatories in the state.

Adopted in 1912 and amended in 1978, this was originally a very detailed section governing prison labor and goods produced by prison labor, and it included a provision requiring the labeling of goods sold in the state as "prison made." The delegates to the 1912 Constitutional Convention proposed this provision, which prohibited the employment of prisoners in private industry, in part, because of pressure from industries that had been complaining about the unfair advantage of having to compete against cheap prison labor. See OCRC, *Final Report,* 51–52.

In 1978, based on a recommendation of the OCRC, the General Assembly recommended and the voters approved a major overhaul of this section to remove its detailed restrictions. See OCRC, *Final Report,* 50–52. The new section simply permitted the General Assembly to enact laws "regulating the occupation and employment of prisoners." The relevant statutes are in Ohio Revised Code chapter 5147.

Section 42

Continuity of government operations in emergencies caused by enemy attack.

The General Assembly shall have the power and the immediate duty to pass laws to provide for prompt and temporary succession to the powers and duties of public offices, of whatever nature and whether filled by election or appointment, the incumbents of which may become unavailable for carrying on the powers and duties of such offices and to pass such other laws as may be necessary and proper for insuring the continuity of governmental operations in periods of emergency resulting from disasters caused by enemy attack.

Adopted in 1961 at the height of the Cold War and amid the national scare of nuclear attack on the United States and never amended, this section provides the General Assembly with the power to enact laws to secure the succession of power and continuity of the Ohio government in emergencies caused by enemy attack. Provisions for the establishment of an emergency interim government are in chapter 161 of the Revised Code.

Article III

Executive

Article III establishes the executive branch of state government, consisting of a governor and key executive offices. The executive branch of Ohio government has undergone significant changes since its creation in 1802, particularly in the powers exercised by the governor. After their experience with the autocratic rule of Northwest Territorial Governor Arthur St. Clair, the Jeffersonians, who dominated the 1802 Constitutional Convention, created an executive branch that had little influence over state government.

Under the 1802 Constitution, the governor was not much more than "an ornamental head of the State." Carrington T. Marshall, ed., *A History of the Courts and Lawyers of Ohio*, vol. III (New York: American Historical Society, Inc., 1934), 829. The governor had the power only to issue pardons, to appoint the adjutant general of the state militia, and to fill certain vacancies in executive offices while the General Assembly was in recess. Although the governor served as commander-in-chief of the state militia, the governor could not veto acts of the legislature. The 1851 Constitution expanded the governor's powers to make appointments and fill vacancies in executive offices, but the governor did not get the veto power until the voters approved an amendment in 1903.

In 1976, the voters approved a major reorganization of this article proposed by the General Assembly and based on the recommendations of the Ohio

The Ohio State Constitution. Steven H. Steinglass and Gino J. Scarselli, Oxford University Press. © Oxford University Press 2022. DOI: 10.1093/oso/9780197619728.003.0005

Constitutional Revision Commission (hereinafter OCRC). See generally Steven H. Steinglass, "Constitutional Revision: Ohio Style," 77 *Ohio St. L. J.* 281 (2016): 334–45.

Section 1

Executive department.

The executive department shall consist of a governor, lieutenant governor, secretary of state, auditor of state, treasurer of state, and an attorney general, who shall be elected on the first Tuesday after the first Monday in November, by the electors of the state, and at the places of voting for members of the General Assembly.

Adopted in 1851 and amended in 1885, this section provides for an executive branch comprising a governor, lieutenant governor, secretary of state, treasurer of state, and attorney general, all of whom are elected officials. The composition of the executive branch has changed significantly since the first constitution. Under the 1802 Constitution, the executive branch consisted of only a governor, who was vested with the supreme executive power of the state (although that did not amount to much at the time), and a secretary of state, who was responsible for recording the official acts of the governor. The 1802 Constitution also referred to a state auditor and to a state treasurer, but these offices were not part of the executive branch. Under the first constitution, the voters elected the governor, while the General Assembly appointed the state auditor, the state treasurer, and the secretary of state.

The 1802 Constitution did not provide for an attorney general or a lieutenant governor. The General Assembly created the office of attorney general in 1846, and from 1846 until 1851, it appointed the attorney general. The 1851 Constitution created these offices and provided that they be elected positions.

The 1885 amendment changed the general election day from the first Tuesday in October to the first Tuesday after the first Monday in November.

Although the constitution defines the power of the governor, see Commentary, Article III, section 5, and the lieutenant governor, see Commentary, Article III, section 1b, it is silent on the powers of the independently elected state constitutional officers—the secretary of state, the auditor of state, the treasurer of state, and the attorney general. But these officials all have a set of powers that were defined by the common law, and it is likely that the framers of the 1851 Constitution recognized and accepted their common-law powers when they created those positions. Indeed, the leading commentary on the history of the office of the Ohio attorney general so concluded:

> Thus it quite cogently appears that the common law was of sufficient strength and clarity in Ohio in 1852 that the framers of the constitution, by employing the

traditional Anglo-American title for the chief law officer of the sovereign, meant to and did establish an attorney general of broad inherent power.

Clinton J. Miller II and Terry M. Miller, "Constitutional Charter of Ohio's Attorney General," 37 *Ohio St. L.J.* 801 (1976).

One appeals court has noted that, "in the absence of constitutional restrictions, courts have recognized that the office of attorney general has all of the powers that attorneys general enjoyed at common law." *State ex rel. Petro v. Marshall* (2006); see also *State ex rel. Cordray v. Marshall* (2009) (noting that nothing in the statutes "appears to abrogate the attorney general's common-law powers within the limited context of this case" and upholding the attorney general's common-law standing).

Section 1a

Joint vote for governor and lieutenant governor.

In the general election for governor and lieutenant governor, one vote shall be cast jointly for the candidates nominated by the same political party or petition. The General Assembly shall provide by law for the nomination of candidates for governor and lieutenant governor.

Adopted in 1976 and never amended, this section provides for the joint election of the governor and lieutenant governor. Before the adoption of this section, political opponents could be elected to the respective offices since the governor and lieutenant governor ran on separate ballots. The OCRC recommended this change, noting the national trend for a joint ballot and stating that "the principal purpose for which the Lieutenant Governor was created—to provide an automatic successor, elected state-wide, to fill any vacancy which may occur in the office of the Governor" and the orderly succession of the lieutenant governor to the office of the governor would be better served if both officials belonged to the same political party. See OCRC, *Recommendations for Amendments to the Ohio Constitution: Final Report* (1977), 137–38 (hereinafter OCRC, *Final Report*).

Section 1b

Duties of lieutenant governor.

The lieutenant governor shall perform such duties in the executive department as are assigned to him by the governor and as are prescribed by law.

Adopted in 1976 and never amended, this section repealed Article III, section 16 of the 1851 Constitution. Under the former section, the lieutenant governor was president of the Senate, and the lieutenant governor's only duty was to cast a vote if the Senate was equally divided. Under the current section, the lieutenant governor no longer casts a deciding vote in the Senate when the Senate is equally divided. If a vote in the Senate results in a tie, the measure fails.

The governor and the General Assembly are now responsible for determining the lieutenant governor's duties. The governor may also assign the lieutenant governor other responsibilities, including the directorship of cabinet-level departments. And under statutory law the lieutenant governor is deputy commander-in-chief of the organized militia and presiding officer of the governor's cabinet when the governor is absent. See O.R.C. sections 108.04–05.

Section 2

Terms of office.

The governor, lieutenant governor, secretary of state, treasurer of state, and attorney general shall hold their offices for four years commencing on the second Monday of January, 1959. Their terms of office shall continue until their successors are elected and qualified. The auditor of state shall hold his office for a term of two years from the second Monday of January, 1961 to the second Monday of January, 1963 and thereafter shall hold his office for a four year term. No person shall hold the office of governor for a period longer than two successive terms of four years. No person shall hold any one of the offices of lieutenant governor, secretary of state, treasurer of state, attorney general, or auditor of state for a period longer than two successive terms of four years. Terms shall be considered successive unless separated by a period of four or more years. Only terms beginning on or after January 1, 1995 shall be considered in determining an individual's eligibility to hold the office of lieutenant governor, secretary of state, treasurer of state, attorney general, or auditor of state.

Adopted in 1851 and amended in 1954 and 1992, this section provides the terms of office for the governor and the other executive branch officers named in section 1. This section replaced Article II, sections 3 and 16 of the 1802 Constitution, which set the terms of office of, respectively, the governor and secretary of state and Article VI, section 2 of the 1802 Constitution, which covered the terms of office of the state treasurer and state auditor. Under the 1802 Constitution, the governor, who was elected by the people, served a two-year term but was not eligible to serve more than six years in any eight-year period. In addition, under the 1802 Constitution the secretary of state, the treasurer of state, and the state auditor, all of whom were appointed by the General Assembly, served three-year terms. The 1802 Constitution also contained an unusual provision applicable only to the secretary of state requiring the secretary to serve under the condition that "he shall so long behave himself well." 1802 Constitution, Article II, section 16.

As adopted in 1851, this section set two-year terms of office for the governor, secretary of state, treasurer of state, and attorney general and a four-year term for the state auditor. No limit was included on the number of terms that a governor could serve, and Ohio's only five-term governor, Governor Frank Lausche, was elected to four consecutive two-year terms from 1948 to 1954 after having lost his initial bid for reelection in 1946 after his first term.

A 1954 amendment to this section proposed by the General Assembly extended the terms of office of the named executive branch officers to four years (although the amendment created a once-only two-year term for the state auditor from January 1961 to January 1963, so the terms of all key executive officers would begin and end the same year).

The 1954 amendment also provided that "[n]o person shall hold the office of governor for a period longer than two successive terms of four years." In 1973, the Ohio Supreme Court resolved an ambiguity in this language, which could have been construed to limit the total number of terms that the governor could serve, see OCRC, *Final Report*, 240, and held that this language applied to successive terms. Therefore, the governor was not barred from serving an unlimited number of terms in office as long as every two successive terms are separated by a period of at least four years. *State ex rel. Rhodes v. Brown* (1973).

The most recent amendment to this section, proposed by initiative petition and approved by the voters in 1992, extended the restriction on serving more than two successive terms to all the executive branch offices named in the constitution. Thus, the governor and the other named executive officers are elected to four-year terms subject to the condition that no person can hold the same office for more than two successive terms. Partial terms in office count as full terms and must be separated by at least four years.

Section 3

Election returns.

The returns of every election for the officers, named in the foregoing section, shall be sealed and transmitted to the seat of government, by the returning officers, directed to the president of the Senate, who, during the first week of the regular session, shall open and publish them, and declare the result, in the presence of a majority of the members of each house of the General Assembly. The joint candidates having the highest number of votes cast for governor and lieutenant governor and the person having the highest number of votes for any other office shall be declared duly elected; but if any two or more have an equal and the highest number of votes for the same office or offices, one of them or any two for whom joint votes were cast for governor and lieutenant governor, shall be chosen by the joint vote of both houses.

Adopted in 1851 and amended in 1976, this section governs the election of the executive branch officers mentioned in the previous section. It provides that the person receiving the highest number of votes shall be elected to that office. This section also gives the General Assembly the power to determine the winner in case an election results in a tie. The 1976 amendment to this section made it consistent with Article III, section 1b, which established joint elections for governor and lieutenant governor.

Section 3 bears some similarity to the Twelfth Amendment to the U.S. Constitution, which gives the U.S. House of Representatives the power to determine who shall serve as president in case no candidate receives a majority of Electoral College votes. In contrast to the Twelfth Amendment, which requires a majority of electoral votes for the president to be elected, this section does not require the winner to receive a majority of votes.

Section 4
Repealed—Presentation of Election Returns.

Adopted in 1851 and repealed in 1976, this section originally provided for election returns to be presented to the secretary of state if the General Assembly was not in session in January following the election.

Section 5
Executive power vested in governor.

The supreme executive power of this State shall be vested in the governor.

Adopted in 1851 and never amended, this section, which is virtually identical to both Article II, section 1, of the 1802 Ohio Constitution and Article II, section 1, of the U.S. Constitution, has remained the same since 1802. Unlike the U.S. Constitution, which vests all executive power in one person, the president, *Touby v. U.S.* (1991), the Ohio Constitution divides executive powers among the governor and the constitutional officers mentioned in Article III, section 1.

The scope of the governor's "executive power" has never been defined, but it encompasses the specific powers granted by the constitution plus ministerial duties conferred upon the governor by statute. *State ex rel. Whiteman v. Chase* (1856). Notwithstanding this section's grant of "supreme executive power," the governor's powers are limited by the powers granted to the secretary of state, state auditor, treasurer, attorney general in the constitution as well as by the powers given to other offices created by the General Assembly. *State ex rel. S. Monroe & Sons Co. v. Baker* (1925).

Section 6
Governor may require written information.

He may require information, in writing, from the officers in the executive department, upon any subject relating to the duties of their respective offices; and shall see that the laws are faithfully executed.

Adopted in 1851 and never amended, this section, which gives the governor authority over other executive department officials, is substantially unchanged from Article II, section 7, of the 1802 Constitution. The last clause is virtually identical to the "Take Care" clause of the U.S. Constitution, which provides that the president "shall take Care that the Laws be faithfully executed." U.S. Constitution, Article II, section 3.

The power to faithfully execute the laws is one of the characteristics of the executive branch and distinguishes it from the other two branches of government under our system of separation of powers. See generally Curtis Rodebush, "Separation of Powers in Ohio: A Critical Analysis," 51 *Clev. St. L. Rev.* 505 (2004).

Although the U.S. Supreme Court has held that there is no federal constitutional requirement that states follow the doctrine of separation of powers, *Sweezy v. New Hampshire* (1957), every state has adopted some form of the doctrine. See Jim Rossi, "Institutional Design and the Lingering Legacy of Antifederalist Separation of Powers Ideals in the States," 52 *Vand. L. Rev.* 1167 (1999).

Section 7

Governor's annual message and recommendations.

He shall communicate at every session, by message, to the General Assembly, the condition of the state, and recommend such measures as he shall deem expedient.

Adopted in 1851 and never amended, this section gives the governor an active role in defining state policy by requiring the governor to inform the General Assembly of the condition of the state and to recommend legislation at every legislative session. See Thomas R. Swisher, ed., *Ohio Constitution Handbook* (Cleveland: Banks-Baldwin Publishing Co., 1990), 305 (hereinafter Swisher, *Ohio Constitution Handbook*). The predecessor to this section, Article II, section 4, of the 1802 Constitution, only required the governor to inform the General Assembly and make recommendations "from time to time," which suggests the lack of importance given to the office of governor under the first constitution. Today, the governor satisfies this mandate by delivering a State of the State address in January at the beginning of each annual legislative session. In addition, in accordance with this section the governor is required by statute to submit a biennial budget to the General Assembly. O.R.C. section 107.03.

Section 8

Governor may convene special session of General Assembly with limited purposes.

The governor on extraordinary occasions may convene the General Assembly by proclamation and shall state in the proclamation the purpose for which such special session is called, and no other business shall be transacted at such special session except that named in the proclamation, or in a subsequent public proclamation or message to the General Assembly issued by the governor during said special session, but the General Assembly may provide for the expenses of the session and other matters incidental thereto.

Adopted in 1851 and amended in 1912, this section addresses when the governor may convene a special session of the General Assembly. The predecessor to this section, Article II, section 9, of the 1802 Constitution, provided that the governor "may, on extraordinary occasions, convene the General Assembly, by proclamation, and shall state to them, when assembled, the purpose for which they shall have been convened." The present section differs significantly from its predecessor by expressly providing that "no other business shall be transacted at such special session except that named in the proclamation . . . ."

Any legislation that is not germane to the purpose of the special session as identified in the proclamation is invalid. *State ex rel. Ach v. Braden* (1932). See also *State ex rel. Ohio Turnpike Commission v. Allen* (1952) ("The provisions of Section 8 of Article III of the Constitution of Ohio requiring the Governor to state in his proclamation the purpose for which a special session of the General Assembly is called are mandatory.") (syllabus). But during a special session the governor may issue a subsequent proclamation broadening the business of the special session, but it is unclear whether a subsequent proclamation may limit its business.

Section 9

When the governor may adjourn the General Assembly.

In case of disagreement between the two houses, in respect to the time of adjournment, he shall have power to adjourn the General Assembly to such time as he may think proper, but not beyond the regular meetings thereof.

Adopted in 1851 and never amended, this section, which is virtually identical to Article II, section 11, of the 1802 Constitution, resolves disputes between the Senate and the House of Representatives over adjournment. Under Article II, section 14, both houses must agree to adjourn for more than five days (two days under Art. I, sec. 15, of the 1802 Const.). If both houses cannot agree, this section permits the governor to intervene and adjourn the General Assembly.

Section 10

Commander-in-chief of militia.

He shall be commander-in-chief of the military and naval forces of the state, except when they shall be called into service of the United States.

Adopted in 1851 and never amended, this section has remained substantially unchanged from Article II, section 10, of the 1802 Constitution. The earlier provision has its roots in section 6 of the Northwest Ordinance, which provided that the governor was to be commander-in-chief of the militia. Statutory provisions govern when the governor may call the "militia" into service. O.R.C. sections 5923.21–.231. These provisions illustrate the interplay between the executive and legislative branches. While the governor is the commander-in-chief and has the power to call the militia into service, the General Assembly may restrict the exercise of that power.

Section 11

Governor may grant reprieves, commutations and pardons.

The governor shall have power, after conviction, to grant reprieves, commutations, and pardons, for all crimes and offenses, except treason and cases of impeachment, upon such conditions as the governor may think proper; subject, however, to such regulations, as to the manner of applying for commutations and pardons, as may be prescribed by law. Upon conviction for treason, the governor may suspend the execution of the sentence, and report the case to the General Assembly, at its next meeting, when the General Assembly shall either pardon, commute the sentence, direct its execution, or grant a further reprieve. The governor shall communicate to the General Assembly, at every regular session, each case of reprieve, commutation, or pardon granted, stating the name and crime of the convict, the sentence, its date, and the date of the commutation, pardon, or reprieve, with the governor's reasons therefor.

Adopted in 1851 and amended in 1995, this section grants the governor the power to exercise executive clemency. This was one of the few powers granted to the governor under Ohio's first constitution. The forerunner of this section, Article II, section 5, of the 1802 Ohio Constitution, was modeled after Article II, section 2, of the U.S. Constitution, and it provided that the governor has "the power to grant reprieves and pardons, after conviction, except in cases of impeachment."

The section refers to three kinds of executive clemency: reprieves (temporary delays in the execution of a sentence), commutations (reductions in sentences), and pardons (permanent releases from punishment for crimes committed). Originally, the governor's clemency power included only the power to grant reprieves and pardons.

The delegates to the 1850–51 Constitutional Convention, influenced by New York's 1846 amendment to its executive clemency provision, proposed adding the power of commutation to the powers of reprieve and pardon. Delegates to the 1851 convention also extended the limitation on executive clemency to cases involving treason and added a clause subjecting the governor's power to grant pardons "to such regulations, as to the manner of applying for commutations and pardons, as may be prescribed by law." The delegates intended this latter clause to provide a safeguard against abuses of the governor's pardon power. See Swisher, *Ohio Constitution Handbook*, 307.

In 1995, the General Assembly proposed and the voters approved an amendment to limit the governor's power to commute sentences, following a public firestorm over a pardon and eight commutations issued by former Governor Richard Celeste. Two days before he left office, Governor Celeste pardoned one inmate and commuted the sentences of eight others, seven of whom were on death row, without the statutorily required Adult Parole Authority (APA) investigations. The Ohio Supreme Court held that the pardon was invalid because the governor's pardon power under the constitution was subject to the statutory procedures governing pardons. The court, however, found no similar constitutional restriction on the governor's commutation power, and it upheld the commutations even though the governor had ignored the statutory procedures. *State ex rel. Maurer v. Sheward* (1994).

Under the 1995 amendment to this section, the statutory procedures governing both pardon and commutation applications must be followed before the governor can grant a pardon or commute a sentence.

The statute regarding pardon and commutation procedures requires all applications to be submitted in writing to the APA, which is to conduct an investigation and report its recommendation for or against clemency to the governor. O.R.C. section 2967.07. Once the statutory provision is satisfied, the constitutional prerequisite is met, and the governor is free to disregard any recommendation. At that point, the governor's discretion to grant or deny executive clemency is not subject to judicial review. *Maurer, supra.*

While a pardon releases the offender from further punishment prescribed for the offense and removes certain disabilities flowing from the conviction, "[a] gubernatorial pardon does not automatically entitle the recipient to have the record of the pardoned conviction sealed." *State v. Boykin* (2013) (syllabus). And the courts lack the inherent authority to seal a criminal record of a pardoned offender. *State v. Radcliff* (2015).

Section 12
Seal of the state.

There shall be a seal of the state, which shall be kept by the governor, and used by him officially; and shall be called "The Great Seal of the State of Ohio."

Adopted in 1851 and never amended, this section concerning the seal of the state is identical to Article II, section 14, of the 1802 Constitution. The seal of Ohio contains the state's coat of arms, which consists of

> a circular shield; in the right foreground of the shield a full sheaf of wheat bound and standing erect; in the left foreground, a cluster of seventeen arrows bound in the center and resembling in form the sheaf of wheat; in the background, a representation of Mount Logan, Ross county, as viewed from Adena state memorial; over the mount, a rising sun three-quarters exposed and radiating thirteen rays to represent the thirteen original colonies shining over the first state in the northwest territory, the

exterior extremities of which rays form a semicircle; and uniting the background and foreground, a representation of the Scioto river and cultivated fields.

O.R.C. section 5.04.

Various offices and departments of state government use the state seal surrounded by the name of the office or department. Below is a picture of the seal used by the Ohio Supreme Court.

Section 13

How grants and commissions issued.

All grants and commissions shall be issued in the name, and by the authority of the state of Ohio, sealed with the great seal; signed by the governor, and countersigned by the secretary of state.

Adopted in 1851 and never amended, this section, which contains the formal requirements for issuing grants and commissions, is almost identical to Article II, section 15, of the 1802 Constitution. These requirements are further spelled out in the state statutes that require judges and other state and county officers to present certificates of their election or appointment and receive a commission from the governor before they are eligible for office. O.R.C. section 107.05.

Section 14

Who is ineligible to serve as governor.

No member of Congress, or person holding office under the authority of this state, or of the United States, shall execute the office of governor, except as herein provided.

Adopted in 1851 and never amended, this section is almost a verbatim restatement of Article II, section 13, of the 1802 Constitution, except for the "as herein provided" clause. The 1851 Constitution permitted the lieutenant governor to hold both offices in case the lieutenant governor had to succeed the governor because of the governor's death, removal, or disability. The present constitution now provides for a replacement in the office of lieutenant governor in such a situation. See Article III, section 17a.

Section 15

Succession in case of vacancy in office of governor.

(A) In the case of the death, conviction on impeachment, resignation, or removal, of the governor, the lieutenant governor shall succeed to the office of governor.

(B) When the governor is unable to discharge the duties of office by reason of disability, the lieutenant governor shall serve as governor until the governor's disability terminates.

(C) In the event of vacancy in the office of governor or when the governor is unable to discharge the duties of office, the line of succession to the office of governor or to the position of serving as governor for the duration of the governor's disability shall proceed from the lieutenant governor to the president of the Senate and then to the speaker of the House of Representatives.

(D) Any person serving as governor for the duration of the governor's disability shall have the powers, duties, and compensation of the office of governor. Any person who succeeds to the office of governor shall have the powers, duties, title, and compensation of the office of governor.

(E) No person shall simultaneously serve as governor and lieutenant governor, president of the Senate, or speaker of the House of Representatives, nor shall any person simultaneously receive the compensation of the office of governor and that of lieutenant governor, president of the Senate, or speaker of the House of Representatives.

Adopted in 1851 and amended in 1976, this section deals with succession to the office of the governor. Under the 1802 Constitution, the office of lieutenant governor did not exist, and the speaker of the Senate succeeded the governor. In the 1851 Constitution, the lieutenant governor became the first successor to the office of governor in case of the governor's death, impeachment, resignation, or removal.

In 1976, the General Assembly, in response to a recommendation from the OCRC, see OCRC, *Final Report*, 226, proposed and the voters approved a revised section 15 to extend the line of succession after the lieutenant governor to the president of the Senate and then to the speaker of the House (subsection (C)). If the lieutenant governor, president of the Senate, and speaker of the House are all unable to serve, succession passes first to the secretary of state and then to the treasurer, auditor, and attorney general by statute. O.R.C. section 161.03.

The OCRC recommendation also distinguished between permanent succession to the office of governor in cases of death, impeachment, resignation, or removal and temporary service by the lieutenant governor when the governor falls under a disability. Under this recommendation, the lieutenant governor would serve as governor on a temporary basis as long as the governor remained under a disability (subsection (B)). The new section did not define the term "disability," consistent with the OCRC's belief that it would be better not to define the term but "to treat as a disability any condition of circumstance that renders the Governor unable to discharge the duties of his office." OCRC, *Final Report*, 226–27. Under Article III, section 22, the Ohio Supreme Court is the ultimate arbiter of whether the governor is under a disability for the purpose of this section.

This section is also applicable when the governor resigns to accept another office. This last occurred in December 1998 when Governor George Voinovich resigned eleven days before the end of his term so he could be sworn in as U.S. senator. His term as governor was not scheduled to end until January 11, 1999, but his term as senator was to begin on January 3, 1999. Because of the preceding section, Article III, section 14, Governor Voinovich could not serve simultaneously as governor and senator and therefore resigned, leading to the appointment of the lieutenant governor, Nancy Hollister, to complete his term as governor.

Section 16

Repealed—Duties of lieutenant governor.

Adopted in 1851 and repealed in 1976, this section named the lieutenant governor as president of the Senate and listed the lieutenant governor's duties.

Section 17

Who shall act if a vacancy occurs in offices of both governor and lieutenant governor.

When a vacancy occurs in both the office of governor and lieutenant governor because of the death, conviction on impeachment, resignation, or removal of the persons elected to those offices prior to the expiration of the first twenty months of a term, a governor and lieutenant governor shall be elected at the next general election occurring in an even-numbered year after the vacancy occurs, for the unexpired portion of the term. The officer next in line of succession' to the office of governor shall serve as governor from the occurrence of the vacancy until the newly elected governor has qualified.

If by reason of death, resignation, or disqualification, the governor-elect is unable to assume the office of governor at the commencement of the gubernatorial term, the lieutenant governor-elect shall assume the office of governor for the full term. If at the commencement of such term, the governor-elect fails to assume the office by reason of disability, the lieutenant governor-elect shall serve as governor until the disability of the governor-elect terminates.

Adopted in 1976 and never amended, this section addresses the situation when a vacancy occurs in both the offices of governor and lieutenant governor. If the vacancy arises early in their terms of office (within the first twenty months), an early election is scheduled for both offices. During the interim, the office of the governor passes first to the president of the Senate and then to the speaker of the House in accordance with Article III, section 15(C).

Section 17a

Filling a vacancy in the office of the lieutenant governor.

Whenever there is a vacancy in the office of the lieutenant governor, the governor shall nominate a lieutenant governor, who shall take office upon confirmation by vote of a majority of the members elected to each house of the General Assembly.

Adopted in 1989 and never amended, this section requires that the governor, with the consent of a majority of the members of both houses, appoint a lieutenant governor in the case of a vacancy.

Section 18

Governor to fill vacancies in elected state offices.

Should the office of auditor of state, treasurer of state, secretary of state, or attorney general become vacant, for any of the causes specified in the fifteenth section of this article, the governor shall fill the vacancy until the disability is removed, or a successor elected and qualified. Such successor shall be elected for the unexpired term of the vacant office at the first general election in an even numbered year that occurs more than forty days after the vacancy has occurred; provided, that when the unexpired term ends within one year immediately following the date of such general election, an election to fill such unexpired term shall not be held and the appointment shall be for such unexpired term.

Adopted in 1851 and amended in 1969, this section limited the General Assembly's power to fill vacancies. Under the 1802 Constitution, the General Assembly had the power to appoint the secretary of state, auditor, and treasurer of state. The governor could appoint successors for these offices but only if a vacancy occurred while the General Assembly was in recess.

The 1851 version of this section gave the governor the power to fill vacancies in the offices of the auditor, treasurer of state, secretary of state, and attorney general no matter when they occur. The person appointed by the governor then fills the vacancy until the official's disability ends or until the voters elect a new official.

In 1969, the General Assembly proposed and the voters approved an amendment to this section to provide for the election of a successor if a year or more remains on the unexpired term. If less than a year remains, the appointed official holds office for the balance of the term.

Section 19

Compensation of key state officers; change during term prohibited.

The officers mentioned in this article shall, at stated times, receive, for their services, a compensation to be established by law, which shall neither be increased nor diminished during the period for which they shall have been elected.

Adopted in 1851 and never amended, this section is derived from Article II, section 6, of the 1802 Constitution, which prohibited the General Assembly from increasing or decreasing the governor's compensation during the governor's term in office. The 1851 Constitution expanded this prohibition to cover the compensation of all officers mentioned in Article III. The prohibition against increasing or decreasing salaries during an officer's term is apparently intended to prevent the General Assembly from attempting to improperly influence executive branch officers. See Swisher, *Ohio Constitution Handbook*, 311.

Section 20

Annual reports of executive officers.

The officers of the executive department, and of the public state institutions shall, at least five days preceding each regular session of the General Assembly, severally report to the governor, who shall transmit such reports, with his message, to the General Assembly.

Adopted in 1851 and never amended, the section requires that the General Assembly be kept informed of the operations of the executive branch. Under it, the officers of the executive department are required to submit a report to the governor five days prior to the opening of each regular session of the General Assembly. With the General Assembly required to hold annual sessions as a result of the 1973 amendment of Article II, section 28, the reporting requirement became an annual obligation of the governor. This annual reporting requirement allows the governor to include these reports in the State of the State address to the General Assembly.

Section 21

Appointments subject to advice and consent of Senate.

When required by law, appointments to state office shall be subject to the advice and consent of the Senate. All statutory provisions requiring advice and consent of the Senate to appointments to state office heretofore enacted by the General Assembly are hereby validated, ratified and confirmed as to all appointments made hereafter, but any such provision may be altered or repealed by law.

No appointment shall be consented to without concurrence of a majority of the total number of Senators provided for by this Constitution, except as hereinafter provided for in the case of failure of the Senate to act. If the Senate has acted upon any appointment to which its consent is required and has refused to consent, an appointment of another person shall be made to fill the vacancy.

If an appointment is submitted during a session of the General Assembly, it shall be acted upon by the Senate during such session of the General Assembly, except that if such session of the General Assembly adjourns sine die within ten days after such submission without acting upon such appointment, it may be acted upon at the next session of the General Assembly.

If an appointment is made after the Senate has adjourned sine die, it shall be submitted to the Senate during the next session of the General Assembly.

In acting upon an appointment a vote shall be taken by a yea and nay vote of the members of the Senate and shall be entered upon its journal. Failure of the Senate to act by a roll call vote on an appointment by the governor within the time provided for herein shall constitute consent to such appointment.

Adopted in 1961 and never amended, this section provides that the General Assembly may subject the appointment of public officers to the advice and consent of the Senate. This section was proposed by the General Assembly in response to an Ohio Supreme Court decision that held (despite the grant of power to the General Assembly to prescribe the *manner* of appointments to public office under Art. II, sec. 27) that the General Assembly could not require the advice and consent of the Senate. *State ex rel. Burns v. DiSalle* (1961).

This section "imposes no right of selection in the Senate but rather the right, where provided by statute, to review the appointment made by the Governor and if dissatisfied therewith to reject such appointment." *State ex rel. Brothers v. Zellar* (1966). In other words, the only power that the Senate has under this section is the power to reject appointments made by the governor. Once a person is appointed by the governor to a particular office, takes the oath of office, and satisfies any other statutory requirements, title to that office vests in the person subject to divesture by the Senate. Ibid. At that time, the appointee has legal authority to begin exercising the duties of the position.

All appointments submitted to the Senate while it is in session must be acted on during that session unless the Senate adjourns without setting a day to return (i.e., sine die) within ten days of the submission. In such cases, the Senate may act on the appointment at the next regular session of the General Assembly. If an appointment is made when the Senate is not in session, the Senate can also wait until the next regular session to act on the appointment. A "session" for the purpose of this section includes both the first and second regular sessions of the General Assembly. *State ex rel. Horner v. Anderson* (1975).

The failure of the Senate to consent to an appointment within the time provided constitutes consent to such appointment. If the Senate rejects the appointment, the appointed officer may serve until the governor appoints another person to the office.

Section 22

Supreme court to determine disability of governor or governor-elect and resolve succession questions.

The Supreme Court has original, exclusive, and final jurisdiction to determine disability of the governor or governor-elect upon presentment to it of a joint resolution by the General Assembly, declaring that the governor or governor-elect is unable to discharge the powers and duties of the office of governor by reason of disability. Such joint resolution shall be adopted by a two-thirds vote of the members elected to each house. The Supreme Court shall give notice of the resolution to the governor and after a public hearing, at which all interested parties may appear and be represented, shall determine the question of disability. The court shall make its determination within twenty-one days after presentment of such resolution.

If the governor transmits to the supreme court a written declaration that the disability no longer exists, the Supreme Court shall, after public hearing at which all interested parties may appear and be represented, determine the question of the continuation of the disability. The court shall make its determination within twenty-one days after transmittal of such declaration.

The Supreme Court has original, exclusive, and final jurisdiction to determine all questions concerning succession to the office of the governor or to its powers and duties.

Adopted in 1976 and never amended, this section gives the Ohio Supreme Court original and exclusive jurisdiction to determine if the governor is unable to continue in office because of a disability. For the court to have jurisdiction, the General Assembly must pass a joint resolution stating that the governor is unable to discharge the powers and duties of the office because of a disability. The joint resolution must be adopted by a two-thirds vote of the members of each house. Once the resolution is submitted to the court, the court must notify the governor and hold a public hearing on the matter. After the hearing, the court must render a decision on the disability of the governor within twenty-one days of receiving the General Assembly's resolution.

The governor is also entitled under this section to submit a declaration to the court stating that the disability no longer exists. In that case, the court must also hold a public hearing and decide the continuation of the governor's disability within twenty-one days from receipt of the governor's declaration.

Article IV

Judicial

Article IV concerns the judicial branch and covers the structure, powers, and jurisdiction of Ohio's "constitutional courts"—the Ohio Supreme Court, the Ohio Courts of Appeals, and the Ohio Courts of Common Pleas—and any "statutory courts" that the General Assembly creates. Problems with Ohio's judicial system, especially its lack of efficiency, were among the principal reasons for the adoption of the 1851 Ohio Constitution. Consistent with changes being made in other states during the wave of constitutional revision in the post-Jacksonian era, the 1851 Constitution also transferred the power to select judges from the General Assembly to the voters, a movement that had begun in New York in 1846. See Jed Handelsman Shugerman, "Economic Crisis and the Rise of Judicial Elections and Judicial Review," 123 *Harv. L. Rev.* 1061 (2010).

Since 1851 the voters have amended this article seventeen times, mostly to address issues of efficiency and organization. In 1912, amendments to this article changed the structure of the court system by creating intermediate courts of appeals to replace the outdated system of circuit courts (which had been created in an 1883 amendment). The 1912 amendments also increased the membership on the Ohio Supreme Court from six to seven justices, with the creation of the position of an elected chief justice; eliminated justices of the peace as constitutional courts (a status given to them in an 1883 amendment); defined the jurisdiction of the courts; and added a supermajority requirement that limited the

The Ohio State Constitution. Steven H. Steinglass and Gino J. Scarselli, Oxford University Press. © Oxford University Press 2022. DOI: 10.1093/oso/9780197619728.003.0006

ability of the Ohio Supreme Court to hold state statutes unconstitutional. See Commentary, Article IV, section 2.

■ MODERN COURTS AMENDMENT

The most sweeping changes to Article IV came in 1968 with the adoption of the Modern Courts Amendment. By the mid-1960s, Ohio had more than 400 judges operating independently, and there was no central authority for assigning judges in districts with relatively light caseloads to districts with heavy caseloads. The Modern Courts Amendment gave the Ohio Supreme Court primary responsibility over the administration and operation of the Ohio judicial system, including the power to adopt rules for the Ohio courts. See generally William W. Milligan and James E. Pohlman, "The 1968 Modern Courts Amendment to the Ohio Constitution," 29 *Ohio St. L. J.* 811 (1968).

The Modern Courts Amendment also included provisions governing the election, compensation, duties, removal, and retirement of judges. And it eliminated the requirement under which the Ohio Supreme Court needed a supermajority vote in order to hold unconstitutional state statutes the constitutionality of which had been upheld by a court of appeals. See Commentary, Article IV, section 2. And in 1973, the General Assembly proposed and the voters approved an amendment that revised portions of sections 1, 4, 5, and 6 of this article.

■ JURISDICTION AND JUSTICIABILITY

Under Article III of the U.S. Constitution, federal courts are courts of limited jurisdiction. As a result, with limited exceptions involving the original jurisdiction of the U.S. Supreme Court, federal courts may only exercise the judicial power identified in the U.S. Constitution when Congress adopts jurisdictional statutes. See Erwin Chemerinsky, *Federal Jurisdiction* (New York: Wolters Kluwer, 6th ed., 2016): 202–3, 696 (hereinafter Chemerinsky, *Federal Jurisdiction*).

In Ohio, on the other hand, the courts of common pleas are courts of general jurisdiction and thus have plenary jurisdiction over cases unless the General Assembly acts affirmatively to assign the cases to special divisions, such as probate or domestic relations, or unless Congress makes the jurisdiction of the federal courts exclusive. And Ohio courts exercise concurrent jurisdiction over nonexclusive federally created civil causes of action such as employment discrimination claims under Title VII of the Civil Rights Act of 1964, see *Manning v. Ohio State Library Board* (1991), and civil rights claims under 42 U.S.C. section 1983, a surviving provision of the Civil Rights Act of 1871. See *Cooperman v. University Surgical Associates* (1987).

Article III of the U.S. Constitution also limits the jurisdiction of federal courts to "cases or controversies," and the U.S. Supreme Court has applied constitutional and prudential limitations on the business of the federal courts through standing, mootness, and other justiciability doctrines. The federal "case or controversy" doctrine, however, is not applicable to the state courts, *State ex rel. Ohio Academy of Trial Lawyers v. Sheward* (1999), and Article IV of the Ohio Constitution does not contain a state "case or controversy" requirement. Nonetheless, the Ohio Constitution limits courts of common pleas to exercising jurisdiction over "justiciable matters," a limitation that does not apply to either the Ohio Supreme Court or the Courts of Appeals. See Commentary, Article IV, section (4)(B).

■ STANDING

Despite the absence of a "case or controversy" requirement in the Ohio Constitution, "Ohio courts have generally chosen to voluntarily follow justiciability doctrines developed by federal courts." Michael E. Solimine, "Recalibrating Justiciability in Ohio Courts," 51 *Clev. St. L. Rev.* 531 (2004): 554 (hereinafter Solimine, "Recalibrating Justiciability"). For example, the court has followed the federal standing model, stating that "[i]t is well established that before an Ohio court can consider the merits of a legal claim, the person seeking relief must establish standing to sue." *Sheward, supra.*

Applying this standard in 2014 in a highly visible case challenging the constitutionality of the JobsOhio legislation, see Commentary, Article VIII, section 4, the court stated that "[t]raditional standing principles require litigants to show, at a minimum, that they have suffered (1) an injury that is (2) fairly traceable to the defendant's allegedly unlawful conduct, and (3) likely to be redressed by the requested relief." *ProgressOhio.org, Inc. JobsOhio* (2014) (internal quotation omitted). And it further stated that "a party wishing to sue must have a direct, personal stake in the outcome of his or her case; ideological opposition to a program or legislative enactment is not enough." Ibid. As a result, the court held that the parties challenging the constitutionality of the JobsOhio legislation did not suffer concrete harm or injury different in manner or degree from that suffered by the general public, and thus did not have standing.

Likewise, the court has held that parties who claimed that they and their communities were negatively affected by gambling did not suffer an injury sufficient to confer standing to challenge the placement of video lottery terminals (i.e., slot machines) at Ohio racetracks. *State ex rel. Walgate v. Kasich* (2016). But the court held that a potential competitor whose naked allegation that he would operate his own casino but for the putative state limitation on the number of casinos to four had plead a sufficient allegation of injury to withstand a motion to dismiss his federal equal protection challenge. Ibid. See also Commentary, Article XV, section 6.

The Ohio Supreme Court has equated the tests for standing under state and federal law, stating that both tests require "an injury in fact, causation, and redressability." In describing the source of these core standing requirements, however, the court has recognized that the federal doctrine is derived from Article III of the U.S. Constitution; but it has described the Ohio doctrine as based on common law standing, see *State ex rel. Walgate v. Kasich* (2016), thus suggesting a role for both the court and the General Assembly in defining the elements of standing.

■ PUBLIC-RIGHTS ACTIONS

Despite its embrace of a standing requirement patterned after federal law, the Ohio Supreme Court has approved an exception, albeit a narrow one, to standing in public-rights actions that seek to vindicate the general public interest. In such cases, the court, exercising its original jurisdiction, may entertain mandamus or prohibition proceedings (but not declaratory judgment actions) brought "to procure the enforcement or protection of a public right" even though the party suing cannot "show any legal right or special individual interest in the result." *Sheward, supra.*

Although the use of "pubic-rights actions" has become more controversial in recent years, the court had long addressed public issues under its original jurisdiction without requiring traditional standing requirements to be met.

> Ordinarily a person is not authorized to attack the constitutionality of a statute, where his private rights have suffered no interference or impairment, but as a matter of public policy a citizen does have such an interest in his government as to give him capacity to maintain a proper action to enforce the performance of a public duty affecting himself and citizens generally. . . . . Where a public right, as distinguished from a purely private right, is involved, a citizen need not show any special interest therein, but he may maintain a proper action predicated on his citizenship relation to such public right. This doctrine has been steadily adhered to by this court over the years.

State ex rel. Newell v. Brown (1954) (prohibition action to prevent election officials from unlawfully placing the names of certain candidates on the ballot); see also *State ex rel. Trauger v. Nash* (1902) (mandamus action to compel the governor to fill a vacancy in the position of lieutenant governor).

In 2014, the court declined to entertain a "public-rights action" in a case challenging the constitutionality of the OhioJobs program. *ProgressOhio.org, Inc. v. JobsOhio* (2014). In so ruling, it discussed the limited availability of "public-rights actions:"

> The public-right doctrine represents an exception to the personal-injury requirement of standing. The doctrine provides that when the issues sought to be litigated are of great importance and interest to the public, they may be resolved in a form of action that involves no rights or obligations peculiar to named parties. To succeed in bringing a public-right case, a litigant must allege rare and extraordinary

> issues that threaten serious public injury. Not all allegedly illegal or unconstitutional government actions rise to this level of importance.

(internal quotations omitted).

■ ADVISORY OPINIONS AND CERTIFIED QUESTIONS

Some states have express authority in their constitutions to permit their courts to render advisory opinions (see, e.g., Mich. Const., Art. III, sec. 8), but Article IV of the Ohio Constitution, like Article III of the U.S. Constitution, is silent as to whether courts may issue advisory opinions The U.S. Supreme Court has interpreted the "case or controversy" requirement to prohibit federal courts from rendering advisory opinions, see Chemerinsky, *Federal Jurisdiction*, 46–54, and the Ohio Supreme Court has a long-standing tradition of also refusing to issue advisory opinions. *BancOhio Nat. Bank v. Rubicon Cadillac, Inc.* (1984). "It has become settled judicial responsibility for courts to refrain from giving opinions on abstract propositions and to avoid the imposition by judgment of premature declarations or advice upon potential controversies." *Fortner v. Thomas* (1970).

The Ohio Supreme Court signaled its unwillingness to issuing advisory opinions in 1882 in *State v. Baughman*. The General Assembly, by joint resolution, had instructed the attorney general to file a quo warranto action against the police commissioners of the City of Xenia seeking answers to four questions concerning their appointments. In concluding that it could not answer two of the questions, the court stated:

> If the judiciary were to assume to decide hypothetical questions of law not involved in a judicial proceeding in a cause before it, even though the decision 'would be of great value to the general assembly' in the discharge of its duties, it would, nevertheless, be an unwarranted interference with the functions of the legislative department that would be unauthorized, and dangerous in its tendency.

Baughman did not refer to advisory opinions by name, but the decision has been seen as having established a prohibition on the rendering of advisory opinions. And the Ohio Supreme Court has elaborated on its refusal to issue advisory opinions. See, for example, *Egan v. National Distillers & Chemical Corp.* (1986) (syllabus) ("[I]t is well-settled that this court will not indulge in advisory opinions."); *Armco, Inc. v. Public Utilities Commission*, (1982) ("Under these circumstances, any opinion this court might express . . . would be purely advisory, and it is well-settled that this court does not indulge itself in advisory opinions.").

The issue of whether the Ohio Supreme Court has authority under the Modern Courts Amendment to adopt a rule permitting the issuance of advisory opinions has not been directly addressed by the court, but in upholding its power to answer questions certified by federal courts, the court held that answering certified questions under the Supreme Court Rules of Practice (now Rule of Practice 9.01) is not an exercise of jurisdiction. See *Scott v. Bank One Trust Co.* (1991) ("If [the certification rule] . . . expanded our jurisdiction, we would have to declare it unconstitutional.").

During the first two decades of this century, the Ohio Supreme Court has been asked approximately forty times to answer questions of state law certified by federal courts, and the court has answered approximately two-thirds of them. The overwhelming majority of these requests have come from district courts, but some have also come from the U.S. Court of Appeals for the Sixth circuit.

In identifying the source of its power to answer certified questions, the Ohio Supreme Court did not rely on the Modern Courts Amendment. Rather, it relied on Ohio's existence as a state in the federal system.

> [t]he Ohio Constitution permits the state to exercise its own sovereignty as far as the United States Constitution and laws permit. Since federal law recognizes Ohio's sovereignty by making Ohio law applicable in federal courts, the state has the power to exercise and the responsibility to protect that sovereignty. Therefore, if answering certified questions serves to further the state's interests and preserve the state's sovereignty, the appropriate branch of state government—this court—may constitutionally answer them.
>
> *Scott v. Bank One Trust Co.* (1991).

The practice of answering certified questions involves all areas of Ohio law, but the court has often used its certification power to interpret the Ohio Constitution. Indeed, many of its most important state constitutional decisions have been in response to questions certified by federal courts. See, for example, *Doe v. Ronan* (2010) (interpreting obligation of contract and bar on retroactive legislation in Art. II, sec. 28); *Mendenhall v. City of Akron* (2008) (interpreting home rule power under Art. XVIII, sec. 3); *Arbino v. Johnson & Johnson* (2007) (interpreting "due course of law" and other provision of Art. I). But the court has also recognized the practical limitations of the certification process, and it has exercised its discretion to decline to answer questions that are too factually specific. *Cooper v. Buckeye Steel Castings* (1993). See also Randall T. Shepard, "Is Making State Constitutional Law through Certified Questions a Good Idea or a Bad Idea?" 38 *Val. U. L. Rev.* 327 (2004).

■ RIPENESS

Sometimes referred to as "standing in time," ripeness refers to the timing of litigation. The Ohio Supreme Court has looked to federal law to define the ripeness doctrine, and most modern Ohio ripeness decisions can be traced back to the court's 1973 decision in *Burger Brewing Co. v. Liquor Control Com., Dep't of Liquor Control* (1973). In *Burger Brewing,* the court stated that it would look to the twofold test developed by the U.S. Supreme Court in *Toilet Goods Association v. Gardner* (1967) "to determine whether the issues tendered are appropriate for judicial resolution, and second to assess the hardship to the parties if judicial relief is denied at that stage."

The Ohio Supreme Court had long refused to hear cases that were premature. For example, in 1941 the court held that "[t]he courts will not interfere with the submission to the electors of a proposed amendment to a city charter, upon a claim that the amendment, if adopted, will contravene the Constitution of Ohio. Such a claim is prematurely asserted." *State ex rel. Kittel v. Bigelow* (1941) (syllabus). And the *Kittel* court expanded how this doctrine applied to cases involving the legislative process.

> This court has repeatedly held that it will not interfere with the legislative process, either by mandamus or by injunction, to prevent the enactment of laws, simply because it is claimed that such legislation when passed will be unconstitutional. . . . This refusal to determine the constitutionality of measures that have not yet been passed is general in its application, extending as well to proposed amendments to the fundamental law of the body politic, as to ordinary statutes and ordinances.

In *Burger Brewing Co., supra,* the court equated ripeness with a justiciability requirement that had its origin in federal law. And in *State ex rel. Jones v. Husted* (2016) (*Jones II*) (plurality opinion), the court stated that "[t]o be justiciable, a claim must be ripe for review" and a claim is not ripe "if it rests on contingent events that may never occur at all" (internal citations omitted).

Finally, in *State v. Maddox* (2022), the court held that a criminal defendant's challenge to the constitutionality of O. R.C. 2967.271, the Reagan Tokes Law, which permits the Ohio Department of Rehabilitation and Correction to administratively extend an incarcerated person's prison term beyond his or her minimum prison term or presumptive earned early-release date but not beyond his or her maximum prison term, is ripe for review under state and federal ripeness standards in a direct appeal of a conviction and prison sentence.

■ MOOTNESS

In 1910, the Ohio Supreme Court, relying on a decision of the U.S. Supreme Court, stated its unwillingness to decide moot cases. "The duty of this court, as of every other judicial tribunal, is to decide actual controversies by a judgment which can be carried into effect, and not to give opinions upon moot questions or abstract propositions, or to declare principles or rules of law which cannot affect the matter in issue in the case before it." *Miner v. Witt* (1910).

Nonetheless, the Ohio Supreme Court has not fully embraced the federal mootness doctrine (which has its roots in the federal case or controversy requirement) and has adopted a more forgiving mootness exception. In federal court, the "capable of repetition yet evading review" mootness exception is limited to cases in which a named party may again be affected. *Weinstein v. Bradford* (1975). In Ohio, on the other hand, the mootness exception applies when the *issue* is capable of repetition for *non-parties* yet evading review. See *Franchise Developers, Inc. v. City of Cincinnati* (1987) (syllabus). ("Although a case may be moot with respect to one of the litigants, this court may hear the appeal where there remains a debatable constitutional question to resolve, or where the matter appealed is one of great public or general interest"). But see *M.R. v. Niesen* (2022) (citing Ohio law but relying on the narrower federal mootness exception to dismiss an appeal in a case raising the serious issue of whether a temporary restraining order that expired acts as a prior restraint on speech, because "[i]t is not enough for an issue to be capable of repetition between some parties; the issue must be capable of repetition between the 'same' parties") (emphasis in original).

■ POLITICAL QUESTION DOCTRINE

The U.S. Supreme Court has recognized a narrow area in which the political question doctrine operates as a basis for declining to exercise jurisdiction. For example, more than a century ago the court refused to hear a Guarantee Clause challenge to Oregon's initiative because of its political nature, *Pacific States Tel. & Tel. Co. v. Oregon* (1912), and it defined and limited the breadth of the political question doctrine in *Baker v. Carr* (1962), when it held that it was not barred from hearing challenges to malapportioned state legislatures.

Though not required to do so, the Ohio courts have sometimes relied on federal cases to apply the political question doctrine to refuse to entertain cases otherwise within their jurisdiction. See Solimine, "Recalibrating Justiciability," 551–55.

But in its most prominent recent decision addressing the doctrine, the controversial *DeRolph* school funding litigation, the court despite a strong dissent by the chief justice refused to apply the political question doctrine to avoid deciding the case on the merits. See *DeRolph v. State* (1997) (Moyer, C. J., dissenting).

■ STATE REMEDIES

Federal law sets minimum federal constitutional requirements that states must meet, but state courts may exercise their independent authority to "fashion state remedial rules that give greater relief than available under federal law." *Danforth v. Minnesota* (2008). This includes the development of *state* remedies for violation of federal rights, and "the remedy a state court chooses to provide its citizens for violations of the Federal Constitution is primarily a question of state law." Ibid. The Ohio Supreme Court, however, has not addressed whether it will use its state remedial authority to provide greater relief under *state* law for violations of the federal constitution than is available under federal law.

State courts have also developed implied rights of action under state constitutional provisions. See, for example, *Godfrey v. State* (2017) (reviewing state policies on implied rights of action under state constitutions throughout the country, and holding that a private claim for damages is available to enforce the equal protection and due process clauses of the Iowa Constitution). See generally Jennifer Friesen, *State Constitutional Law* (LexisNexis, 2007 and 2015 Supp.), chapter 7. But the Ohio Supreme Court has largely rejected this approach, leaving only a small opening for implied rights of action when the General Assembly has not provided other reasonably satisfactory remedies to address the underlying conduct. See *Provens v. Stark County Board of Mental Retardation & Developmental Disabilities* (1992); see also David M. Gareau, "Opening the Courthouse Doors: Allowing a Cause of Action to Arise Directly from a Violation of the Ohio Constitution," 43 *Clev. St. L. Rev.* 459 (1995).

Section 1

Judicial power vested in courts.

The judicial power of the state is vested in a supreme court, courts of appeals, courts of common pleas and divisions thereof, and such others courts inferior to the Supreme Court as may from time to time be established by law.

Adopted in 1851 and amended in 1883, 1912, 1968, and 1973, this section can be traced back to Ohio's first constitution. The 1802 Constitution vested the judicial power in Supreme Court, in a court of common pleas for each county, in justices of the peace, and in other courts that the legislature may create from time to time. See 1802 Constitution, Article III, section 1. The 1851 Constitution added district courts, which functioned largely as appellate courts, and probate courts. Over the years, courts of appeals replaced district courts, probate courts became divisions of common pleas courts, and justices of the peace were abolished as constitutional officers. The 1973 amendment to this article was the final modification of this section.

Though vesting judicial power in enumerated courts, neither this section nor any other section of the Ohio Constitution defines "judicial power." The Ohio Supreme Court, however, has characterized judicial power as the power to hear and determine controversies between adverse parties by applying the law to the facts and rendering a final judgment. *Village of Fairview v. Giffee* (1905). The court has also held that judicial power has to be "determined in the light of the common law, and of the history of our institutions as they existed anterior to and at the time of the adoption of the constitution." *State v. Harmon* (1877). Matters that belong solely to the judiciary include the determination of guilt and the sentencing of defendants in criminal cases, *State ex rel. Bray v. Russell* (2000), and the appellate review of lower court decisions, *City of South Euclid v. Jemison* (1986). In addition, the judicial power includes a court's inherent powers to secure autonomy from the other branches, including the power to order the appropriation of necessary funds and to enforce such order by contempt proceedings. *State ex rel. Edwards v. Murray* (1976).

Judicial Review

The Ohio Supreme Court is the final arbiter of the meaning of Ohio law, including the Ohio Constitution, and in 1807 the court recognized the doctrine of judicial review, thus establishing the primacy of the courts in interpreting the Ohio Constitution. *Rutherford v. M'Fadden* (1807); see The History of the Ohio Constitution, *supra*.

Statutory Courts

Section 1 allows the General Assembly to establish "inferior courts." Under this provision, the General Assembly has established statutory courts, including municipal courts, mayor's courts, small claims courts, and justices of the peace. Having created them, the General Assembly is free to abolish these courts.

The 1968 Modern Courts Amendment "made the probate court a division of the common pleas court," *State v. Brown* (2015), but it left the definition of the jurisdiction and duties of probate courts to the General Assembly. And under the pre-1968 version of this article, the General Assembly had delegated to the probate court the power to establish the confines of park districts and to appoint park commissioners to govern such districts. *State ex rel. Bryant v. Akron Metropolitan Park District for Summit County* (1929).

In *Walker v. City of Toledo* (2014), the court held that neither this section nor the state statute governing the jurisdiction of municipal courts "endow(s) municipal courts with exclusive authority over civil administrative enforcement of traffic-law violations." But, after a change in state law, the court in *State ex rel. Magsig v. City of Toledo* (2020) revisited the issue and held that the General Assembly has the constitutional power to not only create municipal courts but also vest them with exclusive jurisdiction over noncriminal traffic-law adjudications. Thus, cities are now barred from conducting quasi-judicial proceedings for adjudicating liability for violations of municipal traffic ordinances even though they have the home rule power to adopt automated traffic enforcement systems. See Commentary, Article XVIII, section 3.

In 1976, the General Assembly abrogated the state's sovereign immunity and created the Ohio Court of Claims to hear actions for damages against the state. See Commentary, Article I, section 16.

Section 2
Supreme Court.

(A) The Supreme Court shall, until otherwise provided by law, consist of seven judges, who shall be known as the chief justice and justices. In case of the absence or disability of the chief justice, the judge having the period of longest total service upon the court shall be the acting chief justice. If any member of the court shall be unable, by reason of illness, disability or disqualification, to hear, consider and decide a cause or causes, the chief justice or the acting chief justice may direct any judge of any court of appeals to sit with the judges of the Supreme Court in the place and stead of the absent judge. A majority of the Supreme Court shall be necessary to constitute a quorum or to render a judgment.

(B) (1) The Supreme Court shall have original jurisdiction in the following:

(a) Quo warranto;

(b) Mandamus;

(c) Habeas corpus;

(d) Prohibition;

(e) Procedendo;

(f) In any cause on review as may be necessary to its complete determination;

(g) Admission to the practice of law, the discipline of persons so admitted, and all other matters relating to the practice of law.

(2) The Supreme Court shall have appellate jurisdiction as follows:

(a) In appeals from the courts of appeals as a matter of right in the following:

(i) Cases originating in the courts of appeals;

(ii) Cases involving questions arising under the constitution of the United States or of this state.

(b) In appeals from the courts of appeals in cases of felony on leave first obtained,

(c) In direct appeals from the courts of common pleas or other courts of record inferior to the court of appeals as a matter of right in cases in which the death penalty has been imposed.

(d) Such revisory jurisdiction of the proceedings of administrative officers or agencies as may be conferred by law;

(e) In cases of public or great general interest, the Supreme Court may direct any court of appeals to certify its record to the Supreme Court, and may review and affirm, modify, or reverse the judgment of the court of appeals;

(f) The supreme court shall review and affirm, modify, or reverse the judgment in any case certified by any court of appeals pursuant to section 3(B)(4) of this article.

(3) No law shall be passed or rule made whereby any person shall be prevented from invoking the original jurisdiction of the Supreme Court.

(C) The decisions in all cases in the Supreme Court shall be reported, together with the reasons therefor.

Adopted in 1851 and amended in 1883, 1912, 1944, 1968, and 1994, this section provides for the organization and jurisdiction of the Ohio Supreme Court. See also Judicial System Structure (Ohio Supreme Court website).

Since the adoption of the 1802 Constitution, the structure and powers of the Ohio Supreme Court have changed dramatically. The first constitution provided that the court would be both a trial and an appeals court, and it required the justices to hold court annually in every county.

In 1802, Ohio had nine counties and a population of less than 50,000. Although transportation was difficult, it was initially feasible for the court to hear appeals in each county. By 1850 Ohio had eight-seven counties and a population of almost two million, making circuit riding impossible. See F. R. Aumann, "The Development of the Judicial System of Ohio," 41 *Ohio History* 195 (1932): 208–12 (hereinafter Aumann, "The Development of the Judicial System").

During the first fifty years of statehood, the General Assembly enacted a number of laws to address the burdens placed on the Supreme Court by its increasing caseload.

The 1802 Constitution allowed the General Assembly to increase the number of justices from three to four and to divide the state into two circuits. Exercising this authority, the General Assembly in 1808 created two circuits, which effectively created two branches of the Supreme Court: a "Supreme Court in Bank" and a "Supreme Court on Circuit." The Court in Bank decided questions that the justices reserved while on circuit. In 1810, the General Assembly repealed the 1808 law, but in 1823 it reestablished the two circuits. Finally, in 1831, the General Assembly repealed the 1823 law and passed a new law that allowed litigants as well as the justices to reserve questions that arose on circuit. See Aumann, "The Development of the Judicial System," 205–6.

The 1851 Constitution alleviated many of the burdens on the Ohio Supreme Court. It added a fifth justice, eliminated circuit riding, and established the Supreme Court as the court of last appeal. But these changes did not entirely eliminate all of the burdens on the court created by an increasing caseload.

Mounting concern about the caseload, especially after the voters rejected the proposed 1874 Constitution, led the Democrats, the Republicans, and practically all the state's newspapers to support an amendment in 1875 to create a temporary Supreme Court Commission to dispose of cases on the court's docket. See Aumann, "The Development of the Judicial System," 226–27; see also Article IV, section 22, and Commentary.

In 1883, the General Assembly proposed and the voters approved an amendment to allow the General Assembly to increase the number of justices and to again divide the court into two circuits. Acting under the 1883 amendment, the General Assembly in 1892 added a sixth justice and reestablished the circuits.

In 1912, the delegates proposed amendments to reorganize the Ohio Supreme Court in a way that closely resembles today's court. The amendments, which the voters approved, eliminated the authority to establish Supreme Court circuits, and created the position of an elected chief justice, thereby increasing the court to seven justices.

The 1912 amendments also included a cumbersome limitation on the court's power to strike down a law on constitutional grounds. Under this amendment, the Ohio Supreme Court could not hold a law unconstitutional "without the concurrence of at least all but one of the judges, except in the affirmance of a judgment of the court of appeals declaring a law unconstitutional and void." Ohio Constitution, Article IV, section 2 (1913). In other words, if the court of appeals upheld the constitutionality of a law, the Supreme Court could not reverse and hold the law unconstitutional without a supermajority of at least six justices. Despite serious problems with this provision, it survived until the adoption of the Modern Courts Amendment in 1968. See Jonathan L. Entin, "Judicial Supermajorities and the Validity of Statutes: How *Mapp* Became a Fourth Amendment

Landmark instead of a First Amendment Footnote," 52 *Case W. Res. L. Rev.* 441 (2001).

Original Jurisdiction

This section provides the Ohio Supreme Court with original (but not exclusive) jurisdiction over enumerated extraordinary writs, specifically quo warranto, mandamus, habeas corpus, prohibition, and procedendo, see Article IV, section (B), and it further provides that "[n]o law shall be passed or rule made whereby any person shall be prevented from invoking the original jurisdiction of the Supreme Court." Article IV, section 2(B)(3).

The 1802 Ohio Constitution provided that the Ohio Supreme Court "shall have original and appellate jurisdiction both in common law and in chancery, in such cases as shall be directed by law . . . ." (1802 Const. Art. III, sec. 2), but it did not identify the cases in which original jurisdiction was available. The 1851 Constitution, however, was more specific and gave the court original jurisdiction over four of the common law writs--quo warranto, mandamus, habeas corpus, and procedendo--but there was no substantive discussion of why those writs were enumerated or why the General Assembly was not given the power to further define the court's original jurisdiction. See Robert L. Hausser, "The Original Jurisdiction of the Ohio Supreme Court," 7 *Ohio St. L. J.* 27 (1940). Finally, in 1912, the constitutional convention proposed and the voters approved an amendment that added writs of prohibition to the court's original jurisdiction, but the delegates did so without a discussion. Ibid.

The original jurisdiction of the Ohio Supreme Court may not be expanded by the General Assembly, and the General Assembly acted improperly in authorizing the court to exercise original jurisdiction over declaratory judgment actions. *ProgressOhio.org, Inc. v. Kasich* (2011). And the court will go behind the face of a petition for extraordinary relief to determine if it meets the common law requirements for an extraordinary writ or is actually a disguised claim for a declaratory judgment (over which the court lacks original jurisdiction). *State ex rel. JobsOhio v. Goodman* (2012).

In addition to the grant of original jurisdiction in this section, there are other provisions of the Ohio Constitution that provide the court with not only original but also exclusive jurisdiction. See Article II, sections 1e and 1g (ballot issues); Article III, section 2 (gubernatorial disability and succession); Article XI, section 9 (state apportionment); Article XIX, section 3 (congressional redistricting); Article XVI, section 1 (proposed amendments); and Commentaries on these sections.

Modern Courts Amendment

The Modern Courts Amendment made significant changes to this section. Section 2(A) sets the number of Supreme Court justices at seven (subject to legislative alteration) and outlines what is to occur if a justice cannot fulfill his or her term.

Section 2(B), which was amended in 1994 to provide for a direct appeal from trial court decisions imposing the death penalty, defines the court's original and appellate jurisdiction in such cases. Section 2(B) also includes a provision that requires the court to oversee admissions to the Ohio bar and to discipline attorneys. Previously, the Ohio Supreme Court relied on its inherent powers to discipline attorneys admitted to the bar. *Mahoning County Bar Association v. Franko* (1958).

Under section 2(B)(1)(g), the Ohio Supreme Court has original jurisdiction in cases involving the practice of law, and the court has interpreted this section as providing it with "exclusive jurisdiction over all matters related to the practice of law." *Disciplinary Counsel v. Alexicole, Inc.* (2004). But the court has permitted executive branch officials, such as county boards of elections, to determine what constitutes the "practice of law" for purposes of determining whether a judicial candidate's name may be on the ballot. *State ex rel. Emhoff v. Medina County Board of Elections* (2018). The possibility, however, that both the judicial and executive branches would be defining "practice of law" raises the question of whether "under the Ohio Constitution, a board of elections has *any* authority to make the determination whether a candidate engaged in the practice of law." See ibid. (Fischer, J., concurring in judgment only).

Finally, section 2(C) requires that the "decisions in all cases in the Supreme Court shall be reported, together with the reasons therefor."

Death Penalty Appeals

The Ohio Supreme Court has held that a state statute that denied defendants in capital cases the same right to appeal rejections of applications for DNA testing that is available to noncapital defendants violates the equal protection and benefit clause of Article I, section 2, of the Ohio Constitution and the Equal Protection Clause of the Fourteenth Amendment. *State v. Noling* (2016). The court "excised" the offending language from the statute, thus providing an appeal as of right to the Ohio Supreme Court for capital defendants whose application for DNA testing was rejected. Ibid.

Section 3
Court of appeals.

(A) The state shall be divided by law into compact appellate districts in each of which there shall be a court of appeals consisting of three judges. Laws may be passed increasing the number of judges in any district wherein the volume of business may require such additional judge or judges. In districts having additional judges, three judges shall participate in the hearing and disposition of each case. The court shall hold sessions in each county of the district as the necessity arises. The county commissioners of each county shall provide a proper and convenient place for the court of appeals to hold court.

(B) (1) The courts of appeals shall have original jurisdiction in the following:

(a) Quo warranto;

(b) Mandamus;

(c) Habeas corpus;

(d) Prohibition;

(e) Procedendo;

(f) In any cause on review as may be necessary to its complete determination.

(2) Courts of appeals shall have such jurisdiction as may be provided by law to review and affirm, modify, or reverse judgments or final orders of the courts of record inferior to the court of appeals within the district, except that courts of appeals shall not have jurisdiction to review on direct appeal a judgment that imposes a sentence of death. Courts of appeals shall have such appellate jurisdiction as may be provided by law to review and affirm, modify, or reverse final orders or actions of administrative officers or agencies.

(3) A majority of the judges hearing the cause shall be necessary to render a judgment. Judgments of the courts of appeals are final except as provided in section 2(B) (2) of this article. No judgment resulting from a trial by jury shall be reversed on the weight of the evidence except by the concurrence of all three judges hearing the cause.

(4) Whenever the judges of a court of appeals find that a judgment upon which they have agreed is in conflict with a judgment pronounced upon the same question by any other court of appeals of the state, the judges shall certify the record of the case to the Supreme Court for review and final determination.

(C) Laws may be passed providing for the reporting of cases in the courts of appeals.

Adopted in 1968 as part of the Modern Courts Amendment and amended in 1994, this section follows the organization of section 2 but deals with the structure and jurisdiction of the courts of appeals. These appellate courts evolved from the district courts established under Article IV, section 6 of the 1851 Constitution. Before 1851, no true appellate system existed, although the Supreme Court on Circuit functioned as an intermediate court when it reserved questions for the Supreme Court in Bank.

The 1851 Constitution established an intermediate appellate system that contained nine appellate districts with each district comprised of one Supreme Court justice and the common pleas judges of the district. In 1883, the voters approved a modification to Article IV, section 6 that created a circuit court of appeals with judges elected specifically to ride the circuit. See generally Lee E. Skeel, "Constitutional History of Ohio Appellate Courts," 6 *Cleveland-Marshall L. Rev.* 323 (1957).

A constitutional amendment approved in 1912, along with modifications to section 6 in 1945 and 1959, shaped most of the appellate system in place today. These amendments created a system that divided the state into appellate districts consisting of at least three judges per district. Today, the state is divided into twelve appellate districts by statute.

In 1968, the Modern Courts Amendment replaced the former section 6 with this section, which is divided into three subsections.

Section 3(A) provides that all appellate districts shall be drawn with at least three judges. Under this provision, "a valid judgment of a Court of Appeals must have the concurrence of at least two judges." *State v. Pembaur* (1982). Therefore, a judgment is not valid if it depends on the vote of a judge who has retired or is no longer active on the date of disposition. Ibid.

Section 3(B) is divided into four subsections. Section 3(B)(1) deals with the jurisdiction of the court with section 3(B)(2) providing that the courts of appeals have the power to review, affirm, modify, or reverse judgments or final orders of lower courts and administrative agencies. In 1994, however, the voters approved an amendment to section 3(B)(2) proposed by the General Assembly to forbid the courts of appeal from reviewing on direct appeal judgments that impose sentences of death.

Section 3(B)(3) provides that no trial judgment rendered by a jury shall be overturned by an appeals court on the weight of the evidence except by the concurrence of three judges. An appeals court, however, may reverse and grant a directed verdict without a unanimous vote, since the grant of a directed verdict (even though it requires the court to consider the evidence) is a question of law that involves no weighing of evidence. *Ruta v. Breckenridge-Remy Co.* (1982). And section 3(B)(4) requires the Ohio Supreme Court to review cases when two or more appellate districts come to different conclusions on the same issue.

Finally, section 3(C) allows, but does not require, decisions of the courts of appeals to be reported. Criteria governing the reporting of appellate decisions are found in Rule 2 of the Ohio Rules for the Reporting of Opinions.

Death Penalty Appeals

Despite the 1994 amendment to Article IV, section 3(B)(2), which denied jurisdiction to the courts of appeals over death penalty appeals, these courts still have jurisdiction to review trial court decisions denying defense motions for new trials in death penalty cases. And death penalty defendants seeking such appellate review are not limited to appealing such rulings directly to the Supreme Court of Ohio. *State v. Davis* (2011).

Intracircuit Conflicts

The intercircuit certification procedure outlined in Article IV, section 3(B)(4), does not apply to conflicts within an appellate district, but there is a procedure for convening en banc proceedings to resolve intradistrict conflicts. See *In re C.F.* (2007).

Section 4
Common pleas court.

(A) There shall be a court of common pleas and such divisions thereof as may be established by law serving each county of the state. Any judge of a court of common pleas or a division thereof may temporarily hold court in any county. In the interests of the fair, impartial, speedy, and sure administration of justice, each county shall have one or more resident judges, or two or more counties may be combined into districts having one or more judges resident in the district and serving the common pleas courts of all counties in the district, as may be provided by law. Judges serving a district shall sit in each county in the district as the business of the court requires. In counties or districts having more than one judge of the court of common pleas, the judges shall select one of their number to act as presiding judge, to serve at their pleasure. If the judges are unable because of equal division of the vote to make such selection, the judge having the longest total service on the court of common pleas shall serve as presiding judge until selection is made by vote. The presiding judge shall have such duties and exercise such powers as are prescribed by rule of the Supreme Court.

(B) The courts of common pleas and divisions thereof shall have such original jurisdiction over all justiciable matters and such powers of review of proceedings of administrative officers and agencies as may be provided by law.

(C) Unless otherwise provided by law, there shall be a probate division and such other divisions of the courts of common pleas as may be provided by law. Judges shall be elected specifically to such probate division and to such other divisions. The judges of the probate division shall be empowered to employ and control the clerks, employees, deputies, and referees of such probate division of the common pleas courts.

Adopted in 1968 as part of the Modern Courts Amendment and amended in 1973, this section deals with the courts of common pleas, the lowest of the constitutional courts established under the Ohio Constitution.

The 1802 Constitution required the establishment of a common pleas court in each county, see 1802 Constitution, Article III, section 1, but the 1851 Constitution dispensed with this requirement and divided the state into nine districts, one of which encompassed just Hamilton County, and called for each district to be subdivided into three common pleas districts. The 1912 amendment eliminated judicial districts and reinstated the requirement that each county have its own court of common pleas. In 1968, the section took its present form, but the 1973 amendment to it provided that any judge of a court of common pleas may temporarily hold court in any county.

Section 4 is divided into three subsections. Section 4(A) outlines the organization of the courts of common pleas.

Section 4(B) gives the courts of common pleas original jurisdiction over all justiciable matters and such powers of review over administrative officers and agencies as may be provided by law. The Ohio Supreme Court treats this section as providing the General Assembly with exclusive authority to allocate certain cases to specified divisions of the courts of common pleas. See *State v. Aalim* (2017) (*Aalim II*) (on reconsideration) (holding that its initial decision in this case requiring an amenability hearing before the mandatory bindover of juveniles charged with certain serious offenses "usurped the General Assembly's exclusive constitutional authority to define the jurisdiction of the courts of common pleas by impermissibly allowing a juvenile-division judge discretion to veto the legislature's grant of jurisdiction to the general division of a court of common pleas over this limited class of juvenile offenders").

Section (C) allows for the creation of probate and other specialized divisions of the common pleas court. In addition, this subsection requires judges of the specialized divisions to be elected specifically for those divisions.

Today, most courts of common pleas have specialized divisions, which include probate divisions with jurisdiction over decedent estates, care of the mentally ill, adoption issues and marriages, domestic relations divisions that handle divorces, dissolutions, and child custody matters, and juvenile court divisions. The respective jurisdiction of the courts of common pleas and their divisions is not always entirely clear. For example, probate divisions cannot determine by declaratory judgment the validity of a will that claimed to be executed while the person was incompetent. *Corron v. Corron* (1988). Commentators have lamented the confusion caused by the overlapping jurisdiction of common pleas courts and their probate divisions and the lack of clear jurisdictional rules. One commentator has described the existing rules as "ineffective in conserving judicial resources" and as not giving parties "an efficient and economical method to obtain judicial resolution of disputes." John F. Winkler, "The Probate Courts of Ohio," 28 *U. Tol. L. Rev.* 563 (1997).

Justiciable Matters

Under section 4(B), the courts of common pleas "have such original jurisdiction over all justiciable matters." This limitation to "justiciable matters" is not in either the 1802 or 1851 Constitutions or in the 1912 amendments, and it appears to have first been added to the Ohio Constitution in 1968 by the Modern Courts Amendment. But there is no indication in the study that led to the Modern Courts Amendment, see Report of Judicial Administration Study Committee (December 1, 1964), in the relevant Legislative Services Commission Reports, in the leading law review article on the Modern Courts Amendment, or in the ballot language presented to the voters, that the intent of the amendment was to impose a door-closing justiciability requirement on the courts of common pleas. Nonetheless, the Ohio Supreme Court treats this "justiciability" provision as providing a limitation that bars the courts of common pleas, but not the Ohio Supreme Court, from relying on the public-rights exception to standing. *ProgressOhio.Org, Inc. v. JobsOhio* (2011); see also Commentary, Article IV.

Section 5

Other powers of Supreme Court.

(A) (1) In addition to all other powers vested by this article in the Supreme Court, the Supreme Court shall have general superintendence over all courts in the state. Such general superintending power shall be exercised by the chief justice in accordance with rues promulgated by the Supreme Court.

(2) The Supreme Court shall appoint an administrative director who shall assist the chief justice and who shall serve at the pleasure of the court. The compensation and duties of the administrative director shall be determined by the court.

(3) The chief justice or acting chief justice, as necessity arises, shall assign any judge of a court of common pleas or a division thereof temporarily to sit or hold court on any other court of common pleas or division thereof or any court of appeals or shall assign any judge of a court of appeals temporarily to sit or hold court on any other court of appeals or any court of common pleas or division thereof and upon such assignment said judge shall serve in such assigned capacity until the termination of the assignment. Rules may be adopted to provide for the temporary assignment of judges to sit and hold court in any court established by law.

(B) The Supreme Court shall prescribe rules governing practice and procedure in all courts of the state, which rules shall not abridge, enlarge, or modify any substantive right. Proposed rules shall be filed by the court, not later than the fifteenth day of January, with the clerk of each house of the General Assembly during a regular session thereof, and amendments to any such proposed rules may be so filed not later than the first day of May in that session. Such rules shall take effect on the following first day of July, unless prior to such day the General Assembly adopts a concurrent resolution of disapproval. All laws in conflict with such rules shall be of no further force or effect after such rules have taken effect.

Courts may adopt additional rules concerning local practice in their respective courts which are not inconsistent with the rules promulgated by the Supreme Court. The Supreme Court may make rules to require uniform record keeping for all courts of the state, and shall make rules governing the admission to the practice of law and discipline of persons so admitted.

(C) The chief justice of the Supreme Court or any judge of that court designated by him shall pass upon the disqualification of any judge of the courts of appeals or courts of common pleas or division thereof. Rules may be adopted to provide for the hearing of disqualification matters involving judges of courts established by law.

Adopted in 1968 and amended in 1973, this section was probably the most important aspect of the Modem Courts Amendment. See Thomas R. Swisher, ed., *Ohio Constitution Handbook* (Cleveland: Banks-Baldwin Publishing Co., 1990), 366–67 (hereinafter *Ohio Constitution Handbook*). Prior to its adoption, there was no central authority to manage the distribution of the state's judicial resources, which contributed to a growing backlog of cases. Moreover, before 1968, Ohio courts were still using the 1852 Field Code to regulate the civil procedure. Though amended numerous times, the Field Code was inadequate for the tremendous increase in civil litigation that Ohio and the rest of the nation experienced in the twentieth century.

Superintendence over Ohio Courts

Section 5 is divided into three subsections. Section 5(A) provides that the Ohio Supreme Court shall have the power of superintendence over all Ohio courts and requires the court to hire an administrative director. The section also provides that the chief justice may temporarily assign judges to different courts as the need arises. Thus, section 5(A) basically puts the court in charge of the administration of the Ohio courts, and it obviates the need for the court to rely on its inherent power. See *State ex rel. McKean v. Graves* (1914) ("The power to appoint a clerk, when necessary to the convenient and efficient exercise of its functions, is inherent in the court . . . .").

Rule-Making

Section 5(B) gives the Ohio Supreme Court a direct constitutional grant of authority to adopt rules of practice and procedure for all Ohio courts, and it requires the court to promulgate such rules. Under this authority, the court has adopted Rules of Civil Procedure, Rules of Criminal Procedure, Rules of Juvenile Procedure, Traffic Rules, Rules of Appellate Procedure, Rules of Evidence, and the Supreme Court Rules of Practice.

The Ohio Rules of Civil Procedure are modeled after (but not identical to) the Federal Rules of Civil Procedure and, like the federal rules, the state rules are strictly rules of procedure that "shall not abridge, enlarge, or modify any substantive right."

Unlike the rule-making authority of the U.S. Supreme Court, which comes from a federal statute, the Rules Enabling Act (28 U.S.C. section 2072), rather than directly from the U.S. Constitution, the delegation of rule-making authority to the Ohio Supreme Court comes directly from the Ohio Constitution. Therefore, as a result of the constitutional source of the court's rule-making authority, the General Assembly may not change the Ohio Rules of Practice, and the Ohio Supreme Court has struck down procedural statutes intended to govern court proceedings as inconsistent with its rules. See *Rockey v. 84 Lumber Co.* (1993).

Rules proposed by the Ohio Supreme Court, however, may be "vetoed" by the General Assembly by the adoption of a concurrent resolution of disapproval, Article IV, section 5(B), but once a proposed rule goes into effect, the General Assembly cannot amend or override it. *State ex rel. Silcott v. Spahr* (1990); *Rockey v. 84 Lumber Co.* (1993). For a critical review of this exercise of rule-making, see Richard S. Walinksi and Mark D. Wagoner Jr., "Ohio's Modern Courts Amendment Must Be Amended: Why and How," 66 *Clev. St. L. Rev.* 69 (2017).

Section 5(B) allows local courts to establish their own rules of procedure as long as such local rules do not conflict with the rules established by the Ohio Supreme Court, *State ex rel. Henneke v. Davis* (1986), or with statutes enacted by the General Assembly, *Krupansky v. Pascual* (1985).

Finally, section 5(B) also provides that the court may adopt rules to govern the admission and practice of attorneys. For these purposes, the court has promulgated Rules for the Government of the Bar and the Ohio Code of Professional Responsibility.

Disqualification of Judges

Section 5(C) provides the method of disqualification of a judge and allows the chief justice to decide if a judge is qualified to hear a case. Section 5(C) also allows the Supreme Court to adopt rules concerning the disqualification of judges, which have been adopted and are in the Ohio Rules for the Government of the Judiciary.

Section 6

Election of judges; compensation.

(A) (1) The chief justice and the justices of the Supreme Court shall be elected by the electors of the state at large, for terms of not less than six years.

(2) The judges of the courts of appeals shall be elected by the electors of their respective appellate districts, for terms of not less than six years.

(3) The judges of the courts of common pleas and the divisions thereof shall be elected by the electors of the counties, districts, or, as may be provided by law, other subdivisions, in which their respective courts are located, for terms of not less than six years, and each judge of a court of common pleas or division thereof shall reside during his term of office in the county, district, or subdivision in which his court is located.

(4) Terms of office of all judges shall begin on the days fixed by law, and laws shall be enacted to prescribe the times and mode of their election.

(B) The judges of the Supreme Court, courts of appeals, courts of common pleas, and divisions thereof, and of all courts of record established by law, shall, at stated times, receive for their services such compensation as may be provided by law, which shall not be diminished during their term of office. The compensation of all judges of the Supreme Court, except that of the chief justice, shall be the same. The compensation of all judges of the courts of appeals shall be the same. Common pleas judges and judges of divisions thereof, and judges of all courts of record established by law shall receive such compensation as may be provided by law. Judges shall receive no fees or perquisites, nor hold any other office of profit or trust, under the authority of this state, or of the United States. All votes for any judge, for any elective office, except a judicial office, under the authority of this state, given by the General Assembly, or the people shall be void.

(C) No person shall be elected or appointed to any judicial office if on or before the day when he shall assume the office and enter upon the discharge of its duties he shall have attained the age of seventy years. Any voluntarily retired judge, or any judge who is retired under this section, may be assigned with his consent, by the chief justice or acting chief justice of the Supreme Court to active duty as a judge and while so serving shall receive the established compensation for such office, computed upon a per diem basis, in addition to any retirement benefits to which he may be entitled. Laws may be passed providing retirement benefits for judges.

Adopted in 1968 and amended in 1973, this section provides for the election of judges. Under the 1802 Constitution, the General Assembly appointed all judges, except justices of the peace, by joint ballot of both houses for a term of seven years "if so long they behave well." 1802 Constitution, Article 3, sections 8 and 11. Consequently, the judiciary served at the will of the General Assembly, which, in the early years of the state, was not reluctant to exercise its authority over the judiciary. For example, in 1810 the General Assembly passed a "sweeping resolution" that resolved a dispute about the terms of Ohio judges by dismissing all sitting judges and by replacing them with judges more favorable to the legislature. See Carrington T. Marshall, *A History of the Courts and Lawyers of Ohio*, vol. 1 (New York: American Historical Society, 1934), 94–97.

The 1851 Constitution provided for the election of judges, but partisan politics played an important role in their elections since judges were nominated by party conventions and ran on partisan tickets. As a result of a constitutional amendment adopted in 1912, however, party conventions could no longer be used to nominate judges, but judges continued to be nominated through partisan primary elections. And in 2021, the General Assembly adopted a partisan general election judicial ballot for Ohio Supreme Court and Ohio Courts of Appeals elections, thus eliminating the nonpartisan judicial ballot that had been adopted in 1911. See S.B. 80 (134th GA) (2021). See also The History of the Ohio Constitution, *supra*.

The current section resulted from the reorganization of this article under the 1968 Modern Courts Amendment and a minor amendment approved by the voters in 1973.

Section 6(A) provides that judges of the Supreme Court, courts of appeals, and courts of common pleas are elected to terms of not less than six years. Judges on Ohio's municipal and county courts, both of which are created by statute, are elected to office for terms of six years. See O.R.C. sections 1901.06, 1907.11, and 1907.13. Judges on Ohio's Court of Claims, which is also created by statute, are assigned on a temporary basis by the chief justice of the Ohio Supreme Court. See O.R.C. section 2743.03(B).

Periodically, there have been attempts to establish a system of judicial merit selection in which judges are appointed, but none of these efforts have been successful. See The History of the Ohio Constitution, *supra.*

Section 6(B) provides for judicial compensation and forbids judges from holding other elective offices.

Section 6(C) establishes a mandatory retirement age for judges by providing that no person shall be elected or appointed to any judicial office after attaining the age of seventy. Nonetheless, judges may complete terms to which they were elected prior to reaching seventy. Section 6(C) also permits the chief justice to assign cases to voluntarily retired judges (i.e., those who were not defeated in election bids) and judges who had to retire because of age.

The Ohio Supreme Court has upheld Ohio's mandatory retirement age in a challenge under the Equal Protection Clause of the Fourteenth Amendment. *State ex rel. Keefe v. Eyrich* (1986). And in a non-Ohio case the U.S. Supreme Court has upheld a mandatory age requirement for state court judges in a challenge under the Equal Protection Clause of the Fourteenth Amendment and the Age Discrimination in Employment Act of 1967. *Gregory v. Ashcroft* (1991). Most states have adopted mandatory retirement ages for judges. See Christopher R. McFadden, "Judicial Independence, Age-Based BFOQS, and the Perils of Mandatory Retirement Policies for Appointed State Judges," 52 *S. C. Law. Rev.* 81 (2000): 83.

In 2011, the voters rejected an amendment proposed by the General Assembly to extend the judicial retirement age to seventy-five. See Appendix B.

Sections 7–12
Repealed

Adopted in 1851, these sections were repealed at various times. Sections 7, 8, 10, and 12 were repealed in 1968 with the approval of the Modern Courts Amendment. These sections covered probate courts (secs. 7 and 8), the election of judges (sec. 10), and residency requirements for common pleas judges (sec. 12). In 1912, section 9, which dealt with justices of the peace, was repealed. Section 11, which was repealed in 1883, required the first group of five elected Supreme Court justices to draw lots to determine who would serve for a term of one year, who would serve for a term of two years, and so on up to five years.

Section 13

Vacancy in office of judge.

In case the office of any judge shall become vacant, before the expiration of the regular term for which he was elected, the vacancy shall be filled by appointment by the governor, until a successor is elected and has qualified; and such successor shall be elected for the unexpired term, at the first general election for the office which is vacant that occurs more than forty days after the vacancy shall have occurred; provided, however, that when the unexpired term ends within one year immediately following the date of such general election, an election to fill such unexpired term shall not be held and the appointment shall be for such unexpired term.

Adopted in 1851 and slightly modified in 1942, this section, which was not changed by the Modern Courts Amendment, requires the governor to appoint a replacement for any judicial seat that becomes vacant. The appointed successor is to carry on the duties until a replacement is elected at the next general election that takes place more than forty days after the vacancy. If the unexpired term ends within one year of the next general election, the appointed replacement serves for the balance of the term.

Section 14

Repealed—Compensation and holding other offices.

Adopted in 1968 and repealed in 1968 by the Modern Courts Amendment, this section dealt with the compensation of Supreme Court and common pleas judges and prohibited those judges from holding other offices, a prohibition that is now in section 6(B) of this article.

Section 15

Changing number of judges; establishing other courts.

Laws may be passed to increase or diminish the number of judges of the Supreme Court, to increase beyond one or diminish to one the number of judges of the court of common pleas in any county, and to establish other courts, whenever two-thirds of the members elected to each house shall concur therein; but no such change, addition or diminution shall vacate the office of any judge; and any existing court heretofore created by law shall continue in existence until otherwise provided.

Adopted in 1851 and amended in 1912, this section allows the General Assembly to increase or decrease the number of judges on the Supreme Court and courts of common pleas by a two-thirds vote of each house (assuming that the seat is vacant). Section 15 also allows the General Assembly to create statutory courts by a two-thirds vote. The Ohio Supreme Court has interpreted this section as restricting the power of the General Assembly to abolish constitutional courts but not statutory courts. *Geisinger v. Cook* (1977). Thus, the General Assembly may abolish statutory courts with a simple majority vote. Ibid.

Section 16
Repealed—Clerk of courts

Adopted in 1851 and repealed in 1933 as part of the county Home Rule Amendment, see Article X, this section dealt with the election of county clerks of court. As a result, there is nothing in the constitution that requires the election of county clerks of court.

Section 17
Judges removable.

Judges may be removed from office, by concurrent resolution of both houses of the General Assembly, if two-thirds of the members, elected to each house, concur therein; but, no such removal shall be made, except upon complaint, the substance of which, shall be entered on the journal, nor, until the party charged shall have had notice thereof, and an opportunity to be heard.

Adopted in 1851 and never amended, this section prevents the General Assembly from enacting "'sweeping' resolutions to get rid of *persona non grata* in the judicial branch." See Swisher, *Ohio Constitution Handbook*, 378. Section 17 forbids the dismissal of any judge without a resolution of removal and a two-thirds vote of the General Assembly. The resolution of removal must be based on a complaint with proper notice and must give the judge an opportunity to be heard.

Section 17 outlines one of the several ways judges can be removed from office. In addition to removal under this section, judges can be removed by the General Assembly by impeachment and conviction, see Commentary, Article II, sections 23 and 24; under statutes adopted by the General Assembly pursuant to the power given by Article II, section 38, to remove state officials from office "for any misconduct involving moral turpitude or for other cause provided by law," see Commentary, Article II, section 38; and under the Supreme Court Rules for the Government of the Judiciary, Gov. Jud. R. III, 2015.

Section 18
Powers and jurisdiction.

The several judges of the Supreme Court, of the common pleas, and of such other courts as may be created, shall, respectively, have and exercise such power and jurisdiction, at chambers, or otherwise, as may be directed by law.

Adopted in 1851 and never amended, this section allows the General Assembly to determine the power and jurisdiction of judges on the Supreme

Court, common pleas court, and other courts later established by the legislature. This section has lost much of its significance because of the adoption of other amendments that define the powers and jurisdiction of the state courts. See, for example, Article IV, sections 2–4. The Ohio Constitutional Revision Commission (OCRC) recommended repeal of this section in 1976, referring to it as "in one sense unduly limiting and in another sense simply surplusage." OCRC, *Final Report*, 419. But the General Assembly did not propose its repeal to the voters.

Section 19

Courts of conciliation.

The General Assembly may establish courts of conciliation, and prescribe their powers and duties; but such courts shall not render final judgment in any case, except upon submission, by the parties, of the matter in dispute, and their agreement to abide such judgment.

Adopted in 1851 and never amended, this section sought to alleviate judicial backlog by allowing the General Assembly to establish courts of conciliation to resolve disputes without resort to the traditional legal process. The General Assembly, however, has not established specialized courts under this section, though it has established special proceedings, such as arbitration proceedings, O.R.C. chapter 2711, and adjudications before retired judges, O.R.C. section 2701.10. See Swisher, *Ohio Constitution Handbook*, 379.

In 2011, the General Assembly proposed the repeal of this section (along with proposals to repeal the authority to create Supreme Court commissions and to raise the judicial retirement age), but the voters rejected the proposed repeal. In 2015, the Ohio Constitutional Modernization Commission (hereinafter OCMC) recommended its repeal but, to date, the General Assembly has not taken any action to move this proposed repeal to the ballot.

Section 20

Style of process, prosecution, and indictment.

The style of all process shall be, "The state of Ohio;" all prosecutions shall be carried on, in the name, and by the authority, of the state of Ohio; and all indictments shall conclude, "against the peace and dignity of the state of Ohio."

Adopted in 1851 and never amended, this section provides that all prosecutions in state courts will be carried on in the name and authority of the state of Ohio. The section also stipulates that all indictments conclude with the words "against the peace and dignity of the State of Ohio." Notwithstanding this provision, the failure of an indictment to conclude with these words does not necessarily "nullify a conviction otherwise obtained." *Ruch v. State* (1924).

Section 22
Supreme court commission.

A commission, which shall consist of five members, shall be appointed by the governor, with the advice and consent of the Senate, the members of which shall hold office for the term of three years from and after the first day of February, 1876, to dispose of such part of the business then on the dockets of the Supreme Court, as shall, by arrangement between said commission and said court, be transferred to such commission; and said commission shall have like jurisdiction and power in respect to such business as are or may be vested in said court; and the members of said commission shall receive a like compensation for the time being, with the judges of said court. A majority of the members of said commission shall be necessary to form a quorum or pronounce a decision, and its decision shall be certified, entered, and enforced as the judgments of the Supreme Court, and at the expiration of the term of said commission, all business undisposed of shall by it be certified to the Supreme Court and disposed of as if said commission had never existed. The clerk and reporter of said court shall be the clerk and reporter of said commission, and the commission shall have such other attendants not exceeding in number those provided by law for said court, which attendants said commission may appoint and remove at its pleasure.

Any vacancy occurring in said commission, shall be filled by appointment of the governor, with the advice and consent of the Senate, if the Senate be in session, and if the Senate be not in session, by the governor, but in such last case, such appointments shall expire at the end of the next session of the General Assembly. The General Assembly may, on application of the Supreme Court duly entered on the journal of the court and certified, provide by law, whenever two-thirds of such house shall concur therein, from time to time, for the appointment, in like manner, of a like commission with like powers, jurisdiction and duties; provided, that the term of any such commission shall not exceed two years, nor shall it be created oftener than once in ten years.

Adopted in 1875 and never amended, this section was a stopgap measure to relieve the tremendous backlog of cases before the Supreme Court. Under this section, the governor (with the advice and consent of the Senate) was required to appoint a commission of five people for a three-year term beginning in 1876 to hear and decide cases appealed to the Supreme Court. With the creation of this commission, Ohio literally had two supreme courts functioning simultaneously.

This section also contained authority for the creation of additional commissions for two-year terms and, in 1883, the governor appointed a second commission that assisted the Supreme Court with cases until 1885. But this was the last time a commission was appointed.

In 1973, the voters rejected a proposal by the General Assembly (based on a recommendation from the OCRC) to remove legislative authority to create Supreme Court commissions; and in 2011, the voters again rejected a proposal to repeal this section made by the General Assembly (along with proposals to repeal the authority to create courts of conciliation and to raise the judicial retirement age). Finally, the OCMC in 2015 recommended its repeal, but, to date, the General Assembly has not taken any action to move this proposed repeal to the ballot.

This section is sometimes erroneously referred to as section 21, but there has never been a section 21 of Article IV of the 1851 Constitution. Nonetheless, for reasons that are not clear, some commentators treat section 22 as once having been section 21 and use a bracketed citation when referring to it. See, for example, Isaac Franklin Patterson, *The Constitution of Ohio: Amendments and Proposed Amendments* (Cleveland: Arthur H. Clark Co., 1912), 238.

Section 23

Judges in less populous counties; service on more than one court.

Laws may be passed to provide that in any county having less than forty thousand population, as determined by the next preceding federal census, the board of county commissioners of such county, by a unanimous vote or ten percent of the number of electors of such county voting for governor at the next preceding election, by petition, may submit to the electors of such county the question of providing that in such county the same person shall serve as judge of the court of common pleas, judge of the probate court, judge of the juvenile court, judge of the municipal court, and judge of the county court, or of two or more of such courts. If a majority of the electors of such county vote in favor of such proposition, one person shall thereafter be elected to serve in such capacities, but this shall not affect the right of any judge then in office from continuing in office until the end of the term for which he was elected.

Elections may be had in the same manner to discontinue or change the practice of having one person serve in the capacity of judge of more than one court when once adopted.

Adopted in 1965 and never amended, this section provides that county commissioners or the electors of a county with a population of less than 40,000 may decide if the same person may serve more than one judicial post.

Article V

Elective Franchise

Article V concerns voting rights, ballot and election requirements, and term limits. Many of the amendments to this article were adopted to conform to the liberalization of the franchise through amendments to the U.S. Constitution and by U.S. Supreme Court decisions. In 1976, after receiving a recommendation from the Ohio Constitutional Revision Commission (OCRC), the General Assembly proposed a single ballot issue to amend sections 1 and 4 and repeal sections 3 and 5, and the voters approved the proposal. See OCRC, *Recommendations for Amendments to the Ohio Constitution, Final Report, Index to Proceedings and Research* (1977), 253–69 (hereinafter OCRC, *Final Report*). And a 1977 amendment to this section, proposed by initiative petition against a contentious and partisan backdrop, embedded a voter registration requirement in the state constitution for the first time.

Section 1

Who may vote.

Every citizen of the United States, of the age of eighteen years, who has been a resident of the state, county, township or ward, such time as may be provided by law, and has been registered to vote for thirty days, has the qualifications of an elector, and is entitled to vote at all elections. Any elector who fails to vote in at least one election during any period of four consecutive years shall cease to be an elector unless he again registers to vote.

The Ohio State Constitution. Steven H. Steinglass and Gino J. Scarselli, Oxford University Press. © Oxford University Press 2022. DOI: 10.1093/oso/9780197619728.003.0007

Adopted in 1851 and amended in 1923, 1957, 1970, 1976, and 1977, this section now guarantees the right to vote to any U.S. citizen who is eighteen years of age or older, is a resident of the state, and registers to vote at least thirty days before an election. Federal law has been the driving force for the expansion of voting rights since 1851, and this provision differs significantly from its predecessors under the Northwest Ordinance, the 1802 Constitution, and the 1851 Constitution.

■ NORTHWEST ORDINANCE

The Northwest Ordinance limited the right to vote to males who owned a "freehold in fifty acres" and resided in the territory for one or two years, depending on whether the man was a citizen of one of the states. Northwest Ordinance of 1787, section 9. Voters did not have to be citizens of one of the states, and therefore, foreign nationals could vote for representatives to the territorial legislature under the 1787 Ordinance. The 1802 Enabling Act, which set the terms for Ohio's admission into the union, dispensed with the fifty-acre requirement for U.S. citizens. Under the Act, Congress permitted adult male citizens of the United States who paid a territorial or county tax to vote for delegates to the 1802 Constitutional Convention as long as they had resided in the territory for at least a year. Noncitizens who owned a freehold of fifty acres, however, could also vote since the Enabling Act allowed electors who had qualified under the Northwest Ordinance to vote for convention delegates.

■ 1802 CONSTITUTION

As with the Northwest Ordinance and all early state constitutions with the temporary exception of the 1776 New Jersey Constitution, see Robert F. Williams, *The New Jersey State Constitution* (New York: Oxford University Press, 2nd ed., 2012), 9–10, the 1802 Constitution denied women the right to vote.

The 1802 Constitution also expressly limited suffrage to white males, even though nonwhites had not been expressly disenfranchised under the Northwest Ordinance. The delegates to the 1802 Constitutional Convention had initially approved a proposal granting African Americans the right to vote, but on reconsideration they reversed this position with convention president, Edward Tiffin, casting the deciding vote against African American suffrage. See The History of the Ohio Constitution, *supra*.

The 1802 Constitution also imposed residency and taxation requirements. Article IV, section 1, of the 1802 Constitution required voters to reside in the state for at least a year and to pay, or be charged with paying, a state or county tax. This latter requirement appeared to limit the right to vote to property owners since the only state and county taxes in existence at that time were real property taxes. See Thomas R. Swisher, ed., *Ohio Constitution Handbook*

(Cleveland: Banks-Baldwin Publishing Co., 1990), 432. The taxation requirement, however, could be circumvented by work on public roads. Article IV, section 5, of the 1802 Constitution provided that "[n]othing contained in this article shall be so construed as to prevent white male persons, above the age of twenty-one years, who are compelled to labor on the roads of their respective townships or counties, and who have resided one year in the State, from having the right of an elector." Thus, nonproperty owners who met the other voting requirements could vote if they had been compelled to work on township or county roads.

■ 1851 CONSTITUTION

The 1850–51 Constitutional Convention eliminated the taxation requirement but kept the one-year residency requirement. The delegates, however, overwhelmingly rejected the proposals to remove the words "white" and "male" from this section. See The History of the Ohio Constitution, *supra*.

The issue of noncitizen voting was also a contested issue, but the delegates expressly limited the vote to citizens by replacing the 1802 provision that had guaranteed the vote to "all white male *inhabitants*," (emphasis added) Article IV, section 1, with a provision limiting the vote to *citizens*, thus effectively agreeing with an 1817 decision of the Ohio Supreme Court that limited the vote to citizens. See *Johnston v. England* (1817); see also Steven H. Steinglass, "Constitutional Revision: Ohio Style," 77 *Ohio St. L. J.* 281 (2016): 259 n. 59. Prior to *Johnston*, noncitizens participated in Ohio governance during territorial days, in the process leading to the 1802 Convention, and at the constitutional convention. See Jamin B. Raskin, "Legal Aliens, Local Citizens: The Historical, Constitutional, and Theoretical Meanings of Alien Suffrage," 141 *U. Pa. L Rev.* 1391 (1993): 1402–3. The extension of the franchise to noncitizens had been part of the overall policy of encouraging foreigners to settle in the Northwest Territory. Ibid.

In 1863, the Ohio Supreme Court upheld a statute that authorized Ohio civil war soldiers to vote while living outside the state. *Lehman v. McBride* (1863). The 1802 Constitution had limited the voting to the place where the otherwise qualified voter "actually reside[d] at the time of the election," 1802 Constitution, Article IV, section 1, but this provision was not included in the 1851 Constitution.

In 1912, the Ohio Supreme Court rejected the argument that a state statute that provided for the election of judges on a separate (i.e., nonpartisan) ballot (on which straight party ticket voting was not possible) added a literacy requirement to the right to vote. See *State ex rel. Weinberger v. Miller* (1912). In 2021, however, the General Assembly eliminated the nonpartisan judicial ballot for elections to the Ohio Supreme Court and the Ohio Courts of Appeals, thus aligning the general election ballot with the partisan judicial primary ballot.

See S.B. 80 (134th GA) (2021); see also The History of the Ohio Constitution, *supra*.

■ POST-1851 AMENDMENTS

In 1867, prior to the 1870 ratification of the Fifteenth Amendment, Ohio voters rejected a proposed revision of this section to remove "white" and thus extend the right to vote to African Americans. Despite the vitriolic debate on the race issue, the proposal also denied the right to vote to Union draft dodgers and to those who fought for the Confederacy. And the campaign "degenerated into emotional appeals against race equality on the one hand and Copperhead control of State government on the other hand." And the competing slogans included: "Fathers save us from Negro equality" and "Honest Black men are preferable to white traitors." See Eugene H. Roseboom, *The Civil War Era 1850–1873,* in Carl Wittke, ed., *The History of the State of Ohio,* vol. IV (Columbus: Ohio State Archaeological and Historical Society, 1944), 459–60; see also Appendix B.

At the 1873–74 Constitutional Convention, the delegates debated a proposal to submit to the voters a separate issue to remove "white male" from the section on voting. The delegates approved this proposal by a vote of 49–41, but the rules of the convention required a majority of all 105 delegates (or fifty-three votes) for submission to the voters; thus, the proposal failed. See Barbara A. Terzian, "Effusions of Folly and Fanaticism: Race, Gender and Constitution-Making in Ohio, 1802–1923," (Ph.D. dissertation, The Ohio State University, 1999), 259–66.

The 1912 Constitutional Convention, on the other hand, submitted separate proposals to the voters to eliminate the word "male" and the word "white," but these two proposed amendments were among the eight that the voters rejected. And in 1914, the voters also rejected a proposed constitutional amendment that would have extended the vote to women. Nonetheless, acting under the home rule power, some cities gave women the right to vote in local elections, and the Ohio Supreme Court held that a city could permit women to vote in elections for offices not created by the state constitution. *State ex rel. Taylor v. French* (1917).

With respect to African Americans, the proposal to remove "white" from this section in 1874 and the amendment proposed to the voters in 1912 were only symbolic, as African Americans had been guaranteed the right to vote in 1870 with the adoption of the Fifteenth Amendment to the U.S. Constitution.

As with African Americans, women in Ohio secured the right to vote by an amendment to the U.S. Constitution. In 1920, the Nineteenth Amendment to the U.S. Constitution gave women the right to vote in state and national elections. Finally, in 1923, the voters approved an amendment proposed by the General Assembly to remove the words "white" and "male" from this section, three years after women were guaranteed the right to vote and fifty-three years after African Americans secured the franchise.

In 1957, the voters approved an amendment to this section to allow recent Ohio residents who did not meet the state's one-year residency requirement to still vote for electors for the president and vice president of the United States as long as they were not entitled to vote for electors in any other state. In 1970, the voters approved an amendment to this section to reduce the residency requirement to six months and retained the special provision for presidential elections. Finally, in 1976, after the U.S. Supreme Court held that durational residency requirements imposing a waiting period on new residents beyond the time necessary for the state to verify the person's residence were unconstitutional, *Dunn v. Blumstein* (1972), the voters approved another amendment to this section to eliminate the special provision for presidential elections and to give the General Assembly authority to establish residency requirement for all elections. As a result of these changes in federal law, Ohio law now requires a thirty-day residency period as a condition of voting. O.R.C. section 3503.01.

The 1976 amendment also reduced the age requirement for voting in general elections from twenty-one to eighteen to conform to the Twenty-Sixth Amendment to the U.S. Constitution, which the states ratified in 1971. The General Assembly has adopted a statute that further expands those eligible to vote by permitting seventeen-year olds who will be legal electors at the time of the general election to vote in primary elections (O.R.C. sec. 3503.011), and in 2016 a trial court extended this right to vote to presidential primary elections. See *State ex rel. Schwerdtfeger v. Husted* (2016).

■ NONPARTISAN JUDICIAL BALLOT

In 1912, the Ohio Supreme Court rejected the argument that a state statute that provided for the election of judges on a separate (i.e., nonpartisan) ballot added another qualification to the right to vote. The challengers had claimed that the use of the separate ballot (on which straight party ticket voting was not possible) operated as a literacy test, which was not a proper constitutional requirement for voting under this section. See *State ex rel. Weinberger v. Miller* (1912).

■ VOTER REGISTRATION AND PURGES

Beginning with an 1845 statute, Ohio embraced voter registration requirements. See 1845 Ohio Laws 116 (March 13, 1845) ("To provide for registering the names of electors and to prevent fraud at elections").

In 1885, the General Assembly adopted a voter registration law that applied to voters in Ohio's two largest cities—Cincinnati and Cleveland. That same year, however, the Ohio Supreme Court declared the law unconstitutional, because it provided only seven days for registration. *Daggett v. Hudson* (1885). Recognizing that the General Assembly has the power to adopt voter registration laws, the court found the law too restrictive, stating that "[t]here is no provision for registering at pleasure during the earlier part of the year, and no provision for providing his qualifications on election day and voting." And the court asked: "[h]ow many mechanics may be absent pursuing their trades during the seven days!" Finally, the court applied a balancing test stating that "[w]e believe it is an easy task to frame a registry law that, while protecting the election from fraudulent votes, and securing the integrity of the ballot, will in no practical way impede or injuriously restrain the constitutional right of the voter." Ibid.

In 1886, the General Assembly revisited the issue of voter registration, and for most of the twentieth century, voter registration was only required when a municipality reached a population of 16,000. Indeed, in 1952, only seventeen of Ohio's eighty-eight counties were "full registration" counties, and an additional eighteen were "partial registration" counties. That left fifty-three counties without any registration requirement. And by 1972, twenty-eight counties still had no registration requirements. This led to what one commentator has described as "the biggest voter registration fight in Ohio history." See Michael Curtin, "Voter Registration in Ohio" (Teaching Cleveland) (2016).

■ THE 1977 VOTER REGISTRATION CONTROVERSY

In 1977, Democrats, who controlled both houses of the General Assembly, overrode a veto by Republican Governor James A. Rhodes and adopted legislation establishing permanent statewide registration but permitting registration on election day. The law also removed a thirty-day precinct and county residency requirement.

The partisan response was an initiative petition to amend this section by adopting the current thirty-day statewide registration policy. The voters approved this amendment with more than a 60 percent vote, despite opposition that included many rural voters who feared being burdened by voter registration. Thus, the voters put a voter registration requirement in the constitution for the first time.

Under this provision, citizens who have been registered for thirty days are entitled to vote. The section, however, does not bar "same-day" voting as long as the durational registration requirement is met at the time of the election, and the statutory expansion of early in-person voting has created a limited period when registration and voting may take place on the same day.

As currently worded, every otherwise eligible person at least eighteen years of age is entitled to vote, and it is clear that the General Assembly cannot raise the voting age to, for example, twenty-five. But it is unclear—at least textually—whether this section also bars the General Assembly from extending the franchise to otherwise eligible persons who are less than eighteen years of age.

Likewise, this provision gives otherwise eligible persons the right to vote if registered to vote for thirty days, and the General Assembly cannot impose a longer registration requirement. But it is also unclear—at least textually—whether this section also bars the General Assembly from extending the franchise to otherwise eligible persons who were registered for less than thirty days. See generally Joshua A. Douglas, "The Right to Vote under Local Law," 85 *Geo. Wash. L. Rev.* 1039 (2017): 1081 n. 208 (distinguishing the "grant" of the right to vote from a "restriction" on the right).

The 1977 amendment, which placed voter registration in the constitution for the first time, also requires the removal from the voting rolls of any elector who has failed to vote for four consecutive years regardless of the reason, a policy that the U.S. Supreme Court held did not violate federal law. *Husted v. A. Philip Randolph Institute* (2018).

Section 2
By ballot.

All elections shall be by ballot.

Initially adopted in the 1802 Constitution as Article IV, section 2, this provision was incorporated verbatim as Article V, section 2, of the 1851 Constitution, and the voters have never amended it. Nonetheless, there have been significant changes over the years in the nature of the ballots used in elections.

Throughout most of the nineteenth century, political parties prepared and printed the ballots. At the end of the century, however, the states began to reform the way they conducted elections by adopting the Australian or "secret" ballots that are now printed and distributed by the states. In addition, voting moved from a public exercise, and the policy of conducting voting in secret through the use of curtains or voting booths became commonplace. And in 1891 Ohio adopted the Australian ballot legislatively, using what is known as the column format. See Erik J. Engstrom and Jason M. Roberts, "The Politics of Ballot Choice," 77 *Ohio St. L.J.* 839 (2016).

The power of the General Assembly to determine what may go on the ballot includes authority to bar names from appearing more than once on any ballot. And the Ohio Supreme Court has held that nothing in Article V, section 2, or in the equal protection and benefit clause of Article 1, section 2, invalidates a statute that prevented a board of elections from putting candidates on the ballot on both the "Democratic judicial ticket" and the "Lawyers' judicial ticket." *State ex rel. Bateman v. Bode* (1896).

The General Assembly's power over voting, however, is limited by other provisions of the Ohio Constitution, see, for example, Article V, section 2a, by the U.S. Constitution, and by laws enacted by Congress, including the Voting Rights Act of 1965.

■ VOTING MACHINES

In 1909, the Ohio Supreme Court held that this provision barred the use of voting machines. *State ex rel. Karlinger v. Board of Deputy State Supervisors of Elections* (1909).

In response to this decision, the 1912 Constitutional Convention proposed an amendment that would have overruled *Karlinger* by providing that "[a]ll elections shall be either by ballot or by mechanical device, or by both, preserving the secrecy of the vote." See *Proceedings and Debates of the Constitutional Convention of the State of Ohio: Convened January 9, 1912* (Columbus: F. J. Heer Printing, 1912), 2106. But the voters rejected this proposed amendment.

But in 1923, the court revisited this issue, declined to follow *Karlinger*, and expressly held that the "constitutional requirement that all elections be by ballot does not invalidate an otherwise legal enactment providing for the use of voting machines in elections." *State ex rel. Automatic Registering Machine Co. v. Green* (1929). In so ruling, the court stated that "[t]he term 'ballot' designates a method of conducting elections which will insure secrecy, as distinguished from open or viva voce voting." Ibid.

■ SECRET BALLOT

The word "ballot" as used in this section does not refer to a small sheet of paper used to cast votes but to a system or "method of conducting elections which will insure secrecy," and a law authorizing the use of voting machines does not violate this section as long as it ensures secrecy. Ibid.

While the hallmark of this section is secrecy, this section does not create an absolute right to a secret ballot. In *State v. Jackson* (2004), the court reiterated its interpretation of this section as protecting the right of privacy through the use of the secret ballot. But the court held that this section does not prohibit the use of ballots as evidence in a criminal case charging the defendant with ballot tampering and other election law violations.

Section 2a

Names of candidates on ballot.

The names of all candidates for an office at any election shall be arranged in a group under the title of that office. The General Assembly shall provide by law the means by which ballots shall give each candidate's name reasonably equal position by rotation or other comparable methods to the extent practical and appropriate to the voting procedure used. At any election in which a candidate's party designation appears on the ballot, the name or designation of each candidate's party, if any, shall be printed under or after each candidate's name in less prominent type face than that in which the candidate's name is printed. An elector may vote for candidates (other than candidates for electors of president and vice president of the United States, and other than candidates for governor and lieutenant governor) only and in no other way than by indicating his vote for each candidate separately from the indication of his vote for any other candidate.

Proposed by initiative petition and approved by the voters in 1949, and amended in 1975 and 1976, this section required voters to focus on the candidates for office rather than on the candidates' political parties. Before the adoption of this section, voters could cast a straight party ticket vote by marking a single "X" on the ballot. Section 2a rejects that manner of voting by requiring an office-type ballot in which votes are listed in a group under the title of the office being sought, thus requiring votes for candidates for specific offices. The arguments in favor of this amendment stressed the need to reduce the role of political parties, while those opposing the changes argued that the adoption of the amendment would result in a name game under which those candidates with popular ballot names would be most likely to prevail.

Despite the public policy rationale, the 1949 change from the column format to the office bloc format was a partisan-motivated change that removed party emblems from the ballot and barred straight party ticket voting. See Engstrom, "The Politics of Ballot Choice," 854–56.

In 1974, the Ohio Supreme Court ruled that the use of voting machines was not unconstitutional per se, but it further held that this provision did prohibit the use of voting machines and other means of voting that rotated names on a precinct-by-precinct basis. *State ex rel. Roof v. Hardin County Board of Commissioners* (1974). And, in 1975, in response to this decision, the General Assembly proposed and the voters approved an amendment to this section to allow precinct-by-precinct rotation or any other method that gives each candidate's name a "reasonably equal position." In 1976, the General Assembly proposed and the voters approved an amendment that made clear that the ballot should reflect the fact that the governor and the lieutenant governor were being elected on a joint ballot.

The Ohio Supreme Court has held that voting irregularities such as the failure to properly rotate candidate names and problems with voting machines are grounds for setting aside the results of an election. *In re Election of Nov. 6, 1990, for the Office of Attorney General* (1991). Such irregularities, however, must be established by "clear and convincing" evidence—that is, evidence greater than a preponderance of the evidence (more likely than not) but not as great as that required by the criminal law's "beyond a reasonable doubt" standard. *In re Election* involved a challenge to the election for attorney general where the party challenging the initial vote lost by 1,234 votes out of over three million cast. The court held that in order to set aside an election, a challenger had to prove by clear and convincing evidence "(1) that one or more election irregularities occurred, and (2) that the irregularity or irregularities affected enough votes to change or make uncertain the result of the election" (syllabus). Although the challenger proved by clear and convincing evidence that irregularities had occurred, the challenger did not prove that enough votes were affected to either change the result or call the election into question.

Section 3

Repealed—Privilege from arrest

Adopted in 1851 as part of the 1851 Constitution, this section protected voters from arrest for all crimes except treason, felonies, and breaches of the peace. This privilege related to the time they were voting and to the time they were going to and returning from the polls. The General Assembly proposed its repeal in 1976 based on a recommendation from OCRC, and the voters approved the repeal. See OCRC, *Final Report*, 262–64.

Section 4

Exclusion from franchise.

The General Assembly shall have power to exclude from the privilege of voting, or of being eligible to office, any person convicted of a felony.

Adopted in 1851 and amended in 1976, this section addresses the ability of persons convicted of crimes to vote. The 1802 and 1851 Constitutions prevented any person convicted of "bribery, perjury, or other infamous crime" from voting. The 1976 amendment proposed by the General Assembly (based on a recommendation from the OCRC) and approved by the voters eliminated the constitutional bar on voting and gave the General Assembly discretion to deny the franchise to persons convicted of felonies.

Current Ohio law permits a person who has been convicted of a felony under either state or federal law to vote after the person has served his or her sentence or has been granted probation, parole, or a conditional pardon. O.R.C. section 2961.01. Like almost all states, Ohio prohibits persons from voting while serving felony sentences. See National Conference of State Legislatures, *Felon Voting Rights* (2021).

The U.S. Supreme Court has rejected a challenge under the Equal Protection Clause of the Fourteenth Amendment to state statutes that permanently bar those convicted of felonies whether serving sentences or not. *Richardson v. Ramirez* (1974).

Section 5

Repealed—Residence of members of military

Adopted in 1851 and repealed in 1976, this section originally prohibited U.S. military personnel stationed in Ohio from becoming residents of the state. It read: "No person in the military, naval, or marine service of the United States, shall, by being stationed in any garrison, or military, or naval station, within the state, be considered a resident of this state."

In 1976, the General Assembly proposed the repeal of this section, and the voters agreed. The repeal had been recommended by the OCRC, which concluded that the provision denied those living in federal enclaves the right to vote in violation of the Equal Protection Clause of the Fourteenth Amendment, see *Evans v. Cornman* (1970), and because the Commission agreed with the principle of an expanded franchise. See OCRC, *Final Report*, 265–66.

Section 6

Voting by idiots or insane persons.

No idiot, or insane person, shall be entitled to privileges of an elector.

Adopted in 1851 and never amended, this section denies the right to vote to the mentally incompetent, using language that is offensive to the modern ear.

In 1977, the OCRC, believing that this section violated the Due Process and Equal Protection Clauses of the Fourteenth Amendment to the U.S. Constitution, recommended amending the section to delete the words "idiot" and "insane" and replacing them with "person adjudicated mentally incompetent." See OCRC, *Final Report*, 269. The General Assembly did not present this proposed amendment to the voters, but it enacted laws that included the substantive portion of the commission's recommendation. Under Ohio law, an adjudication of incompetence is now required before disqualifying a person from voting because of mental illness. See O.R.C. section 5122.301.

In 2015, the Ohio Constitutional Modernization Commission (hereinafter OCMC) by a vote of 18–8 voted to support a revision of this section to, among other thing, remove the offensive language, but the approval of this recommendation fell short of the statutorily required two-thirds vote needed for a formal recommendation to the General Assembly. Under the failed recommendation, the section would have been revised to read as follows: "The General Assembly shall provide that no person who has been determined under law to lack the mental capacity to vote shall have the rights and privileges of an elector during the time of incapacity." See OCMC, Bill of Rights and Voting Committee, Minutes (April 9, 2015).

Section 7

Primary elections.

All nominations for elective state, district, county and municipal offices shall be made at direct primary elections or by petition as provided by law, and provision shall be made by law for a preferential vote for United States senator; but direct primaries shall not be held for the nomination of township officers or for the officers of municipalities of less than two thousand population, unless petitioned for by a majority of the electors of such township or municipality All delegates from this state to the national conventions of political parties shall be chosen by direct vote of the electors in a manner provided by law. Each candidate for such delegate shall state his first and second choices for the presidency, but the name of no candidate for the presidency shall be so used without his written authority.

Adopted in 1912 and amended in 1975, this section requires the use of primary elections for most state and local elected offices. The exception was for township officers as well as for municipalities with a population of less than 2,000, unless a majority of the electors of the township or municipality petitioned to have direct primaries. The 1912 Constitutional Convention proposed the compulsory use of primary elections to avoid the nomination of candidates by backroom party politics.

The reference to nominations by petitions continued the policy of permitting independent candidates to qualify for the ballot without going through a partisan political process—whether a party convention or a primary.

The preferential vote for U.S. senators, which was also part of the 1912 amendment, was almost immediately rendered obsolete by the 1913 ratification of the Seventeenth Amendment, which provided for the direct election of U.S. senators.

In 1926, the voters rejected by an almost 2:1 margin an amendment proposed by initiative petition to eliminate the compulsory primary, one of the singular accomplishments of the Progressive movement.

In 1975, the General Assembly proposed and the voters approved the addition of the last two sentences regarding national party conventions. This change sought to avoid confusing the voters with "bedsheet" ballots (i.e., ballots containing long lists of candidates). See OCRC, *Final Report*, 269. Prior to 1975, the ballot listed all candidates for delegate to a national party convention with their first and second choices for president. This resulted in the voters being presented with extremely long ballots that at times could not be handled by voting machines. See OCRC, *Final Report*, 269. The 1975 amendment removed the requirement that delegate preferences be printed on the ballot.

Section 8

Term Limits for U.S. Senators and Representatives.

No person shall hold the office of United States Senator from Ohio for a period longer than two successive terms of six years. No person shall hold the office of United States Representative from Ohio for a period longer than four successive terms of two years. Terms shall be considered successive unless separated by a period of four or more years. Only terms beginning on or after January 1, 1993 shall be considered in determining an individual's eligibility to hold office.

Adopted in 1992 and never amended, this section, which was proposed by initiative petition, imposed term limits on members of the U.S. Congress following a national movement to impose term limits on elected officials. In 1995, however, the U.S. Supreme Court struck down term limits for members of Congress, reasoning that states may not impose qualifications for congressional membership in addition to those in the U.S. Constitution. *U.S. Term Limits, Inc. v. Thornton* (1995). Therefore, this section has never had any legal effect.

At the time *Thornton* was decided, Ohio was one of twenty-two states that had adopted terms limits for congressional office. See Sean R. Sullivan, "A Term Limit by Any Other Name? The Constitutionality of State-Enacted Ballot Access Restrictions on Incumbent Members of Congress," 56 *U. Pitt L. Rev.* 845 (1995): 845–46.

Section 9
Eligibility of term-limited officeholders.

In determining the eligibility of an individual to hold an office in accordance with this article, (A) time spent in an office in fulfillment of a term to which another person was first elected shall not be considered provided that a period of at least four years passed between the time, if any, in which the individual previously held that office, and the time the individual is elected or appointed to fulfill the unexpired term; and (B) a person who is elected to an office in a regularly scheduled general election and resigns prior to the completion of the term for which he or she was elected, shall be considered to have served the full term in that office.

Adopted in 1992 with section 8 and also proposed by initiative petition, this section, which has never been amended, addressed whether a previous term counts toward the total time spent in office for purposes of calculating term limits. It provides that a partial term is not counted if at least four years have passed between the time the person is elected or appointed to office and the last time the person held that office. It further provides that when an officeholder resigns before the end of her term, the person is considered to have served a full term in office.

As noted in the previous section, this section has no applicability to members of Congress given the U.S. Supreme Court's decision in *U.S. Term Limits, Inc. v. Thornton* (1995). Nonetheless, the Ohio Constitution contains identical provisions concerning counting of terms for term-limited state executive branch officials, Article III, section 2, and for term-limited members of the General Assembly, Article II, section 2.

Article VI

Education

Ohio's earliest constitutional documents contain references to the importance of education. In the 1785 Land Ordinance the Confederation, Congress set aside land in the Northwest Territory for the creation and support of schools, and the Northwest Ordinance of 1787 promised that "schools and the means of education shall forever be encouraged." Ordinance of 1787, section 14, Article III.

When Ohio became a state, the drafters of the 1802 Ohio Constitution included a provision that reiterated verbatim the promise of the Northwest Ordinance that "religion, morality and knowledge, being essentially necessary to good government and the happiness of mankind, schools and the means of instruction shall forever be encouraged by legislative provision, not inconsistent with the rights of conscience." 1802 Constitution, Article VIII, sections 3, 25. In addition, the 1802 Constitution prohibited laws from being passed that would deprive poor children of an education.

> That no law shall be passed to prevent the poor in the several counties and townships within this state from an equal participation in the schools, academies, colleges and universities within this state, which are endowed, in whole or in part, from the revenue arising from donations made by the United States, for the support of schools and colleges; and the doors of the said schools, academies and universities, shall be open for the reception of scholars, students and teachers, of

The Ohio State Constitution. Steven H. Steinglass and Gino J. Scarselli, Oxford University Press. © Oxford University Press 2022. DOI: 10.1093/oso/9780197619728.003.0008

every grade, without any distinction or preference whatever, contrary to the intent for which said donations were made.

1802 Constitution, Article VIII, section 3.

Although the 1851 Constitution did not include these provisions concerning access to education, the delegates to the 1850–51 Constitutional Convention recognized the importance of education and included a separate article on the subject.

The 1850–51 Convention proposed sections 1 and 2 of this article to require the state to establish a system of common or public schools. And the 1912 Constitutional Convention proposed sections 3 and 4 to give the state administrative control of education and thus "completed the constitutional agenda of the common school movement." See Molly O'Brien and Amanda Woodrum, "The Constitutional Common School," 51 *Clev. St. L Rev.* 581 (2004): 636 (hereinafter O'Brien and Woodrum, "The Constitutional Common School").

Section 1

Funds for religious and educational purposes.

The principal of all funds, arising from the sale, or other disposition of lands, or other property, granted or entrusted to this state for educational and religious purposes, shall be used or disposed of in such manner as the General Assembly shall prescribe by law.

Adopted in 1851 and amended in 1968, this section concerns the proceeds of lands granted to the state of Ohio for educational and religious purposes. The Land Ordinance of 1785 had reserved "lot N 16," or one-thirty-sixth of the land of each township, "for the maintenance of public schools." And in the 1802 Ohio Enabling Act, Congress offered to turn over to the state one-thirty-sixth of the land held by the United States in Ohio to support the public schools. Act of Congress, chapter 40, section 7, 2 Stat. 173, 175 (1802).

The 1802 Constitutional Convention, however, made a counteroffer to the federal government. It proposed that "a like donation, equal to the one thirty-sixth part of the amount of the lands in the United States Military Tract, shall be made for the support of schools." *Propositions from the Ohio Constitutional Convention to the Congress of the United States, Relating to the Admission of Ohio, Ordinance and Resolution Passed in Convention, Nov. 29, 1802,* as reprinted in Daniel J. Ryan, *From Charter to Constitution, Ohio Archaeological and Historical Publications,* 5 *Ohio St. Archaeological and Hist. Soc.* 78 (1897). The federal government accepted the counteroffer, which resulted in Ohio ultimately gaining control of 704,204 acres (or 2.77 percent of its land area) to support public schools. See George W. Knepper, *The Official Ohio Lands Book* (Columbus: Auditor of State, 2002), 57 (hereinafter Knepper, *Ohio Lands Book*).

These land and lands under earlier grants were to be held in trust by the state. In 1826, Congress enacted legislation authorizing the state to sell lands appropriated for schools. See Chapter 6, 4 Stat. 138 (1826) ("An Act to authorize the legislature of the state of Ohio to sell the lands heretofore appropriated for the use of schools in that state."). And in 1833, Congress passed similar legislation authorizing the state to sell lands originally granted to John Cleves Symmes and the Ohio Company for the support of religion. 22 Cong. Ch. 42, 4 Stat. 618 (February 20, 1833).

Proceeds from the sale of these lands were put in a special trust fund known as the "irreducible fund," and the interest from these funds was paid to local schools and religious societies. See Ohio Constitutional Revision Commission (OCRC), *Recommendations for Amendments to the Ohio Constitution: Final Report, Index to Proceedings and Research* (Columbus: The Commission, 1977), 66 (hereinafter OCRC, *Final Report*).

The 1851 Constitution addressed these issues in the original version of this section by requiring that the proceeds from the sale of lands granted for educational or religious purposes must be applied to the objects of the original grants. Article VI, section 1.

■ MINISTERIAL LANDS

In addition to providing land to support education, the federal government allocated land in Ohio to support religion by providing that certain land purchases would be used to support religion. See William E. Peters, *Ohio Lands and Their Subdivision*, 2nd ed. (Athens: W.E. Peters, 1918), 358–66 (hereinafter, Peters, *Ohio Lands*).

The Confederation Congress (in the Ohio Company's First Purchase in 1787) and the United States Congress (in the Symmes Purchase in 1794) had reserved section 29 of certain land purchases for the purpose of religion in what are today Washington, Meigs, Gallia, Lawrence, and Athens counties (from the Ohio Company's First Purchase), and in Butler, Hamilton, and Warren Counties (from the Symmes Purchase). In addition, the Ohio Company on its own reserved section 29 from its Second Purchase in what are now Hocking and Vinton Counties. "'Ministerial land,' as these lands have since been termed, are found nowhere in the United States, except within these three parts of Ohio." Peters, *Ohio Lands,* 364.

The 1802 Constitution addressed these issues by providing in the Bill of Right that "the Legislature which shall secure to each and every denomination of religious societies . . . an equal participation . . . of the profits arising from the land granted by Congress, for the support of religion . . . ." Article VIII, section 26.

The granting of real property for religious purposes has been identified as a "holdover from English and other European traditions where one denomination constituted a state church and received its support and other perquisites from the state." Ohio's "ministerial lands," which totaled 43,525 acres, represented only a small part of the total land originally granted to Ohio by Congress. Knepper, *Ohio Lands Book*, 59–60.

In 1968, after a number of U.S. Supreme Court decisions interpreting the Establishment Clause of the First Amendment called into question the constitutionality of state payments for religious purposes, the state auditor stopped payments to religious societies and requested that Congress address this issue. See OCRC, *Final Report*, 66–67. In May 1968, Congress enacted legislation providing that the monies from the sale of lands authorized by the 1826 and 1833 acts were to be used only "for educational purposes, as the Legislature of the State of Ohio in its discretion shall deem appropriate." Public Law, 90–304 (May 13, 1968). Shortly thereafter, the General Assembly proposed and the voters approved the 1968 amendment to this section, which permitted the General Assembly to disperse money set aside in the trust.

In 1988, the General Assembly transferred supervision of all remaining school and ministerial lands to the board of education in each school district that had been allotted these lands, but title was to be held in trust by the state of Ohio. Knepper, *Ohio Lands Book*, 58–59

In 2015, the OCMC reviewed this section and concluded that it was not obsolete because the state still possessed some "school lands" that were being held in trust for local school districts. OCMC, *Report and Recommendation, Article VI, Section* 1 (Funds for Religious and Educational Purposes) (December 10, 2015).

Section 2

School funds.

The General Assembly shall make such provisions, by taxation, or otherwise, as, with the income arising from the school trust fund, will secure a thorough and efficient system of common schools throughout the state; but no religious or other sect, or sects, shall ever have any exclusive right to, or control of, any part of the school funds of this state.

Adopted in 1851 and never amended, this section embraced the goals of the "common school movement," which began in Massachusetts in the late 1830s under Horace Mann and which called for a tax-supported system of free public schools. See Thomas R. Swisher, ed., *Ohio Constitution Handbook* (Cleveland: Banks-Baldwin Publishing Co., 1990), 388. Although the 1802 Constitution prohibited laws that prevented poor children "from an equal participation" in schools funded or endowed "from the revenue arising from donations made by the United States" and had encouraged schools and the means of instruction (as had the Northwest Ordinance), it contained no provision for the establishment of free public schools.

Establishing free public schools was within the plenary power of the General Assembly under the 1802 Constitution, but the adoption of this section of the 1851 Constitution imposed a requirement on the General Assembly to establish a "thorough and efficient system of common schools throughout the state." This provision expresses the state's commitment to education for all, and it further seeks to protect the common schools by "prohibit[ing] religious sects from controlling or having a right to school funds."

The "thorough and efficient" provision was influenced by an 1837 report about education in England and Europe commissioned by the General Assembly and prepared by Calvin Ellis, a professor of biblical literature at Lane Theological Seminary in Cincinnati. See C. E. Stowe, *Report on Elementary Public Instruction in Europe, Made to the Thirty-Sixth General Assembly of the State of Ohio* (1837). Stowe, the husband of Harriet Beecher Stowe, was a strong supporter of universal public education, and he urged Ohio to follow the Prussian example of state-supported education. His report was widely republished, see Frank Forest Bunker, "Reorganization of the Public School System," 8 *Department of the Interior, Bureau of Education Bulletin* 24 (1916), and twenty-two states have constitutional provisions that include educational standards similar or identical to Ohio's "thorough and efficient" clause. See William E. Thro, "The Role of Language of the State Education Clauses in School Finance Litigation," 79 *Educ. L. Rep.* 19 (1993): 23–24; see *also* O'Brien and Woodrum, "The Constitutional Common School," 584 n. 14.

Despite these similarities, the definition of "common schools" as well as what constitutes a "thorough and efficient" system of education vary widely from state to state due to differences in history, demographics, geography, and other factors. See Paul L. Tractenberg, "Education," in Alan G. Tarr and Robert F. Williams, eds., *State Constitutions for the Twenty-First Century*, vol. 3 (Albany: State University of New York, 2006).

■ A "THOROUGH AND EFFICIENT SYSTEM OF COMMON SCHOOLS"

The 1851 Ohio Constitution was the first state constitution to use the phrase "thorough and efficient" to describe the mandate on the legislature. See Jeremy J. Neff, "A Thorough and Efficient Definition of 'Thorough and Efficient': The Starting Point for Meaningful School Funding Reform," 33 *1 J. of Educ. Fin.* 69 (2007). The drafters of this section did not define the phrase, but the West Virginia Supreme Court noted that "[t]he tenor of the discussion, . . . by those advocating the entire education section as it was finally adopted, leaves no doubt that excellence was the goal, rather than mediocrity; and that education of the public was intended to be a fundamental function of the state government and a fundamental right of Ohioans." *Pauley v. Kelly* (1979). Nonetheless, the Ohio Supreme Court has never held that education is a fundamental right of Ohioans, and it has strongly suggested that it is not. *Cincinnati Board of Education v. Walter* (1979).

The Ohio Supreme Court has long recognized that the General Assembly has primary responsibility over the state's public schools. *Miller v. Korns* (1923), but the Ohio public schools have been controlled by local school districts and supported predominantly by local property taxes. And the court has historically given the General Assembly wide latitude in determining the financing of the state's public schools. See *Walter, supra.*

In 1977, the OCRC reviewed this requirement but did not recommend any changes, concluding that adding specific language to deal with school funding would undermine its view that a constitution should only state general principles and guidelines. See OCRC, *Final Report*, 65–66.

■ *DEROLPH* LITIGATION

In 1973, the U.S. Supreme Court held that the Equal Protection Clause of the Fourteenth Amendment was not available to correct disparities in the funding of public education. *San Antonio Independent School District v. Rodriguez* (1973). This decision, which effectively denied access to a federal remedy to correct school funding disparities, led to a series of state court decisions striking down educational financing statutes on state constitutional grounds. See Jeffrey S. Sutton, *51 Imperfect Solutions: States and the Making of American Constitutional Law* (New York: Oxford University Press, 2018), 27–41.

Concerns about disparities in state support for education led to an unsuccessful effort in the 1970s to challenge the Ohio state funding formula, *Cincinnati Board of Education v. Walter* (1979), but in 1991 a group of public school districts revisited this issue. In a well-resourced suit, they alleged that the General Assembly had failed to meet its constitutional obligation to "secure a thorough and efficient system of common schools throughout the state."

This resulted in the 1997 landmark decision in which the Ohio Supreme Court concluded by a vote of 4–3 that Ohio's system of financing elementary and secondary public schools relied too heavily on local property taxes and violated the mandate that the General Assembly "secure a thorough and efficient system of common schools throughout the state." *DeRolph v. State* (1997) (*DeRolph I*). In so ruling, the court held that a "thorough and efficient" system of public education required sufficient funds for teachers, buildings, and equipment to provide students an educational opportunity and that the Ohio financing system did not meet the constitutional mandate. The decision also resulted in one of the most important (and sometimes heated) disputes between the Ohio Supreme Court and the General Assembly and among the justices in the state's history. For a comprehensive overview of the eleven-year litigation odyssey, see Larry J. Obhof, "*DeRolph v. State* and Ohio's Long Road to an Adequate Education," 2005 *B.Y.U. Educ. & L.J.* 83 (2005).

Although the *DeRolph* court did not reach whether education is a fundamental right or whether the funding system violated the state equal protection guarantee, one of the justices in lengthy concurring opinion reviewed the rich constitutional history of education in Ohio, including the Northwest Ordinance and Ohio's two nineteenth century constitutions. And relying on the proceedings of the 1850–51 Constitutional Convention, he concluded that education was a fundamental right.

> The framers of the 1850–1851 Ohio Constitution clearly acknowledged that education is the foundation upon which all other individual liberties are based. Their debates can lead to no other conclusion than that education is a fundamental right guaranteed to all of Ohio's school-age children.
>
> *DeRolph* I (Douglas, J., concurring).

DeRolph I brought to light evidence that a lack of funding in many districts had resulted in deteriorated school facilities, outdated textbooks, insufficient school supplies, overcrowded classrooms, and other conditions that impeded learning. And the court ordered the General Assembly to "first determine the cost of a basic quality education in both primary and secondary schools in Ohio, and then ensure sufficient funds to provide each student with that education, realizing that local property taxes can no longer be the primary means of providing the finances for a thorough and efficient system of schools."

In response to *DeRolph I*, the General Assembly provided additional funds for schools and proposed a constitutional amendment (which the voters approved in 1999) to allow the state to issue general revenue bonds for school facilities. See Article VIII, sections 2n and 17. The court, however, did not accept these changes as amounting to a "new school financing system." Explaining that a "thorough and efficient" system meant that each school district must have enough funds to provide an adequate education for its students, the court in 2000 held in another 4–3 decision, that the General Assembly had failed to meet the "thorough and efficient" constitutional standard. *DeRolph v. State* (2000) (*DeRolph II*). According to the court, the state, despite its efforts, had failed to address adequately the continued overreliance on property taxes that was responsible for the vast disparities among Ohio's school districts.

The court in *DeRolph II* had identified a number of areas that were still in need of attention, but (as in *DeRolph I*) the court declined to provide the General Assembly with specific guidelines. In response, the General Assembly enacted further measures to increase school funding and to lessen reliance on property taxes. And the court in another 4–3 decision determined that the legislative effort augmented by certain modifications ordered by the court would pass constitutional scrutiny despite the failure to create an entirely new system of school financing. *DeRolph v. State* (2001) (*DeRolph III*). The court in *DeRolph III* also held that given the state's good faith efforts, it was no longer necessary for the court to retain jurisdiction over the case.

But on December 11, 2002, the court, in yet another 4–3 vote, vacated its judgment in *DeRolph III*, reinstated *DeRolph I* and *DeRolph II* as the law of the case, reiterated its earlier ruling that the current school funding system was unconstitutional, and "direct[ed] the General Assembly to enact a school funding scheme that is thorough and efficient." *DeRolph v. State* (2002) (*DeRolph IV*). Nonetheless, despite its conclusion that the current school funding system was still unconstitutional, the court declined to retain jurisdiction, and it returned the case to the Court of Common Pleas for Perry County, the court in which the suit had originally been filed, with "a mandate . . . to carry [the] judgment into execution" (*DeRolph v. State* (2002) (mandate).

Treating the mandate as an opportunity to obtain a determination of compliance with the earlier judicial decree, the plaintiffs sought to continue the proceedings, but on May 16, 2003, the Ohio Supreme Court wrote the final chapter in the *DeRolph* saga. By a 5–2 vote, the court granted the state's petition for a writ of prohibition that barred the court from exercising further jurisdiction over the case. *State ex rel. State v. Lewis* (2003), and in October 2003 the U.S. Supreme Court declined to review the judgment. *DeRolph v. Ohio* (2003).

Commenting on the eleven years of litigation in *DeRolph* and on its apparent end, Cleveland's *Plain Dealer* in 2003 noted the increase in school spending that came as a result of the litigation along with "new attention to accountability and academic standards." *Plain Dealer*, "Stake through DeRolph Heart" (May 20, 2003) (editorial). See also Larry J. Obhof, "School Finance Litigation and the Separation of Powers," 45 *Mitchell Hamline Law Review* 539 (2019) (arguing in support of a "middle approach" to school financing litigation that gives greater respect to separation-of-powers concerns and describing the Ohio litigation as an example of this more deferential approach).

Although the *DeRolph* litigation ended without a judicial determination as to whether the state had complied with the constitutional mandate to provide a "thorough and efficient system of common schools throughout the state," the case brought to light school funding insufficiencies. And the case resulted in the adoption of changes that improved school facilities. But in the view of many school districts and advocates for public schools, the state still has not corrected either the insufficiency of state funding for the public schools or the disparities in the funding of local public school districts. And school voucher programs have been receiving an increasingly larger share of the state school budget.

In the 2021 biennial budget bill, Am. Sub. H.B. 110 (134th GA) (2021), the General Assembly altered the school funding formula and modestly increased the funding for Ohio school districts, but it also continued the significant increase in the proportion of state funding for school vouchers. In response, the same coalition that had successfully organized the *DeRolph* litigation filed a new lawsuit in the Franklin County Court of Common Pleas on January 4, 2022, challenging the state's EdChoice voucher program, which it claims has diverted state funding away from Ohio's public schools and undermined the state's obligation to provide "a thorough and efficient system of common schools throughout the State." *Cf. Simmons-Harris v. Goff* (1999). The case also appears to be asking the Ohio Supreme Court to re-visit the *Simmons* decision in which the court had treated state funding of private education through vouchers as permissible.

■ OHIO CONSTITUTIONAL MODERNIZATION COMMISSION

From to 2013 to 2015, a committee of the Ohio Constitutional Modernization Commission (hereinafter OCMC) intensely reviewed and debated whether changes should be recommended to the "thorough and efficient" mandate in section 2. But the committee was not able to reach any agreement for change, and the full commission adopted the committee's "no change" recommendation and thus submitted no proposal on this section to the General Assembly. OCMC, *Report and Recommendation, Article VI, Section 2* (School Funds) (December 10, 2015).

■ SUPPORT FOR RELIGIOUS SCHOOLS

Section 2 also provides that no religious sect "shall ever have any exclusive right to, or control of, any part of the school funds of this state." This clause predates by more than seven decades the 1875 rejection by Congress of the proposed Blaine Amendment, which would have made the religious clauses of the First Amendment applicable to the states and prohibited the funding of parochial schools. See Steven K. Green, *The Second Disestablishment* (Oxford NY: Oxford University Press, 2010), 294–97. And it also predates the adoption of "Little Blaine" constitutional amendments in more than half of the states in the three decades following the rejection of the proposed federal Blaine Amendment. See Toby J. Heytens, "School Choice and State Constitutions," 86 *Va. L. Rev.* 117 (2000): 123.

The Ohio Supreme Court has interpreted this portion of section 2 as prohibiting direct state aid to private religious schools but not state aid that indirectly benefits religious schools. For example, the court has upheld a statute that required local school districts to provide guidance, testing, and counseling programs for students in religious schools. *Protestants & Other Americans United for Separation of Church & State v. Essex* (1971).

In 1999, the court held that a voucher program created by the state in 1995 for students in the Cleveland school district did not violate this section. *Simmons-Harris v. Goff* (1999). In so ruling, the court relied on the fact that no money flowed directly from the state to a sectarian school and on the fact that no money could reach a sectarian school based solely on its efforts or the efforts of the state. Under the school voucher program, checks were issued to the parents of students in the program and not directly to religious schools; thus, sectarian schools received money that originated in the school voucher program only as the result of independent decisions of parents and students.

The *Simmons-Harris* court, however, struck down a provision of the 1995 school voucher law that gave an admissions priority to a student whose parents belong to a religious group that supported the sectarian school to which the student was applying, and the court severed this provision from the rest of the statute. See ibid.

The *Simmons-Harris* court also held that the obligation of the state to establish a "thorough and efficient system of common schools" did not prohibit the state from establishing and financing a system of nonpublic schools. In so ruling, the court noted the existence of private schools since before the establishment of public schools, and the fact that private schools "have in the past provided and continue to provide a valuable alternative to the public system." Nonetheless, the court stated that the success of private schools "should not come at the expense of our public education system or our public school teachers." And the court qualified its decision to uphold the school voucher program by noting that it "fail(s) to see how the School Voucher Program, *at the current funding level,* undermines the state's obligation to public education." Ibid. (emphasis added).

Despite its conclusion that the 1995 voucher program was valid under this section, the *Simmons-Harris* court struck it down because it violated the "one-subject rule" of Article II, section 15(D). But in 1999 the General Assembly enacted a new statute that created basically the same voucher program, and in June 2002, the U.S. Supreme Court in a 5–4 decision held that the 1999 voucher program did not violate the Establishment Clause of the First Amendment. *Zelman v. Simmons-Harris* (2002).

The Ohio Supreme Court has also held that this section does not prohibit the state from creating community schools (popularly known as charter schools) as part of the state's program of education. *State ex rel. Ohio Congress of Parents & Teachers v. State Board of Education* (2006).

■ SCHOOL SEGREGATION

In 1829, the General Assembly enacted a statute that excluded black and mulatto children from public schools. See Frank U. Quillin, *The Color Line in Ohio: A History of Race Prejudice in a Typical Northern State* (New York: Negro Universities Press, 1913), 82–83 (hereinafter Quillin, *The Color Line*); see also Jonathan L. Entin, "An Ohio Dilemma: Race, Equal Protection, and the Unfulfilled Promise of a State Bill of Rights," 51 *Clev. St. L. Rev.* 395 (2004): 404–10.

In 1848, however, the General Assembly enacted its first law providing for the education of nonwhite students. Under this law, nonwhite students could be admitted to white schools unless whites opposed their admission; in such cases, school districts could establish separate schools paid for by property taxes on nonwhite residents but only if the district contained twenty or more "colored" students. The General Assembly replaced the 1848 law the following year with one that allowed the establishment of nonwhite schools, but again paid for only by taxes on the property of nonwhites. While a proposal to limit free public schools to white children generated heated debate at the 1850–51 Constitutional Convention—as did any issue that touched on race—the delegates ultimately rejected the proposal. See Quillin, *The Color Line*, 82–87; see also *DeRolph I* (Douglas, J., concurring). And, in 1853, the General Assembly enacted a law providing for the education of all children, but the law established a system of segregated schools dividing students into two classes––"white" and "colored."

The Ohio Supreme Court upheld the 1853 act in *Van Camp v. Board of Education of Logan* (1859) without addressing any constitutional issues and despite the fact that nonwhite children would be denied an education if they lived in areas where their numbers were too small to justify a separate school. The court in *Van Camp* also overturned earlier decisions that had held that persons of more than one-half white blood were considered "white" regardless of color. See Barbara A. Terzian, "Effusions of Folly and Fanaticism: Race, Gender and Constitution-Making in Ohio, 1802–1923," (Ph.D. dissertation, The Ohio State University, 1999), 227–36 (hereinafter Terzian, "Effusions of Folly"). Instead, the court held that local communities could use their own standards to determine whether a child was "white," thereby permitting local communities to determine whether nonwhite students could attend the local public schools. In a later case, *State ex rel. Garnes v. McCann* (1871), the court rejected a challenge under the Equal Protection Clause of the Fourteenth Amendment to an act providing for segregated schools. In so holding, the court embraced the doctrine of "separate but equal" twenty-five years before the U.S. Supreme Court adopted the doctrine in *Plessy v. Ferguson* (1896). See Terzian, "Effusions of Folly," 258.

The General Assembly abolished separate schools for nonwhite students in 1887, see *State ex rel. Gibson v. Board of Education of Oxford* (1888), but de jure and de facto segregation continued to exist in Ohio public schools well into the twentieth century, see *Reed v. Rhodes* (1979).

Section 3
Public school system, boards of education.

Provision shall be made by law for the organization, administration and control of the public school system of the state supported by public funds: provided, that each school district embraced wholly or in part within any city shall have the power by referendum vote to determine for itself the number of members and the organization of the district board of education, and provision shall be made by law for the exercise of this power by such school districts.

Adopted in 1912 and never amended, this section created, for the first time, a statewide framework for school governance. It did this by requiring the General Assembly to adopt laws to organize, administer, and control a state public school system. At the same time, it allowed residents living within a city school district to determine by referendum the number of members and the organization of their local boards of education.

■ STATE CONTROL OF THE PUBLIC SCHOOLS

The first clause in this section provides for state supervision of the public schools by requiring that provision "shall be made by law for the organization, administration and control of the public school system . . . ."

This provision was the culmination of many years of work by supporters of an expanded role for the state in education. See generally O'Brien and Woodrum, "The Constitutional Common School," 634–46.

> The delegates did not "contemplate taking out of the hands of the local authorities the control and administration of their local schools, but gave to the state beyond any question, the right to fix the standard and the right to organize an entire system, leaving to each local community the determination of the schools in the system." The vision was "one complete educational system for the schools and all educational institutions supported by public taxation."
>
> Ibid. (quoting George W. Knight) (footnotes omitted).

Supporters of an expanded role of the state in education were concerned that cities, acting under the home rule power authorized by the new article they were also proposing, might interfere with the actions of the state in controlling education. And this section sought to allay those concerns.

George W. Knight of Franklin County, a professor at Ohio State University and a strong supporter of both the education and home rule amendments, described the tension between state control of education and home rule.

> Because the municipal home rule proposal which we have passed is so broad that there is a possibility that unless this is adopted the city of Columbus might have power to do a good deal more in the way of control of its educational system than is desirable it should have. It would be inconsistent with the unified public school system of the state.
>
> *Proceedings and Debates of the Constitutional Convention of the State of Ohio* (Columbus: F. J. Heer, 1929) (hereinafter *1912 Debates*).

During the debates, Mr. Knight made clear his position that the state, not local government, should control education:

> [This provision] must be adopted in order to establish definitely that the state shall for all time, until the constitution is further amended, have complete control over the educational system, and that no city, village or part of territory of the state can withdraw itself, under the guise of a charter, from the public educational system of the state.
>
> *1912 Debates*, 1500.

An earlier version of this provision had extended state control to the "public school and educational system of the state" but the reference to "and educational" was dropped to assuage concerns that the provision might give the state too much control over higher education, which at the time consisted of Ohio University, Miami University, and Ohio State University. In addition, the modification of "public school system of the state," with the addition of the phrase "supported by public funds," made clear that the provision did not extend state control to parochial schools. See *1912 Debates*, 1915–16.

Section 3 gave the state the broad power to embark upon a program of school consolidation. In 1903, there were 2,437 different districts, of which 66 were city districts, 1,036 were village and special districts, and 1,035 were township districts. The boards of education in city districts ranged from 3 members in Wooster and Delaware to 31 in Cincinnati. In some city districts, the voters elected members of the boards at large, in some by wards, and in some by both wards and at large. The boards in the township, village, and special districts ranged from three to six members. See Lewis Bonebrake, "The Public Schools of Ohio." in E. O. Randall, ed., *Complete Proceedings, Ohio Centennial Anniversary Celebration at Chillicothe* (Columbus: F. J. Heer, 1903), 389, 399–400.

As reported by the Ohio School Boards Association in 2013, Ohio now has 613 traditional public school districts, 55 educational service centers, and 49 joint vocational school districts. See remarks to the OCMC by Richard C. Lewis, Executive Director, Ohio School Boards Association (August 8, 2013).

Section 3 allowed the General Assembly to enact legislation authorizing county boards of education to arrange districts and change boundary lines as long as the county boards do not "act unreasonably or in bad faith in effecting the creation of a new district." *Smith v. Board of Education* (1954). And the Ohio Supreme Court has upheld state legislation that required an affirmative vote of 55 percent of the vote in a new district in order to reorganize (unless 75 percent of the voters in any district opposed the reorganization). *State ex rel. Groh v. Board of Education of West Clermont Local School District* (1959) (syllabus).

In 1953, the court summarized the breadth of the power that section 3 gave the state over school districts.

> [T]he General Assembly has the power to provide for the creation of school districts, for changes and modifications thereof, and for the methods by which changes and modifications may be accomplished, and, where it has provided methods by which changes in school districts may be made, no citizen has a vested or contractual right to the continuation of such methods, and if a particular method is abolished or changed by legislative enactment there can be no basis for a claim that a contractual or vested right is impaired.
>
> *State ex rel. Core v. Green* (1953).

The Ohio Supreme Court has held that this section does not prevent the state from creating charter schools as part of the state's program of education. In rejecting a facial challenge to the creation of charter schools, which operate independently of local school districts, the court stated that this section "governs questions of size and organization, not the power and authority, of city school boards." *State ex rel. Ohio Congress of Parents & Teachers v. State Board of Education* (2006).

■ LOCAL BOARDS OF EDUCATION

The second clause in this section addresses the concern that delegates to the 1912 had about the inability or unwillingness of local school boards to address issues concerning their size and organization. For example, according to George W. Harris of Hamilton County, cities of over 50,000 had authority to change (i.e., reduce) the size of school boards only if the local board agreed, but "[t]he larger boards . . . refuse to vote themselves out of office . . . ." *1912 Debates*, 1500. The delegates addressed this issue by requiring that the number of members and the organization of district boards of education should be determined by the voters by referendum. Thus, the constitution gave local voters an explicit role in the organization of their school boards.

Although residents of local school districts may determine the number of members and the organization of their boards of education, this section does not address when the referendum must take place, and the General Assembly has exercised the power to determine the timing of the referendum.

The issue of the timing of the referendum first arose in 1914 after the General Assembly adopted the Jung Small School-Board Act. The act classified and organized city school districts and their respective school board members by using three general categories based on population and by creating a schedule of activities that could delay for two years the referendum on the size and organization of school boards. But the Ohio Supreme Court rejected an argument that the time for a vote specified in the act violated this section. *State ex rel. Ach v. Evans* (1914).

The timing issue arose again in the 1990s in litigation challenging a state statute that reorganized the Cleveland Municipal School District Board of Education to give the mayor authority to appoint a nine-member board. Previously, a seven-member elected board governed the district, but a statute adopted in the wake of the Cleveland school desegregation litigation provided for a referendum in the first even-numbered year occurring at least four years after the board appointed by the mayor assumed control of the district. The statute did not refer to the Cleveland district by name, but it referred to districts under federal desegregation orders (which included only Cleveland). See O.R.C. section 3311.73.

The constitutionality of this statute was challenged on state constitutional grounds in both state and federal courts. Initially, the U.S. Court of Appeals for the Sixth Circuit, relying on the 1914 Ohio Supreme Court decision in *Evans*, held that "the referendum provision did not require that voters approve any legislative change to the organization of the boards of education in Ohio cities before the legislature can enact and implement such changes." *Mixon v. State of Ohio* (1999).

In so ruling, the federal court interpreted *Evans* as permitting a two-year delay in the referendum.

> *Evans* held that the legislature may make such changes without voter pre-approval so long as it provides the voters with an opportunity at a later date to vote on the changes.... Absent a showing of bad faith on the part of the legislature, the court determined that the Jung Bill did not conflict with the referendum provision of the Ohio Constitution because the Jung Bill provided for a referendum within a reasonable time.... *Evans* thus implied that the legislature could wait two years before submitting the school district changes to a referendum.

The residents challenging the legislation brought a parallel action in the Ohio courts, and a state appellate court held, contrary to *Mixon,* that the four-year delay violated the Ohio Constitution. In so ruling, the court treated the two-year time limit in *Evans* as the outside limit for holding a referendum. *Malcolm-Smith v. Goff* (1999). The Ohio Supreme Court, however, reversed that decision on preclusion grounds without discussing the merits of the state constitutional issue. *Malcolm-Smith v. Goff* (2000).

The required referendum was held on November 5, 2002, and more than 70 percent of Cleveland voters supported a plan that permitted the mayor to make appointments to the Board of the Cleveland Municipal School District. The Cleveland Teachers Union and the Cleveland branch of the NAACP supported mayoral control of the board of education. See Cleveland *Plain Dealer* (August 20, 2011) ("Mayoral control of the Cleveland city schools has brought stability but other improvements hard to measure.").

Neither the decision of the Sixth Circuit in *Mixon* nor the reversed decision of the state appellate court is binding precedent; thus *Evans,* though more than a century old, remains the last word from the Ohio Supreme Court on the issue of the timing of the referendum under section 3.

In *State ex rel. Ohio Congress of Parents & Teachers v. State Board of Education* (2006), in the course of rejecting a facial challenge to the validity of the legislation that created charter schools, the court suggested that a statute that "usurped" the power of a city school district would violate this section.

Notwithstanding this suggestion, the court in 2020 in *Youngstown City School District Board of Education v. State of Ohio* (2020) construed this section broadly and stated that the General Assembly "may lawfully influence the authority of school boards in any manner of ways, large and small." This case involved a challenge to a state statute that permitted the state to transfer nearly all the authority of a city school board to a chief executive officer under the control of an academic-distress commission. And the court held that "[t]he limitation in Article VI, Section 3 on the General Assembly's power merely entitles electors to choose the number of members and the organization of the district board of education." Thus, the state appears to have broad power under this section to eliminate elected local school districts or to significantly reduce their power.

■ RURAL SCHOOL DISTRICTS

The power of local school districts to determine their size and organization by referendum did not, however, extend to all school districts. Some representatives of rural districts objected to the application of the provision to them. As explained by Mr. Knight, "it seems that in some portions of the state . . . there is objection to its application to rural school districts." See *1912 Debates*, 1915. Mr. Knight then stated that "[a]s a member of the Convention, I have no desire to force a referendum on any people who do not want it. The cities do want it, and I offer an amendment . . . ." Ibid. Although the nature of the concerns of rural districts was not made clear, to accommodate the rural districts the delegates revised the second clause so that it only applied to those districts "embraced wholly or in part within any city." Thus, the voters in rural school districts that served villages and townships were not given a constitutionally mandated role in determining the size and organization of their school boards. See generally *1912 Debates*, 1914–15.

In 2015 and 2016, a committee of the OCMC reviewed this section, but time ran out before the committee could make a recommendation on it. See OCMC, Education, Public Institutions, and Local Government Committee, *Final Report* (June 30, 2017).

Section 4
State board of education.

There shall be a state board of education which shall be selected in such manner and for such terms as shall be provided by law. There shall be a superintendent of public instruction, who shall be appointed by the state board of education. The respective powers and duties of the board and of the superintendent shall be prescribed by law.

Adopted in 1912 and amended in 1953, this section addresses the role of the state in public education. The provision has its origins in efforts begun early in the nineteenth century to strengthen education in the state.

■ 1851 CONSTITUTIONAL CONVENTION

Prior to the 1850–51 Constitutional Convention, control of the schools was local and fragmented.

> Control of schools was local and fragmented until 1838, when the office of State Superintendent of Common Schools was created. In that year, the creation of

> township and county superintendents and sub-districts gave a degree of organization and leadership to the school system. The office of superintendent, which involved primarily clerical duties, was abolished in 1840 and for the next 14 years the duties of school administration were given to the Secretary of State.
>
> OCRC (1970–77), *Recommendations for Amendments to the Constitution, Part 7, Elections and Suffrage*, 23–25 (March 15, 1975).

Supporters of Ohio common schools were active at the 1850–51 Constitutional Convention, and the key section adopted as a result of their efforts was Article VI, section 2, which required the General Assembly to "make provision . . . [to] secure a thorough and efficient system of common schools throughout the State."

Many of the delegates also sought to establish state responsibility for the system of common schools by creating the constitutional position of state superintendent of common schools. The advantages of having a State Superintendent were seen as the efficiency and uniformity that the Superintendent would bring to the workings of the whole system. The opponents argued against such a mandate, pointing to its expense and to the fact that the General Assembly could create such an office by legislation. Ultimately, the delegates rejected the proposal to create a state superintendent, and the issues concerning the role of the state were left to the General Assembly. See generally O'Brien and Woodrum, "The Constitutional Common School," 623–24.

■ 1912 CONSTITUTIONAL CONVENTION

Section 4 created the state position of superintendent of public instruction to replace the legislatively created state commissioner of common schools, a goal of those supporting a greater role for the state in public education. This provision, which was narrowly adopted by the voters by a 5,000 vote margin, provided as follows:

> A superintendent of public instruction to replace the state commissioner of common schools, shall be included as one of the officers of the executive department to be appointed by the governor, for the term of four years, with the powers and duties now exercised by the state commissioner of common schools until otherwise provided by law, and with such other powers as may be provided by law.
>
> Article VI, section 6 (1912 Const.)

■ POST-1912 HISTORY

In its review of Article VI, the OCRC described the post-1912 history of education, including the work of the School Survey Commission. See OCRC, *Final Report*, 52–67. The School Survey Commission made a comprehensive study of the state's educational system in 1953 and recommended multiple changes in the organization and funding of public education. This included a proposal for an elected state board of education composed of citizens having staggered terms of six years. And in 1953, the voters approved an amendment proposed by the General Assembly to provide for an elected state board of education with the size, the term, and method of selection to be determined by the General Assembly. The board of education was given the responsibility for appointing a superintendent of public instruction.

■ LEGISLATIVE DEVELOPMENTS

The powers and duties of the board and the superintendent are not contained in the constitution but are prescribed in section 3301 of the Ohio Revised Code. In 1955, the General Assembly adopted legislation providing that the state board of education shall consist of one member elected from each of the state's congressional districts.

In the early 1990s, the composition and selection of the board became controversial as Ohio Governor George Voinovich sought legislation that would have established a board exclusively appointed by the governor. The General Assembly rejected this proposal, but it created the current hybrid board with eight members appointed by the governor and the remaining eleven members elected from districts composed of three compact and contiguous senate districts. See ORC, section 3301.01(A) and (B).

In 2015 and 2016, a committee of the OCMC reviewed this section, but time ran out before the committee could make a recommendation on it. See OCMC, Education, Public Institutions, and Local Government Committee, *Final Report* (June 30, 2017).

Section 5

Loans for higher education.

To increase opportunities to the residents of this state for higher education, it is hereby determined to be in the public interest and a proper public purpose for the state to guarantee the repayment of loans made to residents of this state to assist them in meeting the expenses of attending an institution of higher education. Laws may be passed to carry into effect such purpose including the payment, when required, of any such guarantee from moneys available for such payment after first providing the moneys necessary to meet the requirements of any bonds or other obligations heretofore or hereafter authorized by any section of the Constitution. Such laws and guarantees shall not be subject to the limitations or requirements of Article VIII or of Section 11 of Article XII of the Constitution. Amended Substitute House Bill No. 618 enacted by the General Assembly on July 11, 1961, and Amended Senate Bill No. 284 enacted by the General Assembly on May 23, 1963, and all appropriations of moneys made for the purpose of such enactments, are hereby validated, ratified, confirmed, and approved in all respects, and they shall be in full force and effect from and after the effective date of this section, as laws of this state until amended or repealed by law.

Adopted by the voters in 1965 and never amended, this section permits the state to guarantee the repayment of student loans for higher education once the state meets the requirements of any bonds or other obligations. Laws governing student loans are found in chapter 3351 of the Ohio Revised Code, including a law creating a student loan commission to assist educational and financial institutions in carrying out federal student loan programs. See O.R.C. section 3351.07. This section expressly provides that state expenditures for loan guarantees under this section are not subject to the debt limitations of Article VIII or Article XII, section 11. But debt incurred under this section is not backed by the full faith and credit of the state.

The growth of the popular federal direct-lending program and the emergence of private companies offering the same services rendered the state commission obsolete, and the General Assembly dissolved the agency in 1997 and transferred its duties to the Ohio Board of Regents.

Although the OCMC considered this section to be unnecessary for current programs, it voted in 2017 against recommending its repeal because of the possibility that at some time in the future, this section may play a useful role in encouraging state support of funding for higher education. OCMC. *Report and Recommendation, Article VI, Section 5* (March 9, 2017).

Section 6

Tuition credit program.

(A) To increase opportunities to the residents of this state for higher education, it is hereby determined to be in the public interest and a proper public purpose for the state to maintain a program for the sale of tuition credits such that the proceeds of such credits purchased for the benefit of a person then a resident of this state shall be guaranteed to cover a specified amount when applied to the cost of tuition at any state institution of higher education, and the same or a different amount when applied to the cost of tuition at any other institution of higher education, as may be provided by law.

(B) The tuition credits program and the Ohio tuition trust fund previously created by law, which terms include any successor to that program or fund, shall be continued subject to the same laws, except as may hereafter be amended. To secure the guarantees required by division (A) of this section, the General Assembly shall appropriate money sufficient to offset any deficiency that occurs in the Ohio tuition trust fund, at any time necessary to make payment of the full amount of any tuition payment or refund that would have been required by a tuition payment contract, except for the contract's limit of payment to money available in the trust fund. Notwithstanding Section 29 of Article II of this Constitution, or the limitation of a tuition payment contract executed before the effective date of this section, such appropriations may be made by a majority of the members elected to each house of the General Assembly, and the full amount of any such enhanced tuition payment or refund may be disbursed to and accepted by the beneficiary or purchaser. To these ends there is hereby pledged the full faith and credit and taxing power of the state.

All assets that are maintained in the Ohio tuition trust fund shall be used solely for the purposes of that fund. However, if the program is terminated or the fund is liquidated, the remaining assets after the obligations of the fund have been satisfied in accordance with law shall be transferred to the general revenue fund of the state.

Laws shall be passed, which may precede and be made contingent upon the adoption of this amendment by the electors, to provide that future conduct of the tuition credits program shall be consistent with this amendment. Nothing in this amendment shall be construed to prohibit or restrict any amendments to the laws governing the tuition credits program or the Ohio tuition trust fund that are not inconsistent with this amendment.

Adopted by the voters in 1994 and never amended, this section calls for the state to maintain a program of tuition credits for higher education. The purpose of this section is to increase higher educational opportunities for residents of the state by establishing a tuition trust fund backed by the full faith and credit of the state. The fund was established in 1989 as part of Ohio's college savings program (now called "CollegeAdvantage"), which is administered by the Ohio Tuition Authority and which allows tuition credits to be purchased for the benefit of Ohio residents (usually children) to pay future tuition and fees at any Ohio or other institution of higher education.

The General Assembly initially created the program by statute, but a constitutional amendment guaranteeing the full faith and credit of the state was necessary following an Internal Revenue Service ruling that interest earned by the fund was taxable under federal law unless guaranteed by the state. See Ohio Rev. Code Ann. Ohio Const. Article VI, section 6 (Baldwin 2004) (editor's comment).

Ultimately, the federal concerns were resolved by a 1996 change in the federal tax code that confirmed the exempt status of these "529 plans," so named for the Internal Revenue Code section that describes them.

The specific tax advantage of a 529 plan is that distributions (i.e., withdrawals) from this savings plan are tax-free if they are used to pay for qualified higher education expenses. If some or all of the distribution is used to pay for nonqualified expenses, then a portion of the distribution is taxable, and may also be subject to a 10 percent penalty tax. Section 529 plans are very popular and have grown to represent more than $253.2 billion in investments nationwide. As of December 2015, over a half million Ohio accounts are open, with over $9 billion in assets.

The primary goal of this section was to address issues concerning *federal* tax treatment of interest earned under the plans, but the need to address that issue became obsolete with the enactment of section 529. Nonetheless, the section's other purpose was to establish the full faith, and credit backing of the state for the Guaranteed Savings Plan remains viable even though no new Guaranteed Savings Plan account holders have been added since 2003.

In 2017, the OCMC reviewed this section, and concluded that although the changes in federal law resolved the problems the plans had initially been facing, the section should nonetheless be retained because one purpose of the provision was to establish the full faith and credit backing of the state for the higher education savings plans offered by the state. OCMC, *Report and Recommendation, Article VI, Section 6* (March 9, 2007).

Article VII

Public Institutions

Article VII concerns state-supported benevolent institutions for the mentally ill and the visually and hearing impaired. The article also addresses the appointment of directors of benevolent and penal institutions, which have existed in Ohio since before the 1851 Constitution.

Most of the debate in 1851 concerned the respective roles of the General Assembly and the governor in appointing directors of the penitentiary and the trustees of the benevolent and other state institutions.

The voters approved Article VII as part of the 1851 Constitution, and this is the only article of the constitution that the voters have never amended.

In 2017, the Ohio Constitutional Modernization Commission (hereinafter OCMC) recommended the amendment of section 1 and the repeal of sections 2 and 3, but the General Assembly has not taken any action, to date, on this recommendation.

Section 1

Insane, blind, and deaf and dumb.

Institutions for the benefit of the insane, blind, and deaf and dumb, shall always be fostered and supported by the state; and subject to general regulations as may be prescribed by the General Assembly.

The Ohio State Constitution. Steven H. Steinglass and Gino J. Scarselli, Oxford University Press. © Oxford University Press 2022. DOI: 10.1093/oso/9780197619728.003.0009

Adopted in 1851 and never amended, this section created a constitutional mandate that the state foster and support institutions for the benefit of the insane, blind, and deaf and dumb.

Under the 1802 Constitution there was no constitutional mandate or special obligation to create institutions for the benefit of person with mental or physical disabilities, but the General Assembly had plenary legislative authority under the first constitution. 1802 Constitution, Article I, section 1. Nonetheless, Ohio had been providing for the care and treatment of the "insane" since the early 1800s.

Even though this section created a constitutional mandate, the amount of financial support is left to the discretion of the General Assembly. *State ex rel. Price v. Huwe* (1922).

In its consideration of this issue at the 1850–51 Constitutional Convention, the delegates rejected a proposal that would have inserted the word "white" and thus require segregated institutions. The delegates also rejected a proposal on prison labor. The debate focused on the purposes of incarceration, but the delegates did not recommend any provision concerning prison labor. See generally Shari L. O'Neill, *Article VII (Public Institutions) at the 1851 Constitutional Convention* (OCMC) (August 23, 2016).

In requiring support for institutions for the "insane, blind, and deaf and dumb," the language in this section reflects its origins in another era. The proposed 1874 Constitution, which the voters rejected, recommended changing the section as follows:

> Institutions for the benefit of the curable and incurable insane, blind, deaf and dumb, shall be supported by the state. The punitive and reformatory institutions of the state at large shall be a Reform School for Boys, a house of discipline, and a Penitentiary. An asylum for Idiotic and Imbecilic Youth, and a home for Soldiers' and Sailors' Orphans and a Girl's Industrial Home, shall be supported so long as the General Assembly shall deem them necessary. All public institutions shall be subject to such regulations as may be prescribed by law.
>
> Isaac F. Patterson, *The Constitutions of Ohio: Amendments and Proposed Amendments* (Cleveland: Arthur H. Clark Company, 1912), 206–7.

In the 1970s, the Ohio Constitutional Revision Commission (OCRC) considered replacing the language "insane, blind, and deaf and dumb" with "persons who, by reason of disability or handicap." A majority of the OCRC supported amending this section to limit civil commitment to cases where a person posed a risk of harm to themselves or others and to guarantee treatment for those civilly committed, but the OCRC's enabling legislation required a two-thirds majority for proposals to be recommended to the General Assembly. Consequently, these proposals were never submitted to the General Assembly, and the General Assembly did not independently propose them to the voters. See OCRC, *Recommendations for Amendments to the Ohio Constitution: Final Report* (1977), 68–70.

In 2017, the OCMC recommended that section 1 be replaced with the following provision: "Facilities for and services to persons who, by reason of disability, require care or treatment shall be fostered and supported by the state, as may be prescribed by the General Assembly." See OCMC, *Report and Recommendation, Support for Persons with Certain Disabilities* (June 7, 2017). But the General Assembly has not taken any action, to date, on this recommendation.

Section 2

Directors of penitentiary, trustees of benevolent and other state institutions; how appointed.

The directors of the penitentiary shall be appointed or elected in such manner as the General Assembly may direct; and the trustees of the benevolent, and other state institutions, now elected by the General Assembly, and of such other state institutions as may be hereafter created, shall be appointed by the governor, by and with the advice and consent of the Senate, and upon all nominations made by the governor, the question shall be taken by yeas and nays, and entered upon the journals of the Senate.

Adopted in 1851 and never amended, this section addresses the selection of the directors of the state penitentiary. Prior to 1851, the General Assembly selected the directors of the state penitentiary as part of its plenary power.

Much of the debate at the 1850–51 Convention on this article focused on whether directors of the penitentiary should be selected by the General Assembly, appointed by the governor, or directly elected by voters. Some delegates supported allowing the General Assembly to make this determination, but others pointed to the unpopularity of the General Assembly to support giving this power of appointment to the governor. And other delegates argued that the importance of the role of directors of the penitentiary meant that they should be elected, which would have been consistent with a key argument made by those who supported holding the convention. Finally, the delegates supported a compromise that combined appointment by the governor with a requirement for obtaining the advice and consent of the Senate.

Under the compromise, the section contained a bifurcated approach. Directors of penal institutions could be appointed or elected at the discretion of the General Assembly, but the section required that trustees of the benevolent and other state institutions be appointed by the governor with the advice and consent of the Senate. The General Assembly has exercised its discretion under this section by allowing the Director of Rehabilitation and Corrections to be named by the governor with the advice and consent of the Senate. O.R.C. section 121.03. The meaning of "advice and consent" of the Senate is discussed in the Commentary to Article III, section 21.

In 2017, the OCMC concluded that this section was obsolete and recommended that it be repealed. See OCMC, *Report and Recommendation,*

Directors of Public Institutions (June 7, 2017). But the General Assembly has not taken any action, to date, on this recommendation.

Section 3

Vacancies, how filled.

The governor shall have power to fill all vacancies that may occur in the offices aforesaid, until the next session of the General Assembly, and until a successor to his appointee shall be confirmed and qualified.

This section gives the governor the power to appoint an interim head until the next session of the General Assembly if a vacancy occurs in one of the offices mentioned in section 2.

In 2017, the OCMC concluded that this section was obsolete and recommended that it be repealed. See OCMC, *Report and Recommendation, Directors of Public Institutions* (June 7, 2017). But the General Assembly has not taken any action, to date, on this recommendation.

Article VIII

Public Debt and Public Works

Article VIII deals with public debt and public works, and it is the longest and most frequently amended article in the Ohio Constitution. The delegates to the 1850–51 Convention proposed this article to ensure that the state would never again face a debt crisis like the one that resulted from the construction of the state's transportation system beginning in 1825. The delegates did this by imposing a $750,000 limitation on the amount of debt that the state could incur, by restricting the entanglement of public and private money in this article, and by including a provision in Article XII prohibiting expenditures for internal improvements. See Commentary, Article XII, section 6.

There are, however, exceptions to the debt limitation in Article VIII in cases involving military invasions and other emergencies. See Commentary, Article VIII, section 2. And over the years, the voters have overridden the debt limitation by repeatedly adopting amendments to permit bonds to be issued in excess if the limitation for veteran benefits and for a broad array of capital improvement and economic development projects.

In addition to placing a debt limitation on the General Assembly, the delegates prohibited the state from giving or loaning its credit to any association or corporation or becoming a joint owner of any company. See Article VIII, section 4. Finally, the article created a sinking fund to assure that state debt be paid off responsibly. See Article VIII, sections 7, 8, 9, 10, and 11.

The Ohio State Constitution. Steven H. Steinglass and Gino J. Scarselli, Oxford University Press. © Oxford University Press 2022. DOI: 10.1093/oso/9780197619728.003.0010

■ CONSTITUTIONAL CHANGES IN OHIO

States have four distinct approaches to incurring debt. With some exceptions, nine states, including Ohio, only permit the issuance of general obligation debt (or the issuance of general obligation debt in excess of a typically low dollar limitation) through amendments to the state constitution. Twenty states require both legislative approval and voter consent but not constitutional amendments. Fifteen states require legislative approval without voter consent and without an amendment to the state constitution and six states do not have a constitutionally based limitation on incurring general obligation debt, thus leaving the question of whether to issue general obligation debt to the state legislative process. See Ohio Constitutional Modernization Commission (OCMC), Finance, Taxation, and Economic Development Committee, "Review of State Policies on General Obligation Debt" (August 31, 2016), in Meeting Packet (December 10, 2016 Meeting).

Ohio, like nearly every other state, has a balanced budget requirement. See Commentary, Article XII, section 4. This requirement, however, refers to operating budgets and not to expenditures for such items as veteran benefits, highway and housing construction, conservation, revitalization of natural resources, economic development, and technology support. To raise funds for these nonoperating budget items, states, including Ohio, typically issue general obligation bonds—bonds that are backed by the full faith and credit of the state—but some states, also including Ohio, also use revenue bonds that the state does not guarantee.

Since 1851, Ohio voters have approved thirty amendments to Article VIII. The General Assembly proposed forty-three amendments of these amendments, and the voters approved twenty-eight and rejected fifteen. The 1912 Convention proposed three amendments, and the voters approved two of them. The remaining four amendments were proposed by initiative petition, but the voters rejected all of them. Of the thirty approved amendments to Article VIII, twenty-five dealt directly with either increasing state debt or removing limitations on the use of debt.

One of the three amendments proposed by the 1912 Constitutional Convention was a $50 million increase in the level of state indebtedness to support constructing, rebuilding, improving, and repairing intercounty wagon roads. This was the first effort to issue debt in excess of the $750,000 limitation of section 1, but the voters rejected the proposed amendment by only 2018 votes. See Appendix B.

The other two amendments, which the voters approved in 1912, involved county debt (sec. 6) and the selection of the superintendent of public works (sec. 12).

For nearly a hundred years, from the adoption of the 1851 Constitution through 1947, the voters approved only one constitutional amendment authorizing the issuance of debt under Article VIII. That occurred in 1921, when the voters approved section 2a, a provision (since repealed) to create the World War Compensation Fund to provide deferred compensation or bonuses to Ohio veterans of World War 1. The General Assembly sought to avoid the $750,000 limitation in section 1 by including an emergency clause, which provided as follows:

> The people of the state of Ohio hereby declare that they have enacted this special amendment to meet the specific emergency covered thereby and they declare it to be their intention to in no manner affect or change any of the existing provisions of this constitution except as hereby set forth.
>
> Am. S.J.R. 6 (83rd GA) (1921).

The amendment, however, did not identify the specific nature of the emergency. Then, over the sixty-six-year period, from 1948 through 2014, voters approved eighteen amendments to Article VIII authorizing the creation of specific amounts of guaranteed debt as well as five amendments that authorized guaranteed debt under formulaic but not specific dollar ceilings. And five additional amendments dealt with Article VIII issues not involving the authorization of debt.

The pattern of approval of amendments to issue bonds in excess of the debt limitation in Article VIII differed over time, but the common thread that sheds light on the results at the ballot may have been the presence or absence of bipartisan support for the proposed amendment.

From 1913 to 1974, the voters approved fifteen of the eighteen amendments to Article VIII, all of which had been proposed by the General Assembly. But from 1975 to 1980, when there was no longer bipartisan support for bond issues, the voters rejected the eight debt-authorizing amendments proposed by the General Assembly as well as three amendments proposed by initiative petition in 1975 at the behest of the governor. The pattern then changed again, and since 1982, the voters approved thirteen of the sixteen amendments to Article VIII all of which had been proposed by the General Assembly.

Summary of Proposed and Rejected Amendments to Article VIII 1851–2021

Proposed by	Total	Approved	Rejected
General Assembly	43	28	15
Initiative	4	0	4
Convention (1912)	3	2	1
	50	30	20

The political backdrop to the changing success rates of proposed amendments to incur debt under Article VIII had much to do with the policies and politics of Governor James A. Rhodes, Ohio's only governor to serve four four-year terms (though not consecutively), and the loss of bipartisan support for his approach to state debt.

During his first term, Governor Rhodes, who abhorred raising taxes, embraced the use of state debt to support an aggressive infrastructure program that included voter approval of four amendments to Article VIII (secs. 2f, 2g, 2h, and 13). But in 1967, in the first year of his second term, the voters rejected by more than a 2:1 margin what Governor Rhodes viewed as his most important debt-related recommendation. His proposed amendment would have created the Ohio Bond Commission and eliminated the need to amend the constitution to authorize debt. See generally Tom Diemer, Lee Leonard, and Richard G. Zimmerman, *James A. Rhodes: Ohio Colossus* (Kent: Kent State University Press, 2014), 49–51. Instead, the new procedure would have permitted the incurring of debt based on a formula that limited the amount of guaranteed state debt to 6 percent of the general revenue fund of the state. See S.J.R. 29 (107th GA) (1967).

After a brief interregnum during the governorship of John J. Gilligan (when the voters approved three amendments to Article VIII), the third and fourth terms of Governor Rhodes were marked by a complete breakdown of bipartisan support for amendments to Article VIII, and during the six-year period from 1975 to 1980, the voters rejected all eleven proposed amendments to Article VIII. See Appendix B.

■ LENDING-OF-CREDIT LIMITATIONS

In addition to imposing a dollar limitation on the amount of debt that the state could incur, the delegates in the 1850–51 Convention restricted the entanglement of public and private money and the lending of the state and local credit to private entities. But beginning in 1965, debt-authorizing constitutional amendments have routinely overridden the lending-of-credit limitations. See Commentary, Article VIII, sections 4 and 6.

■ BAN ON INTERNAL IMPROVEMENTS

Article XII, section 6, bars the state from contracting debt for internal improvements, but beginning in 1965, the state has made this limitation inapplicable to almost all debt-authorizing amendments. See Commentary, Article XII, section 6.

■ INITIATIVE PETITIONS AND STATE DEBT

The Ohio experience with initiative petitions to amend this article has not been particularly successful. In 1922, the voters rejected a constitutional amendment proposed by initiative petition concerning debt limits for political subdivisions, and in 1975, the voters rejected three amendments proposed by initiative petition concerning highways, housing and health, and local infrastructure.

■ OHIO CONSTITUTIONAL REVISION COMMISSION

While the political controversies over state debt were taking place, the 1970s Ohio Constitutional Revision Commission (OCRC) reviewed Article VIII and made a number of far-reaching recommendations, including a proposal to repeal the $750,000 debt limitation in Article VIII, section 1, and replace it with a provision that would have permitted the state, by a three-fifths vote of the General Assembly and presumably with the approval of the governor, to incur debt for capital improvements. See OCRC, *Recommendations for Amendments to the Ohio Constitution: Final Report, Index to Proceedings and Research* (1977), 150–86 (hereinafter OCRC, *Final Report*). Under this proposal, the debt service was limited by formula to 6 percent of the average annual revenue of the state, a proposal that in a number of ways resembled Governor Rhodes' ill-fated 1967 proposed Ohio Bond Commission. In 1977, the General Assembly embraced this recommendation and included it in a proposed amendment on state debt, but the voters rejected this proposal overwhelmingly by almost a 3:1 margin.

■ OHIO CONSTITUTIONAL MODERNIZATION COMMISSION

In 2016, the OCMC recommended the repeal of sections 2b, 2c, 2d, 2e, 2f, 2g, 2h, 2j, and 2k of this article, because they all involved bonds that were fully issued or paid off or for which bonding authority has lapsed due to the passage of time. See OCMC, *Report and Recommendation, Authorization of Debt Obligations* (September 8, 2016). To protect the holders of any outstanding bonds or obligations issued under the authority of the repealed sections the OCMC also recommended the adoption of new provision that would require that any obligation entered into under the authority of any section of Article VIII that is later repealed remains in full force and effect and continues to be secured in accordance with the original terms of the obligation. Ibid. In addition, the OCMC recommended a new constitutional provision that would convert certain bonds previously issued as revenue bonds under the authority of the fifth paragraph of section 2i to general obligation debt in order to obtain more favorable interest rates. Ibid.

Finally, the OCMC also recommended the repeal of the provisions relating to the sinking fund because of the widespread modern use of bonds to raise funds and because the duties of the sinking fund commission had been assigned to other state officers and agencies. See Commentary Article VIII, sections 7 to 11.

In 2016 and 2017, legislators introduced joint resolutions proposing amendments containing the commission's recommendations on Article

VIII, see H.J.R. 12 (131st GA) (Art. IV); H.J.R. 13 (131st GA) (Art. VIII), but the General Assembly has not taken any steps, to date, to move these recommendations to the ballot.

Section 1

Public debt; limitations.

The state may contract debts to supply casual deficits or failures in revenues, or to meet expenses not otherwise provided for; but the aggregate amount of such debts, direct and contingent, whether contracted by virtue of one or more acts of the General Assembly, or at different periods of time, shall never exceed seven hundred and fifty thousand dollars; and the money, arising from the creation of such debts, shall be applied to the purpose of which it was obtained, or to repay the debts so contracted, and to no other purpose whatever.

Adopted in 1851 and never amended, this section was one of the responses of the delegates to the 1850–51 Convention to the enormous debt that the state had incurred in the second quarter of the nineteenth century. The cost of the construction of the Ohio canal system beginning in 1825 and the subsidies to private canal, turnpike, and railroad companies under the Loan Law of 1837 had resulted in the accumulation of more than $12 million in debt by 1840. See David M. Gold, "Public Aid to Private Enterprises under the Ohio Constitution: Sections 4, 6, and 13 of Article VIII in Historical Perspective," 16 *U. Tol. L. Rev.* 405 (1985): 408–09; see also Ernest Ludlow Bogart, *Internal Improvements and State Debt in Ohio: An Essay in Economic History* (New York: Longmans, Green & Co., 1924), 154–79, 243 (hereinafter Bogart, *Internal Improvements and State Debt in Ohio*).

Section 1 limits the authority of the General Assembly to incur debt. Although it allows the contract of debt to pay for "casual deficits or failures in revenue, or to meet expenses not otherwise provided for," it limits the total amount of debt to $750,000. Such debt is cumulative and not for a single legislative act. And this section further provides that any "money, arising from the creation of such debts, shall be applied to the purpose of which it was obtained, or to repay the debts so contracted, and to no other purpose whatever." Under section 2 of this Article, however, the debt limitation is made inapplicable in certain enumerated emergency situations. And in section 3 the prohibition on the creation of debt is emphatically restated.

In 1857, only six years after the adoption of the new constitution, the Ohio Supreme Court applied section 1 and concluded that a five-year state public works contract, in the absence of revenue or appropriations by the General Assembly to fund the contract, created a debt obligation in violation of Article VIII. *State v. Medbery* (1857).

Though appearing extremely low, especially by today's standards, some states have even lower debt limits. For example, Oregon, Colorado, Nebraska,

Texas, and Arizona have constitutional debt limits ranging from $50,000 (Oregon) to $350,000 (Arizona). The constitutions of four other states—Arkansas, Indiana, Tennessee, and West Virginia—prohibit state debt altogether. See Stewart E. Sterk and Elizabeth S. Goldman, "Controlling Legislative Shortsightedness: The Effectiveness of Constitutional Debt Limitations," 1991 *Wis. L Rev.* 1301 (1991): 1315 nn. 80–81.

The $750,000 limitation and the prohibition on state debt in section 3, however, had little long-term impact in Ohio, because of the adoption of amendments that authorized general obligation debt in excess of the $750,000 limitation.

■ REVENUE BONDS

The $750,000 debt limitation in this section only applies to general obligation debt for which the state has assumed the risk of default. As a result, this limitation and the limitation in section 3 do not apply to debt resulting from lease-appropriation or revenue bonds (i.e., bonds that are paid back solely through income generated from facilities financed by the bonds). See OCRC, *Final Report*, 170.

In 1922, the Ohio Supreme Court described this exception to the debt limitation as follows in *Kasch v. Miller* (1922) (syllabus):

> Where the entire improvement is to be paid for by the issue and sale of bonds in the name of the state, and the principal and interest are to be paid entirely out of the revenues derived from the improvement or from the sale of the corpus in case of default, a state debt is not thereby incurred within the purview of the state Constitution . . . .

And in 1939, the court further described this "special fund" exception to the constitutional debt limitation:

> The debt limitation prescribed by Sections 1 and 3 of Article VIII of the Ohio Constitution does not apply to an indebtedness incurred in the procurement of property or erection of buildings or structures for the use of the state, to be paid for wholly out of revenues or income arising from the use or operation of the particular property for the procurement or construction of which the indebtedness is incurred.
>
> *State, ex rel. Public Institutional Building Authority v. Griffith* (1939) (syllabus) .

The state applied these principles in the 1950s to fund the construction of the Ohio Turnpike with bonds issued by the Ohio Turnpike Commission and secured by revenue from toll receipts. Because the cost of constructing the turnpike was to be repaid entirely from its receipts, the state did not have to commit state funds to turnpike construction and the bonds were not state debt within the meaning of this section. *State ex rel. Ohio Turnpike Commission v. Allen* (1952).

There are limitations, however, on the use of revenue bonds to avoid the state debt limitation. For example, the state does not avoid the limitation by pledging to be the exclusive source of payments for additions and improvements to property that could have initially been acquired through revenue bonds. *State ex rel. Public Institutional Building Authority v. Griffith* (1939). Nor may the state nominally withdraw its obligation to care for the mentally ill by pledging only fees received for their care to pay the rent on a newly constructed facility in light of the constitutional obligation to care for the mentally ill and disabled under section 1 of Article VII. *State ex rel. Public Institutional Building Authority v. Neffner* (1940). And the "special fund" exception for revenue bonds does not permit their being used to repay advances from the federal government for the unemployment compensation fund, even though the proposed fund would be coming from employers who were facing a surcharge on their contributions. *State ex rel. Shkurti v. Withrow* (1987).

■ AVOIDING THE DEBT LIMITATION

The most important exception to the debt limitation in this section is the result of the ability of voters to approve amendments to which the limitation does not apply. *State ex rel. Ohio Funds Management Board v. Walker* (1990). And since 1851, the voters have approved thirty amendments to Article VIII, including twenty amendments that authorized borrowing in excess of the constitutional limitation or that removed limitations on the use of debt.

Debt incurred by short-term borrowing to deal with cash shortages is subject to the limitation of this section. Acting through the Ohio Funds Management Board, the General Assembly had authorized "revenue anticipation notes" for the purpose of dealing with cash flow problems, but the Ohio Supreme Court rejected their use even though the notes would be paid off in the year issued by taxes already collected and deposited in a special repayment fund. *State ex rel. Ohio Funds Management Board v. Walker* (1990). In so ruling, the court described its role as "a watchful guardian of the concern of the framers of these constitutional prohibitions against the creation of state debt not authorized by the Constitution, and [stated that] we feel constrained to again give heed to such concerns." Ibid.

Section 2

State may incur debt for defense or to retire outstanding debts.

In addition to the above limited power, the state may contract debts to repel invasion, suppress insurrection, defend the state in war, or to redeem the present outstanding indebtedness of the state; but the money, arising from the contracting of such debts, shall be applied to the purpose for which it was raised, or to repay such debts, and to no other purpose whatever, and all debts, incurred to redeem the present outstanding indebtedness of the state, shall be so contracted as to be payable by the sinking fund, hereinafter provided for, as the same shall accumulate.

Adopted in 1851 and never amended, this section allows the state to incur debt without regard to the $750,000 limit in emergencies brought about by invasion, insurrection, and war and for the purpose of paying off the present outstanding debt of the state.

With the exception of the amendment authorizing the issuance of bonds in 1921 to provide deferred compensation to World War I veterans (and the corresponding provisions in 1947 and 1956 for World War II and Korean Conflict veterans), the General Assembly has not relied on the "emergency" authority of section 2 when proposing amendments to incur debt in excess of $750,000. No emergency provision was included in the 2009 amendment authorizing compensation for veterans of the Persian Gulf, Afghanistan, and Iraq conflicts.

The phrase "present outstanding debt" in this section refers to the debt that existed in 1851 and not to the present-day debt. *State ex rel. Shkurti v. Withrow* (1987).

The "sinking fund" referred to in the last sentence of this section is a fund specifically designed to pay off the principal and interest on the debt. See Article VIII, section 7.

Section 2a
Repealed—World War I compensation

In 1921, the General Assembly proposed the creation of the World War Compensation Fund to provide bonuses or deferred compensation to veterans of World War I. The voters approved this section, which permitted the state to issue up to $25 million in bonds without regard to the $750,000 limitation in section 1, and this was the first time the constitutional limitation was avoided. To justify the decision to exceed the state debt limit, the amendment relied on the existence of an emergency, stating tautologically that "[t]he people of the state of Ohio hereby declare that they have enacted this special amendment to meet the specific emergency covered thereby . . . ." The emergency provision of section 2 permits the state to exceed the debt limit "to repel invasion, suppress insurrection, [and to] defend the State in war." The 1921 amendment did not identify precise nature of the emergency, and the General Assembly only included emergency provision in amendments approved by the voters in 1947 and 1956.

In 1953, the General Assembly recommended the repeal of section 2a since the funds had been paid out and the bonds had been retired, and the voters approved the repeal. This is the only one of the obsolete bond-authorizing provisions of this article that have been repealed.

Section 2b

World War II compensation.

The board of commissioners created by section 8 of Art. VIII of the Constitution of the state of Ohio, designated therein "The Commissioners of the Sinking Fund," shall, forthwith upon the adoption of this amendment, proceed to issue and sell, from time to time, bonds of the state of Ohio in such amounts of face value as it may deem necessary to provide the funds, or such part thereof, as may be required to pay the compensation and the expenses of administering this section as herein provided for, provided, however, that the aggregate total amount of face value of bonds so issued shall not exceed three hundred million dollars. The full faith and credit of the state of Ohio is hereby pledged for the payment of such bonds. All bonds so issued shall mature in thirty semiannual installments after the respective dates thereof, and the maturities thereof shall be so fixed that the total amounts of payments on account of principal and interest to be paid on each of such semiannual installment payment dates shall be approximately equal, but no such bonds shall be issued or bear dates later than the first day of April, 1951. All bonds so issued shall bear interest at such rates as the commissioners of the sinking fund may fix, which interest shall be payable semiannually. Such bonds, and the interest thereon as income, shall be exempt from all taxes levied by the state of Ohio or any taxing district thereof. The bonds may, at the option of the sinking fund commission, be issued subject to call on any interest payment date at par and accrued interest. All sales of such bonds by the commissioners of the sinking fund shall be in accordance with such regulations as it shall make and promulgate, provided, however, that such bonds shall be sold only to the highest bidder or bidders therefor after notice of such sale shall have been published once each week for three consecutive weeks on the same day of each of such weeks, the first of such notices being published at least twenty-one full days before the date of sale, in a newspaper of general circulation in each of the eight most populous counties in the state of Ohio, and provided that each of such published notices shall state the day, hour and place of the sale, the total face value of the bonds to be sold, their denominations, dates, and the dates of their maturities, information relative to the rates of interest which the bonds will bear, and the dates upon which interest will be payable. The commissioners of the sinking fund shall have the right to reject any or all bids and to re-advertise and re-offer bonds for sale. Out of the proceeds of the sale of all bonds that amount which represents accrued interest, if any, shall be paid into the treasury of the state of Ohio into a fund to be known as the World War II compensation bond retirement fund. The balance shall be paid into the treasury of the state of Ohio into a fund to be known as the World War II compensation fund. The General Assembly of the state of Ohio may appropriate and cause to be paid into the World War II compensation bond retirement fund or the World War II compensation fund, out of the funds in the treasury of the state not otherwise appropriated, such amounts as it may deem proper for use upon order of the commissioners of the sinking fund for the purposes for which such funds are created as herein provided. If the General Assembly should so appropriate any funds to the World War II compensation fund prior to the time the commissioners of the sinking fund shall have issued bonds of the aggregate total amount of face value authorized in this section, the aggregate total amount of face value of bonds so authorized to be issued shall be reduced by the amount of the funds so appropriated.

During the period of fifteen years beginning January 1, 1949, the treasurer of state of the state of Ohio shall, without appropriation thereof by the General Assembly, transfer into said World War II compensation bond retirement fund one million dollars each month out of funds in the state treasury derived from taxes levied by the state for the purpose of providing revenues to defray the expenses of the state, excepting the taxes levied by the state by sections 5527, 5541, and 6291 of the. General Code of Ohio [RC §§ 5735.05, 5735.25, 4503.02] as the same may be in effect on the effective date of this section. To secure such monthly transfer of funds a lien is hereby created upon all funds coming into the state treasury after January 1, 1949, derived from taxes as aforesaid, which lien shall be the first and best lien upon all such funds. It shall be the duty of the treasurer of state to set aside and use for the purpose of making such monthly transfer of funds, part of each dollar received in the state treasury in each calendar year during said period of fifteen years beginning January 1, 1949, derived from taxes as aforesaid, so that the total amount of money so set aside in each of such calendar years shall be twelve million dollars, and so that the ratio which the amount of each dollar so set aside shall bear to one dollar shall be the same as the ratio which the amount of twelve million dollars shall bear to the total amount of money received in the state treasury in such calendar years derived from taxes as aforesaid. The treasurer of state shall set aside part of each such dollar before paying out, transferring, or disposing of in any other manner, such dollar or any part thereof for any other purpose whatsoever, and he shall make the transfer of one million dollars each month to the World War II compensation bond retirement fund, hereinabove provided for, out of said sum of twelve million dollars so set aside in each of such calendar years.

The commissioners of the sinking fund shall, on or before the first day of July in each calendar year, levy and certify to the auditor of the state of Ohio a state tax on all taxable property subject to taxation on the general tax lists of all counties in the state of Ohio for such year at such rate as it shall determine to be necessary to provide, together with other money which will be available in the World War II compensation bond retirement fund, the total amount of funds which will be required in the next following calendar year for the retirement of bonds and the payment of interest payable in such year. Such levy shall be in addition to all other taxes levied now or hereafter within the period during which bonds issued pursuant to the provisions of this section shall be outstanding, by or pursuant to law or any provision of the Constitution of the state of Ohio, and shall not be considered in applying any limitation or aggregate tax rates now or hereafter within the period during which bonds issued pursuant to the provisions of this section shall be outstanding, provided by or pursuant to law or any provision of the Constitution of the state of Ohio. The auditor of state shall certify such levies to the auditor of each county in the state of Ohio, who shall extend the same on the tax lists of his county for the year in which such levy is made and shall place same for collection on the tax duplicates of his county to be collected at the same time and in the same manner as other taxes on such duplicates. Said taxes herein authorized, when collected, shall be paid into the World War II compensation bond retirement fund in the treasury of the state.

The World War II compensation bond retirement fund shall be paid out, without appropriation thereof by the General Assembly of Ohio, upon the order of the commissioners of the sinking fund for the purpose of the payment, or retirement in other manner, of said bonds and interest thereon.

The World War II compensation fund shall be paid out upon order of the commissioners of the sinking fund, without appropriation by the General Assembly of Ohio, in payment of the expenses of administering this section, and as compensation as follows: every person who shall have served in active duty in the armed forces of the United States at any time between December 7, 1941, and September 2, 1945, both dates inclusive, and who, at the time of commencing such service, was and had been a resident of the state of Ohio for at least one year immediately preceding the commencement of such service, and who shall have been separated from such service under honorable conditions, or who is still in such service, or who has been retired, and who was in such service for a period of at least ninety days, shall be entitled to receive compensation of ten dollars for each month during which such person was in active domestic service and fifteen dollars for each month during which such person was in active foreign service within said period of time; provided, however, that any person who was serving in active duty in the armed forces of the United States on the seventh day of December, 1941, and who did not so serve at least ninety days thereafter because of a service-connected injury or death shall be deemed to have served at least ninety days within the period of time commencing December 7, 1941 and ending September 2, 1945; and provided, further, that the maximum amount of compensation payable under this section shall not be in excess of four hundred dollars; and provided, further, that no compensation shall be paid under this section to any person who shall have received from another state a bonus or compensation of a like nature as is provided under this section. No compensation shall be paid under this section to any person for any periods of time spent under penal confinement during the period of active duty. Compensation for a fraction of a month of service shall be paid on the basis of one-thirtieth of the above monthly amounts for each day of such service. Service in the merchant marine of the United States shall not be considered for the purpose of this section. "Domestic service" as used herein means service within the continental limits of the United States (excluding Alaska). "Foreign service" as used herein means service in all other places, including sea duty.

Either the surviving husband or wife, or the surviving child or children, or the surviving parents or parent, of a deceased person shall be paid the same amount of compensation that such deceased person would be entitled to receive under this section, if living; provided, however, that if such deceased person's death was service-connected and in line of duty, his survivors as hereinbefore designated, shall be paid four hundred dollars regardless of the amount of compensation which such deceased person would be entitled to receive under this section, if living; provided further, that the amount of compensation payable to such survivors of such deceased person shall be payable only to one of the three groups of survivors hereinbefore designated in the order in which said groups are herein named; and provided further, that the surviving husband or wife of more than one deceased person who would be entitled to receive compensation under this section, if living, shall be paid only that amount of compensation payable by reason of the first of the deaths of such deceased persons.

No sale or assignment of any right or claim to compensation under this section shall be valid, no claims of creditors shall be enforceable against rights or claims to or payments of compensation under this section, and no fees shall be charged for services in connection with the prosecution of any right or claim to compensation or the collection of any compensation under this section.

The commissioners of the sinking fund shall have complete charge of making payments of the compensation provided for in this section and shall adopt and promulgate regulations governing their procedure in connection therewith, including determinations as to who are proper beneficiaries and the amounts to which such beneficiaries are entitled, determinations as to whether an applicant has the necessary residence requirements, and such other regulations as it may deem necessary and proper; provided, however, that all applications for payment of compensation under this section shall be made to the commissioners of the sinking fund before July 1, 1950.

The commissioners of the sinking fund shall select and appoint such legal counsel and employees as it may deem necessary, fix their compensation and prescribe their duties, and all such appointees shall serve at its pleasure.

The people of the state of Ohio declare that their enactment of this special amendment of the Constitution of the state of Ohio is to meet the specific emergency covered thereby, and they declare it to be their intention to in no manner affect or change any of the existing provisions of the said constitution except as herein set forth. The provisions of this section shall be self executing.

Upon the retirement of all of the bonds that may be issued hereunder and the payment of all valid claims for compensation made within the limitations of time as prescribed herein, the commissioners of the sinking fund shall make a final report to the General Assembly of Ohio, and any balance remaining in any of the funds herein created and referred to shall be disposed of as shall be provided by law.

Adopted in 1947, this section established a system of compensation for World War II veterans and their survivors. The section allowed the state to exceed the $750,000 debt limit through the sale of up to $300 million in state bonds to create World War II retirement and compensation funds. To receive benefits, veterans had to be residents of the state for at least one year before entering service. Qualifying veterans or their survivors could receive up to $400 in benefits. Veterans who served in the Merchant Marine, who were confined in penal institutions, or who were dishonorably discharged were ineligible. This provision required applications for payment to veterans or their survivors to be made before July 1, 1950. It included an emergency clause providing that the "enactment of this special amendment of the Constitution of the state of Ohio is to meet the specific emergency covered thereby."

Section 2c

Construction of state highway system.

The state may contract debts not exceeding five hundred million dollars for the purpose of providing moneys for acquisition of rights-of-way and for construction and reconstruction of highways on the state highway system. Not more than one hundred twenty-five million dollars of the debt authorized by this section shall be contracted within any calendar year, and no part of such debt shall be contracted after the thirty-first day of March, 1962. The principal amount of any part of such debt at any time contracted shall be paid in substantially equal semiannual or annual installments, beginning not later than eighteen months after such debt is contracted, and in such number of installments that the entire debt shall be discharged not later than the year 1972. Securities evidencing the debt authorized by this section shall bear interest and shall be sold upon such terms as may be prescribed by law.

Both the principal of such debt and the interest thereon shall be exempt from taxation by this state or by any taxing subdivision thereof. Moneys raised under the authority of this section shall be expended only to provide adequate highways, including the acquisition of rights-of-way and including participation therein with federal government, municipal corporations, counties and other legally authorized participants, but excluding costs of planning and supervision by the state. All construction shall be done by contract as shall be provided by law. No part of such proceeds shall be appropriated except to meet the requirements of programs or schedules of acquisition of rights-of-way, highway construction and reconstruction which the governor, or other highway authority with the concurrence of the governor, shall submit to the General Assembly before such appropriations are made. Such appropriations shall be made only for major thoroughfares of the state highway system and urban extensions thereof. The debt contracted under the authority of this section shall be paid by revenue bonds issued by the state of Ohio as provided by law, secured by a pledge of moneys derived from fees, excises or license taxes, levied by the state of Ohio, relating to registration, operation, or use of vehicles on public highways, or to fuels used for propelling such vehicles, and a sufficient amount thereof shall be set aside each year, before any other distribution is made, to pay the interest on the outstanding debt and principal of such debt becoming due in that year, without other appropriations, but according to regulations to be established by law.

The General Assembly shall meet on the second Monday in January, 1954, for the sole purpose of enacting laws pursuant to this section.

Adopted in 1953, this section allowed the state to incur debt of up to $500 million through the sale of revenue bonds for the building and improvement of the state highway system. These bonds were not secured by the full faith and credit of the state but by "moneys derived from fees, excises or license taxes, levied by the state of Ohio, relating to registration, operation, or use of vehicles on public highways, or to fuels used for propelling such vehicles." These funds had been constitutionally segregated as a result of a 1947 constitutional amendment proposed by initiative petition. See Commentary, Article XII, section 5a.

The amendment creating this section was the first of four amendments that expressly permitted the state to use highway user receipts to pay off the authorized debt without any further appropriations (referring to the limits under Art. II, sec. 22). See Commentary, Article XII, section 5a. See also Article VIII, sections 2g, 2i, and 2m.

Section 2d

Korean Conflict compensation.

The board of commissioners created by section 8 of Article VIII of the Ohio Constitution designated therein "The Commissioners of the Sinking Fund," shall, forthwith upon the adoption of this amendment, proceed to issue and sell, from time to time, bonds of the state of Ohio in such amounts of face value as are necessary to provide the funds, or such part thereof, as may be required to pay the compensation and the expenses of administering this section as herein provided for, provided that the aggregate total amount of face value of bonds so issued shall not exceed ninety million dollars. The full faith and credit of the state of Ohio is hereby pledged for the payment of such bonds. All bonds so issued shall mature in thirty semiannual installments commencing not later than two years after the respective dates thereof. The maturities thereof shall be so fixed that the total amounts of payments on account of principal and interest to be paid on each of such semiannual installment payment dates shall be substantially equal. No such bonds shall be issued or bear dates later than the first day of April, 1959. All bonds so issued shall bear interest at such rates as the commissioners of the sinking fund may fix, which interest shall be payable semiannually. Such bonds, and the interest thereon as income, shall be exempt from all taxes levied by the state of Ohio or any taxing district thereof.

The bonds may, at the option of the commissioners of the sinking fund, be issued subject to call on any interest payment date at par and accrued interest. All sales of such bonds by the commissioners of the sinking fund shall be in accordance with such regulations as it shall make and promulgate, provided that such bonds shall be sold only to the highest bidder or bidders therefor after notice of such sale shall have been published once each week for three consecutive weeks on the same day of each of such weeks, the first of such notices being published at least twenty-one full days before the date of sale, in a newspaper of general circulation in each of the eight most populous counties in the state of Ohio, and provided that each of such published notices shall state the day, hour and place of the sale, the total face value of the bonds to be sold, their denominations, dates, and the dates of their maturities, information relative to the rates of interest which the bonds will bear, and the dates upon which interest will be payable. The commissioners of the sinking fund shall have the right to reject any or all bids and to re-advertise and re-offer bonds for sale. Out of the proceeds of the sale of all bonds that amount which represents accrued interest, if any, shall be paid into the treasury of the state of Ohio into a fund to be known asThe Korean Conflict Compensation Bond Retirement Fund. The balance shall be paid into the treasury of the state of Ohio into a fund to be known asThe Korean Conflict Compensation Fund. The General Assembly of the state of Ohio may appropriate and cause to be paid into The Korean Conflict Compensation Bond Retirement Fund or The Korean Conflict Compensation Fund, out of the funds in the treasury of the state not otherwise appropriated, such amount as is proper for use upon order of the commissioners of the sinking fund for the purposes for which such funds are created as herein provided. If the General Assembly should so appropriate any funds to The Korean Conflict Compensation Fund prior to the time the commissioners of the sinking fund shall have issued bonds of the aggregate total amount of face value authorized in this section, the aggregate total amount of face value of bonds so authorized to be issued shall be reduced by the amount of the funds so appropriated.

The commissioners of the sinking fund shall, on or before the first day of July in each calendar year, levy and certify to the auditor of the state of Ohio a state tax on all taxable property subject to taxation on the general tax lists of all counties in the state of Ohio for such year at such rate as it shall determine to be necessary to provide, together with other money which will be available in The Korean Conflict Compensation Bond Retirement Fund, the total amount of funds which will be required in the next following calendar year for the retirement of bonds and the payment of interest payable in such year. Such levy shall be in addition to all other taxes levied now or hereafter within the period during which bonds issued pursuant to the provisions of this section shall be outstanding, by or pursuant to law or any provision of the Ohio constitution, and shall not be considered in applying any limitation or aggregate tax rates now or hereafter within the period during which bonds issued pursuant to the provisions of this section shall be outstanding, provided by or pursuant to law or any provision of the Ohio Constitution. The auditor of state shall certify such levies to the auditor of each county in the state of Ohio, who shall extend the same on the tax lists of his county for the year in which such levy is made and shall place the same for collection on the tax duplicates of his county to be collected at the same time and in the same manner as other taxes on such duplicates. Said taxes herein authorized, when collected, shall be paid into The Korean Conflict Compensation Bond Retirement Fund in the treasury of the state. The Korean Conflict Compensation Bond Retirement Fund shall be paid out, without appropriation thereof by the General Assembly of Ohio upon the order of the commissioners of the sinking fund for the purpose of the payment, or retirement in other manner, of said bonds and interest thereon.

The Korean Conflict Compensation Fund shall be paid out upon order of the commissioners of the sinking fund, without appropriation by the General Assembly of Ohio, in payment of the expenses of administering this section, and as compensation as follows: Every person who shall have served on active duty in the armed forces of the United States at any time between June 25, 1950, and July 19, 1953, both dates inclusive, and who, at the time of commencing such service, was and had been a resident of the state of Ohio for at least one year immediately preceding the commencement of such service, and (1) who shall have been separated from such service under honorable conditions or (2) who is still in such service, or (3) who has been retired, shall be entitled to receive compensation of ten dollars for each month during which such person was in active domestic service and of fifteen dollars for each month during which such person was in active foreign service within said period of time; provided that the maximum amount of compensation payable under this section shall not be in excess of four hundred dollars; and provided that no compensation shall be paid under this section to any person who shall have received from another state a bonus or compensation of a like nature as is provided under this section. Compensation for a fraction of a month of service shall be paid on the basis of one-thirtieth of the above monthly amounts for each day of such service. Service in the Merchant Marine of the United States shall not be considered for the purpose of this section. "Domestic service" as used herein, means service within the continental limits of the United States excluding Alaska and sea duty. "Foreign service" as used herein means service in all other places, including sea duty.

No compensation shall be paid under this section to any person for any periods of time spent under penal confinement during the period of active duty.

Either the surviving husband or wife, or the surviving child or children, or the surviving parents or parent, including persons standing in loco parentis for one year preceding commencement of service in the armed forces of the United States, of a deceased person shall be paid the same amount of compensation that such deceased person would have been entitled to receive under this section, if living; provided that if such deceased person's death is determined to have been service-connected by the Veterans Administration of the United States government, his survivors as herein designated, shall be entitled to four hundred dollars regardless of the amount of compensation which such deceased person would have been entitled to receive under this section if living; provided that the amount of compensation payable to such survivors of such deceased person shall be payable only to one of the three groups of survivors herein designated in the order in which said groups are named.

No sale or assignment of any right or claim to compensation under this section shall be valid, no claims or creditors shall be enforceable against rights or claims to or payments of compensation under this section, and no fees shall be charged for services in connection with the prosecution of any right or claim to compensation or the collection of any compensation under this section.

The commissioners of the sinking fund shall have complete charge of making payments of the compensation provided for in this section and shall adopt and promulgate regulations governing their procedure in connection therewith, including determinations as to who are proper beneficiaries and the amounts to which such beneficiaries are entitled, determinations as to whether an applicant has the necessary residence requirements, and such other regulations that are necessary and proper; provided that all applications for payment of compensation under this section shall be made to the commissioners of the sinking fund before January 1, 1959.

The commissioners of the sinking fund shall select and appoint such legal counsel and employees that are necessary, fix their compensation and prescribe their duties, and all such appointees shall serve at its pleasure.

The commissioners of the sinking fund shall permit review of individual records of claims by representatives of recognized veterans organizations when authorized to do so by the applicant.

There is hereby transferred, out of the fund known as the "World War II Compensation Fund," created by section 2b of Article VIII of the Ohio Constitution, the sum of four million dollars, toThe Korean Conflict Compensation Fund, for the purpose of defraying the immediate cost of administration and compensation.

The people of the state of Ohio declare that their enactment of this special amendment of the Ohio Constitution is to meet the specific emergency covered thereby, and they declare it to be their intention to in no manner affect or change any of the existing provisions of the said constitution except as herein set forth. The provisions of this section shall be self executing.

Upon payment of all valid claims for compensation made within the limitations of time as prescribed herein, the commissioners of the sinking fund may transfer any funds inThe Korean Conflict Compensation Fund toThe Korean Conflict Compensation Bond Retirement Fund.

Upon retirement of all of the bonds that may be issued hereunder and the payment of all valid claims for compensation made within the limitations of time as prescribed herein, the commissioners of the sinking fund shall make a final report to the General Assembly of Ohio, and any balance remaining in any of the funds herein created and referred to shall be disposed of as shall be provided by law.

Adopted in 1956, this section concerns the authorization of debt for the payment of compensation for Ohio veterans of the Korean Conflict who served on active duty from June 25, 1950, through July 19, 1953. It authorized the creation of the Korean Conflict Compensation Fund, funded through the sale of up to $90 million in bonds and an initial transfer of $4 million from the World War II fund established under section 2b. It also authorized the fund to retire the debt on the bonds. As with the World War II fund, veterans of the war or their survivors were eligible for benefits; however, veterans who served in the Merchant Marines, who were confined in penal institutions, or who were dishonorably discharged were not. All applications for compensation under this provision had to be made prior to January 1, 1959.

Section 2e
Funds for public building construction

The state may borrow money and issue bonds or other obligations therefor for the purpose of acquiring, constructing, reconstructing and otherwise improving and equipping buildings and structures, excluding highways, and for the purpose of acquiring sites for such buildings and structures, for the penal, correctional, mental, and welfare institutions of the state; for the state supported universities and colleges of the state; for class room facilities to be leased or sold by the state to public school districts unable within limitations provided by law to provide adequate facilities without assistance from the state; and for state offices; provided that the aggregate total amount of such borrowing under authority of this section shall not exceed $ 150,000,000. Not more than thirty million dollars of such borrowing shall be contracted within any calendar year. No part of such borrowing shall be contracted after the last day of December 1964. All bonds or other obligations issued pursuant to this section shall mature within twenty years from date of issue. Not more than $ 75,000,000 of the total expenditure from such borrowing shall be for acquisition, construction, reconstruction and other improvement and equipping of buildings and structures, or for acquisition of sites for such buildings and structures, for the state supported universities and colleges, public school class room facilities and state offices; and not more than $75,000,000 of the total expenditure from such borrowing shall be for acquisition, construction, reconstruction and other improvement and equipping of buildings and structures, or for acquisition of sites for such buildings and structures, for the penal, correctional, mental, and welfare institutions of the state.

The faith and credit of the state are hereby pledged for the payment of such bonds or other obligations and the interest thereon, and they shall be payable from all excises and taxes of the state, except ad valorem taxes on real and personal property, income taxes, and fees, excises, or license taxes relating to registration, operation, or use of vehicles on public highways, or to fuels used for propelling such vehicles.

During the period beginning with the effective date of the first authorization to issue bonds or other obligations under authority of this section and ending on the last day of December 1964, and continuing during such time as such bonds or other obligations are outstanding, and moneys in the capital improvements bond retirement fund are insufficient to pay all interest, principal and charges for the issuance and retirement of such bonds and other obligations, there shall be levied, for the purpose of paying interest, principal, and charges for the issuance and retirement of such bonds and other obligations, an excise tax on sales of cigarettes at the rate of one-half cent on each ten cigarettes or fractional part thereof, and an excise tax on the use, consumption, or storage for consumption of cigarettes by consumers in this state at the rate of one-half cent on each ten cigarettes or fractional part thereof. Such tax on the use, consumption, or storage for consumption of cigarettes by consumers in this state shall not be levied upon cigarettes upon which the tax on sales has been paid. The moneys received into the state treasury from the one-half cent excise tax on sales of cigarettes and from the one-half cent excise tax on the use, consumption or storage for consumption of cigarettes by consumers in this state shall be paid into the capital improvements bond retirement fund. The General Assembly of Ohio shall enact laws providing for the collection of such taxes.

There is hereby created in the state treasury a fund to be known as the capital improvements bond retirement fund. The capital improvements bond retirement fund shall consist of all moneys received by the state from taxes on cigarettes levied under authority of this section, and all other moneys credited to the fund pursuant to law. Such moneys shall be expended, as provided by law, for the purpose of paying interest, principal, and charges for the issuance and retirement of bonds and other obligations issued under authority of this section.

Sufficient amounts of such moneys in the capital improvements bond retirement fund are hereby appropriated for the purpose of paying interest, principal, and charges for the issuance and retirement of bonds or other obligations issued under authority of this section, without other appropriations but according to law.

Any balance remaining in the capital improvements bond retirement fund after payment of all interest, principal, and charges for the issuance and retirement of bonds and other obligations issued under authority of this section, shall be disposed of as shall be provided by law.

As long as any of such bonds or other obligations are outstanding there shall be levied and collected, in amounts sufficient to pay the principal of and the interest on such bonds or other obligations, excises and taxes, excluding those above excepted.

The General Assembly shall meet on the third Monday of January, 1956 for the purpose of enacting laws pursuant to this section.

Adopted in 1955, this section created a capital improvements bond retirement fund to allocate up to $150 million for building and improving structures at state penal, mental, and welfare institutions and at public schools and state-supported colleges and universities. The bonds or other obligations issued under this section had to be issued by December 1964. In addition, this section provided for the establishment of a state excise tax on cigarettes to pay any deficit in the fund.

Despite the title given to this section in some state documents, see Ohio Constitution (Ohio Secretary of State website) ("Providing means for securing funds for highway and public building construction"), this section has nothing to do with securing funds for highway construction. In fact, this section specifically excludes "highways" from the projects that may be funded. And the official ballot presented to the voters correctly described the highway exclusion in this section.

The amendment creating this section was the first to provide that highway user receipts may not be used to pay off bonds issued under it. See Commentary, Article XII, section 5a. Such provisions have become a common feature of future bond-authorizing amendments.

Section 2f

Bonds for public school classrooms, universities, recreation and conservation and state buildings.

In addition to the authorization in Article VIII, Section 2e, the state may borrow not to exceed two hundred fifty million dollars and issue bonds or other obligations therefor, for the purpose of acquiring, constructing, reconstructing, and otherwise improving and equipping buildings and structures, excluding highways; and for the purpose of acquiring lands and interests in lands for sites for such buildings and structures; and for the purpose of assisting in the development of the state, to acquire lands and interests in lands and to develop such lands and interests or other state lands for water impoundment sites, park and recreational uses, and conservation of natural resources; and for use in conjunction with federal grants or loans for any of such purposes. Of said amount, for the purpose of acquiring, constructing, reconstructing, and otherwise improving and equipping buildings and structures, excluding highways, and for the purpose of acquiring lands and interests in lands for sites for such buildings and structures, one hundred seventy-five million dollars shall be issued for the state supported or assisted college or universities including community colleges, municipal universities, and university branches, thirty-five million dollars shall be issued for providing classroom facilities for the public schools to be leased or sold by the state to public school districts unable, within the limitations provided by law, to provide adequate facilities without assistance from the state, and fifteen million dollars shall be issued for state functions, activities, offices, institutions, including penal, correctional, mental, and welfare, and research and development; and for the purpose of assisting in the development of the state by acquiring lands and interests in lands and to develop such lands and interests or other state lands for water impoundment sites, park and recreational uses, and conservation of natural resources twenty-five million dollars shall be issued. Not more than one hundred million dollars of such borrowing shall be contracted within any calendar year. No part of such borrowing shall be contracted after the thirty-first day of December, 1972. All bonds or other obligations issued pursuant to this section shall mature at such time or times not exceeding thirty years from date of issue and in such amounts as shall be fixed by the commissioners of the sinking fund, and shall bear interest and be sold as shall be authorized by law. Both the principal of such debt and the interest thereon shall be exempt from taxation within this state.

The faith and credit of the state are hereby pledged for the payment of such bonds or other obligations, and the interest thereon. They shall be payable from all excises and taxes of the state except ad valorem taxes on real and personal property, income taxes, and fees, excises or license taxes relating to registration, operation, or use of vehicles on public highways or to fuels used for propelling such vehicles. The excises and taxes of the state from which such bonds and other obligations shall be paid shall include an excise tax on sales of cigarettes at the rate of one-half cent on each ten cigarettes or fractional part thereof, and an excise tax on the use, consumption, or storage for consumption of cigarettes by consumers in this state, at the rate of one-half cent on each ten cigarettes or fractional part thereof, which shall be levied during the period beginning with January 1, 1965, and continuing until December 31, 1972, and thereafter as long as any of such bonds and other obligations are outstanding and moneys in the separate and distinct bond retirement fund hereinafter created are insufficient to pay all interest, principal, and charges for the issuance and retirement of such bonds and other obligations. Such tax on the use, consumption, or storage for consumption of cigarettes by consumers in this state shall not be levied upon cigarettes upon which the tax on sales has been paid. The General Assembly of the state of Ohio shall enact laws providing for the collection of such taxes. The moneys received into the state treasury from such one-half cent excise tax on sales of cigarettes and from such one-half cent excise tax on the use, consumption, or storage for consumption of cigarettes by consumers in this state shall be paid into a separate and distinct bond retirement fund hereby created. There shall be transferred in each year from said bond retirement fund to the capital improvements bond retirement fund created by Article VIII, Section 2e of the Constitution of the State of Ohio, from the proceeds of the levy of such excise taxes on cigarettes, such amounts as may be necessary for the payment in such year of the interest, principal, and charges of the bonds or other obligations issued pursuant to said Article VII, Section 2e falling due in such year, to the extent that moneys in said capital improvements bond retirement fund in such year are insufficient to pay such interest, principal, and charges.

The excise taxes on the sale, use, consumption or storage of cigarettes authorized to be levied by Article VIII, Section 2e of the Constitution of the State of Ohio for the payment of bonds and other obligations issued under authority of that section shall not be levied during any period that they are not required to be levied by Article VIII, Section 2e of the Constitution of the State of Ohio.

Sufficient amounts of such moneys remaining in said separate and distinct bond retirement fund created by this section, after such transfers, are hereby appropriated for the purpose of paying interest, principal, and charges for the issuance and retirement of bonds and other obligations issued under authority of this section, without other appropriations but according to law. In the event the moneys in the separate and distinct bond retirement fund created by this section are at any time insufficient to pay the current interest, principal, and charges for the issuance and retirement of bonds and other obligations issued under authority of this section, and such moneys as may be required to pay such current interest, principal, and charges are hereby appropriated for those purposes, without other appropriations but according to law, from the proceeds of all excises and taxes excluding those above excepted. Provision may be made by law for the transfer and the use of any amount in said separate and distinct bond retirement fund in excess of that required in any year for payment of interest, principal, and charges for the issuance and retirement of bonds and other obligations issued under authority of said Article VIII, Section 2e of this section.

Any balance remaining in the separate and distinct bond retirement fund created by this section after payment of all interest, principal, and charges for the issuance and retirement of bonds or other obligations issued under authority of this section shall be disposed of for the purposes enumerated in this section as may be provided by law.

As long as any of such bonds or other obligations are outstanding there shall be levied and collected in amounts sufficient to pay the principal of and interest on such bonds or other obligations, excises and taxes, excluding those above excepted.

Adopted in 1963, this section authorized the issuance of bonds for school classrooms, support for universities, for recreation and conservation, and for state buildings. The section funded many of the same projects referred to in section 2e, including capital improvement projects for state-supported colleges and universities as well as state penal, mental health, and welfare institutions. This also permitted funds to be used for the establishment of parks and recreation areas and for the conservation of natural resources. Obligations issued under this section could not exceed $250 million and had to mature in thirty years or less. The debt raised under this section was to be retired through funds raised by the state's license, fuel, income, and property taxes as well as through the excise tax on cigarettes established under section 2e, which could be collected through December 31, 1972, or until all the debt was retired.

This section provides that highway user receipts may not be used to pay off bonds issued under it. See Commentary, Article XII, section 5a.

Section 2g

Bonds and other obligations for highway construction.

The state may contract debts not exceeding five hundred million dollars for the purpose of providing moneys for acquisition of rights-of-way and for construction and reconstruction of highways on the state highway system and urban extensions thereof. The principal amount of any part of such debt at any time contracted shall be paid at such time or times and in such amounts as shall be fixed by the commissioners of the sinking fund provided that the entire debt shall be discharged not later than the year 1989. The bonds or other obligations evidencing the debt authorized by this section shall bear interest and shall be sold upon such terms as may be prescribed by law. Both the principal of such debt and the interest thereon shall be exempt from taxation within this state. Moneys raised under the authority of this section shall be expended only to provide adequate highways, including engineering and the acquisition of rights-of-way and including participation therein with the federal government, municipal corporations, counties and other legally authorized participants. All construction shall be done by contract as shall be provided by law. No part of such proceeds shall be appropriated except to meet the requirements of programs or schedules or acquisition of rights-of-way, highway construction and reconstruction which the governor, or other highway authority designated by law, with the concurrence of the governor, shall submit to the General Assembly before such appropriations are made. Such appropriations shall be made only for major thoroughfares of the state highway system and urban extension thereof. The debt contracted under the authority of this section shall be evidenced by bonds or other obligations issued by the state of Ohio as provided by law. The faith and credit of the state are hereby pledged for the payment thereof and the interest thereon. Such bonds or other obligations shall be paid from moneys derived from fees, excises, or license taxes, levied by the state of Ohio, relating to registration, operation, or use of vehicles on public highways, or to fuels used for propelling such vehicles, and a sufficient amount thereof, after provision for the amounts required by Article VIII, Section 2c of the Constitution of the State of Ohio for obligations issued pursuant to that section, is hereby appropriated in each year for the purpose of paying the interest on the outstanding debt and the principal of such debt contracted under authority of this section becoming due in that year, without other appropriations, but according to regulations to be established by law. Provision may be made by law for the transfer and the use of any amount of such moneys in excess of that required, in any year, for the payment of interest on and the principal of such debt contracted under authority of this section and said section 2c.

Adopted in 1964, this section allowed the state to acquire debt up to $500 million for highway and road construction. The revenues raised were to be used for the construction and repair of major state thoroughfares and urban extensions in the state's highway system. Retirement of the debt to finance these projects was to be made, in part, through the use of highway user receipts, see Commentary, Article XII, section 5a, without any further appropriation. See Commentary, Article II, section 22.

Section 2h

Bonds for buildings for the state and for state-supported institutions of higher education, and for recreation and natural resources conservation.

The state may, from time to time, borrow not to exceed two hundred ninety million dollars and issue bonds or other obligations thereof for any one or more of the following purposes: acquiring, constructing, reconstructing or otherwise improving and equipping buildings and structures of the state and state supported and assisted institutions of higher education, including those for research and development; acquiring lands and interests in lands for sites for such buildings and structures; assisting in the development of the state, to acquire and develop lands and interests in lands and develop other state lands for water impoundment sites, flood control, parks and recreational uses, or conservation of natural resources; to develop state parks and recreational facilities including the construction, reconstruction and improvement of roads and highways therein; to assist the political subdivisions of the state to finance the cost of constructing and extending water and sewerage lines and mains; for use in conjunction with federal grants or loans for any of such purposes; and for use in conjunction with other governmental entities in acquiring, constructing, reconstructing, improving, and equipping water pipelines, stream flow improvements, airports, historical or educational facilities. The aggregate total amount of such borrowing outstanding under authority of this section shall not, at any time, exceed such sum as will require, during any calendar year, more than $20,000,000 to meet the principal and interest requirements of any such bonds and other obligations, and the charges for the issuance and retirement of such bonds and other obligations, falling due that year. No part of such borrowing shall be contracted after the last day of December, 1970. All bonds or other obligations issued pursuant to this section shall mature within thirty years from the date of issue.

The faith and credit of the state are hereby pledged for the payment of such bonds or other obligations or the interest thereon, and they shall be payable from all excises and taxes of the state, except ad valorem taxes on real and personal property, income taxes, and fees, excises or license taxes relating to the registration, operation, or use of vehicles on the public highways, or to fuels used for propelling such vehicles, after making provision for payment of amounts pledged from such excises and taxes for payment of bonds issued under authority of Sections 2e and 2f of this Article.

During the period beginning with the effective date of the first authorization to issue bonds or other obligations under authority of this section and continuing during such time as such bonds or other obligations are outstanding and so long as moneys in the Development Bond Retirement Fund are insufficient to pay all interest, principal and charges of such bonds or other obligations issued under authority of this section and becoming due in each year, a sufficient amount of moneys derived from such excises and taxes of the state is hereby appropriated in each year for the purpose of paying the interest, principal and charges for the issuance and retirement of bonds or other obligations issued under authority of this section becoming due in that year without other appropriation but according to law. The moneys derived from such excises and taxes and hereby appropriated shall be paid into a distinct bond retirement fund designated "Development Bond Retirement Fund," hereby created. Such moneys shall be expended as provided by law for the purpose of paying interest, principal and charges for the issuance and retirement of bonds and other obligations issued under authority of this section.

Sufficient amounts of such moneys in the Development Bond Retirement Fund are hereby appropriated for the purpose of paying interest, principal and charges for the issuance and retirement of bonds or other obligations issued under authority of this section, so long as any of them are outstanding, without other appropriations but according to law.

Any balance remaining in the Development Bond Retirement Fund after payment of all interest, principal and charges for the issuance and retirement of bonds and other obligations issued under authority of this section, shall be disposed of as shall be provided by law.

As long as any of such bonds or other obligations are outstanding there shall be levied and collected, in amounts sufficient to pay the principal of and the interest on such bonds or other obligations, excises and taxes, excluding those above excepted.

Adopted in 1965, this section allowed the state to raise up to $290 million from the sale of bonds and other obligation to pay for state development projects. More specifically, the section allowed the state to spend funds on state-supported institutions of higher learning with an emphasis on research and development, and for state projects dealing with flood control, state parks, and natural resource conservation. Funds could also be used to assist political subdivisions in building and extending water and sewage lines. The cutoff date for issuing obligations under this section was December 31, 1970, and all obligations issued under this section had to mature in thirty years or less.

This section provides that highway user receipts may not be used to pay off bonds issued under it. See Commentary, Article XII, section 5a.

Section 2i

Capital improvement bonds.

In addition to the authorization otherwise contained in Article VIII of the Ohio Constitution, the General Assembly, in accordance with but subject to the limitations of this section, may authorize the issuance of obligations, including bonds and notes, of the state or of state institutions, boards, commissions, authorities, or other state agencies or instrumentalities for any one or more of the following public capital improvements: the construction, reconstruction, or other improvement of highways, including those on the state highway system and urban extensions thereof, those within or leading to public parks or recreational areas, and those within or leading to municipal corporations, the acquisition, construction, reconstruction, or other improvement of, and provision of equipment for, buildings, structures, or other improvements, and necessary planning and engineering, for water pollution control and abatement, including those for sewage collection, treatment, or disposal, water management, including those for water distribution, collection, supply, storage, or impoundment, and stream flow control, and flood control, state supported or assisted institutions of higher education, technical education, vocational education, juvenile correction, training and rehabilitation, parks and recreation, research and development with respect to transportation, highways and highway transportation, mental hygiene and retardation, police and fire training, airports, and other state buildings and structures, and the acquisition and improvement of real estate and interests therein required with respect to the foregoing, including participation in any such capital improvements with the federal government, municipal corporations, counties, or other governmental entities or any one or more of them which participation may be by grants, loans or contributions to them for any of such capital improvements. It is hereby determined that such capital improvements will directly or indirectly create jobs, enhance employment opportunities, and improve the economic welfare of the people of the state.

The issuance under authority of this section of obligations the holders or owners of which are given the right to have excises and taxes levied by the General Assembly for the payment of the principal thereof or interest thereon, herein called tax supported obligations, shall be subject to the following limitations. Not more than one hundred million dollars principal amount may be issued in any calendar year and not more than five hundred million dollars principal amount may be outstanding at any one time for such capital improvements for highways and research and development with respect to highways and highway transportation, herein called highway obligations, provided that fifty per cent of the proceeds of the first five hundred million dollars of such tax supported highway obligations shall be used for urban extensions of state highways and highways within or leading to municipal corporations. Not more than two hundred fifty nine million dollars aggregate principal amount of such tax supported obligations may be issued for the other capital improvements aforesaid, provided that from the proceeds thereof one hundred twenty million dollars shall be used for water pollution control and abatement and water management, one hundred million dollars shall be used for higher education, technical and vocational education, and juvenile correction, training and rehabilitation, twenty million dollars shall be used for parks and recreation, and nineteen million dollars for airports, and for construction, rehabilitation and equipping of other state buildings and structures, including those for police and fire training. If tax supported obligations are issued under authority of this section to retire tax supported obligations previously issued under authority of this section, such new obligations shall not be counted against such limits to the extent that the principal amount thereof does not exceed the principal amount of the obligations to be retired thereby.

Each issue of tax supported obligations issued pursuant to this section shall mature in not more than thirty years from the date of issuance thereof, or, if issued to retire obligations issued hereunder, within thirty years from the date such debt was originally contracted. If such tax supported obligations are issued as notes in anticipation of the issuance of bonds, provision shall be made by law for setting aside, so long as such notes are outstanding, into a special fund or funds such amounts from the sources authorized for payment of such bonds under this section as would be sufficient for payment of that amount of principal on such bonds that would have been payable during such period if such bonds, maturing during a period of thirty years, had been issued without prior issuance of such notes. Such fund or funds may be used solely for the payment of principal of such notes or of bonds in anticipation of which such notes have been issued.

The faith and credit and excises and taxes of the state, excluding ad valorem taxes on real or personal property and income taxes, shall be pledged to the payment of the principal of and the interest on such tax supported obligations, sinking or bond retirement fund provisions shall be made therefor, and this section shall otherwise be implemented, all in the manner and to the extent provided by law by the General Assembly, including provisions for appropriation of pledged excises and taxes, and covenants to continue their levy, collection and application, to continue so long as such tax supported obligations are outstanding, without necessity for further appropriation notwithstanding Section 22 of Article II, Ohio Constitution; provided that the moneys referred to in Section 5a of Article XII, Ohio Constitution, herein called highway user receipts, shall, after provision for payment of amounts pledged to obligations heretofore or hereafter issued under Sections 2c and 2g of this Article, be pledged to the payment of the principal of and interest on highway obligations authorized by this section but not to other obligations authorized hereby. If excises and taxes other than highway user receipts are pledged to the payment of the principal of or interest on highway obligations authorized by this section, in each year that such highway user receipts are available for such purpose, the same shall be appropriated thereto and the required application of such other excises and taxes shall be reduced in corresponding amount.

The General Assembly also may authorize the issuance of revenue obligations and other obligations, the owners or holders of which are not given the right to have excises or taxes levied by the General Assembly for the payment of principal thereof or interest thereon, for such capital improvements for mental hygiene and retardation, parks and recreation, state supported and state assisted institutions of higher education, including those for technical education, water pollution control and abatement, water management, and housing of branches and agencies of state government, which obligations shall not be subject to other provisions of this section and shall not be deemed to be debts or bonded indebtedness of the state under other provisions of this constitution. Such obligations may be secured by a pledge under law, without necessity for further appropriation, of all or such portion as the General Assembly authorizes of charges for the treatment or care of mental hygiene and retardation patients, receipts with respect to parks and recreational facilities, receipts of or on behalf of state supported and state assisted institutions of higher education, or other revenues or receipts, specified by law for such purpose, of the state or its officers, departments, divisions, institutions, boards, commissions, authorities, or other state agencies or instrumentalities, and this provision may be implemented by law to better provide therefor; provided, however, that any charges for the treatment or care of mental hygiene or retardation patients may be so pledged only to obligations issued for capital improvements for mental hygiene and retardation, any receipts with respect to parks and recreation may be so pledged only to obligations issued for capital improvements for parks and recreation, any receipts of or on behalf of state supported or state assisted institutions of higher education may be pledged only to obligations issued for capital improvements for state supported or state assisted institutions of higher education, and any other revenues or receipts may be so pledged only to obligations issued for capital improvements which are in whole or in part useful to, constructed by, or financed by the department, board, commission, authority, or other agency or instrumentality that receives the revenues or receipts so pledged. The authority provided by this paragraph is in addition to, cumulative with, and not a limitation upon, the authority of the General Assembly under other provisions of this constitution; such paragraph does not impair any law heretofore enacted by the General Assembly, and any obligations issued under any such law consistent with the provisions of this paragraph shall be deemed to be issued under authority of this paragraph.

Both the principal of all obligations authorized under authority of this section and the interest thereon shall be exempt from taxation within this state.

Adopted in 1968, this section allowed the state to raise funds through the issuance of obligations, including bonds and notes, for a wide array of state capital improvements projects, including highway construction, water pollution controls and abatement, sewage treatment, research and development, higher education, and fire and police training. The section sets a $100 million cap as the maximum the state could generate through the issuance of obligations in any one calendar year with a $500 million ceiling on the obligations outstanding at any one time.

This section also allowed the General Assembly to pay off the debt without an appropriation beyond the two-year limit imposed on money drawn from the treasury under Article II, section 22, as long as highway user receipts under Article XII, section 5a, are available after payment of highway debt incurred under sections 2c and 2g of this article.

In addition to issuing general obligation debt, which is supported by the full faith and credit of the state, this section explicitly authorized the issuance of revenue bonds, sometimes referred to as lease-appropriation bonds, which are not supported by the full faith and credit of the state. Specifically, the fifth paragraph of this article authorizes the issuance of "revenue obligations and other obligations, the owners or holders of which are not given the right to have excises or taxes levied by the general assembly for the payment of principal thereof or interest thereon, for . . . capital improvements for mental hygiene and retardation, parks and recreation, and housing of branches and agencies of state government, which obligations . . . shall not be deemed to be debts or bonded indebtedness of the state under other provisions of this Constitution." In lieu of a pledge of the state's taxing power, payment of debt service on these obligations is legally "secured by a pledge under law, without necessity for further appropriation, of all or such portion as the general assembly authorizes of" any charges or other revenues or receipts that the state generates through the facilities that were financed with the debt. Notwithstanding this language, the actual source of payment of debt service on all obligations that have been issued for these purposes under this section has been two-year lease-rental appropriations made by the General Assembly in each biennial state budget.

Section 2j
Vietnam Conflict compensation.

The board of commissioners created by section 8 of Article VIII of the Ohio Constitution shall, forthwith upon the adoption of this amendment, proceed to issue and sell, from time to time, bonds or notes of the state in such amounts of face value as are necessary to provide the funds, or such part thereof, as may be required to pay the compensation and the expenses of administering this section. The aggregate face value of bonds or notes so issued shall not exceed three hundred million dollars. The full faith and credit of the state is hereby pledged for the payment of such bonds or notes.

All bonds or notes so issued shall mature in not more than fifteen years commencing not later than two years after the respective dates thereof. The bonds or notes shall mature according to schedules set forth by the commissioners but shall not mature more than fifteen years after the date of issue. No bonds or notes shall be issued or bear dates later than the first day of April, 1977.

All bonds or notes shall bear interest at such rates as the commissioners determine and shall be payable semiannually. Such bonds or notes, and the interest thereon are exempt from all taxes levied by the state or any taxing district thereof. At the option of the commissioners, the bonds or notes may be issued subject to call on any interest payment date at par and accrued interest.

All sales of such bonds or notes by the commissioners shall be in accordance with such regulations as the commission adopts and promulgates. Such bonds or notes shall be sold only to the highest bidder or bidders after notice of sale has been published once each week for three consecutive weeks on the same day of each week, the first of such notices being published at least twenty-one full days before the date of sale, in a newspaper of general circulation in each of the eight most populous counties in the state. Notices shall state the day, hour and place of the sale, the total face value of the bonds or notes to be sold, their denominations, dates, and the dates of their maturities, information relative to the rates of interest that the bonds or notes will bear, and the dates upon which interest will be payable. The commissioners may reject any or all bids and re-advertise and re-offer bonds or notes for sale.

Out of the proceeds of the sale of all bonds or notes, that amount that represents accrued interest, if any, shall be paid into the state treasury into a fund to be known as the Vietnam Conflict Compensation Bond Retirement Fund, and the balance shall be paid into the state treasury into a fund to be known as the Vietnam Conflict Compensation Fund. The General Assembly may appropriate and cause to be paid into the Vietnam Conflict Compensation Bond Retirement Fund or the Vietnam Conflict Compensation Fund, out of the funds in the treasury not otherwise appropriated, such amount as is proper for use, upon order of the commissioners for the purposes for which such funds are created. If the General Assembly appropriates any funds to the Vietnam Conflict Compensation Fund prior to the time the commissioners have issued bonds or notes of the aggregate amount of face value authorized in this section, the aggregate amount of face value of bonds or notes so authorized to be issued shall be reduced by the amount of the funds so appropriated.

On or before the first day of July in each calendar year, the commissioners shall certify to the auditor of state the total amount of funds it determines is necessary to provide, together with all other money that will be available in the Vietnam Conflict Compensation Bond Retirement Fund, for the retirement of bonds or notes and the payment of interest in the ensuing calendar year. The auditor of state shall transfer from the state general revenue fund to the Vietnam Conflict Compensation Bond Retirement Fund, without appropriation, an amount equal to the amount so certified. The Vietnam Conflict Compensation Bond Retirement Fund shall be paid out without appropriation by the General Assembly, upon the order of the commissioners for the purpose of the payment, or retirement in other manner, of said bonds or notes and interest thereon.

The Vietnam Conflict Compensation Fund shall be paid out upon order of the commissioners, without appropriation by the General Assembly, in payment of the expenses of administering this section, and as compensation as follows: every person, except persons ordered to active duty for training only, who has served on active duty in the armed forces of the United States at any time between August 5, 1964 and July 1, 1973, or who has served on active duty in the armed forces of the United States in Vietnam service, and who, at the time of commencing such service, was and had been a resident of the state for at least one year immediately preceding the commencement of such service, and (1) who was separated from such service under honorable conditions, (2) who is still in such service, or (3) who has been retired, is entitled to receive compensation of ten dollars for each month during which such person was in active domestic service during the compensable period, fifteen dollars for each month during which such person was in active foreign service, but not Vietnam service, during the compensable period, and twenty dollars for each month during which such person was in active Vietnam service. The maximum amount of cash payable to any qualified applicant, unless such applicant qualifies for a payment based upon missing in action or prisoner of war status or unless such applicant qualifies for a survivor's payment, is five hundred dollars. No compensation shall be paid under this section to any person who received from another state a bonus or compensation of a like nature or to any person who has not served on active duty in the armed forces of the United States during the compensable period for at least ninety days unless active duty within such compensable period was terminated as a result of injuries or illness sustained in Vietnam service. Compensation for a fraction of a month of service shall be paid on the basis of one-thirtieth of the appropriate monthly amounts for each day of such service. Persons medically discharged or medically retired from service due to combat related disabilities sustained in Vietnam service shall be paid five hundred dollars. Service in the Merchant Marine of the United States shall not be considered for the purpose of this section. As used in this section "domestic service" means service within the territorial limits of the fifty states, excluding sea duty; "foreign service" means service in all other places, excluding Vietnam service; and "Vietnam service" means military service within the Republic of Vietnam during the period between February 28, 1961 through July 1, 1973 or military service in southeast Asia for which hostile fire pay was awarded pursuant to Title 37, Section 310, United States Code, during the period February 28, 1961 through July 1, 1973.

No compensation shall be paid under this section to any person for any periods of time spent under penal confinement during the period of active duty.

Either the surviving spouse, or the surviving child or children, or the surviving parents, including persons standing in loco parentis for one year preceding commencement of service in the armed forces of the United States, of a deceased person shall be paid the same amount of compensation that the deceased would have been entitled to receive under this section, if living. If such deceased person's death is determined by the Veterans Administration of the United States to have been the result of injuries or illness sustained in Vietnam service his survivors as herein designated, are entitled to one thousand dollars, regardless of the amount of compensation which the deceased would have been entitled to receive under this section, if living. The amount of compensation payable to such survivors shall be payable only to one of the three groups of survivors herein designated in the order in which said groups are named.

Every person designated by the United States Department of Defense as missing in action as a result of honorable service or as held in enemy captivity or who is the spouse, or the child, or the parent, including persons standing in loco parentis for one year preceding commencement of service, of a person designated by the Department of Defense as missing in action as a result of honorable service or held in enemy captivity, is entitled to one thousand dollars in lieu of other cash benefits payable under this section. The amount of compensation payable to such claimants for such missing or captive person shall be payable only to one of the groups of claimants herein designated in the order in which said groups are named. No payment to any survivor of a person designated as missing in action as a result of honorable service or held in enemy captivity, while such person is held captive or is missing in action, shall prevent such missing or captive person from claiming and receiving a bonus of an equal amount upon his being released or located.

The General Assembly shall provide by law for an educational assistance bonus which may be taken in lieu of the cash bonus by any person who served on active duty in the armed forces of the United States and who qualifies for a cash bonus under this section. The educational assistance bonus shall offer financial assistance at any educational institution deemed appropriate by the General Assembly. Such financial assistance shall be equal to twice the amount of the cash bonus for which such person qualifies under this section.

No sale or assignment of any right or claim to compensation under this section shall be valid, no claims of creditors shall be enforceable against rights or claims to or payments of compensation under this section, and no fees shall be charged for services in connection with the prosecution of any right or claim to compensation or the collection of any compensation under this section.

The commissioners shall have complete charge of making payments of the compensation provided for in this section and shall adopt and promulgate regulations governing their procedure in connection therewith, including determinations as to who are proper beneficiaries and the amounts to which such beneficiaries are entitled, determinations as to whether an applicant has the necessary residence requirements, and such other regulations that are necessary and proper. All applications for payment of compensation or educational bonuses under this section shall be made to the commissioners before January 1, 1978.

The commissioners shall select and appoint such legal counsel and employees as are necessary, fix their compensation and prescribe their duties, and all such appointees shall serve at its pleasure. When practical, the commissioners shall employ Vietnam veterans to fill such positions.

The commissioners shall permit review of individual records of claims by representatives of recognized veterans organizations when authorized to do so by the applicant.

There is hereby transferred to the Vietnam Conflict Compensation Fund, for the purpose of defraying the immediate cost of administration and compensation, out of the funds known as the "Korean Conflict Compensation Fund" and the "Korean Conflict Compensation Bond Retirement Fund" created by Section 2d of Article VIII of the Ohio Constitution, the balance remaining after provision for payment of all outstanding bonds or notes, coupons, and charges.

The people of this state declare it to be their intention to in no manner affect or change any of the existing provisions of the constitution except as herein set forth. The provisions of this section shall be self executing.

Upon payment of all valid claims for cash compensation made within the limitations of time as prescribed herein, the commissioners may transfer any funds in the Vietnam Conflict Compensation Fund to the Vietnam Conflict Compensation Bond Retirement Fund.

Upon retirement of all of the bonds or notes that may be issued hereunder and the payment of all valid claims for cash compensation made within the limitations of time as prescribed herein, the commissioners of the sinking fund shall make a final report to the General Assembly, and any balance remaining in any of the funds herein created and referred to shall be disposed of as shall be provided by law.

Adopted in 1973, this section requires the sale of bonds and other obligations to create a compensation fund for Vietnam Conflict veterans and their survivors. To be eligible under this section, Vietnam veterans had to have served on active duty between August 5, 1964, and July 1, 1973, in the Republic of Vietnam or in hostile areas of Southeast Asia. The initial administrative costs of the fund were to be covered from the remaining balancing of the Korean Conflict funds created by section 2d, and the remaining revenues were to be raised through the sale of up to $300 million dollars in bonds and other obligations. No bonds were to be issued after April 1977, and all applications for compensation had to be filed by January 1, 1978. As with the other amendments creating funds for war veterans and their survivors, compensation was not available for veterans who served in the Merchant Marine, were confined in penal institutions, or were dishonorably discharged.

Section 2k

Bonds for local government public infrastructure capital improvements.

(A) In addition to the authorization otherwise contained in Article VIII of the Ohio Constitution, the General Assembly may provide by law, in accordance with but subject to the limitations of this section, for the issuance of bonds and other obligations of the state for the purpose of financing or assisting in the financing of the cost of public infrastructure capital improvements of municipal corporations, counties, townships, and other governmental entities as designated by law. As used in this section, public infrastructure capital improvements shall be limited to roads and bridges, waste water treatment systems, water supply systems, solid waste disposal facilities and storm water and sanitary collection, storage, and treatment facilities, including real property, interests in real property, facilities, and equipment related or incidental thereto. Capital improvements shall include without limitation the cost of acquisition, construction, reconstruction, expansion, improvement, planning, and equipping.

It is hereby determined that such public infrastructure capital improvements are necessary to preserve and expand the public capital infrastructure of such municipal corporations, counties, townships, and other governmental entities, ensure the public health, safety, and welfare, create and preserve jobs, enhance employment opportunities, and improve the economic welfare of the people of this state.

(B)(1) Not more than one hundred twenty million dollars principal amount of bonds and other obligations authorized under this section may be issued in any calendar year, provided that the aggregate total principal amount of bonds and other obligations authorized and issued under this section may not exceed one billion two hundred million dollars. Further limitations may be provided by law upon the amount of bonds that may be issued under this section in any year in order that the total debt charges of the state shall not exceed a proportion of general revenue fund expenditures that would adversely affect the credit rating of the state. If obligations are issued under this section to retire or refund obligations previously issued under this section, the new obligations shall not be counted against those calendar year or total issuance limitations to the extent that their principal amount does not exceed the principal amount of the obligations to be retired or refunded.

(2) Provision shall be made by law for the use to the extent practicable of Ohio products, materials, services, and labor in the making of any project financed, in whole or in part, under this section.

(C) The state may participate in any public infrastructure capital improvement under this section with municipal corporations, counties, townships, or other governmental entities, or any one or more of them. Such participation may be by grants, loans, or contributions to them for any of such capital improvements. The entire proceeds of the bonds shall be used for the public infrastructure capital improvements of municipal corporations, counties, townships, and other governmental entities, except to the extent that the General Assembly provides by law that the state may be reasonably compensated from such moneys for planning, financial management, or other administrative services performed in relation to the bond issuance.

(D) (1) Each issue of obligations issued under this section shall mature in not more than thirty years from the date of issuance, or, if issued to retire or refund other obligations issued under this section, within thirty years from the date the debt was originally contracted. If obligations are issued as notes in anticipation of the issuance of bonds, provision shall be made by law for the establishment and maintenance, during the period in which the notes are outstanding, of a special fund or funds into which shall be paid, from the sources authorized for the payment of such bonds, the amount that would have been sufficient, if bonds maturing during a period of thirty years had been issued without such prior issuance of notes, to pay the principal that would have been payable on such bonds during such period. Such fund or funds shall be used solely for the payment of principal of such notes or of bonds in anticipation of which such notes have been issued.

(2) The obligations issued under this section are general obligations of the state. The full faith and credit, revenue, and taxing power of the state shall be pledged to the payment of the principal of and interest on such obligations as they become due hereinafter called debt service, and bond retirement fund provisions shall be made for payment of debt service. Provision shall be made by law for the sufficiency and appropriation, for purposes of paying debt service, of excises, taxes, and revenues so pledged to debt service, and for covenants to continue the levy, collection, and application of sufficient excises, taxes, and revenues to the extent needed for such purpose. Notwithstanding Section 22 of Article II, Ohio Constitution, no further act of appropriation shall be necessary for that purpose. The obligations and the provision for the payment of debt service and repayment of any loans hereunder by governmental entities are not subject to Sections 5, 6, and 11 of Article XII Ohio Constitution.

(3) The moneys referred to in Section 5a of Article XII, Ohio Constitution, may not be pledged to the payment of debt service on obligations issued under authority of this section.

(4) The obligations issued under authority of this section, the transfer thereof, and the interest and other income therefrom, including any profit made on the sale thereof, shall at all times be free from taxation within the state.

(E) This section shall otherwise be implemented in the manner and to the extent provided by law by the General Assembly.

Adopted in 1987, this section was another amendment used to raise revenue for capital improvements to state and local infrastructures. This section permits the General Assembly to raise not more than $120 million per calendar year, and it provides that the total debt could not exceed $1.2 billion with the condition that all obligations must mature within thirty years.

As with the 1965 *Brand*-fix amendment, see Commentary, Article VIII, section 13, this amendment specifically overrode the Article XII, section 6 prohibition on incurring debt for internal improvements. Moreover, since this section authorized the issuance of general obligation bonds and allowed for their repayment through tax increases, it expressly exempted repayment of the debt from the Article XII, section 5, requirement that new tax laws state their objectives and from the Article XII, section 11, requirement that the General Assembly ensure that there are sufficient taxes to cover annual interest and principal payments on bonds issued and that a sinking fund be provided for the final redemption at maturity of these bonds.

The exemptions from the requirements of Article XII, sections 6 (internal improvements) and 11 (sinking funds), have become standard provisions in debt-authorizing amendments and are in almost all post-1987 debt-authorizing amendments to this article. See Article VIII, section 2l, 2m, 2o, 2p, 2q, 2s, 13, 14, 15, and 16, and Commentaries.

The exemption from Article XII, section 5 (stating objectives of state tax laws) first appeared in this section, and the exemption is also in Article VIII, sections 2l, 2m, 2p, 2s. See Commentaries thereon.

Notwithstanding Article II, section 22 (requiring appropriations of no more than two years), this section provides that no further act of appropriation is necessary to pay the debt service for bonds issued under this section.

This section provides that highway user receipts may not be used to pay off bonds issued under it. See Article XII, section 5a, and Commentary.

This section also provides that debt authorized under it is in addition to debt authorized by this article, presumably the $750,000 debt ceiling in section 1 and the lending-of-credit limitations in sections 4 and 6.

Finally, this section also requires that to the extent practicable Ohio products, materials, services, and labor be used in the making of any projects financed in whole or in part under this section. This is the first use of such a "state products" provision, and similar provisions are in sections 2l, 2m, 2p, and 2s of this article.

Section 2l

Bonds for capital improvements for state and local parks, for land and water recreation facilities, and for preservation of natural resources.

(A) In addition to the authorizations otherwise contained in Article VIII of the Ohio Constitution, the General Assembly shall provide by law, in accordance with and subject to the limitations of this section, for the issuance of bonds and other obligations of the state for the purpose of financing or assisting in the financing of the costs of capital improvements for state and local parks and land

and water recreation facilities; soil and water restoration and protection; land management including preservation of natural areas and reforestation; water management including dam safety, stream and lake management, and flood control and flood damage reduction, fish and wildlife resource management; and other projects that enhance the use and enjoyment of natural resources by individuals. Capital improvements include without limitation the cost of acquisition, construction, reconstruction, expansion, improvement, planning, and equipping.

It is hereby determined that these capital improvements and provisions for them are necessary and appropriate to improve the quality of life of the people of this state, to better ensure the public health, safety, and welfare, and to create and preserve jobs and enhance employment opportunities.

(B)(1) Not more than fifty million dollars principal amount of obligations may be issued under this section in any fiscal year, and not more than two hundred million dollars principal amount may be outstanding at any one time. The limitations of this paragraph do not apply to any obligations authorized to be issued under this section to retire or refund obligations previously issued under this section, to the extent that their principal amount does not exceed the principal amount of the obligations to be retired or refunded.

(2) Each issue of obligations shall mature in not more than twenty-five years from the date of issuance, or, if issued to retire or refund other obligations issued under this section, within twenty-five years from the date the debt was originally contracted. If obligations are issued as bond anticipation notes, provision shall be made, by law or in the proceedings for the issuance of those notes, for the establishment and maintenance while the notes are outstanding of a special fund or funds into which there shall be paid, from the sources authorized for the payment of the bonds, the amount that would have been sufficient, if bonds maturing serially in each year over a period of twenty-five years had been issued without the prior issuance of the notes, to pay the principal that would have been payable on those bonds during that period; such fund or funds shall be used solely for the payment of principal of those notes or of the bonds anticipated.

(C) The state may participate by grants or contributions in financing capital improvements under this section made by local government entities. Of the proceeds of the first two hundred million dollars principal amount in obligations issued under this section for capital improvements, at least twenty per cent shall be allocated to grants or contributions to local government entities for such capital improvements.

(D) The obligations issued under this section are general obligations of the state. The full faith and credit, revenue, and taxing power of the state shall be pledged to the payment of the principal of and interest and other accreted amounts on those obligations as they become due, and bond retirement fund provisions shall be made for payment of that debt service. Provision shall be made by law for the sufficiency and appropriation for purposes of paying that debt service, of excises, taxes, and revenues so pledged to that debt service, and for covenants to continue the levy, collection, and application of sufficient excises, taxes, and revenues to the extent needed for that purpose. Notwithstanding Section 22 of Article II, Ohio Constitution, no further act of appropriation shall be necessary for that purpose. The moneys referred to in section 5a of Article XII, Ohio Constitution, may not be pledged to the payment of that debt service. The obligations and the provisions for the payment of debt service on them are not subject to Sections 5, 6, and 11 of Article XII Ohio Constitution, and, with respect to the purposes to which their proceeds are to be applied, are not subject to sections 4 and 6 of Article VIII, Ohio Constitution.

(E) Obligations issued under authority of this section, the transfer thereof, and the interest and other income and accreted amounts therefrom, including any profit made on the sale thereof, shall at all times be free from taxation within the state.

(F) This section shall be implemented in the manner and to the extent provided by law by the General Assembly.

Adopted in 1993, this section authorizes the issuance of bonds and other obligations to finance capital improvements for state and local parks and land and water recreation facilities; soil and water restoration and protection; land management including preservation of natural areas and reforestation; water management including dam safety, stream and lake management, and flood control and flood damage reduction, fish and wildlife resource management; and other projects that enhance the use and enjoyment of natural resources by individuals.

This section contains a statement of purpose that these capital improvements are necessary and appropriate to improve the quality of life of the people of Ohio, to ensure public health, safety, and welfare, and to enhance employment opportunities

Similar to section 2i, this section limited the outstanding debt that the state could incur at any one time to $250 million. This section also required the state to allocate, through grants or other contributions, at least 25 percent of the first $200 million to local governments for capital improvement projects authorized under this section.

Significantly, the section exempts the bonds issued pursuant to its authority from operation of other constitutional provisions that limit the amount of general obligation debt, or that limit the state's ability to enter into cooperative financial arrangements with private enterprise or local government. Thus, sections 4 and 6 of Article VIII do not apply to debt issued under this section to finance or assist in financing the costs of capital improvements for state and local parks and land and water recreation facilities under this section.

This section also provides that the debt service on bonds issued under its authority is not subject to the requirements of Article XII, sections 5, 6, and 11, see Commentaries thereon, and that the highway user receipts under Article XII, section 5a may not be used to pay off bonds issued under it.

Notwithstanding Article II, section 22 (requiring appropriations of no more than two years), this section provides that no further act of appropriation is necessary to pay the debt service for bonds issued under this section.

Section 2m

Bonds for public infrastructure capital improvement.

(A) In addition to the authorizations otherwise contained in Article VIII of the Ohio Constitution, the General Assembly may provide by law, in accordance with but subject to the limitations of this section, for the issuance of bonds and other obligations of the state for the purpose of financing or assisting in the financing of the cost of public infrastructure capital improvements of municipal corporations, counties, townships, and other governmental entities as designated by law, and the cost of highway capital improvements. As used in this section, public infrastructure capital improvements shall be limited to roads and bridges, waste water treatment systems, water supply systems, solid waste disposal facilities, and storm water and sanitary collection, storage, and treatment facilities, including real property, interests in real property, facilities, and equipment related to or incidental thereto, and shall include without limitation the cost of acquisition, construction, reconstruction, expansion, improvement, planning, and equipping. As used in this section, highway capital improvements shall be limited to highways, including those on the state highway system and urban extensions thereof, those within or leading to public parks or recreation areas, and those within or leading to municipal corporations, and shall include without limitation the cost of acquisition, construction, reconstruction, expansion, improvement, planning, and equipping.

It is hereby determined that such public infrastructure capital improvements and highway capital improvements are necessary to preserve and expand the public capital infrastructure of the state and its municipal corporations, counties, townships, and other governmental entities, ensure the public health, safety, and welfare, create and preserve jobs, enhance employment opportunities, and improve the economic welfare of the people of this state.

(B) Not more than one hundred twenty million dollars principal amount of the infrastructure obligations authorized to be issued under this section, plus the principal amount of infrastructure obligations that in any prior fiscal years could have been but were not issued within the one hundred twenty million dollar fiscal year limit, may be issued in any fiscal year, provided that the aggregate total principal amount of infrastructure obligations issued under this section for public infrastructure capital improvements may not exceed one billion two hundred million dollars; and provided further that no infrastructure obligations shall be issued pursuant to this section until at least one billion one hundred ninety-nine million five hundred thousand dollars aggregate principal amount of obligations have been issued pursuant to Section 2k of Article VIII. Not more than two hundred twenty million dollars principal amount of highway obligations authorized to be issued under this section, plus the principal amount of highway obligations that in any prior fiscal years could have been but were not issued within the two-hundred-twenty-million-dollar fiscal year limit, may be issued in any fiscal year, and not more than one billion two hundred million dollars principal amount of highway obligations issued under this section may be outstanding at any one time. Further limitations may be provided by law upon the amount of infrastructure obligations and highway obligations, hereinafter collectively called obligations, that may be issued under this section in any fiscal year in order that the total debt charges of the state payable from the general revenue fund shall not exceed a proportion of general revenue fund expenditures that would adversely affect the credit rating of the state. If obligations are issued under this section to retire or refund obligations previously issued under this section, the new obligations shall not be counted against those fiscal year or total issuance limitations to the extent that their principal amount does not exceed the principal amount of the obligations to be retired or refunded.

Provision shall be made by law for the use to the extent practicable of Ohio products, materials, services, and labor in the making of any project financed, in whole or in part, under this section.

(C) The state may participate in any public infrastructure capital improvement or highway capital improvement under this section with municipal corporations, counties, townships, or other governmental entities as designated by law, or any one or more of them. Such participation may be by grants, loans, or contributions to them for any such capital improvements. The entire proceeds of the infrastructure obligations shall be used for public infrastructure capital improvements of municipal corporations, counties, townships, and other governmental entities, except to the extent that the General Assembly provides by law that the state may reasonably be compensated from such moneys for planning, financial management, or administrative services performed in relation to the issuance of infrastructure obligations.

(D) Each issue of obligations shall mature in not more than thirty years from the date of issuance, or, if issued to retire or refund other obligations, within thirty years from the date the debt originally was contracted. If obligations are issued as notes in anticipation of the issuance of bonds, provision shall be made by law for the establishment and maintenance, during the period in which the notes are outstanding, of a special fund or funds into which shall be paid, from the sources authorized for the payment of such bonds, the amount that would have been sufficient, if bonds maturing during a period of thirty years had been issued without such prior issuance of notes, to pay the principal that would have been payable on such bonds during such period. Such fund or funds shall be used solely for the payment of principal of such notes or bonds in anticipation of which such notes have been issued.

The obligations are general obligations of the state. The full faith and credit, revenue, and taxing power of the state shall be pledged to the payment of the principal of and premium and interest and other accreted amounts on outstanding obligations as they become due, hereinafter called debt service, and bond retirement fund provisions shall be made for payment of debt service. Provision shall be made by law for the sufficiency and appropriation, for purposes of paying debt service, of excises, taxes, and revenues so pledged to debt service, and for covenants to continue the levy, collection, and application of sufficient excises, taxes, and revenues to the extent needed for such purpose. Notwithstanding Section 22 of Article II, Ohio Constitution, no further act of appropriation shall be necessary for that purpose. The obligations and the provision for the payment of debt service, and repayment by governmental entities of any loans made under this section are not subject to Sections 5, 6, and 11 of Article XII, Ohio Constitution.

The moneys referred to in Section 5a of Article XII, Ohio Constitution may be pledged to the payment of debt service on highway obligations, but may not be pledged to the payment of debt service on infrastructure obligations. In each year that moneys referred to in Section 5a of Article XII, Ohio Constitution pledged to the payment of debt service on highway obligation issued under this section are available for such purpose, such moneys shall be appropriated thereto and the required application of any other excises and taxes shall be reduced in corresponding amount. The obligations issued under authority of this section, the transfer thereof, and the interest, interest equivalent, and other income and accreted amounts therefrom, including any profit made on the sale, exchange, or other disposition thereof, shall at all times be free from taxation within the state.

(E) This section shall otherwise be implemented in the manner and to the extent provided by law by the General Assembly, including provision for the procedure for incurring and issuing obligations, separately or in combination with other state obligations, and refunding, retiring, and evidencing obligations.

(F) The authorizations in this section are in addition to authorizations contained in other sections of Article VIII, Ohio Constitution, are in addition to and not a limitation upon the authority of the General Assembly under other provisions of this constitution, and do not impair any law previously enacted by the General Assembly, except that after December 31, 1996, no additional highway obligation of the state may be issued for any highway purposes under Section 2I of Article VIII, Ohio Constitution, except to refund highway obligations issued under Section 2i that are outstanding on that date.

Adopted in 1995, this section is an updated and modified version of section 2k, which had allowed $1.2 billion to be raised to improve the state and local infrastructure and capital improvement projects (at the rate of not more than $120 million per calendar year) with all obligations required to mature within thirty years

Under section 2m, the state may raise an additional $1.2 billion from bonds and other obligations for state and local infrastructure and capital improvement projects, but the state is prohibited from issuing any new obligations until bonds and notes totaling at least $1,199,500,000 have been issued under section 2k.

As with section 2k, this section provides for the issuance of bonds and other obligations to finance public infrastructure capital improvements of municipal corporations, counties, townships, and other governmental entities, and for highway capital improvements. The section defines "public infrastructure capital improvements" as being limited to roads and bridges, wastewater treatment and water supply systems, solid waste disposal facilities, and storm water and sanitary collection, storage, and treatment facilities, including costs related to real property, facilities, and equipment.

This section provides that the debt service on bonds issued under its authority is not subject to the requirements of Article XII, sections 5 and 11. See Commentaries thereon.

Notwithstanding Article II, section 22 (requiring appropriations of no more than two years), this section provides that no further act of appropriation is necessary to pay the debt service for bonds issued under this section

Under this section, however, highway user receipts under Article XII, section 5a, may be pledged to the payment of debt service on highway obligations, but may not be pledged to the payment of debt service on infrastructure obligations.

This section also requires the use, where practicable, of Ohio products, materials, services, and labor for projects financed in whole or in part under this section.

Section 2n

Bonds for facilities for common schools and state-supported and state-assisted institutions of higher education.

(A) The General Assembly may provide by law, subject to the limitations of and in accordance with this section, for the issuance of bonds and other obligations of the state for the purpose of paying costs of facilities for a system of common schools throughout the state and facilities for state-supported and state-assisted institutions of higher education. As used in this section, "costs" includes, without limitation, the costs of acquisition, construction, improvement, expansion, planning, and equipping.

(B) Each obligation issued under this section shall mature no later than the thirty-first day of December of the twenty-fifth calendar year after its issuance except that obligations issued to refund other obligations shall mature not later than the thirty-first day of December of the twenty-fifth calendar year after the year in which the original obligation to pay was issued or entered into.

(C) Obligations issued under this section are general obligations of the state. The full faith and credit, revenue, and taxing power of the state shall be pledged to the payment of debt service on those outstanding obligations as it becomes due. For purposes of the full and timely payment of that debt service, appropriate provisions shall be made or authorized by law for bond retirement funds, for the sufficiency and appropriation of excises, taxes, and revenues so pledged to that debt service, for which purpose, notwithstanding Section 22 of Article II of the Ohio Constitution, no further act of appropriation shall be necessary, and for covenants to continue the levy, collection, and application of sufficient excises, taxes, and revenues to the extent needed for that purpose. Those obligations and the provisions for the payment of debt service on them are not subject to Sections 5, 6, and 11 of Article XII of the Ohio Constitution.

Moneys referred to in Section 5a of Article XII of the Ohio Constitution may not be pledged or used for the payment of the debt service on those obligations. Moneys consisting of net state lottery proceeds may be pledged or used for payment of debt service on obligations issued under this section to pay costs of facilities for a system of common schools, but not on obligations issued under this section to pay costs of facilities for state-supported and state-assisted institutions of higher education. In the case of the issuance of any of those obligations as bond anticipation notes, provision shall be made by law or in the bond or note proceedings for the establishment and the maintenance, during the period the notes are outstanding, of special funds into which there shall be paid, from the sources authorized for payment of the bonds anticipated, the amount that would have been sufficient to pay the principal that would have been payable on those bonds during that period if bonds maturing serially in each year over the maximum period of maturity referred to in division (B) of this section had been issued without the prior issuance of the notes. Those special funds and investment income on them shall be used solely for the payment of principal of those notes or of the bonds anticipated.

(D) As used in this section, "debt service" means principal and interest and other accreted amounts payable on the obligations referred to.

(E) Obligations issued under this section, their transfer, and the interest, interest equivalent, and other income or accreted amounts on them, including any profit made on their sale, exchange, or other disposition, shall at all times be free from taxation within the state.

(F) This section shall be implemented in the manner and to the extent provided by the General Assembly by law, including provision for the procedure for incurring, refunding, retiring, and evidencing obligations issued as referred to in this section. The total principal amount of obligations issued under this section shall be as determined by the General Assembly, subject to the limitation provided for in Section 17 of this article.

(G) The authorizations in this section are in addition to authorizations contained in other sections of this article, are in addition to and not a limitation upon the authority of the General Assembly under other provisions of this Constitution, and do not impair any law previously enacted by the General Assembly.

Adopted in 1999 in the wake of the Ohio Supreme Court's first decision in *DeRolph v. State* (1997), holding unconstitutional the state's system of financing public schools, see Commentary, Article VI, section 2, this section authorized the General Assembly to issue general obligation bonds and notes to improve the facilities of Ohio's primary and secondary schools and its state-supported and state-assisted institutions of higher education.

There is no fixed dollar amount of debt that can be raised under this section, and the amount is to be determined by the General Assembly, subject to the 5 percent limitation provided in section 17, which was adopted by voters as part of the same amendment. See Commentary, Article VIII, section 17.

This section provides that the debt service on bonds issued under its authority is not subject to the requirements of Article XII, sections 5, 6, and 11, see Commentaries thereon, and that the highway user receipts under Article XII, section 5a may not be used to pay off bonds issued under it. See Commentary, Article XII, section 5a.

Notwithstanding Article II, section 22 (requiring appropriations of no more than two years), this section provides that no further act of appropriation is necessary to pay the debt service for bonds issued under this section.

Section 2o
Bonds for environmental conservation and revitalization.

(A) It is determined and confirmed that the environmental and related conservation, preservation, and revitalization purposes referred to in divisions (A)(1) and (2) of this section, and provisions for them, are proper public purposes of the state and local governmental entities and are necessary and appropriate means to improve the quality of life and the general and economic-well being of the people of this state; to better ensure the public health, safety, and welfare; to protect water and other natural resources; to provide for the conservation and preservation of natural and open areas and farmlands, including by making urban areas more desirable or suitable for development and revitalization; to control, prevent, minimize, clean up, or remediate certain contamination of or pollution from lands in the state and water contamination or pollution; to provide for safe and productive urban land use or reuse; to enhance the availability, public use, and enjoyment of natural areas and resources; and to create and preserve jobs and enhance employment opportunities. Those purposes are:

(1) Conservation purposes, meaning conservation and preservation of natural areas, open spaces, and farmlands and other lands devoted to agriculture, including by acquiring land or interests therein; provision of state and local park and recreation facilities, and other actions that permit and enhance the availability, public use, and enjoyment of natural areas and open spaces in Ohio; and land, forest, water, and other natural resource management projects;

(2) Revitalization purposes, meaning providing for and enabling the environmentally safe and productive development and use or reuse of publicly and privately owned lands, including those within urban areas, by the remediation or clean up, or planning and assessment for remediation or clean up, of contamination, or addressing, by clearance, land acquisition or assembly, infrastructure, or otherwise, that or other property conditions or circumstances that may be deleterious to the public health and safety and the environment and water and other natural resources, or that preclude or inhibit environmentally sound or economic use or reuse of the property.

(B) The General Assembly may provide by law, subject to the limitations of and in accordance with this section, for the issuance of bonds and other obligations of the state for the purpose of paying costs of projects implementing those purposes.

(1) Not more than two hundred million dollars principal amount of obligations issued under this section for conservation purposes may be outstanding in accordance with their terms at any one time. Not more than fifty million dollars principal amount of those obligations, plus the principal amount of those obligations that in any prior fiscal year could have been but were not issued within the fifty-million-dollar fiscal year limit, may be issued in any fiscal year. Those obligations shall be general obligations of the state and the full faith and credit, revenue, and taxing power of the state shall be pledged to the payment of debt service on them as it becomes due, all as provided in this section.

(2) Not more than two hundred million dollars principal amount of obligations issued under this section for revitalization purposes may be outstanding in accordance with their terms at any one time. Not more than fifty million dollars principal amount of those obligations, plus the principal amount of those obligations that in any prior fiscal year could have been but were not issued within the fifty-million-dollar fiscal year limit, may be issued in any fiscal year. Those obligations shall not be general obligations of the state and the full faith and credit, revenue, and taxing power of the state shall not be pledged to the payment of debt service on them. Those obligations shall be secured by a pledge of all or such portion of designated revenues and receipts of the state as the General Assembly authorizes, including receipts from designated taxes or excises, other state revenues from sources other than state taxes or excises, such as from state enterprise activities, and payments for or related to those revitalization purposes made by or on behalf of local governmental entities, responsible parties, or others. The General Assembly shall provide by law for prohibitions or restrictions on the granting or lending of proceeds of obligations issued under division (B)(2) of this section to parties to pay costs of cleanup or remediation of contamination for which they are determined to be responsible.

(C) For purposes of the full and timely payment of debt service on state obligations authorized by this section, appropriate provision shall be made or authorized by law for bond retirement funds, for the sufficiency and appropriation of state excises, taxes, and revenues pledged to the debt service on the respective obligations, for which purpose, notwithstanding Section 22 of Article II of the Ohio Constitution, no further act of appropriation shall be necessary, and for covenants to continue the levy, collection, and application of sufficient state excises, taxes, and revenues to the extent needed for those purposes. Moneys referred to in Section 5a of Article XII of the Ohio Constitution may not be pledged or used for the payment of debt service on those obligations. As used in this section, "debt service" means principal and interest and other accreted amounts payable on the obligations referred to.

(D) (1) Divisions (B) and (C) of this section shall be implemented in the manner and to the extent provided by the General Assembly by law, including provision for procedures for incurring, refunding, retiring, and evidencing state obligations issued pursuant to this section. Each state obligation issued pursuant to this section shall mature no later than the thirty-first day of December of the twenty-fifth calendar year after its issuance, except that obligations issued to refund or retire other obligations shall mature not later than the thirty-first day of December of the twenty-fifth calendar year after the year in which the original obligation to pay was issued or entered into.

(2) In the case of the issuance of state obligations under this section as bond anticipation notes, provision shall be made by law or in the bond or note proceedings for the establishment, and the maintenance during the period the notes are outstanding, of special funds into which there shall be paid, from the sources authorized for payment of the particular bonds anticipated, the amount that would have been sufficient to pay the principal that would have been payable on those bonds during that period if bonds maturing serially in each year over the maximum period of maturity referred to in division (D)(1) of this section had been issued without the prior issuance of the notes. Those special funds and investment income on them shall be used solely for the payment of principal of those notes or of the bonds anticipated.

(E) In addition to projects undertaken by the state, the state may participate or assist, by grants, loans, loan guarantees, or contributions, in the financing of projects for purposes referred to in this section that are undertaken by local governmental entities or by others, including, but not limited to, not-for-profit organizations, at the direction or authorization of local governmental entities. Obligations of the state issued under this section and the provisions for payment of debt service on them, including any payments by local governmental entities, are not subject to Sections 6 and 11 of Article XII of the Ohio Constitution. Those obligations, and obligations of local governmental entities issued for the public purposes referred to in this section, and provisions for payment of debt service on them, and the purposes and uses to which the proceeds of those state or local obligations, or moneys from other sources, are to be or may be applied, are not subject to Sections 4 and 6 of Article VIII of the Ohio Constitution.

(F) The powers and authority granted or confirmed by and under this section, and the determinations and confirmations in this section, are independent of, in addition to, and not in derogation of or a limitation on, powers, authority, determinations, or confirmations under laws, charters, ordinances, or resolutions, or by or under other provisions of the Ohio Constitution including, without limitation, Section 36 of Article II, Sections 2i, 2l, 2m, and 13 of Article VIII, and Articles X and XVIII, and do not impair any previously adopted provision of the Ohio Constitution or any law previously enacted by the General Assembly.

(G) Obligations issued under this section, their transfer, and the interest, interest equivalent, and other income or accreted amounts on them, including any profit made on their sale, exchange, or other disposition, shall at all times be free from taxation within the state.

Adopted in 2000, this section allows the General Assembly to issue bonds and other obligations for the conservation and preservation of natural areas, open spaces, farmlands, state and local parks, and recreation facilities to enhance the availability, public use, and enjoyment of natural areas and open spaces.

This section also permits the General Assembly to incur debt for the "revitalization" of contaminated public and private lands, including abandoned or underused commercial and industrial facilities.

This section limits the principal amount of debt that the state can incur at any one time to $200 million for conservation purposes and $200 million for revitalization purposes under this section. Bonds and notes used for conservation under this section are backed by the full faith and credit of the state, but bonds and notes used for revitalization purposes are not and must be secured by revenues and receipts as provided by the General Assembly. In both cases, the obligations must mature in twenty-five years or less.

Under this section, the state may provide grants, loans, or other support to finance projects undertaken by local government, or by nonprofit organizations at the direction of local government. To accomplish this, the section overrides the prohibitions against lending aid or credit to private entities in Article VIII, sections 4 and 6.

This section also provides that the debt service on bonds issued under its authority is not subject to the requirements of Article XII, sections 6, and 11, see Commentaries thereon, and that the highway user receipts under Article XII, section 5a may not be used to pay off bonds issued under it.

This section, however, does not provide an exemption from the requirement of Article XII, section 5, that laws imposing new taxes state their objective, so any proposals to raise taxes to pay off the debt under this section must clearly indicate that the revenues are to be used for this purpose.

Notwithstanding Article II, section 22 (requiring appropriations of no more than two years), this section provides that no further act of appropriation is necessary to pay the debt service for bonds issued under this section.

Section 2p

Bonds for capital improvements to public infrastructure and for research and development.

(A) It is determined and confirmed that the development purposes referred to in this division, and provisions for them, are proper public purposes of the state and local governmental entities and are necessary and appropriate means to create and preserve jobs and enhance employment and educational opportunities; to improve the quality of life and the general and economic well-being of all the people and businesses in all areas of this state, including economically disadvantaged businesses and individuals; and to preserve and expand the public capital infrastructure; all to better ensure the public health, safety, and welfare. Those purposes are:

(1) Public infrastructure capital improvements, which shall be limited to roads and bridges, waste water treatment systems, water supply systems, solid waste disposal facilities, and storm water and sanitary collection, storage, and treatment facilities, including real property, interests in real property,

facilities, and equipment related to or incidental thereto, and shall include, without limitation, the cost of acquisition, construction, reconstruction, expansion, improvement, planning, and equipping;

(2) Research and development in support of Ohio industry, commerce, and business (hereinafter referred to as "research and development purposes"), which shall include, without limitation, research and product innovation, development, and commercialization through efforts by and collaboration among Ohio business and industry, state and local public entities and agencies, public and private education institutions, or research organizations and institutions, all as may be further provided for by state or local law, but excluding purposes provided for in Section 15 of Article VIII, Ohio Constitution; and

(3) Development of sites and facilities in Ohio for and in support of industry, commerce, distribution, and research and development purposes.

(B) The General Assembly may provide by law, in accordance with but subject to the limitations of this section, for the issuance of general obligation bonds and other obligations of the state for the purpose of financing or assisting in the financing of the cost of projects implementing those purposes.

(1) Not more than one billion three hundred fifty million dollars principal amount of state general obligations may be issued under this section for public infrastructure capital improvements. Not more than one hundred twenty million dollars principal amount of those obligations may be issued in each of the first five fiscal years of issuance and not more than one hundred fifty million dollars principal amount of those obligations may be issued in each of the next five fiscal years of issuance, plus in each case the principal amount of those obligations that in any prior fiscal year could have been but were not issued within those fiscal year limits. No infrastructure obligations may be issued pursuant to this division and division (C) of this section until at least one billion one hundred ninety-nine million five hundred thousand dollars aggregate principal amount of state infrastructure obligations have been issued pursuant to Section 2m of Article VIII, Ohio Constitution.

(2) Not more than one billion two hundred million dollars principal amount of state general obligations may be issued under this section for research and development purposes. Not more than four hundred fifty million dollars principal amount of those obligations may be issued in total from fiscal years 2006 through 2011, not more than two hundred twenty-five million dollars principal amount of those obligations may be issued in the next fiscal year of issuance, and not more than one hundred seventy-five million dollars principal amount of those obligations may be issued in any other fiscal year, plus in each case the principal amount of those obligations that in any prior fiscal year could have been but were not issued.

(3) Not more than one hundred fifty million dollars principal amount of state general obligations may be issued under this section for development of sites and facilities for industry, commerce, distribution, and research and development purposes. Not more than thirty million dollars principal amount of those obligations may be issued in each of the first three fiscal years of issuance, and not more than fifteen million dollars principal amount of those

obligations may be issued in any other fiscal year, plus in each case the principal amount of those obligations that in any prior fiscal year could have been but were not issued.

(C) Each issue of state general obligations for public infrastructure capital improvements or development of sites and facilities shall mature in not more than thirty years from the date of issuance, and each issue of state general obligations for research and development purposes shall mature in not more than twenty years from the date of issuance; or, if issued to retire or refund other obligations, within that number of years from the date the debt being retired or refunded was originally issued. If state general obligations are issued as notes in anticipation of the issuance of bonds, provision shall be made by law for the establishment and maintenance, during the period in which the notes are outstanding, of a special fund or funds into which shall be paid, from the sources authorized for the payment of such bonds, the amount that would have been sufficient, if bonds maturing during the permitted period of years had been issued without such prior issuance of notes, to pay the principal that would have been payable on such bonds during such period. Such fund or funds shall be used solely for the payment of principal of such notes or bonds in anticipation of which such notes have been issued. Notwithstanding anything to the contrary in Section 2k or 2m of Article VIII, obligations issued under this section or Section 2k or 2m to retire or refund obligations previously issued under this section or Section 2k or 2m shall not be counted against the fiscal year or total issuance limitations provided in this section or Section 2k or 2m, as applicable.

The obligations issued under this division and division (B) of this section are general obligations of the state. The full faith and credit, revenue, and taxing power of the state shall be pledged to the payment of the principal of and premium and interest and other accreted amounts on outstanding obligations as they become due (hereinafter called debt service), and bond retirement fund provisions shall be made for payment of that debt service. Provision shall be made by law for the sufficiency and appropriation, for purposes of paying debt service, of excises, taxes, and revenues so pledged or committed to debt service, and for covenants to continue the levy, collection, and application of sufficient excises, taxes, and revenues to the extent needed for that purpose. Notwithstanding Section 22 of Article II, Ohio Constitution, no further act of appropriation shall be necessary for that purpose. The obligations and the provision for the payment of debt service, and repayment by governmental entities of any loans made under this section, are not subject to Sections 5, 6, and 11 of Article XII, Ohio Constitution. Moneys referred to in Section 5a of Article XII, Ohio Constitution may not be pledged or used for the payment of that debt service. Debt service on obligations issued for research and development purposes and for development of sites and facilities shall not be included in the calculation of total debt service for purposes of division (A) of Section 17 of Article VIII, Ohio Constitution.

(D)(1) The state may participate in any public infrastructure capital improvement under this section with municipal corporations, counties, townships, or other governmental entities as designated by law, or any one or more of them. Such participation may be by grants, loans, or contributions to them for any such capital improvements. The entire proceeds of the infrastructure obligations shall be used for public infrastructure capital improvements of municipal corporations, counties, townships, and other governmental entities, except to the extent that the General Assembly provides by law that the state may reasonably be compensated from such moneys for planning, financial management, or administrative services performed in relation to the issuance of infrastructure obligations.

(2)(a) Implementation of the research and development purposes includes supporting any and all related matters and activities, including: attracting researchers and research teams by endowing research chairs or otherwise; activities to develop and commercialize products and processes; intellectual property matters such as copyrights and patents; property interests, including time sharing arrangements; and financial rights and matters such as royalties, licensing, and other financial gain or sharing resulting from research and development purposes. State and local public moneys, including the proceeds of bonds, notes, and other obligations, may be used to pay costs of or in support of or related to these research and development purposes, including, without limitation, capital formation, direct operating costs, costs of research and facilities, including interests in real property therefor, and support for public and private institutions of higher education, research organizations or institutions, and private sector entities. The exercise of these powers by the state and state agencies, including state-supported and state-assisted institutions of higher education, and local public entities and agencies, may be jointly or in coordination with each other, with researchers or research organizations and institutions, with private institutions of higher education, with individuals, or with private sector entities. State and local public participation may be in such manner as the entity or agency determines, including by any one or a combination of grants, loans including loans to lenders or the purchase of loans, subsidies, contributions, advances, or guarantees, or by direct investments of or payment or reimbursement from available moneys, or by providing staffing or other support, including computer or other technology capacity, or equipment or facilities, including interests in real property therefor, and either alone or jointly, in collaborative or cooperative ventures, with other public agencies and private sector entities including not for profit entities. In addition to other state-level monetary participation as referred to in this section or otherwise, state-supported and state-assisted institutions of higher education may, as authorized from time to time by the General Assembly, issue obligations to pay costs of participating in and implementing research and development purposes. In addition to the other obligations authorized in or pursuant to this section, the General Assembly also may authorize the state and state agencies and local public entities and agencies, and corporations not for profit designated by any of them as such agencies or instrumentalities, to issue obligations to borrow and loan or otherwise provide moneys for research and development purposes, including, but not limited to, obligations for which moneys raised by taxation shall not be obligated or pledged for the payment of debt service and which are therefore not subject to Sections 5, 6, and 11 of Article XII, Ohio Constitution.

(b) Implementation of the research and development purposes shall include utilization of independent reviewers to review the merits of proposed research and development projects and to make recommendations concerning which proposed projects should be awarded support from the proceeds of the sale of obligations under this section. Prior to the utilization of an independent reviewer, the state agency proposing to award the support for a project shall provide the name and other descriptive information regarding the independent reviewer to the Governor, the President and Minority Leader of the Senate, and the Speaker and Minority Leader of the House of Representatives. If the recommendations of an independent reviewer with respect to a proposed project are not adopted by the state agency proposing to award the support for the project, the agency shall notify the Governor, the President and Minority Leader of the Senate, and the Speaker and Minority Leader of the House of Representatives of that fact and explain the reasons for not adopting the recommendations.

(c) From the proceeds of the sale of obligations issued under this section, not more than four hundred fifty million dollars may be awarded, promised, or otherwise committed in total for research and development purposes from fiscal years 2006 through 2011, not more than two hundred twenty-five million dollars may be awarded, promised, or otherwise committed for research and development purposes in fiscal year 2012, and not more than one hundred seventy-five million dollars may be awarded, promised, or otherwise committed for research and development purposes in any other fiscal year beginning in fiscal year 2013 and thereafter, plus in each case the amount of the proceeds that in any prior fiscal year could have been but were not awarded.

(3) Development of sites and facilities for and in support of industry, commerce, distribution, and research and development purposes includes acquisition of real estate and interests in real estate, site preparation including any necessary remediation and cleanup, constructing and improving facilities, and providing public infrastructure capital improvements and other transportation and communications infrastructure improvements for and in support of the use of those sites and facilities for those purposes. State and local public moneys, including the proceeds of bonds, notes, and other obligations, may be used to pay costs of those purposes. The exercise of these powers by the state and state agencies and local public entities and agencies, may be jointly or in coordination with each other, and with individuals or private sector business entities. State and local public participation may be in such manner as the entity or agency determines, including by any one or a combination of grants, loans including loans to lenders or the purchase of loans, subsidies, contributions, advances, or guarantees, or by direct investments of or payment or reimbursement from available moneys. In addition to other state-level monetary participation as referred to in this section or otherwise, state-supported and state-assisted institutions of higher education, and local public entities and agencies may, as authorized from time to time by the General Assembly, issue obligations to pay costs of participating in and implementing the development of sites and facilities.

(E) Obligations issued under authority of this section for research and development purposes and site and facility development purposes, provisions for the payment of debt service on them, the purposes and uses to which and the manner in which the proceeds of those obligations or moneys from other exchange, or other disposition thereof, shall at all times be free from taxation within the state.

(F) This section shall otherwise be implemented in the manner and to the extent provided by law by the General Assembly, including provision for the procedure for incurring and issuing obligations, separately or in combination with other obligations, and refunding, retiring, and evidencing obligations; provision for ensuring the accountability of all state funding provided for the development purposes referred to in division (A) of this section; provision for restricting or limiting the taking of private property under Section 19 of Article I for disposition to private sector entities for the purposes identified in divisions (A)(2) and (3) of this section or restricting the disposition of that property to private sector entities or individuals; and provision for the implementation of the development purposes referred to in division (A) of this section to benefit people and businesses otherwise qualified for receipt of funding for the development purposes referred to in division (A) of this section, including economically disadvantaged businesses and individuals in all areas of this state, including by the use to the extent practicable of Ohio products, materials, services, and labor.

(G) The powers and authority granted or confirmed by and under, and the determinations sources are to or may be applied, and other implementation of those development purposes as referred to in this section, are not subject to Sections 4 and 6 of Article VIII, Ohio Constitution. Obligations issued under authority of this section, the transfer thereof, and the interest, interest equivalent, and other income and accreted amounts therefrom, including any profit made on the sale, in, this section are independent of, in addition to, and not in derogation of or a limitation on, powers, authority, determinations, or confirmations under laws or under other provisions of the Ohio Constitution including, without limitation, Section 7 of Article I, Section 5 of Article VI, Sections 2i, 2n, 2o, 13, and 15 of Article VIII, Article X, and of Article XVIII, and do not impair any previously adopted provisions of the Ohio Constitution or any law previously enacted by the General Assembly or by a local public agency.

Adopted in 2005 and amended in 2010, this section created the Third Frontier Program by authorizing the issuance of general obligation bonds for capital improvements to public infrastructure and for research and development in support of Ohio industry, commerce, and business (but not coal technology, which is the subject of sec. 15). These proposals were designed to encourage state economic growth through grants and loans to private industry and educational institutions.

In November 2003, the voters had rejected the precursor to this amendment to Article VIII, which would have given state and local governments authority to issue $500 million in bonds and provide other financial assistance to support science and technology-based research and development.

The 2005 amendment increased the amount of authorized debt to $1.375 billion in bonds for the same purposes as the rejected proposal, and the 2010 amendment authorized the issuance of an additional $700 million in bonds for the same purpose.

Both the rejected and approved amendments made the lending-of-credit limitations in Article VIII, sections 4 and 6, inapplicable and thus permitted state and local governments to invest public money in private business and share in the profits.

This section provides that the debt service on bonds issued under its authority is not subject to the requirements of Article XII, sections 5, 6, and 11, see Commentaries thereon, and that the highway user receipts under Article XII, section 5a may not be used to pay off bonds issued under it. See Commentary, Article XII, section 5a.

In addition, this section provides that the debt service issued on obligations issued for research and development purposes and for development of sites and facilities pursuant to this section is not subject to the 5 percent limitation in section 17(A) of this article.

Notwithstanding Article II, section 22 (requiring appropriations of no more than two years), this section provides that no further act of appropriation is necessary to pay the debt service for bonds issued under this section

This provision also required the use, to the extent practicable, of Ohio products, materials, services, and labor.

Section 2q

Bonds for environmental revitalization and conservation.

(A) It is determined and confirmed that the environmental and related conservation, preservation, and revitalization purposes referred to in divisions (A)(1) and (2) of this section, and provisions for them, are proper public purposes of the state and local governmental entities and are necessary and appropriate means to improve the quality of life and the general and economic well-being of the people of this state; to better ensure the public health, safety, and welfare; to protect water and other natural resources; to provide for the conservation and preservation of natural and open areas and farmlands, including by making urban areas more desirable or suitable for development and revitalization; to control, prevent, minimize, clean up, or remediate certain contamination of or pollution from lands in the state and water contamination or pollution; to provide for safe and productive urban land use or reuse; to enhance the availability, public use, and enjoyment of natural areas and resources; and to create and preserve jobs and enhance employment opportunities. Those purposes are:

(1) Conservation purposes, meaning conservation and preservation of natural areas, open spaces, and farmlands and other lands devoted to agriculture, including by acquiring land or interests therein; provision of state and local park and recreation facilities, and other actions that permit and enhance the availability, public use, and enjoyment of natural areas and open spaces

in Ohio; and land, forest, water, and other natural resource management projects;

(2) Revitalization purposes, meaning providing for and enabling the environmentally safe and productive development and use or reuse of publicly and privately owned lands, including those within urban areas, by the remediation or clean up, or planning and assessment for remediation or clean up, of contamination, or addressing, by clearance, land acquisition or assembly, infrastructure, or otherwise, that or other property conditions or circumstances that may be deleterious to the public health and safety and the environment and water and other natural resources, or that preclude or inhibit environmentally sound or economic use or reuse of the property.

(B) The General Assembly may provide by law, subject to the limitations of and in accordance with this section, for the issuance of bonds and other obligations of the state for the purpose of paying costs of projects implementing those purposes.

(1) Not more than two hundred million dollars principal amount of obligations issued under this section for conservation purposes may be outstanding in accordance with their terms at any one time. Not more than fifty million dollars principal amount of those obligations, plus the principal amount of those obligations that in any prior fiscal year could have been but were not issued within the fifty-million-dollar fiscal year limit, may be issued in any fiscal year. Those obligations shall be general obligations of the state and the full faith and credit, revenue, and taxing power of the state shall be pledged to the payment of debt service on them as it becomes due, all as provided in this section.

(2) Not more than two hundred million dollars principal amount of obligations issued under this section for revitalization purposes may be outstanding in accordance with their terms at any one time. Not more than fifty million dollars principal amount of those obligations, plus the principal amount of those obligations that in any prior fiscal year could have been but were not issued within the fifty-million-dollar fiscal year limit, may be issued in any fiscal year. Those obligations shall not be general obligations of the state and the full faith and credit, revenue, and taxing power of the state shall not be pledged to the payment of debt service on them. Those obligations shall be secured by a pledge of all or such portion of designated revenues and receipts of the state as the General Assembly authorizes, including receipts from designated taxes or excises, other state revenues from sources other than state taxes or excises, such as from state enterprise activities, and payments for or related to those revitalization purposes made by or on behalf of local governmental entities, responsible parties, or others. The general assembly shall provide by law for prohibitions or restrictions on the granting or lending of proceeds of obligations issued under division (B)(2) of this section to parties to pay costs of cleanup or remediation of contamination for which they are determined to be responsible.

(C) For purposes of the full and timely payment of debt service on state obligations authorized by this section, appropriate provision shall be made or authorized by law for bond retirement funds, for the sufficiency and appropriation of state excises, taxes, and revenues pledged to the debt service on the respective obligations, for which purpose, notwithstanding Section 22 of Article II of the Ohio Constitution, no further act of appropriation shall be necessary, and for covenants to continue the levy, collection, and application of sufficient state excises, taxes, and revenues to the extent needed for those purposes. Moneys referred to in Section 5a of Article XII of the Ohio Constitution may not be pledged or used for the payment of debt service on those obligations.

As used in this section, "debt service" means principal and interest and other accreted amounts payable on the obligations referred to.

(D)(1) Divisions (B) and (C) of this section shall be implemented in the manner and to the extent provided by the General Assembly by law, including provision for procedures for incurring, refunding, retiring, and evidencing state obligations issued pursuant to this section. Each state obligation issued pursuant to this section shall mature no later than the thirty-first day of December of the twenty-fifth calendar year after its issuance, except that obligations issued to refund or retire other obligations shall mature not later than the thirty-first day of December of the twenty-fifth calendar year after the year in which the original obligation to pay was issued or entered into.

(2) In the case of the issuance of state obligations under this section as bond anticipation notes, provision shall be made by law or in the bond or note proceedings for the establishment, and the maintenance during the period the notes are outstanding, of special funds into which there shall be paid, from the sources authorized for payment of the particular bonds anticipated, the amount that would have been sufficient to pay the principal that would have been payable on those bonds during that period if bonds maturing serially in each year over the maximum period of maturity referred to in division (D)(1) of this section had been issued without the prior issuance of the notes. Those special funds and investment income on them shall be used solely for the payment of principal of those notes or of the bonds anticipated.

(E) In addition to projects undertaken by the state, the state may participate or assist, by grants, loans, loan guarantees, or contributions, in the financing of projects for purposes referred to in this section that are undertaken by local governmental entities or by others, including, but not limited to, not-for-profit organizations, at the direction or authorization of local governmental entities. Obligations of the state issued under this section and the provisions for payment of debt service on them, including any payments by local governmental entities, are not subject to Sections 6 and 11 of Article XII of the Ohio Constitution. Those obligations, and obligations of local governmental entities issued for the public purposes referred to in this section, and provisions for payment of debt service on them, and the purposes and uses to which the proceeds of those state or local obligations, or moneys from other sources, are to be or may be applied, are not subject to Sections 4 and 6 of Article VIII of the Ohio Constitution.

(F) The powers and authority granted or confirmed by and under this section, and the determinations and confirmations in this section, are independent of, in addition to, and not in derogation of or a limitation on, powers, authority, determinations, or confirmations under laws, charters, ordinances, or resolutions, or by or under other provisions of the Ohio Constitution including, without limitation, Section 36 of Article II, Sections 2i, 2l, 2m, 2o, and 13 of Article VIII, and Articles X and XVIII, and do not impair any previously adopted provision of the Ohio Constitution or any law previously enacted by the General Assembly.

(G) Obligations issued under this section, their transfer, and the interest, interest equivalent, and other income or accreted amounts on them, including any profit made on their sale, exchange, or other disposition, shall at all times be free from taxation within the state.

Adopted in 2008, this section continues the Clear Ohio Program created with the adoption of section 2o in 2000 by authorizing general obligation and revenue bonds for conservation and revitalization purposes. The section authorizes the issuance of up to $200 million in general obligation bonds for conservation and preservation of natural areas, farmlands, park and recreation facilities, and to support other natural areas and natural resource management projects. The provision also authorizes the issuance of up to $200 in revenue bonds for environmental revitalization and cleanup projects.

Section 2q limits the amount borrowed in any one fiscal year to $50 million in general obligation bonds and $50 million in revenue bonds, plus the principal amount of obligations that, in any prior fiscal year, could have been issued for either category of bonds but were not.

This section provides that the debt service on bonds issued under its authority is not subject to the requirements of Article XII, sections 6 and 11, see Commentaries thereon, and that the highway user receipts under Article XII, section 5a may not be used to pay off bonds issued under it. See Commentary, Article XII, section 5a.

Notwithstanding Article II, section 22 (requiring appropriations of no more than two years), this section provides that no further act of appropriation is necessary to pay the debt service for bonds issued under this section.

Section 2r

Persian Gulf, Afghanistan, and Iraq Conflict compensation.

(A) Upon the request of the department of veterans services, the Ohio public facilities commission shall proceed to issue and sell, from time to time, bonds or other obligations of the state in such amounts as are necessary to provide all or part of the funds as may be required to pay the compensation established by, and the expenses of administering, this section. The original principal amount of obligations so issued shall not exceed two hundred million dollars, provided that obligations issued under this section to retire or refund obligations previously issued under this section shall not be counted against that issuance limitation. The full faith and credit, revenue, and taxing power of the state is hereby pledged for payment of debt service on such obligations issued under this section, and the state covenants to continue the levy, collection, and application of sufficient state excises, taxes, and revenues to the extent needed for those purposes; provided that moneys referred to in Section 5a of Article XII of the Constitution of the State of Ohio may not be pledged or used for the payment of debt service. As used in this section, "debt service" means principal and interest and other accreted amounts payable on the obligations authorized by this section.

Each obligation so issued shall mature not later than the thirty-first day of December of the fifteenth calendar year after its issuance, except that obligations issued to refund obligations under this section shall mature not later than the thirty-first day of December of the fifteenth calendar year after the year in which the original obligation was issued. Except for obligations issued under this section to retire or refund obligations previously issued under this section, no obligations shall be issued under this section later than December 31, 2013.

In the case of the issuance of any obligations under this section as bond anticipation notes, provision shall be made in the bond or note proceedings for the establishment, and the maintenance during the period the notes are outstanding, of special funds into which there shall be paid, from the sources authorized for payment of the bonds anticipated, the amount that would have been sufficient to pay the principal that would have been payable on those bonds during that period if bonds maturing serially in each year over the maximum period of maturity referred to in this section had been issued without the prior issuance of the notes. Those special funds and investment income on them shall be used solely for the payment of debt service on those notes or the bonds anticipated.

The obligations issued under this section, their transfer, and the interest, interest equivalent, and other income thereon, including any profit made on their sale, exchange, or other disposition, shall at all times be free from taxation within the state.

Such obligations may be sold at public or private sale as determined by the Ohio public facilities commission.

(B) Out of the proceeds of the sale of all obligations, except those issued to refund or retire obligations previously issued under this section, the amount that represents accrued interest, if any, shall be paid into the state treasury into the Persian gulf, Afghanistan, and Iraq conflicts compensation bond retirement fund, which is hereby created. As determined at the time of sale, the amount that represents premium shall be paid into either the Persian gulf, Afghanistan, and Iraq conflicts compensation bond retirement fund or the Persian gulf, Afghanistan, and Iraq conflicts compensation fund, which is hereby created in the state treasury. The balance of the proceeds shall be paid into the Persian gulf, Afghanistan, and Iraq conflicts compensation fund. All proceeds of the sale of any obligations issued under this section to refund or retire obligations previously issued under this section shall be paid into the Persian gulf, Afghanistan, and Iraq conflicts compensation bond retirement fund and used to pay debt service on those outstanding obligations so refunded. The general assembly may appropriate and cause to be paid into the Persian gulf, Afghanistan, and Iraq conflicts compensation bond retirement fund or the Persian gulf, Afghanistan, and Iraq conflicts compensation fund, out of money in the treasury not otherwise appropriated, such amount as is proper for use for the purposes for which such funds are created. Except for amounts advanced by the general assembly to the Persian gulf, Afghanistan, and Iraq conflicts compensation fund with the express expectation of reimbursement from the proceeds of obligations paid into that fund, and except for amounts transferred under division (E) of this section for the purpose of defraying the immediate cost of administration and compensation, if the general assembly appropriates any funds to the Persian gulf, Afghanistan, and Iraq conflicts compensation fund prior to the time obligations have been issued in the original principal amount authorized in this section, that original principal amount authorized in this section shall be reduced by the amount of funds appropriated.

(C) On or before the fifteenth day of July of each fiscal year, the Ohio public facilities commission shall certify, or cause to be certified, to the director of budget and management the total amount of money required during the current fiscal year, together with all other money that will be available in the Persian gulf, Afghanistan, and Iraq conflicts compensation bond retirement fund, to meet in full all debt service and related financing costs on the obligations issued under this section. The director shall transfer from the general revenue fund to the Persian gulf, Afghanistan, and Iraq conflicts compensation bond retirement fund, without necessity of appropriation by the general assembly, an amount equal to the amount so certified, and those funds shall be used for the payment of the debt service.

(D)(1) The Persian gulf, Afghanistan, and Iraq conflicts compensation fund shall be paid out upon the order of the department of veterans services, without necessity of appropriation by the general assembly, in payment of the expenses of administering this section and as compensation as follows to each person who meets all of the following requirements:

(a) The person has served in active duty in the United States armed forces, except active duty for training only, at any time between August 2, 1990, and March 3, 1991, at any time between October 7, 2001, and the date determined by the president of the United States as the end of involvement of the United States armed forces in Afghanistan, or at any time between March 19, 2003, and the date determined by the president of the United States as the end of the involvement of the United States armed forces in Iraq.

(b) The person was an Ohio resident at the start of active duty service and is currently an Ohio resident.

(c) The person was separated from the United States armed forces under honorable conditions, is still serving in active duty service, or remains in any reserve component of the United States armed forces or in the Ohio national guard after serving on active duty.

A person who meets the requirements of divisions (D)(1)(a), (b), and (c) of this section is entitled to, and may apply to receive, compensation of fifty dollars for each month of active domestic or foreign service and one hundred dollars for each month of Persian gulf, Afghanistan, or Iraq service during the compensable periods.

A person who is medically discharged or medically retired from service due to combat-related disabilities sustained during Persian gulf, Afghanistan, or Iraq service is entitled to, and may apply to receive, compensation of one thousand dollars. The maximum amount of cash payable to any person in active domestic or foreign service is five hundred dollars and the maximum amount of cash payable to any person in Persian gulf, Afghanistan, or Iraq service is one thousand dollars, unless the person qualifies for a survivor's payment or a payment based on missing in action or prisoner of war status under division (D)(2) or (D)(3) of this section. Compensation for a fraction of a month of service shall be paid on the basis of one-thirtieth of the appropriate monthly amount for each day of service.

(2) The surviving spouse, surviving child or children, or surviving parent or parents, including a person or persons standing in loco parentis for at least one year preceding commencement of service in the United States armed forces, is entitled to, and may apply to receive, the same amount of compensation that the person who served in the armed forces would have received under division (D)(1) of this section. If the United States department of veterans' affairs determines that the person's death was the result of injuries or illness sustained in Persian gulf, Afghanistan, or Iraq service, the person's survivors are entitled to, and may apply for, a survivor's payment of five thousand dollars, regardless of the amount of compensation that the deceased would have been entitled to receive under this section, if living. The survivor's payment shall be made to the surviving spouse. If there is no surviving spouse, the payment shall go to the surviving child or children. If there are no surviving children, the payment shall go to the surviving parent or parents or person or persons standing in loco parentis for at least one year preceding commencement of service in the United States armed forces.

(3) A person designated by the United States department of defense as missing in action as a result of honorable service or held in enemy captivity, or the spouse, child, or parent, including a person standing in loco parentis for at least one year preceding commencement of service in the United States armed forces, of a person designated as missing in action or held in enemy captivity, is entitled to, and may apply for, a payment of five thousand dollars. This payment replaces any other cash benefit payable under this section. While the person is missing or held captive, the payment shall be made to the person's spouse. If there is no spouse to claim the payment, payment shall be made to the person's child or children. If the person does not have children, payment shall be made to the person's parent or parents or person or persons standing in loco parentis for at least one year preceding commencement of service in the United States armed forces.

No payment to a spouse, child, parent, or person in loco parentis of a person designated as missing in action as a result of honorable service or held in enemy captivity, while the person is missing in action or held captive, shall prevent the missing or captive person from claiming and receiving a bonus of an equal amount on the person's release or location.

(4) Compensation shall not be paid under this section as follows:

(a) To any person who received from another state a bonus or compensation of a similar nature;

(b) To any person who served less than ninety days in the United States armed forces, unless active duty was terminated as a result of injuries or illness sustained during Persian gulf, Afghanistan, or Iraq service during the compensable period;

(c) To any person for any time period spent under penal confinement during the compensable period.

(5) No sale or assignment of any right or claim to compensation under this section shall be valid. No claims of creditors shall be enforceable against rights or claims to or payments of compensation under this section. No fees shall be charged for services in connection with the prosecution of any right or claim to compensation or the collection of any compensation under this section.

(6) All applications for payment of compensation under this section shall be made to the department of veterans services according to the following schedule:

(a) For Persian gulf service, not later than December 31, 2013;

(b) For Afghanistan service, not later than three years after the date determined by the president of the United States as the end of involvement of the United States armed forces in Afghanistan;

(c) For Iraq service, not later than three years after the date determined by the president of the United States as the end of involvement of the United States armed forces in Iraq.

(7) As used in this section:

"Afghanistan service" means military service within Afghanistan during the period between October 7, 2001, and the date determined by the president of the United States as the end of the involvement of the United States armed forces in Afghanistan.

"Domestic service" means service within the territorial limits of the fifty states.

"Foreign service" means service in locations other than the territorial limits of the fifty states, excluding Persian gulf, Afghanistan, or Iraq service.

"Iraq service" means military service within Iraq during the period between March 19, 2003, and the date determined by the president of the United States as the end of the involvement of the United States armed forces in Iraq.

"Persian gulf service" means military service within the Persian gulf theater of operations during the period between August 2, 1990, and March 3, 1991.

"United States armed forces" includes the army, air force, navy, marine corps, and coast guard; any active reserve component of such forces; and members of the Ohio national guard serving on active duty.

(E) The department of veterans services (hereinafter referred to as the "department") shall have complete charge of making payment of compensation under division (D) of this section and shall adopt rules, including rules regarding the amounts to which beneficiaries are entitled, residency requirements for purposes of division (D)(1)(b) of this section, and any other rules necessary to implement this section. These rules shall be adopted in accordance with Chapter 119 of the Revised Code.

The department shall select and appoint legal counsel and employees as are necessary and fix their compensation and prescribe their duties. All appointees shall serve at the pleasure of the director of veterans services. When practical, the department shall employ Persian gulf, Afghanistan, and Iraq conflict veterans to fill such positions. The general assembly shall transfer necessary funds to the Persian gulf, Afghanistan, and Iraq conflicts compensation fund and to the department's operating budget, for the purpose of defraying the immediate cost of administration and compensation. Any funds so transferred shall not reduce the original principal amount of obligations that may be issued under this section.

On payment of all valid claims for cash compensation made within the time limitations under this section, the department may transfer any funds remaining in the Persian gulf, Afghanistan, and Iraq conflicts compensation fund to the Persian gulf, Afghanistan, and Iraq conflicts compensation bond retirement fund.

On retirement of all of the obligations issued under this section and payment of all valid claims for cash compensation made within the time limitations under this section, the department shall make a final report to the general assembly. Any balance remaining in the Persian gulf, Afghanistan, and Iraq conflicts compensation fund or the Persian gulf, Afghanistan, and Iraq conflicts compensation bond retirement fund shall be transferred or disposed of as provided by law.

Notwithstanding any other provision of this section to the contrary, valid claims for cash compensation made within the time limitations under this section shall be paid only if adequate funds remain in the Persian gulf, Afghanistan, and Iraq conflicts compensation fund.

(F) The people of this state declare it to be their intention that this amendment in no manner affects or changes any of the existing provisions of the Constitution except as set forth in this section. The provisions of this section shall be self-executing.

(G) Debt service on obligations issued pursuant to this section shall not be included in the calculation of total debt service for purposes of division (A) of Section 17 of Article VIII of the Constitution of the State of Ohio.

(H) As provided in divisions (C) and (D)(1) of this section, no further act of appropriation is necessary, notwithstanding Section 22 of Article II of the Constitution of the State of Ohio.

(I) Any reference in this section to a public office, officer, or body shall include any successor thereto.

Adopted in 2009, this section authorized the issuance of general obligation bonds to provide compensation to the veterans of the Persian Gulf, Afghanistan, and Iraq conflicts and their survivors. To be eligible for compensation, veterans had to have served on active duty in one or more of those locations during the specified time periods. Unlike previous war veteran compensation amendments, this section authorizes the Public Facilities Commission (rather than the sinking fund commission) to issue and sell bonds and other obligations to fund payment, pledging the state's full faith and credit, revenue, and taxing power to pay the debt service. Additionally, the section gives responsibility to the Ohio Department of Veterans Services for paying compensation and adopting rules regarding amounts, residency, or other relevant factors.

This section provides that highway user receipts may not be used to pay off bonds issued under it. See Commentary, Article XII, section 5a.

Notwithstanding Article II, section 22 (requiring appropriations of no more than two years), this section provides that this section is inapplicable and thus no further act of appropriation is necessary to pay the debt service for bonds issued under this section.

Debt service on obligations issued pursuant to this section is not subject to the 5 percent limitation in section 17(A) of this article. And no further act of appropriation is necessary, notwithstanding Article II, section 22.

Section 2s

Issuance of bonds for public infrastructure capital improvements.

(A) In addition to the authorizations otherwise contained in Article VIII of the Ohio Constitution, the General Assembly may provide by law, in accordance with and subject to the limitations of this section, for the issuance of bonds and other obligations of the state for the purpose of financing or assisting in the financing of the cost of public infrastructure capital improvements of municipal corporations, counties, townships, and other governmental entities as designated by law. As used in this section, public infrastructure capital improvements shall be limited to roads and bridges, waste water treatment systems, water supply systems, solid waste disposal facilities, and storm water and sanitary collection, storage, and treatment facilities, including real property, interests in real property, facilities, and equipment related to or incidental thereto, and shall include, without limitation, the cost of acquisition, construction, reconstruction, expansion, improvement, planning, and equipping.

It is hereby determined that such public infrastructure capital improvements are necessary to preserve and expand the public capital infrastructure of such municipal corporations, counties, townships, and other governmental entities, ensure the public health, safety, and welfare, create and preserve jobs, enhance employment opportunities, and improve the economic welfare of the people of this state.

(B) Not more than one billion eight hundred seventy-five million dollars principal amount of state general obligations may be issued under this section for public infrastructure capital improvements. Not more than one hundred seventy-five million dollars principal amount of those obligations may be issued in each of the first five fiscal years of issuance and not more than two hundred million dollars principal amount of those obligations may be issued in each of the next five fiscal years of issuance, plus in each case the principal amount of those obligations that in any prior fiscal year could have been but were not issued within those fiscal year limits. No obligations may be issued pursuant to this section until all of the state infrastructure obligations authorized under Section 2p of Article VIII, Ohio Constitution have been issued.

(C) Each issue of obligations issued under this section shall mature in not more than thirty years from the date of issuance, or, if issued to retire or refund other obligations, within that number of years from the date the debt being retired or refunded was originally issued. If state general obligations are issued as notes in anticipation of the issuance of bonds, provision shall be made by law for the establishment and maintenance, during the period in which the notes are outstanding, of a special fund or funds into which shall be paid, from the sources authorized for the payment of such bonds, the amount that would have been sufficient, if bonds maturing during the permitted period of years had been issued without such prior issuance of notes, to pay the principal that would have been payable on such bonds during such period. Such fund or funds shall be used solely for the payment of principal of such notes or bonds in anticipation of which such notes have been issued. Obligations issued under this section to retire or refund obligations previously issued under this section or Section 2k, 2m, or 2p shall not be counted against the fiscal year or total issuance limitations provided in this section or Section 2k, 2m, or 2p, as applicable.

(D) The obligations issued under this section are general obligations of the state. The full faith and credit, revenue, and taxing power of the state shall be pledged to the payment of the principal of and premium and interest and other accreted amounts on outstanding obligations as they become due (hereinafter called debt service), and bond retirement fund provisions shall be made for payment of that debt service. Provision shall be made by law for the sufficiency and appropriation, for purposes of paying debt service, of excises, taxes, and revenues so pledged or committed to debt service, and for covenants to continue the levy, collection, and application of sufficient excises, taxes, and revenues to the extent needed for that purpose. Notwithstanding Section 22 of Article II, Ohio Constitution, no further act of appropriation shall be necessary for that purpose. The obligations and the provision for the payment of debt service, and repayment by governmental entities of any loans made under this section, are not subject to Sections 5, 6, and 11 of Article XII, Ohio Constitution. Moneys referred to in Section 5a of Article XII, Ohio Constitution may not be pledged to the payment of that debt service.

(E) The state may participate in any public infrastructure capital improvement under this section with municipal corporations, counties, townships, or other governmental entities as designated by law, or any one or more of them. Such participation may be by grants, loans, or contributions to them for any such capital improvements. The entire proceeds of the infrastructure obligations shall be used for public infrastructure capital improvements of municipal corporations, counties, townships, and other governmental entities, except to the extent that the General Assembly provides by law that the state may reasonably be compensated from such moneys for planning, financial management, or administrative services performed in relation to the issuance of infrastructure obligations.

(F) Obligations issued under authority of this section, the transfer thereof, and the interest, interest equivalent, and other income and accreted amounts therefrom, including any profit made on the sale, exchange, or other disposition thereof, shall at all times be free from taxation within the state.

(G) This section shall otherwise be implemented in the manner and to the extent provided by law by the General Assembly, including provision for the procedure for incurring and issuing obligations, separately or in combination with other obligations, and refunding, retiring, and evidencing obligations, and provision for the use to the extent practicable of Ohio products, materials, services, and labor in the making of any project financed, in whole or in part, under this section.

(H) The powers and authority granted or confirmed by and under, and the determinations in, this section are independent of, in addition to, and not in derogation of or a limitation on, powers, authority, determinations, or confirmations under laws or under other provisions of the Ohio Constitution and do not impair any previously adopted provisions of the Ohio Constitution or any law previously enacted by the General Assembly or by a local public agency.

Adopted in 2014, this section authorized the General Assembly to issue up to $1.875 billion in general obligation bonds to finance public infrastructure capital improvements of municipal corporations, counties, townships, and other governmental entities, with the improvements being limited to roads and bridges, wastewater treatment and water supply systems, solid waste disposal facilities, and storm water and sanitary collection, storage, and treatment ties. With broad, nearly unanimous bipartisan support in the General Assembly, the voters approved this amendment by an almost 2:1 margin.

Of the $1.875 billion in bonds authorized under this section, not more than $175 million may be issued in each of the first five fiscal years of issuance and not more than $200 million in each of the next five fiscal years, plus in each case the principal amount of those obligations that in any prior fiscal year could have been but were not issued within those fiscal year limits. No obligations may be issued pursuant to this section until all of the state infrastructure obligations authorized under section 2p of Article VIII, Ohio Constitution have been issued.

This section provides that the debt service on bonds issued under its authority is not subject to the requirements of Article XII, sections 5, 6, and 11, see Commentaries thereon, and that the highway user receipts under Article XII, section 5a may not be used to pay off bonds issued under it. See Commentary, Article XII, section 5a.

Notwithstanding section 22 of Article II, Ohio Constitution, no further act of appropriation shall be necessary for that purpose. Obligations issued under this section are not subject to sections 4 and 6 of Article VIII and sections 5, 6, and 11 of Article XII.

This provision also required the use to the extent practicable of Ohio products, materials, services, and labor in the making of any project financed, in whole or in part, under this section.

Section 3

The state to create no other debt.

Except the debts above specified in sections 1 and 2 of this article, no debt whatever shall hereafter be created by, or on behalf of the state.

Adopted in 1851, this section provides that no debt can be created by the state unless it falls within the $750,000 limitation of section 1 or the exceptions under section 2. Together with section 1, this section appeared to have placed a strict limit on the debt that the state can incur. But this impression is belied by the judicially established special fund exception for revenue bonds, see Commentary, Article VIII, section 1, by the recognition in the 1851 Constitution that the limitation can be avoided by amendments for internal improvements, see Commentary, Article XII, section 6, and by the numerous voter-approved debt-authorizing amendments to Article VIII, see Commentary, Article VIII.

Section 4

Credit of state; the state shall not become joint owner or stockholder.

The credit of the state shall not, in any manner, be given or loaned to, or in aid of, any individual association or corporation whatever; nor shall the state ever hereafter become a joint owner, or stockholder, in any company or association, in this state, or elsewhere, formed for any purpose whatever.

Adopted in 1851 and never amended, this section reflects the general distrust that delegates to the constitutional convention had over the entanglement of private and public money. The state had become heavily involved in ventures with private investors in the late 1830s and 1840s, particularly after passage of the 1837 Loan Law, which required the state to finance private canal, turnpike, and railroad companies. See David M. Gold, "Public Aid to Private Enterprises under the Ohio Constitution: Sections 4, 6, and 13 of Article VIII in Historical Perspective," 16 *U. Tol. L. Rev.* 405 (1985): 408–9 (hereinafter Gold, "Public Aid to Private Enterprise"); Bogart, *Internal Improvements and State Debt in Ohio,* 165–78.

Many of these investments went bad, and by 1850, there was strong public pressure against the investment of state funds in private enterprises. See Thomas R. Swisher, ed., *Ohio Constitution Handbook* (Cleveland: Banks-Baldwin Publishing Co., 1990), 410. The delegates were aware of the problems created by joint ventures and investments, and they approved section 4 with only six dissenting votes. Gold, "Public Aid to Private Enterprise," 413

Section 4 expressly forbids the state from giving or loaning money to "any individual association or corporation" or from becoming "a joint owner, or stockholder, in any company or association . . . formed for any purpose whatever." Notwithstanding this language, which would seem to preclude all financial involvement with private entities, as the Ohio Supreme Court held in 1871 in banning all "business partnerships" when construing the companion provision in section 6, *Walker v. City of Cincinnati* (1871), the court subsequently approved a number of exceptions to the prohibition.

In 1922, however, the court held that this section (along with companion sec. 6 similarly limiting local government) did not forbid financial aid or the loan of the credit of the state to an agricultural fair that is a public institution designed for public instruction, the advancement of learning, and the dissemination of useful knowledge. *State ex rel. Leaverton v. Kerns* (1922).

And in 1955, the court concluded that sections 4 and 6 do not prevent state and local governments from providing funds to nonprofit war veterans' organizations for the public purposes of rehabilitating veterans and promoting patriotism. *State ex rel. Dickman v. Defenbacher* (1955).

The court has also interpreted this section to permit aid to for-profit corporations where the government transactions being financed involved a public purpose such as a sale for market value of property acquired through "slum clearance," *State ex rel. Bruestle v. Rich* (1953), or leases to private corporations of a publicly owned grain elevator for an adequate rental, *State ex rel. McElroy v. Baron* (1959).

In 1964, however, the Ohio Supreme Court in *State ex rel. Saxbe v. Brand* (1964) held that the law that created the Ohio Development Financing Commission violated Article VIII, section 4. The law had authorized the selling of $10 million in revenue bonds with the proceeds to be used for loans to private for-profit borrowers to spur economic development, but the court held that section 4 prohibited such a giving or loaning of the state's credit even though the law involved no direct or contingent indebtedness of the state.

Though never amended, section 4 lost much of its force as a result of a series of amendments approved after the *Brand* decision.

In 1965, the General Assembly proposed and the voters approved section 13 of this article, which expressly exempted state financial support of economic development projects from the limitations in sections 4 and 6. See Commentary, Article VIII, section 13. And in subsequent years, the state adopted the practice of expressly making the lending-of-credit limitations inapplicable to debt-authorizing amendments. See Commentaries, Article VIII, sections 2k, 2l, 2o, 2p, 2q, 2s, 14, 15, and 16.

In 1968, subsequent to the *Brand* amendment, the court held that section 6 (sec. 4's companion provision) did not prohibit a city from constructing a stadium, from lending its credit to support spending on a proposed stadium, or from lending the city's credit to a public organization (such as the county) to support the construction of a stadium. *Bazell v. City of Cincinnati* (1968).

But in 1976, the court changed direction and strictly construed section 13, holding that the state may not lend its credit to developers unless one of the exceptions in section 13 applied. *State ex rel. Brown v. Beard* (1976).

This led to a series of bond-authorizing amendments designed to avoid *Beard,* see Article VIII, section 2k, 14, 15, and 16, but in 1991 the court again changed direction, overruled *Beard,* and held that subsidies for the construction of for-profit, multiunit, low- and moderate-income rental housing fell within the exception for economic development in Article VIII, section 13. See Commentary, Article VIII, section 13.

The court has also recognized that section 4 does not bar providing state loans to community schools for buildings and other facilities because the schools are public organizations created to advance a public purpose—the state's public school system. *State ex rel. Ohio Congress of Parents & Teachers v. State Board of Education* (2006).

■ JOBSOHIO

The lending-of-credit issue was central to the litigation challenging the 2011 JobsOhio Act, which created a nonprofit publicly funded corporation for "the purposes of promoting economic development, job creation, job retention, job training, and the recruitment of business" to Ohio.

An array of parties challenged this litigation in an original action in the Ohio Supreme Court, claiming inter alia that the act violated this section. The court, however, initially rejected this challenge on jurisdictional grounds because the General Assembly had unconstitutionally sought to expand the court's original jurisdiction. *ProgressOhio.org, Inc. v. Kasich* (2011). And in subsequent decisions, the court refused to exercise original jurisdiction over a putative writ of mandamus, *State ex rel. JobsOhio v. Goodman* (2012), and found a lack of standing in an action that had originally been brought in the court of common pleas, *ProgressOhio.org, Inc. v. JobsOhio* (2014). See Commentary, Article IV.

The *JobsOhio* challengers, relying on *Walker,* claimed that section 4 prohibited joint ventures between the state and private companies and barred the state from directly or indirectly taking equity positions in private companies. The state responded by pointing to post-*Walker* decisions and arguing that section 4 did not bar joint ventures with private nonprofit organizations; they also disputed the claim that the state would be taking an equity position with JobsOhio, while asserting that section 4 did not bar it from subsequently investing in private companies. But given the court's jurisdictional rulings, it is doubtful whether the court will ever directly address the JobsOhio/lending-of-credit issue on the merits.

Section 5

No assumption of debt by the state.

The state shall never assume the debts of any county, city, town, or township, or of any corporation whatever, unless such debt shall have been created to repel invasion, suppress insurrection, or defend the state in war.

Adopted in 1851 and never amended, this section requires political subdivisions to be accountable for all debt created at the local level. It forbids the state from assuming the debts of political subdivisions and corporations except in times of war and civil unrest, the same exceptions that apply to debt incurred directly by the state (see sec. 2).

Section 6

Counties, cities, towns, or townships, not authorized to become stockholders; regulation of insurance.

No laws shall be passed authorizing any county, city, town or township, by vote of its citizens, or otherwise, to become a stockholder in any joint stock company, corporation, or association whatever; or to raise money for, or to loan its credit to, or in aid of, any such company, corporation, or association: provided, that nothing in this section shall prevent the insuring of public buildings or property in mutual insurance associations or companies. Laws may be passed providing for the regulation of all rates charged or to be charged by any insurance company, corporation or association organized under the laws of this state, or doing any insurance business in this state for profit.

Adopted in 1851 and amended in 1912, this section applies a lending-of-credit limitation to local governments. The Ohio Supreme Court has construed both sections 4 and 6 similarly, but the unlike the limitations in sections 1, 2, and 3 on the amount and type of *state* debt, no such limitations apply to *local* debt. *Walker v. City of Cincinnati* (1871). Thus, Cincinnati, which was prevented from lending its credit for the construction and operation of a railroad that it wanted badly, was not barred from constructing and operating railroad itself. See Gold, "Public Aid to Private Enterprise," 424–27. But the court subsequently struck down a state statute that permitted counties to issue bonds backed by their credit for building railroads because the county could sell the railroad at any time for virtually any consideration, in effect, authorizing the railroad "to use the public bonds to construct a work which becomes the property of the purchaser as fast as it is built." *Taylor v. Commissioners of Ross County* (1872).

And in *Alter v. City of Cincinnati*, 1897, the Ohio Supreme Court held that a plan to join public and private water-supply facilities conflicted with section 6, and thus "effectively outlawed joint ventures between government and private business, regardless of who loaned credit to whom or whether there was a lending of credit at all." Gold, "Public Aid to Private Enterprise," 436.

In 1912, the voters approved an amendment to this section to allow local governments to insure public buildings and public property and to allow the state to regulate insurance rates. The delegates to the 1912 Convention proposed this amendment in response to an opinion of the attorney general questioning the authority for these insurance-related activities. See The Constitutional History of Ohio, 85–86.

In 1989, the court stated that sections 4 and 6 do not prohibit aid to private parties for public purposes. In a case involving the proposed sale of $20 million of housing construction revenue notes by the City of Cleveland to support the construction of housing, the court upheld the issuance of the notes, stating that "[h]istorically, Sections 4 and 6 of Article VIII have not been applied to programs undertaken for public welfare. Rather, these sections have been uniformly held to prohibit governmental involvement only in ventures that subsidize commerce or industry." *State ex rel. Tomino v. Brown* (1989).

As with the frequently adopted exceptions to the lending-of-credit limitation in section 4, see Commentary, Article VIII, section 4, it has become standard drafting procedure to include exceptions to the lending-of-credit limitation of this section in bond-authorizing amendments.

Section 7
Sinking fund.

The faith of the state being pledged for the payment of its public debt, in order to provide therefor, there shall be created a sinking fund, which shall be sufficient to pay the accruing interest on such debt, and, annually, to reduce the principal thereof, by a sum not less than one hundred thousand dollars, increased yearly, and each and every year, by compounding, at the rate of six per cent per annum. The said sinking fund shall consist, of the net annual income of the public works and stocks owned by the state, of any other funds or resources that are, or may be, provided by law, and of such further sum, to be raised by taxation, as may be required for the purposes aforesaid.

Sections 7–11 were adopted as part of the 1851 Constitution to provide a mechanism for paying off the state debt. Section 7 authorized the creation of a "sinking fund," a fund designed to accumulate money to pay off the principal of the debt, to pay the interest on the debt as it accrues, and to reduce the principal annually by at least $100,000 in the first year and $100,000 plus 6 percent compounded annually thereafter. Revenue for the fund would come from the net annual income generated from the state's public works projects and any other funds or resources, including, if necessary, additional taxes.

Section 8
The commissioners of the sinking fund.

The governor, treasurer of state, auditor of state, secretary of state, and attorney general, are hereby created a board of commissioners to be styled, "The Commissioners of the Sinking Fund."

Adopted in 1851 and amended in 1947, this section established a board of commissioners known as "The Commissioners of the Sinking Fund" to administer the sinking fund. The board initially consisted of the auditor of state, the secretary of state, and the attorney general. In 1947, the General Assembly proposed and the voters approved an amendment to add the governor and the state treasurer to the board.

Section 9

Biennial report of sinking fund commissioners.

The commissioners of the sinking fund shall, immediately preceding each regular session of the General Assembly, make an estimate of the probable amount of the fund, provided for in the seventh section of this article, from all sources except from taxation, and report the same, together with all their proceedings relative to said fund and the public debt, to the governor, who shall transmit the same with his regular message, to the General Assembly; and the General Assembly shall make all necessary provision for raising and disbursing said sinking fund, in pursuance of the provisions of this article.

Adopted in 1851 and never amended, this section requires that the commissioners of the sinking fund present a biennial report on the public debt and an estimate of the amount of money in the sinking fund to the governor, who is to present it to the General Assembly at the beginning of each regular session. The report must include information about the amount in the fund from all sources except taxation. Relying on this information, the General Assembly is directed to make all necessary provision for raising and disbursing the fund in pursuance of the provisions of Article VIII.

Section 10

Application of sinking fund.

It shall be the duty of the said commissioners faithfully to apply said fund, together with all moneys that may be, by the General Assembly, appropriated to that object, to the payment of the interest, as it becomes due, and the redemption of the principal of the public debt of the state, excepting only, the school and trust funds held by the state.

Adopted in 1851 and never amended, this section gives the commissioners of the sinking fund the responsibility for administering the sinking fund. This includes applying the fund, along with other moneys appropriated by the General Assembly, to the payment of interest as due as well as to the redemption of the principal of the public debt. Section 10 excludes the school and trust funds held by the state. See Commentary, Article VI, section 2.

Section 11
Semiannual report of sinking fund commissioners.

The said commissioners shall, semiannually, make a full and detailed report of their proceedings to the governor, who shall, immediately, cause the same to be published, and shall also communicate the same to the General Assembly, forthwith, if it be in session, and if not, then at its first session after such report shall be made.

Adopted in 1851 and never amended, this section requires the commissioners of the sinking fund to prepare a detailed report describing the proceedings of the sinking fund commission twice a year and present it to the governor, who is required to have it published and presented to the General Assembly. This report is in addition to the biennial report required by section 9.

Beginning with the adoption of Article VIII, section 2k, in 1987, the state has adopting the practice of making the requirements of the sinking fund inapplicable to most debt-authorizing amendments. See Article VIII, sections 2l, 2m, 2o, 2p, 2q, 2s, 13, 14, 15, and 16, and Commentaries thereon.

Section 12
Repealed—Superintendent of public works

Adopted in 1851, this section established a board of public works elected by the voters to supervise state public works projects. In 1912, the voters approved an amendment to this section to create a superintendent of public works appointed by the governor to replace the board. In 1974, the voters approved an amendment proposed by the General Assembly to repeal this section.

Section 13
Economic development.

To create or preserve jobs and employment opportunities, to improve the economic welfare of the people of the state, to control air, water, and thermal pollution, or to dispose of solid waste, it is hereby determined to be in the public interest and a proper public purpose for the state or its political subdivisions, taxing districts, or public authorities, its or their agencies or instrumentalities, or corporations not for profit designated by any of them as such agencies or instrumentalities, to acquire, construct, enlarge, improve, or equip, and to sell, lease, exchange, or otherwise dispose of property, structures, equipment, and facilities within the State of Ohio for industry, commerce, distribution, and research, to make or guarantee loans and to borrow money and issue bonds or other obligations to provide moneys for the acquisition, construction, enlargement, improvement, or equipment, of such property, structures, equipment and facilities. Laws may be passed to carry into effect such purposes and to authorize for such purposes the borrowing of money by, and the issuance of bonds or other obligations of, the state, or its political subdivisions, taxing districts, or public authorities, its or their agencies or instrumentalities, or corporations not for profit designated by any of them as such agencies or instrumentalities, and to authorize the making of guarantees and loans and the lending of aid and credit, which laws, bonds, obligations, loans, guarantees, and lending of aid and credit shall not be subject to the requirements, limitations, or prohibitions of any other section of Article VIII, or of Article XII, Sections 6 and 11, of the Constitution, provided that moneys raised by taxation shall not be obligated or pledged for the payment of bonds or other obligations issued or guarantees made pursuant to laws enacted under this section.

Except for facilities for pollution control or solid waste disposal, as determined by law, no guarantees or loans and no lending of aid or credit shall be made under the laws enacted pursuant to this section of the constitution for facilities to be constructed for the purpose of providing electric or gas utility service to the public.

The powers herein granted shall be in addition to and not in derogation of existing powers of the state or its political subdivisions, taxing districts, or public authorities, or their agencies or instrumentalities or corporations not for profit designated by any of them as such agencies or instrumentalities.

Any corporation organized under the laws of Ohio is hereby authorized to lend or contribute moneys to the state or its political subdivisions or agencies or instrumentalities thereof on such terms as may be agreed upon in furtherance of laws enacted pursuant to this section.

Adopted in 1965 and amended in 1974, this section was initially a response to the 1964 decision of the Ohio Supreme Court in *State ex rel. Saxbe v. Brand* (1964), in which the court held that the law that created the Ohio Development Financing Commission violated Article VIII, section 4. The law had authorized the selling of $10 million in revenue bonds with the proceeds to be used to make loans to private borrowers to spur economic development, but the court held that section 4 prohibited giving or loaning of state's credit even though the law involved no direct or contingent indebtedness of the state.

The 1965 amendment addressed the *Brand* issue by providing an exception to the lending-of-credit limitations of Article VIII, sections 4 and 6 for bonds issued to "create or preserve jobs and employment opportunities, to improve the economic welfare of the people of the state." It also provided that the other limitations in Article VIII as well as the requirements of Article XII, sections 6 (banning debt for internal improvements) and 11 (requiring a sinking fund) do not apply to debt issued under this section.

The 1965 amendment creating this section was the first amendment to expressly make the requirements of Article VIII (including the lending-of-credit limitations) and the requirements of Article XII, sections 6 and 11, inapplicable to bonds that met its requirements. The section also sought to assure that tax money not be used to pay off these bonds by providing "that moneys raised by taxation shall not be obligated or pledged for the payment of bonds or other obligations issued or guarantees made pursuant to laws enacted under this section."

Provisions creating exceptions to the lending-of-credit limitations of Article VIII, sections 4 and 6, have become standard provisions in debt-authorizing amendments to this article (other than those authorizing debt for veterans compensation) and are also contained in almost all of the post-1987 debt-authorizing amendments to this article, specifically sections 2l, 2o, 2p, 2q, 2s, 14, 15, and 16.

The exemptions from the requirements of sections 6 and 11 of Article XII have also become standard provisions in debt-authorizing amendments (other than those authorizing debt for veterans compensation) and are also contained in almost all of the post-1987 debt-authorizing amendments to this article, specifically sections 2l, 2m, 2o, 2p, 2q, and 2s, 14, 15, and 16.

■ THE 1974 AMENDMENT

As initially approved in 1965, the purpose of this section was "[t]o create or preserve jobs and employment opportunities, to improve the economic welfare of the people of the state," and the amendment barred guarantees or loans "for facilities to be constructed for the purpose of providing electric or gas utility service to the public." But the 1974 amendment proposed by the General Assembly and approved by the voters expressly provided that the bonds could be used to "to control air, water, and thermal pollution, or to dispose of solid waste." But the amendment did not remove the prohibition on the lending of aid or credit "for facilities to be constructed for the purpose of providing electric or gas utility service to the public."

■ COURT DECISIONS

This section has been the subject of frequent litigation as to whether specific bond proposals are justified by the broad purposes of this section and thus fall within the exception from the lending-of-credit limitations of sections 4 and 6 of Article VIII.

Despite its origin as a response to the court's 1964 decision in *Brand,* this section was also the subject of future litigation. In 1976 in *State ex rel. Brown v. Beard,* the Ohio Supreme Court held that the issuance and sale of revenue bonds to provide funds for mortgage loans to developers for construction and rehabilitation of low and moderate income rental housing were not directly related to purposes enumerated in this section and thus was a lending of the state's credit in violation of section 4.

But in the 1980s, the court appeared to change direction. In 1981, it held that the pledge of profits from the state's liquor enterprise for the payment of debt service on bonds issued to make loans for economic development projects was authorized under this section and thus did not violate the lending-of-credit limitation of section 4. *State ex rel. Duerk v. Donahey* (1981). And, in 1984, it held that the sale of industrial revenue bonds for the assistance of a farmer's business is also permissible under this section. *State ex rel. Preble County Board of Commissioners v. Mong* (1984).

Finally, in 1991, fifteen years after *Beard*, the court overruled *Beard* and held that "[t]he construction of for-profit, multiunit, low- and moderate-income rental housing constitutes the construction of facilities for industry and commerce under section 13 . . . ." *State ex rel. Lake County Board of Commissioners v. Zupancic* (1991) (syllabus).

As a result of *Zupancic*, the court seemed to have dramatically weakened the lending-of-credit limitations in sections 4 and 6. By giving the terms "industry" and "commerce" a broad interpretation, it appeared that public funds could be used to finance any project that was in any way related to one of the broad public purposes identified at the beginning of section 13.

But in 2000 the court appeared to have returned to the stricter approach of its earlier decisions and required this section be construed narrowly. In *C.I.V.I.C. Group v. City of Warren* (2000), the court held that loans to a private developers to build a "street containing two cul-de-sacs and related improvements does not meet the definition of industry and commerce [since] . . . [o]nce construction is complete no one is benefited except the residential property owners." Ibid. Thus, it appears that debt incurred under this section must be used for enumerated public purposes that benefit more than a few individuals.

Section 14

Bonds for housing programs.

To create or preserve opportunities for safe and sanitary housing and to improve the economic welfare of the people of the state, it is hereby determined to be in the public interest and a proper public purpose for the state to borrow money and issue bonds and other obligations to make available financing, at reasonable interest rates to consumers substantially reflecting savings in the cost of money to lenders resulting from the implementation of this section, for the acquisition, construction, rehabilitation, remodeling, and improvement of privately owned multiple-unit dwellings used and occupied exclusively by persons sixty-two years of age and older, and privately owned, owner occupied single family housing by providing loans to, or through the agency of, or originated by, or purchasing loans from, persons regularly engaged in the business of making or brokering residential mortgage loans, all as determined by or pursuant to law. Laws may be passed to carry into effect such purpose and to authorize for such purpose the borrowing of money by, and the issuance of bonds or other obligations of the state and to authorize the making of such loans, which laws, bonds, obligations, and loans shall not be subject to the requirements, limitations, or prohibitions of any other section of Article VIII, or sections 6 and 11 of

Article XII, Ohio Constitution, provided that moneys raised by taxation shall not be obligated or pledged for the payment of bonds or other obligations issued pursuant to laws enacted under this section.

The powers granted in this section shall be in addition to and not in derogation of existing powers of the state.

Any corporation organized under the laws of this state may lend or contribute moneys to the state on such terms as may be agreed upon in furtherance of laws enacted pursuant to this section.

Adopted in 1982 during a period of high interest rates, this section allows the state to borrow money and issue bonds to assist lenders and mortgage brokers in providing financing for privately owned multiunit housing used exclusively by persons sixty-two years and older and for owner-occupied single-family housing. The state may borrow money from in-state corporations for the purpose of this section, but it cannot pay off debt incurred under this section through the use of tax revenues.

The General Assembly proposed this amendment after the decision of the Ohio Supreme Court in *State ex rel. Brown v. Beard* (1976) held that the issuance of bonds by the Ohio Housing Development Board to provide funds for mortgage loans to developers for the construction and rehabilitation of low and moderate income rental housing was not within the scope of section 13 of Article VIII and thus violated section 4 of Article VIII.

Consistent with the pattern begun in 1965, this section expressly provides an exemption from the limitation-of-credit and other requirements of Article VIII as well as from the requirements of sections 6 and 11 of Article XII, Ohio Constitution.

Section 15

Bonds for development of coal technology.

Laws may be passed authorizing the state to borrow money and to issue bonds and other obligations for the purpose of making grants and making or guaranteeing loans for research and development of coal technology that will encourage the use of Ohio coal, to any individual, association, or corporation doing business in this state, or to any educational or scientific institution located in this state, notwithstanding the requirements, limitations, or prohibitions of any other section of Article VIII or of sections 6 and 11 of article XII of the constitution. The aggregate principal amount of the money borrowed and bonds and other obligations issued by the state pursuant to laws passed under this section shall not exceed one hundred million dollars outstanding at any time. The full faith and credit of the state may be pledged for the payment of bonds or other obligations issued or guarantees made pursuant to laws passed under this section.

Laws passed pursuant to this section also may provide for the state to share in any royalties, profits, or other financial gain resulting from the research and development.

Adopted in 1985, this section permits the state to incur general obligation debt to support research into more efficient and environmentally friendly uses of Ohio's high sulfur coal. This section allows the state to issue bonds and other obligations for grants and loans to any entity within the state for research and development in coal technology. The section limits the amount of outstanding debt to $100 million and authorizes the legislature to enact laws that permit the state to share profits from this research and development.

This section also provides that the requirements, limitations, or prohibitions of "any other section of article VIII" (including but not expressly identifying the lending-of-credit limitation of section 4) and the limitations Article XII, sections 6 and 11, do not apply to general obligation bonds issued under this section.

Section 16

Bonds and other assistance for housing programs.

To enhance the availability of adequate housing in the state and to improve the economic and general well-being of the people of the state, it is determined to be in the public interest and a proper public purpose for the state or its political subdivisions, directly or through a public authority, agency, or instrumentality, to provide, or assist in providing, by grants, loans, subsidies to loans, loans to lenders, purchase of loans, guarantees of loans, or otherwise as determined by the General Assembly, housing, including shelters to provide temporary housing in the state for individuals and families by the acquisition, financing, construction, leasing, rehabilitation, remodeling, improvement, or equipping of publicly or privately owned housing, including the acquisition of real property and interests in real property. Laws, including charters, ordinances, and resolutions, may be passed to carry into effect those purposes, including but not limited to the authorization of the making of grants, loans, subsidies to loans, loans to lenders, purchase of loans, and guarantees of loans by the state or its political subdivisions, directly or through a public authority, agency, or instrumentality, which laws, charters, ordinances, resolutions, grants, loans, subsidies to loans, loans to lenders, purchase of loans, guarantees of loans, and any other actions authorized by the General Assembly shall not be subject to the requirement, limitations, or prohibitions of any other section of Article VIII, or Sections 6 and 11 of Article XII, Ohio Constitution.

The General Assembly also may authorize the issuance by the state, directly or through its public authorities, agencies, or instrumentalities, of obligations to provide moneys for the provision of or assistance in the provision of housing, including shelters to provide temporary housing, in the state for individuals and families, which obligations are not supported by the full faith and credit of the state, and shall not be deemed to be debts or bonded indebtedness of the state under other provisions of this Constitution. Such obligations may be secured by a pledge under law, without necessity for further appropriation, of all or such portion as the General Assembly authorizes of revenues or receipts of the state or its public authorities, agencies, or instrumentalities, and this provision may be implemented by law to better provide therefor.

The powers granted under this section are independent of, in addition to, and not in derogation of other powers under laws, charters, ordinances, resolutions, or this Constitution, including the powers granted under Section 14 of Article VIII and Articles X and XVIII, and the provision of any capital improvements under Section 2i of Article VIII, Ohio Constitution. The powers granted under this section do not impair any law, charter, ordinance, or resolution enacted prior to the effective date of this section or any obligations issued under such law, charter, ordinance, or resolution. The powers granted under this section are subject to the power of the General Assembly to regulate taxation and debt of political subdivisions, including the regulation of municipal taxation and debt pursuant to Section 6 of Article XIII and Section 13 of Article XVIII, Ohio Constitution.

The powers granted to political subdivisions under this section shall be operative on and after September 1, 1991, or on an earlier date that an act of the General Assembly declares such powers shall be operative.

Adopted in 1990, this section, along with section 14, is aimed at helping families and individuals acquire affordable housing. This section authorizes grants and loans for permanent and temporary housing (including funds for emergency shelters). This section allows the state and its political subdivisions to issue obligations backed by the state in accordance with laws enacted by the General Assembly to finance, acquire, remodel, and construct private residences and public facilities. It also allows funds to be used to provide, and assist people in finding, housing, or shelter, but funds for those purposes are not general obligation debt and thus are not backed by the full faith and credit of the state.

This section also provides that neither the lending-of-credit and other limitations of Article VIII or Article XII, sections 6 and 11, apply to debt incurred or credit extended under this section.

There is no dollar cap on the amount of bonds that can be issued under this section, but the section is subject to the 5 percent debt service limitation of section 17(A).

Section 17

Limitations on obligations state may issue.

(A) Direct obligations of the state may not be issued under this article if the amount required to be applied or set aside in any future fiscal year for payment of debt service on direct obligations of the state to be outstanding in accordance with their terms during such future fiscal year would exceed five per cent of the total estimated revenues of the state for the General Revenue Fund and from net state lottery proceeds during the fiscal year in which the particular obligations are to be issued. As used in this division, "debt service" includes the debt service on the bonds to be issued under this article that are direct obligations of the state plus, if the obligations to be issued are bond anticipation notes, the debt service on the bonds anticipated, plus the debt service on all other outstanding bonds that are direct obligations of the state, to the extent that debt service on all those bonds and bonds anticipated is to be paid from the General Revenue Fund or net state lottery proceeds.

(B) The limitations of division (A) of this section shall not apply to a particular issue or amount of obligations if the limitations are waived as to that particular issue or amount by the affirmative vote of at least three-fifths of the members of each house of the General Assembly, or to obligations issued to retire bond anticipation notes that were issued when the requirements of division (A) of this section were originally met as estimated for the bonds anticipated.

(C) For purposes of division (A) of this section, debt contracted by the state pursuant to Section 2 of Article VIII of the Ohio Constitution to repel invasion, suppress insurrection, or to defend the state in war, shall not be included in the calculation of total debt service.

(D) For purposes of division (A) of this section, the General Assembly shall provide by law for computing the amounts required for payment of debt service, and may provide for estimating payments of debt service on bonds anticipated by notes, for including payments of debt service on obligations issued to refund or retire prior obligations in lieu of such payments on the prior refunded or retired obligations, and for the method of computing payments of debt service on any obligations required to be retired or for which sinking fund deposits are required prior to stated maturity. The Governor or the Governor's designee for such purpose shall determine and certify the fiscal year amounts required to be applied or set aside for payment of debt service, the obligations to which that debt service relates, the total estimated revenues of the state for the state General Revenue Fund and from net state lottery proceeds during the particular fiscal year, other financial data necessary for the purposes of computations under division (A) of this section, and the permitted latest maturity of obligations. That certification shall be conclusive for the purposes of the validity of any obligations issued under this article.

(E) As used in this section:

(1) "Fiscal year" means the state fiscal year.

(2) "Debt service" means principal and interest and other accreted amounts payable on the obligations referred to.

(3) "Direct obligations of the state" means obligations issued by the state on which the state of Ohio is the primary or only direct obligor

Adopted in 1999 as part of the same ballot issue in which the voters approved the adoption of section 2n to authorize general obligation bonds for educational facilities, this section establishes a formula-based annual debt service limitation. Under this limitation, the state is prohibited from issuing direct obligations (which includes general obligation and bond anticipation notes that are paid from the state's general revenue fund) that would require payments for debt service in any future fiscal year of an amount that exceeds 5 percent of the total estimated revenues for the general revenue fund plus net state lottery proceeds for the fiscal year of issuance. This formula-based approach is similar to the one included in the ill-fated 1967 proposal to create an Ohio Bond Commission and in the unsuccessful 1977 proposal of the OCRC. See Commentary, Article VIII.

Under this section, the General Assembly may waive the 5 percent limitation by a three-fifths vote in each house (apparently without the approval of the governor).

The 5 percent limitation inapplicable to all or parts of selected constitutional amendments, see Article VIII, sections 2p and 2r, and it does not apply to debt incurred because of civil unrest and the other emergencies described in Article VIII, section 2.

For fiscal year 2019, the total revenue of the state for the general revenue fund and net lottery proceeds was $34,921,508,000. The annual debt service payment was $1,402,757,299, which is 4.02 percent of the state's total revenue (and well under the five percent limit of this section). See Ohio Office of Budget and Management, State Debt Profile; see also Constitution Article VIII, section 17 Determination and Certification by Governor's Designee (Ohio Office of Budget and Management) (September 10, 2019) (listing debt service requirements).

Article IX

Militia

The militia existed in Ohio well before statehood. The Northwest Ordinance provided for the appointment of the governor as the commander-in-chief of the militia with the power to appoint all officers below the rank of general. See Ordinance of 1787, section 6. The present constitution retains the governor's position as commander-in-chief of the militia, Article III, section 10, and the strict subordination of the militia to civilian power, Article I, section 4. See generally John Kulewicz, "The Relationship between Military and Civil Power in Ohio," 28 *Clev. St. L. Rev.* 611 (1979).

Article IX gives the governor the power to call forth the militia and describes who is subject to service in the militia. The organization of the state's militia and exemptions for service are found in chapters 5913–5924 of the Ohio Revised Code.

Section 1

Who shall perform military duty.

All citizens, residents of this state, being seventeen years of age, and under the age of sixty-seven years, shall be subject to enrollment in the militia and the performance of military duty, in such manner, not incompatible with the Constitution and laws of the United States, as may be prescribed by law.

The Ohio State Constitution. Steven H. Steinglass and Gino J. Scarselli, Oxford University Press. © Oxford University Press 2022. DOI: 10.1093/oso/9780197619728.003.0011

Adopted in 1851, and amended in 1953 and 1961, this section defines who is subject to enrollment in the militia. Both amendments were proposed by the General Assembly and approved by the voters.

From 1851 to 1953, the section provided as follows: "All white male citizens, residents of the state, being eighteen years of age, and under the age of forty-five years, shall be enrolled in the militia, and perform military duty, in such manner, not incompatible with the Constitution and laws of the United States, as may be prescribed by law." The 1953 amendment eliminated the racial restriction by replacing the phrase "all white male citizens" with "all male citizens," and the 1961 amendment dropped the gender limitation and increased the age limitation from forty-five to sixty-seven.

The Ohio militia today comprises an organized militia, which consists of the Ohio National Guard, the Ohio naval militia, and the Ohio military reserve, and an unorganized militia, which consists of every citizen of the state between the ages of eighteen and sixty-seven who is not a member of the organized militia. O.R.C. section 5923.01. Ohio law requires that the organized militia be called to duty before the unorganized militia, O.R.C. section 5923.21(B), and further provides certain exemptions from service for persons who are defined by statute as handicapped. Additionally, Ohio law provides exemptions for various persons who can be excused upon request, including judicial and executive officers of the state and the federal governments, members of the Ohio General Assembly (but not members of Congress), members of the U.S. armed forces, postal workers, and anyone who claims an exemption "because of religious belief or other moral conviction held as a matter of conscience." O.R.C. section 5923.02.

Section 2
Repealed—Election of certain officers

Adopted in 1851 and repealed in 1953, this section provided for the election of certain militia officers.

Section 3
Officers to be appointed by the governor.

The governor shall appoint the adjutant general and such other officers and warrant officers, as may be provided for by law.

Adopted in 1851 and amended in 1953, this section addresses the appointment of the adjutant general (the administrative head of the organized militia) and other officers of the militia.

Under the 1802 Ohio Constitution, the governor had the power to appoint the adjutant general, but the system of selecting military officers has changed dramatically since 1802. The first constitution devoted seven sections to the election and appointment of military officers and went into great detail, including, for example, the election of majors by captains and subalterns of the battalions.

The 1851 Constitution did away with the election of military officers, but it included a clause in this section requiring major generals, brigadier generals, colonels, and commandants to appoint their staff, and captains to appoint their noncommissioned officers. In 1961, the voters modified this section to its current form under which the governor retains the authority to appoint the adjutant general and is given the power to appoint other officers as provided by law.

Section 4

Power of governor to call forth militia.

The governor shall have the power to call forth the militia, to execute the laws of the state, to suppress insurrection, to repel invasion, and to act in the event of a disaster within the state.

Adopted in 1851 and amended in 1961, this section originally gave the governor the power to commission all officers of the line and staff. The 1961 amendment dropped this power, but it left the governor with the power to call forth the militia.

Under section 923.21 of the Ohio Revised Code, the governor may call the organized militia by issuing a proclamation, "to execute the laws of this state, suppress insurrection, repel invasion, act in the event of a disaster, and promote the health, safety and welfare of the citizens."

Ohio law allows the militia to aid civil authorities in times of martial law, but it only permits the military to arrest civilians "for the purpose of escorting such civilians to civil authorities." O.R.C. section 5923.231.

Section 5

Public Arms.

The General Assembly shall provide, by law, for the protection and safekeeping of the public arms.

Adopted in 1851 and never amended, this section requires the General Assembly to provide for the protection and safekeeping of the public arms. Its supporting legislation is in chapter 5911 of the Ohio Revised Code.

Article X

County and Township Organizations

Counties and townships existed in Ohio before statehood. The Northwest Ordinance referred to both in directing the territorial governor "to lay out the parts of the district in which the Indian titles shall have been extinguished, into counties and townships, subject, however, to such alterations as may thereafter be made by the legislature." Ordinance of 1787, section 8. Unlike municipalities, which under Ohio law include cities and villages (see Art. XVIII, sec. 1), counties and townships are agencies or administrative arms of the state and have no inherent powers independent of the General Assembly. This article, however, allows counties (but not townships) to adopt charters by which they may exercise powers of local self-government analogous to the home rule powers conferred on municipalities under Article XVIII.

Article X has its origins in the 1851 Ohio Constitution, but, despite its having seven sections, it was a bare-bones article giving the General Assembly the power to create counties and townships but not defining their powers other than giving them "the power of local taxation for public purposes, as may be prescribed by law." Article X, section 7. In 1933, however, the voters approved a constitutional amendment, proposed by initiative petition, to restructure this article completely, to repeal all its existing sections, and to give counties the option of adopting home rule. Townships also have the option of adopting limited home rule, but the General Assembly has given them this option, see O.R.C. sections

The Ohio State Constitution. Steven H. Steinglass and Gino J. Scarselli, Oxford University Press. © Oxford University Press 2022. DOI: 10.1093/oso/9780197619728.003.0012

504.01–17. See generally Stephen Cianca, "Home Rule in Ohio Counties: Legal and Constitutional Perspectives," 19 *U. Dayton L. Rev.* 533 (1994).

Under the 1851 Constitution, the clerk of the court of common pleas was elected in each county for a three-year term, see 1851 Constitution, Article IV, section 16, but the voters repealed this provision in 1933, when they approved the county home rule amendment. Nothing in the Ohio Constitution expressly requires or bars the election of local clerks of court.

Although the General Assembly can create new counties, the 1851 Constitution requires that proposals to do so must be approved by the voters of the affected counties, see Article II, section 30. Not surprisingly, Ohio continues to have the eighty-eight counties that it had in 1851. The state also has 1,491 townships. *Baldwin's Ohio Township Law* (Cleveland: Banks-Baldwin Publishing Co., 2018), section 1:11.

Section 1

Organization and government of counties; county home rule; submission.

The General Assembly shall provide by general law for the organization and government of counties, and may provide by general law alternative forms of county government. No alternative form shall become operative in any county until submitted to the electors thereof and approved by a majority of those voting thereon under regulations provided by law. Municipalities and townships shall have authority, with the consent of the county, to transfer to the county any of their powers or to revoke the transfer of any such power, under regulations provided by general law, but the rights of initiative and referendum shall be secured to the people of such municipalities or townships in respect of every measure making or revoking such transfer and to the people of such county in respect of every measure giving or withdrawing such consent.

Adopted in 1933 and never amended, this section requires the General Assembly to provide by general law for the organization and government of counties. The General Assembly has created a general form of county government consisting of an elected board of county commissioners, various other elected officials, and a network of boards and commissions. The General Assembly is also permitted under this section to provide alternative forms of county government and has created an elected county executive plan and an "appointive county executive plan," O.R.C. section 302.02, but no county in Ohio has chosen an alternative form of government.

Under this section, the General Assembly may also delegate limited legislative powers to county governments (including the delegation of the power to fix the salaries of county officers) as long as the delegations do not interfere with the constitutional power of townships or municipalities. *Blacker v. Wiethe* (1968). Section 1, however, permits townships and municipalities to transfer some or all of their powers to counties in accordance with laws prescribed by the General Assembly. Therefore, this provision allows smaller townships and municipalities without adequate resources to rely on the county to supply government services. See Harvey Walker, "County Home Rule in Ohio," 1 *L.J. Ohio St. Student B.A.* 11 (1935). Such transfers, however, must be approved by the voters of both the county and the subdivision (i.e., the township or municipality). Additionally, townships and municipalities may revoke any transfer of their powers to a county, but as with transfers, any revocations must be approved by the voters of both the county and the subdivision.

The earlier version of this section was adopted in 1851 but repealed in 1933 (as part of the proposed initiative to create a new Art. X) provided in its entirety that "[t]he general assembly shall provide, by law, for the election of such county and township officers as may be necessary."

Section 2

Township officers; election; power.

The General Assembly shall provide by general law for the election of such township officers as may be necessary. The trustees of townships shall have such powers of local taxation as may be prescribed by law. No money shall be drawn from any township treasury except by authority of law.

Adopted in 1933 and never amended, this section requires the General Assembly to enact legislation for the election of township officers. It also allows the General Assembly to adopt legislation giving township trustees the power to collect taxes and spend township funds. Laws covering the election and duties of township officers and trustees are found in chapters 503 and 505 of the Ohio Revised Code.

Earlier versions of this section, which were adopted in 1851, amended in 1885, and repealed in 1933, established the date of elections.

Section 3

County charters; approval by voters.

The people of any county may frame and adopt or amend a charter as provided in this article but the right of the initiative and referendum is reserved to the people of each county on all matters which such county may now or hereafter be authorized to control by legislative action. Every such charter shall provide the form of government of the county and shall determine which of its officers shall be elected and the manner of their election. It shall provide for the exercise of all powers vested in, and the performance of all duties imposed upon counties and county officers by law. Any such charter may provide for the concurrent or exclusive exercise by the county, in all or in part of its area, of all or of any designated powers vested by the constitution or laws of Ohio in municipalities; it may provide for the organization of the county as a municipal corporation; and in any such case it may provide for the succession by the county to the rights, properties, and obligations of municipalities and townships therein incident to the municipal power so vested in the county, and for the division of the county into districts for purposes of administration or of taxation or of both. Any charter or amendment which alters the form and offices of county government or which provides for the exercise by the county of power vested in municipalities by the constitution or laws of Ohio, or both, shall become effective if approved by a majority of the electors voting thereon. In case of conflict between the exercise of powers granted by such charter and the exercise of powers by municipalities or townships, granted by the constitution or general law, whether or not such powers are being exercised at the time of the adoption of the charter, the exercise of power by the municipality or township shall prevail. A charter or amendment providing for the exclusive exercise of municipal powers by the county or providing for the succession by the county to any property or obligation of any municipality or township without the consent of the legislative authority of such municipality or township shall become effective only when it shall have been approved by a majority of those voting thereon (1) in the county, (2) in the largest municipality, (3) in the county outside of such municipality, and (4) in counties having a population, based upon the latest preceding federal decennial census of 500,000 or less, in each of a majority of the combined total of municipalities and townships in the county (not included within any township any part of its area lying within a municipality).

Adopted in 1933 and amended in 1957, this is the key section of Article X. It allows counties to exercise powers of local self-government and other home rule powers analogous to the powers granted to municipalities under Article XVIII, sections 3 and 7. This section, however, requires counties to adopt charters before they can exercise home rule powers. Absent a charter, counties may exercise only those powers expressly granted by the General Assembly. *Geauga County Board of Commissioners v. Munn Road Sand & Gravel* (1993). In contrast, since the adoption of the municipal home rule amendment in 1912, municipalities have possessed the constitutional power of local self-government and may exercise control over their internal affairs regardless of whether they have adopted a charter Ibid. See Commentary to Article XVIII, section 3.

Under this section, every county charter must provide a form of county government and must determine which county officers shall be elected and the manner of their election. In addition, every charter must continue to provide all the powers and duties conferred on counties and county officers under state law. Beyond these minimal requirements, a county charter may also "provide for the concurrent or exclusive exercise by the county, in all or in part of its area, of all or of any designated powers vested by the constitution or laws of Ohio in municipalities." If, however, the exercise of powers granted by a county charter conflicts with the exercise of powers granted to a municipality or township, this section provides that the municipality or township prevails.

All charters that change the form and offices of county government or provide for the exercise of municipal powers must be approved by a majority of the county electors voting on the question. Before the 1957 amendment, county charters that vested *any* municipal power in counties had to be approved by four separate majorities: (1) a majority of the voters in the county; (2) a majority of the voters in the largest city in the county; (3) a majority of voters outside the largest city; and (4) a majority of the county's cities, villages, and townships.

In 1935, an elected Cuyahoga County Charter Commission proposed a charter that would have provided for a county manager and a county council elected by proportional representation, but the proposed charter vested some municipal powers in the county (though it did not divest municipalities of those powers). The requisite majority of the voters in Cuyahoga County and in the City of Cleveland approved the proposed charter, but it failed to obtain the requisite majority vote in the county outside Cleveland. Nor did a majority of the county's cities, villages, and townships support the charter, and the Ohio Supreme Court upheld the refusal of the county commissioners to certify the charter. *State ex rel. Howland v. Krause* (1936).

Subsequently, the 1957 amendment to this section modified the four-majority requirement by eliminating the requirement that a majority of the combined total of municipalities and townships support the charter in counties having a population of 500,000 or more. More important, the 1957 amendment eliminated the language applying the four-majority requirement whenever the charter vested any municipal power in the county, and under the amended section the four-majority requirement only applies when the charter provides for the *exclusive* exercise of municipal powers by the county.

Although county home rule has been advanced as a great opportunity to make local government more efficient, Summit County and Cuyahoga County are the only counties in the state that have adopted charters.

This section also reserves the "right of the initiative and referendum" to the "people of each county" but the secretary or state may keep off the ballot proposed charters that do not provide for the election or appointment of a county executive or for any meaningful change in the structure of county government. *State ex rel. Walker v. Husted* (2015). And to appear on the ballot a proposed charter must "provide for the exercise of all powers vested in, and the performance of all duties imposed upon counties and county officers by law." *State ex rel. McGinn v. Walker* (2017). See Commentary, Article II, section 1f.

The General Assembly has adopted two mutually exclusive statutory proceedings for reviewing decisions by election officials to place or to refuse to place proposed charter or charter amendments on the ballot, and (where these procedures are not adequate) the Ohio Supreme Court may exercise original (but not exclusive) jurisdiction over extraordinary writs seeking to review the actions of election officials. See *State ex rel. Jones v. Husted* (2016) (*Jones I*).

An earlier version of this section adopted in 1851 but repealed in 1933 provided that sheriff and county treasurer could not serve in their offices for more than four years in any period of six years.

Section 4

County charter commission; duties; election.

The legislative authority (which includes the Board of County Commissioners) of any county may by a two-thirds vote of its members, or upon petition of eight per cent of the electors of the county as certified by the election authorities of the county shall forthwith, by resolution submit to the electors of the county the question, "Shall a county charter commission be chosen?" The question shall be voted upon at the next general election, occurring not sooner than ninety-five days after certification of the resolution to the election authorities. The ballot containing the question shall bear no party designation. Provision shall be made thereon for the election to such commission from the county at large of fifteen electors if a majority of the electors voting on the question have voted in the affirmative.

Candidates for such commission shall be nominated by petition of one per cent of the electors of the county.

The petition shall be filed with the election authorities no less than seventy-five days prior to such election. Candidates shall be declared elected in the order of the number of votes received, beginning with the candidate receiving the largest number; but not more than seven candidates residing in the same city or village may be elected. The holding of a public office does not preclude any person from seeking or holding membership on a county charter commission nor does membership on a county charter commission preclude any such member from seeking or holding other public office, but not more than four officeholders may be elected to a county charter commission at the same time. The legislative authority shall appropriate sufficient sums to enable the charter commission to perform its duties and to pay all reasonable expenses thereof.

The commission shall frame a charter for the county or amendments to the existing charter, and shall, by vote of a majority of the authorized number of members of the commission, submit the same to the electors of the county, to be voted upon at the next general election next following the election of the commission. The commission shall certify the proposed charter or amendments to the election authorities not later than seventy-five days prior to such election. Amendments to a county charter or the question of the repeal thereof may also be submitted to the electors of the county in the manner provided in this section for the submission of the question whether a charter commission shall be chosen, to be voted upon at the first general election occurring not sooner than sixty days after their submission. The legislative authority or charter commission submitting any charter or amendment shall, not later than thirty days prior to the election on such charter or amendment, mail or otherwise distribute a copy thereof to each of the electors of the county as far as may be reasonably possible, except that, as provided by law, notice of proposed amendments may be given by newspaper advertising. Except as provided in Section 3 of this Article, every charter or amendment shall become effective if it has been approved by the majority of the electors voting thereon. It shall take effect on the thirtieth day after such approval unless another date be fixed therein. When more than one amendment, which shall relate to only one subject but may affect or include more than one section or part of a charter, is submitted at the same time, they shall be so submitted as to enable the electors to vote on each separately. In case more than one charter is submitted at the same time or in case of conflict between the provisions of two or more amendments submitted at the same time, that charter or provision shall prevail which received the highest affirmative vote, not less than a majority. If a charter or amendment submitted by a charter commission is not approved by the electors of the county, the charter commission may resubmit the same one time, in its original form or as revised by the charter commission, to the electors of the county at the next succeeding general election or at any other election held throughout the county prior thereto, in the manner provided for the original submission thereof.

The legislative authority of any county, upon petition of ten per cent of the electors of the county, shall forthwith, by resolution, submit to the electors of the county, in the manner provided in this section for the submission of the question whether a charter commission shall be chosen, the question of the adoption of a charter in the form attached to such petition.

Laws may be passed to provide for the organization and procedures of county charter commissions, including the filling of any vacancy which may occur, and otherwise to facilitate the operation of this section. The basis upon which the required number of petitioners in any case provided for in this section shall be determined, shall be the total number of votes cast in the county for the office of governor at the last preceding general election therefor.

The foregoing provisions of this section shall be self-executing except as herein otherwise provided.

Adopted in 1933 and amended in 1978, this section outlines the two ways in which a county charter may be drafted and submitted to the voters: through an elected county charter commission or directly by the voters.

The county's legislative body by a two-thirds vote may adopt a resolution asking "Shall a county charter commission be chosen?" Alternatively, a petition signed by 8 percent of the county electors may present the same question to the voters.

If the issue is approved by a majority of the voters voting on it, the voters then elect a charter commission that is responsible for drafting a charter. The charter is then submitted to the voters for approval. A charter may also be submitted directly to the voters by a petition signed by 10 percent of the county electors.

The 1978 amendment revised multiple aspects of this section. These changes included modifying the one-subject rule for any proposed charter amendments, modifying the conflict-resolution provision for conflicting petitions approved in the same election, permitting a county charter commission to resubmit a failed proposal a second time, providing for the appropriation of funds for circulating a proposal, authorizing the General Assembly to pass laws regulating county commissions, changing the deadline to submit a proposal from sixty days to ninety-five days before an election, changing the time at which a person must file to qualify as a candidate for member of the county charter commission, permitting up to four public office holders to be elected as members of a fifteen-member county charter commission, permitting members of a county charter commission to run for public office, reducing the number of signatures needed to place an amendment or a proposal to create a charter commission on the ballot from 10 percent to 8 percent, and adding a method for electors to place a proposed charter directly on the ballot by submitting a petition signed by 10 percent of the electors to the county commission. In addition, the amendment added a provision to allow electors to hold a vote on whether to repeal a measure upon a vote of two-thirds of the county commissioners or 8 percent of the county's electors. Finally, the amended section rejected an Ohio Attorney General Opinion that had taken the position that newspaper advertising did not meet the "mail or otherwise distribute" requirement. The new language expressly provided that notice of proposed charter amendments may be given by newspaper advertising if provided by law and published in the newspapers at least thirty days before the election.

Sections 5–7
Repealed

Adopted in 1851 and repealed in 1933, these sections addressed, respectively, the withdrawal of funds from county and township treasuries (sec. 5), the removal of justices of the peace and county and township officers (sec. 6), and powers of local taxation (sec. 7).

Article XI

Apportionment

Article XI governs the apportionment of seats in the Ohio General Assembly, one of the most important and controversial issues in Ohio constitutional and political history.

In 2015, the voters approved an amendment recommended by the General Assembly to repeal and replace the prior article with a bipartisan commission-based process and strong antigerrymandering provisions. The ballot language had advised voters that the goal of the proposed amendment was to "end the partisan process for drawing Ohio House and Senate districts, and replace it with a bipartisan process with the goal of having district boundaries that are compact and politically competitive." See Issue 1, *Ballot Issues for the 2015 November Election* (Ohio Secretary of State website).

Then, in 2018 the General Assembly (against the backdrop of a threatened proposed redistricting initiative) recommended and the voters approved an amendment that revised this article by expanding the duties of the Ohio Redistricting Commission to include a backup role in congressional redistricting and that adopted an entirely new article, Article XIX, to govern congressional redistricting. The overwhelmingly favorable votes on these proposed amendments (both of which were approved by the voters by more than 2:1 margins) suggest a broad public commitment to reducing the extreme partisanship that historically has characterized legislative apportionment and congressional redistricting in Ohio.

The Ohio State Constitution. Steven H. Steinglass and Gino J. Scarselli, Oxford University Press. © Oxford University Press 2022. DOI: 10.1093/oso/9780197619728.003.0013

The effective date for both the 2015 and the 2018 changes was January 1, 2021.

■ BACKGROUND

Under the 1802 Constitution, the General Assembly had total control over the apportionment of seats in the Ohio House and Senate, and the number of seats and their apportionment largely depended upon the party in power. *State ex rel. Herbert v. Bricker* (1942). See Thomas R. Swisher, ed., *Ohio Constitution Handbook* (Cleveland: Banks-Baldwin Law Publishing Co., 1990), 427. Apportionment was initially based only on counties, and the 1802 Constitution provided that the house would have between twenty-four and thirty-six members until the state had 22,000 white male inhabitants above twenty-one years of age; at that time the General Assembly was required to provide that the number of house members would be between thirty-six and seventy-two. 1802 Constitution, Article I, section 2. The number of members of the Senate, which was also left to the General Assembly, was between one-third and one-half of the number of House members. 1802 Constitution, Article I, section 6. And the constitution required a new enumeration and apportionment every four years. 1802 Constitution, Article I, section 2.

Gerrymandering was a common practice in the first fifty years of statehood, and the 1851 Ohio Constitution sought to address this issue by transferring responsibility for apportionment from the General Assembly to a board consisting of the governor, the state auditor, and the secretary of state. The resulting apportionments, which took place every ten years, were still characterized by districts drawn along county lines, and in 1903 the voters constitutionalized the county-based approach to apportionment by approving the Hanna Amendment, which provided "that each county shall have [at least] one representative [regardless of population]." Ohio Constitution, Article XI, section 2 (1903).

In 1967, the voters completely reorganized this article in response to decisions by the federal courts. In *Baker v. Carr* (1962), the U.S. Supreme Court had limited the political question doctrine and permitted challenges to the drawing of state legislative districts. And in *Reynolds v. Sims* (1964), the Court held that the Equal Protection Clause of the Fourteenth Amendment required state legislative districts to have substantially equivalent populations under the "one person, one vote" principle. Finally, in the wake of *Reynolds*, the Court reversed a district court decision that had upheld the amended version of this article. *Nolan v. Rhodes* (1964).

In 2012, the Ohio Supreme Court rejected a challenge to the apportionment plan adopted in 2011 by the state apportionment board (which had been expanded to five members in 1967). In *Wilson v. Kasich* (2012), the court looked to the text and stated that "[t]he words used in Article XI do not explicitly require political neutrality, or for that matter, politically competitive districts or representational fairness, in the apportionment board's creation of state legislative districts." It then held that "[t]he Ohio Constitution does not mandate political neutrality in the reapportionment of house and senate districts, but partisan considerations cannot prevail over the nonpartisan requirements . . . ." (syllabus). Finally, the court held that the board retained discretion to decide which of the multiple apportionment requirements should apply. See also Commentary, Article XI, section 6. This set the table for the 2015 proposal to adopt an entirely new article to govern apportionment.

■ 2022 LITIGATION

The voters' approval of new constitutional standards and procedures for state redistricting led to one of the most contentious chapters in the history of Ohio constitutional litigation.

On January 12, 2022, in its first case construing this article, the Ohio Supreme Court in *League of Women Voters of Ohio v Ohio Redistricting Commission* (2022) (*League I*), held that the four-year state redistricting plan adopted by the commission on a 5-2 strictly partisan vote violated the nonpartisanship and proportionality requirements of sections 6(A) and 6(B). In so ruling, the court held that these requirements were enforceable not just aspirational; that the proportionality requirement in section 6(B) referred to the voting preferences of voters and not to the results of elections; that stand-alone violations of section 6 were actionable; and that four-year plans were subject to judicial review.

In her concurring opinion, Ohio Supreme Court Chief Justice Maureen O'Connor (perhaps anticipating what would be happening in this contentious litigation) pointed out that there were alternative methods to address redistricting in which partisanship is removed from the process, and she specifically pointed to the independent redistricting commissions operating in Arizona, California and Michigan.

> Having now seen firsthand that the current Ohio Redistricting Commission—comprised of statewide elected officials and partisan legislators—is seemingly unwilling to put aside partisan concerns as directed by the people's vote, Ohioans may opt to pursue further constitutional amendment to replace the current commission with a truly independent, nonpartisan commission that more effectively distances the redistricting process from partisan politics.
>
> *League I* (O'Connor, C.J, concurring).

On February 7, 2022, in *League of Women Voters of Ohio v Ohio Redistricting Commission* (2022) (*League II*), the court held that the second four-year state redistricting plan adopted by the commission did not remedy the defects identified by the court. In rejecting the second plan in its entirety, the court read sections 6(A) and 6(B) *in pari materia* to conclude that the plan violated the nonpartisanship standard by treating Democratic and Republican districts differently, thus favoring one political party. And on March 16, 2022, in *League of Women Voters of Ohio v Ohio Redistricting Commission* (2022) (*League III*), the court held that the third four-year state redistricting plan submitted by the commission did not remedy the constitutional defects identified in the court's earlier decisions. In rejecting this plan, the court concluded that the plan (which met the 54–46 per cent proportionality standard) was nonetheless invalid because "a disproportionate number of toss-up districts are labeled Democratic-leaning." The court also stated that the "gross and unnecessary disparity in the allocation of close districts is what offends Article XI, Section 6(B)." Finally, the court criticized the failure of the Republican legislative leaders on the commission to work with the Democrats and the other commission members, and it ordered the members of the commission to work together to draft a state redistricting plan through a transparent process and to retain an independent map drawer answerable to all commission members to assist in drafting a new plan. *Ibid.* On March 28, 2022, however, the commission adopted a fourth four-year state redistricting plan that made only minor tweaks in the plan that had been rejected by the state court.

On April 14, 2022, the Ohio Supreme Court rejected the fourth redistricting plan but declined to order the adoption of a specific redistricting plan to avoid a violation of federal law, relying, in part, on the "no court" language in sections 9(D)(1) and (2). *League of Women Voters of Ohio v Ohio Redistricting Commission* (2022) (*League IV*). These limitations, however, should not tie the court's hands (any more than they limit the power of federal courts) when a proposed redistricting plan violates both state and federal law. See Commentary on Art. XI, sec.9(D)(1) and (2).

Meanwhile, on April 20, 2022, a three-judge federal district court in a case filed to get the federal court to adopt a state redistricting plan that had been rejected by the Ohio Supreme Court joined the fray. In a major departure from principles of judicial federalism under which state courts are the final arbiters of the meaning of state constitutions, the three-judge court announced that it would order the adoption of the third state redistricting plan for a two-year period if the commission did not adopt a compliant plan by May 28, 2022. *See Gonidakis v Ohio Redistricting Commission* (2022).

Finally, on May 9, 2022, the commission submitted its fifth redistricting plan, which consisted of a re-submission of the state-court-rejected third state redistricting plan, thus making it likely that the federal court would order the use in the 2022 election of a redistricting plan that had been rejected by the Ohio Supreme Court, unless the court used its contempt power to force the commission and its members to comply with the requirements of its earlier decisions and the Ohio Constitution.

Section 1
Ohio redistricting commission.

(A) The Ohio redistricting commission shall be responsible for the redistricting of this state for the general assembly. The commission shall consist of the following seven members:

(1) The governor;

(2) The auditor of state;

(3) The secretary of state;

(4) One person appointed by the speaker of the house of representatives;

(5) One person appointed by the legislative leader of the largest political party in the house of representatives of which the speaker of the house of representatives is not a member;

(6) One person appointed by the president of the senate; and

(7) One person appointed by the legislative leader of the largest political party in the senate of which the president of the senate is not a member.

No appointed member of the commission shall be a current member of congress.

The legislative leaders in the senate and the house of representatives of each of the two largest political parties represented in the general assembly, acting jointly by political party, shall appoint a member of the commission to serve as a co-chairperson of the commission.

(B)(1) Unless otherwise specified in this article or in Article XIX of this constitution, a simple majority of the commission members shall be required for any action by the commission.

(2)(a) Except as otherwise provided in division (B)(2)(b) of this section, a majority vote of the members of the commission, including at least one member of the commission who is a member of each of the two largest political parties represented in the general assembly, shall be required to do any of the following:

(i) Adopt rules of the commission;

(ii) Hire staff for the commission;

(iii) Expend funds.

(b) If the commission is unable to agree, by the vote required under division (B)(2)(a) of this section, on the manner in which funds should be expended, each co-chairperson of the commission shall have the authority to expend one-half of the funds that have been appropriated to the commission.

(3) The affirmative vote of four members of the commission, including at least two members of the commission who represent each of the two largest political parties represented in the general assembly shall be required to adopt any general assembly district plan. For the purposes of this division and of Section 1 of Article XIX of this constitution, a member of the commission shall be considered to represent a political party if the member was

appointed to the commission by a member of that political party or if, in the case of the governor, the auditor of state, or the secretary of state, the member is a member of that political party.

(C) At the first meeting of the commission, which the governor shall convene only in a year ending in the numeral one, except as provided in Sections 8 and 9 of this article and in Sections 1 and 3 of Article XIX of this constitution, the commission shall set a schedule for the adoption of procedural rules for the operation of the commission.

The commission shall release to the public a proposed general assembly district plan for the boundaries for each of the ninety-nine house of representatives districts and the thirty-three senate districts. The commission shall draft the proposed plan in the manner prescribed in this article. Before adopting, but after introducing, a proposed plan, the commission shall conduct a minimum of three public hearings across the state to present the proposed plan and shall seek public input regarding the proposed plan. All meetings of the commission shall be open to the public. Meetings shall be broadcast by electronic means of transmission using a medium readily accessible by the general public.

The commission shall adopt a final general assembly district plan not later than the first day of September of a year ending in the numeral one. After the commission adopts a final plan, the commission shall promptly file the plan with the secretary of state. Upon filing with the secretary of state, the plan shall become effective.

Four weeks after the adoption of a general assembly district plan or a congressional district plan, whichever is later, the commission shall be automatically dissolved.

(D) The general assembly shall be responsible for making the appropriations it determines necessary in order for the commission to perform its duties under this article and Article XIX of this constitution.

Adopted in 2015 and amended in 2018, this section replaced prior section 1 to make several noteworthy changes in how the General Assembly is apportioned and to eliminate partisan gerrymandering. Like the repealed section, the new section requires the creation of ninety-nine house districts and thirty-three senate districts every ten years.

First, the new section replaced the five-member apportionment board with a seven-member Ohio Redistricting Commission and transferred responsibility for apportioning the state to this commission. The commission now consists of three statewide elected officials––the governor, the auditor, and the secretary of state––and four persons appointed by the majority and minority leaders of the General Assembly. These four persons include one chosen by the speaker of the House, one chosen by the president of the Senate, one chosen by the minority leader of the House, and one chosen by the minority leader of the Senate. In contrast, the apportionment board under the 1967 predecessor consisted of the three statewide elected officials and two legislators from different houses and different political parties. The new section also added a bipartisan cochairperson requirement under which the legislative leaders of the two largest political parties in the General Assembly, acting jointly by political party, appoint a member of the commission to serve as cochairperson.

Second, the new section makes important procedural changes in the apportionment process. Under the repealed version, a simple majority of members present was sufficient to approve any action. The new version retains the simple majority vote for most subjects, but for votes to adopt rules, to hire staff, or to expend funds it requires that there be a bipartisan majority vote with at least two of the four votes coming from members of opposing political parties. The General Assembly is responsible for approving the necessary appropriations for the commission, but if a stalemate results on the manner of expending funds, each cochairperson assumes the power to expend half of the appropriated funds.

Third, the new section seeks to ensure transparency during the process. The commission must make all of its meetings open to the public, and it must conduct at least three public hearings across the state to present the plan to the public. At these hearings, the commission must seek public input regarding the proposed plan. In addition, the commission must publicly broadcast the meetings electronically using a medium readily accessible by the general public.

Fourth, the new section reduces the role of the governor by eliminating gubernatorial control over the choice of the date, time, and place of meetings. It also continues the prior policy of not permitting the governor to exercise the veto power by providing that the plan be filed promptly with the secretary of state and that the plan becomes effective upon this filing. And the inclusion of an effective date precludes the use of the referendum under Article II, section 1d, to challenge a general assembly redistricting plan.

Fifth, the new section requires the commission to set a schedule for adopting procedural rules at its first meeting and to adopt a final plan, by bipartisan vote, no later than September 1 of the year ending in one. Once adopted, the commission must file the plan promptly with the secretary of state, and the plan becomes effective upon this filing.

Finally, section 1 provides that four weeks after adopting a general assembly district plan or a congressional district plan, whichever is later, the commission shall automatically dissolve.

In 2018, the voters approved an amendment of the yet-to-be-effective section 1 to add provisions on congressional redistricting. See Article XIX, sections 1 and 2, and Commentaries thereon. One new provision prohibits the General Assembly from appointing a current member of the U.S. Congress to serve as a member of the commission.

On January 12, 2022, in its first case construing this article, the Ohio Supreme Court in *League of Women Voters of Ohio v. Ohio Redistricting Commission* (2022), held that in suits challenging state apportionment plans under this article, the commission is "the only necessary respondent, but the better practice, . . . is to name the commission's members as respondents, too" (internal quotations omitted). In this case, the court held that the four-year plan adopted by the commission on a 5-2 partisan vote violated the nonpartisanship and proportionality requirements of section 6(A) and 6(B).

In her concurring opinion in *League of Women Voters,* Ohio Supreme Court Chief Justice Maureen O'Connor pointed out that there were alternative methods to address redistricting in which partisanship is removed from the process, and she specifically pointed to the independent redistricting commissions operating in Arizona, California, and Michigan.

> Having now seen firsthand that the current Ohio Redistricting Commission—comprised of statewide elected officials and partisan legislators—is seemingly unwilling to put aside partisan concerns as directed by the people's vote, Ohioans may opt to pursue further constitutional amendment to replace the current commission with a truly independent, nonpartisan commission that more effectively distances the redistricting process from partisan politics.
>
> *League of Women Voters of Ohio v. Ohio Redistricting Commission* (2022) (O'Connor, C.J, concurring).

■ PRIOR PROVISIONS FOR APPORTIONING SEATS

The predecessors to the 1967 version of this section did not divide the House or the Senate into a specific number of districts. Instead, they created a "ratio of representation," or apportionment ratio, equal to one one-hundredth of the population of the state determined by the last federal census. The public officials designated to apportion the state then used that ratio to determine the number of districts on a county-by-county basis.

Prior to 1967, as a result of the 1903 Hanna Amendment, each county was entitled to at least one representative in the house. Based on that requirement and on a complex formula for allocating additional seats under which counties with less than one and three-fourths of the ratio were entitled to only a single representative, people living in rural counties with small populations had a distinct political advantage. For example, in 1960 the state's population was 9,706,397, and the ratio of representation was 97,064. As a result, counties with less than 169,862 inhabitants (ratio times one and three-fourths) were entitled to one representative. Because every county had to have a representative, counties with populations less than but close to 169,862 were treated the same as counties with much smaller populations. Thus, Vinton County with a 1960 population of 10,274 and Clark County with a population of 131,440 each had only one representative. *Nolan v. Rhodes* (1963).

In response to the U.S. Supreme Court's decision in *Nolan v. Rhodes* (1964) summarily reversing a federal district court decision that had upheld the state's 1960 apportionment plan, the General Assembly proposed an amendment to revise Article XI; but in 1965 the voters rejected it. In 1967, the General Assembly proposed another amendment to revise Article XI, which the voters approved.

Under the 1967 amendment, each county was no longer entitled to a representative. Instead, the public officials designated to apportion the state divide the state's population by ninety-nine (the number of seats in the House of Representatives) to determine the representation ratio for the House and by thirty-three (the number of seats in the Senate) to determine the representation ratio for the state Senate. These ratios represent the "ideal populations" of house and senate districts, and officials were required to use them to determine the permissible district population ranges. But despite the repeal of the Hanna Amendment, preference was still given to districts drawn along county lines.

Section 2

Number of representatives per district.

Each house of representatives district shall be entitled to a single representative in each general assembly. Each senate district shall be entitled to a single senator in each general assembly.

Originally adopted as section 5 in the 1967 reorganization of this article, this section provides that there be a single representative for each house district and a single senator for each senate district. The 2015 revision of this article kept this section unchanged and simply moved it to section 2.

Prior to the 1967 reorganization, Ohio had a "curious combination of single-member and multiple member districts" with the most populated counties having more than one state representative and more than one state senator. David King, "The Ohio General Assembly," in Harvey Walker, ed., *An Analysis and Appraisal of the Ohio State Constitution 1851–1951* (Cincinnati: The Stephen H. Wilder Foundation, 1951). In 1950, for example, Cuyahoga County, which consisted of a single house and senate district, elected six senators and eighteen representatives at large. Ibid.

Section 3

Ratio of representation; requirements for general assembly house districts; splitting of counties, municipal corporations, and townships.

(A) The whole population of the state, as determined by the federal decennial census or, if such is unavailable, such other basis as the general assembly may direct, shall be divided by the number "ninety-nine" and by the number "thirty-three" and the quotients shall be the ratio of representation in the house of representatives and in the senate, respectively, for ten years next succeeding such redistricting.

(B) A general assembly district plan shall comply with all of the requirements of division (B) of this section.

(1) The population of each house of representatives district shall be substantially equal to the ratio of representation in the house of representatives, and the population of each senate district shall be substantially equal to the ratio of representation in the senate, as provided in division (A) of this section. In no event shall any district contain a population of less than ninety-five per cent nor more than one hundred five per cent of the applicable ratio of representation.

(2) Any general assembly district plan adopted by the commission shall comply with all applicable provisions of the constitutions of Ohio and the United States and of federal law.

(3) Every general assembly district shall be composed of contiguous territory, and the boundary of each district shall be a single nonintersecting continuous line.

(C) House of representatives districts shall be created and numbered in the following order of priority, to the extent that such order is consistent with the foregoing standards:

(1) Proceeding in succession from the largest to the smallest, each county containing population greater than one hundred five per cent of the ratio of representation in the house of representatives shall be divided into as many house of representatives districts as it has whole ratios of representation. Any fraction of the population in excess of a whole ratio shall be a part of only one adjoining house of representatives district.

(2) Each county containing population of not less than ninety-five per cent of the ratio of representation in the house of representatives nor more than one hundred five per cent of the ratio shall be designated a representative district.

(3) The remaining territory of the state shall be divided into representative districts by combining the areas of counties, municipal corporations, and townships. Where feasible, no county shall be split more than once.

(D)(1)(a) Except as otherwise provided in divisions (D)(1)(b) and (c) of this section, a county, municipal corporation, or township is considered to be split if any contiguous portion of its territory is not contained entirely within one district.

(b) If a municipal corporation or township has territory in more than one county, the contiguous portion of that municipal corporation or township that lies in each county shall be considered to be a separate municipal corporation or township for the purposes of this section.

(c) If a municipal corporation or township that is located in a county that contains a municipal corporation or township that has a population of more than one ratio of representation is split for the purpose of complying with division (E)(1)(a) or (b) of this section, each portion of that municipal corporation or township shall be considered to be a separate municipal corporation or township for the purposes of this section.

(2) Representative districts shall be drawn so as to split the smallest possible number of municipal corporations and townships whose contiguous portions contain a population of more than fifty per cent, but less than one hundred per cent, of one ratio of representation.

(3) Where the requirements of divisions (B), (C), and (D) of this section cannot feasibly be attained by forming a representative district from whole municipal corporations and townships, not more than one municipal corporation or township may be split per representative district.

(E)(1) If it is not possible for the commission to comply with all of the requirements of divisions (B), (C), and (D) of this section in drawing a particular representative district, the commission shall take the first action listed below that makes it possible for the commission to draw that district:

(a) Notwithstanding division (D)(3) of this section, the commission shall create the district by splitting two municipal corporations or townships whose contiguous portions do not contain a population of more than fifty per cent, but less than one hundred per cent, of one ratio of representation.

(b) Notwithstanding division (D)(2) of this section, the commission shall create the district by splitting a municipal corporation or township whose contiguous portions contain a population of more than fifty per cent, but less than one hundred per cent, of one ratio of representation.

(c) Notwithstanding division (C)(2) of this section, the commission shall create the district by splitting, once, a single county that contains a population of not less than ninety-five per cent of the ratio of representation, but not more than one hundred five per cent of the ratio of representation.

(d) Notwithstanding division (C)(1) of this section, the commission shall create the district by including in two districts portions of the territory that remains after a county that contains a population of more than one hundred five per cent of the ratio of representation has been divided into as many house of representatives districts as it has whole ratios of representation.

(2) If the commission takes an action under division (E)(1) of this section, the commission shall include in the general assembly district plan a statement explaining which action the commission took under that division and the reason the commission took that action.

(3) If the commission complies with divisions (E)(1) and (2) of this section in drawing a district, the commission shall not be considered to have violated division (C)(1), (C)(2), (D)(2), or (D)(3) of this section, as applicable, in drawing that district, for the purpose of an analysis under division (D) of Section 9 of this article.

The 2015 amendment to this article created a detailed and lengthy section that combined and replaced portions of prior sections 2, 3, 4, 7, 8, 9, and 10.

Section 3(A), previously section 2, describes the method of apportioning seats in the General Assembly. It requires the commission to divide the state's population by ninety-nine (the number of seats in the Ohio House of Representatives) to determine the representation ratio in the House and to divide the state's population by thirty-three (the number of seats in the Ohio Senate) to determine the representation ratio for the state Senate. These ratios represent the "ideal populations" of house and senate districts, which the commission then uses to determine the permissible district population ranges.

Section 3(B) sets out the basic requirements for any general assembly district. Section 3(B)(1) combines the previous sections 3 and 4 of this article to provide the permissible population ranges for house and senate districts. It provides that the population of each house district must substantially equal the house representation ratio (i.e., the "ideal" house district population), which is 1/99 of the population of the state at the last federal census, and the population of each senate district must substantially equal the senate ratio, which is 1/33 of the population of the state at the last federal census. It also permits districts to vary slightly from the ideal ratio, but no district can have a population less than 95 percent or greater than 105 percent of the ideal district size. Section 3(B)(2) requires any proposed apportionment plan to comply with the Ohio Constitution, the U.S. Constitution, and all federal laws. Finally, section 3(B)(3), previously section 7(A), requires the commission to draw every general assembly district from contiguous territory with a continuous, nonintersecting boundary line.

Section 3(C) provides for the creation and numbering of house of representative districts. Thus, it combines the substantive standards from the prior sections 3, 4, 7, 8, and 9, with the procedural standards in the prior section 10 into one streamlined section. Section 3(C)(1), previously section 8, provides that the commission must divide any county containing a population greater than 105 percent of a whole ratio of representation into as many districts as it has whole ratios of representation. Next, the commission must take any remaining fraction of the population in excess of a whole ratio and make it part of an adjoining house district. The commission must divide the counties in this way on a county-by-county basis, starting with the largest county and proceeding in succession from the largest county to the smallest county. Thus, the amendment removed any ambiguity over whether the apportionment board had discretion over which counties to look to first when creating house districts.

Section 3(C)(2), previously section 9, provides that the commission must designate a county as a representative district if its population falls within 95 percent and 105 percent of the ratio of representation, removing any language granting the commission discretion over whether to follow this requirement.

Section 3(C)(3) modifies and replaces sections 7 and 10. This section instructs the commission to divide the remaining territory of the state into districts by combining the areas of counties, municipal corporations, and townships. This section states that the commission shall not split a county more than once where feasible. Section 3(D)(1)(a) explains that the commission may consider a county "split" if any contiguous portion of the county's territory is not contained entirely within one district. Sections 3(D)(1)(b) and (c) explain how the commission must treat a municipal corporation or township that has territory in more than one district for purposes of apportionment. Section 3(D)(2) instructs the commission to draw representative districts so as to split the smallest possible number of municipal corporations and townships with populations between 50 and 100 percent of a ratio of representation. Finally, section 3(D)(3) gives the commission the discretion to split a municipal corporation or township if the commission cannot feasibly form a district without doing so after complying with all the requirements of sections 3(B), (C), and (D); however, the commission may not split more than one municipal corporation or township per representative district under this provision.

Section 3(E)(1) gives the commission instructions if it is "not possible" for the commission to comply with all the requirements of sections (B), (C), and (D) when drawing representative districts. This section favors splitting two less populous municipal corporations or townships. See Article XI, section 3(E)(1)(a). If not possible, this section then favors splitting a larger municipal corporation or township. See Article XI, section 3(E)(1)(b). If the commission cannot resolve the issue through splitting a township or municipal corporation, only then can the commission resort to splitting a county, and the commission must split a less populous county before a more populous one. See Article XI, sections 3(E)(1)(c)–(d). Previously, the apportionment board had almost unreviewable discretion over which governmental units to split and in which order. Now, the express language of this section substantially limits the commission's discretion.

Section 3(E)(2) requires the commission to include a written statement in a proposed apportionment plan if it took any action under section 3(E)(1) and to explain the reason for taking that action. This requirement helps avoid the evidentiary problems faced in *Wilson v. Kasich* (2012) by having the commission create a reliable record of any splitting of governmental units in advance of any litigation. The amended version also added an incentive for the commission to comply with this requirement in section 3(E)(3). It states that a court of competent jurisdiction will not consider the commission to have violated sections 3(C)(1), (C)(2), (D)(2), or (D)(3) in a constitutional challenge if the commission complies with all of section 3(E)'s requirements, which includes the written record requirement. Thus, if the commission fails to make such a written record, it cannot later avail itself of section 3(E)(3)'s protection.

■ PRIOR POPULATION RANGES

Prior to the 2015 revision of this article, the 10 percent population range for the ninety-nine house districts was not an absolute requirement, and district lines could vary from the representation ratio to avoid dividing certain counties into more than one district. See Article XI, former section 9.

Because of this exception, the "total" or "maximum" deviation between the districts with the highest and lowest populations could exceed 10 percent, and in *Voinovich v. Quilter* (1993), the U.S. Supreme Court held that Ohio's apportionment plan following the 1990 census gave rise to a prima facie violation of equal protection because the total deviation between districts exceeded 10 percent.

Under that plan, the largest house district had a deviation of 104.91 percent of the representation ratio and the smallest district had a deviation of 91.10 percent, for a total deviation of 13.81 percent (104.91 percent minus 91.10 percent). Although the court noted that minor differences in total deviations were permissible, it returned the case to the district court for a ruling on whether the deviation was rationally related to the state policy of preserving county borders and on whether the total deviation exceeded constitutional limits. On remand, the district court upheld the plan finding that it was rationally related to the state policy of preserving county borders and that the total deviation of 13.81 percent did not exceed federal constitutional limits. *Quilter v. Voinovich* (1994).

Section 4

Composition and numbering of senate districts.

(A) Senate districts shall be composed of three contiguous house of representatives districts.

(B)(1) A county having at least one whole senate ratio of representation shall have as many senate districts wholly within the boundaries of the county as it has whole senate ratios of representation. Any fraction of the population in excess of a whole ratio shall be a part of only one adjoining senate district.

(2) Counties having less than one senate ratio of representation, but at least one house of representatives ratio of representation, shall be part of only one senate district.

(3) If it is not possible for the commission to draw representative districts that comply with all of the requirements of this article and that make it possible for the commission to comply with all of the requirements of divisions (B)(1) and (2) of this section, the commission shall draw senate districts so as to commit the fewest possible violations of those divisions. If the commission complies with this division in drawing senate districts, the commission shall not be considered to have violated division (B)(1) or (2) of this section, as applicable, in drawing those districts, for the purpose of an analysis under division (D) of Section 9 of this article.

(C) The number of whole ratios of representation for a county shall be determined by dividing the population of the county by the ratio of representation in the senate determined under division (A) of Section 3 of this article.

(D) Senate districts shall be numbered from one through thirty-three and as provided in Section 5 of this article.

The 2015 amendment to this article repealed section 11 and replaced it with this section. The new section 4 governs the drawing of senate districts and continues to provide that each senate district shall be composed of three contiguous house districts. But it also contains greater detail than its predecessor to govern the process of creating senate districts.

Under this section, each county having a population greater than the senate representation ratio (1/33 of the population of the state) must contain as many senate districts as "whole" ratios of representation. The commission determines the number of whole ratios of representation for a county by dividing the county's population by 1/33 of the state's population and discarding the remainder. The commission must place the remainder or excess population into only one adjoining senate district. Counties having populations less than one senate ratio of representation but more than one house district may also only be a part of one senate district.

Section 4(B)(3) also creates an internal order of preference if the commission finds that it cannot comply with all the provisions in this section, thus removing the discretion to choose which provision to apply in the event of a conflict between constitutional provisions. Section 4(B)(3) provides that if the commission cannot draw senate districts that comply with all the requirements of sections 4(B)(1) and 4(B)(2), it must attempt to draw senate districts in a manner so as to minimize the number of violations to as few possible. If the commission follows this mandate, a court with jurisdiction to review the plan under section 9 will not find that the commission violated section 4(B)(1) or 4(B)(2) in an analysis of applicable remedies under section 9(D).

■ POPULATION IN SENATE DISTRICTS

The predecessor to this section was the Senate equivalent of section 3. Adopted in 1967, it called for the use of the senate representation ratio (1/33 of the state population determined at the last federal census) and a 95/105 percent deviation range.

Despite the mandatory language of this section's predecessor, the Ohio Supreme Court held that an apportionment plan could avoid the 95/105 deviation range if compliance with the range meant violating other provisions of Article XI. *Voinovich v. Ferguson* (1992). In *Ferguson*, the court upheld the apportionment of a district that had a population below the permissible range. Senate District 32 contained only 93.99 percent of the senate representation ratio because of constraints imposed by prior sections 9 and 11 of this article. Under prior section 9, when a population of a county is at least 90 percent of the ratio of representation, public officials designated to apportion the state must make a reasonable effort to create a house district containing the whole county. Under prior section 11, counties having less than one senate ratio of representation but at least one house seat could only be a part of one senate district. The Ohio Supreme Court ruled the apportionment of Senate District 32 "was unavoidable because irreconcilable conflicts with Sections 9 and 11 . . . prevented adding population from adjacent territory." Ibid. According to the court, public officials were not required to correct one constitutional problem by violating others.

Section 5

Change in boundaries of senate districts.

At any time the boundaries of senate districts are changed in any general assembly district plan made pursuant to any provision of this article, a senator whose term will not expire within two years of the time the plan becomes effective shall represent, for the remainder of the term for which the senator was elected, the senate district that contains the largest portion of the population of the district from which the senator was elected, and the district shall be given the number of the district from which the senator was elected. If more than one senator whose term will not so expire would represent the same district by following the provisions of this section, the plan shall designate which senator shall represent the district and shall designate which district the other senator or senators shall represent for the balance of their term or terms.

Originally adopted in 1967 as section 12, the 2015 amendment of this article moved the provision to section 5. The section provides a contingency plan for how to determine senate representation in the event that lawmakers change district boundaries before a senator's four-year term expires. If the senator at the time the district boundaries changed has two or more years remaining on his or her term, the senator shall represent the new district that contains the largest portion of the population of the former district. If the change results in more than one senator representing the same district, the Ohio Redistricting Commission shall designate in the plan which senator shall represent which district for the remainder of their terms.

Section 6

Nonpartisan, proportional, and compact assembly districts.

The Ohio redistricting commission shall attempt to draw a general assembly district plan that meets all of the following standards:

(A) No general assembly district plan shall be drawn primarily to favor or disfavor a political party.

(B) The statewide proportion of districts whose voters, based on statewide state and federal partisan general election results during the last ten years, favor each political party shall correspond closely to the statewide preferences of the voters of Ohio.

(C) General assembly districts shall be compact.

Nothing in this section permits the commission to violate the district standards described in Section 2, 3, 4, 5, or 7 of this article.

In addition to the bipartisan political process, this section contains three substantive standards (two of which were not part of the pre-2015 article) that the Ohio Redistricting Commission must follow in developing a general assembly district plan.

First, the commission is barred from drawing a general assembly district plan "to favor or disfavor a political party." In 2012, the Ohio Supreme Court held that "Article XI does not prevent the board from considering partisan factors in its apportionment decision" because "[t]he words used in Article XI do not explicitly require political neutrality." *Wilson v. Kasich* (2012). In response to this holding, section 6(a) explicitly provides that the commission must not draw a plan "drawn primarily to favor or disfavor a political party." This standard appears to address not only the effect of the plan but also the motivation of its drafters. This section also eliminates the protection provided incumbents by dropping the requirement that new apportionment plans follow district boundaries already in existence.

Second, the commission must draw a plan that "correspond(s) closely to the statewide preferences of the voters of Ohio." Known as a proportionality requirement, this provision requires the commission to look to statewide state and federal partisan general election results during the last ten years and draw a district plan that corresponds to the statewide voting preferences. When the voters approved the 2015 amendment, Ohio became the first state to add a proportionality requirement to its constitution. See generally National Conference of State Legislatures, "Redistricting Criteria."

Third, the commission must draw compact general assembly districts. This standard appears to simply recodify the compactness requirement that had been in the prior section 7.

Finally, this section prevents the commission from attempting to use these three standards to justify violating the other requirements set forth in section 2, 3, 4, 5, or 7 of this article. If such a situation arises, the commission must first adhere to sections 2, 3, 4, 5, and 7, and then attempt to comply with the three standards in this section.

Prior to the adoption of this section, its predecessor required that house districts be compact and contiguous, that the splitting of counties and other governmental units be minimized, and that a new apportionment plan follow district boundaries already in existence (sec. 7).

The 2012 Ohio Supreme Court decision upholding the 2010 apportionment plan held that the order of paragraphs in the prior section 7 did not create a hierarchy that had to be followed in a specific order. *Wilson v. Kasich* (2012). Thus, it rejected the view that the preference for following existing district lines, which is sometimes referred to as representational continuity or incumbent protection, in prior section 7(D) is subservient to the mandates earlier in the section to create compact districts and to minimize the splitting of counties and other governmental units. Instead, the *Wilson* court held that the requirements were coequal provisions, and as such, the board was empowered to apply whichever sections it deemed proper to resolve a conflict among them.

In *League of Women Voters of Ohio v. Ohio Redistricting Commission* (2022) (*League I*), the Ohio Supreme Court rejected the argument that the "shall attempt" language in section 6 made this section aspirational, and it held that stand-alone violations of section 6 were actionable. The court then interpreted the reference in section 6(B) to "election results" as referring to voter preferences and not to the number of elections in which candidates prevailed. Finally, it ruled that the plan adopted by the Ohio Redistricting Commission on a 5-2 partisan vote did not comply with the section 6(A) nonpartisanship requirement and the section 6(B) proportionality requirement.

Section 7

Creation of district boundaries based on decennial census.

Notwithstanding the fact that boundaries of counties, municipal corporations, and townships within a district may be changed, district boundaries shall be created by using the boundaries of counties, municipal corporations, and townships as they exist at the time of the federal decennial census on which the redistricting is based, or, if unavailable, on such other basis as the general assembly has directed.

Adopted in 2015, this section requires the Ohio Redistricting Commission to draw the house and senate district boundaries according to the boundaries of political subdivisions and city wards. This section also mandates that officials cannot change house and senate district boundaries until the next federal census even though the boundaries of counties, municipal corporations, and townships may change in the interim. This new section is a slightly modified version of section 6 of the 1967 reorganization of this article.

Section 8

Proceedings when Ohio redistricting commission fails to timely adopt final general assembly district plan.

(A)(1) If the Ohio redistricting commission fails to adopt a final general assembly district plan not later than the first day of September of a year ending in the numeral one, in accordance with Section 1 of this article, the commission shall introduce a proposed general assembly district plan by a simple majority vote of the commission.

(2) After introducing a proposed general assembly district plan under division (A)(1) of this section, the commission shall hold a public hearing concerning the proposed plan, at which the public may offer testimony and at which

the commission may adopt amendments to the proposed plan. Members of the commission should attend the hearing; however, only a quorum of the members of the commission is required to conduct the hearing.

(3) After the hearing described in division (A)(2) of this section is held, and not later than the fifteenth day of September of a year ending in the numeral one, the commission shall adopt a final general assembly district plan, either by the vote required to adopt a plan under division (B)(3) of Section 1 of this article or by a simple majority vote of the commission.

(B) If the commission adopts a final general assembly district plan in accordance with division (A)(3) of this section by the vote required to adopt a plan under division (B)(3) of Section 1 of this article, the plan shall take effect upon filing with the secretary of state and shall remain effective until the next year ending in the numeral one, except as provided in Section 9 of this article.

(C)(1)(a) Except as otherwise provided in division (C)(1)(b) of this section, if the commission adopts a final general assembly district plan in accordance with division (A)(3) of this section by a simple majority vote of the commission, and not by the vote required to adopt a plan under division (B)(3) of Section 1 of this article, the plan shall take effect upon filing with the secretary of state and shall remain effective until two general elections for the house of representatives have occurred under the plan.

(b) If the commission adopts a final general assembly district plan in accordance with division (A)(3) of this section by a simple majority vote of the commission, and not by the vote required to adopt a plan under division (B) of Section 1 of this article, and that plan is adopted to replace a plan that ceased to be effective under division (C)(1)(a) of this section before a year ending in the numeral one, the plan adopted under this division shall take effect upon filing with the secretary of state and shall remain effective until a year ending in the numeral one, except as provided in Section 9 of this article.

(2) A final general assembly district plan adopted under division (C)(1)(a) or (b) of this section shall include a statement explaining what the commission determined to be the statewide preferences of the voters of Ohio and the manner in which the statewide proportion of districts in the plan whose voters, based on statewide state and federal partisan general election results during the last ten years, favor each political party corresponds closely to those preferences, as described in division (B) of Section 6 of this article. At the time the plan is adopted, a member of the commission who does not vote in favor of the plan may submit a declaration of the member's opinion concerning the statement included with the plan.

(D) After a general assembly district plan adopted under division (C)(1)(a) of this section ceases to be effective, and not earlier than the first day of July of the year following the year in which the plan ceased to be effective, the commission shall be reconstituted as provided in Section 1 of this article, convene, and adopt a new general assembly district plan in accordance with this article, to be used until the next time for redistricting under this article. The commission shall draw the new general assembly district plan using the same population and county, municipal corporation, and township boundary data as were used to draw the previous plan adopted under division (C) of this section.

Adopted in 2015, this section contains a contingency plan if the commission fails to adopt a plan by September 1 of a year in which it convenes. Section 8(A)(1) allows the commission to approve a proposal for a plan after September 1 by a simple majority vote. Once it approves such a plan, the commission must hold a public hearing on that plan, and the commission may amend it. See Article XI, section 8(A)(2). Although all commission members "should attend the hearing," section 8(A)(2) provides that the commission needs only a quorum of its members (i.e., four of seven) to conduct the required public hearing.

Section 8(A)(3) sets a tight set of deadlines for when the commission must hold the public hearing because it requires the commission to adopt a final plan no later than September 15. Thus, the commission must hold the public hearing within the two-week period after the September 1 deadline. The commission can adopt this final contingency plan by the bipartisan vote required under section 1(B)(3) or by a simple majority vote. If the commission approves the final plan under the bipartisan vote requirement, the plan becomes effective until the next decennial apportionment. See Article XI, section 8(B).

If the commission only approves the plan by a simple majority of its members, the plan remains effective from the date of filing with the secretary of state until two general elections for the House of Representatives have taken place. After two general elections, a new commission must be reconstituted to draw a new apportionment plan, see Article XI, section 8(D). This new commission must use the same population, county, municipal corporation, and township boundary data to draw its plan as was used by the prior commission. If the newly constituted commission also fails to adopt a plan by the requisite bipartisan vote, section 8(C)(1)(b) provides that the new plan remains in effect until the next apportionment year subject to any court orders issued under section 9.

Section 8(C)(2) requires the commission to include a statement explaining what numbers and conclusions the commission relied upon to determine the statewide voting preferences under section 6's proportionality provision. This section also allows a dissenting member of the commission to submit a declaration of opinion concerning the adopted plan at this time.

In *League of Women Voters of Ohio v. Ohio Redistricting Commission* (2022) (*League I*), the Ohio Supreme Court rejected the argument that a four-year plan adopted by the Ohio Redistricting Commission on a 5-2 partisan vote was not subject to judicial review.

Section 9

Supreme court jurisdiction; proceedings upon determination of invalidity by court order.

(A) The supreme court of Ohio shall have exclusive, original jurisdiction in all cases arising under this article.

(B) In the event that any section of this constitution relating to redistricting, any general assembly district plan made by the Ohio redistricting commission, or any district is determined to be invalid by an unappealed final order of a court of competent jurisdiction then, notwithstanding any other provisions of this constitution, the commission shall be reconstituted as provided in Section 1 of this article, convene, and ascertain and determine a general assembly district plan in conformity with such provisions of this constitution as are then valid, including establishing terms of office and election of members of the general assembly from districts designated in the plan, to be used until the next time for redistricting under this article in conformity with such provisions of this constitution as are then valid.

(C) Notwithstanding any provision of this constitution or any law regarding the residence of senators and representatives, a general assembly district plan made pursuant to this section shall allow thirty days for persons to change residence in order to be eligible for election.

(D)(1) No court shall order, in any circumstance, the implementation or enforcement of any general assembly district plan that has not been approved by the commission in the manner prescribed by this article.

(2) No court shall order the commission to adopt a particular general assembly district plan or to draw a particular district.

(3) If the supreme court of Ohio determines that a general assembly district plan adopted by the commission does not comply with the requirements of Section 2, 3, 4, 5, or 7 of this article, the available remedies shall be as follows:

(a) If the court finds that the plan contains one or more isolated violations of those requirements, the court shall order the commission to amend the plan to correct the violation.

(b) If the court finds that it is necessary to amend not fewer than six house of representatives districts to correct violations of those requirements, to amend not fewer than two senate districts to correct violations of those requirements, or both, the court shall declare the plan invalid and shall order the commission to adopt a new general assembly district plan in accordance with this article.

(c) If, in considering a plan adopted under division (C) of Section 8 of this article, the court determines that both of the following are true, the court shall order the commission to adopt a new general assembly district plan in accordance with this article:

(i) The plan significantly violates those requirements in a manner that materially affects the ability of the plan to contain districts whose voters favor political parties in an overall proportion that corresponds closely to the statewide political party preferences of the voters of Ohio, as described in division (B) of Section 6 of this article.

(ii) The statewide proportion of districts in the plan whose voters, based on statewide state and federal partisan general election results during the last ten years, favor each political party does not correspond closely to the statewide preferences of the voters of Ohio.

Adopted in 2015, this section, which deals with the jurisdiction of the Ohio Supreme Court, includes modified versions of most of the provisions that had been in section 13 and moves them to this section.

Sections 9(A), 9(B), and 9(C) contain only slight changes from their earlier counterparts, but 9(D) added several new provisions to govern a court's authority under this section. In addition, the new section eliminated a provision that gave the governor the power to set the date, time, and place of any meetings held pursuant to this section.

Section 9(A) provides the Ohio Supreme Court with original and exclusive jurisdiction in matters concerning this article. This provision bars lower state courts from entertaining cases arising under this article, but it does not (and could not) prevent lower federal courts from exercising original jurisdiction over cases arising under federal law or supplemental jurisdiction over cases arising under this article. An exercise of supplemental jurisdiction, however, is very unlikely under the federal supplemental jurisdictional statute. See 28 U.S.C. section 1367(c).

Section 9(B) contains a contingency plan in the event that any "court of competent jurisdiction" (presumably the Ohio Supreme Court, the U.S. Supreme Court, or lower federal courts) invalidates a plan for redistricting the General Assembly or invalidates a provision of the constitution relating to redistricting. In such cases, the commission shall be reconstituted (consistent with sec. 1), convene, and establish a new general assembly districting plan in line with the valid sections of Article XI.

Section 9(C) requires that any general assembly redistricting plan made pursuant to this section allow representatives and senators at least thirty days to change their residence to become eligible for election in a new district.

Section 9(D)(1) bars courts from ordering the state to enforce or implement a districting plan that the commission has not approved, and section 9(D)(2) bars courts from ordering the commission to adopt or approve a particular plan or to draw a particular district. Properly and narrowly construed, however, these provisions should not prevent the court from adopting a plan not approved by the commission when the court rejects a proposed redistricting plan that violates both state and federal law. *Cf.* Haywood v. Drown (2009) (state courts must entertain federal claims unless their refusal is based on a neutral rule of judicial administration).

Section 9(D)(3), which by its terms is directed only to the Ohio Supreme Court, seeks to cabin the discretion typically available to courts by defining in great detail the steps the court should take if it determines that a redistricting plan for the General Assembly fails to comply with section 2, 3, 4, 5, or 7 of Article XI.

Section 9(D)(3)(a) provides that in the case of isolated violations of these sections, the court shall order the commission to amend the plan to correct the violation.

Section 9(D)(3)(b) provides that the court shall declare a plan invalid and order the commission to adopt a new plan if it determines that six or more house districts or two or more senate districts do not comply with these sections.

Section 9(D)(3)(c) complements the new nonpartisanship and proportionality requirements of this article. This section requires the court to order the commission to create a new plan if it finds that a plan adopted under section 8(C) by a simple majority of the commission significantly violates the requirements of section 2, 3, 4, 5 or 7 in a way that materially affects the plan's ability to adhere to the proportionality requirement of section 6(B) *and* does not correspond closely to the statewide preferences of the voters of Ohio. When the standards of this provision are not met, however, the court still has the power to enforce the nonpartisanship, proportionality, and compactness requirements of section 6.

On January 12, 2022, in *League of Women Voters of Ohio v. Ohio Redistricting Commission* (2022) (*League I*), the Ohio Supreme Court ruled that the provisions in this section governing the remedial power of the court when there were violations of the technical requirements of sections 2, 3, 4, 5, and 7 did not deprive the court of jurisdiction to review stand-alone violations of section 6. And the court held that the four-year plan adopted by the Ohio Redistricting Commission on a partisan 5-2 vote violated the section 6(A) nonpartisanship requirement and the section 6(B) proportionality requirement.

This section gives the Ohio courts exclusive jurisdiction to determine whether a plan meets the requirements of the article, but it does not (nor could it) divest federal courts of jurisdiction over claims that a general assembly district plan violates federal law.

Section 10
Severability.

The various provisions of this article are intended to be severable, and the invalidity of one or more of such provisions shall not affect the validity of the remaining provisions.

Adopted in 1967 as section 15, this section, which was moved in 2015 to section 10, makes the provisions of Article XI severable if a court holds some but not all of its provisions unconstitutional. The severability provision effectively affirmed the holding of the Ohio Supreme Court in *State ex rel. King v. Rhodes* (1967).

Section 11
Repealed

Adopted in 1967 and modified and moved to a new section 4 in 2015, this section governed the drawing of senate districts.

Section 12
Repealed

Adopted in 1967 and moved to a new section 5 in 2015, this section provided rules for senate representation if the public officials designated to apportion the state changed district boundaries before a senator's four-year term expired.

Section 13
Repealed

Adopted in 1967 and modified and moved to a new section 9 in 2015, this section provided that the Ohio Supreme Court had original and exclusive jurisdiction in matters concerning Article XI.

Section 14
Repealed

Adopted in 1967 and repealed in 2015 because it was obsolete, this section called for the carrying over of state legislative boundaries in existence prior to the November 1967 election on a new Article XI and provided for an interim plan if a court decision should find the apportionment plan existing at the time unconstitutional before the 1970 general election.

Section 15
Repealed

Adopted in 1967 and moved largely unchanged to a new section 10, this section 15 provided for the severability of Article XI's provisions in the event that a court decision found one of its provisions unconstitutional to ensure that the rest of Article XI would remain enforceable.

Article XII

Finance and Taxation

The 1802 Ohio Constitution gave the General Assembly a virtually unqualified power to tax. The current Article XII, adopted as part of the 1851 Constitution, limited the state's taxing powers and ended the common practice of financing private corporations—a practice that many believed contributed to the debt crisis that resulted from the construction of the state's transportation system.

Voters have amended Article XII fourteen times, more times than any article save Article VIII, which deals with public debt. Commentators have described Article XII, and Ohio's tax system in general, as "a hodge-podge of sacred cows" and "constitutional provisions and statutes resulting from the demands for revenue and the pressures for exemption." V. E. Carlson, "Finance and Taxation in Ohio," in Harvey Walker, ed., *An Analysis and Appraisal of the Ohio State Constitution 1851–1951* (Cincinnati: The Stephen H. Wilder Foundation, 1951), 59; Lloyd E. Fisher Jr., "Charities and the Ohio Tax Laws," 18 *Ohio St. L. J.* 228 (1957).

Section 1

Poll tax.

No poll tax shall ever be levied in this state, or service required, which may be commuted in money or other thing of value.

The Ohio State Constitution. Steven H. Steinglass and Gino J. Scarselli, Oxford University Press. © Oxford University Press 2022. DOI: 10.1093/oso/9780197619728.003.0014

Adopted in 1851 and amended in 1912, this section bars the use of poll or "head" taxes, which are taxes levied on persons (rather than on their property or income) and levied irrespective of the taxpayer's ability to pay. *Marion Foundry Co. v. Landes* (1925). Poll taxes were common in the original states that formed the union, see *Harper v. Virginia State Bd. of Elections* (1966) (Harlan, J., dissenting), but Ohio has never had a poll tax and was one of the first states to include a prohibition against them in its constitution. See Ohio Constitutional Revision Commission (OCRC), *Recommendations for Amendments to the Ohio Constitution: Final Report, Index to Proceedings and Research* (1977), 195 (hereinafter OCRC, *Final Report*). The 1802 Constitution provided in the Bill of Rights that "the levying [of] taxes by the poll is grievous and oppressive; therefore the Legislature shall never levy a poll tax for county or State purposes." 1802 Constitution, Article VIII, section 23. The 1851 Constitution moved this provision from the Bill of Rights to this article, dropped the prefatory language, but continued to bar the levying of poll taxes.

Although not necessarily tied to voting, poll taxes have an infamous history of being used to disfranchise voters. A number of southern states began using poll taxes in the late 1800s to disenfranchise African Americans. See generally Frederic D. Ogden, *The Poll Tax in the South* (Tuscaloosa: University of Alabama Press, 1958). The ratification in 1964 of the Twenty-Fourth Amendment to the U.S. Constitution barred the use of poll taxes as a prerequisite to voting in federal elections, and the U.S. Supreme Court subsequently held in *Harper* that the use of poll taxes in state elections violated the Equal Protection Clause of the Fourteenth Amendment.

Although Ohio has never required the payment of a specific tax before voting, the state placed financial limitations in the path of those who sought to vote. Under the 1802 Constitution, the right to vote was restricted to white male residents twenty-one or older who were responsible for the payment of state or county taxes or who worked on public roads. 1802 Constitution, Article IV, sections 1, 5. Beginning in 1804, the General Assembly enacted laws that required all adult males to work on public roads or contribute to the public road fund. See OCRC, *Final Report*, 195. The 1851 Constitution eliminated the taxation and roadwork restrictions on voting, but it did not prohibit compulsory roadwork statutes despite the belief of many delegates at the 1850–51 Constitutional Convention that these statutes amounted to "hidden" poll taxes. Ibid. "[T]he obligation to labor on the highway is really and truly a poll tax" (quoting *Report of the Debates and Proceedings of the Convention for the Revision of the Constitution of the State of Ohio, 1850–51*, vol. 2 (1851), 745) (hereinafter *1850–51 Debates*). And one delegate stated as follows.

> Under our present system of laws, there is but one manner in which a tax by the poll is levied—for road purposes. This law enforces upon every citizen the obligation to perform a given amount of labor on the public highway, and this, without

regard to the amount of property he may possess, or, in fact whether he have property or not.

1850–51 Debates, vol. 2, 34–35.

Nonetheless, in 1894, the Ohio Supreme Court held that a compulsory roadwork statute that required two days labor or an annual fee of four dollars was not a poll tax and thus was not prohibited by this section. *Dennis v. Simon* (1894).

In 1912, the convention proposed and the voters approved an amendment to this section to bar expressly the requirement of "service." In 1921, the voters overwhelmingly rejected by almost a 3:1 margin a constitutional amendment proposed by the General Assembly to authorize the levying of a poll tax. See Appendix B.

Section 2

Limitation on tax rate; exemption.

No property, taxed according to value, shall be so taxed in excess of one per cent of its true value in money for all state and local purposes, but laws may be passed authorizing additional taxes to be levied outside of such limitation, either when approved by at least a majority of the electors of the taxing district voting on such proposition, or when provided for by the charter of a municipal corporation. Land and improvements thereon shall be taxed by uniform rule according to value, except that laws may be passed to reduce taxes by providing for a reduction in value of the homestead of permanently and totally disabled residents, residents sixty-five years of age and older, and residents sixty years of age or older who are surviving spouses of deceased residents who were sixty-five years of age or older or permanently and totally disabled and receiving a reduction in the value of their homestead at the time of death, provided the surviving spouse continues to reside in a qualifying homestead, and providing for income and other qualifications to obtain such reduction. Without limiting the general power, subject to the provisions of Article I of this constitution, to determine the subjects and methods of taxation or exemptions therefrom, general laws may be passed to exempt burying grounds, public school houses, houses used exclusively for public worship, institutions used exclusively for charitable purposes, and public property used exclusively for any public purpose, but all such laws shall be subject to alteration or repeal; and the value of all property so exempted shall, from time to time, be ascertained and published as may be directed by law.

Adopted in 1851 and amended eight times, this section (not including a 1918 initiated amendment that the Ohio Supreme Court struck down) placed limitations on the power of the state to tax real and personal property and expressly required taxation "by uniform rule according to value." Under the 1802 Constitution the power of the General Assembly to tax was unrestricted except for the prohibition against poll taxes.

Prior to the 1912 Convention, there were seven attempts to amend this section, and they all failed with the exception of the 1905 proposal. See Appendix

B. After the 1912 Convention, the voters began to approve amendments to this section, and, according to the OCRC, no provision of this article "has occupied a more prominent place in the history of taxation in Ohio." OCRC, *Final Report*, 199.

In its current form, last revised in 1990, this section contains two general restrictions on the power of state and local authorities to tax property. Subject to certain exceptions, this section prohibits the taxing of real property in excess of 1 percent or "ten mill" of its "true value in money" and requires the classification of real property for tax purposes by "uniform rule." It also contains authority for specific exemptions from taxation.

■ ONE PERCENT LIMITATION

The 1851 version of this section required taxing by "uniform rule," but it did not place a limitation on the amount of such taxation.

In 1929, the General Assembly proposed and the voters approved an amendment that imposed a 1.5 percent limitation on the amount of tax that could be levied under this section, but in 1933, in the midst of the Great Depression, the voters lowered this amount to 1 percent by approving an amendment proposed by initiative petition. The 1 percent limit, however, is not an absolute ceiling, and property may be taxed at a higher rate if the voters approve the higher rate or if a municipal charter permits a higher rate.

■ REAL PROPERTY CLASSIFICATIONS AND EXEMPTIONS

The second limitation in this section is a prohibition against classifying real property for tax purposes. With certain exceptions, section 2 requires that all real property and improvements to real estate must be taxed at a "uniform rule according to value."

When adopted in 1851, the "uniform rule" applied to both real and personal property. It also permitted the General Assembly to exempt from taxation certain charitable, educational, and religious property as well as personal property valued at less than $200. And in 1905, the voters approved an amendment that continued the permissive exemption for charitable, educational, and religious property and personal property valued at less than $200; but it included a mandatory exemption of state, local, and school bonds from taxation.

The uniform taxation rule was the subject of a heated debate between business groups and proponents of the rule at the 1912 Constitutional Convention.

Business groups lobbied for its repeal because they believed that the elimination of the bar on classification would result in lower taxes for property owned by businesses as well as lower taxes for intangible property such as stocks and bonds. OCRC, *Final Report*, 197–98; see also Lloyd Sponholtz, "The 1912

Constitutional Convention in Ohio: The Call-Up and Nonpartisan Selection of Delegates," 79 *Ohio History* 209 (1970).

Proponents, including most Progressives, argued that the uniform rule was the only way to ensure that all property would be taxed equally. The Progressives also supported the taxation of all bonds, including those given a mandatory exemption in 1906. The proponents prevailed, and the amendment on taxation proposed by the 1912 Convention and approved by the voters retained the "uniform rule," limited the exemption of bonds to those previously exempt and outstanding, reworded the permissive charitable exemption, and increased the permissive $200 personal property exemption to $500. See OCRC, *Final Report*, 197–98.

In 1918, the voters approved conflicting amendments to this section proposed by the General Assembly and by initiative petition. The former received the most affirmative votes, and thus became part of the constitution under the conflict-resolution requirement of Article II, section 1b. The adopted amendment permitted the General Assembly to pass laws "to provide against the double taxation that results from the taxation of both the real estate and the mortgage or the debt secured" upon it. The rejected amendment would have cut back on the permitted exemptions in the section and returned to the more limited exemption language of the 1851 section; additionally, it did not authorize the passage of laws barring double taxation. *State ex rel. Greenlund v. Fulton* (1919).

In 1929, the voters approved an amendment proposed by the General Assembly not only to place a 1.5 percent limit on real estate taxes (see above), but also to limit the "uniform rule" to real property. The 1929 amendment also made bonds sold pursuant to Article VIII, section 2a to support the World War Compensation Fund exempt from taxation, and removed the $500 ceiling on the personal property exemption.

Since the last major revision of this section in 1929, the voters approved amendments proposed by the General Assembly to modify the "uniform rule" in 1933 (see above), 1970, 1974, and 1990.

The uniform rule requires that all real property "be assessed on the basis of the same uniform percentage of actual value," where "actual value" refers to the property's fair market value (i.e., "the amount which such property should bring if sold on the open market"). *State ex rel. Park Investment Co. v. Board of Tax Appeals* (1964). In other words, under the uniform rule the tax basis (i.e., percentage of fair market value on which taxes are calculated) of all real property—residential, commercial, and agricultural—must be the same throughout the state. Consistent with this requirement, Ohio law provides that real property cannot be assessed at more than 35 percent of its actual value. See O.R.C. section 5715.01.

The 1970 amendment to this section added a "homestead" exemption that allowed a reduction in the assessed value of the homestead of senior citizens age sixty-five or older. In 1974 and 1990, respectively, amendments to this section extended the homestead exemption to permanently and totally disabled residents and to certain surviving spouses age sixty or older.

■ TAX EXEMPTIONS

Since its adoption in 1851, this section has allowed the General Assembly and local taxing authorities to exempt certain property from taxation. This includes exemptions for "burying grounds, public school houses, houses used exclusively for public worship, institutions used exclusively for charitable purposes, and public property used exclusively for any public purpose."

In 1965, in *Denison University v. Board of Tax Appeals* (1965), however, the Ohio Supreme Court abandoned more than hundred years of case law that had interpreted this section as limiting the General Assembly to exempting only the five enumerated categories of property from taxation. See Karen Bond Coriell, "Chaos, Contradiction and Confusion: Ohio's Real Property Tax Exemptions," 53 *Ohio St. L. J.* 265 (1992): 267. In *Denison*, the court held that a private university was entitled to exemptions for a farm, guesthouses, and other university property that was not used "exclusively" for charitable or public purposes. In abandoning the "used exclusively" limitation in section 2, the court stated that the General Assembly "has a power to determine exemptions from taxation that is limited only by the provisions of Article I of the Ohio Constitution." Ibid. (syllabus). *Denison* led to the legislative adoption of a public college tax exemption, which has been the subject of considerable litigation. See, for example, *Equity Dublin Associates v. Testa* (2014); *Case Western Reserve University v. Wilkins* (2005); *Cleveland State University v. Perk* (1971).

In 2009, the court addressed the exemption for charities. Noting that despite "its apparent breadth, the definition of charity does not encompass public worship," the court held that there was no exemption for property used as the administrative headquarters for a church or congregation. *Church of God in N. Ohio, Inc. v. Levin* (2009).

Section 2a

Authority to classify real estate for taxation, two classes; procedures.

(A) Except as expressly authorized in this section, land and improvements thereon shall, in all other respects, be taxed as provided in Section 36, of Article II and Section 2 of this article.

(B) This section does not apply to any of the following:

(1) Taxes levied at whatever rate is required to produce a specified amount of tax money or an amount to pay debt charges;

(2) Taxes levied within the one per cent limitation imposed by Section 2 of this article;

(3) Taxes provided for by the charter of a municipal corporation.

(C) Notwithstanding Section 2 of this article, laws may be passed that provide all of the following:

(1) Land and improvements thereon in each taxing district shall be placed into one of two classes solely for the purpose of separately reducing the taxes charged against all land and improvements in each of the two classes as provided in division (C)(2) of this section. The classes shall be:

(a) Residential and agricultural land and improvements;

(b) All other land and improvements.

(2) With respect to each voted tax authorized to be levied by each taxing district, the amount of taxes imposed by such tax against all land and improvements thereon in each class shall be reduced in order that the amount charged for collection against all land and improvements in that class in the current year, exclusive of land and improvements not taxed by the district in both the preceding year and in the current year and those not taxed in that class in the preceding year, equals the amount charged for collection against such land and improvements in the preceding year.

(D) Laws may be passed to provide that the reductions made under this section in the amounts of taxes charged for the current expenses of cities, townships, school districts, counties, or other taxing districts are subject to the limitation that the sum of the amounts of all taxes charged for current expenses against the land and improvements thereon in each of the two classes of property subject to taxation in cities, townships, school districts, counties, or other types of taxing districts, shall not be less than a uniform per cent of the taxable value of the property in the districts to which the limitation applies. Different but uniform percentage limitations may be established for cities, townships, school districts, counties, and other types of taxing districts.

Adopted in 1980 and never amended, this section, which was proposed by the General Assembly and approved by the voters, contains an exemption to the "uniform rule" requirement of Article XII, section 2, by allowing reductions in the assessed value of residential and agricultural property. The purpose of this section was to alleviate what was perceived as an unfair tax burden on homeowners and farmers as a result of spiraling inflation in the late 1970s. *State ex rel. Swetland v. Kinney* (1982).

Section 3
Imposition of taxes.

Laws may be passed providing for:

(A) The taxation of decedents' estates or of the right to receive or succeed to such estates, and the rates of such taxation may be uniform or may be graduated based on the value of the estate, inheritance, or succession. Such tax may also be levied at different rates upon collateral and direct inheritances, and a portion of each estate may be exempt from such taxation as provided by law.

(B) The taxation of incomes, and the rates of such taxation may be either uniform or graduated, and may be applied to such incomes and with such exemptions as may be provided by law.

(C) Excise and franchise taxes and for the imposition of taxes upon the production of coal, oil, gas, and other minerals; except that no excise tax shall be levied or collected upon the sale or purchase of food for human consumption off the premises where sold.

Adopted in 1976 and never amended, this section is a consolidation of sections 7, 8, 10, and 12 of Article XII, each of which was repealed when the voters approved section 3. This section, which was proposed by the General Assembly and which addresses the taxes that the General Assembly may levy, was the subject of a recommendation by the OCRC. See OCRC, *Final Report*, 192–218.

Section 3(A) is derived from section 7, which in turn was adopted in 1912 to allow for a graduated estate tax, thus overruling the Ohio Supreme Court decision in *State ex rel. Schwartz v. Ferris* (1895). Like its predecessor, this section specifically gives the General Assembly the power to enact either a uniform or graduated estate tax. Subsection (A), however, differs from its predecessor by allowing the General Assembly to exempt any portion of the estate from taxation. Section 7 had limited the exemption to $20,000.

Section 3(B), which was derived from prior section 8, which in turn was adopted in 1912, gives the General Assembly the power to create a uniform or graduated income tax. The 1912 provision had allowed the General Assembly to exempt up to $3,000 annually from income but this section now incorporates a 1973 amendment that allowed the exemption of any amount of income from taxation.

Section 3(C) allows for the creation of excise and franchise taxes. It is a combination of repealed section 10, which was adopted in 1912, and repealed section 12, which was adopted in 1936. An "excise" is a tax imposed on the performance of an act, the engaging in an occupation, or the enjoyment of a privilege. *Saviers v. Smith* (1920).

Section 3(C) also allows for the imposition of taxes on gas, coal, oil, and minerals, but it prohibits the collection of an excise tax on food consumed off the premises where it is sold. The part of section 3(C) concerned with taxation on fossil fuels and minerals is derived from repealed section 10, which the voters had approved in 1912. The part forbidding taxation on food consumed off the premises is derived from repealed section 12, which was proposed by initiative petition and approved by the voters in 1936.

Under section 3(C), the state has imposed taxes on public utilities gross receipts, which the court viewed as a tax upon the privilege of doing business, *State ex rel. Cleveland v. Kosydar* (1973), and on food purchased at a drive-in retail establishment but consumed away from the building, *Ilersich v. Schneider* (1964).

The policy of the state in compelling vendors to collect sales taxes from the purchasers of goods does not violate either the Ohio or the U.S. Constitution. *Fox v. Frank* (1935).

Section 4
Revenue.

The General Assembly shall provide for raising revenue, sufficient to defray the expenses of the state, for each year, and also a sufficient sum to pay principal and interest as they become due on the state debt.

Adopted in 1851 and amended in 1976, this section was a response to the enormous state debt incurred from financing the construction of the state's transportation system beginning in 1825. See Commentary, Article VIII, section 1. After the passage of the 1837 Loan Law, which authorized unlimited financial aid to private transportation companies, the state debt ballooned to nearly $20 million, and the state had to borrow money simply to meet the interest on the debt. See Ernest Ludlow Bogart, *Internal Improvements and State Debt in Ohio: An Essay in Economic History* (New York: Longmans, Green and Co., 1924), 58–63, 165–78; see also J. E. Hagerty, C. P. McClelland, and C. C. Huntington, *History of the Ohio Canals: Their Construction, Cost, Use and Partial Abandonment* (Columbus: Ohio State Archaeological and Historical Society, 1905), 81–84, 87–92. This experience resulted in a number of provisions in the 1851 Constitution, including the limitations on state debt in Article VIII, and in section 6 of this article, and this provision, which requires the General Assembly to raise sufficient revenue annually to pay the state debt.

In 1976, the General Assembly proposed and the voters approved an amendment to this section to require the legislature to raise sufficient revenues annually to pay off the principal as it becomes due. The original version only required revenues annually to pay the interest on the state debt. The 1976 amendment resulted from a recommendation of the OCRC to reflect modern debt financing. Because most modern debt financing is serial, that is, payments on the principal are due over the course of the loan rather than in one lump sum at the end of the term, the commission believed that sufficient revenues should be raised each year to pay off that part of the principal that became due as well as the annual interest on the debt. See OCRC, *Final Report*, 207–8.

Section 5
Levying of taxes.

No tax shall be levied, except in pursuance of law; and every law imposing a tax shall state, distinctly, the object of the same, to which only, it shall be applied.

Adopted in 1851 and never amended, this section provides that every statute authorizing a tax shall distinctly state the purpose of the tax and ensure that the tax will only be used for that purpose. The General Assembly can satisfy this section even if the statute authorizing the new tax does not state its *objective* as long as the objective is otherwise apparent. *Ashley v. Ryan* (1892). The 1850–51 Constitutional Convention proposed this section to protect people from paying taxes for which no specific purpose had been identified and to hold legislators accountable for raising taxes and for the use of the tax revenues. Ibid.

Since 1987, the state has adopted the practice of making this section inapplicable to selected debt-authorizing provisions, including sections 2k, 2l, 2m, 2p, and 2s.

The funding of charter schools through the state's complex educational financing formula is not a diversion of local tax dollars in violation of this section. *State ex rel. Ohio Congress of Parents & Teachers v. State Bd. of Educ.* (2006).

Section 5a

Use of motor vehicle license and fuel taxes restricted.

No moneys derived from fees, excises, or license taxes relating to registration, operation, or use of vehicles on public highways, or to fuels used for propelling such vehicles, shall be expended for other than costs of administering such laws, statutory refunds and adjustments provided therein, payment of highway obligations, costs for construction, reconstruction, maintenance and repair of public highways and bridges and other statutory highway purposes, expense of state enforcement of traffic laws, and expenditures authorized for hospitalization of indigent persons injured in motor vehicle accidents on the public highways.

Adopted in 1947 and never amended, this section concerns taxes and fees on the registration, operation, and use of motor vehicles. In 1934, the voters narrowly rejected two constitutional amendments proposed by initiative petition to prohibit taxes on motor vehicles entirely and to limit the use of motor vehicle license fees and excise taxes on fuel to improvements of public thoroughfares. Thirteen years later, the voters approved section 5a, which was proposed by another initiative petition. The approved language somewhat loosened the restrictions that had been rejected earlier, and the voters approved the amendment by more than a 3:2 margin. See Appendix B.

This section provides that revenues from fees, excises, licensing taxes, and other taxes on fuel and motor vehicles must be used to maintain, build, or repair public highways and bridges. It also authorizes the use of these revenues to offset the cost of hospitalization for indigents injured in motor vehicle accidents on public roads.

Applying this provision, the Ohio Supreme Court has rejected efforts to use highway user revenues for non-highway related purposes. See, for example,

Grandle v. Rhodes (1957) (on reconsideration) (stating that highway improvement funds may only be used for purposes "directly connected with the construction, maintenance and repair of highways and the enforcement of traffic laws" and enjoining their use to support construction of a parking garage); see also *Knox County Board of Commissioners v. Knox County Engineer* (2006) (barring use of highway improvement funds to pay County Risk Sharing Authority insurance premiums). But see, for example, *Stockberger v. Henry* (2012) (permitting the use of highway improvement funds for joint self-insurance pool); *State ex rel. Walter v. Vogel* (1959) (permitting the use of highway improvement funds to maintain lighting systems for urban portions of limited access highways).

The court has also held that a fee charged by the Bureau of Motor Vehicles for a driver license abstract did not relate to the "operation or use of vehicles on public highways" and thus such revenues could be spent for nonhighway purposes. *Ohio Trucking Association v. Charles* (2012).

But in a case of first impression dealing with the substantial amount of money accumulated under Ohio's Commercial Activity Tax from the application of the tax to motor-vehicle-fuel sales, the court concluded that the expenditure of these funds is limited to the highway-related purposes specified in this section. *Beaver Excavating Co. v. Testa* (2012).

In *Village of Put-in-Bay v. Mathys* (2020), the court held the imposition of a "license fee" by a municipality on vehicles that are made available for hire and use within the municipality was not barred by this section. See also *Village of Put-in-Bay* (Fischer, J., concurring) (discussing the history of this section and concluding that it limited *state-imposed* fees, excises, and license taxes but not those imposed by municipalities).

Beginning with the 1953 approval of Article VIII, section 2c to authorize debt for highways, the state has selectively included provisions in the debt-authorizing amendments to permit the use of section 5a highway user receipts to pay off debt incurred under the various sections. See Article VIII, sections 2c, 2g, and 2i. But most of the debt-authorizing amendments to Article VIII (other than those providing for veterans compensation) include provisions that bar the use of section 5a highway user receipts to pay off debt incurred under those sections. See Article VIII, sections 2e, 2f, 2h, 2k, 2l, 2m, 2n, 2o, 2p, 2q, 2r, and 2s. Article VIII, section 2m, which authorized bonds for highways and infrastructure, permits highway user receipts to be used to pay off highway but not infrastructure bonds.

Section 6

Debt for internal improvement.

Except as otherwise provided in this constitution the state shall never contract any debt for purposes of internal improvement.

Adopted in 1851 and amended in 1912, this section seeks to prevent the state from incurring debt for internal improvements. As originally adopted in the 1851 Constitution this provision was a complete bar on the prohibited use of state debt, and read as follows: "The state shall never contract any debt for purposes of internal improvement." But in 1912, the constitutional convention recommended and the voters approved an exception to this section to allow the state to incur such debt "as otherwise provided in this constitution."

For more than fifty years this exception was not relied upon. But beginning in 1965 with the adoption of Article VIII, section 13, the state has included language making the bar on incurring debt for internal improvements inapplicable to all debt-authorizing amendments with the exceptions of the 1973 and 2009 amendments for veterans' compensation (secs. 2j and 2r) and the 1999 amendment on educational facilities and the debt service cap (secs. 2n and 17).

Section 7

Repealed—Inheritance tax

Adopted in 1912 but repealed in 1976 and moved to section 3(A), this section authorized the adoption of a tax on estates.

Section 8

Repealed—Income tax

Adopted in 1912, this section, which authorized the establishment of an income tax, was repealed in 1976 and moved to section 3(B).

Section 9

Apportionment of income, estate, and inheritance taxes.

Not less than fifty per cent of the income, estate, and inheritance taxes that may be collected by the state shall be returned to the county, school district, city, village, or township in which said income, estate, or inheritance tax originates, or to any of the same, as may be provided by law.

Adopted in 1912 and amended in 1930 and 1976, this section required that not less than 50 percent of income and inheritance taxes be returned to the city, village, or township in which the taxes originated. In 1930, the General Assembly proposed and the voters approved an amendment that added counties and school districts to the list of local subdivisions eligible to receive these payments but that also gave the General Assembly discretion to determine which political subdivisions would receive revenues.

The 1930 amendment was proposed in response to the 1929 revision of Article XII, section 2, which removed personal property from the uniform rule of taxation. This removal was seen as detrimental to public schools and county governments. As a result, the amendment to this section sought to soften the blow to schools and counties from the previous year's amendment. The 1930 amendment, however, did not guarantee an influx of money for schools and counties because the amendment included a clause, "or to any of the same, as may be provided by law" that gave the General Assembly the power to determine which political subdivisions received revenues. See OCRC, *Final Report, 214*.

In 1976, an amendment to this section proposed by the General Assembly and approved by the voters revised this section by requiring that 50 percent of estate taxes to be returned to the school district or local government.

Section 10

Repealed—Excise and franchise taxes

Adopted in 1912, this section originally provided for excise and franchise taxes on fossil fuel and minerals. In 1976 this section was repealed and replaced by section 3(C) of this article.

Section 11

Sinking fund.

No bonded indebtedness of the state, or any political subdivisions thereof, shall be incurred or renewed unless, in the legislation under which such indebtedness is incurred or renewed, provision is made for levying and collecting annually by taxation an amount sufficient to pay the interest on said bonds, and to provide a sinking fund for their final redemption at maturity.

Adopted in 1912 and never amended, this section requires the state and municipalities that issue bonds to make provisions in the bond-generating legislation for taxation to pay the interest on the obligations. Similar in purpose to Article VIII, sections 7 and 4 of this article, this section is designed to force governmental entities to make sufficient provisions to pay off their debt.

This section requires that state and local governments pay off the interest and principal on their debt before meeting current operating expenses. *State ex rel. National City Bank v. Board of Education* (1977).

This section also functions as an indirect limit on the amount of debt that the state and local governments can incur. In *State ex rel. Portsmouth v. Kountz* (1935), the Ohio Supreme Court held that the amount of taxation that could be levied under this section was subject to the 1 percent limit found in section 2 of this article. In other words, state and local governments must be able to pay the interest on any debt they incur within the 1 percent limit imposed by section 2 unless otherwise exempted by that section.

Finally, this section requires governmental entities to establish a sinking fund (i.e., a fund to accumulate money for the payment of a debt in one lump sum at the end of its term) before issuing bonds or other obligations.

But sinking funds are no longer used for this purpose, and beginning in 1965 with the adoption of the original version of section 13, the state has adopted the practice of specifically making this section inapplicable to bonds issued under Article VIII. See Article VIII, sections 2k, 2l, 2m, 2o, 2p, 2q, 2s, 13, 14, 15, and 16. And the state's 2009 bond-authorizing amendment for compensating veterans (Art. VIII, sec. 2r) expressly identified the Public Facilities Commission, rather than the sinking fund commission, as the state agency responsible for the financial management of the state debt incurred under that provision.

Section 12

Repealed—Excise tax on sales or purchase of food prohibited

Adopted in 1936, this section prohibited the imposition of excise taxes on the sale of food or beverages consumed off premises. This section was repealed in 1976 and replaced by section 3(C) of this article.

Section 13

Wholesale taxes on foods.

No sales or other excise taxes shall be levied or collected (1) upon any wholesale sale or wholesale purchase of food for human consumption, its ingredients or its packaging, (2) upon any sale or purchase of such items sold to or purchased by a manufacturer, processor, packager, distributor or reseller of food for human consumption, or its ingredients, for use in its trade or business; or (3) in any retail transaction, on any packaging that contains food for human consumption on or off the premises where sold. For purposes of this section, food for human consumption shall include nonalcoholic beverages. This section shall not affect the extent to which the levy or collection of sales or other excise taxes on the retail sale or retail purchase of food for human consumption is permitted or prohibited by Section 3(C) of this Article.

Adopted in 1994 and never amended, this section, which was proposed by initiative petition and approved by the voters, this section prohibits sales or other excise taxes on the wholesale sale or purchase of foods for human consumption and on foods sold or purchased by a manufacturer, processor, distributor, or reseller. It also prohibits retail sales or other excise taxes on packaging that contains food for human consumption.

This section defines "food" to include soft drinks and other nonalcoholic beverages, and it was popularly referred to as the "pop tax" amendment. It was proposed at the behest of the soft drink industry to invalidate a wholesale tax on soft drinks. It does not, however, prohibit retail sales taxes on soft drinks or any other foods consumed on the premises where they are sold as permitted by section 3(C).

In 2009, the Ohio Supreme Court considered whether a commercial activity tax constituted an "excise tax" under sections 3 and 13 of this article. In *Ohio Grocers Association v. Levin* (2009), the court held that a proposed "commercial activity tax" was not a proscribed excise tax because the tax was imposed on the person enjoying the privilege-of-doing-business rather than on the sale of food. Furthermore, the court allowed for the measurement of the tax by gross receipts, which included the proceeds from the sale of food. In effect, this decision expanded the power of the General Assembly to impose taxes on grocery stores and other entities engaged in the sale of food.

Article XIII

Corporations

Under Ohio law, private and municipal corporations are "creatures of the state," owing their existence to state law. *State ex rel. Kohler v. Cincinnati, W. & B. Railway Co.* (1890). Article XIII deals with the formation of corporations and with the power of the state to regulate them. The 1851 Constitution adopted this article in response to the abuses involved in the incorporation of private and municipal corporations under the 1802 Constitution.

Section 1

Special acts conferring corporate powers prohibited.

The General Assembly shall pass no special act conferring corporate powers.

Adopted in 1851 and never amended, this section forbids the General Assembly from passing special acts "conferring corporate powers." This prohibition was the response to the practice of creating corporations and conferring corporate powers by special legislative acts. Its companion provision, Article XIII, section 6, authorized the organization of cities by general law.

Under the 1802 Constitution, the General Assembly formed all corporations through the passage of special legislation, resulting in the General Assembly spending an inordinate amount of time incorporating businesses. See generally

The Ohio State Constitution. Steven H. Steinglass and Gino J. Scarselli, Oxford University Press. © Oxford University Press 2022. DOI: 10.1093/oso/9780197619728.003.0015

Ohio Constitutional Revision Commission (OCRC), *Recommendations for Amendments to the Ohio Constitution: Final Report, Index to Proceedings and Research* (Columbus: The Commission, 1977), 82 (hereinafter OCRC, *Final Report*). Many viewed this process as unfair and subject to abuse because the General Assembly often included special privileges in corporate charters, thereby giving some corporations an advantage over their competitors. Moreover, the broad grants of power often written into corporate charters by promoters and approved by special legislation led to risky financial ventures for which the state was ultimately responsible, particularly in connection with the building of the state's transportation system in the 1820s and 1830s. See generally Thomas R. Swisher, *Ohio Constitution Handbook* (Cleveland: Banks-Baldwin Law Publishing Co., 1990) (hereinafter, Swisher, *Ohio Constitution Handbook*), 459.

A "special act" for purposes of this section is "one that is local and temporary in its operation." *State ex rel. Kauer v. Defenbacher* (1950). The prohibition in this section extends to special acts of the General Assembly conferring corporate powers on municipal as well as private corporations. *State ex rel. Attorney General v. City of Cincinnati* (1872). This section, however, does not apply to county and township organizations and state agencies. *State ex rel. Saxbe v. Alexander* (1959). Nor does it apply to state universities and their boards of trustees. *Neil v. Board of Trustees of the Ohio Agriculture and Mechanical College* (1876).

Section 2

Corporations, how formed.

Corporations may be formed under general laws; but all such laws may, from time to time, be altered or repealed. Corporations may be classified and there may be conferred upon proper boards, commissions or officers, such supervisory and regulatory powers over their organization, business and issue and sale of stocks and securities and over the business and sale of the stocks and securities of foreign corporations and joint stock companies in this state, as may be prescribed by law. Laws may be passed regulating the sale and conveyance of other personal property, whether owned by a corporation, joint stock company or individual.

Adopted in 1851 and amended in 1912, this section provides that business organizations seeking access to the corporate form may incorporate under the general laws of the state, which laws the state may alter or repeal from time to time. Read in connection with section 1's prohibition on establishing corporations and conferring corporate powers through special acts, this section in effect requires corporations to be formed under general laws. Title 17 of the Ohio Revised Code contains Ohio's general laws governing the formation and powers of corporations (and other business entities).

As originally adopted, this section contained only the first sentence of the current version. This provision prevented the conferring of special benefits on particular corporations (often to the disadvantage of other corporations) and to the general public (because many of these special benefits included tax breaks). It also sought to address the inefficiency of the General Assembly. Prior to the 1851 Constitution, special legislation occupied nearly all the time of the legislature and resulted in an extraordinary number of laws largely due to the General Assembly giving itself the responsibility for all acts of incorporating private and municipal corporations. As Isaac F. Patterson described:

> As early as 1833 the work of the General Assembly for one year was represented by the passage of two hundred and fifty local laws and only thirty general laws. But the local acts and resolutions passed by the General Assembly of 1849 . . . fill seven hundred and forty-six pages of the *Laws of Ohio* for that year, and include seventy-five acts relating to plank roads, sixty-seven to railroads, and seventy-eight to turnpikes. The legislature of 1851, the one in session at the time the new Constitution was being framed, broke all records. It was a veritable bargain sale rush. The local acts and resolutions for that year cover eight hundred and seventeen pages and include forty charters and amendments of charters of insurance companies; sixty-six charters and amendments of charters of plank roads; seventy-four charters and amendments of charters of turnpikes; and eighty-nine acts relating to railroads.
>
> Isaac F. Patterson, *The Constitutions of Ohio: Amendments, and Proposed Amendments* (Cleveland: The Arthur H. Clark Co., 1912), 19–20.

In the first session of the General Assembly following adoption of the 1851 Constitution, the General Assembly "passed a total of only twenty-four local acts on all subjects." Ibid.

The delegates to the 1851 Constitution included the reservation clause in the first sentence to allow the General Assembly to amend or repeal general laws. This was in part a response to the U.S. Supreme Court's ruling in *Trustees of Dartmouth College v. Woodward* (1819), holding that a corporate charter was a contract between the corporation and the state that could not be altered absent specific language in the charter. See OCRC, *Final Report*, 82; see also Commentary, Article I, section 2.

Other provisions of the Ohio Constitution limit the General Assembly's power to amend or repeal corporate charters and general laws governing corporations, such as Article I, section 19, which restricts the state's power of eminent domain, and Article II, section 28, which prohibits the General Assembly from passing retroactive laws and laws that impair the obligation of contracts. *Wheatley v. A.I. Root Co.* (1946).

In 1912, the voters approved a proposal made by the 1912 Constitutional Convention to amend this section to confer power to corporate management to manage and sell securities. The final sentence of the section, also adopted in 1912, allows the General Assembly to pass legislation to regulate the sale and conveyance of other personal property.

Section 3

Dues from corporations; how secured; inspection of private banks.

Dues from private corporations shall be secured by such means as may be prescribed by law, but in no case shall any stockholder be individually liable otherwise than for the unpaid stock owned by him or her. No corporation not organized under the laws of this state, or of the United States, or person, partnership or association shall use the word "bank," "banker" or "banking," or words of similar meaning in any foreign language, as a designation or name under which business may be conducted in this state unless such corporation, person, partnership or association shall submit to inspection, examination and regulation as may hereafter be provided by the laws of this state.

Adopted in 1851 and amended in 1903, 1912, and 1937, this section combines a prohibition against imposing personal liability on stockholders beyond their share of stock in a corporation and a restriction on the use of the term "bank" and similar words.

As originally adopted in 1851, this section provided that stockholders could be liable up to double the amount of stock they owned plus any amount of money they had not yet paid for their shares. In 1852, the General Assembly passed the first general corporate law, the Corporation Act of May 1, 1852, imposing double liability on stockholders. See *Everard v. Kroeger* (1938). The purpose of permitting stockholders to be held doubly liable was to protect the creditors of a corporation.

In 1903, the voters approved an amendment proposed by the Ohio General Assembly to amend this section by adding the word "private" and thus limit the applicability of this section to private corporations. The amendment had the effect of excluding schools, libraries, state banks, and other publicly funded corporations from its reach. In addition, the amendment removed double liability for stockholders and thus limited the individual liability of stockholders to the amount of unpaid stock they owned.

In 1912, the voters approved an amendment proposed by the 1912 Constitutional Convention to amend this section to reintroduce additional liability beyond the amount of unpaid stock in corporations that were "authorized to receive money on deposit" (e.g., banks). Under the 1912 amendment, stockholders of a bank could be held individually liable on a pro rata share for the debts of the bank. The purpose of this amendment was to protect depositors as well as creditors and to restore and maintain confidence in the banking system. *State ex rel. Squire v. Harris* (1938). The 1912 amendment also added the provision prohibiting individuals, partnerships, associations, and foreign corporations from using the words "bank," "banker," or "banking" in their names unless they submit to inspection, regulation, and examination by state regulators.

After passage of the Federal Deposit Insurance Act of 1933, the General Assembly proposed and the voters approved an amendment in 1936 to limit the additional liability of stockholders of banking and other depository corporations to the amount of unpaid stock they owned in the corporation. See Lloyd A. Helms, "Corporations under the Ohio Constitution," in Harvey Walker, ed., *An Analysis and Appraisal of the Ohio State Constitution 1851–1951* (Cincinnati: The Stephen H. Wilder Foundation, 1951).

Section 4

Corporate property subject to taxation.

The property of corporations, now existing or hereafter created, shall forever be subject to taxation, the same as the property of individuals.

Adopted in 1851 and never amended, this section provides that corporate property shall be subject to the same taxation as property owned by individuals. The 1851 Convention proposed this section in response to the General Assembly's practice of exempting the property of certain corporations from taxation. See OCRC, *Final Report*, 83. It does not, however, prohibit tax exemptions on corporate property if the exemptions also apply to the property of individuals. *State ex rel. Struble v. Davis* (1937). Franchise taxes levied on corporations for the privilege of doing business in the state, however, are not property taxes, *Southern Gum Co. v. Laylin* (1902), and thus this section does not apply to franchise taxes.

Section 5

Rights of way; full compensation; jury trial.

No right of way shall be appropriated to the use of any corporation; until full compensation therefor be first made in money or first secured by a deposit of money, to the owner, irrespective of any benefit from any improvement proposed by such corporation, which compensation shall be ascertained by a jury of twelve men, in a court of record, as shall be prescribed by law.

Adopted in 1851 and never amended, this section placed limitations on the power of eminent domain exercised by railroad, canal, and turnpike companies.

Under the 1802 Constitution it was common for the state to grant corporations the power of eminent domain in order for the state to encourage the construction of a transportation system. Although property owners were entitled to compensation when their property was taken by eminent domain, the 1802 Constitution contained no provision for determining the amount of compensation. Court-appointed commissioners decided how much compensation was due, and "[m]any landowners felt that they had been cheated by pro-railroad commissioners appointed by pro-railroad courts and that they were left completely without recourse." OCRC, *Final Report*, 479.

This section continued to allow corporations to acquire property through eminent domain but required property owners to receive full compensation before their property was taken.

The current language in this section, like Article I, section 19, which deals with the taking of private property by the state, requires a jury to determine the amount of compensation. But, unlike Article I, section 19, this section requires a jury of "twelve men" to fix the amount of compensation.

In 1929, a property owner challenged the amount of compensation he received from a railroad company that had taken his property because the jury contained men and women. The Ohio Supreme Court did not disturb the award holding that the word "men" related to the mode of trial and not to the qualifications of jurors. The court further observed that this section uses the word "men" generically, and that women, who are now electors, meet the qualifications to serve as jurors. *Thatcher v. Pennsylvania, O. & D.R. Co.* (1929).

This section permits the delegation of the eminent domain power to private corporations. But because this is a delegation of sovereign power, the Ohio Supreme Court in *Currier v. Marietta and Cincinnati Railroad Co.* (1860) required that such delegations be strictly limited to their stated purposes and terms:

> There is no rule more familiar or better settled than this: that grants of corporate power, being in derogation of common right, are to be strictly construed; and this is especially the case where the power claimed is a delegation of the right of eminent domain-one of the highest powers of sovereignty pertaining to the State itself, and interfering most seriously, and often vexatiously, with the ordinary rights of property.

Although the language of this section contains more explicit protections of property rights than those provided in Article I, section 5, in the 1970s the OCRC concluded that "these differences have been almost entirely eliminated by court decisions" and declined to recommend any change in the section other than the removal of the requirement that a jury consist "of twelve men," preferring to leave the number of jurors flexible as is the case for other civil juries. But the General Assembly did not submit any proposed constitutional amendment of this section to the voters.

Section 6

Organization of cities; limitations of power.

> The General Assembly shall provide for the organization of cities, and incorporated villages; by general laws, and restrict their power of taxation, assessment, borrowing money, contracting debts and loaning their credit, so as to prevent the abuse of such power.

Adopted in 1851 and never amended, this section requires the General Assembly to organize cities and incorporated villages according to general laws. The delegates to the convention proposed this section, in part, to end the practice of incorporating cities and villages by special acts of legislation—the same practice that the General Assembly used to incorporate private corporations. See OCRC, *Final Report,* 311–12, 325. To prevent abuses of power by municipalities, this section gives the General Assembly the power to limit the ability of municipalities to levy taxes and assessments, to borrow money, and to loan funds.

In 1912, the supporters of the Home Rule Amendment apparently meant to repeal this section because of its overlap with a number of sections of Article XVIII, including section 13, which also permits the General Assembly to restrict the power of municipalities to levy taxes and incur debt. OCRC, *Final Report,* 325 (citing *Proceedings and Debates of the Constitutional Convention of the State of Ohio* (Columbus: The F. J. Heer Printing Co., 1912), 1434–35, 1493–94). The delegates at the 1912 Convention made no proposal, however, to repeal this section, and the Ohio Supreme Court subsequently held that the adoption of the Home Rule Amendment did not implicitly repeal this section. *Berry v. City of Columbus* (1922).

Ohio courts have relied on both this section and Article XVIII, section 13 to limit municipal taxing and borrowing powers.

Unlike Article XVIII, section 13, this section also allows the state to limit municipal power to levy assessments—a power specifically granted to municipalities by Article XVIII, section 11—in cases where the appropriation of property for public improvements benefits other property.

Legislation adopted by the General Assembly under this section prevails in conflicts with local assessment laws adopted under Article XVIII, section 11. See *Berry, supra.* Thus, where a city charter or local ordinance authorizing assessments conflicts with a general law of the state, the general law prevails. Ibid.

Section 7

Association with banking powers.

No act of the General Assembly, authorizing associations with banking powers, shall take effect until it shall be submitted to the people, at the general election next succeeding the passage thereof, and be approved by a majority of all the electors, voting at such election.

Adopted in 1851 and never amended, this section prohibits the General Assembly from passing legislation "authorizing associations with banking powers" without the approval of the voters. The delegates to the 1851 Constitution apparently understood the term "banking powers" to refer only to the power to issue bank notes as a form of currency and not to other banking functions, such as receiving deposits and loaning money. See *Dearborn v. Northwestern Savings Bank* (1885).

The panics of 1819 and 1837 were widely blamed on banks that issued notes above and beyond their assets, see Swisher, *Ohio Const. Handbook,* 468, and one of the delegates to the 1850–51 convention commented that the convention looked "upon that function which empowers banks to issue their own notes to circulate as money, as the nuisance which [the delegates] desire should be abated." *1850–51 Debates*, vol. 2, 416. This provision, had the effect of forbidding the General Assembly from allowing banks and other institutions to issue notes that circulate as currency unless approved by the voters, *Dearborn, supra*, was viewed as "a compromise between advocates of the gold standard and advocates of an easy money policy." OCRC, *Final Report*, 85.

States are apparently not prohibited from authorizing private banks to issue their own paper currency, but beginning with the 1863 National Bank Act, a series of federal laws imposing taxes on private notes effectively abolished private banks. See Lewis D. Solomon, "Local Currency: A Legal and Policy Analysis," *Kan. J. L. & Pub. Pol.* 5 (Winter 1996); see also David G. Oedel, "Why Regulate Cybermoney?" 46 *Am. U. L. Rev.* 1075 (1997).

In the 1970s, the OCRC recommended the repeal of this section given the dominance of the U.S. currency, see OCRC, *Final Report*, 85, but the General Assembly did not submit a proposed constitutional amendment of this section to the voters.

Article XIV

Ohio Livestock Care Standards Board

JURISPRUDENCE

Prior to the 2009 adoption of an article creating the Ohio Livestock Care Board, this article had been a placeholder with no operative provisions since 1953.

Under the 1851 Constitution, the original Article XIV, which was repealed in 1953, contained an article on jurisprudence, which created a mechanism for revising the rules of procedure used in civil as contrasted to criminal cases in the Ohio courts. The original article required the General Assembly to establish a committee of three commissioners to

> revise, reform, simplify and abridge the practice, pleadings, forms and proceedings of the courts of record . . . and, as far as practicable and expedient . . . provide for the abolition of the distinct forms of action at law, now in use, and for the administration of justice by a uniform mode of proceeding, without reference to any distinction between law and equity.
>
> 1851 Ohio Constitution, Article XIV, section 2.

The commissioners, appointed in March 1852, took less than a year to submit a report to the General Assembly recommending the adoption of a system of procedure that was modeled on New York's "Field Code," and that abolished the ancient common law forms of action in favor of a single cause of

The Ohio State Constitution. Steven H. Steinglass and Gino J. Scarselli, Oxford University Press. © Oxford University Press 2022. DOI: 10.1093/oso/9780197619728.003.0016

action characterized by the pleading of facts rather than statements of law. See generally James Fleming Jr., and Geoffrey C. Hazard Jr., *Civil Procedure,* 3d ed. (Boston: Little, Brown & Co., 1985), 18.

In March 1853, the General Assembly accepted the commissioners' recommendation and adopted the Ohio Code of Civil Procedure. See Charles M. Hepburn, *The Historical Development of Code Pleading in America and England* (Cincinnati: W.H. Anderson & Co., 1897), 100–1. The Ohio Code, with minor modifications in 1879, governed civil practice in Ohio courts until 1970 when the Ohio Supreme Court, acting under the authority of the Modern Courts Amendment, revised Ohio's rules to conform more closely to the Federal Rules of Civil Procedure. See Commentary, Article IV, section 5. See also Josiah H. Blackmore II, "Not from Zeus's Head Full-Blown: The Story of Civil Procedure in Ohio," in *The History of Ohio Law* (Athens: Ohio University Press, 2004).

In 1953, the voters repealed the jurisprudence article in its entirety, and in 2009, the General Assembly selected this empty article as the place for a new article creating the Ohio Livestock Care Standards Board.

■ OHIO LIVESTOCK CARE STANDARDS BOARD

(A) There is hereby created the Ohio Livestock Care Standards Board for the purpose of establishing standards governing the care and well-being of livestock and poultry in this state. In carrying out its purpose, the Board shall endeavor to maintain food safety, encourage locally grown and raised food, and protect Ohio farms and families. The Board shall be comprised of the following thirteen members:

(1) The director of the state department that regulates agriculture who shall be the chairperson of the Board;

(2) Ten members appointed by the Governor with the advice and consent of the Senate. The ten members appointed by the Governor shall be residents of this state and shall include the following:

(a) One member representing family farms;

(b) One member who is knowledgeable about food safety in this state;

(c) Two members representing statewide organizations that represent farmers;

(d) One member who is a veterinarian who is licensed in this state;

(e) The State Veterinarian in the state department that regulates agriculture;

(f) The dean of the agriculture department of a college or university located in this state;

(g) Two members of the public representing Ohio consumers;

(h) One member representing a county humane society that is organized under state law.

(3) One member appointed by the Speaker of the House of Representatives who shall be a family farmer;

(4) One member appointed by the President of the Senate who shall be a family farmer.

Not more than seven members appointed to the Board at any given time shall be of the same political party.

(B) The Board shall have authority to establish standards governing the care and well-being of livestock and poultry in this state, subject to the authority of the General Assembly. In establishing those standards, the Board shall consider factors that include, but are not limited to, agricultural best management practices for such care and well-being, biosecurity, disease prevention, animal morbidity and mortality data, food safety practices, and the protection of local, affordable food supplies for consumers.

(C) The state department that regulates agriculture shall have the authority to administer and enforce the standards established by the Board.

(D) The General Assembly may enact laws that it deems necessary to carry out the purposes of this section, to facilitate the execution of the duties of the Board and the state department that regulates agriculture under this section, and to set the terms of office of the Board members and conditions for the Board members' service on the Board.

(E) If any part of this section is held invalid, the remainder of this section shall not be affected by that holding and shall continue in full force and effect.

Proposed by the General Assembly in 2009 and approved by the voters that year, this article created the Ohio Livestock Care Standards Board for the purpose of establishing standards governing the care and well-being of livestock and poultry in the state.

The board consists of thirteen members, who are appointed by the governor, the president of the Senate, and the speaker of the House of Representatives, and the board must include the director of the Ohio Department of Agriculture, three family farmers, a food safety expert, two members from a statewide farming organization, two veterinarians, a dean of an Ohio college of agriculture, two consumers, and one local humane society representative.

The catalyst behind this amendment was the announced effort of the Humane Society of the United States to push Ohio to adopt a policy similar to the recently enacted (through the statutory initiative) California Prevention of Farm Animal Cruelty Act, which had required "that calves raised for veal, egg-laying hens and pregnant pigs be confined only in ways that allow these animals to lie down, stand up, fully extend their limbs and turn around freely."

In this century, federal legislation focusing on animal welfare has been replaced by state legislation that focused not on animal welfare but rather on animal rights. One trend in recent years involves legislation controlling livestock housing, and Ohio's agricultural community was not happy with the proposals being made.

Choosing to be proactive rather than work with the Humane Society, Ohio agricultural groups united formed a political action committee and urged the creation of the Ohio Livestock Care Standards Board. The board was described by its proponents as an unbiased group of industry experts responsible for overseeing livestock care in Ohio.

The state's major newspapers opposed this proposed amendment. The Cleveland *Plain Dealer, The Columbus Dispatch, The Dayton Daily News,* and *The Toledo Blade* endorsed a "No" vote, generally citing opposition to including the board in the Ohio Constitution. See Hannah N. Thompson, "Agricultural Issues on the Ballot: The 2009 Ohio Issue 2 Campaign" (Honor Project) (Presented in Partial Fulfillment of the Requirements for the Degree of Bachelor of Science in the College of Food, Agricultural, and Environmental Sciences at the Ohio State University) (2011) (Ohio State Universities Knowledge Bank) (website).

The voters approved the proposed amendment by a 63.7 percent to 36.3 percent vote, which led the Humane Society to begin the process of initiating a constitutional amendment that would have blunted some of the provisions of the approved amendment. But ultimately there was a meeting of the minds, and the otherwise adverse parties agreed on a number of the standards that were adopted by the newly appointed board.

Article XV

Miscellaneous

Article XV includes a number of miscellaneous provisions, addressing such matters as the location of the state capital in Columbus, the authorization of a state lottery and casino gambling, oaths of office, and the civil service. Proposed amendments to this article that the voters rejected in recent years include an amendment to require legislative approval of nuclear power plant safety features (1976), an amendment to raise the drinking age for beer to twenty-one (1983), and four amendments to allow casino gambling (1990, 1996, 2006, and 2008).

Section 1
Seat of Government.

Columbus shall be the seat of government, until otherwise directed by law.

Adopted in the 1851 Constitution and never amended, this section provides that Columbus is the seat of government, but it permits the General Assembly to change its location.

The Constitution of 1802 had named Chillicothe, which had been the capital of the eastern section of the Northwest Territory, as the seat of government (or state capital) of the new state but only until 1808. 1802 Constitution, Article VII, section 4. This section did not specify where the state capital would

The Ohio State Constitution. Steven H. Steinglass and Gino J. Scarselli, Oxford University Press. © Oxford University Press 2022. DOI: 10.1093/oso/9780197619728.003.0017

subsequently be located, and the General Assembly moved the seat of government to Zanesville, where it remained from 1809 to 1816, when it was briefly returned to Chillicothe. Finally, the General Assembly moved it to (what was to become) Columbus in order to have it near the geographic center of the state. See Ohio Constitutional Revision Commission, *Recommendations for Amendments to the Ohio Constitution: Final Report, Index to Proceedings and Research* (1977), 86 (hereinafter OCRC, *Final Report*).

Though there has been very little litigation concerning this section, an appeals court held that the state board of optometry is required to maintain a central office in Columbus. But it is unclear whether this decision is based on this constitutional provision or on a statute that required the maintenance of a central office in Columbus. *State v. Barhorst* (1959).

Section 2
Repealed—Public printing

Adopted in 1851 but repealed in 1976, this section concerned contracts for the printing of bills, laws, and other legislative documents for each house of the General Assembly and for the executive branch of government. The original version required that such printing be "let, on contract, to the lowest responsible bidder." In 1912, the voters approved an amendment proposed by the constitutional convention to permit the state to do the printing itself.

Section 3
Receipts and expenditures.

An accurate and detailed statement of the receipts and expenditures of the public money, the several amounts paid, to whom, and on what account, shall, from time to time, be published, as shall be prescribed by law.

Adopted in 1851 and never amended, this section requires the General Assembly to pass legislation mandating that a financial statement of state expenditures and receipts be made on a regular basis. A proposal requiring annual publication was removed during the 1851 Constitutional Convention when it was brought to the attention of the delegates that the proposal, if adopted, would require the annual disclosure of the salaries of public officials. OCRC, *Final Report*, 86–87

Section 4
Officers to be qualified electors.

No person shall be elected or appointed to any office in the state unless possessed of the qualifications of an elector.

Adopted in 1851 and amended in 1913 and 1953, this section provides that any person eligible to vote may hold office.

The 1802 Constitution set distinct qualifications for various public officials in different sections of the constitution. For example, officials appointed to any office within a county had to be citizens and residents of the county; representatives had to be citizens of the United States, residents of the state, and at least twenty-five years old; senators had to be citizens of the United States, residents of the county or district from which they were elected, and at least thirty years old; and the governor had to be a citizen of the United States for twelve years, a resident of the state for four years, and at least thirty years old. 1802 Constitution, Article I, sections 4, 7, 27, and Article II, section 3.

The current section is now virtually identical to the 1851 version, which provided that "[n]o person shall be elected or appointed to any office in the state, unless he possesses the qualifications of an elector." Since women, African Americans, and members of other racial minorities were not permitted to vote in 1851, all public officials were white men over the age of twenty-one.

In 1913, the voters approved an amendment to this section proposed by the General Assembly to remove the male pronoun and thus to allow women (who were still denied the franchise as a result of the defeat of the proposed amendment on women's suffrage in 1912) to serve on boards and in departments and institutions "involving the interests of care of women or children or both." The 1913 amendment, which was proposed by the General Assembly, was the only one of five amendments that the voters approved that year (four of which had been proposed by the General Assembly), and it was the first amendment adopted after the 1912 Constitutional Convention.

With the extension of suffrage to women in 1920 as a result of the ratification of the Nineteenth Amendment to the U.S. Constitution, this special provision concerning the governmental service of women became obsolete, and in 1953, the voters approved an amendment proposed by the General Assembly to delete the special reference to women.

Section 5
Repealed—Duelists ineligible for office

Adopted in 1851 but not repealed until 1976, this section prohibited persons who had fought in a duel or had assisted someone in a duel (the person's "second," for example) from holding public office. Duelists, however, may still be ineligible for public office under Article V, section 4, which allows the General Assembly to prohibit anyone who has been convicted of a felony from holding office.

Section 6
Lotteries, charitable bingo, casino gaming.

Except as otherwise provided in this section, lotteries, and the sale of lottery tickets, for any purpose whatever, shall forever be prohibited in this state.

(A) The General Assembly may authorize an agency of the state to conduct lotteries, to sell rights to participate therein, and to award prizes by chance to participants, provided that the entire net proceeds of any such lottery are paid into a fund of the state treasury that shall consist solely of such proceeds and shall be used solely for the support of elementary, secondary, vocational, and special education programs as determined in appropriations made by the General Assembly.

(B) The General Assembly may authorize and regulate the operation of bingo to be conducted by charitable organizations for charitable purposes.

(C)(1) Casino gaming shall be authorized at four casino facilities (a single casino at a designated location within each of the cities of Cincinnati, Cleveland, and Toledo, and within Franklin County) to create new funding for cities, counties, public school districts, law enforcement, the horse racing industry and job training for Ohio's workforce.

(2) A thirty-three percent tax shall be levied and collected by the state on all gross casino revenue received by each casino operator of these four casino facilities. Except as otherwise provided in section 6(C), no other casino gaming-related state or local fees, taxes, or other charges (however measured, calculated, or otherwise derived) may be, directly or indirectly, applied to, levied against, or otherwise imposed upon gross casino revenue, casino operators, their operations, their owners, or their property.

(3) The proceeds of the tax on gross casino revenue collected by the state shall be distributed as follows:

(a) Fifty-one percent of the tax on gross casino revenue shall be distributed among all eighty-eight counties in proportion to such counties' respective populations at the time of such distribution. If a county's most populated city, as of the 2000 United States census bureau census, had a population greater than 80,000, then fifty percent of that county's distribution will go to said city.

(b) Thirty-four percent of the tax on gross casino revenue shall be distributed among all eighty-eight counties in proportion to such counties' respective public school district student populations at the time of such distribution. Each such distribution received by a county shall be distributed among all public school districts located (in whole or in part) within such county in proportion to each school district's respective student population who are residents of such county at the time of such distribution to the school districts. Each public school district shall determine how its distributions are appropriated, but all distributions shall only be used to support primary and secondary education.

(c) Five percent of the tax on gross casino revenue shall be distributed to the host city where the casino facility that generated such gross casino revenue is located.

(d)Three percent of the tax on gross casino revenue shall be distributed to fund the Ohio casino control commission.

(e) Three percent of the tax on gross casino revenue shall be distributed to an Ohio state racing commission fund to support purses, breeding programs, and operations at all existing commercial horse racetracks permitted as of January 1, 2009. However, no funding under this division shall be distributed to operations of an Ohio commercial horse racetrack if an owner or operator of the racetrack holds a majority interest in an Ohio casino facility or in an Ohio casino license.

(f) Two percent of the tax on gross casino revenue shall be distributed to a state law enforcement training fund to enhance public safety by providing additional training opportunities to the law enforcement community.

(g) Two percent of the tax on gross casino revenue shall be distributed to a state problem gambling and addictions fund which shall be used for the treatment of problem gambling and substance abuse, and related research.

Tax collection, and distributions to public school districts and local governments, under sections 6(C)(2) and (3), are intended to supplement, not supplant, any funding obligations of the state. Accordingly, all such distributions shall be disregarded for purposes of determining whether funding obligations imposed by other sections of this Constitution are met.

(4) There is hereby created the Ohio casino control commission which shall license and regulate casino operators, management companies retained by such casino operators, key employees of such casino operators and such management companies, gaming-related vendors, and all gaming authorized by section 6(C), to ensure the integrity of casino gaming.

Said commission shall determine all voting issues by majority vote and shall consist of seven members appointed by the governor with the advice and consent of the senate. Each member of the commission must be a resident of Ohio. At least one member of the commission must be experienced in law enforcement and criminal investigation. At least one member of the commission must be a certified public accountant experienced in accounting and auditing. At least one member of the commission must be an attorney admitted to the practice of law in Ohio. At least one member of the commission must be a resident of a county where one of the casino facilities is located. Not more than four members may be affiliated with the same political party. No commission member may have any affiliation with an Ohio casino operator or facility.

Said commission shall require each initial licensed casino operator of each of the four casino facilities to pay an upfront license fee of fifty million dollars ($50,000,000) per casino facility for the benefit of the state, for a total of two hundred million dollars ($200,000,000). The upfront license fee shall be used to fund state economic development programs which support regional job training efforts to equip Ohio's workforce with additional skills to grow the economy.

To carry out the tax provisions of section 6(C), and in addition to any other enforcement powers provided under Ohio law, the tax commissioner of the State and the Ohio casino control commission, or any person employed by the tax commissioner or said commission for that purpose, upon demand, may inspect books, accounts, records, and memoranda of any person subject to such provisions, and may examine under oath any officer, agent, or employee of that person.

(5) Each initial licensed casino operator of each of the four casino facilities shall make an initial investment of at least two hundred fifty million dollars ($250,000,000) for the development of each casino facility for a total minimum investment of one billion dollars ($1,000,000,000) statewide. A casino operator: (a) may not hold a majority interest in more than two of the four licenses allocated to the casino facilities at any one time; and (b) may not hold a majority interest in more than two of the four casino facilities at any one time.

(6) Casino gaming authorized in section 6(C) shall be conducted only by licensed casino operators of the four casino facilities or by licensed management companies retained by such casino operators. At the discretion of each licensed casino operator of a casino facility: (a) casino gaming may be conducted twenty-four hours each day; and (b) a maximum of five thousand slot machines may be operated at such casino facility.

(7) Each of the four casino facilities shall be subject to all applicable state laws and local ordinances related to health and building codes, or any related requirements and provisions. Notwithstanding the foregoing, no local zoning, land use laws, subdivision regulations or similar provisions shall prohibit the development or operation of the four casino facilities set forth herein, provided that no casino facility shall be located in a district zoned exclusively residential as of January 1, 2009.

(8) Notwithstanding any provision of the Constitution, statutes of Ohio, or a local charter and ordinance, only one casino facility shall be operated in each of the cities of Cleveland, Cincinnati, and Toledo, and in Franklin County.

(9) For purposes of this section 6(C), the following definitions shall be applied:

"Casino facility" means all or any part of any one or more of the following properties (together with all improvements situated thereon) in Cleveland, Cincinnati, Toledo, and Franklin County:

(a) Cleveland:

Being an approximate 61 acre area in Cuyahoga County, Ohio, as identified by the Cuyahoga County Auditor, as of 02/27/09, as tax parcel numbers 004-28-001, 004-29-004A, 004-29-005, 004-29-008, 004-29-009, 004-29-010, 004-29-012, 004-29-013, 004-29-014, 004-29-020, 004-29-018, 004-29-017, 004-29-016, 004-29-021, 004-29-025, 004-29-027, 004-29-026, 004-28-008, 004-28-004, 004-28-003, 004-28-002, 004-28-010, 004-29-001, 004-29-007 and 004-04-017 and all lands and air rights lying within and/or above the public rights of way adjacent to such parcels.

Being an approximate 8.66 acre area in Cuyahoga County, Ohio, being that parcel identified by the Cuyahoga County Auditor, as of 02/27/09, as tax parcel number 101-21-002 and all lands and air rights lying within and/or above the public rights of way adjacent to such parcel.

Being an approximate 2.56 acre area in Cuyahoga County, Ohio, being that parcel identified by the Cuyahoga County Auditor, as of 02/27/09, as tax parcel number 101-21-002 and all lands and air rights lying within and/or above the public rights of way adjacent to such parcel.

Being an approximate 7.91 acre area in Cuyahoga County, Ohio, being that parcel identified by the Cuyahoga County Auditor, as of 02/27/09, as tax parcel number 101-23-050A and all lands and air rights lying within and/or above the public rights of way adjacent to such parcel.

All air rights above the parcel located in Cuyahoga County, Ohio identified by the Cuyahoga County Auditor, as of 02/27/09, as tax parcel number 101-22-003.

Being an approximate 1.55 acre area in Cuyahoga County, Ohio, as identified by the Cuyahoga County Auditor, as of 02/27/09, as tax parcel numbers 122-18-010, 122-18-011 and 122-18-012 and all lands and air rights lying within and/or above the public rights of way adjacent to such parcels.

Being an approximate 1.83 acre area in Cuyahoga County, Ohio, as identified by the Cuyahoga County Auditor, as of 02/27/09, as tax parcel numbers 101-30-002 and 101-30-003 and all lands and air rights lying within and/or above the public rights of way adjacent to such parcels.

Consisting of floors one through four, mezzanine, basement, sub-basement, Parcel No. 36-2, Item III, Parcels First and Second, Item V, Parcel A, and Item VI, Parcel One of the Higbee Building in Cuyahoga County, Ohio, as identified by the Cuyahoga County Auditor, as of 2/29/091, as tax parcel numbers 101-23-002 and 101-23-050F and all lands and air rights lying within and/or above the public rights of way adjacent to such parcels.

(b) Franklin County:

Being an approximate 113.794 acre area in Franklin County, Ohio, as identified by the Franklin County Auditor, as of 01/19/10, as tax parcel number 140-003620-00.

(c) Cincinnati:

Being an approximate 20.4 acre area in Hamilton County, Ohio, being identified by the Hamilton County Auditor, as of 02/27/09, as tax parcel numbers 074-0002-0009-00, 074-0001-0001-00, 074-0001-0002-00, 074-0001-0003-00, 074-0001-0004-00, 074-0001-0006-00, 074-0001-0008-00, 074-0001-0014-00, 074-0001-0016-00, 074-0001-0031-00, 074-0001-0039-00, 074-0001-0041-00, 074-0001-0042-00, 074-0001-0043-00, 074-0002-0001-00, 074-0004-0001-00, 074-0004-0002-00, 074-0004-0003-00 and 074-0005-0003-00.

(d) Toledo:

Being an approximate 44.24 acre area in the City of Toledo, Lucas County, Ohio, as identified by the Lucas County Auditor, as of 03/05/09, as tax parcel numbers 18-76138 and 18-76515.

"Casino gaming" means any type of slot machine or table game wagering, using money, casino credit, or any representative of value, authorized in any of the states of Indiana, Michigan, Pennsylvania and West Virginia as of January 1, 2009, and shall include slot machine and table game wagering subsequently authorized by, but shall not be limited by subsequent restrictions placed on such wagering in, such states. Notwithstanding the aforementioned definition, "casino gaming" does not include bingo, as authorized in article XV, section 6 of the Ohio Constitution and conducted as of January 1, 2009, or horse racing where the pari-mutuel system of wagering is conducted, as authorized under the laws of Ohio as of January 1, 2009.

"Casino operator" means any person, trust, corporation, partnership, limited partnership, association, limited liability company or other business enterprise that directly holds an ownership or leasehold interest in a casino facility. "Casino operator" does not include an agency of the state, any political subdivision of the state, or any person, trust, corporation, partnership, limited partnership, association, limited liability company or other business enterprise that may have an interest in a casino facility, but who is legally or contractually restricted from conducting casino gaming.

"Gross casino revenue" means the total amount of money exchanged for the purchase of chips, tokens, tickets, electronic cards, or similar objects by casino patrons, less winnings paid to wagerers.

"Majority interest" in a license or in a casino facility (as the case may be) means beneficial ownership of more than fifty percent (50%) of the total fair market value of such license or casino facility (as the case may be). For purposes of the foregoing, whether a majority interest is held in a license or in a casino facility (as the case may be) shall be determined in accordance with the rules for constructive ownership of stock provided in Treas. Reg. § 1.409A-3(i)(5)(iii) as in effect on January 1, 2009.

"Slot machines" shall include any mechanical, electrical, or other device or machine which, upon insertion of a coin, token, ticket, or similar object, or upon payment of any consideration, is available to play or operate, the play or operation of which, whether by reason of the skill of the operator or application of the element of chance, or both, makes individual prize determinations for individual participants in cash, premiums, merchandise, tokens, or any thing of value, whether the payoff is made automatically from the machine or in any other manner.

"Table game" means any game played with cards, dice, or any mechanical, electromechanical, or electronic device or machine for money, casino credit, or any representative of value.

(10) The General Assembly shall pass laws within six months of the effective date of section 6(C) to facilitate the operation of section 6(C).

(11) Each provision of section 6(C) is intended to be independent and severable, and if any provision of section 6(C) is held to be invalid, either on its face or as applied to any person or circumstance, the remaining provisions of section 6(C), and the application thereof to any person or circumstance

other than those to which it is held invalid, shall not be affected thereby. In any case of a conflict between any provision of section 6(C) and any other provision contained in this Constitution, the provisions of section 6(C) shall control.

(12) Notwithstanding the provisions of section 6(C)(11), nothing in this section 6(C) (including, without limitation, the provisions of sections 6(C)(6) and 6(C)(8)) shall restrict or in any way limit lotteries authorized under section 6(A) of this article or bingo authorized under section 6(B) of this article. The provisions of this section 6(C) shall have no effect upon activities authorized under sections 6(A) and/or (6)(B) of this article.

Adopted in 1851 and amended five times, this section initially only provided that "[l]otteries, and the sale of lottery tickets, for any purpose whatever, shall forever be prohibited in this state."

Before statehood, "any species of gaming, play or pastime whatsoever" was prohibited in the Northwest Territory, and the use of billiard tables "or other gaming tables, or any other machine" for gambling was prohibited. See Salmon P. Chase, "A Preliminary Sketch of the History of Ohio," in *Statutes of Ohio and the Northwestern Territory, vol. I.* Cincinnati: Corey & Fairbank, 105.

The 1802 Constitution did not refer to gambling or lotteries, but the General Assembly in the first decade of the century adopted legislation prohibiting lotteries and most forms of gambling. Nonetheless it frequently approved special legislation permitting the use of lotteries to raise state funds for public improvements. This widespread use of lotteries by the state engendered strong public opposition, and in 1830 the General Assembly broadly prohibited "any lottery, or scheme of chance, of any kind . . . by whatever name." 28 Ohio Laws 37 (1830).

■ THE 1850–51 CONSTITUTIONAL CONVENTION

There was only limited discussion of lotteries at the 1850–51 Constitutional Convention. The delegates equated lotteries with other evils such as prostitution and liquor sales, but they singled out lotteries and the sale of lottery tickets for special treatment without directly addressing gambling. Mr. McCormick of Adams County, recognizing that the delegates had incorporated legislative subjects in the fundamental law, observed that they had barred "lotteries and lottery tickets, without embracing any other species of gambling." *Report of the Debates and Proceedings of the Convention for the Revision of the Constitution of the State Of Ohio 1850–51* (Columbus: S. Medary, 1851) (hereinafter *1850–51 Debates*), vol. 2, 719 (February 25, 1851). And the Ohio Supreme Court, noting that the constitutional prohibition was against lotteries and the sale of lottery tickets only, has observed that "the adverse attitude of the General Assembly toward the use of gambling machines or devices was so pronounced, and their use so adverse to the policy of the state, that it apparently was thought unnecessary to write any prohibition thereof into the Constitution." *Mills-Jennings of Ohio, Inc. v. Department of Liquor Control* (1982).

THE INTERREGNUM

The 1851 Constitution did not define lotteries, and the lottery prohibition is self-executing but only "to the extent that it is a declarative limitation upon the plenary legislative power of the Ohio General Assembly with respect to lotteries and the sale of lottery tickets . . . ." *City of Columbus v. Barr* (1953). The General Assembly, however, has broad power to prescribe penalties for violations of the constitutional provisions and to regulate nonlottery gambling. *State v. Parker* (1948). And over the years, it has exercised this power to prohibit various forms of gambling, including policy, numbers, betting on the outcome of elections, pinball, craps (dice), poker, and keno. Under the prevailing legislative distinction, lotteries, which were considered games of chance, were barred as a result of the constitutional provision, while other games of chance and games of skill were barred by state statutes and not by the constitution.

The statutory prohibitions on gambling typically barred schemes that included consideration, chance, and a prize. For example, a newspaper promotion that required a payment or 50 cents with 24 cents going toward a subscription and the 26 cents balance providing a pool for prizes for correctly guessing (or coming the closest to guessing) the vote in the 1902 secretary of state race was an illegal gambling game. See *Stevens v. Cincinnati Times-Star Co.* (1905) ("[W]here the players make up by payment of money, or other thing of value, a purse which affords the prizes, as in the ordinary raffle, the game is a gambling game, whether skill enters into the result or not.").

The Ohio Supreme Court, however, has recognized that lotteries and gambling are not synonymous, and the court has held that "[t]he term 'gambling' includes a lottery but is broader and may encompass more than the term 'lottery.'" *Westerhaus Co. v. City of Cincinnati* (1956) (syllabus). Nonetheless, the court has viewed the constitutional prohibition on lotteries as explaining the state's antigambling policy, but it has acknowledged that the courts have "seldom relied solely on the Constitution in antigambling litigation, [but] it was repeatedly invoked as evidencing a strong public policy against gambling." *Mills-Jennings of Ohio, Inc. v. Department of Liquor Control* (1982).

Notwithstanding the lottery prohibition, there has been widespread acquiescence and in some cases explicit state approval of various gambling activities since 1851. For example, county fairs have been the venue for horse racing and gambling since the nineteenth century, and in 1933 the General Assembly created the Ohio State Racing Commission to regulate the racing industry, include harness and thoroughbred racing at county fairs and racetracks. Moreover, gambling sponsored by religious, veterans, and other nonprofit groups was common, and the General Assembly regulated those activities through the criminal law. Finally, the state effectively recognized the *constitutionality* of charitable bingo but subjected it (unevenly) to regulation (through the criminal law) before the voters approved an amendment on charitable bingo in 1975.

Thus, despite the antigambling sentiment in the state and the conclusion that the lottery prohibition applies to some games of chance that are not "traditional" lotteries or raffles, neither the decisions of the Ohio Supreme Court nor the historical record supports the conclusion that the Ohio Constitution bars gambling.

■ THE OHIO LOTTERY

In 1937, proponents of a state lottery submitted a petition for a constitutional amendment to the attorney general in which they sought to make the constitutional bar on lotteries inapplicable to state-operated lotteries. The attorney general certified the summary as fair truthful, see Ohio Attorney General Reports and Opinions 1937 (1937), 1464, but, for whatever reason, the proponents did not bring the proposal to the ballot.

In 1973, the voters approved an amendment proposed by the General Assembly to permit the creation of a state lottery with all proceeds going to the state's general revenue fund. This amendment authorized the General Assembly to authorize a state agency "to conduct lotteries, to sell rights to participate therein, and to award prizes by chance to participants."

And in 1987, the voters approved an amendment proposed by the General Assembly to require that all lottery proceeds be used to support education programs. The net proceeds of any such lottery are to be paid into the state treasury and used "solely for the support of elementary, secondary, vocational, and special education programs."

In 2001, the General Assembly gave the Ohio Lottery Commission permission to join a multistate lottery, and gambling opponents challenged the state's decision to participate in the multistate lottery, widely known as "Mega Millions." An Ohio appellate court rejected the argument that the constitution only permitted a lottery operated exclusively by the state, but it barred the state from using the proceeds from the multistate lottery to resolve the state's budget problem. This decision was based on the 1987 amendment to this section, which had required the state to use the "entire net proceeds" of state-conducted lotteries solely for the support of education. See *Ohio Roundtable v. Taft* (2003).

■ CHARITABLE BINGO

The express prohibition on lotteries in the 1851 Constitution made clear that a constitutional amendment was necessary to permit the creation of the state lottery. It is less clear, however, whether it was also necessary to amend this section in 1975 to authorize charitable bingo, but there was strong support for the view that bingo was a form of lottery. See generally Patricia Ravenscraft and Elizabeth Reilly, Comment, "Perspectives on Ohio Bingo Regulation: An Historical Analysis and Proposal for Change," 10 *Akron L. Rev.* 646 (1977). The proponents of charitable bingo clearly thought that a constitutional amendment was necessary, especially in light of criminal prosecutions of churches and other nonprofit organizations that sponsored charitable bingo.

Thus, even though the Ohio Supreme Court had not authoritatively addressed this issue, proponents of charitable bingo sought a constitutional amendment to remove any uncertainty about the constitutionality of permitting charitable bingo. As a result, in 1975 the General Assembly proposed and the voters approved by a narrow 53.8 percent vote a revision of this section to allow charitable bingo subject to regulations established by the General Assembly.

■ CASINO GAMING

Beginning in the late 1980s, there were repeated attempts to introduce casino gambling (or casino gaming) in Ohio.

In 1989, the Ohio House, apparently believing that a constitutional amendment was not required, approved a bill to authorize a five-year pilot project for a casino and resort hotel in Lorain, where there would be games of chance, including games by electronic and mechanical devices. H.B. 128, 118th G.A. The Ohio Senate, however, did not act, and the proponents responded by proposing an amendment by initiative petition to authorize the Lorain casino. The voters rejected the proposal in 1990 with only 38 percent favoring it.

In 1996, the voters rejected by the same margin an amendment also proposed by initiative petition to authorize "games and schemes of chance" at eight permanently moored riverboat sites.

In 2006, the voters rejected with a 43 percent favorable vote an amendment proposed by initiative petition to permit up to 31,500 slot machines at Ohio's seven racetracks and at two nonrace track Cleveland locations in order to provide moneys for scholarships and education funding. The proposal expressly excluded "live games associated with casinos, including, but not limited to roulette, card games, and dice games" at the racetracks, but such live games could be conducted at the nontrack facilities in Cleveland and at the two commercial horse racing tracks in Cuyahoga County.

And in 2008, the voters rejected with a 37 percent favorable vote an amendment proposed by initiative petition to permit one privately owned casino in Chester Township near Wilmington, Ohio, to "conduct any game permitted in the State of Nevada, or any state adjacent to Ohio, including any type of card or table games, slot machines, and electronic gaming devices, except bets on races or sporting events."

Finally, in 2009, a different group of gambling proponents (including some who had opposed earlier efforts by their competitors) had more luck (or at least a better sense of timing) and mounted a well-funded campaign for a constitutional amendment to authorize casino gaming. Proposed by initiative petition in the midst of the most severe economic downturn since the depression, the proponents of the amendment defined it as a jobs and tax proposal. And the voters approved the amendment with a 53 percent favorable vote, the lowest approval percentage of any initiated amendment since 1918. See Table of Initiated Constitutional Amendments Approved by Ohio Voters, Ohio Constitution—Law and History (CM Law Website).

■ 2009 CASINO GAMING AMENDMENT

The 2009 amendment approved casino gaming at four locations identified by parcel numbers in Cincinnati, Cleveland, Columbus, and Toledo. But in 2010, the General Assembly—bowing to public opposition to the location of the Columbus casino—proposed an amendment (subsequently approved by 68.4 percent of the voters) to move the Columbus casino to a site in Franklin County outside Columbus. Subsequently, Columbus and Franklin Township agreed that Columbus would annex the parcel, and Columbus did, resulting in the Franklin County casino ending up in Columbus albeit at a different location in the city.

The 2009 amendment created a new and detailed section 6(C) to authorize casino gaming in the four identified sites and to provide for the distribution of funds to all Ohio counties from a 33 percent tax "on all gross casino revenue received by each casino operator of these four casino facilities."

The 2009 amendment defined "casino gaming" as "any type of slot machine or table game wagering, using money, casino credit, or any representative of value, authorized in any of the states of Indiana, Michigan, Pennsylvania and West Virginia as of January 1, 2009, and shall include slot machine and table game wagering subsequently authorized by . . . such states."

The 2009 amendment did not prevent the General Assembly from expanding the gambling activities permitted at the approved casinos, but it expressly excluded "bingo, as authorized in article XV, section 6 of the Ohio Constitution and conducted as of January 1, 2009, . . . [and] horse racing where the pari-mutuel system of wagering is conducted, as authorized under the laws of Ohio as of January 1, 2009."

But was the 2009 constitutional amendment necessary to authorize casino gaming in Ohio? Not if one interprets lottery narrowly more akin to traditional raffles. But regardless of the proper interpretation, the proponents of casino gaming obviously saw an amendment as politically necessary in light of the broad opposition to casino gaming in the General Assembly. The question, however, is of more than theoretical importance. If an amendment was constitutionally required, the four constitutionally identified casinos would have a constitutional monopoly; but if the issue is one that the General Assembly could have addressed, it would be free to authorize additional casinos in Ohio. And the amendment seemed to contemplate such legislative expansions by not expressly prohibiting any such expansions and by providing that "only one casino facility shall be operated in each of the cities of Cleveland, Cincinnati, and Toledo, and in Franklin County."

■ CHALLENGES TO VIDEO LOTTERY TERMINALS AND CASINO GAMING

In 2009, the General Assembly approved legislation that authorized the Ohio Lottery Commission to operate slot machines, dubbed video lottery terminals ("VLTs"), 2009 Am. Sub. H.B. 1, and the commission issued administrative rules limiting VLT licenses to those with permits to conduct horse races. To justify these VLTs the state simply treated the slot machines as lotteries subject to regulation by the Lottery Commission.

Opponents of VLTs and casino gaming challenged the constitutionality of this legislation, but, consistent with its decision in the *JobsOhio* case (see Commentary on Art. IV), the Ohio Supreme Court rejected the challenge because the plaintiffs lacked standing to raise the state constitutional claims. Nonetheless, the court held that one of the plaintiffs had standing to challenge the "special and exclusive privilege to engage in casino gaming in Ohio [given] to two gaming corporations" on the ground that this limitation created a monopoly in violation of the Equal Protection Clause of the Fourteenth Amendment. *State ex rel. Walgate v. Kasich* (2016). On remand, a state court of appeals rejected this federal challenge on the merits, and the Ohio Supreme Court and the U.S. Supreme Court declined to review the decision. See *State ex rel. Walgate v. Kasich* (2018).

■ WHAT EXACTLY IS A LOTTERY?

The most important question that must be answered to understand the scope of the constitutional prohibition on lotteries (and its implication for gambling in general) is "what exactly is a lottery?"

The Ohio Supreme Court has recognized that the constitutional prohibition "was against lotteries and the sale of lottery tickets only." *Mills-Jennings of Ohio, Inc. v. Department of Liquor Control* (1982). And despite "the adverse attitude of the General Assembly toward the use of gambling machines or devices," ibid., it would be a significant stretch to go beyond the constitutional text and interpret the bar on lotteries as a general bar on nonlottery forms of gambling. In any case, the constitutional text bars only lotteries, and the Ohio Supreme Court has never held that it also bars nonlottery forms of gambling.

■ SPORTS GAMBLING

The interpretation of the breadth of the Ohio constitutional prohibition on lotteries has been at the center of a debate over whether (or how) the state will permit sports gambling. Until 2017, both Ohio and federal laws barred sports gambling, but in that year the U.S. Supreme Court struck down the federal bar as a violation of the Tenth Amendment to the U.S. Constitution. *Murphy v. National Collegiate Athletic Association* (2018). This left the states, including Ohio, the question of whether to permit sports gambling.

If the state constitutional prohibition on lotteries is interpreted narrowly, the General Assembly is free to authorize sports gambling and to create the applicable administrative mechanism and tax rate. This could include giving responsibility for regulating sports gambling to the Lottery Commission, to the Casino Control Commission, or to a new state agency.

On the other hand, if the constitutional bar on lotteries is construed broadly to reach all gambling except the state lottery or the four casinos authorized by this section, a constitutional amendment will be needed to authorize sports gambling.

Recognizing the potential constitutional problem, some proponents of sports gambling sought to characterize sports gambling as a "sports gaming lottery" and to place it under the administrative authority of the Ohio Lottery Commission. See H.B. 194 (133rd GA) (passed House on May 28, 2020).

But other proponents of sports gambling avoided this approach and sought to place sports gambling under the administrative authority of the Ohio Casino Control Commission. Under this approach, casino operators and racetracks that operate VLTs would be able to offer sports gambling at their current facilities and online. See S.B. 176 (134th GA) (passed Senate on June 16, 2021).

In December 2021, the General Assembly enacted comprehensive legislation that expanded the availability of sports gambling at state casinos, racetracks, bars, and mobile betting platforms. The new legislation, which also authorized some online sports gambling, gave primary administrative authority to the Ohio Casino Control Commission with a secondary role going to the Ohio Lottery Commission. See H.B. 29 (134th G.A.)

Assuming opponents of gambling can meet state the standing requirements that prevented them from challenging earlier expansions of gambling, see *State ex rel. Walgate v. Kasich* (2016), and Commentary on Article IV, the courts will have to resolve whether this section requires that gambling may only be extended by constitutional amendment.

■ HAS THE OHIO CONSTITUTION ALREADY APPROVED SPORTS GAMBLING?

An alternative approach, apparently advocated by some proponents of sports gambling, is that sports gambling is a form of "casino gaming" and thus has already been approved by the Ohio Constitution. To reach this result, one must argue that sports gambling meets the definition of casino gaming, which is constitutionally defined as a "type of slot machine or table game wagering, using money, casino credit, or any representative of value, authorized in any of the states of Indiana, Michigan, Pennsylvania and West Virginia." And since Pennsylvania and West Virginia permit sports gambling at their casinos, the argument is that Ohio has already approved sports gambling, and thus there is no need to amend the constitution. But even if this argument is accepted, it would still be necessary to amend the constitution if the proponents of sports gambling wanted to avoid application of the constitutionally embedded 33 percent tax rate on casino gaming.

More importantly, it is unlikely that the courts would shoehorn sports gambling into the Ohio Constitution based on the practice in other states. It is highly unusual for a state to give up even a portion of its sovereignty and delegate construction of its constitution to decision makers in other states; thus, to respect the sovereignty of the state, any use of such an approach should be embraced only narrowly, if at all. Finally, this approach would be at odds with the ejusdem generis canon of construction (i.e., of the same kind) under which a general reference after an enumerated list should be interpreted to be of the same type as the items earlier in the list. Thus, the general reference to the gambling practices of the neighboring states should not be construed as including items that are dissimilar from those in the earlier enumerated list of items (i.e., a "type of slot machine or table game wagering").

Section 7
Oath of officers.

Every person chosen or appointed to any office under this state, before entering upon the discharge of its duties, shall take an oath or affirmation, to support the Constitution of the United States, and of this state, and also an oath of office.

Adopted in 1851 and never amended, this section is based on a very similar provision in Article VII, section 1 of the 1802 Constitution. This section requires every person elected or appointed to an office in Ohio to take an oath of office and an oath or affirmation to support the Ohio and U.S. Constitutions. No particular words are necessary. The oath of office may be "sworn in any form he deems binding on his conscience," O.R.C. section 3.21, and may also be stated as an affirmation, O.R.C. section 3.20, if a person objects to talking oaths.

Section 8
Repealed—Bureau of statistics

Adopted in 1851 and repealed in 1976, this section established a bureau of statistics in the secretary of state's office.

Section 9
Repealed—Intoxicating Liquor

This section concerned liquor and liquor trafficking. The original version, adopted in 1851, forbade the state from regulating the sale or distribution of liquor ("No license to traffic in intoxicating liquors shall hereafter be granted in this state") but permitted the General Assembly to enact laws "against evils resulting therefrom." In 1918, with the beginning of national prohibition, the section was amended to prohibit the "sale and manufacture for sale of intoxicating liquors" within the state except "for medicinal, industrial, scientific, sacramental, or other non-beverage purposes." The General Assembly proposed the repeal of this section in 1933, the same year the Twenty-first Amendment was ratified to repeal the Eighteenth Amendment and end prohibition, and the voters approved the repeal of this section.

Section 9a
Repealed—Intoxicating Liquor

Adopted in 1914 and repealed four years later when prohibition went into effect, this section forbade laws from being passed that prohibited the sale of liquor throughout the state and forbade local authorities from prohibiting the sale of liquor without the consent of the local electorate.

Section 10
Civil service.

Appointments and promotions in the civil service of the state, the several counties, and cities, shall be made according to merit and fitness, to be ascertained, as is practicable, by competitive examinations. Laws shall be passed providing for the enforcement of this provision.

Adopted in 1912 amid the wave of progressive reform sweeping the nation and never amended, this section required the adoption of merit-based civil service systems for hiring and promoting public employees at both the state and local levels. Reformers at the 1912 Convention wanted state employees to be selected on their ability and not their political affiliation and believed that public employees would serve better if they were politically neutral. The section calls for the appointment and promotion of state, county, and city civil service employees by competitive examination. In 1913, the General Assembly began enacting legislation to implement a competitive civil service system for certain public employees. The present-day rules governing civil service are found in chapter 124 of the Ohio Revised Code.

Section 11
Marriage.

Only a union between one man and one woman may be a marriage valid in or recognized by this state and its political subdivisions. This state and its political subdivisions shall not create or recognize a legal status for relationships of unmarried individuals that intends to approximate the design, qualities, significance or effect of marriage.

Proposed by initiative petition and approved by the voters in 2004, a presidential election year, this section barred same-sex marriages by providing that "[o]nly a union between one man and one woman may be a marriage valid in or recognized by this state and its political subdivisions."

Despite opposition from gay and lesbian organizations, private industry, and many public officials, including the governor and both of Ohio's U.S. senators, the voters approved this amendment by more than a 3:2 margin. This was one of eleven "gay marriage" amendments to state constitutions adopted throughout the country in the November 2004 general election for reasons that, in part, relate to ginning up the turnout of conservative voters in the presidential election of that year.

The first sentence of this section bans marriages between same-sex couples. The second sentence appears to ban civil unions by providing that the "state and its political subdivisions shall not create or recognize a legal status for relationships of unmarried individuals that intends to approximate the design, qualities, significance or effect of marriage."

In June 2015, the U.S. Supreme Court in *Obergefell v. Hodges* (2015) held that this provision violated the Fourteenth Amendment to the U.S. Constitution, reasoning that "the right to marry is a fundamental right inherent in the liberty of the person, and under the Due Process and Equal Protection Clauses of the Fourteenth Amendment couples of the same-sex may not be deprived of that right and that liberty."

In addition, applying the requirements of the Full Faith and Credit Clause of Article IV, section 1, of the U.S. Constitution, the court held that "there is no lawful basis for a State to refuse to recognize a lawful same-sex marriage performed in another State on the ground of its same-sex character." Thus, this provision of the Ohio Constitution cannot be used as a basis for refusing to recognize same-sex marriages entered into in other states or any way interfering with marriage equality.

Article XVI

Amendments

Article XVI contains two of the three ways the Ohio Constitution can be amended. Under this article, proposed constitutional amendments can be submitted to the voters by the General Assembly (sec. 1) or by a constitutional convention, which may be called at any time by a two-thirds vote of both houses of the General Assembly (sec. 2) or by an affirmative vote on a mandatory statewide referendum every twenty years (sec. 3). The third way, by initiative petition, is described in Article II, sections 1 and la. Unlike the 1802 Constitution, which was not submitted to the voters for approval, all changes in the Ohio Constitution since 1802, including all amendments, must be approved by the voters.

Amending the constitution is much easier today than it was under Ohio's first constitution. Under the 1802 Constitution, only a constitutional convention could propose amendments, and constitutional conventions could be called only if two-thirds of the General Assembly voted to submit a proposal for a convention to the electorate and a majority of those voting for representatives voted in favor of the proposed constitutional convention.

The 1851 Constitution allowed the General Assembly to submit amendments directly to the voters, but until the 1912 amendments to this article, amendments proposed by the General Assembly (but not by conventions) had to be approved by a majority of all persons voting in the election rather than by a simple majority of those voting on the amendments.

The Ohio State Constitution. Steven H. Steinglass and Gino J. Scarselli, Oxford University Press. © Oxford University Press 2022. DOI: 10.1093/oso/9780197619728.003.0018

In 2017, a committee of the Ohio Constitutional Modernization Commission (OCMC) reviewed a comprehensive analysis of issues under this article, but time ran out before the committee or the commission could make any recommendations relating to this article. See OCMC, *Constitution Revision and Updating Committee, Issues Concerning Article XVI and the Amendment Process* (June 8, 2017), and OCMC, Constitution Revision and Updating Committee, Minutes (June 8, 2017).

Section 1

How constitution to be amended; Supreme Court jurisdiction.

Either branch of the General Assembly may propose amendments to this constitution, and, if the same shall be agreed to by three-fifths of the members elected to each house, such proposed amendments shall be entered on the journals, with the yeas and nays, and shall be filed with the secretary of state at least ninety days before the date of the election at which they are to be submitted to the electors, for their approval or rejection. They shall be submitted on a separate ballot without party designation of any kind, at either a special or a general election as the General Assembly may prescribe.

The ballot language for such proposed amendments shall be prescribed by a majority of the Ohio ballot board, consisting of the secretary of state and four other members, who shall be designated in a manner prescribed by law and not more than two of whom shall be members of the same political party. The ballot language shall properly identify the substance of the proposal to be voted upon. The ballot need not contain the full text nor a condensed text of the proposal. The board shall also prepare an explanation of the proposal, which may include its purpose and effects, and shall certify the ballot language and the explanation to the secretary of state not later than seventy-five days before the election. The ballot language and the explanation shall be available for public inspection in the office of the secretary of state.

The Supreme Court shall have exclusive, original jurisdiction in all cases challenging the adoption or submission of a proposed constitutional amendment to the electors. No such case challenging the ballot language, the explanation, or the actions or procedures of the General Assembly in adopting and submitting a constitutional amendment shall be filed later than sixty-four days before the election. The ballot language shall not be held invalid unless it is such as to mislead, deceive, or defraud the voters.

Unless the General Assembly otherwise provides by law for the preparation of arguments for and, if any, against a proposed amendment, the board may prepare such arguments.

Such proposed amendments, the ballot language, the explanation, and the arguments, if any, shall be published once a week for three consecutive weeks preceding such election, in at least one newspaper of general circulation in each county of the state, where a newspaper is published. The General Assembly shall provide by law for other dissemination of information in order to inform the electors concerning proposed amendments. An election on a proposed constitutional amendment submitted by the General Assembly shall not be enjoined nor invalidated because the explanation, arguments, or other information is faulty in any way. If the majority of the electors voting on the same shall adopt such amendments the same shall become a part of the constitution. When more than one amendment shall be submitted at the same time, they shall be so submitted as to enable the electors to vote on each amendment, separately.

Adopted in 1851 and amended in 1912 and 1974, this section outlines the most commonly used process for revising the constitution. Under this section either house of the General Assembly may propose a constitutional amendment through a joint resolution. The proposed amendment must be approved by at least a three-fifths vote of the members of each house and be filed with the secretary of state at least ninety days before it can be submitted to the voters. The governor cannot veto a joint resolution proposing a constitutional amendment. If approved by a majority of the voters who voted on the particular amendment, the amendment immediately becomes part of the constitution unless the amendment presented to the voters has a later date. *City of Euclid v. Heaton* (1968).

The most important amendment to this section was adopted in 1912, when the voters approved an amendment proposed by the 1912 Convention to change the method of counting votes on proposed amendments. Under this amendment, the majority vote required to approve an amendment proposed by the General Assembly was changed from a majority of those who voted in the election to a majority of the votes on the proposed amendment (a change that was consistent with the requirement that laws and amendments proposed by initiative petition receive "an affirmative majority of the votes cast thereon"). See Article II, section 1g.

Prior to this change, nineteen of the twenty-six General Assembly-proposed amendments that the voters "rejected" from 1851 to 1912 received more positive than negative votes. Still, these amendments failed because of the supermajority requirement, which required the amendments to receive a majority of the votes of those voting in the election. In fact, some amendments that failed had wide margins voting in their favor. For example, a proposed tax amendment in 1903 received 326,622 votes in its favor and only 43,563 against it, but it did not receive a majority of the 877,203 votes cast in the election. See Appendix B; see also Steven H. Steinglass, "Constitutional Revision: Ohio Style," 77 *Ohio St. L. J.* 281 (2016): 309–10.

This change in the method of counting votes significantly increased the percentage of amendments adopted by the voters. From 1851 to 1912, the voters approved 11 of 37, or only 29.7 percent, of the amendments submitted to them by the General Assembly, but from 1913 to 2018, the voters approved 94 of 141, or 66.7 percent, of the amendments proposed by the General Assembly. Ibid.

■ BALLOT BOARD

The 1974 amendment to this section created the Ohio Ballot Board and gave the board responsibility for drafting the ballot language for proposed amendments.

The constitution does not require the ballot to contain the actual text of proposed amendments, but the ballot must include a nonargumentative explanation of the substance of the amendment. And under this section "[t]he ballot language shall not be held invalid [by the Ohio Supreme Court] unless it is such as to mislead, deceive, or defraud the voters."

In interpreting this standard, the Ohio Supreme Court in *State ex rel. Bailey v. Celebrezze* (1981) stated that "the text of a ballot statement . . . must fairly and accurately present the question or issue to be decided in order to assure a free, intelligent and informed vote by the average citizen affected" (internal quotations omitted). The court then issued a writ ordering the Ballot Board to redraft the ballot language for a proposed workers' compensation amendment because it found that the ballot explanation was slanted against the amendment. The proposed language had provided that "[t]his proposed amendment would change the existing non-profit Ohio Workers' compensation system by requiring the General Assembly to pass laws permitting insurance companies to sell Workers' Compensation coverage in Ohio at rates determined by those insurance companies under the regulation of the Ohio Department of Insurance."

In addition to drafting an explanation of the proposed amendment, the Ballot Board, if permitted by the General Assembly, is responsible for drafting arguments for and against the amendment. The ballot language, explanation, and arguments must be published in a newspaper of general circulation in every county once a week for three weeks before the election.

A 1978 amendment to Article II, section 1g, applied the requirements of this section relating to ballot language to amendments proposed by initiative petition. See Commentary, Article II, section 1g; Commentary, Article II, section 1g.

■ OHIO SUPREME COURT JURISDICTION

The 1974 amendment to this section also provided the Ohio Supreme Court with original and exclusive jurisdiction in all cases challenging the adoption or submission of proposed constitutional amendments as long as the challenge is made at least sixty-four days before the election. Previously such cases could be brought under the original jurisdiction of the court through extraordinary writs, but the cases could originate in the lower courts as well. The 1974 amendment had the effect of divesting the lower state courts of original jurisdiction to hear these cases.

This grant of original and exclusive jurisdiction under this section, by its terms, applies to proposed constitutional amendments but not to proposed initiated statutes.

Though appearing in a section that primarily addresses amendments proposed by the General Assembly, the grant of original and exclusive jurisdiction under this section is not limited by its terms to amendments proposed by joint resolutions, and it was arguably applicable to amendments proposed by initiative petition. But the 2008 amendments to Article II, section 1g obviated the need to reach this issue by expressly providing for original and exclusive jurisdiction in cases involving not only proposed initiated amendments but also proposed initiated statutes and referenda. See Commentary, Article II, section 1g.

■ PRE-ELECTION SUBSTANTIVE JUDICIAL REVIEW

The Ohio Supreme Court has historically rejected the availability of pre-election substantive judicial review to challenge proposed amendments on the ground that, if adopted, the amendments would be unconstitutional. This position was first developed by the court in cases involving challenges to amendments proposed by initiative petition, see Commentary, Article II, section 1g, but there is no reason to believe that the court would not similarly bar pre-election substantive judicial review in cases involving amendments proposed by the General Assembly.

■ ONE AMENDMENT, SEPARATE VOTE REQUIREMENT

The 1851 Constitution included a one amendment, separate vote requirement under which constitutional amendments proposed by the General Assembly (as contrasted to those proposed by constitutional conventions) had to be submitted to the voters in such a way "as to enable the electors to vote on each amendment separately." The delegates at the 1912 Convention made a minor punctuation change in this section but, more importantly, they did not include the one amendment, separate vote requirement in the language creating the constitutional initiative. See Article II, section 1g, and Commentary.

Despite its rejection of pre-election *substantive* judicial review, the Ohio Supreme Court has acted as a gatekeeper and provided pre-election judicial review in cases alleging noncompliance with the one amendment, separate vote requirement. For example, in 1972 the court struck from the ballot the initial proposal of the Ohio Constitutional Revision Commission for violating the one amendment, separate vote requirement. *State ex rel. Roahrig v. Brown* (1972). The case involved amendments proposed by the General Assembly to three sections of the constitution to provide for the joint election of the governor and lieutenant governor, to repeal a provision barring persons convicted of embezzlement of public funds from holding public office, and to repeal the authorization for supreme court commissions. In removing the proposed amendment from the ballot, the court stated that: "a proposal consists of one amendment to the Constitution only so long as each of its subjects bears some reasonable relationship to a single *general* object or purpose." Ibid.

In *State ex rel. Liberty Council v. Brunner* (2010), in the course of rejecting a decision of the Ballot Board to divide an initiated amendment on healthcare into two separate amendments, the court identified the purpose of the one amendment, separate vote requirement:

> The constitutional mandate that multifarious amendments shall be submitted separately has two great objectives. The first is to prevent imposition upon or deceit of the public by the presentation of a proposal which is misleading or the effect of which is concealed or not readily understandable. The second is to afford the voters freedom of choice and prevent "logrolling" or the combining of unrelated proposals in order to secure approval by appealing to different groups which will support the entire proposal in order to secure some part of it although perhaps disapproving of other parts.

In ruling that the one amendment, separate vote requirement (whether of statutory or constitutional origin), see Commentary, Article II, section 1g, applied to amendments proposed both by the General Assembly and by initiative petition, the court in *Ohio Liberty Council* defined the requirement as follows:

> [T]he applicable test for determining compliance with the separate-vote requirement of Section 1, Article XVI, is that "a proposal consists of one amendment to the Constitution only so long as each of its subjects bears some reasonable relationship to a single general object or purpose. . . . Thus, where an amendment to the Constitution relates to a single purpose or object and all else contained therein is incidental and reasonably necessary to effectuate the purpose of the amendment, such amendment is not violative of the provisions of Section 1, Article XVI." Courts have generally taken a "liberal [view] in interpreting what such a single general purpose or object may be."

(alterations in original; emphasis omitted).

Under this test, proposed amendments need not relate to a *single subject* but need only relate to a "single general object or purpose." Thus, the standard is more forgiving than the "one-subject" requirement, which limits the ability of the General Assembly to put unrelated subjects in a single statute. See Commentary, Article II, section 15(D).

This section, however, does not bar the General Assembly from proposing multiple constitutional amendments in a single joint resolution as long as the amendments appear separately on the ballot. See *State ex rel. Slemmer v. Brown* (1973) ("Section 1, Article XVI, Ohio Constitution, requiring that electors be enabled to vote separately on each of several proposed amendments to such Constitution, places no limitation upon the General Assembly with respect to proposing more than one amendment in a single joint resolution.") (syllabus).

■ EFFECTIVE DATE OF AMENDMENTS

Under this section, constitutional amendments proposed by the General Assembly take effect when approved by the voters, see *City of Euclid v. Heaton*

(1968), but amendments approved through the initiative process do not take effect until thirty days after the election at which the voters approved them, see Article II, section 1b.

An amendment proposed by the General Assembly may go into effect at a later date, but only if the language postponing the effective date is also submitted to the voters and approved by them. *State ex rel. McNamara v. Campbell* (1916).

Section 2
Convention.

Whenever two-thirds of the members elected to each branch of the General Assembly shall think it necessary to call a convention to revise, amend, or change this constitution, they shall recommend to the electors to vote on a separate ballot without party designation of any kind at the next election for members to the General Assembly, for or against a convention; and if a majority of all the electors, voting for and against the calling of a convention, shall have voted for a convention, the General Assembly shall, at their next session, provide, by law, for calling the same. Candidates for members of the constitutional convention shall be nominated by nominating petitions only and shall be voted for upon one independent and separate ballot without any emblem or party designation whatever. The convention shall consist of as many members as the House of Representatives, who shall be chosen as provided by law, and shall meet within three months after their election, for the purpose, aforesaid.

Adopted in 1851 and amended in 1912, section 2 permits the General Assembly to place the question of whether to hold a constitutional convention on the ballot. A proposal to hold a convention must be approved by a two-thirds vote of each house. If the voters approve the proposal, the General Assembly at its next session must provide for the calling of a convention. Candidates for delegate may only be nominated by petition and cannot have any party designation next to their names on the election ballot. Once elected, the delegates must meet within three months to begin the convention.

The original version of this section, which was adopted as part of the 1851 Constitution, differed from its predecessor in three ways. First, the 1802 Constitution expressly prohibited any amendment to the constitution that would introduce slavery or involuntary servitude. The 1851 Constitution dropped this provision, although retaining a prohibition against slavery in the Bill of Rights. See Commentary, Article I, section 6. Second, the 1802 Constitution did not address whether the two-thirds vote in the General Assembly to put a convention call on the ballot was a two-thirds vote of each house or a joint ballot. The 1851 Constitution removed this ambiguity and expressly provided that the two-thirds vote was required in each house. Third, under the 1802 Constitution, the holding of a convention required an affirmative vote of all those voting for representatives to the General Assembly. The 1851 Constitution, on the other hand, required an affirmative vote of a majority of electors voting in the election. The 1912 amendment repealed this supermajority requirement to permit conventions to be called by a majority of electors voting on the specific question of whether to hold a constitutional convention rather than a majority of electors voting at the election.

The General Assembly twice submitted proposals for constitutional conventions under the 1802 Constitution. In 1819, the voters rejected the call for a convention by a vote of 6,897 to 29,315. In 1849, with the support of the Democratic Party and a Whig governor, the electorate approved calling a constitutional convention, Ohio's second, by a vote of almost 3:1 See The Constitutional History of Ohio, *supra****25–28.

Ohio's third constitutional convention, the 1873–74 Constitutional Convention, was not called pursuant to the authority of this section but rather pursuant to a vote taken under the authority of Article XVI, section 3, which requires a mandatory twenty-year referendum on whether to hold a constitutional convention.

The General Assembly has twice proposed constitutional conventions under the 1851 version of this section. Proposed by joint resolution in 1896, the first proposal primarily addressed continued concern about the tax system. This proposal was not submitted to the voters because the joint resolution contained not only the proposal for a constitutional convention but also a change in the election laws to authorize straight party ticket voting under which political parties could endorse convention calls. The Ohio Supreme Court held that the General Assembly could not change the election laws by joint resolution since the change, which amounted to a repeal of a prior act of legislation, had to satisfy all the requirements for a bill to become law. *State ex rel. Attorney General Kinney* (1897). Since the change to the election laws was "intimately connected with the recommendation for calling a convention," the court invalidated the entire joint resolution.

The second proposal under this section, submitted in 1910, was approved by the voters by more than a 10:1 margin under a state law that permitted straight party ticket votes to be counted as supportive of political party endorsements of the convention call. And this resulted in the 1912 Constitutional Convention, the last convention held in Ohio. See The History of the Ohio Constitution, *supra*.

■ HOW WOULD A CONVENTION WORK?

The limited guidance concerning a constitutional convention provided under this section includes the requirement that delegates be elected at general elections on nonpartisan ballots and a requirement for the exclusive use of nominating petitions. Additional details, including the financing of conventions.

This section does not identify the districts from which delegates are elected, but in 1911 the General Assembly used the districts used for members of the House of Representatives. Given that the number of delegates must be the same as the number of members of the House of Representatives, there seems to be an assumption that the General Assembly will use House districts for the election of convention delegates.

The constitution is silent as to when a proposed new constitution (or convention-proposed amendments) will go on the ballot. The 1912 Convention, however, strategically presented its proposed amendments to the voters at a special election held on September 3, 1912, the day after Labor Day. See *Proceedings and Debates of the Constitutional Convention of the State of Ohio: Convened January 9, 1912* (Columbus: F. J. Heer Printing Co., 1912), 308.

Some states have used limited constitutional conventions, but there is no Ohio authority directly on point. Nonetheless, it is likely that the General Assembly is permitted to propose a limited convention.

A constitutional convention is not limited to only proposing a new constitution. In 1851 and 1874 the conventions proposed new constitutions as well as separate amendments. And in 1912, the convention did not propose a new constitution but rather proposed forty-two different amendments.

There is no authority for Ohio voters to initiate a constitutional convention. The delegates at the 1912 Convention discussed the possibility of giving the voters this power, but they rejected this proposal by a vote of 68–29.

Section 3

Question of constitutional convention to be submitted periodically.

At the general election to be held in the year one thousand nine hundred and thirty-two, and in each twentieth year thereafter, the question: "Shall there be a convention to revise, alter, or amend the constitution[,]" shall be submitted to the electors of the state; and in case a majority of the electors, voting for and against the calling of a convention, shall decide in favor of a convention, the General Assembly, at its next session, shall provide, by law, for the election of delegates, and the assembling of such convention, as is provided in the preceding section; but no amendment of this constitution, agreed upon by any convention assembled in pursuance of this article, shall take effect, until the same shall have been submitted to the electors of the state, and adopted by a majority of those voting thereon.

Adopted in 1851 and amended in 1912, this section provides that every twenty years the voters will be asked whether to hold a constitutional convention. In 1910 the General Assembly submitted the question to the voters one year before the question would have had been submitted to the voters.

In 1912, the voters approved an amendment to this section to change the required vote on the constitutional call from a majority of votes cast in the election to a majority of votes on the specific question of whether to hold a convention. The first vote under the amended section took place in 1932.

The constitution specifies the precise question that must be presented to the voters at the mandatory convention call, and there is a strong argument that the General Assembly may not modify the precise question presented to the voters, for example, by making it a call for a limited convention. Nonetheless, this required constitutional call does not prevent the General Assembly from proposing conventions at other times and from limiting the questions before such conventions.

The only time the voters approved a convention call under this section was in 1871. In 1891, the voters rejected a proposal to hold a constitutional convention, and since 1912, they rejected proposed conventions in 1932, 1952, 1972, 1992, and 2012, with the rejections coming in overwhelming votes since 1952. See Appendix A.

Article XVII

Elections

Article XVII governs the time for holding elections and contains general provisions covering terms of office and the filling of vacancies in offices. Provisions concerning terms of office and vacancies for specific offices are in Articles II, III, IV, and V. Provisions concerning the elective franchise, election requirements, and term limits are also in Article V.

Adopted in 1905, the voters proposed a reorganization of this article in 1976 based on a recommendation of the Ohio Constitutional Revision Commission (OCRC).

Section 1

Time for holding.

Elections for state and county officers shall be held on the first Tuesday after the first Monday in November in even numbered years; and all elections for all other elective officers shall be held on the first Tuesday after the first Monday in November in the odd numbered years.

The term of office of all elective county, township, municipal, and school officers shall be such even number of years not exceeding four as may be prescribed by law or such even number of years as may be provided in municipal or county charters.

The Ohio State Constitution. Steven H. Steinglass and Gino J. Scarselli, Oxford University Press. © Oxford University Press 2022. DOI: 10.1093/oso/9780197619728.003.0019

The term of office of all judges shall be as provided in Article IV of this constitution or, if not so provided, an even number of years not exceeding six as provided by law.

The General Assembly may extend existing terms of office as to effect the purpose of this section.

Adopted in 1905 and amended in 1954 and 1976, this section sets the times for election of public officials. Elections for state and county offices take place on the first Tuesday after the first Monday in November in even-numbered years. All other elections for government officials are held on the first Tuesday after the first Monday in November in odd-numbered years.

This section also provides that the election of county, township, and school officials shall be in even-numbered years and that terms for those officials shall not exceed four years unless specified otherwise in a municipal or county charter. Under this section, judges' terms are to be specified under Article IV but cannot exceed six years. Section 1 applies only to regularly occurring elections and has no effect on special elections to fill vacancies in municipal offices.

The 1954 amendment to this section was part of a proposal that extended the terms of the governor, lieutenant governor, secretary of state, treasurer of state, and attorney general to four years. These changes were contained in amended Article III, section 2; the provisions in this section addressed some of the transitional issues in moving to the longer terms. See Commentary, Article III, section 2.

The 1976 amendment to this section, recommended by the OCRC and proposed to the voters by the General Assembly, did not make any substantive changes. The purpose of the proposal was to improve the constitutional drafting and to attempt to have all relevant information in the same section. Part of this involved deleting provisions that already were in other parts of the constitution but retaining provisions that did not appear elsewhere, such as the terms of office of elective county, township, municipal, and school officers. To accomplish this, the proposal moved two sentences from section 2 to this section. See OCRC, *Recommendations for Amendments to the Ohio Constitution: Final Report*, 1977, 269–70.

The 1976 amendment to this section also expressly gave the General Assembly the power to extend the terms of existing offices should the terms be changed, a power that the General Assembly had exercised without express constitutional authority. Ibid.

Section 2
Terms of officers, vacancies.

Any vacancy which may occur in any elective state office created by Article II or III or created by or pursuant to Article IV of this constitution shall be filled only if and as provided in such articles. Any vacancy which may occur in any elective state office not so created, shall be filled by appointment by the governor until the disability is removed, or a successor elected and qualified. Such successor shall be elected for the unexpired term of the vacant office at the first general election in an even numbered year that occurs more than forty days after the vacancy has occurred; provided, that when the unexpired term ends within one year immediately following the date of such general election, an election to fill such unexpired term shall not be held and the appointment shall be for such unexpired term. All vacancies in other elective offices shall be filled for the unexpired term in such manner as may be prescribed by this constitution or by law.

Adopted in 1905 and amended in 1947, 1954, 1970, and 1976, this section provides that vacancies that occur in offices governed by Articles II, III, or IV shall be filled as provided by those articles. See also Article II, section 27.

Initially, the section contained a detailed list of offices and provisions for filling vacancies in them. The current version provides that vacancies in state elective offices not covered in Articles II, III, or IV are filled by the governor. In such cases, the governor appoints a successor who serves until the first general election in an even-numbered year that occurs more than forty days after the vacancy has occurred unless the unexpired term ends within a year of the next general election. In that case, the appointed successor serves for the rest of the term.

In 1947, 1954, and 1970, the General Assembly proposed and the voters approved technical amendments involving terms of offices and the filling of vacancies. See OCRC, *Recommendations for Amendments to the Ohio Constitution: Final Report* (1977), 272.

The 1976 amendment was the result of a proposal by the OCRC to eliminate duplication and inconsistent language without making any substantive changes. Ibid.

Section 2 also provides that vacancies in local elective officers are filled as prescribed by either the constitution or the law. *State ex rel. Toledo v. Lucas County Board of Elections* (2002). For example, a municipal charter may prescribe the manner of filling vacancies in elective municipal offices. *Jones v. City of Cleveland* (1932).

Section 3
Repealed—Present incumbents

Adopted in 1905 and repealed in 1953, this section provided that elected officials holding office when terms of office were changed would continue to serve for the remainder of their terms. In 1953, the General Assembly proposed that this section and two others be repeated as obsolete, and the voters agreed.

Article XVIII

Municipal Corporations

In 1912, the voters approved Article XVIII, known as the "Home Rule Amendment," which has only been amended twice. Home rule was one of the highest priorities of the Progressives, who wanted to give municipalities the power to govern themselves. In describing this proposal, Herbert S. Bigelow, the president of the 1912 Constitutional Convention, stated that "[i]t is second only to the initiative and referendum in importance. Its adoption will bring a great, peaceful, and beneficent revolution. It will set the cities of Ohio free." Herbert S. Bigelow, *New Constitution for Ohio* (June 5, 1912) (U.S. House of Representatives) (69th Cong. 2d Sess.) (Doc. No. 863): 10–11. See Commentary, Article II, section 1f.

In 1902, the Ohio Supreme Court in *State ex rel. Knisely v. Jones* had declared unconstitutional the system of classifying cities and legislating differently in order to adopt city-specific legislation, in this case the board of commissioners of the City of Toledo. The system of classification placed each of the state's twelve major cities in classifications and grades of their own, and the court concluded that state law violated the provision of the 1851 Constitution barring the General Assembly from passing any "special act conferring corporate powers." Article XIII, section 1. The General Assembly responded to the ensuing crisis in local governance by adopting the Municipal Code of 1902, but supporters of the cities believed that the code was inadequate, thus beginning a decade

The Ohio State Constitution. Steven H. Steinglass and Gino J. Scarselli, Oxford University Press. © Oxford University Press 2022. DOI: 10.1093/oso/9780197619728.003.0020

of political activity in support of a constitutional provision on home rule. See Harvey Walker, "Municipal Government in Ohio before 1912," 9 *Ohio St. L.J.* 1 (1948) (hereinafter Walker, "Municipal Government before 1912").

Before the adoption of this article, Ohio law treated municipalities as creatures of the state, and under the prevailing Dillon's Rule municipalities could exercise only those powers delegated to them by the General Assembly. See *Bloom v. City of Xenia* (1877). See also Walker, "Municipal Government in Ohio."

George W. Knight of Franklin County, a professor at Ohio State University, opened the 1912 debate with a lengthy statement in favor of the Home Rule Amendment followed by a section-by-section review of the proposal and then by a broader discussion of it. See *Proceedings and Debates of the Constitutional Convention of the State of Ohio: Convened January 9, 1912* (Columbus: F. J. Heer Printing Co., 1912), 1433–42 (hereinafter *1912 Debates*).

Initially, Mr. Knight identified the three key purposes of the proposal. First, it provided for the organization of municipalities.

> [T]he first thing that the proposal undertakes to do is to provide that municipalities . . . shall have the right, if they so desire, to frame charters for themselves, to provide each for itself the type or form of organization for municipal business as it desires.
>
> Ibid., 1433.

Second, it reversed the presumption against the power of municipalities exercising power (the so-called Dillon's Rule). He stated:

> So the presumption would now become a presumption in favor of the lawfulness of the municipalities' act, and that presumption would only be overcome by showing that the power had been denied to the municipalities or that it was against the general laws of the state.
>
> Ibid.

Third, it expressly empowered municipalities to operate public utilities:

> [T]he proposal expressly undertakes to make clearer or make broader the power of municipalities to control, either by leasing, constructing, or acquiring from corporations now owning or operating the public utilities within the corporation and serving the corporation, the water supply the lighting and heating supply and the other things—without specifying—which come within the purview of municipal public utilities, thus removing once and far all, all legitimate questions as to the authority of municipalities to undertake and carry on essential municipal activities.
>
> Ibid.

Mr. Knight then concluded: "These three things are the fundamental things which are undertaken by the proposal, and these three things taken together certainly constitute what may be termed, and rightly termed, municipal home rule." Ibid.

Most of the debate on home rule concerned section 3, and the debate was characterized by repeated efforts by home rule opponents to adopt amendments designed to undercut home rule. See *1912 Debates,* 1483 (Mr. Crosser). The split on these issues reflected not only an urban-rural split but also divisions between home rule supporters from Cleveland and Cincinnati, according to Lloyd Luther Sponholtz, one of the foremost authorities on the 1912 Convention. See Lloyd Luther Sponholtz, *Progressivism in Microcosm: An Analysis of the Political Forces at Work in the Ohio Constitutional Convention of 1912* (Ph.D. dissertation, University of Pittsburgh, 1969), 156.

Section 1

Classification of cities and villages.

Municipal corporations are hereby classified into cities and villages. All such corporations having a population of five thousand or over shall be cities; all others shall be villages. The method of transition from one class to the other shall be regulated by law.

Adopted in 1912 and never amended, this section deals with the classification of municipal corporations. It divides municipalities into cities and villages according to population. Cities consist of 5,000 or more residents, and villages consist of less than 5,000 residents. This section, which retained the statutory classifications that were in place under the Ohio Municipal Code in 1912, allows cities and villages to continue to operate, if they desire, under the general statutory laws. Section 1 is not self-executing, and it required the General Assembly to pass laws providing for the transition of villages to cities. *Christensen v. Hagedorn* (1962). These laws are in O.R.C. sections 703.01–703.011.

Section 2

General and additional laws.

General laws shall be passed to provide for the incorporation and government of cities and villages; and additional laws may also be passed for the government of municipalities adopting the same; but no such additional law shall become operative in any municipality until it shall have been submitted to the electors thereof, and affirmed by a majority of those voting thereon, under regulations to be established by law.

Adopted in 1912 and never amended, this section requires the General Assembly to pass general laws for the incorporation of municipalities and the organization of municipal government. This section also allows the General Assembly to adopt "additional laws" that provide optional forms of government, but such optional forms of government must be approved by a majority of municipal voters voting on the submission. The original version of this section authorized the General Assembly to "enact *special* laws for the government of municipalities" but the use of the phrase "special laws" was changed to "additional laws" in the final draft. See Walker, "Municipal Government before 1912."

Section 7 of this article also allows municipalities to choose a form of government through the adoption of municipal charters.

Under current Ohio law, the General Assembly has established three optional plans for the organization of municipal governments: a "commission plan" under which the municipality is governed by a board of commissioners; a "city manager plan" under which the municipality is governed by an elected council headed by a city manager; and a "federal plan," which is similar to the general statutory plan of a mayor and city or village council established under the general laws. Thus, a municipal government can be organized in five different ways: under the general statutory plan, O.R.C. chapters 731 and 733; under one of the three optional plans, O.R.C. chapter 705; or under a municipal charter adopted in accordance with Article XVIII, section 7.

Section 3

Municipal powers of local self-government.

Municipalities shall have authority to exercise all powers of local self-government and to adopt and enforce within their limits such local police, sanitary and other similar regulations, as are not in conflict with general laws.

Adopted in 1912 and never amended, this section is the source of municipal home rule power, and it grants municipalities "all powers of local self-government" as well as the power "to adopt and enforce local police, sanitary and other similar regulations, as are not in conflict with general laws." Section 3 is self-executing, and therefore, the powers it confers on municipalities do not depend on the General Assembly to enact state legislation. *Village of Perrysburg v. Ridgway* (1923). Nor is this grant of power limited to municipalities that adopt city charters. See Commentary, Article XVIII, section 7.

By rejecting Dillon's Rule and giving municipalities plenary power over local self-government, this section made express delegations of power to municipalities unnecessary. But the delegates chose to include express authorizations in selected areas, thus avoiding years of litigation over the power of municipalities to act under this section. See, for example, Article XVIII, section 4 (ownership and operation of public utilities); Article XVIII, section 6 (sale of surplus utility services to noninhabitants).

This section defines the relationship between municipal and state power. The power to exercise "all powers of local self-government" is distinguishable from the power "to adopt and enforce local police, sanitary and other similar regulations." The latter phrase refers to a municipality's police power, that is, its power to protect the public's health, safety, and morals. *Cleveland Telephone Co. v. City of Cleveland* (1918). This distinction is important because the concluding phrase––"not in conflict with general laws"––only modifies the phrase "local police, sanitary and other similar regulations." *Fitzgerald v. City of Cleveland* (1913). Thus, a municipality may exercise all power over local affairs except to the extent that its exercise of police power conflicts with general state law. And it "appears to be well-settled" that this no-conflict limitation only applies to a municipality's police power. See John E. Gotherman, Harold W. Babbit, and James F. Lang, *Local Government Law—Municipal* (Baldwin's Ohio Practice) (Thomson Reuters, 2019), section 3.7 (hereinafter *Local Government Law*).

The question of whether an enactment by the General Assembly overrides a municipal law is one of the most frequently litigated issues under the Ohio Constitution, and there have been more than a hundred Ohio Supreme Court decisions addressing it. *City of Dayton v. State* (2017) (DeWine, J., dissenting). And it is an issue that is arising throughout the country as state legislatures seek to rein in cities that they believe are exhibiting too much independence. See generally Richard Briffault, "The Challenge of the New Preemption," 70 *Stan. L. Rev.* 1995 (2018).

■ THE CONFLICT APPROACH

The delegates to the 1912 Convention adopted a conflict approach to determine whether state law overrode a municipal ordinance. As proposed by the Committee on Municipal Government, the Home Rule Amendment (Proposal No. 272) would have made all exercise of municipal power "subject to general laws." See *1912 Debates,* 1313. But as finally approved, the proposal gave municipalities broad authority "to exercise all powers of local self-government" but limited municipal power to permit only "local police, sanitary and other similar regulations, as are not in conflict with general laws."

Recognized by the Ohio Supreme Court in 1913, see *Fitzgerald v. City of Cleveland, supra,* the conflict approach (and its general law corollary) continues to be the court's prevailing approach to resolving conflicts between state and local laws. And a conflict between a municipal ordinance and a general law exists when an "ordinance permits or licenses that which the statute forbids and prohibits, and vice versa." *Struthers v. Sokol* (1923).

In describing the operation of the conflict approach, the court in 2002 synthesized its earlier decisions and adopted a four-part cumulative test, which it summarized in *City of Canton v. State* (2002), for determining when a state statute is a general law that could trump a local law.

> To constitute a general law for purposes of home-rule analysis, a statute must (1) be part of a statewide and comprehensive legislative enactment, (2) apply to

> all parts of the state alike and operate uniformly throughout the state, (3) set forth police, sanitary, or similar regulations, rather than purport only to grant or limit legislative power of a municipal corporation to set forth police, sanitary, or similar regulations, and (4) prescribe a rule of conduct upon citizens generally.
>
> (syllabus).

In *Canton,* the court upheld a municipal ordinance in the face of a state statute that prohibited municipalities from excluding manufactured homes from certain areas. In so ruling, it concluded that the provisions of the relevant state statute were not general laws because they only restricted a municipality's police power and thus were not part of a comprehensive legislative enactment. See also *City of Youngstown v. Evans* (1929) (striking down a statute that limited municipal authority to set punishments for misdemeanor violations of municipal ordinances, because the statute was "not a general law in the sense of prescribing a rule of conduct upon citizens generally. It is a limitation upon law making by municipal legislative bodies."); but see *City of Cleveland v. State* (2019) (DeWine, J., concurring in judgment) (rejecting the *Canton* general law analysis and concluding that a state statute that barred cities and other public authorities from requiring contractors to employ a requisite percentage of residents on public contracts was a general law even though it functioned as a limitation upon law-making by municipal legislative bodies and did not prescribe a rule of conduct upon citizens).

Since *Canton,* there has been a torrent of Ohio Supreme Court decisions applying the conflict approach both to expand and to limit the home rule power of municipalities. Cities have been permitted to impose civil penalties for violations captured by traffic cameras as long as their ordinances do not alter statewide traffic regulations. *City of Dayton v. State* (2017); *Mendenhall v. City of Akron* (2008); to adopt ordinances to license, register, and regulate entities that tow motor vehicles, *City of Cleveland v. Ohio* (2014); and to limit the capacity of semiautomatic weapons to ten rounds despite a state statute that prohibited possession of semiautomatic firearms capable of firing more than thirty-one cartridges without reloading, *City of Cincinnati v. Baskin* (2006).

In most cases, however, the Ohio Supreme Court has ruled against the home rule claims of cities. For example, a city ordinance prohibiting firearms in municipal parks was found to conflict with a statewide comprehensive legislative enactment and thus was not enforceable, *Ohioans for Concealed Carry, Inc. v. City of Clyde* (2008), and a state law displacing municipal firearm ordinances was part of a comprehensive statewide legislative enactment applicable uniformly across the state, and thus did not unconstitutionally infringe municipal authority, *City of Cleveland v. State* (2010). Cities have also been prevented from regulating predatory lending, *American Financial Services Association v. City of Cleveland* (2006), from regulating the drilling of oil and gas wells, *State ex rel. Morrison v. Beck Energy Corp.* (2015), and from providing a bonus to private contractors that employed a designated percentage of city residents on public projects, *City of Cleveland v. State* (2019) (plurality).

And in *Walker v. City of Toledo* (2014), the court held "that Ohio municipalities have home-rule authority to establish administrative proceedings, including administrative hearings, related to civil enforcement of traffic ordinances, and that these administrative proceedings must be exhausted before offenders or the municipality can pursue judicial remedies." But, in *State ex rel. Magsig v. City of Toledo* (2020), the court (without reaching the constitutional/home rule issue) held that an amended state statute gave municipal courts exclusive jurisdiction over noncriminal traffic-law adjudications, thus barring cities from conducting quasi-judicial proceedings for adjudicating liability for violations of municipal traffic ordinances.

The *Canton* approach and the centrality of the general law inquiry has not been without controversy, as illustrated in a recent decision in which the court struck down a statute that sought to regulate when municipalities could use traffic cameras to monitor compliance with speed limits and traffic signals. In *City of Dayton v. State* (2017), a plurality of the court concluded that under the third prong of the *Canton* test, a statute that expressly limited the legislative power of a municipal corporation to set forth police, sanitary, or similar regulations "without serving an overriding statewide interest" violated the Home Rule Amendment. Meanwhile, a concurring opinion rejected this conclusion, but opined that "under the fourth prong of the *Canton* test, a statute must 'prescribe a rule of conduct upon citizens generally' to qualify as a general law." Thus, a statute that barred or limited the municipal use of traffic cameras did not regulate citizens or (more particularly) drivers but rather improperly limited the power of municipalities. *City of Dayton v. State* (2017) (French, J., concurring in judgment only). Finally, one member of the *Dayton* court concluded that "the *Canton* test has proved unworkable" and has urged the court to "return to the language of the Home Rule Amendment."); Ibid. (DeWine, J., dissenting). See also Matthew Mahoney, "Home Rule in Ohio: General Laws, Conflicts, and the Failure of the Courts to Protect the Ohio Constitution," 67 *Clev. St. L. Rev.* 117 (2019) (suggesting that the *Canton* approach be modified to provide greater protection for home rule through a balancing approach).

■ STATEWIDE CONCERN DOCTRINE

The Ohio Supreme Court has limited a municipality's power under the "statewide concern" doctrine. Under this doctrine, a municipality cannot "infringe on matters of general and statewide concern." *State ex rel. Evans v. Moore* (1982). A local regulation that has "significant extraterritorial effects" or concerns a matter that "affects the general public of the state as a whole more than it does the local inhabitants" is a matter of statewide concern and is superseded by state law. Ibid.

The court, however, has recognized that "the doctrine is relevant only in deciding, as a preliminary matter, whether a particular issue is not a matter of merely local concern, but is of statewide concern, and therefore not included within the power of local self-government." *American Financial Services Association v. City of Cleveland* (2006) (internal quotations omitted).

The court has relied upon the statewide concern doctrine in striking down municipal ordinances in cases involving the regulation of watercraft, *State ex rel. McElroy v. Akron* (1962); hazardous waste disposal, *Clermont Environmental Reclamation Co. v. Wiederhold* (1982); public employee collective bargaining, *Kettering v. State Employment Relations Board* (1986); and prevailing wage for workers on public improvement projects, *State ex rel. Evans v. Moore* (1982).

On the other hand, "[t]he manner of regulating the civil service of a city is peculiarly a matter of municipal concern . . . [and] [o]ne of the powers of local self-government . . . " *State ex rel. Lentz v. Edwards* (1914). And the court has held that the makeup and jurisdiction of local civil service commissions are not matters of statewide concern, and thus state civil service laws do not preempt otherwise applicable local ordinances. *State Personnel Board of Review v. Bay Village Civil Service Commission* (1986); *Ohio Association of Public School Employees v. Twinsburg* (1988). But see Commentary, Article II, section 34.

A leading commentator has argued that the statewide concern doctrine has undermined the home rule of municipalities and that "there is no place in Ohio's constitutional arrangement of state-local relations for a matter to be of statewide concern unless it is exclusively within state authority." See George D. Vaubel, "Toward Principles of State Restraint upon the Exercise of Municipal Power in Home Rule," 20 *Stetson L. Rev.* 845 (1991). But the court appears committed to the statewide concern doctrine, which it has viewed as evolving. See *State ex rel. McElroy v. Akron* (1962) ("Due to our changing society, many things which were once considered a matter of purely local concern and subject strictly to local regulation, if any, have now become a matter of statewide concern, creating the necessity for statewide control.").

■ CONFLICT AND IMPLIED PREEMPTION

Although the conflict approach with its general law corollary is the established approach to this section, the suggestion has been made that a greater role be accorded to the doctrine of preemption. In an opinion concurring in the judgment in a case rejecting a municipality's attempt to regulate predatory lending, a member of the court urged the court to look to the "well-settled" federal law of preemption and interpret this section "to permit the General Assembly to preempt by an explicit statement of preemption certain areas of law not exclusively reserved to the municipalities." *American Financial Services Association v. City of Cleveland* (2006) (O'Connor, J., concurring in judgment only). Under this proposal, preemption would only apply if the statewide concern threshold is met and if "the General Assembly passes express preemption language accompanying statewide regulation . . . ." Ibid.

Federal preemption law, however, is one of the most confusing areas of federal law, and it is far from "well-settled." See generally Erwin Chemerinsky, *Constitutional Law: Principles and Policies* (New York: Wolters Kluwer, 6th ed., 2019), section 5.2, 430–61. And the subsequent more careful review of the changes in the language of section 3 during the 1912 debates by the proponent of an increased use of preemption (despite a favorable comment about implied preemption) concluded "that the delegates rejected the concept of conflict purely by implication."

> The change in the section's language during the Constitutional Convention shows that the delegates rejected the concept of conflict purely by implication. The delegates believed that as long as the state legislature did not indicate intent to occupy the field or to prevent a stricter standard, a municipality could freely pass any ordinance stricter than state legislation, as long as the ordinance could coexist with state legislation.
>
> *City of Cincinnati v. Baskin* (O'Connor, J.) (concurring in judgment only).

Finally, the rejection of implied preemption (or as it is sometimes described, conflict by implication) in the area of home rule is consistent with the court's rejection of implied preemption in other areas. See Commentary, Article XVIII, section 13 (rejecting implied preemption in the tax area).

1912 DEBATES AND PREEMPTION

A review of the 1912 debates also supports the conclusion that the delegates did more than simply reject the doctrine of implied preemption. Instead, they adopted a conflict approach, which is reflected in the text and history of section 3 and which is consistent with their overarching goal of increasing the power of municipalities vis-a-vis the state.

George W. Knight of Franklin County, who presented the arguments in favor of the Home Rule Amendment, also made clear that an important purpose of section 3 had been to assure that the General Assembly did not pass special laws "under the guise of general laws," *1912 Debates,* 1442 ("The committee was of opinion that a general law was one that in fact and in form touched the subject that affected the state universally.").

In its proposal to the convention, the Committee on Municipal Government sought to empower municipalities, but the committee also recognized that state interests would sometimes overrule local ones. They sought to thread this needle by including an "affecting the welfare" clause to limit the power of the General Assembly to adopt laws that trumped municipal exercises of the police power. But the proposal also expressly permitted the General Assembly to wall off areas in which municipalities could not act by giving the General Assembly a grant of preemptive power under which it could "by general law, affecting the state as a whole, . . . specifically deny all municipalities the right to act thereon." Ibid. See also *1912 Debates,* 1463. Thus the proposal granted broad power to municipalities while also establishing a limitation on its exercise.

The committee's original proposal had begun as follows: "Municipalities shall have the power to enact and enforce within their limits such local police, sanitary, and other similar regulations, *as are not in conflict with general laws,* affecting the welfare of the state as a whole." *1912 Debates,* 1313 (emphasis added). It then expressly permitted the General Assembly to wall off areas in which municipalities could not act by giving the General Assembly a grant of preemptive power under which it could "by general law, affecting the state as a whole, . . . specifically deny all municipalities the right to act thereon." Ibid. See also *1912 Debates,* 1463.

The full text of the committee's *original* proposed section 3 provided as follows:

> Municipalities shall have the power to enact and enforce within their limits such local police, sanitary, and other similar regulations, as are not in conflict with general laws, affecting the welfare of the state as a whole. No such regulations shall by reason of requirements therein, in addition to those fixed by law, be deemed in conflict therewith unless the general assembly, by general law, affecting the welfare of the state as a whole, shall specifically deny all municipalities the right to act thereon.
>
> *1912 Debates,* 1313.

Despite their desire to provide a constitutional grant of home rule to municipalities, the home rule proponents recognized that their proposal––although reversing Dillon's Rule––would still give the state the power to trump local exercises of the police power. The issue was when and how could this happen. And of particular concern was not letting the issue of home rule get mixed up with the liquor question (which was also under consideration). See *1912 Debates,* 1468–69 (Mr. Redington).

Edward W. Doty of Cuyahoga County, an ally of Bigelow and the clerk of the state Senate, argued that the "welfare of the state as a whole" clause was unnecessary, and the delegates ultimately approved the Doty Amendment, which dropped not only the two "welfare of the state as a whole" clauses but also the preemptive "specifically deny" language from what became the final version of section 3. See *1912 Debates,* 1472–74.

In the robust but often confusing debate on the "welfare of the state as a whole" clause, the delegates said little directly about preemption. But one delegate, Humphrey Jones of Fayette County, a strong supporter of the townships, recognized the significance of the "specifically deny" clause and argued that its adoption would invite a new flood of special legislation, as "those who are opposed to . . . [a municipality acting under home rule] will be driven to the legislature to get legislation to prevent or nullify the action of the municipality." *1912 Debates,* 1472.

Ultimately, the delegates rejected the preemption language when they adopted the Doty Amendment and gave final approval to the Home Rule Amendment by a vote of 104 to 6. See *1912 Debates*, 1496.

The rejection of the "specifically deny" clause suggests that the delegates did not want the General Assembly to strike down local ordinances simply because it wanted to do so. Instead, the delegates adopted a more nuanced approach in which the conflict must arise because general (as opposed to special) state law addressed the issue. And this history provides support for the *Canton* approach to general law under which general law only prevails in a conflict with a municipal regulation when the general law is "part of a statewide and comprehensive legislative enactment."

■ OTHER LIMITATIONS ON MUNICIPALITIES

A municipality's "powers of local self-government" and its police power may be limited by the General Assembly under constitutional provisions independent of Article XVIII. For example, under Article IV, section 1, the General Assembly has the power to create courts, *State ex rel. Cherrington, Pros. Atty., v. Hutsinpiller* (1925), and this includes the power to define their jurisdiction, to provide for their maintenance, and to require suitable quarters for them, *State ex rel. Ramey v. Davis* (1929).

The General Assembly is also authorized by Article XIII, section 6 (as well as by sec. 13 of this article) to pass laws that limit a municipality's power to levy taxes and incur debt and to require reports from municipalities as to their financial condition and transactions. A municipality, however, may not rely on section 3 to impose fees on building permits to provide the city with additional revenue because such fees constitute an unconstitutional tax under Article XII, section 2. *Drees Co. v. Hamilton Township* (2012); see *also* Commentary, Article XII, section 2. In addition, Article II, section 1f, limits the municipality's powers of initiative and referendum. *Buckeye Community Hope Foundation v. City of Cuyahoga Falls* (1998).

■ EMPLOYEE RIGHTS

In the area of employee rights, the broad power of the state over employee-welfare legislation in Article II, section 34, has resulted in the use of the supremacy clause of that section to approve statutes that deny municipalities the right to exercise their powers of "local self-government" to determine the compensation of their employees. *City of Rocky River v. State Employment Relations Board* (1989); *City of Cincinnati v. Ohio Council 8* (1991), the right to require municipal employees to reside in the municipality, *City of Lima v. Ohio* (2009), and the right to require public contractors to employ a certain percentage of city residents for municipally funded construction projects, *City of Cleveland v. State*

(2019) (plurality). And in 2016, the General Assembly relied on this provision of Article II to adopt a statute that bars municipalities from establishing minimum wage levels within their jurisdictions. But the reach of Article II, section 34, has effectively been limited by the court's split decision in *City of Cleveland v. State* (2019) (plurality). See Commentary, Article II, section 34.

■ NEW CAUSES OF ACTION

State criminal law represents an area of statewide concern, and the Ohio Supreme Court has stated that "[t]he power to define and classify and prescribe punishment for felonies committed within the state is lodged in the General Assembly" (*State ex rel. Sensible Norwood v. Hamilton County Bd. of Elections* (2016)). In *City of Youngstown v. Evans* (1929), however, the court struck down a statute that had limited the authority of municipalities to set punishments for violations of a municipal misdemeanor ordinance. In so ruling the court stated that the statute was "not a general law in the sense of prescribing a rule of conduct upon citizens generally. It is a limitation upon law making by municipal legislative bodies." Ibid. And state law now expressly permits a municipality to "make the violation of any of its ordinances a misdemeanor, and provide for the punishment thereof by fine or imprisonment, or both." *Sensible Norwood* (quoting O.R.C. sec. 715.67).

The Ohio Supreme Court has not determined if municipalities have the authority to create new civil causes of action to enforce existing obligations. But given the ability of municipalities to supplement the enforcement of municipal ordinances by making violations of their ordinances misdemeanors, there is a strong argument that municipalities may also use their home rule power to create new causes of action to enforce existing municipal obligations.

In *Drewes Farms Partnership v. City of Toledo* (2020), a federal district court struck down Toledo's voter-approved charter amendment, which adopted the Lake Erie Bill of Rights, on the ground that it was unconstitutionally vague under the Due Process Clause of the Fourteenth Amendment and beyond the power of municipalities under Article XVIII, section 3, of the Ohio Constitution.

Section 4

Acquisition of public utility; contract for service; condemnation.

Any municipality may acquire, construct, own, lease and operate within or without its corporate limits, any public utility the product or service of which is or is to be supplied to the municipality or its inhabitants, and may contract with others for any such product or service. The acquisition of any such public utility may be by condemnation or otherwise, and a municipality may acquire thereby the use of, or full title to, the property and franchise of any company or person supplying to the municipality or its inhabitants the service or product of any such utility.

Adopted in 1912 and never amended, this section grants municipalities broad power to own and operate public utilities. Under this section, a municipality may acquire, own, lease, or construct a public utility. The Ohio Supreme Court has defined a "public utility" as one in which "the devotion to public use must be of such character that the product and service is available to the public generally and indiscriminately or there must be the acceptance by the utility of public franchises or calling to its aid the police power of the state." *Southern Ohio Power Co. v. Public Utilities Commission* (1924).

Prior to the 1912 Convention, municipalities often owned and operated public utilities but only with the approval of the General Assembly. The abolition of Dillon's Rule and the broad grant of power given to municipalities under section 3 were probably sufficient to permit municipalities to own and operate utilities without section 4, but the inclusion of section 4 made this municipal power explicit and eliminated the litigation that would have taken place had municipalities acted without the authority of this section. See *1912 Debates,* 1482.

During the 1912 debates the delegates rejected two substantive amendments that they saw as placing too many burdens on the municipal ownership and operation of public utilities. These included proposals to subject municipalities to state regulation and to bar sales of utility service below cost. See *1912 Debates,* 1482, 1491–92.

The powers granted to a municipality under this section are "plenary," *Village of Lucas v. Lucas Local School District* (1982), but can be restricted by the General Assembly in limited circumstances for public health or safety reasons, *State ex rel. Toledo Edison Co. v. City of Clyde* (1996). Thus, municipalities have the exclusive power to contract for public utility services, but they cannot avoid a state law requiring public utilities to fluoridate water. *City of Canton v. Whitman* (1975).

There are other limitations on the power that municipalities have under this section. For example, a municipality may sell only a limited amount of utility service to nonresidents. See Article XVIII, section 6, and Commentary. And a municipality may not use excess surplus utility revenues to pay for general municipal expenses because such a use of revenues constitutes a tax, which is subject to regulation by the General Assembly. *City of Cincinnati v. Roettinger* (1922). Nor does the power of a municipality to condemn land extend to the appropriation of the public streets of another municipality. *Village of Blue Ash v. City of Cincinnati* (1962).

Nonetheless, a municipality may acquire a utility through condemnation and even acquire land through eminent domain outside the municipality's corporate limits to establish a public utility. But a municipality has no authority to exercise its power of eminent domain beyond its corporate limits other than the power under this section to acquire property to operate a public utility to serve its own residents. *Clifton v. Blanchester* (2012); *Britt v. City of Columbus* (1974).

Section 5

Referendum on acquiring or operating municipal utility.

Any municipality proceeding to acquire, construct, own, lease or operate a public utility, or to contract with any person or company therefor, shall act by ordinance and no such ordinance shall take effect until after thirty days from its passage. If within said thirty days a petition signed by ten per centum of the electors of the municipality shall be filed with the executive authority thereof demanding a referendum on such ordinance it shall not take effect until submitted to the electors and approved by a majority of those voting thereon. The submission of any such question shall be governed by all the provisions of section 8 of this article as to the submission of the question of choosing a charter commission.

Adopted in 1912 and never amended, this section provides that a municipal ordinance allowing for the construction, ownership, lease, or operation of a public utility will not go into effect if (within thirty days of its passage) 10 percent of the electorate sign a petition demanding a referendum. Once the petition is properly signed and filed, the ordinance will not become effective unless approved by a majority of those voting on the referendum. According to the Ohio Supreme Court, this section must be read *in pari materia* with section 14 of this article, and therefore, the 10 percent requirement for signing petitions refers to 10 percent of the electors who voted in the preceding general municipal election and not to 10 percent of all the electors of a municipality. *State ex rel. Huebner v. West Jefferson Village Council* (1996).

This section does not apply to ordinances related to utilities already in operation; nor does it limit emergency ordinances necessary for the immediate preservation of the public health or safety. *State ex rel. City of Fostoria v. King* (1950); *Shryock v. City of Zanesville* (1915).

Section 6

Sale of surplus product of municipal utility.

Any municipality, owning or operating a public utility for the purpose of supplying the service or product thereof to the municipality or its inhabitants, may also sell and deliver to others any transportation service of such utility and the surplus product of any other utility in an amount not exceeding in either case fifty per cent of the total service or product supplied by such utility within the municipality, provided that such fifty per cent limitation shall not apply to the sale of water or sewage services.

Adopted in 1912 and amended in 1959, this section allows a municipality that owns or operates a utility to sell the surplus service or product as long as the surplus does not exceed 50 percent of the total service or product used by the municipality owning or operating the utility. The delegates proposed this provision to limit the extent to which municipal utilities could sell services to nonresidents.

In 1959, the voters approved an amendment proposed by the General Assembly to exempt water and sewage services from the 50 percent limit. See Appendix B.

Although a municipality may sell surplus services or products to nonresidents, it is not bound to do so under this section absent an express contract, even if the municipality has provided surplus products or services in the past. *Fairway Manor, Inc. v. Board of Commissioners of Summit County* (1988).

A municipality may require its extraterritorial utility service customers to agree to annexation in exchange for the continuation of services. *Bakies v. Perrysburg* (2006).

In *Toledo Edison v. City of Bryan* (2000), the Ohio Supreme Court read sections 4 and 6 *in pari materia* and held that a municipality was barred by these sections from creating an artificial electricity surplus by purchasing electricity solely for the purpose of reselling the entire amount to an entity outside the municipality's geographic boundaries. The *Toledo Edison* court, however, did not address whether municipalities, acting under the broad power of section 3, had this power. But in *Cleveland Electric Illuminating Co. v. City of Cleveland* (2021) (plurality opinion), the court recognized that a municipal utility may acquire and sell outside its municipal boundaries surplus electricity acquired for such purposes as lowering its costs, subject to the 50 percent limitation in this section. Two dissenting justices, however, would have revisited *Toledo Edison* and rejected the "artificial surplus" doctrine.

Section 7

Home rule; municipal charter.

Any municipality may frame and adopt or amend a charter for its government and may, subject to the provisions of section 3 of this article, exercise thereunder all powers of local self-government.

Adopted in 1912 and never amended, this section gives municipalities the power to adopt charters and, subject to section 3, exercise thereunder all powers of local self-government. Mr. Knight identified this section as one of the three principal features of the Home Rule Amendment. See *1912 Debates*, 1433.

This section allows a municipality to adopt a charter by which it can choose its own form of government, see Article XVIII, section 2, and provide for, among other things, the election and appointment of municipal officers, the hiring of employees, and the procedures for enacting ordinances. Typically, the court "will construe municipal charters to give effect to all separate provisions and to harmonize them with statutory provisions whenever possible." *State ex rel. Murray v. Scioto County Board of Elections* (2010). If there is a conflict between a charter provision and a state law over a matter of local self-government, the charter provision will generally prevail. *State ex rel. Bardo v. City of Lyndhurst* (1988); *Fitzgerald v. City of Cleveland* (1913).

Section 7 is not a source of the municipal power of local self-government, but it gives municipalities certain control over local matters that they would not otherwise have. See *Local Government Law*, section 3.2.

Municipalities need not adopt a charter in order to exercise the powers of home rule granted in section 3. *Village of Perrysburg v. Ridgway* (1923). Although charter and noncharter municipalities have the same powers of local self-government over matters of substantive law under section 3, charter municipalities also have control over organizational and procedural matters. *Northern Ohio Patrolmen's Benevolent Association v. City of Parma* (1980). Thus, municipalities that have not adopted a charter must follow procedures prescribed by the General Assembly in passing legislation.

The procedure/substance distinction adopted by the Ohio Supreme Court in *City of Parma* has created some confusion. For example, in *City of Parma* the court held that an ordinance passed by a noncharter city deducting military compensation from the pay of city employees on military leave was a matter of substantive law, and therefore, the ordinance superseded a conflicting state law. The court, however, has treated noncharter city ordinances dealing with qualifications for local offices and employee layoff provisions as procedural and, therefore, preempted by state law. *State ex rel. Ziegler v. Hamilton County Board of Elections* (1993); *Treska v. Trumble* (1983).

Section 8

Submission and adoption of proposed charter; referendum.

The legislative authority of any city or village may by a two-thirds vote of its members, and upon petition of ten per centum of the electors shall for with, provide by ordinance for the submission to the electors, of the question, "Shall a commission be chosen to frame a charter." The ordinance providing for the submission of such question shall require that it be submitted to the electors at the next regular municipal election if one shall occur not less than sixty nor more than one hundred and twenty days after its passage; otherwise it shall provide for the submission of the question at a special election to be called and held within the time aforesaid. The ballot containing such question shall bear no party designation, and provision shall be made thereon for the election from the municipality at large of fifteen electors who shall constitute a commission to frame a charter; provided that a majority of the electors voting on such question shall have voted in the affirmative. Any charter so framed shall be submitted to the electors of the municipality at an election to be held at a time fixed by the charter commission and within one year from the date of its election, provision for which shall be made by the legislative authority of the municipality in so far as not prescribed by general law. Not less than thirty days prior to such election the clerk of the municipality shall mail a copy of the proposed charter to each elector whose name appears upon the poll or registration books of the last regular or general election held therein. If such proposed charter is approved by a majority of the electors voting thereon it shall become the charter of such municipality at the time fixed therein.

Adopted in 1912 and never amended, this section governs the process of adopting municipal charters. The section provides that by a two-thirds vote of a municipality's legislative authority or by a petition signed by 10 percent of the electors (voting in the last preceding general municipal election) a municipality must submit the following question to the electorate: "Shall a commission be chosen to frame a charter?" No party designation can be affixed to the question once it is placed on the ballot, and the ballot must include a provision for the election of a fifteen-member charter commission.

The charter commission must complete the proposed charter within one year of the election and set a date to submit the proposed charter to the voters. Thirty days prior to the election, the clerk of the municipality must mail every registered voter a copy of the proposed charter. The charter becomes effective only if approved by a majority of the electorate voting on the proposal. The procedures set forth in this section are mandatory. *Billington v. Cotner* (1971).

Section 9
Amendment of charter; referendum.

Amendments to any charter framed and adopted as herein provided may be submitted to the electors of a municipality by a two-thirds vote of the legislative authority thereof, and, upon petitions signed by ten per centum of the electors of the municipality setting forth any such proposed amendment, shall be submitted by such legislative authority. The submission of proposed amendments to the electors shall be governed by the requirements of section 8 as to the submission of the question of choosing a charter commission; and copies of proposed amendments may be mailed to the electors as hereinbefore provided for copies of a proposed charter, or pursuant to laws passed by the General Assembly, notice of proposed amendments may be given by newspaper advertising. If any such amendment is approved by a majority of the electors voting thereon, it shall become a part of the charter of the municipality. A copy of said charter or any amendment thereto shall be certified to the secretary of state, within thirty days after adoption by a referendum vote.

Adopted in 1912 and amended in 1970, section 9 provides that amendments to a municipal charter may be submitted to the electors of a municipality for approval by two-thirds of the municipality's legislative or by petition signed by 10 percent of the electors voting in the last preceding general municipal election. Section 9 expressly requires compliance with the provisions of section 8 of this article for any proposed charter amendment submitted to the voters. *State ex rel. Committee for Charter Amendment Petition v. City of Maple Heights* (2014).

Section 8 also imposes a constitutional duty on city councils to submit initiatives for city charter amendments to the voters "forthwith," and city councils have only a limited authority to review the sufficiency of the petition—not its substance. Thus, a city council violates this duty if it does not place a petition before the voters at least sixty days before the election. *State ex rel. Committee for Charter Amendment Petition v. City of Maple Heights* (2014).

In 2018, the court ruled that this section imposes clear procedural requirements on municipal legislatures upon receipt of petitions for charter amendments: (1) to pass an ordinance "forthwith" to submit a proposal with sufficient valid signatures to the electors; and (2) to provide in that ordinance that the matter be submitted at the next regular municipal election if one will occur no more than 120 days and no less than 60 days after the passage of the ordinance. *State ex rel. Maxcy v. Saferin* (2018); see also *State ex rel. Hinchliffe v. Gibbons* (1927).

Proposed amendments must be ratified by a majority of the electors voting on the proposal, and they must be filed with the secretary of state within thirty days of ratification.

The General Assembly proposed the 1970 amendment in response to an opinion of the Attorney General that had concluded that that newspaper advertising was insufficient. The amendment authorized the General Assembly to enact laws to permit notice of proposed charter amendments by newspaper advertising rather than exclusively through the mails.

In 2014, the Ohio Supreme Court held that a city council exceeded its constitutional authority under Article XVIII, section 9, when it refused to place a proposed charter amendment on the ballot because the council concluded that the proposal was unconstitutional, a role that is reserved to the courts alone. *State ex rel. Ebersole v. Powell* (on reconsideration) ("The proper time for an aggrieved party to challenge the constitutionality of the charter amendment is after the voters approve the measure, assuming they do so.").

A city charter cannot require a higher number of signatures in order to get a proposed charter amendment on the ballot than the 10 percent requirement in this section. *State ex rel. Wilen v. Kent* (2015).

In 2018, the court concluded that a county board of elections had no authority under Article II, section 1f to review the substance of proposed municipal charter amendments. Because Article XVIII, section 9 was a specific provision and Article II, section 1f was a general provision, the court held that section 9 controls in the event of a conflict between the two. *State ex rel. Maxcy v. Saferin* (2018).

Section 10

Appropriation in excess of public use.

A municipality appropriating or otherwise acquiring property for public use may in furtherance of such public use appropriate or acquire an excess over that actually to be occupied by the improvement, and may sell such excess with such restrictions as shall be appropriate to preserve the improvement made.

Bonds may be issued to supply the funds in whole or in part to pay for the excess property so appropriated or otherwise acquired, but said bonds shall be a lien only against the property so acquired for the improvement and excess, and they shall not be a liability of the municipality nor be included in any limitation of the bonded indebtedness of such municipality prescribed by law.

Adopted in 1912 and never amended, this section allows a municipality that is acquiring property for public use to acquire excess property that it can later sell. The appropriation of excess property, however, must be in furtherance of a public use. A municipality has reasonable discretion to determine the amount of excess property it wants to appropriate, but courts will not "sanction an arbitrary and unreasonable taking of excess private property for the contemplated use, under the guise that it is necessary [in furtherance of the contemplated use] . . . where the weight of the evidence shows it to be otherwise." *City of East Cleveland v. Nau* (1931). Thus, under this section a municipality "is required not only to define specifically the purpose of the appropriation in its legislation" but also to "sustain such requirement by proof of its necessity." Ibid.

This section also allows a municipality to issue bonds to finance the purchase of excess property. The bonds, however, can only be held as a lien against the purchased property.

Section 11
Assessments for cost of appropriating property.

Any municipality appropriating private property for a public improvement may provide money therefor in part by assessments upon benefited property not in excess of the special benefits conferred upon such property by the improvements. Said assessments, however, upon all the abutting, adjacent, and other property in the district benefited, shall in no case be levied for more than fifty per centum of the cost of such appropriation.

Adopted in 1912 and never amended, this section allows a municipality appropriating private property for a public improvement to levy assessments on property benefited by the public improvement. The 1912 Convention proposed this section to overturn an Ohio Supreme Court case, *City of Dayton v. Bauman* (1902), which held that special assessments cannot be levied to pay for the cost of appropriating private property. See *1912 Debates*, 1476. Under this section, the assessments levied on property benefited by the public improvement cannot be in excess of the benefits conferred by the improvement and cannot include more than 50 percent of the cost of appropriating private property. See *Thomas v. City of Beavercreek* (1995).

Section 12

Bonds for public utilities.

Any municipality which acquires, constructs or extends any public utility and desires to raise money for such purposes may issue mortgage bonds therefore beyond the general limit of bonded indebtedness prescribed by law; provided that such mortgage bonds issued beyond the general limit of bonded indebtedness prescribed by law shall not impose any liability upon such municipality but shall be secured only upon the property and revenues of such public utility, including a franchise stating the terms upon which, in case of foreclosure, the purchaser may operate the same, which franchise shall in no case extend for a longer period than twenty years from the date of the sale of such utility and franchise on foreclosure.

Adopted in 1912 and never amended, this section allows a municipality to acquire, construct, or extend a public utility with funds raised from the sale of mortgage bonds beyond any debt limit imposed by law. Bonds issued beyond the general limit of bonded indebtedness, however, cannot impose liability on the municipality and must be secured by the revenues and property of the public utility.

This section is self-executing and self-sufficient, and utility mortgage bonds created and issued strictly within its terms are not affected by other parts of the constitution or by laws passed under section 13 to limit a municipality's power to incur debt. *City of Middletown v. City Commission of Middletown* (1941). And the Ohio Supreme Court has interpreted the section to mean that the bonds may be secured not only by the property acquired or constructed with the sale of such bonds but also by any proceeds or property directly connected with the utility, including property already owned by the utility. Ibid. Notwithstanding this section, a municipality may issue general obligation bonds (subject to the debt limits prescribed by law) as well as general revenue bonds to acquire, construct, or operate public utilities.

Section 13

Taxation, debts, reports and accounts.

Laws may be passed to limit the power of municipalities to levy taxes and incur debts for local purposes, and may require reports from municipalities as to their financial condition and transactions, in such form as may be provided by law, and may provide for the examination of the vouchers, books and accounts of all municipal authorities, or of public undertakings conducted by such authorities.

Adopted in 1912 and never amended, this section, like Article XIII, section 6, allows the General Assembly to limit the power of municipalities to tax and incur debt. Under this section, the General Assembly may also require municipalities to file financial reports with the state and to allow their financial records to be open for state inspection.

The municipal taxing power is one of the "powers of local self-government." But in 1925, the Ohio Supreme Court rejected a city occupational tax because the field had already been occupied by the state, which had adopted state excise taxes on railroads, telephone, and telegraph companies. *City of Cincinnati v. American Tel. & Tel. Co.* (1925).

The court applied this approach, sometimes referred to as implied preemption, to restrict a city's power to levy certain taxes until 1998, when it rejected nearly seventy-five years of precedent and held that "[t]he mere enactment of state legislation that results in an occupation of a field of taxation is not sufficient to constitute an exercise of the General Assembly's constitutional power to limit municipal taxation." *Cincinnati Bell Tel. Co. v. City of Cincinnati* (1998). Thus, to limit the power of municipalities to adopt taxes, an express act of the General Assembly is required.

In *Village of Put-in-Bay v. Mathys* (2020) the court held that a municipality could require owners of vehicles that are made available for hire and use within the municipality to pay a "license fee" on those vehicles, and it further held that the fee was not preempted by state law and not barred by Article XII, section 5a.

Although the General Assembly can limit a city's power to tax, it cannot require a city to impose a tax. Thus, a state statute that defined net profit for purposes of municipal income tax did not invalidate a city ordinance that contained a contrasting definition of net profit for purposes of the municipal income tax. *Gesler v. City of Worthington Income Tax Board of Appeals* (2013).

In *City of Athens v. McClain* (2020), the Ohio Supreme Court held that (despite cities' constitutional power of local self-government) this section permits the adoption of a state-administered, centralized system for reporting and collecting municipal net profit taxes on businesses. But the court further held that the state did not have authority to impose a 0.5 percent charge for state administrative services related to the tax.

Section 14

Municipal elections.

All elections and submissions of questions provided for in this article shall be conducted by the election authorities prescribed by general law. The percentage of electors required to sign any petition provided for herein shall be based upon the total vote cast at the last preceding general municipal election.

Adopted in 1912 and never amended, this section requires that all elections under this article be conducted in accordance with general election laws. In situations where this article calls for a petition, see sections 5, 8, and 9, the percentage of electors required to sign the petition is based on the number of electors who voted in the last preceding general municipal election rather than the total number of electors registered in the municipality. *State ex rel. Huebner v. West Jefferson Village Council* (1996). "The intention and effect of the plain language of Section 14, when read with the other sections of Article XVIII, are to encourage citizens to place issues on the ballot. By reducing the base number of electors from which the ten percent of required signatures is calculated, Section 14 allows the individual easier access to the political process in presenting important issues for consideration and possible approval by the electorate." *State ex rel. Lewis v. Hamilton County Bd. of Elections* (1995) (Moyer, C. J., concurring).

Article XIX

Congressional Redistricting

Congressional redistricting had been the responsibility of the General Assembly since the adoption of the 1802 Constitution, but in 2018 the voters approved an amendment to revise completely the process for drawing congressional district lines. Though continuing to rely in the first instance on the General Assembly, the new amendment included a supermajority bipartisan voting requirement, detailed standards for drawing district lines, and a back-up role for the 2015-created Ohio Redistricting Commission.

The new amendment reflected not only the unwillingness of the General Assembly to give up completely its role in congressional redistricting but also the desire of reform proponents to limit the broad discretion the General Assembly once possessed. The resulting compromise gave the General Assembly initial responsibility for drawing congressional district lines, but it also included detailed procedural and substantive standards and compressed deadlines to govern the entire process.

Proponents of the 2018 amendment sought to end partisan gerrymandering and to create what they described as a fair, bipartisan, and transparent process for congressional redistricting. And the ballot language further advised voters that the goal of the amendment was to "end the partisan process for drawing congressional districts, and replace it with a process with the goals of promoting bipartisanship, keeping local communities together, and having district boundaries

The Ohio State Constitution. Steven H. Steinglass and Gino J. Scarselli, Oxford University Press. © Oxford University Press 2022. DOI: 10.1093/oso/9780197619728.003.0021

that are more compact." The proponents also sought to promote transparency through mandatory public hearings and a process under which members of the public had an opportunity to submit their own congressional redistricting proposals. See Issue 1, *Ballot Issues for the May 2018 Primary Election* (Ohio Secretary of State website).

The 2018 amendment was the culmination of many years of effort by those who had sought what they characterized as fairer and less partisan apportionment and redistricting.

Despite the rejection of a proposed commission to draw legislative and congressional lines in 2012 (and earlier rejections in 1981 and 2005), efforts to obtain change through the political process continued, and in 2014 and 2015, state legislative apportionment and congressional redistricting seemed to be moving in tandem. But the congressional redistricting proposal ran into political opposition as well as an argument that the use of congressional redistricting commissions violated the Elections Clause of the U.S. Constitution. See Article I, section 4, clause 1 ("[T]he Times, Places and Manner of holding Elections for Senators and Representatives shall be prescribed in each State by the Legislature thereof; but the Congress may at any time by Law make or alter such Regulations . . . ."). As a result, the 2015 constitutional amendment on state apportionment, see Article XI, did not include any changes in congressional redistricting.

On June 29, 2015, however, the U.S. Supreme Court decided *Arizona State Legislature v. Arizona Independent Redistricting Commission* (2015) and upheld the use of initiated independent redistricting commissions to draw boundaries for congressional districts. The 5-4 decision turned, in part, on whether the word "Legislature" in the Elections Clause refers literally to the representative body that makes the laws or more broadly to the legislative process.

The removal of the potential federal impediment put congressional redistricting back into play, but legislative agreement on a joint resolution did not come until early 2018 and only after good government advocates, including the League of Women Voters of Ohio and Common Cause Ohio, began moving forward with a proposed initiated amendment. At that point, the General Assembly proposed an amendment on congressional redistricting, and the voters approved by almost a 3:1 margin a single ballot measure to revise Article XI and to adopt Article XIX to govern congressional redistricting. See Appendix B. The effective date of this amendment was January 1, 2021.

The decision of the U.S. Supreme Court in *Rucho v. Common Cause* (2019), which held that partisan gerrymandering is a nonjusticiable political question under federal law, underscores the wisdom of the path chosen in Ohio for addressing apportionment and redistricting.

On January 14, 2022, in its first case construing this article, the Ohio Supreme Court in *Adams v. DeWine* (2022), permitted two suits challenging a congressional redistricting plan adopted by the general assembly to proceed against the secretary of state in his official capacity, against the speaker of the House in his official capacity, and against the president of the Senate in his official capacity. The court dismissed the actions against the Ohio Redistricting Commission, against the seven members of the commission in their official capacities, and against the governor in his official capacity.

On the merits, the *Adams* court held "that the [four-year] congressional-district plan adopted by the General Assembly without a bipartisan majority in November 2022 is invalid in its entirety because it unduly favors the Republican Party and disfavors the Democratic Party. . . ."

In describing the evil of gerrymandering, the court stated:

> Gerrymandering is the antithetical perversion of representative democracy. It is an abuse of power—by whichever political party has control to draw geographic boundaries for elected state and congressional offices and engages in that practice—that strategically exaggerates the power of voters who tend to support the favored party while diminishing the power of voters who tend to support the disfavored party. Its singular allure is that it locks in the controlling party's political power while locking out any other party or executive office from serving as a check and balance to power.

Section 1

Adoption of congressional district plan.

(A) Except as otherwise provided in this section, the general assembly shall be responsible for the redistricting of this state for congress based on the prescribed number of congressional districts apportioned to the state pursuant to Section 2 of Article I of the Constitution of the United States.

Not later than the last day of September of a year ending in the numeral one, the general assembly shall pass a congressional district plan in the form of a bill by the affirmative vote of three-fifths of the members of each house of the general assembly, including the affirmative vote of at least one-half of the members of each of the two largest political parties represented in that house. A congressional district plan that is passed under this division and becomes law shall remain effective until the next year ending in the numeral one, except as provided in Section 3 of this article.

(B) If a congressional district plan is not passed not later than the last day of September of a year ending in the numeral one and filed with the secretary of state in accordance with Section 16 of Article II of this constitution, then the Ohio redistricting commission described in Article XI of this constitution shall adopt a congressional district plan not later than the last day of October of that year by the affirmative vote of four members of the commission, including at least two members of the commission who represent each of the two largest political parties represented in the general assembly. The plan shall take effect upon filing with the secretary of state and shall remain effective until the next year ending in the numeral one, except as provided in Section 3 of this article.

(C)(1) If the Ohio redistricting commission does not adopt a plan not later than the last day of October of a year ending in the numeral one, then the general assembly shall pass a congressional district plan in the form of a bill not later than the last day of November of that year.

(2) If the general assembly passes a congressional district plan under division (C)(1) of this section by the affirmative vote of three-fifths of the members of each house of the general assembly, including the affirmative vote of at least one-third of the members of each of the two largest political parties represented in that house, and the plan becomes law, the plan shall remain effective until the next year ending in the numeral one, except as provided in Section 3 of this article.

(3) If the general assembly passes a congressional district plan under division (C)(1) of this section by a simple majority of the members of each house of the general assembly, and not by the vote described in division (C)(2) of this section, all of the following shall apply:

(a) The general assembly shall not pass a plan that unduly favors or disfavors a political party or its incumbents.

(b) The general assembly shall not unduly split governmental units, giving preference to keeping whole, in the order named, counties, then townships and municipal corporations.

(c) Division (B)(2) of Section 2 of this article shall not apply to the plan. The general assembly shall attempt to draw districts that are compact.

(d) The general assembly shall include in the plan an explanation of the plan's compliance with divisions (C)(3)(a) to (c) of this section.

(e) If the plan becomes law, the plan shall remain effective until two general elections for the United States house of representatives have occurred under the plan, except as provided in Section 3 of this article.

(D) Not later than the last day of September of the year after the year in which a plan expires under division (C)(3)(e) of this section, the general assembly shall pass a congressional district plan in the form of a bill by the affirmative vote of three-fifths of the members of each house of the general assembly, including the affirmative vote of at least one-half of the members of each of the two largest political parties represented in that house. A congressional district plan that is passed under this division and becomes law shall remain effective until the next year ending in the numeral one, except as provided in Section 3 of this article.

A congressional district plan passed under this division shall be drawn using the federal decennial census data or other data on which the previous redistricting was based.

(E) If a congressional district plan is not passed not later than the last day of September of the year after the year in which a plan expires under division (C)(3)(e) of this section and filed with the secretary of state in accordance with Section 16 of Article II of this constitution, then the Ohio redistricting commission described in Article XI of this constitution shall be reconstituted and reconvene and shall adopt a congressional district plan not later than the last day of October of that year by the affirmative vote of four members of the commission, including at least two members of the commission who represent each of the two largest political parties represented in the general assembly. A congressional district plan adopted under this division shall take effect upon filing with the secretary of state and shall remain effective until the next year ending in the numeral one, except as provided in Section 3 of this article.

A congressional district plan adopted under this division shall be drawn using the federal decennial census data or other data on which the previous redistricting was based.

(F)(1) If the Ohio redistricting commission does not adopt a congressional district plan not later than the last day of October of the year after the year in which a plan expires under division (C)(3)(e) of this section, then the general assembly shall pass a congressional district plan in the form of a bill not later than the last day of November of that year. A congressional district plan adopted under this division shall be drawn using the federal decennial census data or other data on which the previous redistricting was based.

(2) If the general assembly passes a congressional district plan under division (F)(1) of this section by the affirmative vote of three-fifths of the members of each house, including the affirmative vote of at least one-third of the members of each of the two largest political parties represented in that house, and the plan becomes law, it shall remain effective until the next year ending in the numeral one, except as provided in Section 3 of this article.

(3) If the general assembly passes a congressional district plan under division (F)(1) of this section by a simple majority vote of the members of each house of the general assembly, and not by the vote described in division (F)(2) of this section, all of the following shall apply:

(a) The general assembly shall not pass a plan that unduly favors or disfavors a political party or its incumbents.

(b) The general assembly shall not unduly split governmental units, giving preference to keeping whole, in the order named, counties, then townships and municipal corporations.

(c) Division (B)(2) of Section 2 of this article shall not apply to the plan. The general assembly shall attempt to draw districts that are compact.

(d) The general assembly shall include in the plan an explanation of the plan's compliance with divisions (F)(3)(a) to (c) of this section.

(e) If the plan becomes law, the plan shall remain effective until the next year ending in the numeral one, except as provided in Section 3 of this article.

(G) Before the general assembly passes a congressional district plan under any division of this section, a joint committee of the general assembly shall hold at least two public committee hearings concerning a proposed plan. Before the Ohio redistricting commission adopts a congressional district plan under any division of this section, the commission shall hold at least two public hearings concerning a proposed plan.

(H) The general assembly and the Ohio redistricting commission shall facilitate and allow for the submission of proposed congressional district plans by members of the public. The general assembly shall provide by law the manner in which members of the public may do so.

(I) For purposes of filing a congressional district plan with the governor or the secretary of state under this article, a congressional district plan shall include both a legal description of the boundaries of the congressional districts and all electronic data necessary to create a congressional district map for the purpose of holding congressional elections.

(J) When a congressional district plan ceases to be effective under this article, the district boundaries described in that plan shall continue in operation for the purpose of holding elections until a new congressional district plan takes effect in accordance with this article. If a vacancy occurs in a district that was created under the previous district plan, the election to fill the vacancy for the remainder of the unexpired term shall be held using the previous district plan.

Adopted in 2018, this section sets forth the general framework for congressional redistricting. Section 1(A) gives the General Assembly initial responsibility for drawing the boundaries of the districts apportioned to Ohio under federal law. This section also provides that the General Assembly must pass a bill for congressional redistricting by at least a three-fifths vote in each house no later than September 30 of years ending in the numeral one. The affirmative vote must include at least one-half of the members of the two largest political parties in each house. For example, if twenty-four members of the Ohio Senate belong to the majority political party and nine members belong to the minority political party, an affirmative vote on the bill must contain at least twenty votes with at least twelve votes from the majority political party and at least five votes from the minority political party. Any plan so approved (and signed by the governor) becomes law and remains in effect for the next ten years, except as provided in section 3 (which refers to a judicial determination that the plan is invalid). See Article XIX, section 3(B)(1).

If the General Assembly fails to adopt a plan before the September 30 deadline or fails to timely file a plan in accordance with Article II, section 16, of the Ohio Constitution, section 1(B) provides that the Ohio Redistricting Commission, the body responsible for apportioning the General Assembly under Article XI, assumes responsibility for adopting a congressional redistricting plan. This section requires the commission to adopt a congressional redistricting plan no later than October 31 of a year ending in one by a vote of at least four of the commission's seven members with at least two votes from commission members who represent each of the two largest political parties in the General Assembly. Any plan adopted in this way becomes effective upon its being filed with the secretary of state and remains in effect for the next ten years, except as provided in section 3 (which refers to a judicial determination that the plan is invalid). See Article XIX, section 3(B)(1). And unlike congressional redistricting plans adopted by the General Assembly (which are in the form of a bill), redistricting plans adopted by the commission are effective immediately upon filing with the secretary of state and are not subject either to a veto by the governor under Article II, section 16, or to a referendum under Article II, section 1d.

Section 1(C)(1) further provides that if the commission fails to adopt a plan by October 31, responsibility shifts back to the General Assembly, which will have a second chance to adopt a congressional redistricting plan during the month of November. This time, the affirmative three-fifths vote need only contain at least one-third of the members of the two largest parties in that house. For example, if the Ohio Senate's thirty-three members had twenty-four members from one party and nine members from another, under section 1(C)(1), a plan needs at least twenty votes to pass of which at least eight votes must come from the majority party and at least three votes must come from the minority party.

If the General Assembly only approves a congressional redistricting plan in its November vote by a simple majority, that plan is only effective for four years, that is, until the passing of two elections for members of the U.S. House of Representative. And such plan must meet the additional requirements of section 1(C)(3), which do not apply to plans approved by the General Assembly that meet the supermajority bipartisan voting requirement or to plans adopted by the Ohio Redistricting Commission that meet the bipartisan voting requirement.

First, the plan must not unduly favor or disfavor a political party or its incumbents. See section 1(C)(3)(a). Second, the plan must not unduly split governmental units and must give preference to keeping counties, townships, and municipal corporations whole, in that order. See section 1(C)(3)(b). Third, the General Assembly must *attempt* to draw compact districts (and thus need not comply with the strict compactness requirement of sec. 2(B)(2)). See section 1(C)(3)(c). Fourth, the General Assembly must include in the plan a written explanation of how its plan complies with each of these elements.

In the wake of *Wilson v. Kasich* (2012), this section's express mandates reflect a desire to limit discretion and restrict the ability of lawmakers to pick and choose which constitutional provisions to apply. But unlike the requirements for state legislative apportionment, the requirements for congressional redistricting do not include a proportionality requirement. See Commentary, Article XI, section 6(B).

Section 1(D) provides that after September 30 of the year following a plan's expiration under section 1(C)(3)(e) (i.e., after two elections), the General Assembly must pass another congressional redistricting plan by a three-fifths vote with the support of at least one-half of each of the two largest political parties. For example, if the General Assembly adopts a plan under section 1(C)(3)(e) in November 2021, the General Assembly has until September 30, 2025, to pass a new congressional redistricting plan in accordance with this section, and this plan must rely on the same data used to draw the previous congressional districting plan. Once passed, the new plan remains in effect until the next year ending in the numeral one.

Section 1(E) provides that if the General Assembly fails to approve a replacement plan by the September 30 deadline in section 1(D), responsibility for drawing a congressional districting plan again shifts to the Ohio Redistricting Commission. And the commission must adopt a new congressional redistricting plan no later than October 31 of the same year by a vote of at least four of the seven commission members (including at least two members who represent each of the two largest political parties represented in the General Assembly). Such a plan remains in effect until the next year ending in the numeral one.

If the commission fails to adopt a replacement plan by the October 31 deadline, responsibility again shifts to the General Assembly under section 1(F)(1). The General Assembly has until November 30 to adopt a plan. This time, an affirmative vote requires three-fifths of the members of each house, which must include at least one-third of the members of the two largest political parties. If that effort fails as well, section 1(F)(3) allows approval of a congressional redistricting plan by only a simple majority vote (with no bipartisan vote requirement) but *only* if the plan satisfies each element listed in section 1(F)(3). First, the plan must not unduly favor or disfavor a political party or its incumbents. Second, the plan must not unduly split governmental units, giving preference to keeping counties, townships, and municipal corporations whole, in the order named. Third, the General Assembly must attempt to draw compact districts. Fourth, the plan must include a written explanation of how it meets each of these elements. Finally, a plan so enacted remains in effect until the next year ending in the numeral one.

Section 1(G) has a public hearing requirement. It mandates that a joint committee of the General Assembly hold at least two public hearings concerning any plan proposed by the General Assembly prior to a final vote on the plan. This section also imposes the same public hearing requirement on the Ohio Redistricting Commission for any plan it proposes.

Section 1(H) requires both the General Assembly and the commission to "facilitate and allow" members of the public to submit proposals for congressional redistricting plans. This section also gives the General Assembly the power to establish laws to control the manner in which the public may submit such proposals.

Section 1(I) contains an evidentiary requirement. This section requires that any plan proposed under this article must include both a legal description of the map's boundaries and all relevant data needed to create a congressional redistricting.

Finally, section 1(J) provides that the boundaries in a congressional redistricting plan will remain in effect until a new plan is approved in accordance with this article. In addition, this section makes clear that any election to fill a vacancy that occurs under a previous plan will be held under that previous plan.

2022 LITIGATION

In *Adams v. DeWine* (2022), the Ohio Supreme Court held that the four-year congressional redistricting plan adopted by the General Assembly and signed by the governor was invalid in its entirety for unduly favoring one party and for unduly splitting three of the state's more populous counties—Cuyahoga (Cleveland), Hamilton (Cincinnati), and Summit (Toledo). In so ruling, the court (without adopting the proportionality standard that appears only in Article XI) considered the likely results of the redistricting plan (which would have given one party approximately 80% of Ohio's fifteen congressional seats) as an evidentiary matter. The court also made clear that the standard was not whether the new districts were more competitive than the prior ones but whether they unduly favored one political party. Finally, the court ruled that the splitting of twelve counties, though below the twenty-three permitted by section 2(B), was invalid because the county splits unduly favored one political party.

On March 1, 2022, after the General Assembly choose not to act, the Ohio Redistricting Commission adopted a four-year congressional redistricting plan in a partisan vote. On March 18, 2022, the court denied the petitioners' motion to enforce the court's order and their motion to amend the complaint, because the court had dismissed the commission from the suit and had not retained continuing jurisdiction. In so ruling, the court permitted the filing of a new original action to challenge the constitutionality of the second congressional redistricting plan, and two groups of petitioners almost immediately filed such actions. The court consolidated the cases on March 29, 2022, but the briefing schedule set up by the court left the second redistricting plan in place for the 2022 congressional elections though subject to further proceedings before the 2024 elections. See *Neiman v. LaRose* (2022).

Section 2

Requirements for a congressional district plan.

(A)(1) Each congressional district shall be entitled to a single representative in the United States house of representatives in each congress.

(2) The whole population of the state, as determined by the federal decennial census or, if the federal decennial census is unavailable, another basis as directed by the general assembly, shall be divided by the number of congressional districts apportioned to the state pursuant to Section 2 of Article I of the Constitution of the United States, and the quotient shall be the congressional ratio of representation for the next ten years.

(3) Notwithstanding the fact that boundaries of counties, municipal corporations, and townships within a district may be changed, district boundaries shall be created by using the data from the most recent federal decennial census or from the basis directed by the general assembly, as applicable.

(B) A congressional district plan shall comply with all of the following requirements:

(1) The plan shall comply with all applicable provisions of the constitutions of Ohio and the United States and of federal law, including federal laws protecting racial minority voting rights.

(2) Every congressional district shall be compact.

(3) Every congressional district shall be composed of contiguous territory, and the boundary of each district shall be a single nonintersecting continuous line.

(4) Except as otherwise required by federal law, in a county that contains a population that exceeds the congressional ratio of representation, the authority drawing the districts shall take the first of the following actions that applies to that county:

(a) If a municipal corporation or township located in that county contains a population that exceeds the congressional ratio of representation, the authority shall attempt to include a significant portion of that municipal corporation or township in a single district and may include in that district other municipal corporations or townships that are located in that county and whose residents have similar interests as the residents of the municipal corporation or township that contains a population that exceeds the congressional ratio of representation. In determining whether the population of a municipal corporation or township exceeds the congressional ratio of representation for the purpose of this division, if the territory of that municipal corporation or township completely surrounds the territory of another municipal corporation or township, the territory of the surrounded municipal corporation or township shall be considered part of the territory of the surrounding municipal corporation or township.

(b) If one municipal corporation or township in that county contains a population of not less than one hundred thousand and not more than the congressional ratio of representation, that municipal corporation or township shall not be split. If that county contains two or more such municipal corporations or townships, only the most populous of those municipal corporations or townships shall not be split.

(5) Of the eighty-eight counties in this state, sixty-five counties shall be contained entirely within a district, eighteen counties may be split not more than once, and five counties may be split not more than twice. The authority drawing the districts may determine which counties may be split.

(6) If a congressional district includes only part of the territory of a particular county, the part of that congressional district that lies in that particular county shall be contiguous within the boundaries of the county.

(7) No two congressional districts shall share portions of the territory of more than one county, except for a county whose population exceeds four hundred thousand.

(8) The authority drawing the districts shall attempt to include at least one whole county in each congressional district. This division does not apply to a congressional district that is contained entirely within one county or that cannot be drawn in that manner while complying with federal law.

(C)(1) Except as otherwise provided in division (C)(2) of this section, for purposes of this article, a county, municipal corporation, or township is considered to be split if, based on the census data used for the purpose of redistricting, any contiguous portion of its territory is not contained entirely within one district.

(2) If a municipal corporation or township has territory in more than one county, the contiguous portion of that municipal corporation or township that lies in each county shall be considered to be a separate municipal corporation or township for purposes of this section.

Adopted in 2018, this section establishes the standards for congressional redistricting plans whether adopted by the General Assembly or the Ohio Redistricting Commission.

Section 2(A)(1) permits only one-member districts. Section 2(A)(2) sets forth the method for deriving the congressional ratio of representation (i.e., the state's whole population divided by the number of state congressional districts). And section 2(A)(3) specifies what data the General Assembly must use to determine counties, townships, and municipal corporation boundaries, while acknowledging that such boundaries may change.

Section 2(B) contains the required standards for any congressional redistricting plan. First, the plan must comply with all applicable provisions of the Ohio Constitution, the U.S. Constitution, and federal laws (explicitly referring to laws protecting racial minority voting rights). See section 2(B)(1). The requirement in section 2(B)(1) that a congressional district plan comply with all applicable provisions of the U.S. Constitution presumably refers to the "one man one vote" principle of the Equal Protection Clause of the Fourteenth Amendment. See *Wesberry v. Sanders* (1964) ("[A]s nearly as is practicable one man's vote in a congressional election is to be worth as much as another's.").

Federal law, however, does not require absolute population equality, and no such requirement is included in this article. Indeed, this section recognizes the inevitability of departures from absolute population equality by acknowledging that the congressional ratio of representation may be exceeded and by specifying the steps that must be taken in such cases. Finally, this recognition of deviations from absolute equality is consistent with the prevailing federal doctrine, which permits deviations in order to achieve other legitimate objectives. See *Tennant v. Jefferson County Commission* (2012) (noting that the "as nearly as is practicable" standard does not require that congressional districts be drawn with "precise mathematical equality" and approving a .79 percent deviation between the largest and smallest districts.

Under sections 2(B)(2)–(3), the compact and contiguous requirements are addressed in a bifurcated way. All congressional districts must be composed of contiguous territory, separated by a single nonintersecting continuous line. But the compactness requirement of section 2(B)(2) is not applicable to plans adopted by a simple majority vote under section 1(C)(1). Under this watered-down version of the compactness requirement, the General Assembly need only "attempt to draw districts that are compact." But the prohibitions on drawing unduly partisan districts and unduly splitting governmental units are applicable to redistricting plans that are adopted by a simple majority vote of the General Assembly under section 1(C)(1).

Section 2(B)(4) contains specific procedures that must be followed when there is a county with a population in excess of a congressional ratio of representation. Unless federal law provides otherwise, the authority drawing the district lines (either the General Assembly or the commission) must adhere to the following: if a township or municipality in a particular county has a population that exceeds a congressional ratio of representation, the drafters must try to include a "significant portion" of that entity in a single congressional district. Furthermore, the drafters may include within that district residents from other municipalities or townships in that county whose residents have "similar interests" to the residents of that congressional district. In her dissent in *Wilson v. Kasich* (2012), Justice McGee Brown observed that some noncontiguous political subdivisions share common issues, services, political concerns, and elected representatives. In such instances, this provision gives the drafters discretion to make appropriate accommodations. Section 2(B)(4)(a) also provides that the drafters must treat a township or municipal corporation that lies entirely within the territory of another such entity as part of that larger surrounding municipal corporation or township.

Section 2(B)(4)(b) provides that the drafters not split a municipal corporation or township that contains a population of 100,000 or more but less than one congressional ratio. If such an entity contains multiple townships or municipalities, the drafters must not split the most populous municipal corporations or townships.

Section 2(B)(5) provides unambiguously that the drafters must place at least sixty-five of Ohio's eighty-eight counties entirely within a congressional district. Furthermore, the drafters may split no more than five counties more than twice and no more than eighteen counties more than once. Within these limitations, the drafters retain discretion to determine which counties to split to meet the requirements of this article.

Section 2(B)(6) requires that if a congressional district includes territory from another county, the part of that district that lies in that other county must be contiguous within the boundaries of the county. Section 2(B)(7) provides that no two districts may share portions of territory of more than one county except for a county with a population that exceeds 400,000. These two measures, in effect, prevent the drafters from carving out small pockets of noncontiguous territories from other counties to favor or disfavor a particular party or candidate.

Section 2(B)(8) requires the drafters to attempt to include at least one whole county within the boundaries of every congressional district, but this provision does not apply to districts contained entirely within a single county or when doing so would violate federal law.

Section 2(C)(1) defines a "split" broadly for purposes of congressional redistricting. Thus, a governmental unit is considered split if any contiguous portion of its territory is not contained entirely within one congressional district. Thus, drafters cannot avoid the numerosity requirements for splits in section 2(B)(5) by redefining the term "split." Finally, section 2(C)(2) provides that if a governmental unit contains territory in more than one county, the drafters must treat the contiguous portion of that unit in each county as a separate municipal corporation or township for purposes of this section.

Section 3

Jurisdiction; legal challenges; procedures upon invalidation of congressional district plan.

(A) The supreme court of Ohio shall have exclusive, original jurisdiction in all cases arising under this article.

(B)(1) In the event that any section of this constitution relating to congressional redistricting, any congressional district plan, or any congressional district or group of congressional districts is challenged and is determined to be invalid by an unappealed final order of a court of competent jurisdiction then, notwithstanding any other provisions of this constitution, the general assembly shall pass a congressional district plan in accordance with the provisions of this constitution that are then valid, to be used until the next time for redistricting under this article in accordance with the provisions of this constitution that are then valid.

The general assembly shall pass that plan not later than the thirtieth day after the last day on which an appeal of the court order could have been filed or, if the order is not appealable, the thirtieth day after the day on which the order is issued.

A congressional district plan passed under this division shall remedy any legal defects in the previous plan identified by the court but shall include no changes to the previous plan other than those made in order to remedy those defects.

(2) If a new congressional district plan is not passed in accordance with division (B)(1) of this section and filed with the secretary of state in accordance with Section 16 of Article II of this constitution, the Ohio redistricting commission shall be reconstituted and reconvene and shall adopt a congressional district plan in accordance with the provisions of this constitution that are then valid, to be used until the next time for redistricting under this article in accordance with the provisions of this constitution that are then valid.

The commission shall adopt that plan not later than the thirtieth day after the deadline described in division (B)(1) of this section.

A congressional district plan adopted under this division shall remedy any legal defects in the previous plan identified by the court but shall include no other changes to the previous plan other than those made in order to remedy those defects.

Adopted in 2018, section 3 provides the basic framework for legal challenges to congressional redistricting plans, including the available remedies. As with state apportionment challenges, this article expressly provides that the Ohio Supreme Court has original and exclusive jurisdiction over all cases arising under this article. It also implicitly recognizes that a federal court (i.e., a court of competent jurisdiction) may also review the validity of congressional redistricting plans under federal law. See also Commentary, Article XI, section 9.

Section 3(B)(1) gives the General Assembly the authority to pass a new redistricting plan in accordance with Article XIX's procedures if the Ohio Supreme Court or a court of competent jurisdiction determines that a particular plan is invalid. But the General Assembly must pass the new plan on or before the thirtieth day after the order becomes final or the time for an appeal expires. Furthermore, this section requires that a substitute plan must remedy any legal defects that the Ohio Supreme Court or a court of competent jurisdiction identified, but the plan may not change any other parts of the previous plan. If the General Assembly fails to adopt a substitute plan on or before the thirty-day deadline, section 3(B)(2) requires the Ohio Redistricting Commission to reconstitute and reconvene to adopt a suitable plan. The commission then has thirty days from the General Assembly's prior deadline to adopt a plan that remedies the legal defects while leaving the remaining valid provisions unchanged.

In *Adams v. DeWine* (2022), the Ohio Supreme Court interpreted this section as recognizing that congressional plans that contain isolated defects may be subject to remediation by simply correcting the defects in the affected district or districts. But the court stated that:

> when a congressional-district plan contains systemic flaws such that constitutional defects in the drawing of some district boundaries have a consequential effect on the district boundaries of other contiguous districts, such a plan is incapable of being remediated with the surgical precision necessary to correct only isolated districts while leaving the rest of the plan intact.

On July 19, 2022, in Neiman v. LaRose (2022), the Ohio Supreme Court by a 4-3 vote held that the revised congressional redistricting plan adopted by the Commission on March 2, 2022, "unduly favors the Republican Party and disfavors the Democratic Party in violation of Article XIX, Section 1(C)(3)(a) . . . by packing Democratic voters into a few dense Democratic-leaning districts, thereby increasing the Republican vote share of the remaining districts." The court then ordered the General Assembly to pass a compliant congressional redistricting plan within 30 days. Finally, the court order provided that if the General Assembly fails to pass a compliant plan within that period, the Commission is required to adopt a compliant plan within 30 days.

This ruling came too late to affect the 2022 congressional election, but the litigation will continue with a focus on the 2024 congressional elections.

SCHEDULES TO THE OHIO CONSTITUTION

Schedules, though not a part of the constitution, include important information, such as the method of submitting amendments to the voters, the effective date of proposed amendments if adopted by the voters, and the effect of adopted amendments on existing law. The Ohio Supreme Court treats schedules as binding, see *State ex rel. Evans v. Dudley* (1853), and schedules can contain substantive provisions. For example, this was done in 1851 when the delegates to the Ohio Constitutional Convention of 1850–51 submitted a proposed amendment on liquor licensing as a schedule subject to a separate vote to avoid the risk that the voters would reject the entire constitution. The voters approved the new constitution but rejected the proposal on liquor licensing.

The schedule that accompanied the proposed 1912 amendments made clear that the requirement that constitutional amendments be adopted by a majority of votes cast in the election and not a simple majority vote on each proposed amendment was not applicable to amendments proposed by a constitutional convention.

Below are the schedules to the 1802 and 1851 Constitutions, as well as all schedules that accompanied amendments that the voters approved since 1851.

1802 CONSTITUTION

Section 1. That no evils or inconveniencies may arise, from the change of a territorial government to a permanent State government, it is declared by this convention, that all rights, suits actions, prosecutions, claims and contracts, both as it respects individuals and body corporate, shall continue, as if no change had taken place in the government.

Section 2. All fines, penalties and forfeitures, due and owing to the territory of the United States, northwest of the river Ohio, shall inure to the use of the State. All bonds executed to the Governor, or any other officer in his official capacity, in the territory, shall pass over to the Governor and other officers of the State, and their successors in office, for the use of the State, or by him or them to be respectively assigned over to the use of those concerned, as the case may be.

Section 3. The Governor, secretary and judges, and all other officers under the territorial government, shall continue in the exercise of the duties of their respective departments until the said officers are superseded under the authority of this constitution.

Section 4. All laws, and parts of laws, now in force in this territory, not inconsistent with this constitution, shall continue and remain in full effect, until repealed by the legislature, except so much of the act entitled, "An act regulating the admission and practice of attorneys and counsellors-at-law", and of the act made amendatory thereto, as related to the term of time which the applicant shall have studied law, his residence within the territory, and the term of time which he shall have practiced as an attorney-at-law, before he can be admitted to the degree of a counsellor-at-law.

Section 5. The Governor of the State shall make use of his private seal, until a State seal be procured.

Section 6. The President of the convention shall issue writs of election to the sheriffs of the several counties, requiring them to proceed to the election of a Governor, members of the General Assembly, sheriffs and coroners, at the respective election districts in each county, on the second Tuesday of January next; which election will be conducted in the manner prescribed by the existing election laws of the territory; and the members of the General Assembly, then elected, shall continue to exercise the duties of their respective offices, until the next annual or biennial election thereafter, as prescribed in this constitution, and no longer.

Section 7. Until the first enumeration shall be made, as directed in the second section the first article of the constitution, the county of Hamilton, shall be entitled to four Senators and eight Representatives; the county of Clermont, one Senator and two Representatives; the county of Adams, one Senator and three Representatives; the county of Ross, two Senators and four Representatives; the county of Fairfield, one Senator and two Representatives; the county of Washington, two Senators and three Representatives; the county of Belmont, one Senator and two Representatives; the county of Jefferson, two Senators and four Representatives, and the county of Trumbull, one Senator and two Representatives.

■ 1851 CONSTITUTION

Of prior laws. All laws of this state, in force on the first day of September one thousand eight hundred and fifty-one, not inconsistent with this constitution, shall continue in force, until amended, or repealed.

The first election of members of General Assembly. The first election for members of the General Assembly, under this constitution, shall be held on the second Tuesday of October, one thousand eight hundred and fifty-one

For state officers. The first election for governor, lieutenant governor, auditor, treasurer, and secretary of state and attorney general, shall be held on the second Tuesday of October, one thousand eight hundred and fifty-one. The persons, holding said offices on the first day of September, one thousand eight hundred and fifty-one, shall continue therein, until the second Monday of January, one thousand eight hundred and fifty-two.

For judges, clerks, etc. The first election for judges of the Supreme Court, courts of common pleas, and probate courts, and clerks of the courts of common pleas, shall be held on the second Tuesday of October, one thousand eight hundred and fifty-one, and the official term of said judges and clerks, so elected, shall commence on the second Monday of February, one thousand eight hundred and fifty-two. Judges and clerks of the courts of common pleas and Supreme Court, in office on the first day of September, one thousand eight hundred and fifty-one, shall continue in office with their present powers and duties, until the second Monday of February, one thousand eight hundred fifty-two. No suit or proceeding, pending in any of the courts of this state, shall be affected by the adoption of this constitution.

Officers to continue in office until the expiration of their terms. The register and receiver of the land office, directors of the penitentiary, directors of the benevolent institutions of the state, the state librarian, and all other officers, not otherwise provided for in this constitution in office on the first day of September, one thousand eight hundred and fifty-one, shall continue in office, until their terms expire, respectively, unless the General Assembly shall otherwise provide.

Certain courts. The superior and commercial courts of Cincinnati, and the superior court of Cleveland, shall remain, until otherwise provided by law, with their present powers and jurisdiction; and the judges and clerks of said courts, in office on the first day of September, one thousand eight hundred and fifty-one, shall continue in office, until the expiration of their terms of office, respectively, or, until otherwise provided by law; but neither of said courts shall continue after the second Monday of February, one thousand eight hundred and fifty-three; and no suits shall be commenced in said two first mentioned courts, after the second Monday of February, one thousand eight hundred and fifty-two, nor in said last mentioned court, after the second Monday in August, one thousand eight hundred and fifty-two; and all business in either of said courts, not disposed of within the time limited for their continuance as aforesaid, shall be transferred to the court of common pleas.

County and township officers. All county and township officers and justices of the peace, in office on the first day of September, one thousand eight hundred and fifty-one, shall continue in office until their terms expire, respectively,

Vacancies. Vacancies in office, occurring after the first day of September, one thousand eight hundred and fifty-one, shall be filled, as is now prescribed by law, and until officers are elected or appointed, and qualified, under this constitution.

When constitution shall take effect. This constitution shall take effect, on the first day of September, one thousand eight hundred and fifty-one.

Term of office. All officers shall continue in office, until their successors shall be chosen and qualified.

Transfer of suits, Supreme Court. Suits pending in the Supreme Court in bank, shall be transferred to the Supreme Court provided for in this constitution, and be proceeded in according to law.

Transfer of suits, district courts. The district courts shall, in their respective counties, be the successors of the present Supreme Court; and all suits, prosecutions, judgments, records, and proceedings, pending and remaining in said Supreme Court, in the several counties of any district, shall be transferred to the respective district courts of such counties, and be proceeded in, as though no change had been made in said Supreme Court.

Transfer of suits, courts of common pleas. The said courts of common pleas, shall be the successors of the present courts of common pleas in the several counties, except as to probate jurisdiction; and all suits, prosecutions, proceedings, records and judgments, pending or being in said last mentioned courts, except as aforesaid, shall be transferred to the courts of common pleas created by this constitution, and proceeded in, as though the same had been therein instituted.

Transfer of suits, probate courts. The probate courts provided for in this constitution, as to all matters within the jurisdiction conferred upon said courts, shall be the successors, in the several counties, of the present courts of common pleas; and the records, files, and papers, business and proceedings, appertaining to said jurisdiction, shall be transferred to said courts of probate, and be there proceeded in, according to law.

Judges and clerks, how elected, etc. Until otherwise provided by law, elections for judges and clerks shall be held, and the poll books returned, as is provided for governor, and the abstract therefrom, certified to the secretary of state, shall be by him opened, in the presence of the governor, who shall declare the result, and issue commissions to the persons elected.

Election returns, when sent. Where two or more counties are joined in a senatorial, representative, or judicial district, the returns of elections shall be sent to the county, having the largest population.

Constitution submitted to the electors of the state. The foregoing constitution shall be submitted to the electors of the state, at an election to be held on the third Tuesday of June, one thousand eight hundred and fifty-one, in the several election districts of this state. The ballots at such election shall be written or printed as follows: Those in favor of the constitution, "New Constitution, Yes;" those against the constitution, "New Constitution, No." The polls at said election shall be opened between the hours of eight and ten o'clock a.m., and closed at six o'clock p.m.; and the said election shall be conducted, and the returns thereof made and certified, to the secretary of state, as provided by law for annual elections of state and county officers. Within twenty days after such election, the secretary of state shall open the returns thereof, in the presence of the governor; and, if it shall appear that a majority of all the votes, cast at such election, are in favor of the constitution, the governor shall issue his proclamation, stating that fact, and said constitution shall be the constitution of the state of Ohio, and not otherwise.

Note: The result of this election, excluding the returns of two counties, Defiance and Auglaize, which were not received in the twenty days specified, was as follows:

"New Constitution, Yes"	125,564
"New Constitution, No"	109,276

Because a majority of all votes cast at this election were in favor of the new constitution, the Constitution of 1851 was adopted.

License to traffic in intoxicating liquors. At the time when the votes of the electors shall be taken for the adoption or rejection this constitution, the additional section, in the words following, to wit: "No license to traffic in intoxicating liquors shall hereafter be granted in this state; but the General Assembly may, by law, provide against evils resulting therefrom," shall be separately submitted to the electors for adoption or rejection, in form following, to wit: A separate ballot may be given by every elector and deposited in a separate box. Upon the ballots given for said separate amendment shall be written or printed, or partly written and partly printed, the words: "License to sell intoxicating liquors, Yes;" and upon the ballots given against said amendment, in like manner, the words: "License to sell intoxicating liquors, No." If, at the said election, a majority of all the votes given for and against said amendment, shall contain the words: "License to sell intoxicating liquors, No," then the said amendment shall be a separate section of article fifteen of the constitution.

Authors' Note: The election result:

"License to sell intoxicating liquors, Yes"	104,255
"License to sell intoxicating liquors, No"	113,237

Because a majority of votes on this amendment were "no" votes, under the strange voting procedure of this schedule, the proposed constitutional language barring the granting of licenses to traffic in intoxicating liquors was approved and became Article XV, section 9 of the 1851 Constitution.

Apportionment for House of Representatives. The apportionment of the House of Representatives, during the first decennial period under this constitution, shall be as follows:

The counties of Adams, Allen, Athens, Auglaize, Carroll, Champaign, Clark, Clinton, Crawford, Darke, Delaware, Erie, Fayette, Gallia, Geauga, Greene, Hancock, Harrison, Hocking, Holmes, Lake, Lawrence, Logan, Madison, Marion, Meigs, Morrow, Perry, Pickaway, Pike, Preble, Sandusky, Scioto, Shelby and Union, shall, severally, be entitled to one representative, in each session of the decennial period.

The counties of Franklin, Licking, Montgomery, and Stark, shall each be entitled to two representatives, in each session of the decennial period.

The counties of Ashland, Coshocton, Highland, Huron, Lorain, Mahoning, Medina, Miami, Portage, Seneca, Summit, and Warren, shall, severally, be entitled to one representative, in each session; and one additional representative in the fifth session of the decennial period.

The counties of Ashtabula, Brown, Butler, Clermont, Fairfield, Guernsey, Jefferson, Knox, Monroe, Morgan, Richland, Trumbull, Tuscarawas, and Washington, shall severally, be entitled to one representative, in each session; and two additional representatives, one in the third, and one in the fourth session of the decennial period.

The counties of Belmont, Columbiana, Ross and Wayne, shall, severally, be entitled to one representative, in each session; and three additional representatives, one in the first, one in the second, and one in the third session of the decennial period.

The county of Muskingum shall be entitled to two representatives, in each session; and one additional representative, in the fifth session, of the decennial period.

The county of Cuyahoga shall be entitled to two representatives, in each session; and two additional representatives, one in the third, and one in the fourth session, of the decennial period.

The county of Hamilton shall be entitled to seven representatives, in each session; and four additional representatives, one in the first, one in the second, one in the third, and one in the fourth session, of the decennial period.

The following counties, until they shall have acquired a sufficient population to entitle them to elect, separately, under the fourth section of the eleventh article, shall form districts in manner following, to wit: The counties of Jackson and Vinton, one district; the counties of Lucas and Fulton, one district; the counties of Wyandot and Hardin, one district; the counties of Mercer and Van Wert, one district; the counties of Paulding, Defiance, and Williams, one district; the counties of Putnam and Henry, one district; and the counties of Wood and Ottawa, one district; each of which districts shall be entitled to one representative, in every session of the decennial period.

■ 1912

General schedule. The several amendments passed and submitted by this convention when adopted at the election shall take effect on the first day of January,

1913, except as otherwise specifically provided by the schedule attached to any of said amendments. All laws then in force, not inconsistent therewith shall continue in force until amended or repealed; provided that all cases pending in the courts on the first day of January, 1913, shall be heard and tried in the same manner and by the same procedure as is now authorized by law. Any provision of the amendments passed and submitted by this convention and adopted by the electors, inconsistent with, or in conflict with, any provision of the present constitution, shall be held to prevail.

Method of submission. The several proposals duly passed by this convention shall be submitted to the electors as separate amendments to the constitution at a special election to be held on the third day of September, 1912. The several amendments shall be designated on the ballot by their proper article and section numbers and also by their approved descriptive titles and shall be printed on said ballot and consecutively numbered in the manner and form hereinafter set forth. The adoption of any amendment by its title shall have the effect of adopting the amendment in full as finally passed by the convention. Said special election shall be held pursuant to all provisions of law applicable thereto including special registration. Ballots shall be marked in accordance with instructions printed thereon. Challengers and witnesses shall be admitted to all polling places under such regulations as may be prescribed by the secretary of state. Within ten days after said election the boards of deputy state supervisors of elections of the several counties shall forward by mail in duplicate sealed certified abstracts of the votes cast on the several amendments, one to the secretary of state and one to the auditor of state at Columbus. Within five days thereafter such abstracts shall be opened and canvassed by the secretary of state and auditor of state in the presence of the governor who shall forthwith, by proclamation, declare the results of said election. Each amendment on which the number of affirmative votes shall exceed the number of negative votes shall become a part of the constitution.

Schedule to Article II, sections 1, 1a, 1b, 1c, 1d, 1e, 1f, and 1g. The foregoing amendment, if adopted by the electors shall take effect on October 1, 1912.

Schedule to Article IV, sections 1, 2, 3, 6, 7, 12, and 15. If the foregoing amendment shall be adopted by the electors, the judges of the courts of common pleas in office, or elected thereto prior to January first, 1913, shall hold their offices for the term for which they were elected and the additional judges provided for herein, shall be elected at the general election in the year 1914; each county shall continue as a part of its existing common pleas district and sub- division thereof, until one resident judge of the court of common pleas is elected and qualified therein.

Schedule to Article VI, sections 3 and 4. If the foregoing amendment be adopted by the electors it shall take effect ad become part of the constitution on the second Monday of July, 1913.

Schedule to Article XVIII, sections 1–14. If the foregoing amendment to the constitution be adopted by the electors and become a part of the constitution, it shall take effect on November 15th, 1912.

■ 1918

Schedule to Article XV, section 9. If the proposed amendment be adopted, it shall become section 9 of Article XV of the constitution, and it shall take effect on the 27th day of May of the year following the date of the election at which it is adopted, at which time original sections 9 and 9a of Article XV of the constitution and all statues inconsistent with the foregoing amendment shall be repealed.

■ 1929

Schedule to Article XII, sections 2 and 3. If the votes for the proposal shall exceed those against it, the amendment shall go into effect January 1, 1931, and original sections 2 and 3 of article XII of the constitution of the state of Ohio shall be repealed and annulled; but all levies for interest and sinking fund or retirement of bonds issued, or authorized prior to said date which are not subject to the statutory limitation of fifteen mills on the aggregate rate of taxation then in force, and all tax levies provided for by the conservancy act of Ohio and the sanitary district act of Ohio, as said laws are in force on said date, for the purposes of conservancy districts and sanitary districts organized prior to said date, and all tax levies for other purposes authorized by the General Assembly prior to said date or by vote of the electors of any political subdivision of the state, pursuant to laws in force on said date, to be made outside said statutory limitation for and during a period of years extending beyond said date, to be made outside said statutory limitation for and during a period of years extending beyond said date, or provided for by the charter of a municipal corporation pursuant to laws in force on said date, shall not be subject to the limitation of fifteen mills established by said amendment; and levies for interest and sinking fund or retirement of bonds issued or authorized prior to said date, shall be outside of said limitation to the extent required to equalize any reduction in the amount of taxable property available for such levies, or in the rate imposed upon such property, effected by laws thereafter passed.

■ 1931

Schedule to Article XII, sections 2 and 3. If the votes for the proposal shall exceed those against it, the amendment shall go into effect January 1, 1931, and original sections 2 and 3 of article XII of the constitution of the state of Ohio shall be repealed and annulled; but all levies for interest and sinking fund or retirement of bonds issued, or authorized prior to said date which are not subject to the statutory limitation of fifteen mills on the aggregate rate of taxation then in force, and all tax levies provided for by the conservancy act of Ohio and the sanitary district act of Ohio, as said laws are in force on said date, for the purposes of conservancy districts and sanitary districts organized prior to said date, and all tax levies for other purposes authorized by the General Assembly prior to said date or by vote of the electors of any political subdivision of the state, pursuant to laws in force on said date, to be made outside said statutory limitation for and during a period of years extending beyond said date, or provided for by the charter of a municipal corporation pursuant to laws in force on said date, shall not be subject to the limitation of fifteen mills established by said amendment; and levies for interest and sinking fund or retirement of bonds issued or authorized prior to said date, shall be outside of said limitation of the extent required to equalize any reduction in the amount of taxable property available for such levies, or in the rate by laws thereafter passed.

■ 1934

Schedule to Article XII, section 2. If the votes for the proposal shall exceed those against it, the amendment shall go into effect January 1, 1934, and existing Section 2 of Article XII of the Constitution of the state of Ohio shall be repealed and annulled, but the following exuberated levies shall not be subject to the limitation of one per cent established by such amendment: (1) All levies for interest and sinking fund or retirement of bonds issued or authorized prior to said date which are not subject to the present limitation of one and one-half per cent imposed by Section 2 of Article XII and the schedule thereto as approved by the electors of the state on November 5, 1929; (2) All tax levies provided for by the conservancy act of Ohio or the sanitary district act of Ohio, as said laws are in force on January 1, 1934, for the purpose of conservancy districts and sanitary districts organized prior to said date; (3) All tax levies authorized prior to said date by vote of the electors of any political subdivision of the state, pursuant to laws in force at the time of such vote, to be made for or during a period of years extending beyond January 1, 1934, which levies are outside of the present limitation of one and one-half per cent imposed by Section 2 of Article XII ad the schedule thereto as approved on November 5, 1929; and (4) All tax levies provided for by the charter of a municipal corporation pursuant to law and which were authorized prior to January 1, 1934, and are not subject to the present limitation of one and one-half per cent imposed by said section and schedule as approved on November 5, 1929.

■ 1953

Schedule to Article VI, section 4. If the vote for the proposal shall exceed those against it, the foregoing shall take immediate effect and existing section 4 of article

VI of the constitution shall be repealed and annulled. The superintendent of public instruction, in office when the foregoing amendment takes effect, shall continue therein until the superintendent of public institution for whom provision is made under the foregoing amendment shall have been appointed and shall have qualified.

1968

Schedule to Article IV, sections 1–14 and Article XI, sections 12 and 13. If adopted by a majority of the electors voting on this amendment, the amendment except paragraph (b) of the Schedule shall take effect January 10, 1970, and existing sections 1 and 2, and sections 3, 4, 6, 7, 8, 10, 12, and 14 of Article IV of the Constitution of Ohio shall be repealed from such effective date. Paragraph (b) of the Schedule and the repeal of sections 12 and 13 of Article XI adopted in 1851, shall become effective immediately upon the adoption of this amendment by the electors of this state. Upon the effective date of this amendment:

(A) Provision shall be made by law for the disposition of all pending cases in accordance with the procedural law in effect at the time of the effective date of this amendment.

(B) In accordance with the provisions of this article, the General Assembly shall enact such laws and the Supreme Court shall promulgate such rules as will give effect to the provisions herein.

(C) All laws and rules of court in existence upon the effective date of this amendment shall continue in effect until superseded or changed in the manner authorized by this amendment.

(D) All judges of the probate courts shall become judges of the courts of common pleas.

(E) Any judge who is holding office on December 31, 1969, and who would be eligible for re-election in 1970 for a term beginning in 1971 except for his age and the provisions of division (C) of Section 6, Article IV, shall be eligible nevertheless to be re-elected in 1970 for one additional term as judge of the same court.

1976

Schedule to Article III, sections lb and 16. Section lb of Article III authorizing the governor to assign duties in the executive department to the lieutenant governor and the repeal of section 16 of Article III shall not take effect until the second Monday in January, 1979.

Schedule to Article III, section 22. If, on the effective date of this amendment, section number 16 is already assigned to a section of Article III of the Constitution of Ohio, the secretary of state shall assign section number 22 to the section in Article III that would be numbered section 16 by this amendment, and such number shall be the official number of such section and shall be so published in any publication of the constitution and shall be cited and referred to by such number.

Schedule to Article XII, section 9. If, on the effective date of this amendment, section number 6 is already assigned to a section in Article XII that would be amended by this amendment to include a renumbering of the section from section 9 to section 6, and such number shall be the official number of such section and shall be so published in any publication of the constitution and shall be cited and referred to by such number.

■ 1982

Schedule to Article VIII, section 14. If, on the effective date of this amendment, section number 14 is already assigned to a section in Article VIII of the Constitution of Ohio, the Secretary of State shall assign section number 15 to the section in Article VIII that would be numbered section 14 by this amendment, and such number shall be the official number of such section and shall be so published in any publication of the Constitution and such section shall be cited and referred to by such number.

■ 1987

Schedule to Article XV, section 6. It is the intent of the General Assembly that the question of this proposed constitutional amendment shall be state ballot issue number one at the 1987 general election.

■ 1990

Schedule to Article VIII, section 16. If there is more than one question to be submitted to the electors throughout the state at the general election to be held on the first Tuesday after the first Monday in November, 1990, the Secretary of State shall place the question of the adoption of this amendment as the first such question on the ballot.

■ 1992

Schedule to Article II, section 2; Article III, section 2; and Article V, sections 8 and 9. If adopted by a majority of electors voting on this amendment, each provision of this amendment shall be deemed severable from the others, and a finding that a provision is invalid shall not affect the other provisions.

■ 1994

Schedule to Article IV, sections 2 and 3. Upon the adoption of the amendment to Sections 2 and 3 of Article IV of the Constitution of the State of Ohio, the General Assembly shall amend the Revised Code of Ohio to implement the direct appeals of death sentences to the Ohio Supreme Court.

The amendments to Sections 2 and 3 of Article IV of the Constitution of Ohio regarding the direct appeal of a sentence of death apply only to cases in which a sentence of death is imposed for an offense committed on or after January 1, 1995. A direct appeal of a sentence of death imposed for an offense committed prior to January 1, 1995, shall be taken in the same manner as if the amendment had not been adopted.

■ 1997

Schedule to Article I, section 9. Until the General Assembly enacts standards to determine whether a person who is charged with a felony where the proof is evident or the presumption great poses a substantial risk of serious physical harm to any person or to the community, bail or the denial of bail shall be determined as if the amendment of Section 9 of Article I of the Constitution of the State of Ohio had not been adopted.

■ 2015

Schedule to Article II, section 1e. Division (B)(1) of Section 1e of Article II of the Constitution of the State of Ohio, as amended by this proposal, does not apply to any provision of the Constitution of the State of Ohio in effect prior to the effective date of that amendment.

■ 2018

Schedule to Articles XI and XIX. If adopted by a majority of the electors voting on this proposal, the version of Section 1 of Article XI amended by this proposal and Sections 1, 2, and 3 of Article XIX of the Constitution of the State of Ohio enacted by this proposal take effect January 1, 2021, and the existing version of Section 1 of Article XI of the Constitution of the State of Ohio that is scheduled to take effect January 1, 2021, is repealed from that effective date.

APPENDIX A

Table of Votes on Holding Constitutional Conventions under the 1802 and 1851 Constitutions

Under Article XVI, section 3, of the 1851 Constitution, the question of whether to hold a constitutional convention is presented to the voters every twenty years. Owing to strong public support, the General Assembly submitted the question to the voters one year earlier in 1910. Table A lists the votes on whether to hold a constitutional convention and includes the pre-1851 rejection of a call for a constitutional convention in 1819 and the approval of one in 1849.

Table of Votes on Proposed Constitutional Conventions

Date of Election	Result	Vote for	Vote against
1802 Constitution			
10-12-1819	Failed	6,987	29,315
10-9-1849	Passed	145,698	51,167
1851 Constitution			
10-10-1871	Passed	267,618	104,231
11-3-1891	Failed	99,789	161,722
11-8-1910	Passed	693,263	67,718
11-8-1932	Failed	853,619	1,056,855
11-4-1952	Failed	1,020,235	1,977,313
11-7-1972	Failed	1,291,267	2,142,534
11-3-1992	Failed	1,672,373	2,660,270
11-6-2012	Failed	1,523,239	3,248,142

■ APPENDIX B

Table of Proposed Constitutional Amendments and Votes

Table B, Proposed Constitutional Amendments, was originally published in Thomas R. Swisher, ed., *Ohio Constitution Handbook* (Cleveland: Banks-Baldwin Law Publishing Co., 1990), 597, and also appears in Baldwin's *Ohio Revised Code Annotated Constitution of the State of Ohio, Table of Proposed Amendments to Ohio Constitution* (West Group, 2002) (hereinafter *West Table of Proposed Amendments*). The table has been updated and modified to include the vote totals, which (prior to 1912) are taken from Isaac F. Patterson, *The Constitutions of Ohio: Amendments and Proposed Amendments* (Cleveland: Arthur H. Clark Co., 1912), and (subsequently) from historical election data on file with the Ohio secretary of state. Table B is reprinted in this modified form with the permission of West Publishing, a Thomson business.

Abbreviations: GA = General Assembly; CC = constitutional convention; IP = initiative petition. Bracketed notes in superscript (e.g., [x]) following some of the entries are explained at the end of the table.

The asterisks (*) following the results of a number of amendments from 1857 through 1908 indicate that the amendment received a majority of votes cast in its favor but did not meet the constitutional requirement in effect at the time under Article XVI, section 1. Under that provision, an amendment proposed by the General Assembly had to receive a majority of votes cast in the election and not simply a majority of the votes cast on the proposed amendment. Of the twenty-six amendments that failed during this period, nineteen would have been adopted but for this supermajority requirement.

Appendix B Table of Proposed Constitutional Amendment and Votes

Date of Election	Proposed by	Subject	Art. & Sec. Affected	Result	Votes
10-13-1857	GA	Annual sessions of the General Assembly	II:25	Failed*	151,202 to 31,890
	GA	Changes to district courts	IV:5, 6	Failed*	156,646 to 30,039
	GA	Equal taxation for banks and individuals	XII:2–3	Failed*	160,470 to 20,609
	GA	Grant General Assembly greater control over corporations	XIII:1–2	Failed*	123,229 to 35,973
	GA	Single legislative districts	XI	Failed*	147,260 to 32,657
10-11-1859	GA	Annual sessions of the General Assembly	II:25	Failed*	101,178 to 75,394
10-8-1867	GA	Deny right to vote to union draft dodgers and deserters, and persons who fought for Confederacy and to repeal the provision limiting the vote to whites	V:1	Failed	216,987 to 255,340
8-18-1874	CC	Adopt new constitution to replace 1851 Constitution		Failed	102,885 to 250,169
	CC	Minority representation on Supreme Court and circuit courts		Failed	73,615 to 259,415
	CC	Aid to railroads		Failed	45,416 to 296,658
	CC	License of liquor traffic		Failed	172,252 to 179,538
10-12-1875	GA	Commission to help dispose of Supreme Court's case backlog	IV:22	Approved	339,076 to 98,561
	GA	Provide for tax on dogs	XII:7	Failed*	278,005 to 73,801
10-9-1877	GA	Reorganize court system	IV:1, 3, 5–8, 12, 14–16, 18; XI:12–13	Failed	54,896 to 268,478
10-14-1879	GA	Modify district court organization	IV:3, 5	Failed	159,630 to 163,639
	GA	Change time for the election of members of the General Assembly	II:2 [a]	Failed*	166,285 to 158,642
	GA	Change time for the election of state officers	III:l [a]	Failed*	162,728 to 155,257
	GA	Change time for the election of township trustees	X:4 [a]	Failed*	197,223 to 130,455

10-9-1883	GA	Replace district courts with circuit courts; modify organization of Supreme Court	IV:1–2, 5–6	Approved	400,919 to 144,335
	GA	Regulation and taxation of liquor traffic [b]	XV:9	Failed	99,238 to 288,605
	GA	Prohibit manufacture of and traffic in liquor [b]	XV:9	Failed*	323,129 to 226,595
10-13-1885	GA	Change election day to 1st Tuesday after 1st Monday in November for members of the General Assembly	II:2[c]	Approved	538,858 to 53,177
	GA	Change election day to 1st Tuesday after 1st Monday in November for state officers	III:1[c]	Approved	536,273 to 53,223
	GA	Change election day to 1st Tuesday after 1st Monday in November for county officers	X:2[c]	Approved	534,660 to 53,629
	GA	Provide three-year terms for township officers	X:4	Approved	469,113 to 59,929
11-5-1889	GA	Apportion General Assembly into single districts	XI:1–11	Failed	245,444 to 259,420
	GA	Re: taxing power of General Assembly	XII:2	Failed	245,438 to 273,268
	GA	Provide for biennial elections	II:25; III:18; IV:2, 6–7, 9, 11–13, 16; VIII:12;X:2, 4; XVI:3	Failed*	257,662 to 254,215
11-3-1891	GA	Taxation of real estate, and tangible and intangible personal property; exemptions	XII:2	Failed*	303,177 to 65,014
11-7-1893	GA	Apportion General Assembly into single districts	XI:1–11	Failed*	322,887 to 81,481
	GA	Taxation of real estate, and tangible and intangible personal property; exemptions	XII:2	Failed*	322,422 to 82,281
11-3-1903	GA	Classify cities as 1st, 2nd, and 3rd class by population	XIIL:6	Failed	21,664 to 32,110
	GA	Stockholders liable only for unpaid stock	XIII:3	Approved	751,783 to 29,383
	GA	Classification of property for tax purposes	XII:2	Failed*	326,622 to 43,563
	GA	Confer veto power on governor	11:16	Approved	458,681 to 338,317

(*continued*)

Appendix B Table of Proposed Constitutional Amendment and Votes —(Continued)

Date of Election	Proposed by	Subject	Art. & Sec. Affected	Result	Votes
	GA	Apportionment of General Assembly giving each county at least one representative	XI:2	Approved	757,505 to 26,497
11-7-1905	GA	Election of state and county officers in even years, other officers in odd years; terms; vacancies; incumbents	XVII:1–3	Approved	702,699 to 90,762
	GA	Taxation; state, local, and school bonds exempt	XII:2	Approved	655,508 to 139,062
11-3-1908	GA	Modify governor's veto power	II:16, 18	Failed*	323,770 to 61,754
	GA	When sessions of General Assembly to begin	II:25	Failed*	328,362 to 63,006
	GA	General Assembly's power to tax; classification of property for taxation	XII:2	Failed*	339,747 to 95,867
9-3-1912[d]	CC	Remove double liability of stockholders; inspection of private banks	XIII:3	Approved	377,272 to 156,688
	CC	Provide for land title registration and warranty	II:40	Approved	346,373 to 171,807
	CC	Investigations by each house of General Assembly	II:8	Approved	348,779 to 175,337
	CC	Mandate direct primaries for most elective offices	V:7	Approved	349,801 to 183,112
	CC	Provide for laws re: work hours, minimum wage, and comfort, health, safety, and general welfare of employees	II:34	Approved	353,588 to 189,728
	CC	Provide alternate procedure for removal of officials for misconduct	II:38	Approved	347,333 to 185,986
	CC	Prohibit limiting wrongful death damages	I:19a	Approved	355,605 to 195,216
	CC	Regulate expert testimony in criminal cases	II:39	Approved	336,987 to 185,458
	CC	Allow civil verdicts on concurrence of 3/4 of jury	1:5	Approved	345,686 to 203,953
	CC	Regulate state printing	XV:2	Approved	319,612 to 192,378
	CC	Governor to limit purpose of special session of General Assembly	III:8	Approved	319,100 to 192,130
	CC	Promote conservation of natural resources	II:36	Approved	318,192 to 191,893
	CC	Regulate insurance	VIII:6	Approved	321,388 to 196,628
	CC	Abolish prison contract labor	II:41	Approved	333,034 to 215,208

CC	Provide for workmen's compensation system	II:35	Approved	321,558 to 211,772
CC	Adopt civil service; competitive examinations; merit promotion	XV:10	Approved	306,767 to 204,580
CC	Require eight-hour day on public works	11:37	Approved	333,308 to 232,899
CC	Allow waiver of sovereign immunity	I:16	Approved	306,764 to 216,634
CC	Regulate corporations; sale of personal property	XIII:2	Approved	300,466 to 212,704
CC	Provide for municipal home rule	XVIII:1–14	Approved	301,861 to 215,120
CC	Organization of boards of education	VI:3	Approved	298,460 to 213,337
CC	License liquor traffic	XV:9	Approved	273,361 to 188,825
CC	Abolish board of public works	VIII:12	Approved	296,635 to 214,829
CC	Adopt initiative and referendum	11:1, la–lg	Approved	312,592 to 231,312
CC	Common pleas judge for each county	IV:3, 7, 12, 15	Approved	301,891 to 223,287
CC	Allow depositions in criminal cases and comment on defendant's failure to testify	I:10	Approved	291,717 to 227,547
CC	Schedule of effective dates	Schedules	Approved	275,062 to 213,979
CC	Permit mechanics' and materialmen's liens	II:33	Approved	278,582 to 242,385
CC	Modify governor's veto power	II:16	Approved	282,412 to 254,186
CC	Methods of amending constitution	XVI:1–3	Approved	271,827 to 246,687
CC	Reorganize court system; substitute courts of appeals for circuit courts	IV:1, 2, 6	Approved	264,922 to 244,375
CC	Taxation; state and local government bonds; inheritance, income, franchise, and severance taxes	XII:1, 2, 6–11	Approved	269,039 to 249,864
CC	Abolish justices of peace in certain cities	IV:9	Approved	264,832 to 252,936
CC	Superintendent of public instruction to replace commissioner of common schools	VI:4	Approved	256,615 to 251,946
CC	Regulate outdoor advertising	XV:11	Failed	261,361 to 262,440

(continued)

Appendix B Table of Proposed Constitutional Amendment and Votes —(Continued)

Date of Election	Proposed by	Subject	Art. & Sec. Affected	Result	Votes
	CC	Expand bonded debt limit for intercounty roads	VIII:1	Failed	272,564 to 274,582
	CC	Limit contempt proceedings and injunctions in labor cases	IV:21	Failed	240,896 to 257,302
	CC	Allow women to hold certain offices	XV:4	Failed	261,806 to 284,370
	CC	Delete word "white" from voter qualifications	V:1	Failed	242,735 to 265,693
	CC	Abolish capital punishment	I:9	Failed	258,706 to 303,246
	CC	Allow use of voting machines	V:2	Failed	242,342 to 288,652
	CC	Give women right to vote	V:l	Failed	249,420 to 336,875
11-4-1913	GA	Short ballot for state officers	III:1–3	Failed	239,126 to 461,555
	GA	Short ballot for county and township officers	X:l, 2	Failed	217,875 to 449,493
	GA	Exempt state and local bonds from taxation	XII:12	Failed	312,232 to 340,570
	GA	Women eligible to serve on boards or commissions affecting women and children	XV:4	Approved	435,222 to 255,036
	IP	Provide for smaller legislature	XI:1–5	Failed	240,237 to 418,114
11-3-1914	IP	Home rule re: liquor	XV:9a	Approved	559,872 to 547,254
	IP	Limit tax rate; classification of property for taxation	XIX:1–2	Failed	223,873 to 551,760
	IP	Give women right to vote	V:l	Failed	335,390 to 518,295
	IP	Prohibit manufacture, importation, and sale of alcoholic	XV:9	Failed	504,177 to 588,329
11-2-1915	IP	Prohibit manufacture and sale of alcoholic beverages	XV:9	Failed	484,969 to 540,377
	IP	Four-year elective terms for all county officers; retroactive re: incumbents	X:2	Failed	207,435 to 604,463
	IP	Limit elections on twice failed constitutional amendments	XVI:4	Failed	417,384 to 482,275
	GA	Exempt state and local bonds from taxation	XII:12	Failed	337,124 to 401,083

11-6-1917	IP	Prohibit manufacture and sale of intoxicating liquor	XI:9	Failed	522,590 to 588,382
11-5-1918	IP	Referendum; voters may approve/reject action of legislature ratifying any proposed amendment to U.S. Constitution	II:1	Approved	508,282 to 315,030
	IP	Prohibit manufacture and sale of alcoholic beverages	XV:9	Approved	463,354 to 437,895
	IP	General Assembly to classify property for taxation	XII:2	Approved [e]	336,616 to 304,399
	GA	General Assembly may provide against double taxation of real estate and mortgage or secured debt on real estate	XII:2	Approved [e]	479,420 to 371,176
11-4-1919	IP	Define the phrase "intoxicating liquor"	XV:1, 9	Failed	474,907 to 504,688
	IP	Repeal statewide prohibition	XV:9	Failed	454,933 to 496,876
	GA	Classification of property for taxation	XII:2	Failed	439,987 to 517,245
11-8-1921	GA	Provide for veterans' bonuses	VIII:2a	Approved	949,109 to 324,447
	GA	Reapportion General Assembly with twenty-six senate districts	XI:7	Failed	336,574 to 518,524
	GA	Authorize poll tax	XII:1	Failed	244,509 to 672,581
11-7-1922	IP	Permit low-alcohol (2.75%) beverages	XV:1, 9	Failed	719,050 to 908,522
	IP	Provide for debt limit for political subdivisions	VIII:13	Failed	499,203 to 691,471
	IP	Provide unvoted tax rate of fifteen millions; limit state tax rate to one	XII:1	Failed	475,740 to 720,237
11-6-1923	GA	Expand Industrial Commission's power re: workmen's compensation	11:35	Approved	588,851 to 528,572
	GA	Delete "white male" from voter qualifications	V:l	Approved	536,762 to 421,744
	GA	Authorize notice by publication of proposed constitutional amendments and laws	II:lg	Failed	351,513 to 493,786
11-3-1925	GA	Debt restrictions on political subdivisions	VIII:13	Failed	450,218 to 535,251
	GA	Taxation by uniform rule of real estate and tangible property except motor vehicles	XII:2	Failed	435,944 to 501,221

(*continued*)

Appendix B Table of Proposed Constitutional Amendment and Votes —(Continued)

Date of Election	Proposed by	Subject	Art. & Sec. Affected	Result	Votes
	GA	Four-year terms for state and county officers	III:2; X:2–3; XVII:2	Failed	325,451 to 543,183
8-10-1926	GA	Authorize municipalities to levy assessments for entire cost of public improvements	XVIII:11	Failed	234,754 to 352,301
11-2-1926	IP	Eliminate compulsory primaries	V:7–8	Failed	405,152 to 743,313
11-6-1928	IP	Revise judges' compensation	IV:14	Failed	704,248 to 1,197,324
11-5-1929	GA	Fifteen-million limit on unvoted real estate taxes	XIL2–3	Approved	710,538 to 510,874
11-4-1930	GA	Distribution of income and inheritance taxes	XII:9	Approved	930,914 to 574,017
11-3-1931	GA	Permit state to contract debts for welfare institutions	VIII:2b	Failed	487,459 to 766,057
11-7-1933	GA	Repeal of statewide prohibition	XV:9	Approved	1,250,923 to 578,035
	IP	Ten-million limit on unvoted real estate taxes	XII:2	Approved	979,061 to 661,151
	IP	Home rule for counties	IV:16; X:1–7	Approved	846,594 to 742,925
11-6-1934	IP	No taxation of motor vehicles on which license tax paid; restrictions on license use	XII:5a	Failed	825,157 to 883,373
	IP	Motor vehicle fuel taxes; use	XII:5b	Failed	760,589 to 859,525
11-3-1936	GA	Eliminate additional liability of stockholders of banking and other depository corporations	XIIL:3	Approved	1,078,170 to 824,968
	IP	Prohibit sales tax on food for consumption off premises	XII:12	Approved	1,585,327 to 719,966
11-8-1938	IP	Appoint instead of electing Supreme Court and court of appeals judges	IV:1, la-lg, 2, 6, 10, 13–15, 18	Failed	621,011 to 1,237,443
11-7-1939	GA	Changes re: state board of education	IV:4	Failed	747,545 to 1,137,054
	IP	Re: old age pensions	XII:13	Failed	464,670 to 1,546,207
	IP	Change requirements for initiative petitions	II:lh	Failed	406,612 to 1,485,919
11-3-1942	GA	Re: vacancies in judicial office	IV:13	Approved	954,704 to 448,981

11-7-1944	GA	Permit temporary or substitute judges in the Supreme Court	IV:2	Approved	1,429,635 to 611,276
	GA	Re: jurisdiction of courts of appeals	IV:6	Approved	1,279,216 to 633,813
11-4-1947	GA	Provide veterans' bonuses	VIII:2b	Approved	1,497,804 to 478,701
	GA	Six-year term for probate judges; delete requirement that compensation be paid from county treasury	IV:7; XVIT.2	Approved	855,106 to 692,061
	GA	Expand Sinking Fund Commission to include governor and treasurer of state	VIII.-8	Approved	782,158 to 762,129
	IP	Limit use of motor vehicle license and fuel taxes for road and related purposes	XII:5a	Approved	1,037,650 to 669,718
11-8-1949	GA	Permit more than one probate judge per county	IV:7	Failed	874,291 to 876,647
	IP	Adopt office-type ballot	V:2a	Approved	1,007,693 to 750,206
11-6-1951	GA	Permit more than one probate judge per county	IV:7	Approved	875,083 to 696,672
11-3-1953	GA	Authorize bond issue for highway system	VIII:2c	Approved	1,035,869 to 676,496
	GA	Create state board of education with power to appoint superintendent of public instruction	VI:4	Approved	913,134 to 693,624
	GA	Delete "white" re: males eligible or required to serve in state militia	IX:1	Approved	905,059 to 650,567
	GA	Eliminate conflicts with U.S. Constitution	11:1, 27	Approved	1,004,862 to 405,210
	GA	Eliminate obsolete provisions re: eligibility of women for office	XV:4	Approved	1,092,268 to 500,380
	GA	Adjusted compensation for World War II veterans	VIII:2a	Approved	984,014 to 616,113
	GA	Repeal provision for electing militia officers	IX:2	Approved	755,725 to 622,245
	GA	Repeal obsolete provisions re: 1851 commission to modernize court procedure	XIV:1–3	Approved	789,511 to 541,477
	GA	Repeal obsolete provision re: incumbents in office in 1905	XVII:3	Approved	835,195 to 493,099
11-2-1954	GA	Four-year terms for governor, lieutenant governor, attorney general, and secretary of state; limit governor to two successive terms	III:2; XVII:1–2	Approved	1,165,650 to 933,716

(*continued*)

Appendix B Table of Proposed Constitutional Amendment and Votes —(Continued)

Date of Election	Proposed by	Subject	Art. & Sec. Affected	Result	Votes
	GA	Four-year terms for senators and representatives	XI:1, 3, 6, 9–11	Failed	945,373 to 1,081,099
11-8-1955	GA	Authorize bond issue for construction program for public buildings	VIII:2e	Approved	1,154,976 to 909,030
	GA	Permit officer's compensation to be changed during term	11:20	Failed	793,384 to 1,142,738
	GA	Permit judge's compensation to be changed during term	IV:14	Failed	849,677 to 1,107,646
11-6-1956	GA	Korean veterans' bonuses	VIII:2d	Approved	2,202,510 to 889,245
	GA	Four-year terms for state senators	11:2; XI:1, 6, 9–11	Approved	1,636,449 to 1,214,643
11-5-1957	GA	Permit appointment to state offices of persons not qualified as electors	XV:4	Failed	696,372 to 1,040,638
	GA	Allow new Ohio residents to vote for president and vice president	V:l	Approved	1.072,396 to 658,244
	GA	Permit adoption of county charters	X:3	Approved	832,912 to 799,094
11-4-1958	GA	Permit county voters to form metropolitan federations	X:5	Failed	1,108,383 to 1,410,277
	IP	Forbid closed-shop union contracts (so-called right to work amendment)	I:la	Failed	1,160,324 to 2,001,512
11-3-1959	GA	Remove limitation on extraterritorial sale of water and sewer services by municipalities	XVIII:6	Approved	1,085,378 to 775,610
	GA	Permit General Assembly to increase number of court of appeals judges in districts where needed	IV:6	Approved	1,028,914 to 809,957
11-7-1961	GA	Change method of filling vacancies in General Assembly	11:2	Approved	1,251,105 to 650,064
	GA	Continuity of state government in case of attack	11:42	Approved	1,394,429 to 516,992
	GA	Increase militia age limits; calling militia in disaster; conform to federal law	IX:1, 3–4	Approved	947,130 to 944,705
	GA	Provide for advice and consent of Senate re: appointments to office	111:21	Approved	1,168,831 to 642,512
11-6-1962	IP	Limit state's power re: Sunday closing laws	1:21	Failed	1,274,792 to 1,697,433
11-5-1963	GA	Authorize bond issue for public improvements	VIII:2f	Approved	1,397,971 to 922,687

5-5-1964	GA	Authorize bond issue for highways	VIII:2g	Approved	1,011,817 to 538,684
5-4-1965	GA	Guarantee college loans for Ohio residents	VI:5	Approved	847,927 to 438,945
	GA	Authorize bond issue for state development	VIII:2h	Approved	715,642 to 548,557
	GA	Revise apportionment of Ohio House	XI:1, 3–5, 8, 10–11	Failed	595,288 to 681,283
	GA	Guarantee loans for industrial development	VIII:13	Approved	711,031 to 542,802
11-2-1965	GA	Authorize same judge to serve more than one court in counties under 40,000	IV:23	Approved	1,194,966 to 1,073,671
	GA	Create urban service authority	X:5–6	Failed	892,657 to 1,346,597
5-2-1967	GA	Create Ohio Bond Commission	VIII:21	Failed	508,364 to 1,022,078
	GA	Change apportionment of Ohio House and Senate	II:3; XI:1–10	Failed	699,021 to 850,068
11-7-1967	GA	Apportion Ohio House and Senate into single-member districts	II:2–3; XI:1–15	Approved	1,315,736 to 908,010
5-7-1968	GA	Disposition of school and ministerial lands trust funds	VI:	Approved	847,861 to 695,368
	GA	Filling vacancies in Ohio House	II:11	Approved	1,020,500 to 487,938
	GA	Revise administration and organization of Ohio court system (so-called Modern Courts Amendment)	IV:l-8, 10, 12, 14; XI:12–13	Approved	925,481 to 556,530
11-5-1968	GA	Authorize bond issue for highways and other capital improvements	VIII:2i	Approved	1,732,512 to 1,550,959
	GA	Taxation; homestead exemption	XII:2	Failed	1,382,016 to 1,825,615
11-4-1969	GA	Lower voting age from twenty-one to nineteen	V:l	Failed	1,226,592 to 1,274,334
	GA	Dispense with short-term elections to fill vacancies	III:18; XVII:2	Approved	1,432,960 to 795,813
11-3-1970	GA	Real estate tax homestead reduction for residents sixty-five and older	XII:2	Approved	2,115,557 to 711,761
	GA	Reduce voter residence requirement from one year to six months	V:l	Approved	1,702,600 to 1,073,058
	GA	Permit notice by publication instead of mail of proposed municipal charter amendments	XVIII:9	Approved	1,326,818 to 1,212,814
11-2-1971	GA	Require notice by publication of constitutional amendments and laws proposed by initiative and referendum	II:lg	Approved	1,645,961 to 900,549

(*continued*)

Appendix B Table of Proposed Constitutional Amendment and Votes —(Continued)

Date of Election	Proposed by	Subject	Art. & Sec. Affected	Result	Votes
11-7-1972	IP	Re: levy or increase in income tax (except municipal income tax) without voter approval	XII:8	Failed	1,164,653 to 2,571,516
5-8-1973	GA	Authorize state lottery	XV:6	Approved	973,956 to 547,655
	GA	Allow taking before payment in appropriation of property for water and sewer purposes	I:19	Failed	405,035 to 993,245
	GA	Repeal disqualification from office for embezzling public funds; delete accounting before taking legislative seat	II:5	Failed	530,232 to 848,743
	GA	Repeal provision for commission to help dispose of Supreme Court's case backlog	IV:22	Failed	563,919 to 692,623
	GA	Method of amending Supreme Court rules of practice and procedure	IV:5	Failed	580,106 to 679,223
	GA	Re: compensation of judges	IV:6	Failed	646,384 to 677,787
	GA	Revise organization, administration and procedures of General Assembly	II:4, 6–9, 11, 14–19, 25	Approved	680,870 to 572,980
11-6-1973	GA	Tax valuation of farmland according to agricultural use	II:36	Approved	1,810,630 to 567,189
	GA	Authorize General Assembly to provide for amount of income exempt from taxation	XII:8	Approved	1,299,882 to 883,123
	GA	Re: court organization and administration	IV:1, 4–6	Approved	1,317,379 to 778,466
	GA	Vietnam veterans' bonuses	VIII:2j	Approved	1,650,120 to 647,629
5-7-1974	GA	Re: compensation of public officers and legislators	II:20, 31	Failed	611,726 to 747,518
	GA	Allow compensation increases for public officers with more than two years remaining in term	II:20a	Failed	365,921 to 992,978
	GA	Preparing ballot language and informing voters re: proposed constitutional amendments	XVI:1	Approved	964,885 to 376,022

11-5-1974	GA	Real estate tax: homestead reduction for disabled	XII:2	Approved	2,266,355 to 492,813
	GA	Repeal requirement that governor appoint public works superintendent for one-year term	VIII:12	Approved	1,463,408 to 995,748
	GA	Re: industrial development revenue bonds and loan guarantee programs	VIII:13	Approved	1,613,444 to 882,778
11-4-1975	IP	Authorize tax incentives to industrial plants	XII:13	Failed	573,874 to 2,164,957
	IP	Authorize bond issue for highway purposes, payable from gas tax, other highway funds, and general revenue	VIII:2k	Failed	439,041 to 2,304,854
	IP	Re: providing state, county, or municipal assistance for housing and healthcare	VIII:14	Failed	869,437 to 1,882,454
	IP	Authorize bonds for capital improvements for political subdivisions, payable from increased sales and use taxes and general revenue	VIII:21	Failed	487,326 to 2,219,093
	GA	Tax valuation of recreational land	II:36a	Failed	1,014,425 to 1,539,423
	GA	Give candidates reasonably equal treatment on ballot, by name rotation or otherwise	V:2a	Approved	1,619,219 to 915,599
	GA	Voters to elect delegates to national party conventions	V:7	Approved	1,653,931 to 906,156
	GA	State or subdivisions or may lend credit to reorganize state rail system; tax reduction for railroad property	VIII:14	Failed	871,726 to 1,614,597
	GA	Permit charitable bingo	XV:6	Approved	1,405,453 to 1,205,009
6-8-1976	GA	Require joint election of governor and lieutenant governor; revise lieutenant governor's duties	III:1a, lb, 16; V:2a	Approved	1,085,175 to 689,244
	GA	Provide rail transportation services	VIII:14	Failed	775,697 to 953,322
	GA	Authorize bonds for conservation of energy and energy resources	VIII:13	Failed	819,424 to 833,454
	GA	Re: qualifications of electors; remove unconstitutional and unnecessary language	V:1, 3–5	Approved	975,916 to 743,060

(*continued*)

Appendix B Table of Proposed Constitutional Amendment and Votes —(Continued)

Date of Election	Proposed by	Subject	Art. & Sec. Affected	Result	Votes
	GA	Re: elections, terms of office, and vacancies; remove unnecessary language	XVII:1–2	Approved	954,446 to 668,159
	GA	Permit political subdivisions to pay debt from sources other than tax levies; specify property tax limitations	XIL:7, 11	Failed	675,012 to 890,896
	GA	Require at least 50 percent of estate taxes to be returned to political subdivisions	XII:4, 9	Approved	951,310 to 699,823
	GA	Consolidate provisions for imposing taxes; clarify language	XII:3, 7–8, 10, 12	Approved	918,450 to 712,489
11-2-1976	IP	Limit rates for gas and electricity furnished to residential consumers	XIX	Failed	1,247,388 to 2,334,816
	IP	Representation of residential consumers re: utility regulatory actions	XX	Failed	1,092,781 to 2,557,265
	IP	Procedures for legislative hearings and approval of safety features for nuclear power plants	XV:11	Failed	1,150,360 to 2,462,000
	IP	Simplify initiative and referendum procedures	II:1, la–lg; XIV	Failed	1,175,410 to 2,407,960
	GA	Succession in case of disability or vacancy in office of governor or lieutenant governor	III:15–17	Approved	2,388,184 to 1,048,967
	GA	Repeal obsolete provisions on public printing, dueling, and bureau of statistics	XV:2, 5, 8	Approved	2,284,178 to 1,129,165
	GA	Re: declaration of election results for state officers at next regular General Assembly session	III:3–4	Approved	2,297,422 to 1,103,822
11-8-1977	IP	Person entitled to vote if registered for thirty days; elector failing to vote at least once in four years must reregister	V:l	Approved	1,964,361 to 1,225,852
	IP	Prohibit leghold or other traps causing prolonged suffering	XIX	Failed	1,169,068 to 2,027,642
	GA	Authorize state and political subdivisions to lend aid and credit and issue bonds for housing	VIII:14	Failed	1,120,885 to 1,773,779
	GA	Revise limitations on state debt	VIII:1, 2, 2b–2h, 3, 7, 9–10; XIL:6	Failed	759,327 to 1,999,791

6-6-1978	GA	Ballot Board to write language for state issues; advertising proposals; initiative and referendum petitions	II:lg	Approved	720,661 to 379,067
11-7-1978	GA	Modify procedures to adopt, amend, or repeal county charter	X:4	Approved	1,297,846 to 1,039,259
	GA	General Assembly to regulate prison labor; remove constitutional restrictions on sale of prison-made goods	II:41	Approved	1,281,941 to 1,083,814
6-3-1980	GA	Authorize public financing and operation of electric utilities through nonprofit corporations	VIII:14	Failed	793,256 to 1,124,596
	GA	State and subdivisions may borrow money to subsidize private, low cost housing	VIII:14 or l5	Failed	797,020 to 1,137,028
	GA	Authorize bond issue for highway improvements	VIII:2k	Failed	815,011 to 1,084,438
	GA	Change method for delivering proposed municipal or county charters or amendments to voters	X:4; XVIII:8	Failed	868,199 to 956,204
11-4-1980	GA	Authorize General Assembly to classify real property for taxation	XII:2a	Approved	1,973,344 to
11-3-1981	IP	Authorize private companies to sell workers' compensation insurance	11:35	Failed	572,227 to 3,000,028
	IP	Change apportionment methods for General Assembly and congressional districts	II:2; XI	Failed	1,093,485 to 1,513,502
11-2-1982	GA	Authorize bonds to subsidize low-cost housing	VIII:14	Approved	1,827,453 to 1,356,336
	GA	High speed rail system financed by 1 percent sales tax	VIII:14	Failed	708,605 to 2,420,593
	IP	Members of Public Utilities Commission to be elected; public financing of campaigns	XIX	Failed	1,053,274 to 2,175,893
11-8-1983	IP	Raise drinking age to twenty-one	XV:11	Failed	1,386,959 to 1,965,469
	IP	Require 3/5 majority of General Assembly to raise taxes	II:15	Failed	1,354,320 to 1,967,129
	IP	Repeal all taxes approved since 1982	XII:3a	Failed	1,452,061 to 1,883,270
11-5-1985	GA	Authorize bond issue to finance coal research	VIII:15	Approved	1,439,344 to 807,647
11-3-1987	GA	Entire net proceeds of state lottery to be used for support of education	XV:6	Approved	1,984,905 to 564,421

(*continued*)

Appendix B Table of Proposed Constitutional Amendment and Votes —(Continued)

Date of Election	Proposed by	Subject	Art. & Sec. Affected	Result	Votes
	GA	Permit state to finance local governments to improve roads, water, sewer, and waste collection and treatment facilities	VIII:2k	Approved	1,674,913 to 689,383
	IP	Appoint instead of elect Supreme Court and court of appeals judges	IV:6, 7, 13	Failed	878,683 to 1,600,588
11-7-1989	GA	Method for filling vacancy in office of lieutenant governor	III:17a	Approved	1,641,719 to 873,114
11-6-1990	GA	Authorize public financial support for low-cost housing	VIII:16	Approved	1,705,528 to 1,517,466
	GA	Extend homestead exemption to surviving spouses	XII:2	Approved	2,967,935 to 372,950
	IP	License casino gambling with voter approval	XV:6	Failed	1,270,387 to 2,098,725
11-3-1992	IP	Terra limits for state senators and representatives	II:2; V:9	Approved	2,982,285 to 1,378,009
	IP	Term limits for state executive branch officers other than governor	III:2; V:9	Approved	3,028,288 to 1,349,244
	IP	Term limits for U.S. senators and representatives	V:8;V:9 [f]	Approved	2,897,123 to 1,476,461
11-2-1993	GA	Authorize bond issue for capital improvements for parks	VIII:21	Approved	1,547,841 to 1.008.172
11-8-1994	GA	Protect rights of crime victims	I:10a	Approved	2,447,260 to 704,650
	GA	Eliminate intermediate appeal and provide for direct appeal to Supreme Court in death penalty cases	IV:2–3	Approved	2,199,791 to 936,323
	GA	Protect viability of prepaid tuition program and prevent federal taxation of program income	VI:6	Approved	1,816,087 to 1,191,116
	IP	Repeal soft drink excise tax	XII:13	Approved	2,228,874 to 1,126,728
11-7-1995	GA	Limit unrestricted power of governor to commute sentences	III:11	Approved	1,816,213 to 742,590
	GA	Public works and highways; issuance of obligations	VIII:2m	Approved	1,408,834 to 865,698
11-5-1996	IP	Allow river boat casino gambling	XV:6	Failed	1,639,955 to 2,659,076
11-4-1997	GA	Denial of bail to persons charged with certain felonies	1:9	Approved	2,168,949 to 803,658
5-5-1998	GA	Authorize the state to issue bonds for school facilities	VIII:2n, 17	Failed [g]	714,823 to 1,101,625

11-2-1999	GA	Authorize the state to issue bonds for school facilities	VIII:2n, 17	Approved [g]	1,285,277 to 828,426
11-7-2000	GA	Issuance of bonds for environmental conservation	VIII:2o	Approved	2,196,068 to 1,628,022
11-5-2002	IP	Treatment in lieu of incarceration for certain drug offenders	IV:24	Failed	1,012,682 to 2,048,770
11-4-2003	GA	Authorize the state to issue bonds for science and technology	VII:2p	Failed	1,235,323 to 1,195,706
11-4-2004	IP	Ban on same-sex marriage, civil unions	XV:11	Approved	3,329,335 to 2,065,462
11-8-2005	GA	Create jobs and stimulate economic growth in Ohio	VIII:2p	Approved	1,512,669 to 1,282,571
	IP	Expand to all Ohio registered voters the option to vote up to thirty-five days prior to election day by mail or in person at the appropriate local board of elections	XVII:6	Failed	1,065,109 to 1,840,658
	IP	Restore confidence, level the playing field, and reduce the influence of big money contributors in politics by significantly limiting campaign contributions to statewide and state legislative candidates and political parties	XVII:5	Failed	955,334 to 1,927,502
	IP	Restore competitiveness to congressional and state legislative races in Ohio.	XI	Failed	871,898 to 2,005,952
	IP	Create a bipartisan and independent state board of elections supervisors to administer elections similar to the county boards of elections.	XVII:4	Failed	854,918 to 2,001,983
11-7-2006	IP	Raise the state minimum wage	II:34a	Approved	2,205,850 to 1,687,996
	IP	Provide moneys for scholarships/education funding by permitting limited gaming.	XV:12	Failed	1,753,452 to 2,286,840
	IP	Provide a smoking ban in enclosed areas with certain exceptions.	XV:12	Failed	1,450,164 to 2,590,448
11-4-2008	GA	Provide for earlier filing deadlines for statewide ballot issues	II:1a, 1b, 1c, 1g	Approved	3,261,912 to 1,489,311
	GA	Authorize the state to issue bonds to continue the Clear Ohio program for environmental revitalization and conservation	VIII:2q	Approved	3,418,883 to 1,530,843

(*continued*)

Appendix B Table of Proposed Constitutional Amendment and Votes —(Continued)

Date of Election	Proposed by	Subject	Art. & Sec. Affected	Result	Votes
	GA	Protect private property rights in ground water, lakes, and other watercourses	I:19b	Approved	3,485,895 to 1,359,697
	IP	For a casino near Wilmington in Southwest Ohio and distribute to all Ohio counties a tax on the casino	XV:6a	Failed	1,981,490 to 3,352,931
11-3-2009	GA	Authorize the state to issue bonds to provide compensation to the veterans of the Persian Gulf, Afghanistan, and Iraq conflicts	VIII:2r	Approved	2,277,479 to 876,498
	GA	Create the Ohio Livestock Care Standards Board	XIV:1	Approved	2,020,804 to 1,148,519
	IP	Amend the constitution to allow for one casino each in Cincinnati, Cleveland, Columbus, and Toledo and distribute to all Ohio counties a tax on the casinos	XV:6	Approved	1,713,255 to 1,519,605
5-4-2010	GA	Extend the Ohio Third Frontier Program by authorizing the issuance of additional general obligation bonds to promote economic growth	VIII:2p	Approved	1,050,265 to 650,988
	GA	Change the location of the Columbus casino facility authorized by previous statewide vote	XV:6	Approved	1,154,504 to 534,013
11-8-2011	GA	Increase the age limit for judicial office, to eliminate the authority of the General Assembly to create courts of conciliation and supreme court commissions	IV:6, 19, 22	Failed	1,273,536 to 2,080,207
	IP	Freedom to choose healthcare	Add I:21	Approved	2,268,470 to 1,190,385
11-6-2012	IP	Ohio Citizens Independent Redistricting Commission amendment	Art. XI	Failed	1,800,073 to 3,088.353
5-6-2014	GA	Capital improvements—general obligation bonds	VIII:2s	Approved	797,207 to 427,273
11-3-2015	GA	Ohio legislative redistricting reform	Art XI	Approved	2,073,563 to 827,971
	GA	Restrict special interest amendments to the Ohio Constitution	II:1e	Approved	1,587,060 to 1,489,703
	IP	Marijuana Legalization Amendment	XV:12	Failed	1,122,386 to 2,003,641

11-7-2017	IP	Rights for crime victims	Art. I:10a	Approved	1,921,172 to 404,957
5-8-2018	GA	Congressional Redistricting Procedures Amendment	XI:1; XIX:1, 2, 3	Approved	1,178,468 to 395,088
11-6-2018	IP	Reduce penalties for crimes of obtaining, possessing, and using illegal drugs	XV:12	Failed	1,623,933 to 2,769,140

NOTES TO APPENDIX B

a. These three amendments proposed in 1879 are not listed in Swisher, *Ohio Constitution Handbook*, 597 or in the *West Table of Proposed Amendments*, but they are included in Patterson, *The Constitutions of Ohio*, 245–46.

b. The *West Table of Proposed Amendments* and the Swisher, *Ohio Constitution Handbook* do not include either of these amendments proposed in 1883. But see Patterson, *The Ohio Constitutions*, 249–50.

c. The *West Table of Proposed Amendments* and the Swisher, *Ohio Constitution Handbook* list these three amendments proposed in 1885 as a single amendment, but Patterson lists them as a single amendment submitted as three separate propositions. See Patterson, *The Ohio Constitutions*, 254. The above table lists them separately since each was subject to a separate vote.

d. The above table lists the proposed amendments resulting from the 1912 Convention in order of the percentage of votes cast in favor of the amendment at the September 3, 1912, election. The amendment removing double liability for stockholders is listed first as 71 percent of the electorate voted in favor of its adoption. The amendment on women's suffrage is listed last since it received only a 43 percent favorable vote.

e. The voters adopted both of the proposed 1918 amendments to Article XII, section 2, and the table lists both as having been adopted. However, the Ohio Supreme Court held that the amendment proposed by the General Assembly would take effect over the conflicting amendment proposed by initiative petition because, pursuant to Article II, section lb, the former received a larger number of affirmative votes. See *State ex rel. Greenlund v. Fulton* (1919).

f. The 1992 amendment establishing term limits for U.S. senators and representatives from Ohio never went into effect because the U.S. Supreme Court in *U.S. Term Limits, Inc. v. Thornton* (1995) held unconstitutional state limitations on the terms for U.S. senators and representatives. This decision, however, did not address term limits for state officials, and term limits for state senators, state representatives, and state executive branch officers remain in effect.

g. The *West Table of Proposed Amendments* lists two separate amendments in 1998 and 1999 on school financing. The *West Table* divides each year's amendment into two parts, one dealing with facilities for schools and institutions of higher education, Article VIII, section 2n, and one dealing with limitations on the debt issued by the state, Article VIII, section 17. The above table lists each year's proposed amendments as single proposals for the years 1998 and 1999, because only one amendment was submitted to the voters each year.

■ BIBLIOGRAPHICAL ESSAY AND SELECTED BIBLIOGRAPHY

Constitutional Texts and Convention Proceedings

The Ohio Constitution of 1802 and the Ohio Constitution of 1851, as originally adopted, are in Swindler's multivolume *Sources and Documents of United States Constitutions* and in Patterson's *The Constitutions of Ohio: Amendments and Proposed Amendments.* Patterson's book, published in 1912 on the eve of Ohio's fourth constitutional convention, also includes the proposed constitution of 1874, which the voters rejected. The 1802 Constitution, the Northwest Ordinance, the 1802 Enabling Act, and the journal of first constitutional convention are all in Ryan's "From Charter to Constitution," a 1897 compilation of fundamental documents published in the *Ohio Archaeological and Historical Quarterly,* one of the precursors to *Ohio History.*

The Ohio Constitutions of 1802 and 1851, the journal of Ohio's first constitutional convention, and the proceedings and debates of the 1850–51 Convention, the 1873–74 Convention, and the 1912 Convention, as described below, are available online in searchable formats.

General History

There are a number of excellent general sources on Ohio history. Roseboom and Weisenberger's *A History of Ohio,* first published in 1934 and in a second edition in 1953, is the best one-volume state history. It covers the history of the state from the first Native Americans and contains a series of exceptional bibliographic essays. Wittke's six-volume work, *The History of the State of Ohio,* which includes volumes by Bond, Roseboom, and Utter, is the most comprehensive treatment of Ohio history through the 1930s. For other general histories of Ohio, see Randall and Ryan's five-volume *History of Ohio* published in 1912 and Galbreath's five-volume *History of Ohio* published in 1925. All three of these multivolume histories include chapters or portions of chapters on the Northwest Ordinance, the movement to statehood, and the state's constitutional conventions.

For works that focus on Ohio's early history, see Chaddock's *Ohio before 1850,* Downes' *Frontier Ohio,* Hurt's *The Ohio Frontier, Crucible of the Old Northwest,* and Smith's *An Ohio Reader: 1750 to the Civil War.* Downes' *Frontier Ohio* is especially strong on the people and events leading to Ohio's admission into the union. Two important early nineteenth-century histories are Chase's "A Preliminary Sketch of the History of Ohio" in his statutory compilation,

Statutes of Ohio and the Northwestern Territory and Atwater's *History of the State of Ohio,* the first book on Ohio history. Regarding Ohio's admission into the union and the controversy over the date of admission, see Pershing's "The Admission of Ohio to the Union." The political and ideological history of Ohio from 1780 to 1825 is covered in Cayton's *The Frontier Republic,* and the early history of political parties is examined in Ratcliffe's "The Experience of Revolution and the Beginning of Party Politics in Ohio."

For biographies on important figures surrounding the movement for statehood, see Cole's *Thomas Worthington,* Sears' *Thomas Worthington: Father of Ohio Statehood,* Julia Perkins Cutler's *Life and Times of Ephraim Cutler,* Gilmore's *Life of Edward Tiffin,* David Mead Massie's *Nathaniel Massie,* West's "Arthur St. Clair," and Smith's introduction in *The St. Clair Papers.* For an interesting article on the dismissal of Arthur St. Clair as territorial governor, see Downes' "Thomas Jefferson and the Removal of Governor St. Clair in 1802." For biographical sketches of Ohio's early political leaders, see Milligan's *Ohio's Founding Fathers.*

For a review of the development of the state's system of canals and other internal improvements, the financing of which contributed to the calling of the second constitutional convention, see Bogart's *Internal Improvements and State Debt in Ohio,* Haggerty et al.'s *History of the Ohio Canals,* and Scheiber's *Ohio Canal Era: A Case Study.* And for a review of the role of Rufus P. Ranney, a leading figure at the 1850–51 Convention, see Gold's *The Jacksonian Conservatism of Rufus P. Ranney.*

For a comprehensive history of the Progressive movement in Ohio and its role in the calling of Ohio's fourth constitutional convention and the convention itself, see Hoyt Landon Warner's *Progressivism in Ohio 1897–1917.*

The foremost journal focusing on the history of Ohio is *Ohio History,* which was first published in 1887 and is the scholarly journal of the Ohio Historical Society. Originally published as the *Ohio Archaeological and Historical Quarterly* (1887–1954; vols. 1–43), it was renamed *The Ohio State Archaeological and Historical Quarterly* (1935–54; vols. 44–63) and *The Ohio Historical Quarterly* (1955–61; vols. 64–70) before finally settling on *Ohio History* in 1962 with volume 71. No issues were published from 2004 to 2007, and in 2007 (with volume 114) the journal was transferred to Kent State University Press. It is now an online, open access publication available back to 2007 on the Kent State University Press website, and from 1887 to 2003 on the Ohio History website. (See online resources below.) The references in this bibliography are to the name the journal used when the relevant article was published.

Constitutional and Legal History and Analysis

Important sources of information on the Ohio Constitution include Swisher's *Ohio Constitution Handbook,* the Ohio Constitutional Revision Commission's

(OCRC's) eleven-volume review of the Ohio Constitution, and the materials developed by the Ohio Constitutional Modernization Commission (OCMC).

Swisher's work, published in 1990 by Banks-Baldwin, contains an excellent short history of the Ohio Constitution, commentary on each section, and amendments and case annotations through March 1, 1990. The OCRC, created in 1969 by the General Assembly to recommend changes to the Ohio Constitution, issued a series of reports from 1970 to 1977. The commission's *Final Report* (which is volume 11) includes all of its earlier reports, which contain commentary on virtually all sections of the constitution along with a long list of proposed changes. The first ten volumes contain a treasure trove of the proceedings of the OCRC, including committee and commission minutes and research memoranda on numerous issues relating to the Ohio Constitution. And the OCMC, created by the General Assembly in 2011 to replicate the work of the OCRC, closed its doors on June 30, 2017, four years in advance of its original sunset date, but its research and deliberations are an invaluable source of information about selected aspects of the Ohio Constitution.

The most detailed analysis of the 1802 and 1851 Constitutions and the events leading to them is McDonald's 1916 dissertation, "A Study in Constitution Making-Ohio: 1802–1874." Parkinson's dissertation, "Antebellum State Constitution-Making: Retention, Circumvention, Revision," examines antebellum state constitution-making in general, and it reviews the events leading to the calling of Ohio's second constitutional convention, including the threat of a circumvention convention. For a review of the politics leading to the second constitutional convention, see Holt's three articles. And for the work of Samuel Medary, the leading polemicist for the 1850–51 Convention, see his twenty-six-issue biweekly publication, *The New Constitution* (1849–50).

Patterson's introduction to *The Constitutions of Ohio* and Galbreath's *Constitutional Conventions of Ohio* also make important contributions. Both review the constitutions and conventions up to the fourth constitutional convention in 1912. Galbreath's work, published in December 1911, also includes a list of the delegates to all four Ohio constitutional conventions, including the delegates who had been elected in the fall of 1911 to serve at the 1912 Convention.

For a review of the Ohio Constitution at the halfway mark of the twentieth century, see Walker's *An Analysis and Appraisal of the Ohio Constitution 1851–1951*. For a brief overview of the various articles of the current constitutions of Ohio and other states, see Maddex's *State Constitutions of the United States*. For a brief but excellent review of the history of the Ohio Constitution from the Northwest Ordinance to the present, see Terzian's "Ohio's Constitutions: An Historical Perspective" in the 2004 symposium issue of the *Cleveland State Law Review*.

For a history of Ohio's first fundamental document, the Northwest Ordinance, see Barrett's *Evolution of the Ordinance of 1787.* For the political and social climate leading to the adoption of the Northwest Ordinance and the importance of the ordinance on the development of the nation, see Onuf's *Statehood and Union* and "For the Common Benefit." An excellent history of events leading to statehood and the early constitutions of the states in the Ohio valley is Barnhart's *Valley of Democracy.* Barnhart's chapter on Ohio is especially good on the influences of other state constitutions on the 1802 Constitution.

For an inventory of the papers of early Ohio political leaders, including St. Clair, Tiffin, Huntington, and Worthington, see *The Papers of Thirteen Early Ohio Political Leaders* (Columbus: Ohio Historical Society, 1977).

For works focusing specifically on the 1802 Constitution, see Downes' "Ohio's First Constitution," Ryan's speech "The First Constitution: What Influenced Its Adoption and Its Influence on Ohio," delivered at Ohio's centennial celebration and published in 1897, and Tarr's "The Ohio Constitution of 1802: An Introduction," a short monograph.

The best general reviews of the second constitutional convention and the adoption of the 1851 Constitution are the works by McDonald, Patterson, and Galbreath as well as Downes' "Ohio's Second Constitution." There are also several scholarly reviews of portions of the 1850–51 debates in work on specific topics such as education (O'Brien and Woodrum), home rule (Vaubel), race and gender (Terzian), and the special privileges clause (Gold on Ranney).

There are a number of works that focus specifically on the 1912 Convention. See, for example, Warner's article "Ohio's Constitutional Convention of 1912" and Sponholtz's dissertation "Progressivism in Microcosm." The proceedings of the 1912 Convention and the politics leading to the convention are also covered in greater depth in Warner's *Progressivism in Ohio*, the most comprehensive treatment of Progressivism in Ohio. Bigelow's *New Constitution for Ohio* is a review of the proposed amendments resulting from the 1912 Convention by the Progressive leader and president of the convention. Votes on the proposed amendments by the electors in each county are given in Graves' *The Constitution of the State of Ohio*, and Sponholtz's dissertation includes a great amount of demographic data that he correlates with votes on issues addressed at the convention.

There is an extensive literature on the history of the Ohio judiciary. The most valuable early twentieth-century works are Aumann's "The Development of the Judicial System of Ohio" and volume 1 of Carrington T. Marshall's *A History of the Courts and Lawyers of Ohio.* Marshall's work, published in 1934 by a former chief justice of the Ohio Supreme Court, includes a history of the judiciary article of the Ohio Constitution beginning in 1802 and descriptions of important Ohio Supreme Court cases. Other works on the early history of the judiciary include Utter's "Judicial Review in Early Ohio" and Downes' "Judicial Review under the Ohio Constitution of 1802." Pollack's *Ohio Unreported Judicial Decisions, Prior to 1823* contains the opinions in *Rutherford v. M'Fadden* (1807), the case that established judicial review in Ohio and led to the impeachment of Judge Pease and Justice Tod. For a detailed review of the ensuing judicial review/impeachment controversy, see Melhorn's *Lest We Be Marshall'd: Judicial Powers and Politics in Ohio, 1806–1812.* And for a detailed collection of cases exercising the power of judicial review in the nineteenth and very early twentieth centuries, see Hixson's 1922 master's thesis, "The Judicial Veto in Ohio." A review of judicial selection is contained in Solimine and Saphire's "The Selection of Judges in Ohio." Finally, for information about the politics of judicial selection in Ohio, see works by Baum, and for data concerning expenditures in political races, including judicial elections, see *FollowtheMoney.org—Election Overview* (National Institute on Money in Politics) (website).

For a history of Ohio's lower courts, see Skeel's "Constitutional History of Ohio Appellate Courts" and Winkler's "The Probate Courts of Ohio." Jonathan Entin's article "Judicial Supermajorities and the Validity of Statutes" concerns the requirement adopted in 1912 to prohibit the Ohio Supreme Court from holding a law unconstitutional in many cases without the concurrence of all but one Supreme Court justice. Milligan and Pohlman's article on the Modern Courts Amendment covers the adoption of the 1968 amendments that restructured the Ohio judiciary, and Fischer et al. examine the Modern Courts Amendment on its fiftieth anniversary.

For a history of the interactions among and between the judicial, legislative, and executive branches see Woodbridge's "A History of Separation of Powers in Ohio" and Rodebush's "Separations of Powers in Ohio: A Critical Analysis."

There is also an extensive literature on the constitutional history of race. The best work on the constitutional treatment of race is the dissertation by Terzian "Effusions of Folly and Fanaticism: Race, Gender and Constitution—Making in Ohio, 1802–1923." Terzian's dissertation also includes an extensive bibliography. On the broader subject of race and the status of African Americans, see Hickock's *The Negro in Ohio, 1802–1870*; Quillin's *The Color Line in Ohio*; Thurston's "The 1802 Constitutional Convention and Status of the Negro"; and Entin's "An Ohio Dilemma: Race, Equal Protection, and the Unfulfilled Promise of a State Bill of Rights," which covers the definition of "white" in the Ohio Constitution and the history of segregated schools. Finkelman's "Race, Slavery and Law in Antebellum Ohio" reviews broadly the role of race in early nineteenth-century Ohio. On women's suffrage and the 1912 Convention, see the Terzian dissertation and her chapter in *The History of Ohio Law* and Shilling's 1916 article on "Women's Suffrage in the Constitutional Convention of Ohio."

For a collection of primary source documents, including the Virginia Act of Cession, the Ordinance of 1784, the Land Ordinance of 1785, the Northwest Ordinance, the 1802 Constitution, excerpts from the proceedings of the 1850–51 Constitutional Convention on race, gender, and governmental reform, and excerpts from the Proceedings of the 1912 Constitutional Convention on home rule, direct democracy, and the initiative, see Shriver and Wunderlin's *The Documentary Heritage of Ohio.*

Though not focusing on the Ohio Constitution, *Ohio Politics,* edited by Alexander P. Lamis and Brian Usher, discusses many state constitutional issues in its review of the terms of Ohio governors since 1945.

For a general discussion of the development of state constitutions, a good starting point is Tarr's *Understanding State Constitutions.* Another good source of information about state constitutions are law school casebooks by Williams and Friedman, *State Constitutional Law: Cases and Materials,* and by Sutton, Holland, McAllister, and Shaman, *State Constitutional Law: The Modern Experience,* as well as the treatises by Williams, *The Law of American State Constitutions,* and by Friesen, *State Constitutional Law: Litigating Individual Rights, Claims, and Defenses.* And for a national review of direct democracy and the role and politics of the constitutional amendment process, see Dinan's *State Constitutional Politics: Governing by Amendment in the American States.*

The occasion of Ohio's bicentennial in 2003 led to two important collections of scholarly work on the Ohio Constitution and Ohio law. In 2004, shortly before the publication of first edition of this book, the *Cleveland State Law Review* published a collection of articles presented at a symposium that addressed the Ohio Constitution, "Symposium: The Ohio State Constitution—Then and Now: An Examination of the Law and History of the Ohio Constitution on the Occasion of Its Bicentennial." This double-issue of the law review, edited by O'Neill, includes important articles by several of the authors cited in this book, including Bettman, Terzian, Entin, Hoffer and McDade Rodebush, O'Brien and Woodrum, O' Reilly, Saphire, Solimine, and Williams.

And later in 2004, after the publication of first edition of this book, funding by the Ohio Bicentennial Commission led to the publication of a two-volume set of articles on *The History of Ohio Law,* edited by Benedict and Winkler. Several of the articles deal directly or indirectly with the Ohio Constitution, and this edition relies on important contributions in this publication by Benedict, Finkelman, Pierce, Kulewicz, Terzian, and Winkler.

In addition to Ohio-focused scholarship, there is a rich national literature on state constitutional law and its role in a federal judicial system. Efforts to expand interest nationally in state constitutional law, especially as it relates to protecting individual rights, have been undertaken by two influential federal court judges, U.S. Supreme Court Justice William J. Brennan Jr., beginning with his influential 1977 Harvard Law Review article, and more recently by UChief Judge Jeffrey S. Sutton of the United States Court of Appeals for the

Sixth Curcuit in his book *51 Inflexible Solutions*, and by many state court judges, including most notably Shirley S. Abrahamson (Wisconsin), Hans A. Linde (Oregon), Goodwin Liu (California), and Robert F. Utter (Washington). Some of their nonjudicial writings are included in the bibliography.

Political scientists, once the principal academics, looking at state constitutions as part of their study of public law have returned to this topic, and the work of Tarr and Dinan provide a national, historical, and political context in which to view state constitutions. Baum has addressed the politics of state judicial selection, and Zackin's *Looking for Rights in All the Wrong Places: Why State Constitutions Contain America's Positive Rights* looks at the availability of positive rights under state constitutions, with a focus on education, labor, and environmental rights.

Unpublished dissertations, though sometimes difficult to obtain, provide useful information about the Ohio Constitution, and the book relies on dissertations by McDonald, Parkinson, Sponholtz, and Terzian.

Specific Sections and Topics

Other works on specific topics and provisions of the Ohio Constitution include the following:

On religious freedom and the difference between Ohio's free exercise clause (Art. 1, sec. 7) and that of the federal constitution, see Robert Williams' article on the new judicial federalism, which reviews *Humphrey v. Lane*, the landmark Ohio Supreme Court case, and Jeffrey Williams' article on *Humphrey v. Lane.*

On a comparison of Ohio constitutional law on search and seizures, Article I, section 14, and the Fourth Amendment and a discussion of the Ohio Supreme Court case *State v. Robinette* (1997), see Lassiter's "Eliminating Consent from the Lexicon of Traffic Stop Interrogations," Saphire's "Ohio Constitutional Interpretation," and Bettman's "Ohio Joins the New Judicial Federalism Movement: A Little To-Ing and a Little Fro-Ing."

On the constitution's open courts provision, Article I, section 16, see Harrison's "How Open Is Open? The Development of the Public Access Doctrine." On the tension between the provision and sovereign immunity, Article I, section 16, see Schnopp's "*Garrett v. Sandusky:* Justice Pfeifer's Fight for Full and Fair Legal Redress."

On constitutional restrictions on the General Assembly's law-making power, see Kulewicz's "The History of the One-Subject Rule of the Ohio Constitution," Schuck's "Returning the 'One' to Ohio's 'One-Subject' Rule," and Hoffer and McDade's "Of Dignity and Logrolling: Ohio's One-Subject Rule and the Very Evils It Was Designed to Prevent." On general laws and the uniformity requirement (Art. II, sec. 26), see Magrish's "Ohio Constitutional Requirement That Laws of a General Nature Shall Have Uniform Operation throughout the State" and Mallison's "General versus Special Statutes in Ohio."

On the initiative and referendum, Article II, see Chesley's "The Current Use of Initiative and Referendum in Ohio and Other States" and Steinglass' "Constitutional Revision: Ohio Style."

On commission-based constitutional revision, see the documents generated by the OCRC and the OCMC.

On state and municipal debt and the prohibition against government aid to corporations, Article VIII, see Sterk and Goldman's "Controlling Legislative Shortsightedness" and Gold's "Public Aid to Private Enterprises under the Ohio Constitution."

On the militia, Article IX, see Kulewicz's "The Relationship between Military and Civil Power in Ohio."

On taxation, Article XI, see Coriell's "Chaos, Contradiction and Confusion: Ohio's Real Property Tax Exemptions."

On education and the *DeRolph* case, Article VI, see Hawk's "As Perfect as Can Be Devised," Haynes' "Tension in the Judicial-Legislative Relationship," O'Neil's "Ohio's School Funding Dilemma," and Owsiany's "The General Assembly v. the Supreme Court: Who Makes Public Policy in Ohio?" On the history of educational provisions in Ohio and other states' constitutions, see Eastman's "When Did Education Become a Civil Right?" and O'Brien and Woodrum's "The Constitutional Common School." For a review of the *DeRolph* litigation and educational financing, see Obhof, "*DeRolph v. State and Ohio's Long Road to an Adequate Education.*" See also Larry J. Obhof, "School Finance Litigation and the Separation of Powers," 45 *Mitchell Hamline Law Review* 539 (2019).

On tort reform, see Clayborn's "Ohio's 'Employment Intentional Tort,'" Werber's "Ohio Tort Reform versus the Ohio Constitution" and "Ohio Tort Reform in 1998," and O'Reilly's "Writing Checks or Righting Wrongs: Election Funding and the Tort Decisions of the Ohio Supreme Court."

On home rule, Article XVIII, see Vaubel's many articles and Walker's "Municipal Government in Ohio before 1912." On county home rule (Art. X, sec. 1), see Walker's "County Home Rule in Ohio" and Cianca's "Home Rule in Ohio Counties."

On the Ohio Supreme Court's response to the "New Judicial Federalism"—the name given to the approach of state courts to look to their state bills of rights rather than the U.S. Constitution to protect individual rights—the *Cleveland State Law Review*'s issue on the state's bicentennial contains articles on the new judicial federalism by Abrahamson, Bettman, Saphire, and Williams.

Online Resources

Constitutions and Constitutional Conventions

Most of the primary source and other documents cited in this bibliography are available online. The web pages listed below were last visited in June 2020. If online access no longer works, the website can usually be found by "googling" the name of the website's host.

Ohio Constitutions and Constitutional Conventions

The Journal of the 1802 Ohio Constitutional Convention and other fundamental documents are collected in Ryan's "From Charter to Constitution," which was published in 1897 by the *Ohio Archaeological and Historical Quarterly*, the precursor of *Ohio History*.
<https://resources.ohiohistory.org/ohj/browse/indexbrowse.php> [last visited June 7, 2020] https://perma.cc/5UXQ-NAAD>

The original 1802 Ohio Constitutions is available on the Ohio History Connection website. <https://ohiohistorycentral.org/w/Ohio_Constitution_of_1803_(Transcript)?rec=1858> [last visited June 9, 2020] https://perma.cc/93EJ-FCBU

The original 1851 Ohio Constitutions is available on the *Ohio Constitution: Law and History* website.
<https://www.law.csuohio.edu/sites/default/files/lawlibrary/ohioconlaw/1851constitution.pdf> [last visited June 9, 2020] https://perma.cc/5AEM-NDCA

The current Ohio Constitution, the Ohio Constitution of 1851, as amended, is available on the websites maintained by the General Assembly.
<https://www.legislature.ohio.gov/laws/ohio-constitution> [last visited June 8, 2020] https://perma.cc/7HUL-YH5J
and by the secretary of state
<https://www.sos.state.oh.us/globalassets/publications/election/constitution.pdf> [last visited June 8, 2020] https://perma.cc/HKL9-34L4

The Proceedings and Debates of the 1850–51 Convention are available through Google and on the University of Michigan's Making of America Books website.
<https://quod.lib.umich.edu/m/moa/aey0639.0002.001?view=toc> [last visited June 9, 2020] https://perma.cc/6BZ7-PP9S

The Proceedings and Debates of the 1873–74 Convention are available through Google and on the University of Michigan's Making of America Books website.
https://quod.lib.umich.edu/m/moa/AEW7721.0001.001?rgn=full+text;view=toc;q1=ohio+convention> [last visited June 9, 2020] https://perma.cc/2FXC-HH5T

The Proceedings and Debates of the 1912 Conventions are available on the Ohio Supreme Court's website.
<http://www.supremecourt.ohio.gov/LegalResources/LawLibrary/resources/1912Convention.asp> [last visited June 8, 2020] https://perma.cc/W7QA-F6KL

Other Online Resources—National

The Council of State Governments annually publishes *Book of the States,* which contains tables on state constitutions and the amendment process. <http://knowledgecenter.csg.org/kc/content/book-states-2019-chapter-1-state-constitutions> [last visited June 9, 2020] https://perma.cc/V3YZ-VCGY

The National Conference of State Legislatures has information on its website with a range of state governmental topics, including the initiative and referendum.
<https://www.ncsl.org/aboutus.aspx> [last visited June 18, 2020] https://perma.cc/GA3K-DDZX

The National Institute on Money in Politics website, Followthemoney.org collects information on state election expenditures, including judicial elections and constitutional and other ballot issues.
<https://www.followthemoney.org/at-a-glance?y=2020&s=OH> [last visited June 7, 2020] https://perma.cc/5J9L-BTWC

Oxford University Press has published *Oxford Commentaries on the State Constitutions of the United States,* a fifty-volume series of commentaries on state constitutions that is available to subscribers online.

Rutgers Center for State Constitutional Studies has a website that contains a number of articles on state constitutional law, including Tarr's "The Ohio Constitution of 1802: An Introduction" <https://statecon.camden.rutgers.edu> [last visited June 7, 2020] https://perma.cc/J77K-MHKK

Other Online Resources—Ohio

The Ohio Attorney General's website maintains a *List of Petitions Submitted to the Attorney General's Office,* which includes submissions for the "fair and truthful determination."
<https://www.ohioattorneygeneral.gov/Legal/Ballot-Initiatives/Petitions-Submitted-to-the-Attorney-General-s-Offi> [last visited June 6, 2020] https://perma.cc/6UUH-2G9W

The website of the Ohio Legislative Service Commission contains an overview of Ohio state government, including the legislative, executive, and judicial branches.
<https://www.lsc.ohio.gov/pages/general/aboutus.aspx?active=idA>
[last visited on June 8, 2020] https://perma.cc/C48E-78W6

This website also contains *A Guidebook for Ohio Legislators*
<https://www.lsc.ohio.gov/pages/reference/current/guidebookforlegislators.aspx [last visited June 8, 2020] https://perma.cc/R5UK-D7TM

The OCRC's relevant documents are on the Legislative Services Commission website.
<https://www.lsc.ohio.gov/pages/reference/current/generalreference.aspx?active=idOCRCR> [last visited June 6, 2020] https://perma.cc/BM43-RTGP

The OCMC's relevant documents are on the following website: http://ocmc.ohio/gov/home

The Ohio secretary of state's website contains current and historical information on Ohio elections, including documents relevant to the Ballot Board. <https://www.sos.state.oh.us/legislation-and-ballot-issues/> [last visited June 6, 2020] https://perma.cc/7J4B-SWDS

It also lists all constitutional amendments proposed to the voters since 1913 and the vote on such proposals. <https://www.sos.state.oh.us/globalassets/elections/historical/issuehist.pdf> [last visited on June 7, 2020] https://perma.cc/A8ZE-5YEL

The Ohio Supreme Court's website contains many documents on the court, including a timeline of significant Supreme Court decisions, a chart showing the organization of Ohio's judicial system, biographies of all Ohio Supreme Court justices, the proceedings from the 1912 Constitutional Convention, and an online docket that provides access to the briefs in recent and pending cases. <http://www.supremecourt.ohio.gov>/ [last visited June 6, 2020] https://perma.cc/N77Z-LP76

For a collection of documents relating to the 2013–14 effort to reform Ohio judicial elections, see <http://ohiojudicialreform.org/about-ohiojudicialreform-org/> [last visited June 14, 2020] https://perma.cc/L7DJ-9FJ8

Articles from the *Northwest Ohio Quarterly*, including Downes' articles on the first and second constitution, are available at the University of Toledo's "Attic" website. <https://toledosattic.org/resources/nwohiohistory> [last visited June 7, 2020] https://perma.cc/ND92-J5M8

Ohio History Connection (formerly operating as the Ohio Historical Society) maintains a website that provides online access to many primary source documents as well as the issues of the Ohio Historical Society's scholarly journal from 1887 to 2003, which was first published as *Ohio Archaeological and Historical Quarterly* and since 1962 as *Ohio History*. <https://resources.ohiohistory.org/ohj/browse/indexbrowse.php> [last visited June 7, 2020] https://perma.cc/5UXQ-NAAD

Issues of *Ohio History* since 2007 are available from Kent State University Press. <http://oaks.kent.edu/ohj> [last visited June 15, 2020] https://perma.cc/G9FY-8G45

The most comprehensive free access to primary sources and other documents relating to the Ohio Constitution is provided on the *Ohio Constitution: Law and History* website, which was created by Dean Steinglass and is maintained by the Law Library at the Cleveland-Marshall College of Law, Cleveland State University. It includes links to all relevant primary source documents, including the 1802 and 1851 Constitutions, the proceedings for the 1850–51, 1872–74, and 1912 Constitutional Convention, and such difficult to find items as, Samuel Medary's *The New Constitution* (1849–50), the dissertations by

McDonald and Parkinson, the 1897 compilation of fundamental documents by Ryan, and publications of the Ohio Constitutional Modernization Commission that are not on the Commission website:
<http://guides.law.csuohio.edu/ohioconstitution> [last visited June 6, 2020] https://perma.cc/RJV6-BVYE

Primary Sources—Constitutions and Constitutional Conventions

Ohio Constitution of 1802 (1802).

Ohio Constitution of 1851 (1851).

Journal of the Convention, of the Territory of the United States North-west of the Ohio, begun and held at Chillicothe, on Monday the First Day of November, A.D., 1802 (1802).

Report of the Debates and Proceedings of the Convention for the Revision of the Constitution of the State of Ohio, 1850–51, 2 vols. (Columbus: S. Medary, 1851).

Official Report of the Proceedings and Debates of the Third Constitutional Convention of Ohio, 2 vols. (Cleveland: W. S. Robison & Co., 1873–74).

Proceedings and Debates of the Constitutional Convention of the State of Ohio: Convened January 9, 1912, 2 vols. (Columbus: F. J. Heer Printing Co., 1912).

"Review of Fourth Ohio Constitutional Convention by Contributing Members and Amendments Adopted by the People in 1912" published in Mercer, James K., *Ohio Legislative History 1909–1913.* (Columbus: Edward T. Miller Co., 1913), 409–48.

Secondary and Other Sources

Abrahamson, Shirley S. "State Constitutional Law, New Judicial Federalism, and the Rehnquist Court," 51 *Clev. St. L. Rev.* 339 (2004).

Atwater, Caleb. *A History of the State of Ohio, Natural and Civil.* Cincinnati: Glezen & Shepard, 1838.

Aumann, Francis R. "The Selection, Tenure, Retirement and Compensation of Judges in Ohio," 5 *U. Cin. L. Rev.* 408 (1931).

______. "The Development of the Judicial System of Ohio," 41 *Ohio Arch. and Hist. Q.* 195 (1932).

Barber, Kathleen L. "Ohio Judicial Elections—Nonpartisan Premises with Partisan Results," 32 *Ohio St. L. J.* 762 (1971).

Barnhart, John D. *Valley of Democracy: The Frontier versus the Plantation in the Ohio Valley, 1775–1818.* Bloomington: Indiana University Press, 1953.

Barrett, Jay A. *Evolution of the Ordinance of 1787.* New York: Arno Press, 1971.

Baum, Lawrence. "Judicial Election & Appointment at the State Level," 77 *Ky. L. J.* 645 (1988–89).

______. "Judicial Elections and Judicial Independence: The Voter's Perspective," 64 *Ohio St. L. J.* 13 (2003).

Benedict, Michael Les. "Civil Liberty in Ohio," in Michael Les Benedict and John F. Winkler, eds., *The History of Ohio Law*. Athens: Ohio University Press, 2004.

______, and John F. Winkler, eds. *The History of Ohio Law.* Athens: Ohio University Press, 2004.

Bettman, Marianna Brown. "Ohio Joins the New Judicial Federalism Movement: A Little To-Ing and a Little Fro-Ing," 51 *Clev. St. L. Rev.* 491 (2004).

Biber, Eric. "The Price of Admission: Causes, Effects, and Patters of Conditions Imposed on States Entering the Union," 46 *Am. J. Legal Hist.* 119 (2004).

Bigelow, Herbert S. *New Constitution for Ohio: An Explanation of the Work of Ohio's Fourth Constitutional Convention.* Washington, DC: [s.n.], July 5, 1912.

Blackmore II, Josiah H. "Not from Zeus's Head Full-Blown: The Story of Civil Procedure in Ohio," in Michael Les Benedict and John F. Winkler, eds., *The History of Ohio Law*. Athens: Ohio University Press, 2004.

Bogart, Ernest Ludlow. *Internal Improvements and State Debt in Ohio: An Essay in Economic History*. New York: Longmans, Green & Co., 1924.

Bond, Beverley W., Jr. "The Foundations of Ohio," in Carl Wittke, ed., *The History of the State of Ohio*, vol. I. Columbus: Ohio State Archaeological and Historical Society, 1941.

Book of the States (Council of State Governments). <http://knowledgecenter.csg.org/kc/content/book-states-2019-chapter-1-state-constitutions> (June 9, 2020) <https://perma.cc/V3YZ-VCGY>

Brennan, William J., Jr. "State Constitutions and the Protection of Individual Rights," 90 *Harv. L. Rev.* 489 (1977).

Briffault, Richard. "The Challenge of the New Preemption," 70 *Stan. L. Rev.* 1995 (2018).

Broder, David S. *Democracy Derailed: Initiative Campaigns and the Power of Money*. New York: Harcourt Inc., 2000.

Bunker, Frank Forest. *Reorganization of the Public School System*, Department of the Interior, Bureau of Education Bulletin No. 8, 24 (1916).

Burnet, Jacob. *Notes on the Early Settlement of the North-Western Territory.* Cincinnati: Derby, Bradley & Co., 1847.

Carlson, V. E. "Finance and Taxation in Ohio," in Harvey Walker, ed., *An Analysis and Appraisal of the Ohio State Constitution 1851–1951*. Cincinnati: The Stephen H. Wilder Foundation, 1951, 58–67.

Cayton, Andrew R. L. *The Frontier Republic: Ideology and Politics in the Ohio Country, 1780–1825*. Kent: Kent State University Press, 1986.

______. "Law and Authority in the Northwest Territory," in Michael Les Benedict and John F. Winkler, eds., *The History of Ohio Law*. Athens: Ohio University Press, 2004.

Chaddock, Robert E. *Ohio before 1850: A Study of the Early Influence of Pennsylvania and Southern Populations in Ohio*. New York: Longmans, Green & Co., 1908.

Chambers II, John Whiteclay. *The Tyranny of Change: America in the Progressive Era, 1900–1917*. New York: St. Martin's Press, 1980.

Charles, Patrick J. *The Second Amendment: The Intent and Its Interpretation by the States and the Supreme Court*. Jefferson NC: McFarland Publishing, 2009.

Chase, Salmon P. "A Preliminary Sketch of the History of Ohio," in *Statutes of Ohio and the Northwestern Territory*, vol. I. Cincinnati: Corey & Fairbank, 1833, 9–48.

Chemerinsky, Erwin. *Constitutional Law: Principles and Policies*, 6th ed. New York: Wolters Kluwer, 2019.

______. *Federal Jurisdiction*, 6th ed. New York: Wolters Kluwer, 2016.

Chesley, Richard A. "The Current Use of Initiative and Referendum in Ohio and Other States," 53 *U. Cin. L. Rev.* 541 (1984).

Cianca, Stephen. "Home Rule in Ohio Counties: Legal and Constitutional Perspectives," 19 *U. Dayton L. Rev.* 533 (1994).

Clayborn, Mark A. "Ohio's 'Employment Intentional Tort': A Workers' Compensation Exception, or the Creation of an Entirely New Cause of Action?" 44 *Clev. St. L. Rev.* 381 (1996).

Cole, Frank P. "Thomas Worthington,"12 *Ohio Archaeological and Historical Publications* 339 (1903).

Coriell, Karen Bond. "Chaos, Contradiction and Confusion: Ohio's Real Property Tax Exemptions," 53 *Ohio St. L. J.* 265 (1992).

Curtin, Michael. "Voter Registration in Ohio," *Teaching Cleveland* (2016).

Cutler, Julia Perkins. *Life and Times of Ephraim Cutler*. Cincinnati: Robert Clark & Co., 1890 (reprinted New York: Arno Press, 1971).

Diemer, Tom, Lee Leonard, and Richard G. Zimmerman. James A. *Rhodes: Ohio Colossus*. Kent: Kent State University Press, 2014.

Dinan, John. "Framing a 'People's Government': State Constitution-Making in the Progressive Era," 30 *Rutgers L. J.* 933 (1999).

______. *State Constitutional Politics: Governing by Amendment in the American States*. Chicago: University of Chicago Press, 2018.

Douglas, Joshua A. "The Right to Vote under Local Law," 85 *Geo. Wash. L. Rev.* 1039 (2017).

Downes, Randolph C. *Frontier Ohio, 1788–1803*. Columbus: Ohio Historical Society, 1935.

______. "Judicial Review under the Ohio Constitution of 1802," 18 *Northwest Ohio Quarterly* 140 (October 1946).

______. "Ohio's First Constitution," 25 *Northwest Ohio Quarterly* 12 (Winter 1953).

______. "Ohio's Second Constitution," 26 *Northwest Ohio Quarterly* 71 (Spring 1953).

______. "Thomas Jefferson and the Removal of Governor St. Clair in 1802," 36 *Ohio Archaeological and Historical Society Publications* 62 (1927).

Eastman, John C. "When Did Education Become a Civil Right? An Assessment of State Constitutional Provisions for Education 1776–1900," 42 *Am. J. Legal Hist.* 1 (January 1998).

Engstrom, Erik J., and Jason M Roberts. "The Politics of Ballot Choice," 77 *Ohio St. L. J.* 839 (2016).

Entin, Jonathan L. "An Ohio Dilemma: Race, Equal Protection, and the Unfulfilled Promise of a State Bill of Rights," 51 *Clev. St. L. Rev.* 395 (2004).

______. "Judicial Supermajorities and the Validity of Statutes: How Mapp Became a Fourth Amendment Landmark Instead of a First Amendment Footnote," 52 *Case W. Res. L. Rev.* 441 (2001).

Finkelman, Paul. "Race, Slavery and Law in Antebellum Ohio," in Michael Les Benedict and John F. Winkler, eds., *The History of Ohio Law*. Athens: Ohio University Press, 2004.

Fino, Susan P. *The Michigan State Constitution*. New York: Oxford University, 2011.

Fischer, Patrick, David Hejmanowski, Kylie Conley, Paul Kerridge, and Ronad Wadlinger. "The Modern Courts Amendment at 50," 33 *Ohio Lawyer* 10 (October–December 2019).

Fisher, Lloyd E., Jr. "Charities and the Ohio Tax Laws," 18 *Ohio St. L. J.* 228 (1957).

FollowtheMoney.org—Election Overview (National Institute on Money in Politics). <https://www.followthemoney.org/at-a-glance?y=2020&s=OH> (June 7, 2020) https://perma.cc/5J9L-BTWC

Forte, David F., and Matthew Spalding, eds. *The Heritage Guide to the Constitution*, 2nd ed. Washington, DC: The Heritage Foundation, 2014.

Friesen, Jennifer. *State Constitutional Law: Litigating Individual Rights, Claims, and Defenses*, 4th ed. New York: LEXIS Law Pub., 2006 and 2015 Supp.

Galbreath, C. B. *Constitutional Conventions of Ohio*. Columbus: Stoneman Press, 1911.

______. *History of Ohio*, 5 vols. New York & Chicago: The American Historical Society, 1925.

Gareau, David M. "Opening the Courthouse Doors: Allowing a Cause of Action to Arise Directly from a Violation of the Ohio Constitution," 43 *Clev. St. L. Rev.* 459 (1995).

Garner, Richard. "Flexible Predictability: Stare Decisis in Ohio," 48 *Akron L. Rev.* 15 (2015).

Gillman, Howard. *The Constitution Besieged: The Rise and Fall of Lochner Era Police Powers Jurisprudence*. Durham: Duke University Press, 1993.

Gilmore, William. *Life of Edward Tiffin*. Chillicothe: Homey & Son, 1897.

Gold, David M. *Democracy in Session: A History of the Ohio General Assembly*. Athens: Ohio University Press, 2009.

______. "The General Assembly and Ohio's Constitutional Culture," in Michael Les Benedict and John F. Winkler, eds., *The History of Ohio Law*. Athens: Ohio University Press, 2004.

______. *The Jacksonian Conservatism of Rufus P. Ranney*. Athens: Ohio University Press, 2017.

______. "Public Aid to Private Enterprises under the Ohio Constitution: Sections 4, 6, and 13 of Article VIII in Historical Perspective," 16 *U. Tol L. Rev.* 405 (1985).

Graves, Charles S. *The Constitution of the State of Ohio and the Several Amendments Submitted at the Election of September 3, 1912, with the Proclamation of the Governor and the Vote by Counties on Each Amendment.* Columbus: F. J. Heer Printing Co., 1913.

Green, Steven K. *The Second Disestablishment.* New York: Oxford University Press, 2010.

Hack, Julie Ann. *"Misdemeanor[s]" Worthy of Judicial Impeachment in Early Ohio Constitutional History.* Ohio Constitution: Law and History, Spring 2009 (CM Law Website).

Hagerty, J. E., C. P. McClelland, and C. C. Huntington. *History of the Ohio Canals: Their Construction, Cost, Use and Partial Abandonment.* Columbus: Ohio State Archaeological and Historical Society, 1905 (clarified and copyrighted by Arthur W. McGraw, 1992).

Harrison, Jack B. "How Open Is Open? The Development of the Public Access Doctrine under State Open Court Provisions," 60 *U. Cin. L Rev.* 1307 (1992).

Hawk, Morris L. "'As Perfect as Can Be Devised': *DeRolph v. State of Ohio* and the Right to Education in Ohio," 45 *Case W. Res. L. Rev.* 679 (1995).

Haynes, Anne M. "Tension in the Judicial-Legislative Relationship: *DeRolph v. State*," 32 *U. Tol. L .Rev.* 611(2001).

Hern, Robert. "A Statistical Approach to Ohio's Constitutional History . . . And a Calculation of Its Future," in *Book of the States*, The Council of State Governments, 2012, 18–36.

Hershkoff, Helen. "Just Words: Common Law and the Enforcement of State Constitutional Social and Economic Rights," 62 *Stan. L. Rev.* 1521 (2010).

Heytens, Toby J. "School Choice and State Constitutions," 86 *Va. L. Rev.* 117 (2000).

Hickock, Charles T. *The Negro in Ohio, 1802–1870.* Cleveland: Williams Publishing & Electric Co., 1896 (reprinted New York: AMS Press, 1975).

Hixson, J. H. "The Judicial Veto in Ohio." Master's thesis, Ohio State University, 1922.

Hoffer, Stephanie, and Travis McDade. "Of Dignity and Logrolling: Ohio's One-Subject Rule and the Very Evils It Was Designed to Prevent," 51 *Clev. St. L. Rev.* 557 (2004).

Holt, Edgar Allan. "Party Politics in Ohio, 1840–50," 37 *Ohio Archaeological and Historical Quarterly* 439 (1928); 38 *Ohio Archaeological and Historical Quarterly* 47 (1929); and 38 *Ohio Archaeological and Historical Quarterly* 260 (1929).

Howard, A. E. Dick. *Commentaries on the Constitution of Virginia*, 2 vols. Charlottesville: University Press of Virginia, 1974.

______. *The Road from Runnymede*. Charlottesville: The University Press of Virginia, 1968.

Hurt, R. Douglas. *The Ohio Frontier, Crucible of the Old Northwest, 1720–1830*. Bloomington: Indiana University Press 1996.

Judicial Selection in the States: Appellate and General Election Courts. American Judicature Society, 2013.

Katz, Lewis R., John Martin, and Jay Macke. *Baldwin's Ohio Practice Criminal Law*, 3rd ed. Thomson Reuters, 2021.

Knepper, George W. *The Official Ohio Lands Book*. Columbus: Auditor of State, 2002.

Kulewicz, John J. "The History of the One-Subject Rule of the Ohio Constitution," 45 *Clev. St. L. Rev.* 591 (1997).

______. "Reinventing the Governor: A History of Executive Power under Ohio Law," in Michael Les Benedict and John F. Winkler, eds., *The History of Ohio Law*. Athens: Ohio University Press, 2004.

_____. "The Relationship between Military and Civil Power in Ohio," 28 *Clev. St. L. Rev.* 611 (1979).

Lamis, Alexander P., and Brian Usher, eds. *Ohio Politics*. Kent: Kent State University Press, 2007 (revised and updated).

Lang, James F. *Local Government Law—Municipal*. Baldwin's Ohio Practice. Thomson Reuters, 2019.

Lassiter, Christo. "Eliminating Consent from the Lexicon of Traffic Stop Interrogations," 27 *Cap. U. L. Rev.* 79 (1998).

Levy, Leonard. *Origins of the Fifth Amendment*. New York: Oxford University Press, 1968.

Linde, Hans A. "Without Due Process: Unconstitutional Law in Oregon," 49 *Or. L. Rev.* 125 (1970).

______. "First Things First: Rediscovering the States' Bills of Rights," 9 *U. Balt. L. Rev.* 379 (1980).

Liu, Goodwin. "State Constitutions and the Protection of Individual Rights: A Reappraisal," 92 *N.Y.U. L. Rev.* 1307 (2017).

Long, Justin. "State Constitutional Prohibitions on Special Laws," 60 *Clev. St. L. Rev.* 719 (2012).

Maddex, Robert L. *State Constitutions of the United States*. Washington, DC: Congressional Quarterly, Inc., 1998.

Maddox, Rolland W. "Minority Control of Court Decisions in Ohio," 24 *American Political Science Review* 638 (August 1930).

Magrish, James L. "Ohio Constitutional Requirement that Laws of a General Nature Shall Have Uniform Operation throughout the State," 3 *U. Cin. L. Rev.* 344 (1929).

Mahoney, Matthew. "Home Rule in Ohio: General Laws, Conflicts, and the Failure of the Courts to Protect the Ohio Constitution," 67 *Clev. St. L. Rev.* 117 (2019).

Mallison, W. T., Jr. "General versus Special Statutes in Ohio," 11 *Ohio St. L. J.* 464 (1950).

Marshall, Carrington T. *A History of the Courts and Lawyers of Ohio.* New York: American Historical Society, 1934.

Martzoloff, C. L. "Ohio: Changes in the Constitution," 6 *American Political Science Review* 573 (November 1912).

Massie, David Mead. *Nathaniel Massie: A Pioneer of Ohio: A Sketch of His Life and Selections from His Correspondence.* Cincinnati: Robert Clark, 1896.McCullough, David. *The Pioneers: The Heroic Struggle of the Settlers Who Brought the American Ideal West.* New York: Simon & Schuster, 2019.

McDonald, Howard. "A Study in Constitution Making—Ohio: 1802–1874." Ph.D. dissertation, University of Michigan, 1916.

McFadden, Christopher R. "Judicial Independence, Age-Based BFOQS, and the Perils of Mandatory Retirement Policies for Appointed State Judges," 52 *S. C. Law. Rev.* 81 (2000).

Medary, Samuel. *The New Constitution.* Columbus, 1849–50. <https://www.law.csuohio.edu/lawlibrary/ohioconstitution/medary> (June 7, 2020) https://perma.cc/H2CM-AWY9

Melhorn, Donald F., Jr. *Lest We Be Marshall'd: Judicial Powers and Politics in Ohio, 1806–1812.* Akron: University of Akron Press, 2003.

Mercer, James K. *Ohio Legislative History 1909–1913.* Columbus: Edward T. Miller Co., 1913.

Miller II, Clinton J., and Terry M Miller. "Constitutional Charter of Ohio's Attorney General," 37 *Ohio St. L. J.* 801 (1976).

Milligan, Fred J. *Ohio's Founding Fathers.* Lincoln, NE: iUniverse, Inc., 2003.

Milligan, William W., and James E. Pohlman. "The 1968 Modern Courts Amendment to the Ohio Constitution," 29 *Ohio St. L. J.* 811 (1968).

National Conference of State Legislatures. "Initiative and Referendum in the 20th Century." 2002. <https://www.ncsl.org/research/elections-and-campaigns/task-force-report.aspx> (June 7, 2020) https://perma.cc/K7YY-B8DU

______. "Redistricting Criteria." https://www.ncsl.org/research/redistricting/redistricting- criteria.aspx (June 17, 2020) https://perma.cc/L9BS-Y23Y

O'Brien, Molly, and Amanda Woodrum. "The Constitutional Common School," 51 *Clev. St. L. Rev.* 581 (2004).

O'Connor, Maureen. *A Proposal for Strengthening Judicial Elections.* Ohio Courts, May 2013. <http://ohiojudicialreform.org/wp-content/uploads/2017/11/Plan13.pdf> (June 14, 2020) https://perma.cc/2T8S-ZJVN

_____. *A Plan to Elevate Judicial Elections.* Ohio Courts, 2014. http://ohiojudicialreform.org/resources/ (June 14, 2020) https://perma.cc/8YRQ-MWHL

O'Neil, Cindy M. "Ohio's School Funding Dilemma: A Review of *DeRolph v. State*," 27 *Cap. U. L. Rev.* 891 (1999).

O'Neill, Kevin Francis. "The Road Not Taken: State Constitutions as an Alternative Source of Protection for Reproductive Rights," 11 *N.Y.L. Sch. J. Hum. Rts.* 1 (1993).

_____. "Foreword: The Ohio Constitution on the Occasion of Its Bicentennial," 51 *Clev. St. L. Rev.* 333 (2004).

O'Reilly, James T. "Writing Checks or Righting Wrongs: Election Funding and the Tort Decisions of the Ohio Supreme Court," 51 *Clev. St. L. Rev.* 643 (2004).

Obhof, Larry J. "*DeRolph v. State* and Ohio's Long Road to an Adequate Education," 2005 *B.Y.U. Educ. & L. J.* 83 (2005).

Oedel, David G. "Why Regulate Cybermoney?" 46 *Am. U. L. Rev.* 1075 (1997).

Ogden, Frederic D. *The Poll Tax in the South.* Tuscaloosa: University of Alabama Press, 1958.

Ohio Constitutional Modernization Commission. *Final Reports.* 2017 (LSC website).

Ohio Constitutional Revision Commission. *Recommendations for Amendments to the Ohio Constitution: Final Report, Index to Proceedings and Research.* Columbus: The Commission, 1977 (LSC website).

Ohio Historical Society. *The Papers of Thirteen Early Ohio Political Leaders.* Columbus: Ohio Historical Society, 1977.

Onuf, Peter S. *Statehood and Union: A History of the Northwest Ordinance.* Bloomington: Indiana University Press, 1987.

_____. "For the Common Benefit," 5 *Ohio Historical Society* 2 (April–May 1988).

Owsiany, David J. "The General Assembly v. the Supreme Court: Who Makes Public Policy in Ohio?" 32 *U. Tol. L. Rev.* 549 (2001).

Parkinson, Jr., George Phillip. "Antebellum State Constitution-Making: Retention, Circumvention, Revision." Ph.D. dissertation, University of Wisconsin, 1972.

Patricia, Ravenscraft, and Elizabeth Reilly, Comment, "Perspectives on Ohio Bingo Regulation: An Historical Analysis and Proposal for Change," 10 *Akron L. Rev.* 646 (1977).

Patterson, Isaac F. *The Constitutions of Ohio: Amendments and Proposed Amendments.* Cleveland, Arthur H. Clark Co., 1912.

Pershing, Benjamin H. "The Admission of Ohio to the Union," 63 *Ohio Archaeological and Hisorical Quarterly* 240 (July 1955).

Peters, William E. *Ohio Lands and Their Subdivision,* 2nd ed. Athens: W.E. Peters, 1918.

Pierce, Michael. "Organized Labor and the Law in Ohio," in Michael Les Benedict and John F. Winkler, eds., *The History of Ohio Law.* Athens: Ohio University Press, 2004.

______. *Striking with the Ballot: Ohio Labor and the Populist Party.* DeKalb: Northern Illinois University Press, 2010.

Pollack, Ervin H., ed. *Ohio Unreported Judicial Decisions, Prior to 1823.* Indianapolis: Allen Smith Company, 1952.

Porter, Mary Cornelia, and G. Alan Tarr. "The New Judicial Federalism and the Ohio Supreme Court: Anatomy of a Failure," 45 *Ohio St. L. J.* 143 (1984).

Post, Albert. "The Anti-gallows Movement in Ohio," 54 *The Ohio State Archaeological and Historical Quarterly* (April–June 1945): 104–12.

Progress Report. *Judicial Impartiality: The Next Steps* (January 2004).

Quillin, Fran. *The Color Line in Ohio: A History of Race Prejudice in a Typical Northern State.* New York: Negro Universities Press, 1913.

Randall, Emilius O., and Daniel J. Ryan. *History of Ohio*, 5 vols. New York: Century History Company, 1912.

Raskin, Jamin B. "Legal Aliens, Local Citizens: The Historical, Constitutional, and Theoretical Meanings of Alien Suffrage," 141 *U. Pa. L. Rev.* 1391 (1993).

Ratcliffe, Donald J. "The Experience of Revolution and the Beginning of Party Politics in Ohio, 1776–1816," 85 *Ohio Hist* (1976): 186–230.

Rodebush, Curtis. "Separation of Powers in Ohio: A Critical Analysis," 51 *Clev. St. L. Rev.* 505 (2004).

Roseboom, Eugene H. "The Civil War Era: 1850–1873," in Carl Wittke, ed., *The History of the State of Ohio*, vol. IV. Columbus: Ohio State Archaeological and Historical Society, 1944.

_____, and Francis P. Weisenburger. *A History of Ohio*, 2nd ed. Columbus: Ohio Historical Society, 2012.

Rossi, Jim. "Institutional Design and the Lingering Legacy of Antifederalist Separation of Powers Ideals in the States," 52 *Vand. L. Rev.* 1167 (1999).

Ryan, Daniel J. "From Charter to Constitution: Being a Collection of Public Documents Pertaining to the Territory of the Northwest and the State of Ohio, from the Charters of James I, to and including the First Constitution of Ohio, and the State Papers Relating to Its Admission to the Union, Showing Thereby the Historical Chain of Title of Said State from 1606 to 1803," 5 *Ohio Archaeological and Historical Quarterly* (1897): vii–164.

______. "The First Constitution: What Influenced Its Adoption and Its Influence on Ohio?" 12 *Ohio Archaeological and Historical Quarterly* (1903): 11–23.

_______. "The Influence of Socialism on the Ohio Constitution," 196 *North American Review* 665–72 (1912): 665–72.

______, and Charles Sawyer. "The Ohio Constitution: A Reply and a Rejoinder," 197 *The North American Review* 275–80 (1913): 275–80.

Saphire, Richard B. "Ohio Constitutional Interpretation," 51 *Clev. St. L. Rev.* 437 (2004).

Scheiber, Harry N. *Ohio Canal Era: A Case Study of Government and the Economy, 1820–1861.* Athens: Ohio University Press, 1987.

Schnopp, Stefan. "*Garrett v. Sandusky:* Justice Pfeifer's Fight for Full and Fair Legal Redress: Does Sovereign Immunity Violate Ohio's 'Open Court' Provision?" 27 *U. Tol L. Rev.* 729 (1996).

Schuck, James Preston. "Returning the 'One' to Ohio's 'One-Subject' Rule," 28 *Cap. U. L. Rev.* 899 (2000).

Schwartz, Bernard. *The Bill of Rights: A Documentary History*. New York: Chelsea House Publishers, 1971.

Sears, Alfred Byron. *Thomas Worthington: Father of Ohio Statehood*. Columbus: The Ohio State University Press, 1958.

Shaman, Jeffrey M. *Equality and Liberty in the Golden Age of State Constitutional Law*. New York: Oxford University Press, 2008.

Shepard, Randall T. "Is Making State Constitutional Law through Certified Questions a Good Idea or a Bad Idea Valparaiso," 38 *Val. U. L. Rev.* 327 (2004).

Shilling, D. C. "Women's Suffrage in the Constitutional Convention of Ohio," 25 *Ohio Hist.* (1916): 166–74.

Shriver, Phillip P., and Clarence E. Wunderlin, Jr., *The Documentary Heritage of Ohio*. Athens: Ohio University Press, 2000.

Shugerman, Jed, "Economic Crisis and the Rise of Judicial Elections and Judicial Review," 123 *Harv. L. Rev.* 1061 (2010).

Skeel, Lee E. "Constitutional History of Ohio Appellate Courts," 6 *Cleveland-Marshall L. Rev.* 323 (1957).

Smith, Thomas H., ed. *An Ohio Reader: 1750 to the Civil War*. Grand Rapids: William B. Eerdmans Publishing Company, 1975.

Smith, William Henry. *The St. Clair Papers*. Cincinnati: Robert Clarke & Co., 1882.

Solimine, Michael E. "Recalibrating Justiciability in Ohio Courts," 51 *Clev. St. L. Rev.* 531 (2004).

______, and Richard B. Saphire. "The Selection of Judges in Ohio," in Michael Les Benedict and John F. Winkler, eds., *The History of Ohio Law*. Athens: Ohio University Press, 2004.

Solomon, Lewis D. "Local Currency: A Legal and Policy Analysis," 5 *Kan. J. L. & Pub. Pol.* 59 (Winter 1996).

Sponholtz, Lloyd. "Progressivism in Microcosm: An Analysis of the Political Forces at Work in the Ohio Constitutional Convention of 1912." Ph.D. dissertation, University of Pittsburg, 1969.

______. "The 1912 Constitutional Convention in Ohio: The Call-up and Nonpartisan Selection of Delegates," 79 *Ohio History* (1970): 209–10.

Steinglass, Steven H. "Constitutional Revision: Ohio Style," 77 *Ohio St. L. J.* 281 (2016).

Sterk, Stewart E., and Elizabeth S. Goldman. "Controlling Legislative Shortsightedness: The Effectiveness of Constitutional Debt Limitations," 1991 *Wis. L Rev.* 1301 (1991).

Sullivan, Sean R. "A Term Limit by Any Other Name? The Constitutionality of State-Enacted Ballot Access Restrictions on Incumbent Members of Congress," 56 *U. Pitt L. Rev.* 845 (1995).

Sutton, Jeffrey S. "What Does—and Does Not—Ail State Constitutional Law," 59 *U. Kan. L. Rev.* 687, 707 (2011).

______. *51 Imperfect Solutions: States and the Making of American Constitutional Law*. New York: Oxford University Press, 2018.

______, Randy J. Holland, Stephen R. McAllister, and Jeffrey M. Shaman. *State Constitutional Law: The Modern Experience*, 3rd ed. St. Paul: Thomson Reuters, 2020.

Swindler, William F., ed. *Sources and Documents of United States Constitutions*, vol. 7. New York: Oceana Publications Inc., 1978.

Swisher, Thomas R., ed. *Ohio Constitution Handbook*. Cleveland: Banks-Baldwin Law Publishing Co., 1990.

Tarr, G. Alan. *Understanding State Constitutions*. Princeton: Princeton University Press, 1998.

______. *The Ohio Constitution of 1802: An Introduction*. Rutgers University Center for State Constitutional Studies, 2000 (Rutgers website).

______, and Mary Cornelia Porter. "Ohio: Partisan Justice," in *State Supreme Courts in State and Nation*. New Haven: Yale University Press, 1988, 124–83.

Terzian, Barbara A. "Effusions of Folly and Fanaticism: Race, Gender and Constitution—Making in Ohio, 1802–1923." Ph.D. dissertation, Ohio State University, 1999.

______. "Ohio's Constitutions: An Historical Perspective," 51 *Clev. St. L. Rev.* 357 (2004).

______. "Ohio's Constitutional Conventions and Constitutions," in Michael Les Benedict and John F. Winkler, eds., *The History of Ohio Law*. Athens: Ohio University Press, 2004.

______. "'Let Us Agitate': Woman Suffrage at Ohio's Constitutional Conventions: 1850–1913," in Michael Les Benedict and John F. Winkler, eds., *The History of Ohio Law*. Athens: Ohio University Press, 2004.

Thompson, Hannah N. "Agricultural Issues on the Ballot: The 2009 Ohio Issue 2 Campaign." Honor Project, Presented in Partial Fulfillment of the Requirements for the Degree of Bachelor of Science in the College of Food, Agricultural, and Environmental Sciences at the Ohio State University, 2011.

Thro, William E. "The Role of Language of the State Education Clauses in School Finance Litigation," 79 *Educ. L. Rep.* 19 (1993).

Thurston, Helen M. "The 1802 Constitutional Convention and Status of the Negro," 81 *Ohio History* (Winter 1972): 15–37.

Trafford, Kathleen. "City of Norwood v. Horney—Much More Than Eminent Domain: A Forceful Affirmation of the Independent Authority of the Ohio Constitution and the Court's Power to Enforce It," 48 *Akron L. Rev.* 35 (2015).

Utter, William T. "The Frontier State 1803–1825," in Carl Wittke, ed., *The History of the State of Ohio*, vol. II. Columbus: Ohio State Archaeological and Historical Society, 1942.

Vaubel, George D. "Judicial Review in Early Ohio," 14 *Mississippi Valley Historical Review* (June 1927): 3–24.

______. "Municipal Home Rule in Ohio Part IV," 3 *Ohio N. U. L. Rev.* 1106 (1976).

_____. "Municipal Home Rule in Ohio (1976–1995)," 22 *Ohio N.U. L Rev.* 143 (1995).
______. *Municipal Home Rule in Ohio.* Buffalo: William S. Hein & Co., Inc., 1978.
______. "Toward Principles of State Restraint upon the Exercise of Municipal Power in Home Rule," 20 *Stetson L. Rev.* 845 (1991).
Walinksi, Richard S., and Mark D. Wagoner, Jr. "Ohio's Modern Courts Amendment Must Be Amended: Why and How," 66 *Clev. St. L. Rev.* 69 (2017).
Walker, Harvey, ed. *An Analysis and Appraisal of the Ohio Constitution 1851–1951.* Cincinnati: Stephen J. Wilder Foundation, 1951.
_____. "County Home Rule in Ohio," 1 *Ohio St. Student Bar Assn. L. J.* 11 (1935).
_____. "Municipal Government in Ohio before 1912," 9 *Ohio St. L. J.* 1 (1948).
Walker, James L. "The Ohio Constitution," in George E. Connor and Christopher W. Hammons, eds., *The Constitutionalism of American States.* Columbus and London: University of Missouri Press, 2008, 447–59.
Warner, Hoyt Landon."Ohio's Constitutional Convention of 1912," 61 *Ohio State Archaeological and Hist. Q.* (1952): 11–31.
______. *Progressivism in Ohio 1897–1917.* Columbus: Ohio State University Press, 1964.
Werber, Stephen J. "Ohio Tort Reform versus the Ohio Constitution," 69 *Temple L. Rev.* 1155 (1996).
_____. "Ohio Tort Reform in 1998: The War Continues," 45 *Clev. St. L. Rev.* 539 (1997).
West, J. Martin. "Arthur St. Clair," 5 *Timeline* 52 (April–May 1988).
Williams, Jeffery D. "*Humphrey v. Lane:* The Ohio Constitution's David Slays the Goliath of *Employment Division, Department of Human Resources of Oregon v. Smith,*" 34 *Akron L. Rev.* 919 (2001).
Williams, Robert F. "The Brennan Lecture: Interpreting State Constitutions as Unique Legal Documents," 27 *Okla. City U. L Rev.* 189 (2002).
______. *The Law of American State Constitutions.* New York: Oxford University Press, 2011.
______. *The New Jersey State Constitution,* 2nd ed. New York: Oxford University Press, 2012.
______. "The New Judicial Federalism in Ohio: The First Decade," 51 *Clev. St. L. Rev.* 415 (2004).
______, and Lawrence Friedman. *State Constitutional Law: Cases and Materials,* 5th ed. Charlottesville, VA: Lexis Law Pub., 2015.
Winkler, John. "The Legal Literature of Ohio," in Michael Les Benedict and John F. Winkler, eds., *The History of Ohio Law.* Athens: Ohio University Press, 2004.
______. "The Probate Courts of Ohio," 28 *U. Tol. L. Rev.* 563 (1997).
Wittke, Carl, ed. *The History of the State of Ohio.* Columbus: Ohio State Archaeological and Historical Society, 1941.

Woodbridge, Frederick. "A History of Separation of Powers in Ohio: A Study in Administrative Law," 13 *U. Cin. L. Rev.* 191 (1939).

Zimmerman, Richard G. "Rhodes's First Eight Years: 1963–1971," in Alexander P. Lamis and Brian Usher, eds., *Ohio Politics*. Kent: Kent State University Press, 2007, 85–108 (revised and updated).

■ ABOUT THE AUTHORS

STEVEN H. STEINGLASS is Dean Emeritus and Professor Emeritus at Cleveland State University's Cleveland-Marshall College of Law, where he was on the faculty from 1980 to 2011. He has had visiting appointments at Case Western Reserve University School of Law, Widener University School of Law, St. Louis University School of Law, and the University of Wisconsin Law School; from 2013 to 2017 he served as Senior Policy Advisor for the Ohio Constitutional Modernization Commission. Dean Steinglass received his undergraduate degree from the University of Pennsylvania and his law degree from the Columbia Law School. He has written law review articles and book chapters about state courts and federal civil rights litigation as well as an annually updated two-volume treatise on civil rights litigation, *Section 1983 Litigation in and Federal* (revised ed. 2021-2022) (Thomson Reuters). He has argued two cases before the U.S. Supreme Court.

GINO J. SCARSELLI is an attorney in private practice in Cleveland, Ohio. He graduated magna cum laude from Cleveland State University's Cleveland-Marshall College of Law in 1993 and holds a master's degree in philosophy from Ohio State University. He has served as law clerk for Judge Solomon Oliver Jr., of the U.S. District Court for the Northern District of Ohio and as Assistant Legal Director of the American Civil Liberties Union of Ohio.

■ TABLE OF CASES

A

Adair v. United States, 208 U.S. 161 (1908), 179
Adamsky v. Buckeye Local School District, 73 Ohio St.3d 360, 653 N.E.2d 212 (1995), 119
Adams v. DeWine, ____ Ohio St.3d, N.E.3d ___, 2022 WL 129092 (Jan. 14, 2022), 554–55, 566
Adkins v. Children's Hospital, 261 U.S. 525 (1923), 179
Adler v. Whitbeck, 44 Ohio St. 539, 9 N.E. 672 (1887), 175
Aetna Life Insurance Co. v. Schilling, 67 Ohio St.3d 164, 616 N.E.2d 893 (1993), 251–52
Alter v. City of Cincinnati, 56 Ohio St. 47, 46 N.E. 69 (1897), 423
American Association of University Professors v. Central State University, 87 Ohio St.3d 55, 717 N.E.2d 286 (1999), 111, 121
American Financial Services Association v. City of Cleveland, 112 Ohio St.3d 170, 858 N.E.2d 776 (2006), 536–37, 538–39
American Publishing Co. v. Fisher, 166 U.S. 464 (1897), 131–32
Anderson v. Millikin, 9 Ohio St. 568 (1859), 50n.241
Anderson v. Poindexter, 6 Ohio St. 622 (1856), 132–33
Arbino v. Johnson & Johnson, 116 Ohio St. 3d 468, 880 N.E.2d 420 (2007), 94, 94n.359, 95–96, 121, 130, 131, 177, 294
Arizona State Legislature v. Arizona Independent Redistricting Commission, 135 S.Ct. 2652 (2015), 554
Armco, Inc. v. Public Utilities Commission, 69 Ohio St. 2d 401, 433 N.E.2d 923 (1982), 293
Arnold v. City of Cleveland, 67 Ohio St.3d 35, 616 N.E.2d 163 (1993), 81, 81n.324, 82, 95, 96, 97, 106, 107, 112, 119–20, 122, 127–28, 141, 178
Ashley v. Ryan, 49 Ohio St. 504, 31 N.E. 721 (1892), 480
Ashwander v. Tennessee Valley Authority, 297 U.S. 288 (1936), 108
Atkins v. Virginia, 536 U.S. 304 (2002), 142
Auditor of Lucas County v. State ex rel. Boyles, 75 Ohio St. 114 (1906), 50–51, 58, 114
Austintown Board of Trustees v. Tracy, 76 Ohio St.3d 353, 667 N.E.2d 1174 (1996), 120–21, 247

B

Baker v. Beckwith, 29 Ohio St. 314 (1876), 37–38
Baker v. Carr, 369 U.S. 186 (1962), 296, 448
Bakies v. Perrysburg, 108 Ohio St.3d 361, 843 N.E.2d 118 (2006), 545
BancOhio Nat. Bank v. Rubicon Cadillac, Inc., 11 Ohio St.3d 32, 462 N.E.2d 1379 (1984), 293
Barker v. Wingo, 407 U.S. 514 (1972), 150
Bartlett v. State, 73 Ohio St. 54, 75 N.E. 939 (1905), 254
Bazell v. City of Cincinnati, 13 Ohio St. 2d 63, 233 N.E.2d 864 (1968), 421
Beaver Excavating Co. v. Testa, 134 Ohio St.3d 565, 983 N.E.2d 1317 (2012), 481
Belding v. State ex rel. Heifher, 121 Ohio St. 393, 169 N.E. 301 (1929), 129
Berry v. City of Columbus, 104 Ohio St. 607, 136 N.E. 824, (1922), 493

Bielat v. Bielat, 87 Ohio St.3d 350, 721 N.E.2d 28 (2000), 250
Billington v. Corner, 25 Ohio St.2d 140, 267 N.E.2d 410 (1971), 547
Bingham v. Miller, 17 Ohio 445 (1848), 254
Blacker v. Wiethe, 16 Ohio St.2d 65, 242 N.E.2d 655 (1968), 440–41
Blankenship v. Cincinnati Milacron Chemicals, Inc., 69 Ohio St.2d 608, 433 N.E.2d 572 (1982), 264
Blanton v. North Las Vegas, 489 U.S. 538 (1989), 129–30
Blockburger v. United States, 284 U.S. 299 (1932), 155
Bloom v. City of Xenia, 32 Ohio St. 461 (1877), 532
Blue Cross of Northeast Ohio v. Ratchford, 64 Ohio St.2d 256, 416 N.E.2d 614 (1980), 143
Board of Regents v. Roth, 408 U.S. 564 (1972), 177–78
Bogen v. Clemmer, 125 Ohio St. 186, 180 N.E. 710 (1932), 193–94
Brady v. Safety-Kleen Corp., 61 Ohio St.3d 624, 576 N.E.2d 722 (1991), 258, 263–64
Branzburg v. Hayes, 408 U.S. 665 (1972), 144–45
Brennaman v. R.M.I. Co., 70 Ohio St.3d 460, 639 N.E.2d 425 (1994), 173
Britt v. City of Columbus, 38 Ohio St.2d 1, 309 N.E.2d 412 (1974), 543
Brown v. Rogers, 71 Ohio St.3d 570, 645 N.E.2d 1241 (1995), 137
Browning-Ferris Industries of Vermont, Inc. v. Kelco Disposal, Inc., 492 U.S. 257 (1989), 143
Buckeye Community Hope Foundation v. City of Cuyahoga Falls, 81 Ohio St.3d 559, 692 N.E.2d 997 (1998), 211, 212, 541
Buckley v. American Constitutional Law Foundation, 525 U.S. 182 (1999), 219
Burger Brewing Co. v. Liquor Control Com., Dep't of Liquor Control, 34 Ohio St. 2d 93, 296 N.E.2d 261 (1973), 295
Burgess v. Eli Lilly & Co., 66 Ohio St.3d 59, 609 N.E.2d 140 (1993), 173
Burke v. City of Cincinnati, 10 Ohio Dec. 542, 8 Ohio N.P. 109 (1900), 129, 231
Burks v. United States, 473 U.S. 1 (1978), 156
Butler v. Jordan, 92 Ohio St.3d 354, 750 N.E.2d 554 (2001), 129

C

C.I.V.I.C. Group v. City of Warren, 88 Ohio St.3d 37, 723 N.E.2d 106 (2000), 429
California v. Beheler, 463 U.S. 1121(1983), 152–53
Carchedi v. Rhodes, 560 F.Supp. 1010 (S.D. Ohio 1982), 164–65
Case Western Reserve University v. Wilkins, 105 Ohio St.3d 276, 825 N.E.2d 146 (2005), 476
Cassidy v. Glossip, 12 Ohio St.2d 17, 231 N.E.2d 64 (1967), 130, 131
Chapel State Theatre Co. v. Hooper, 123 Ohio St. 322, 175 N.E. 450 (1931), 255
Christensen v. Hagedorn, 174 Ohio St. 98, 186 N.E.2d 848 (1962), 533
Church of God in N. Ohio, Inc. v. Levin, 124 Ohio St. 3d 36, 918 N.E.2d 981 (2009), 476
Cincinnati Bell Telephone Co. v. City of Cincinnati, 81 Ohio St.3d 599, 693 N.E.2d 212 (1998), 551
Cincinnati Board of Education v. Minor, 23 Ohio St. 211 (1872), 77n.309, 136
Cincinnati Board of Education v. Walter, 58 Ohio St.2d 368, 390 N.E.2d 813 (1979), 119–20, 335–36
Cincinnati, Wilmington & Zanesville RR Co. v. Clinton County Commissioners, 1 Ohio St. 77 (1852), 29, 29n.139
Citizens in Charge, Inc. v. Husted, 2015 WL 12748275 (S.D. Ohio March 16, 2015), *rev'd on other grounds*, 810 F.3d 437 (6th Cir. 2016), 219
Citizens United v. Federal Election Commission, 558 U.S. 310 (2010), 91
City of Akron v. Mingo, 169 Ohio St. 511, 160 N.E.2d 225 (1959), 234
City of Athens v. McClain, 163 Ohio St.3d 61, 168 N.E.3d 411 (2020), 551

City of Canton v. State, 95 Ohio St.3d 149, 766 N.E.2d 963 (2002), 535, 536, 537, 541
City of Canton v. Whitman, 44 Ohio St.2d 62, 337 N.E.2d 766 (1975), 543
City of Centerville v. Knab, 162 Ohio St.2d 623, 166 N.E.3d 167 (2020), 161
City of Cincinnati v. American Tel. & Tel. Co., 112 Ohio St. 493, 147 N.E. 806 (1925), 551
City of Cincinnati v. Baskin, 112 Ohio St.3d 279, 859 N.E.2d 514 (2006), 536, 539
City of Cincinnati v. Bawtenheimer, 63 Ohio St.3d 260, 586 N.E.2d 1065 (1992), 152
City of Cincinnati v. Coates, 402 U.S. 611 (1971), 126–27
City of Cincinnati v. Correll, 141 Ohio St. 535, 49 N.E.2d 412 (1943), 176
City of Cincinnati v. DeGolyer, 25 Ohio St.2d 101, 267N.E.2d 282 (1971), 170
City of Cincinnati v. Hillenbrand, 103 Ohio St. 286, 133 N.E. 556 (1921), 212
City of Cincinnati v. Ohio Council 8, 61 Ohio St.3d 658, 576 N.E.2d 745 (1991), 90n.345
City of Cincinnati v. Roettinger, 105 Ohio St. 145, 127 N.E. 6 (1922), 543
City of Cleveland v. Anderson, 13 Ohio App.2d 83, 234 N.E.2d 304 (1968), 126
City of Cleveland v. Clements Brothers Construction Co., 67 Ohio St. 197, 65 N.E. 885 (1902), 50, 58, 114, 266
City of Cleveland v. State, 128 Ohio St.3d 135, 942 N.E.2d 370 (2010), 536–37
City of Cleveland v. Ohio, 138 Ohio St.3d 232, 5 N.E.3d 644 (2014), 536
City of Cleveland v. State, 157 Ohio St.3d 330, 136 N.E.3d 466 (2019), 256–57, 536–37, 541–42
City of Columbus v. Barr, 160 Ohio St. 209, 115 N.E.2d 391 (1953), 508
City of Dayton v. Bauman, 66 Ohio St. 379, 64 N.E. 433 (1902), 549
City of Dayton v. State, 151 Ohio St.3d 168, 87 N.E.3d 176 (2017), 12, 14, 15
City of East Cleveland v. Nau, 124 Ohio St. 433, 179 N.E. 187(1931), 549
City of Euclid v. Heaton 11 Ohio St.2d 65, 238 N.E.2d 790 (1968), 519, 522–23
City of Lima v. State, 122 Ohio St.3d 155, 909 N.E.2d 616 (2009), 256–57, 541–42
City of Middletown v. City Commissioners of Middletown, 138 Ohio St. 596, 37 N.E.2d 609(1941), 550
City of Middletown v. Ferguson, 25 Ohio St.3d 71, 495 N.E.2d 380 (1986), *Cert. denied*, 479 U.S. 1034 (1987), 251–52
City of Norwood v. Horney, 110 Ohio St.3d 353, 853 N.E.2d 1115 (2006), 97, 98–99, 107, 111, 178, 186
City of Piqua v. Hinger, 15 Ohio St.2d 110, 238 N.E.2d 766 (1968), 152
City of Seven Hills v. Aryan Nations, 76 Ohio St.3d 304, 667 N.E.2d 942 (1996), 163
City of South Euclid v. Jemison, 28 Ohio St.3d 157, 503 N.E.2d 136 (1986), 193–94, 297
City of Toledo v. Sims, 84 Ohio Law Abs. 476, 169N.E.2d 516 (Mun. Ct. 1960), 126
Clark v. Southview Hospital & Family Health Center, 68 Ohio St.3d 435, 628 N.E.2d 46 (1994), 93
Clermont Environmantal Reclamation Co. v. Wiederhold, 2 Ohio St.3d 44, 442 N.E.2d 1278 (1982), 538
Cleveland Electric Illuminating Co. v. City of Cleveland, _____ Ohio St.3d _____, _____ N.E.3d _____, 2022 WL 6016475 (Dec. 21, 2021), 545
Cleveland State University. v. Perk, 26 Ohio St.2d 1, 268 N.E.2d 577 (1971), 476
Cleveland Telephone Co. v. City of Cleveland, 98 Ohio St. 358, 121 N.E. 701 (1918), 534–35
Clifton v. Blanchester, 131 Ohio St.3d 287, 964 N.E.2d 414 (2012), 543
Clinton v. State, 33 Ohio St. 27 (1877), 135–36
Conlan v Haskins, 177 Ohio St. 65, 202 N.E.2d 419 (1964), 145
Cook v. Maxwell, 2 Ohio St.2d 107, 206 N.E.2d 558 (1965), 137
Cooper v. Buckeye Steel Castings, 67 Ohio St. 2d 563, 621 N.E.2d 396 (1993), 294
Cooperman v. University Surgical Associates, 32 Ohio St. 3d 191, 513 N.E.2d 288 (1987), 303
Corron v. Corron, 40 Ohio St.3d 75, 531 N.E.2d 708 (1988), 306
Costanzo v. Gaul, 62 Ohio St.2d 106, 403 N.E.2d 979 (1980), 234

Coy v. Iowa, 487 U.S. 1012 (1988), 148
Cramer v. Petrie, 70 Ohio St.3d 131, 637 N.E.2d 882 (1994), 170
Crist v. Bretz, 437 U.S. 28 (1978), 156
Currier v. Marietta and Cincinnati Railroad Co., 11 Ohio St. 228 (1860), 492

D

Daggett v. Hudson, 43 Ohio St. 548, 3 N.E. 538 (1885), 77n.311, 321–22
Danforth v. Minnesota, 552 U.S. 264 (2008), 296
Daniels v. Williams, 474 U.S. 327 (1986), 177–78
Dardinger v. Anthem Blue Cross & Blue Shield, 98 Ohio St.3d 77, 781 N.E.2d 121 (2002), 143
Davidson v. Rogers, 281 Or. 219, 574 P.2d 624 (1978), 172
Davis v. Hildebrant, 241 U.S. 565 (1915), 206
Dearborn v. Northwestern Savings Bank, 42 Ohio St. 617 (1885), 493–94
Decker v. State, 113 Ohio St. 512, 150 N.E. 74 (1925), 149
Denison University v. Bd. of Tax Appeals, 2 Ohio St.2d 17,205 N.E.2d 896 (1965), 78n.314, 476
Dennis v. Simon, 51 Ohio St. 233, 36 N.E. 832 (1894), 473
DeRolph v. Ohio, 540 U.S. 966 (2003), 338
DeRolph v. State, 78 Ohio St.3d 193, 677 N.E.2d 733 (1997) (*DeRolph I*), 80, 296, 336––39, 340–41, 398
DeRolph v. State, 89 Ohio St.3d 1, 728 N.E.2d 993 (2000) (*DeRolph II*), 337––38
DeRolph v. State, 93 Ohio St.3 309, 754 N.E.2d 1184 (2001) (*DeRolph III*), 337, 338
DeRolph v. State, 97 Ohio St.3d 1477, 780 N.E.2d 282 (2002 (mandate), 338
DeRolph v. State, 97 Ohio St.3d 434,780 N.E.2d 529 (2002) (*DeRolph IV*), 15, 80
Desenco, Inc. v. City of Akron, 84 Ohio St.3d 535, 706 N.E.2d 323 (1999), 247
Dimick v. Schiedt, 293 U.S. 474 (1935), 129
Direct Plumbing Supply Co. v. City of Dayton, 138 Ohio St. 540, 38 N.E.2d 70 (1941), 78, 79, 107, 176, 180, 185
Disciplinary Counsel v. Alexicole, Inc., 153 Ohio St.3d 313, 106 N.E.3d 21 (2004), 302
District of Columbia v. Heller, 554 U.S. 570 (2008), 128
Doe v. Ronan, 127 Ohio St.3d 188, 937 N.E.2d 556 (2010), 251, 294
Donnelly v. Fairview Park, 13 Ohio St.2d 1, 233 N.E.2d 500 (1968), 211
Drees Co. v. Hamilton Township, 132 Ohio St.3d 186, 970 N.E.2d 916 (2012), 541
Drewes Farms Partnership v. City of Toledo, 2020 WL 966628 (N.D. Ohio Feb. 27, 2020), 542
DuBose v. McGuffey, _____ Ohio St.3d _____, _____ N.E.3d _____ 2022 WL 34730 (Jan. 4, 2022), 139
Dunn v. Blumstein, 405 U.S. 330 (1972), 73, 321

E

E. W. Scripps Co. v. Fulton, 100 Ohio App. 157, 125 N.E.2d 896 (1955), 171
Eastwood Mall, Inc. v. Slanco, 68 Ohio St.3d 221, 626 N.E.2d 59 (1994), 163
Egan v. National Distillers & Chemical Corp., 25 Ohio St. 3d 176, 495 N.E.2d 904 (1986), 293
Employment Division, Oregon Department of Human Resources v. Smith, 494 U.S. 872 (1990), 134–35
Equity Dublin Associates v. Testa, 142 Ohio St.3d 152, 28 N.E.3d 1206 (2014), 476
Evans v. Cornman, 398 U.S. 419 (1970), 327

Evans v. Mannix, 90 Ohio St. 355, 107 N.E. 763 (1914), 188–89
Everard v. Kroeger, 60 Ohio App. 123, 19 N.E.2d 964 (1938), 490
Ex parte Bushnell, 9 Ohio St. 77 (1859), 133
Ex parte Lockhart, 1 Disn. 105, 12 Ohio Dec. Reprint 515 (Super. Ct. 1855), 164–65

F

Fabrey v. McDonald Village Police Department, 70 Ohio St.3d 351, 639 N.E.2d 31 (1994), 174, 180
Fairway Manor, Inc. v. Board of Commissioners of Summit County, 36 Ohio St.3d 85, 521 N.E.2d 818 (1988), 545
Fay v. Noia, 372 U.S. 391 (1963), 136–37
FirstEnergy Solutions Corp. v. Ohioans against Corporate Bailouts, 157 Ohio St.3d 1500, 134 N.E.3d 1225 (2019) (Table), 205, 206
Fitzgerald v. City of Cleveland, 88 Ohio St. 338, 103 N.E. 512 (1913), 78n.314, 534–35, 545–46
Fortner v. Thomas, 22 Ohio St.2d 13, 257 N.E.2d 371 (1970), 293
Fox v. Fox, 24 Ohio St. 335 (1873), 184–85
Fox v. Frank, 52 Ohio App. 483, 3 N.E.2d 996 (1935), 479
Franchise Developers, Inc. v. City of Cincinnati, 30 Ohio St.3d 28, 505 N.E.2d 966 (1987), 295–96
Friedman v. Johnson, 18 Ohio St.3d 85, 480 N.E.2d 82 (1985), 183–84
Furman v. Georgia 408 U.S. 238 (1972), 140

G

Gallimore v. Children's Hospital Medical Center, 67 Ohio St.3d 244, 617 N.E.2d 1052 (1993), 93
Gamble v. United States, 139 S.Ct. 1960 (2019), 157–58
Garrett v. Sandusky, 68 Ohio St.3d 139, 624 N.E.2d 704 (1993), 184
Geauga County Board of Commissioners v. Munn Road Sand & Gravel, 67 Ohio St.3d 579, 621 N.E.2d 696 (1993), 442
Geisinger v. Cook, 52 Ohio St.2d 51, 369 N.E.2d 477 (1977), 312–13
Gertz v. Robert Welch, Inc., 418 U.S. 323 (1974), 164
Gesler v. City of Worthington Income Tax Board of Appeals, 138 Ohio St.3d 76, 3 N.E.3d 1177 (2013), 551
Gideon v. Wainwright, 372 U.S. 335 (1963), 145
Gitlow v. New York, 268 U.S. 652 (1925), 179
Godfrey v. State, 898 N.W.2d 844 (Iowa 2017), 296–97
Gonidakis v. LaRose, _____ F.Supp.3d ______, 2022 WL 1175617 (S.D. Ohio April 20, 2022), 451
Gonidakis v. LaRose, _____ F.Supp.3d ______, 2022 WL 1709146 (S.D. Ohio May 27, 2022), 451
Goshorn v. Purcell, 11 Ohio St. 641 (1860), 251
Grandle v. Rhodes, 166 Ohio St. 197, 140 N.E.2d 897 (1957), 480–81
Great Southern Fire Proof Hotel Co. v. Jones, 193 U. S. 532 (1904), 255
Green v. State Civil Service Commission, 90 Ohio St. 252, 107 N.E. 531 (1914), 184–85
Gregory v. Ashcroft, 501 U.S. 452 (1991), 311
Gregory v. Flowers, 32 Ohio St.2d 48, 290 N.E.2d 181 (1972), 250
Griffin v. California, 380 U.S. 609 (1965), 153
Griffith v. Commissioners of Crawford County, 20 Ohio St. 609 (1851), 28n.138

H

Haas v. Hayslip, 51 Ohio St.2d 135, 364 N.E.2d 1376 (1977), 183, 184
Hardy v. VerMeulen, 32 Ohio St.3d 45, 512 N.E.2d 626 (1987), 79, 94n.358, 173–74
Harmon v. State, 66 Ohio St. 249 (1902), 50, 117–18
Harper v. Virginia State Board of Elections, 383 U.S. 663 (1966), 472
Haverlack v. Portage Homes, Inc., 2 Ohio St.3d 26, 442 N.E.2d 74 (1982), 184
Hawke v. Smith, 253 U.S. 221 (1920), 66–67, 67n.293, 193, 206
Haywood v. Drown, 556 U.S. 729 (2009), 468
Heath v. Alabama, 474 U.S. 82 (1985), 157–58
Hibbard v. State, 65 Ohio St 574 (1901), 23, 50, 58, 114
Hile v. City of Cleveland, 107 Ohio St. 144, 141 N.E. 35 (1923), 184–85
Hill v. Higdon, 5 Ohio St. 243 (1855), 110
Hixson v. Burson, 54 Ohio St. 470, 43 N.E. 1000 (1896), 246, 247
Hocking Val. Coal Co. v. Rosser, 53 Ohio St. 12, 41 N.E. 263, (1895), 110, 117–18
Holeton v. Crouse Cartage Co., 92 Ohio St.3d 115, 748 N.E.2d 1111 (2001), 264, 265, 266
Home Telephone & Telegraph Co. v. City of Los Angeles (1913), 109
Hoover v. Bd. of County Commissioners, 19 Ohio St.3d 1, 482 N.E.2d 575 (1985), 236–37, 238, 239
Hout v. Hout, 20 Ohio St. 119 (1870), 251
Humphrey v. Lane, 89 Ohio St.3d 62, 728 N.E.2d 1039 (2000), 96, 134–35
Husted v. A. Philip Randolph Institute, 138 S.Ct. 1833 (2018), 74n.307, 323

I

Ilersich v. Schneider, 176 Ohio St. 255, 199 N.E.2d 388 (1964) 478
Illinois v. Perkins, 496 U.S. 292 (1990), 152–53
In re A.G., 148 Ohio St.3d 118, 69 N.E.3d 646 (2016), 155, 157
In re B.C., 141 Ohio St.3d 55, 21 N.E.3d 308 (2014), 177
In re Bostwick, 43 Ohio App. 76, 181 N.E. 905 (1931), 267
In re Bostwick, 125 Ohio St. 182, 180 N.E. 713 (1932), 245, 268
In re C.F., 113 Ohio St.3d 73, 862 N.E.2d 816 (2007), 304–5
In re C.P., 131 Ohio St.3d 513, 967 N.E.2d 729 (2012), 141, 142, 181
In re Election of Nov. 6, 1990, for the Office of Attorney General, 58 Ohio St.3d 103, 569N.E.2d 447 (1991), 325–26
In re Estate of Fiore v. DiPrima, 16 Ohio App.3d 473, 476 N.E.2d 1093 (1984), 165
In re Fisher, 39 Ohio St.2d 71, 313 N.E.2d 851 (1974), 137
In re Gault, 387 U.S. 1 (1967), 181
In re Locket, 157 Ohio St. 192, 105 N.E.2d 35 (1952), 137
In re Nowak, 104 Ohio St.3d 466, 820 N.E.2d 335 (2004), 238–39
In re Proposed Annexation by Columbus City School Dist, 45 Ohio St.2d 117, 341 N.E.2d 589 (1976), 248
In re Protest Filed by Citizens for the Merit Selection of Judges, Inc., 49 Ohio St.3d 102, 551 N.E.2d 150(1990), 220
In re Suburban Motor Freight, Inc., 998 F.2d 338 (6th Cir. 1993), 264
In re T. R., 52 Ohio St.3d 6, 556 N.E.2d, 439 (1990), 171–72
Inwood v. State, 42 Ohio St. 186 (1884), 129–30
Isaac v. Intercoast Sales Corp., 132 Ohio St. 289, 7 N.E.2d 216 (1937), 183
Ives v. South Buffalo Railway Co., 94 N.E. 431 (N.Y. 1911), 51, 263

J

Johnson v. BP Chems., Inc., 85 Ohio St.3d 298, 707 N.E.2d 1107 (1999), 258–59, 264–65
Johnson v. Timmerman-Cooper, 93 Ohio St.3d 614, 757 N.E.2d 1153 (2001), 137
Johnston v. England (1817) (printed in Ervin H. Pollack ed., Ohio Unreported Judicial Decisions Prior to 1823 (1952)), 319
Jones v. City of Cleveland, 124 Ohio St. 544, 179 N.E. 741 (1932), 529
Jones v. VIP Development Co., 15 Ohio St.3d 90, 472 N.E.2d 1046 (1984), 264

K

Kaminski v. Metal & Wire Products Company, 125 Ohio St.3d 250, 927 N.E.2d 1066 (2010), 258–59, 265
Kasch v. Miller, 104 Ohio St. 281, 135 N.E. 813 (1922), 363
Kastigar v. United States, 406 U.S. 441 (1972), 152
Kennedy v. Byers, 107 Ohio St. 90 140 N.E. 630 (1923), 187
Kettering v. State Employment Relations Board, 26 Ohio St.3d 50, 496 N.E.2d 983 (1986), 538
Kilbreath v. Rudy, 16 Ohio St.2d 70, 242 N.E.2d 658 (1968), 250
King v. Safford, 19 Ohio St. 587 (1869), 42–43
Kinney v. Kaiser Aluminum & Chemical Corp., 41 Ohio St.2d 120, 322 N.E.2d 880 (1975), 136
Klein v. Leis, 146 Ohio App.3d 526, 767 N.E.2d 286 (2002), 128
Kneisley v. Lattim-Stevens Co., 40 Ohio St.3d 354, 533 N.E.2d 743 (1988), 130
Knox County Board of Commissioners. v. Knox County Engineer, 109 Ohio St.3d 353, 847 N.E.2d 1206 (2006), 480–81
Krause v. State, 31 Ohio St.2d 132, 285 N.E.2d 736 (1972), 183
Krupansky v. Pascual, 27 Ohio App. 3d 90, 499 N.E.2d 899(1985), 309

L

Lafferty v. Shinn, 38 Ohio St. 46 (1882), 173
Lansdowne v. Beacon Journal Publishing Co., 32 Ohio St.3d 176, 512 N.E.2d 979 (1987), 164
Lassiter v. Department of Social Services, 452 U.S. 18 (1981), 178
League of Women Voters of Ohio v. Ohio Redistricting Commission, ___ Ohio St.3d ___, ___ N.E.3d ____, 2022 WL 110261 (Jan. 12, 2022) (League I), 451, 453–54, 464, 466, 469
League of Women Voters of Ohio v. Ohio Redistricting Commission, ___ Ohio St. 3d ____, ____N.E.3d ____, 2022 WL 1665325 (May 25, 2022) (League V), 451
League of Women Voters of Ohio v. Ohio Redistricting Commission, ____ Ohio St.3d ____, ___N.E.3d ____, 2022 WL 354619 (Feb. 7, 2022) (League II), 451
League of Women Voters of Ohio v. Ohio Redistricting Commission, ___ Ohio St.3d ___, ___N.E.3d ____, 2022 WL 803033 (March 16, 2022) (League III), 451
League of Women Voters of Ohio v. Ohio Redistricting Commission, 166 Ohio St. 3d 1460, ____N.E.3d ____, 2022-Ohio-1235 (April 14, 2022) (League IV), 451
Lefkowitz v. Turley, 414 U.S. 70 (1973), 151
Lehman v. McBride, 15 Ohio St. 573 (1863), 239, 319
Lemon v. Kurtzman, 403 U.S. 602 (1971), 134
Liming v. Damos, 133 Ohio St.3d 509, 979 N.E.2d 297 (2012), 178
Lockhart v. Nelson, 488 U.S. 33 (1988), 156
Lucas v. Carney, 167 Ohio St. 416, 149 N.E.2d 238 (1958), 186

M

M.R. v. Niesen, ____ Ohio St.3d ____, ____N.E.3d ____, 2022 WL 1019608 (April 6, 2022), 295–96
MacNab v. Board of Park Commissioners, 108 Ohio St. 497, 141 N.E. 332 (1923), 265–66
McClain v. State, 64 Ohio St.3d 1460 (2022) (Table), 130
Mahoning County Bar Association v. Franko, 168 Ohio St. 17, 151 N.E.2d 17 (1958), 302
Maloney v. Rhodes, 45 Ohio St.2d 319, 345 N.E.2d 407 (1976), 239–40
Malcolm-Smith v. Goff, 1999 WL 961495 (Ohio Ct. App. Oct. 21, 1999), 345
Malcolm-Smith v. Goff, 90 Ohio St.3d 316, 738 N.E.2d 793 (2000), 345
Manning v. Ohio State Library Board, 62 Ohio St.3d 24, 577 N.E.2d 650 (1991), 183–84, 290
Mapp v. Ohio, 367 U.S. 643 (1961), 78n.315, 168
Marbury v. Madison, 5 U.S. (1 Cranch) 137 (1803), 26–27, 112–13
Marion Foundry Co. v. Landes, 112 Ohio St. 166, 147 N.E. 302 (1925), 472
Maryland v. Craig, 497 U.S. 836 (1990), 148
Mason v. State ex rel. McCoy, 58 Ohio St. 30, 50 N.E. 6 (1898), 130
Matheny v. Golden, 5 Ohio St. 361 (1856), 125
Mathews v. Eldridge, 424 U.S. 319 (1976), 177–78
Matter of Adoption of Y.E.F., 163 Ohio St.3d 521, 171 N.E.3d 302 (2020), 123
McConneil v. Federal Election Commission, 124 S.Ct. 619 (2003), 91
McCrone v. Bank One Corp., 107 Ohio St.3d 272, 839 N.E.2d 1 (2005), 119
McDonald v. City of Chicago, 561 U.S.742 (2010), 127–28
McMillan's Lessee v. Robbins, 5 Ohio 28 (1831), 165
Mendenhall v. City of Akron, 117 Ohio St.3d 33, 881 N.E.2d 255 (2008), 294, 536
Meyer v. Nebraska, 262 U.S. 290 (1923), 179
Milan and Richland Plank Rd. Co. v. Husted, 3 Ohio St. 578, 583 (1854), 125
Milkovich v. Lorain Journal Co., 497 U.S. 1 (1990), 164
Miller v. Alabama, 567 U.S. 460 (2012), 141–42
Miller v. Hixson, 64 Ohio St. 39, 59 N.E. 749 (1901), 250
Miller v. Korns, 107 Ohio St. 287, 140 N.E. 773 (1923), 78, 336
Miller v. State, 3 Ohio St. 475 (1854), 29, 29n.140, 81
Mills-Jennings of Ohio, Inc. v. Department of Liquor Control, 70 Ohio St.2d 95, 435 N.E.2d 407 (1982), 507, 508, 512
Miner v. Witt, 82 Ohio St. 237, 92 N.E. 21 (1910), 295
Minneapolis & St. L.R. Co. v. Bombolis, 241 U.S. 211 (1916), 129
Minnesota v. Murphy, 465 U.S. 420 (1984), 152–53
Miranda v. Arizona, 384 U.S. 436 (1966), 152–53
Mixon v. State of Ohio, 193 F.3d 389 (6th Cir. 1999), 344––45
Mominee v. Scherbarth, 28 Ohio St.3d 270, 503 N.E.2d 717 (1986), 79, 176
Monroe v. Collins, 17 Ohio St. 665 (1868), 50n.241
Morris v. Savoy, 61 Ohio St.3d 684, 576 N.E.2d 765 (1991), 79–80, 176
Morrison v. Olson, 487 U.S. 654 (1988), 193–94
Murphy v. National Collegiate Athletic Association, 138 S.Ct. 1461 (2018), 512–13

N

Nader v. Blackwell, 545 F.3d 459 (6th Cir. 2008), 219
National Federation of Independent Business v. Sebelius, 567 U.S. 519 (2012), 189
Neil v. Board of Trustees of the Ohio Agriculture and Mechanical College, 31 Ohio St. 15 (1876), 488

Neiman v. LaRose,—N.E.3d—, 2022 WL 2812895 (July 19, 2022), 566
Neiman v. LaRose, 166 Ohio St.3d 1452, 2022 WL 908387 (Table) (2022), 561
New York Times Co. v. Sullivan, 376 U.S. 254 (1964), 163
New York v. Belten, 453 U.S. 454 (1981), 167
Nolan v. Rhodes, 218 F. Supp. 953 (S.D. Ohio 1963), *rev'd*, 378 U.S. 556 (1964), 454
Nolan v. Rhodes, 378 U.S. 556 (1964), *reversing* 218 F. Supp. 953 (S.D. Ohio 1963), 455
Northern Ohio Patrolmen's Benevolent Association v. City of Parma, 61 Ohio St.2d 375, 402 N.E.2d 519 (1980), 546

O

O'Neill v. Coughlan, Case No. 04CV1612 (N.D. Ohio Sept. 14, 2004), 92n.355
Obergefell v. Hodges, 135 S. Ct. 2584 (2015), 516
Ohio Association of Public School Employees v. Twinsburg, 36 Ohio St.3d 180, 522 N.E.2d 532 (1988), 538
Ohio ex rel. Bryant v. Akron Metropolitan Park District, 281 U.S. 74 (1930), 77
Ohio Grocers Association v. Levin, 123 Ohio St.3d 303, 916 N.E.2d 446 (2009), 112–13, 485
Ohio Manufacturers' Association v. Ohioans for Drug Price Relief Act, 149 Ohio St.3d 250, 74 N.E.3d 399 (2016), 200, 224
Ohio Trucking Association v. Charles, 134 Ohio St.3d 502, 983 N.E.2d 1262 (2012), 481
Ohio v. Gallagher, 425 U.S. 257 (1976), 153
Ohio v. Johnson, 67 U.S. 493 (1984). 82n.330
Ohio v. Reiner, 532 U.S. 17 (2001), 82n.330
Ohio v. Robinette, 519 U.S. 33 (1996), 82n.330
Ohio v. Johnson, 467 U.S. 493 (1984), 82n.330
Ohio Valley Radiology Associates Inc. v. Ohio Valley Hospital Association, 28 Ohio St.3d 118, 502 N.E.2d 599 (1986), 177
Ohioans Against Corp. Bailouts v. LaRose, 157 Ohio St. 3d 1518, 136 N.E.3d 522 (2019), 203–4
Ohioans Against Corp. Bailouts v. LaRose, 157 Ohio St. 3d 1559, 138 N.E.3d 1151 (2020) (Table), 203–4
Ohioans Against Corp. Bailouts v. LaRose, 417 F. Supp. 3d 962 (S.D. Ohio 2019), *appeal dismissed*, 2020 WL 858155 (6th Cir. Jan. 22, 2020), 203
Ohioans for Concealed Carry, Inc. v. City of Clyde, 120 Ohio St.3d 96, 896 N.E.2d 967 (2008), 536–37

P

Pacific States Tel. & Tel. Co. v. Oregon, 223 U.S. 118 (1912), 296
Palmer v. Tingle, 55 Ohio St. 423, 45 N.E. 313 (1896), 50, 58, 106, 113, 114, 115, 117–18, 255
Parratt v. Taylor, 451 U.S. 527 (1981), 177–78
Paul v. Davis, 424 U.S. 693 (1976), 178–79
Pauley v. Kelly, 162 W.Va. 672, 255 S.E.2d 859 (W. Va. 1979), 335–36
Pegan v. Crawmer, 76 Ohio St.3d 97, 666 N.E.2d 1091 (1996), 137
Pennhurst State School & Hospital v. Halderman, 465 U.S. 89 (1984), 184
Pfeifer v. Graves, 88 Ohio St. 473, 104 N.E. 529 (1913), 199, 223
Pim v. Nicholson, 6 Ohio St. 176 (1856), 237–38
Planned Parenthood of Southeastern Pennsylvania v. Casey, 505 U.S. 833 (1992), 180
Plessy v. Ferguson, 163 U.S. 537 (1896)
Press-Enterprise Co. v. Superior Court, 484 U.S. 510 (1984) (*Press-Enterprise I*), 172
Press-Enterprise Co. v. Superior Court, 478 U.S. 1 (1986) (*Press-Enterprise II*), 172

Preterm–Cleveland, Inc. v. Kasich, 153 Ohio St.3d 157, 102 N.E.3d 461(2018), 239
Primes v. Tyler, 43 Ohio St.2d 195, 331 N.E.2d 723 (1975), 119, 125
ProgressOhio.org, Inc. v. JobsOhio, 139 Ohio St.3d 520, 13 N.E.3d 1101 (2014), 291, 292, 306–7, 422
ProgressOhio.org, Inc. v. Kasich, 129 Ohio St.3d 449, 953 N.E.2d 329 (2011), 301, 422
Protestants & Other Americans United for Separation of Church & State v. Essex, 28 Ohio St.2d 79, 275 N.E.2d 603 (1971), 339
Provens v. Stark County Board of Mental Retardation & Developmental Disabilities, 64 Ohio St.3d 252, 594 N.E.2d 959 (1992), 296–97
Pruneyard Shopping Center v. Robbins, 447 U.S. 74 (1980), 112–13
Put-In-Bay Island Taxing District Authority v. Colonial, Inc., 65 Ohio St.3d 449, 605 N.E.2d21 (1992), 247

Q

Quilter v. Voinovich, 857 F. Supp. 579 (N. D. Ohio 1994), 460

R

City of Rocky River v. State Employment Relations Bd., 43 Ohio St.3d 1, 539 N.E.2d 103 (1989) (on rehearing), 94, 256–57, 263–64, 266, 541–42
Raudabaugh v. State, 96 Ohio St. 513, 118 N.E. 102 (1917), 183
Redman v. Ohio Dept. of Industrial Relations, Ohio St.3d 399, 662 N.E.2d 352 (1996), 194–95
Reed v. Rhodes, 607 F.2d 714 (6th Cir. 1979), 341
Republican Party of Minnesota v. White, 536 U.S. 765 (2002), 96
Reynolds v. Sims, 377 U.S. 533 (1964), 71, 448
Richardson v. Ramirez, 418 U.S. 24 (1974), 326
Richmond Newspapers, Inc. v. Virginia, 448 U.S. 555 (1980), 126, 171–72
Ritzman v Campbell, 93 Ohio St. 246, 112 N.E. 591 (1915), 231
Robins v. Pruneyard Shopping Center, 23 Cal.3d 899, 153 Cal.Rptr. 854, 592 P.2d 341 (1979), 163
Robinson v. California, 370 U.S. 660 (1962), 139
Rockey v. 84 Lumber Co., 66 Ohio St.3d 221, 611 N.E.2d 789 (1993), 308–9
Roe v. Wade, 410 U.S. 113 (1973), 85
Roper v. Simmons, 543 U.S. 551 (2005), 142
Ross v. Farmers Insurance Group of Companies, 82 Ohio St.3d 281, 695 N.E.2d 732 (1998), 251–52
Ruch v. State, 111 Ohio St. 580, 146 N.E. 67 (1924), 314
Rucho v. Common Cause, 139 S.Ct. 2484 (2019), 554
Ruta v. Breckenridge-Remy Co., 69 Ohio St.2d 66, 430 N.E.2d 935 (1982), 304
Ruther v. Kaiser, 134 Ohio St.3d 408, 983 N.E.2d 291 (2012), 94n.358, 173–74
Rutherford v. M'Fadden (1807) (printed in Ervin H. Pollack ed., Ohio Unreported Judicial Decisions Prior to 1823 (1952)), 26–27, 27n.125,244, 297

S

Salt Creek Valley Turnpike Co. v. Parks, 50 Ohio St. 568, 35 N.E. 304 (1893), 175
San Antonio Independent School District v. Rodriguez, 411 U.S. 1 (1973), 121, 336
Saviers v. Smith, 101 Ohio St. 132, 128 N.E. 269 (1920), 478

Schafer v. Haller, 108 Ohio St. 322, 140 N.E. 517 (1923), 114
Schaller v. Rogers, 2008 WL 4078446 (Ohio Ct. App. Sept. 4, 2008), 203, 220–21
Scott v. Bank One Trust Co., 62 Ohio St.3d 39, 577 N.E.2d 1077 (1991), 293–94
Scott-Pontzer v. Liberty Mutual fire Insurance Co. 85 Ohio St.3d 660, 710 N.E.2d 1161 (2004), 93--94
Second Nat. Bank v. Becker, 62 Ohio St. 289, 56 N.E. 1025 (1900), 170
Shie v. Leonard, 84 Ohio St.3d 160, 702 N.E.2d 419 (1998), 137
Shimko v. Lobe, 103 Ohio St.3d 59, 813 N.E.2d 669 (2004), 130
Shryock v. City of Zanesville, 92 Ohio St. 375, 110 N. E. 937 (1915), 544
Simmons-Harris v. Goff, 86 Ohio St.3d 1,711 N.E.2d 203 (1999), 111, 134, 238, 338–40
Singer v. City of Fairborn, 73 Ohio App.3d 809, 598 N.E.2d 806 (1991), 127
Singer v. United States, 384 U.S. 24 (1965), 131
Smith v. Board of Education, 97 Ohio App. 507, 127 N.E.2d 623 (1954), 343
Smith v. Leis, 106 Ohio St.3d 309, 857 N.E.2d 138 (2005), 138
Smothers v. Gresham Transfer, Inc., 332 Or. 83, 110, 23 P.3d 333 (2001), 173
Sogg v. Zurz, 121 Ohio St.3d 449, 905 N.E.2d 187 (2009), 186
Sorrell v. Thevenir, 69 Ohio St.3d 415, 633 N.E.2d 504 (1994), 94n.359, 130, 177
Sorrentino v. Ohio National Guard, 53 Ohio St.3d 214, 560 N.E.2d 186 (1990), 243
Southern Gum Co. v. Laylin, 66 Ohio St. 578, 64 N.E. 564 (1902), 491
Southern Ohio Power Co. v. Public Utilities Commission, 110 Ohio St. 246, 143 N.E. 700 (1924), 543
State ex rel. Abernathy v. Lucas County Board of Elections, 156 Ohio St.3d 238, 125 N.E.3d 832 (2019), 213, 215
State ex rel. Ach v. Braden, 125 Ohio St. 307, 181 N.E. 138 (1932), 278
State ex rel. Ach v. Evans, 90 Ohio St. 243, 107 N.E. 537 (1914), 344
State ex rel. Akron Education Association v. Essex, 47 Ohio St.2d 47, 351 N.E.2d 118 (1976), 241
State ex rel. Attorney General v. City of Cincinnati, 20 Ohio St. 18 (1870), 112–13
State ex rel. Attorney General v. City of Cincinnati, 23 Ohio St. 445 (1872), 488
State ex rel. Attorney General v. Covington, 29 Ohio St. 102 (1876), 188–89
State ex rel. Attorney General v. Guilbert, 56 Ohio. St. 575 (1897), 50, 59, 269
State ex rel. Attorney General v. Kennon, 7 Ohio St. 546 (1857), 249
State ex rel. Attorney General v. Kinney, 56 Ohio St.721, 47 N.E. 569 (1897), 47, 77n.312, 195–96, 223, 524
State ex rel. Automatic Registering Machine Co. v. Green, 121 Ohio St. 301, 168 N.E. 131 (1929), 324
State ex rel. Bailey v. Celebrezze, 67 Ohio St.2d 516, 426 N.E.2d 493 (1981), 520
State ex rel. Bardo v. City of Lyndhurst, 37 Ohio St.3d 106, 524 N.E.2d 447 (1988), 545–46
State ex rel. Barren v. Brown, 51 Ohio St.2d 169, 365 N.E.2d 887 (1977), 202
State ex rel. Bateman v. Bode, 55 Ohio St. 224, 45 N.E. 195 (1896), 118, 323
State ex rel. Beard v. Hardin, 153 Ohio St.3d 571, 109 N.E.3d 1174 (2018), 215–16
State ex rel. Bray v. Russell, 89 Ohio St.3d 132, 729 N.E.2d 359 (2000), 297
State ex rel. Brothers v. Zellar, 7 Ohio St.2d 109, 218 N.E.2d 729 (1966), 286
State ex rel. Brown v. Beard, 48 Ohio St.2d 290, 358 N.E.2d 569 (1976), 421, 430
State ex rel. Brown v. Ferguson, 32 Ohio St.2d 245, 291 N.E.2d 434 (1972), 241
State ex rel. Bruestle v. Rich, 159 Ohio St. 13, 110 N.E. 778 (1953), 421
State ex rel. Bryant v. Akron Metropolitan Park District for Summit County, 120 Ohio St. 464, 166 N.E. 407 (1929), 298
State ex rel. Burns v. DiSalle, 172 Ohio St. 363, 176 N.E.2d 428 (1961), 78n.314, 286
State ex rel. Carriger v. City of Galion, 53 Ohio St.3d 250, 560 N.E.2d 194 (1990), 133

State ex rel. Cherrington, Pros. Atty., v. Hutsinpiller, 112 Ohio St. 468, 147 N. E. 647 (1925), 541
State ex rel. Citizens Action for a Livable Montgomery v. Hamilton County Board of Elections, 115 Ohio St.3d 437, 875 N.E.2d 902 (2007), 215–16
State ex rel. City Loan & Savings Co. of Wapakoneta v. Moore, 124 Ohio St. 256, 177 N.E. 910 (1931), 229
State ex rel. City of Fostoria v. King, 154 Ohio St. 213, 94 N.E.2d 697 (1950), 544
State ex rel. City of Portsmouth v. Kountz, 129 Ohio St. 272, 194 N.E. 869 (1935), 483
State ex rel. Cleveland Right to Life v. State of Ohio Controlling Board, 138 Ohio St.3d 57, 3 N.E.3d 185 (2013), 195, 241
State ex rel. Cook v. Cook, 66 Ohio St. 566, 64 N.E. 7 (1902), 170
State ex rel. Cordray v. Helms, 192 Ohio App.3d 426, 949 N.E.2d 522 (2011), 188
State ex rel. Cordray v. Marshall, 123 Ohio St.3d 229, 915 N.E.2d 633 (2009), 273
State ex rel. Core v. Green, 160 Ohio St. 175, 115 N.E.2d 157 (1953), 343
State ex rel. Cramer v. Brown, 7 Ohio St.3d 5, 454 N.E.2d 132 (1983), 223
State ex rel. Davis Invest. Co. v. Columbus, 175 Ohio St. 337, 194 N.E.2d 859 (1963), 206
State ex rel. Dayton Fraternal Order of Police Lodge No. 44 v. State Employment Relations Board, 22 Ohio St.3d 1,488 N.E.2d 181 (1986), 120, 247
State ex rel. Dickman v. Defenbacher, 164 Ohio St. 142, 128 N.E.2d 59 (1955), 112, 421
State ex rel. Dix v. Celeste, 11 Ohio St.3d 141, 464 N.E.2d 153 (1984), 238
State ex rel. Doerfler v. Price, 101 Ohio St. 50, 128 N.E. 173 (1920), 144
State ex rel. Donahey v. Edmonson, 89 Ohio St. 93, 105 N.E. 269 (1913), C0.P31 n.46
State ex rel. Duclos v. Hamilton Cty. Bd. of Elections, 145 Ohio St. 3d 254, 48 N.E.3d 543 (2016), 224
State ex rel. Duerk v. Donahey, 67 Ohio St.2d 216, 423 N.E.2d 429 (1981), 428–29
State ex rel. Duffy v. Sweeney, 152 Ohio St. 308, 89 N.E.2d 641 (1949), 201
State ex rel. Durell v. Celebrezze, 63 Ohio App.2d 125, 409 N.E.2d 1044 (1979), 208
State ex rel. Ebersole v. Powell, 141 Ohio St.3d 17, 21 N.E.3d 274 (2014), 548
State ex rel. Edwards v. Murray, 48 Ohio St.2d 303, 358 N.E.2d 577 (1976), 297
State ex rel. Emhoff v. Medina County Board of Elections, 153 Ohio St.3d 313, 106 N.E.3d 21 (2018), 302.
State ex rel. Espen v. Wood County Board of Elections, 154 Ohio St.3d 1, 110 N.E.3d 1222 (2017), 214
State ex rel. Ethics First—You Decide Ohio Political Action Committee v. DeWine, 147 Ohio St.3d 373, 66 N.E.3d 689 (2016), 220, 222
State ex rel. Evans v. Dudley, 1 Ohio St. 437 (1853), 567
State ex rel. Evans v. Moore, 69 Ohio St.2d 88, 431 N.E.2d 31 (1982), 537, 538
State ex rel. Field v. Williams, 34 Ohio St. 218 (1877), 252
State ex rel. Flak v. Betras, 152 Ohio St.3d 244, 95 N.E.3d 329 (2017), 213
State ex rel. Fleming v. Fox, 158 Ohio St.3d 244, 141 N.E.3d 138 (2019), 215
State ex rel. Cleveland v. Kosydar, 36 Ohio St.2d 183, 305 N.E.2d 803 (1973), 478
State ex rel. Garnes v. McCann, 21 Ohio St. 198 (1871), 118, 341
State ex rel. Gibson v. Board of Education of Oxford, 45 Ohio St. 555, 16 N.E. 373 (1888), 341
State ex rel. Glander v. Ferguson, 148 Ohio St. 581, 76 N.E.2d 373 (1947), 243
State ex rel. Gottlieb v. Sulligan, 175 Ohio St. 238, 193 N.E.2d 270 (1963), 249
State ex rel. Greenlund v. Fulton, 99 Ohio St. 168, 124 N.E. 172 (1919), 88, 475
State ex rel. Groh v. Board Education of West Clermont Local School District, 169 Ohio St. 54, 157 N.E.2d 325 (1959), 343
State ex rel. Harbage v. Ferguson, 68 Ohio App. 189, 36 N.E.2d 500 (1941), 253
State ex rel. Jones v. Husted, 147 Ohio St.3d 341, 65 N.E.3d 733 (2016) (*Jones I*), 223–24, 443
State ex rel. Jones v. Husted, 149 Ohio St.3d 110, 73 N.E.3d 463 (2016) (*Jones II*), 295

State ex rel. Heller v. Miller, 61 Ohio St.2d 6, 399 N.E.2d 66 (1980), 99n.367, 110, 120, 176, 178
State ex rel. Henneke v. Davis, 25 Ohio St.3d 23, 494 N.E.2d 1133 (1986), 289–316
State ex rel. Herbert v. Bricker, 139 Ohio St. 499, 41 N.E.2d 377 (1942), 448
State ex rel. Herbert v. Ferguson, 142 Ohio St. 496, 52 N.E.2d 980 (1944), 191–270
State ex rel. Herron v. Smith, 44 Ohio St. 348, 7 N.E. 447 (1886), 231
State ex rel. Hinchliffe v. Gibbons, 116 Ohio St. 390, 156 N.E. 455 (1927), 548
State ex rel. Hinkle v. Franklin County Board of Elections, 62 Ohio St.3d 145, 580 N.E.2d 767 (1991), 238
State ex rel. Hodges v. Taft, 64 Ohio St.3d 1, 591 N.E.2d 1186 (1992), 205, 230
State ex rel. Hoel v. Brown, 105 Ohio St. 479, 138 N.E. 230 (1922), 268
State ex rel. Horner v. Anderson, 41 Ohio St.2d 166, 324 N.E.2d 572 (1975), 286
State ex rel. Howard v. Ferreri, 70 Ohio St.3d 587, 639 N.E.2d 1189 (1994), 178
State ex rel. Howland v. Krause, 130 Ohio St. 455, 200 N.E. 512 (1936), 78n.314, 443
State ex rel. Hubbell v. Bettman, 124 Ohio St. 24, 176 N.E. 664 (1931), 221, 222
State ex rel. Huebner v. West Jefferson Village Council, 75 Ohio St.3d 381, 662 N.E.2d 339(1996), 544, 551–52
State ex rel. Hughes, v. Brown, 31 Ohio St.2d 41, 285 N.E.2d 376 (1972), 267
State ex rel. Jackman v. Cuyahoga County Court of Common Pleas, 9 Ohio St.2d 159, 224 N.E.2d 906 (1967), 193
State ex rel. JobsOhio v. Goodman, 133 Ohio St.3d 297, 978 N.E.2d 153 (2012), 301, 422
State ex rel. Karlinger v. Board of Deputy State Supervisors of Elections, 80 Ohio St. 471 (1909), 51, 324
State ex rel. Kauer v. Defenbacher, 153 Ohio St. 268, 91 N.E.2d 512 (1950), 243, 488
State ex rel. Kear v. Lucas County Court of Common Pleas, 67 Ohio St.2d 189, 423 N.E.2d 427(1981), 130
State ex rel. Keller v. Forney, 108 Ohio St. 463, 141 N.E. 16 (1923), 205
State ex rel. Khumprakob v. Mahoning County Board of Elections, 153 Ohio St.3d 581, 109 N.E.3d 1184 (2018) 213, 214
State ex rel. King v. Rhodes, 11 Ohio St.2d 95, 228 N.E.2d 653 (1967), 469
State ex rel. Kittel v. Bigelow, 138 Ohio St. 497, 7 N.E.2d 41 (1941), 295
State ex rel. Knisely v. Jones, 66 Ohio St. 453 (1902), 50, 56, 59, 246, 531–32
State ex rel. Kohler v. Cincinnati, W. & B. Ry. Co.,47 Ohio St. 130, 23 N.E. 928 (1890), 487
State ex rel. Koren v. Grogan, 68 Ohio St.3d 590, 629 N.E.2d 446 (1994), 152
State ex rel. Krieg v. Matia, 138 Ohio St. 504, 37 N.E.2d 53 (1941), 248
State ex rel. Lake County Board of Commissioners v. Zupancic, 62 Ohio St.3d 297, 581 N.E.2d 1086 (1991), 429
State ex rel. Landis v. Board of County Commissioners, 95 Ohio St. 157, 115 N.E. 919 (1917), 226–27
State ex rel. Leaverton v. Kerns, 104 Ohio St. 550, 136 N.E. 217 (1922), 390
State ex rel. Lentz v. Edwards, 90 Ohio St. 305, 107 N.E. 768 (1914), 538
State ex rel. LetOhioVote.org v. Hon. Jennifer Brunner, 123 Ohio St.3d 322, 916 N.E.2d 462 (2009), 192
State ex rel. Lewis v. Hamilton County Bd. of Elections, 74 Ohio St.3d 1201, 655 N.E.2d 177(1995), 551–52
State ex rel. Liberty Council v. Brunner, 125 Ohio St.3d 315, 928 N.E.2d 410 (2010), 522
State ex rel. Magsig v. City of Toledo, 160 Ohio St.3d 342, 156 N.E.3d 899 (2020), 298, 537
State ex rel. Maurer v. Sheward, 71 Ohio St.3d 513, 644 N.E.2d 369 (1994), 27n.125, 76, 280
State ex rel. Maxcy v. Saferin, 155 Ohio St.3d 496, 122 N.E.3d 1165 (2018), 211, 213, 548
State ex rel. McCann v. Delaware County Bd. of Elections, 155 Ohio St. 3d 14, 118 N.E.3d 224 (2018), 195

State ex rel. McElroy v. Baron, 169 Ohio St 439, 160 N.E.2d 10(1959), 421
State ex rel. McGinn v. Walker, 151 Ohio St.3d 199, 87 N.E.3d 204 (2017), 213–14, 443
State ex rel. McKean v. Graves, 91 Ohio St. 23 (1914), 308
State ex rel. McNamara v. Campbell, 94 Ohio St. 403, 115 N.E. 29 (1916), 243, 523
State ex rel. Meshel v. Keip, 66 Ohio St.2d 379, 423 N.E.2d 60 (1981), 194–95, 226–27
State ex rel. Miller v. Anthony, 72 Ohio St.3d 132, 647 N.E.2d 1368 (1995), 165
State ex rel. Morrison v. Beck Energy Corp., 143 Ohio St.3d 271, 37 N.E.3d 128 (2015), 536–37
State ex rel. Murray v. Scioto County Board of Elections, 127 Ohio St.3d 280, 939 N.E.2d 157 (2010), 545
State ex rel. National City Bank v. Board of Education of Cleveland City School District, 52 Ohio St.2d 81, 369 N.E.2d 1200 (1977), 483
State ex rel. Newell v. Brown, 162 Ohio St. 147 (1954), 292
State ex rel. Nolan v. ClenDening, 93 Ohio St. 264, 112 N.E. 1029 (1915), 202
State ex rel. Ohio Academy of Trial Lawyers v. Sheward, 86 Ohio St.3d 451, 715 N.E.2d 1062 (1999), 79–80, 173, 237, 238, 290–91, 292
State ex rel. Ohio AFL-CIO v. Ohio Bur. of Workers' Compensation, 97 Ohio St.3d 504, 780 N.E.2d 981 (2002), 96
State ex rel. Ohio AFL-CIO v. Voinovich, 69 Ohio St.3d 225, 631 N.E.2d 582 (1994), 205, 236–37, 238
State ex rel. Ohio Civil Serv. Employees Association v. State, 146 Ohio St.3d 315, 56 N.E.3d 913 (2016), 239
State ex rel. Ohio Civil Service Employees Association v. State Emp. Relations Bd., 104 Ohio St.3d 122, 818 N.E.2d 688 (2004), 238–39
State ex rel. Ohio Congress of Parents & Teachers v. State Board of Education, 111 Ohio St. 3d 568, 857 N.W.2d 1148 (2006), 340,343–44, 345
State ex rel. Ohio Funds Management Board v. Walker, 55 Ohio St.3d 1, 561 N.E.2d 927 (1990), 364
State ex rel. Ohio General Assembly v. Brunner, 114 Ohio St.3d 386, 872 N.E.2d 912 (2006), 242
State ex rel. Ohio Gen. Assembly v. Brunner, 115 Ohio St.3d 103, 873 N.E.2d 1232 (2007), 203, 522
State ex rel. Ohio Liberty Council v. Brunner, 125 Ohio St.3d 315, 928 N.E.2d 410 (2010), 222
State ex rel. Ohio Roundtable v. Taft, 2003 WL 21470307 (Ohio Ct. App. June 26, 2003), 509
State ex rel. Ohio Turnpike Commission v. Allen, 158 Ohio St. 168, 107 N.E.2d 345 (1952), 278, 363
State ex rel. Ohioans for Fair Districts v. Husted, 130 Ohio St.3d 240, 957 N.E.2d 277 (2011), 205
State ex rel. Oster v. Lorain County Board of Elections, 93 Ohio St.3d 480, 756 N.E.2d 649(2001), 219
State ex rel. OTR v. Columbus, 76 Ohio St.3d 203, 607 N.E.2d 8 (1996), 186
State ex rel. Park Investment Co. v. Board of Tax Appeals, 175 Ohio St. 410, 195 N.E.2d 908(1964), 475
State ex rel. Patton v. Myers, 127 Ohio St. 95, 186 N.E. 872 (1933), 203
State ex rel. Petro v. Marshall, 2006-Ohio-5357, 2006 WL 2924762 (Ohio Ct. App. Oct. 10, 2006), 273
State ex rel. Pirman v. Money, 69 Ohio St.3d 591, 635 N.E.2d 26 (1994), 137
State ex rel. Preble County Board of Commissioners v. Mong, 12 Ohio St.3d 66, 465 N.E.2d 428 (1984), 428–29
State ex rel. Price v. Huwe, 105 Ohio St. 304, 137 N.E. 167 (1922), 354
State ex rel. Public Institutional Building Authority v. Griffith, 135 Ohio St. 604, 22 N.E.2d 200(1939), 363, 364

State ex rel. Public Institutional Building Authority v. Neffner, 137 Ohio St. 390, 30 N.E.2d 705 (1940), 364
State ex rel. Ramey v. Davis, 119 Ohio St. 596, 165 N.E. 298 (1929), 541
State ex rel. ResponsibleOhio v. Ohio Ballot Bd., No. 2015-1411, 2015 Ohio LEXIS 2391 (Ohio Sept. 16, 2015), 208
State ex rel. Rhodes v. Brown, 34 Ohio St.2d 101, 296 N.E.2d 538 (1973), 78n.314, 275
State ex rel. Roahrig v. Brown, 30 Ohio St.2d 82, 282 N.E.2d 584 (1972), 223, 228, 521
State ex rel. Roof v. Hardin County Board of Commissioners, 39 Ohio St.2d 130, 314 N.E.2d 172(1974), 325
State ex rel. S. Monroe & Sons Co. v. Baker, 112 Ohio St. 356, 147 N.E. 501 (1925), 276
State ex rel. Saxbe v. Alexander, 168 Ohio St. 404, 155 N.E.2d 678 (1959), 488
State ex rel. Saxbe v. Brand, 176 Ohio St. 44, 197 N.E.2d 328 (1964), 78n.314, 421, 427
State ex rel. Schorr v. Kennedy, 132 Ohio St. 510, 9 N.E.2d 278 (1937), 206
State ex rel. Schwartz v. Ferris, 53 Ohio St. 314 (1895), 50, 117, 120–21, 478
State ex rel. Schwerdtfeger v. Husted, Case No. 16CV-2348 (Franklin Co. CCP 2016), 321
State ex rel. Ohioans for Secure and Fair Elections v. LaRose, 159 Ohio St.3d 568 152 N.E.3d 267 (2020), 203, 222
State ex rel. Sensible Norwood v. Hamilton County Bd. of Elections, 148 Ohio St.3d 176, 69 N.E.3d 696 (2016), 213, 215, 542
State ex rel. Sheets v. Laylin, 68 Ohio St. 1, 68 N.E. 574 (1903), 49
State ex rel. Shemo v. City of Mayfield Heights., 95 Ohio St.3d 59, 765 N.E.2d 345 (2002), *Cert. denied*, 538 U.S. 906 (2003), 186
State ex rel. Shkurti v. Withrow, 32 Ohio St.3d 424, 513 N.E.2d 1332 (1987), 364, 365
State ex rel. Silcott v. Spahr, 50 Ohio St.3d 110, 552 N.E.2d 926 (1990), 309
State ex rel. Singer v. Cartledge, 129 Ohio St. 279, 195 N.E. 237 (1935), 211
State ex rel. Slemmer v. Brown, 34 Ohio App. 2d 27, 295 N.E.2d 434 (1973), 522
State ex rel. Spirko v. Judges of Court of Appeals, 27 Ohio St. 3d 13, 501 N.E.2d 625 (1986), 183
State ex rel. Squire v. Harris, 59 Ohio App. 165, 17 N.E.2d 425 (1938), 490
State ex rel. State v Lewis, 99 Ohio St.3d 97, 789 N.E.2d 195, *cert. denied*, 540 U,S, 966 (2003), 96, 338
State ex rel. Struble v. Davis, 132 Ohio St. 555, 9 N.E.2d 684 (1937), 491
State ex rel. Suwalski v. Peeler, ___ Ohio St.3d _____, ___ N.E.3d _____, 2021 WL 5364386 (Nov. 18, 2021), 161
State ex rel. Sylvester v. Neal, 140 Ohio St.3d 47, 14 N.E.3d 1024 (2014), 138, 248
State ex rel. Taft v. Franklin County Court of Common Pleas, 81 Ohio St.3d 480, 692 N.E.2d 560 (1998), 248
State ex rel. Taylor v. French, 96 Ohio St. 172, 117 N.E. 173 (1917), 320
State ex rel. The Cincinnati Post v. Second District Court of Appeals, 65 Ohio St.3d 378, 604 N.E.2d 153 (1992), 172
State ex rel. The Repository v. Unger, 28 Ohio St.3d 418, 504 N.E.2d 37 (1986), 79, 172
State ex rel. Thomas v. McGinty, 164 Ohio St.3d 167, 172 N.E.3d 824 (2020), 161
State ex rel. Toledo Blade Co. v. Henry County Court of Common Pleas, 125 Ohio St.3d 149, 926 N.E.2d 634 (2010), 163, 172
State ex rel. Toledo Edison Co. v. City of Clyde, 76 Ohio St.3d 508, 668 N.E.2d 498 (1996), 543
State ex rel. Toledo v. Lucas County Board of Elections, 95 Ohio St.3d 73, 765 N.E.2d 854 (2002), 529
State ex rel. Tomino v. Brown, 47 Ohio St.3d 119, 549 N.E.2d 505 (1989), 424
State ex rel. Trauger v. Nash, 66 Ohio St. 612 (1902), 292
State ex rel. Tulley v. Brown, 29 Ohio St.2d 235, 281 N.E.2d 187 (1972), 203

State ex rel. Turner v. U. S. Fid. & Guar. Co. of Baltimore, Md., 96 Ohio St. 250, 117 N.E. 232 (1917), 58n.271
State ex rel. Twitchell v. Saferin, 155 Ohio St.3d 52, 119 N.E.3d 365 (2018), 214
State ex rel. Walgate v. Kasich, 139 S. Ct. 108 (2018), *denying cert. to* 93 N.E.3d 417 (Ohio Ct. App. 2017), 512
State ex rel. Walgate v. Kasich, 147 Ohio St.3d 1, 59 N.E.3d 1240 (2016), 291–92, 512, 513
State ex rel. Walker v. Husted, 144 Ohio St.3d 361, 43 N.E.3d 419 (2015), 212, 443
State ex rel. Walter v. Vogel, 169 Ohio St. 368, 159 N.E.2d 892 (1959), 480–81
State ex rel. Weaver v. Board of Trustees, 126 Ohio St. 290, 185N.E. 196 (1933), 78, 118
State ex rel. Weinberger v. Miller, 87 Ohio St. 12, 99 N.E. 1078 (1912), 112–13, 319–20, 321
State ex rel. Whiteman v. Chase, 5 Ohio St. 528 (1856), 276
State ex rel. Wilen v. Kent, 144 Ohio St.3d 121, 41 N.E.3d 390 (2015), 548
State ex rel. Wright v. Ohio Adult Parole Authority, 75 Ohio St.3d 82, 661 N.E.2d 728 (1996), 166–67
State ex rel. Yaple v. Creamer, 85 Ohio St. 349, 97 N.E. 602 (1912), 51, 263
State ex rel. City of Youngstown v. Mahoning Cty. Bd. of Elections, 144 Ohio St.3d 239, 41 N.E.3d 1229 (2015), 212
State ex rel. Zeigler v. Zumbar, 129 Ohio St.3d 240, 951 N.E.2d 405 (2011), 268
State ex rel. Ziegler v. Hamilton County Board of Elections, 67 Ohio St.3d 588, 621 N.E.2d 1199(1993), 546
State ex rel. Zupancic v. Limbach, 58 Ohio St.3d 130, 568 N.E.2d 1206 (1991), 247
State ex rel. Carney v. Brown, 11 Ohio App. 2d 239, 230 N.E.2d 350 (1967), 232
State Farm Mutual Automobile Insurance Co. v. Campbell, 123 S. Ct. 1513 (2003), 143
State Personnel Board of Review v. Bay Village Civil Service Commission, 28 Ohio St.3d 214, 503 N.E.2d 518 (1986), 538
State v. Aalim, 150 Ohio St.3d 463, 83 N.E.3d 862 (2016) (Aalim I), 182
State v. Aalim, 150 Ohio St.3d 489, 83 N.E.3d 883 (2017) (Aalim II) (on reconsideration), 180, 182, 306
State v. Adkins, 129 Ohio St.3d 287, 951 N.E.2d 766 (2011), 250–51
State v. Anderson, 148 Ohio St.3d 74, 68 N.E.3d 790 (2016), 157, 177
State v. Arnold, 126 Ohio St.3d 290, 933 N.E.2d 775 (2010), 148
State v. Barhorst, 106 App. 335, 153 N.E. 2d 514 (1959), 500
State v. Baughman, 38 Ohio St. 455 (1882), 293
State v. Bembry, 90 N.E.3d 891, 151 Ohio St.3d 502 (2017), 169
State v. Bethel, 110 Ohio St.3d 416, 854 N.E.2d 150 (2006), 149–50
State v. Bevacqua, 147 Ohio St. 20, 22, 67 N.E.2d 786 (1946), 138
State v. Bode, 144 Ohio St.3d 155, 41 20153d 1156 (2015), 98n.364, 181
State v. Bodyke, 126 Ohio St.3d 266, 933 N.E.2d 753 (2010), 94, 194
State v. Boykin, 138 Ohio St.3d 97, 4 N.E.3d 980 (2013), 280
State v. Brewer, 121 Ohio St.3d 202, 903 N.E.2d 284 (2009), 156
State v. Broom, 146 Ohio St.3d 60, 51 N.E.3d 620 (2016), 142, 157
State v. Brown, 2 Ohio App.3d 321, 441 N.E.2d 1126 (1981), 157–58
State v. Brown, 38 Ohio St.3d 305, 528 N.E.2d 523 (1988), 144
State v. Brown, 63 Ohio St.3d 349, 588 N.E.2d 113 (1992), 167
State v. Brown, 64 Ohio St.3d 649, 597 N.E.2d 510 (1992), 81–82, 149
State v. Brown, 99 Ohio St.3d 323, 792 N.E.2d 175 (2003), 96, 168
State v. Brown, 142 Ohio St.3d 92, 28 N.E.3d 81(2015), 298
State v. Brown, 143 Ohio St.3d 444, 39 N.E.3d 496 (2015), 98n.364, 169
State v. Buckley, 16 Ohio St.2d 128, 243 N.E.2d 66 (1968), 119
State v. Carter, 89 Ohio St.3d 593, 734 N.E.2d 345 (2000), 140

State v. Chaffin, 30 Ohio St.2d 13, 282 N.E.2d 46 (1972), 139
State v. Coleman, 45 Ohio St.3d 298, 544 N.E.2d 622 (1989), 140
State v. D.H., 120 Ohio St.3d 540, 901 N.E.2d 209 (2009), 181
State v. Davis, 131 Ohio St.3d 1, 959 N.E.2d 516 (2011), 304
State v. Evans, 144 Ohio App.3d 539, 760 N.E.2d 909 (2001), 152
State v. Farris, 109 Ohio St.3d 519, 849 N.E.2d 985 (2006), 153
State v. Ferguson, 175 Ohio St. 390, 195 N.E.2d 794 (1964), 155
State v. Fletcher, 26 Ohio St.2d 221, 271 N.E.2d 567 (1971), 157–58
State v. Gallagher, 46 Ohio St.2d 225, 348 N.E.2d 336 (1976), 111, 153
State v. Gardner, 58 Ohio St. 599, 51 N.E. 136 (1898), 50, 117–18
State v. Geraldo, 68 Ohio St.2d 120, 429 N.E.2d 141 (1981), 166–67
State v. Greer, 66 Ohio St.2d 139, 420 N.E.2d 982 (1981), 145
State v. Gustafson, 76 Ohio St.3d 425, 668 N.E.2d 435 (1996), 154, 156
State v. Hairston, 118 Ohio St.3d 289, 888 N.E.2d 1073 (2008), 139
State v. Hand, 149 Ohio St.3d 94, 73 N.E.3d 448 (2016), 181
State v. Harmon, 31 Ohio St. 250 (1877), 297
State v. Harris, 58 Ohio St.2d 257, 389 N.E.2d 1121 (1979), 155
State v. Hensley, 75 Ohio St. 255, 79 N.E. 462 (1906), 149–50
State v. Heston, 29 Ohio St.2d 152, 280 N.E.2d 376 (1972), 152
State v. Hill, 92 Ohio St.3d 191, 749 N.E.2d 274 (2001), 150–51
State v. Hipp, 38 Ohio St. 199 (1882), 66, 77n.310
State v. Hochhausler, 76 Ohio St.3d 455, 668 N.E.2d 457 (1996), 178, 254
State v. Hubbard, ___ Ohio St.3d ___, ___ N.E.3d ____, 2021 WL 4898587 (Oct. 21, 2021), 251
State v. Jackson, 102 Ohio St.3d 380, 811 N.E.2d 68 (2004), 324
State v. Jenkins, 15 Ohio St.3d 164, 473 N.E.2d 264 (1984), 140
State v. Johnson, 141 Ohio St.3d 136, 22 N.E.3d 1061 (2014), 169
State v. Jordan, ___ Ohio St.3d ___, ___ N.E.3d ____, 2021 WL 5182447 (Nov.9, 2021), 169
State v. Kareski, 137 Ohio St.3d 92, 998 N.E.2d 410 (2013), 156–57
State v. Keich, 76 Ohio Law Abs. 180, 145 N.E.2d 532 (1956), 129–30
State v. Kelley, 57 Ohio St.3d 127, 566 N.E.2d 658 (1991), 150
State v. King, 70 Ohio St.3d 158, 637 N.E.2d 903 (1994), 150
State v. Kirk, 72 Ohio St.3d 564, 651 N.E.2d 981 (1995), 149
State v. Lane, 60 Ohio St.2d 112, 397 N.E.2d 1338 (1979), 150–51, 171
State v. Lang, 129 Ohio St.3d 512, 954 N.E.2d 596 (2011), 142, 159
State v. Lathrop, 93 Ohio St. 79, 112 N.E. 209 (1915), 204
State v. Lindway, 131 Ohio St. 166, 2 N.E.2d 490 (1936), 78n.315, 168
State v. Long, 138 Ohio St.3d 478, 8 N.E.3d 890 (2014), 141–42
State v. Lovejoy, 79 Ohio St.3d 440, 683 N.E.2d 1112 (1997), 156
State v. Lundgren, 73 Ohio St.3d 474, 653 N.E.2d 304 (1995), 151
State v. Lynn, 5 Ohio St.2d 106, 214 N.E.2d 226 (1966), 153
State v. Maddox, _____ Ohio St.3d _____, _____ N.E.3d _____, 2022 WL 790470 (March 16, 2022), 295
State v. Madison, 64 Ohio St.2d 322, 415 N.E.2d 272 (1980), 147
State v. Mapp, 170 Ohio St. 427, 166 N.E.2d 387 (1960), *rev'd*, 367 U.S. 643 (1961), 78n.315
State v. Medbery, 7 Ohio St. 522 (1857), 243, 362
State v. Meeker, 26 Ohio St.2d 9, 268 N.E.2d 589 (1971), 150
State v. Mole, 149 Ohio St.3d 215, 74 N.E.3d 368 (2016), 98–99, 98n.364, 99n.366, 119, 122–23

State v. Moore, 149 Ohio St.3d 557, 76 N.E.3d 1127 (2016), 120
State v. Moss, 69 Ohio St.2d 515, 433 N.E.2d 181 (1982), 154
State v. Murrell, 94 Ohio St.3d 489, 764 N.E.2d 986 (2002), 168
State v. Mutter, 150 Ohio St.3d 429, 82 N.E.3d 1141(2017), 155, 157
State v. Nieto, 101 Ohio St. 409, 130 N.E. 663 (1920), 78n.314, 128
State v. Noling, 149 Ohio St.3d 327, 75 N.E.3d 141 (2016), 120, 302
State v. O'Brien, 30 Ohio St.3d 122, 508 N.E.2d 144 (1987), 145, 150
State v. Orr, 91 Ohio St.3d 389, 745 N.E.2d 1036 (2001), 167–68
State v. Parker, 150 Ohio St. 22, 80 N.E.2d 490 (1948), 508
State v. Patrick, 164 Ohio St.3d 309, 172 N.E.3d 952 (2020), 142
State v. Pembaur, 69 Ohio St.2d 110, 430 N.E.2d 1331 (1982), 304
State v. Peters, 112 Ohio St. 249, 147 N.E. 81 (1924), 266
State v. Radcliff, 142 Ohio St.3d 78, 28 N.E.3d 69 (2015), 280
State v. Roberts, 32 Ohio St.3d 225, 513 N.E.2d 720 (1987), 153
State v. Roberts, 137 Ohio St.3d 230, 998 N.E.2d 1100 (2013), 141
State v. Robinette, 80 Ohio St.3d 234, 685 N.E.2d 762 (1997), 82, 98, 111, 167–68
State v. Rohrer, 54 N.E.3d 654 (Ohio Ct. App. 2015), 189–90
State v. Scott, 92 Ohio St.3d 1, 748 N.E.2d 11 (2001), 140--41
State v. Self, 56 Ohio St.3d 73, 564 N.E.2d 446 (1990), 147, 148
State v. Selvage, 80 Ohio St.3d 465, 687 N.E.2d 433 (1997), 150
State v. Sinks, 42 Ohio St. 345 (1884), 66, 77n.310
State v. Storch, 66 Ohio St.3d 280, 612 N.E.2d 305 (1993), 81–82, 147–48, 167
State v. Stricklen, 63 Ohio St.2d 47, 406 N.E.2d 1110 (1980), 146
State v. Sullivan, 90 Ohio St.3d 502, 739 N.E.2d 788 (2001), 239
State v. Thompkins, 75 Ohio St.3d 558, 664 N.E.2d 926 (1996), 180
State v. Thompson, 92 Ohio St.3d 584, 752 N.E.2d 276 (2001), 254
State v. Thompson, 95 Ohio St.3d 264, 767 N.E.2d 251 (2002), 118, 119
State v. Tolbert, 60 Ohio St.3d 89, 573 N.E.2d 617 (1991), 155
State v. Warner, 55 Ohio St.3d 31, 564 N.E.2d 18 (1990), 210
State v. Welch, 53 Ohio St.2d 47, 372 N.E.2d 346 (1978), 148
State v. Wellman, 37 Ohio St.2d 162, 309 N.E.2d 915 (1974), 145
State v. White, 82 Ohio St.3d 16, 693 N.E.2d 772 (1998), 150–51
State v. White, 85 Ohio St.3d 433, 709 N.E.2d 140 (1999), 159
State v. Williams, 6 Ohio St.3d 281, 452 N.E.2d 1323 (1983), 148
State v. Williams, 88 Ohio St.3d 513, 728 N.E.2d 342 (2000), 114, 179
State v. Williams, 126 Ohio St.3d 65, 930 N.E.2d 770 (2010), 121
State v. Williams, 129 Ohio St.3d 344, 952 N.E.2d 1108 (2011), 250–51
State v. Wilmoth, 22 Ohio St.3d 251, 490 N.E.2d 1236 (1986), 169
State v. Wing, 66 Ohio St. 407, 65 N.E. 514 (1902), 146
State v. Wogenstahl, 75 Ohio St.3d 344, 662 N.E.2d 311 (1996), 98n.362
State v. Wyant, 64 Ohio St.3d 566, 597 N.E.2d 450 (1992), 162–63
State v. Wyant, 68 Ohio St.3d 162, 624 N.E.2d 722 (1994), 162–63
State v. Zucal, 82 Ohio St.3d 215, 694 N.E.2d 1341 (1998), 139
State v. Zuern, 32 Ohio St.3d 56, 512 N.E.2d 585 (1987), 150–51
Steele v. Hamilton County Community Mental Health Bd., 90 Ohio St.3d 176, 736 N.E.2d 10 (2000), 110 C1.P49, 189–90
Stevens v. Cincinnati Times-Star Co., 72 Ohio St. 112, 73 N.E. 1058 (1905), 508
Stockberger v. Henry, 134 Ohio St.3d 213, 981 N.E.2d 807 (2012), 480–81

Stolz v. J & B Steel Erectors, Inc., 155 Ohio St. 3d 567, 122 N.E.3d 1228 (2018), 109, 123
Strader v. Graham, 51 US 82 (1850), 12n.46
Strain v. Southerton, 148 Ohio St. 153, 74 N.E.2d 69 (1947), 247–48, 256
Strattman v. Studt, 20 Ohio St.2d 95, 253 N.E.2d 749 (1969), 170
Struthers v. Sokol, 108 Ohio St. 263, 140 N.E. 519 (1923), 535
Sweezy v. New Hampshire, 354 U.S. 234 (1957), 277
Swetland v. Kinney, 69 Ohio St.2d 567, 433 N.E.2d 217 (1982), 477

T

Taylor v. Academy Iron & Metal Co., 36 Ohio St.3d 149, 522 N.E.2d 464 (1988), 263
Taylor v. Commissioners of Ross County, 23 Ohio St. 22 (1872), 423
Tennant v. Jefferson County Commission, 567 U.S. 758 (2012), 563
Thatcher v. Pennsylvania, O. & D.R. Co. 121 Ohio St. 205, 167 N.E. 682 (1929), 492
Thomas v. City of Beavercreek, 105 Ohio App. 3d 350, 663 N.E.2d 1333 (1995), 549
Thomas v. Mills, 117 Ohio St. 114 (1927), 183
Thrailkill v. Smith, 106 Ohio St. 1, 138 N.E. 532 (1922), 208
Thurston v. Maxwell, 3 Ohio St.2d 92, 209 N.E.2d 204 (1965), 146
Timbs v. Indiana, 139 S.Ct. 682 (2019), 139
Toilet Goods Association v. Gardner 387 U.S. 158 (1967), 294
Toledo City Board. of Education v. State Board of Education, 146 Ohio St.3d 356, 56 N.E.3d 950 (2016), 251
Toledo Edison v. City of Bryan, 90 Ohio St.3d 288, 737 N.E.2d 529 (2000), 545
Touby v. U.S., 500 U.S. 160 (1991), 276
Treska v. Trumble, 4 Ohio St.3d 150, 447 N.E.2d 1283 (1983), 546
Trustees of Dartmouth College v. Woodward, 17 U.S. (4 Wheat.) 518 (1819), 124–25, 489

U

U.S. Term Limits, Inc. v. Thornton, 514 U.S. 779 (1995), 328–29
U.S. Trust Co. of New York v. New Jersey, 431 U.S. 1, 25 (1977), 251–52
U.S. v. MacDonald, 456 U.S. 1 (1982), 149
U.S. v. Valenzuela-Bernal, 458 U.S. 858 (1982), 149
U.S. v. Carolene Products, Co., 304 U.S. 144 (1938), 181

V

Vail v. The Plain Dealer Publishing Co., 72 Ohio St.3d 279, 649 N.E.2d 182 (1995), 164
Van Camp v. Board of Education of Logan, 9 Ohio St. 406 (1859), 341
Van Fossen v. Babcock & Wilcox Co., 36 Ohio St.3d 100, 522 N.E.2d 489 (1988), 79, 250
Village of Blue Ash v. City of Cincinnati, 173 Ohio S, 182 N.E.2d 557 (1962), 543
Village of Fairview v. Giffee, 73 Ohio St. 183, 76 N.E. 865 (1905), 193–94, 253–54, 297
Village of Lucas v. Lucas Local School District, 2 Ohio St.3d 13, 442 N.E.2d 449 (1982), 543
Village of Perrysburg v. Ridgway, 108 Ohio St. 245, 140 N.E. 595 (1923), 534, 546
Village of Put-In-Bay v. Mathys, 163 Ohio St.3d 1, 167 N.E.3d 922 (2020), 481, 551
Voinovich v. Ferguson, 63 Ohio St.3d 198, 586 N.E.2d 1020 (1992), 461–62
Voinovich v. Quilter, 507 U.S. 146 (1993), 460

W

Walker v. City of Cincinnati, 21 Ohio St. 14 (1871), 420–21, 423
Walker v. City of Toledo, 143 Ohio St.3d 420, 39 N.E.3d 474 (2014), 298, 537
Wampler v. Higgins, 93 Ohio St.3d 111, 752 N.E.2d 962 (2001), 111, 164
Weeks v. United States, 232 U.S. 383 (1914), 168
Weil v. Taxicabs of Cincinnati, Inc., 139 Ohio St. 198, 39 N.E.2d 148 (1942), 250
Weinland v. Fulton, 99 Ohio St. 10, 121 N.E. 816 (1918), 223
Weinstein v. Bradford, 423 U.S. 147 (1975), 295–96
Wesberry v. Sanders, 376 U.S. 1 (1964), 563
Westerhaus Co. v. City of Cincinnati, 165 Ohio St. 327, 135 N.E.2d 318 (1956), 508
Westfield Insurance Co. v. Galatis, 100 Ohio St.3d 216, 707 N.E.2d 1256 (2003), 93--94
Weyandt v. Davis, 112 Ohio App. 3d 717, 679 N.E.2d 1191 (1996), 269
Williams v. Marion Rapid Transit, Inc., 152 Ohio St. 114, 87 N.E.2d 334 (1949), 173
Williamson v. U.S., 207 U.S. 425 (1908), 234
Wilson v. Kasich, 134 Ohio St.3d 221, 981 N.E.2d 814 (2012), 112–13, 448–49, 459, 463–64, 559, 564
Wisconsin v. Mitchell, 508 U.S. 476 (1993), 162–63

Y

Youngstown City School District Board of Education v. State of Ohio, 165 Ohio St.3d 240, 177 N.E.3d 267 (2020), 237, 345–46
Youngstown v. Aiello, 156 Ohio St. 32, 100 N.E.2d 62 (1951), 206

Z

Zelman v. Simmons-Harris, 122 S.Ct. 2460 (2002), 134, 340
Zoppo v. Homestead Insurance Co., 71 Ohio St.3d 552, 644 N.E.2d 397 (1994), 130

INDEX

For the benefit of digital users, indexed terms that span two pages (e.g., 52–53) may, on occasion, appear on only one of those pages.

Tables are indicated by *t* following the page number

advice and consent of Senate, 71, 78n.314, 194, 285–86, 315, 355, 496, 503
advisory opinions, 293–94
African Americans
- colonization of, 12, 15, 18, 31, 35, 36–37, 105
- deletion of "white," 30, 35–37, 45–46, 61, 67–68, 319, 320, 340–41, 354
- first convention debates on equal rights, 18–19
- militia, 9, 36–37, 45–46
- school segregation, 37, 78, 118, 340–41, 344
- second convention debates on equal rights, 35–37
- slavery, 132–33, 141, 174, 536
- voting rights, 18–19, 318, 319, 320

age of Ohio Constitution, 3n.1
alcoholic beverages. *See* liquor
amendments
- Article XVI, 517–26
- before 1912, 47–49
- since 1912, 62–76
- through commissions (*see* Constitutional Modernization Commission; Constitutional Revision Commission)
- through constitutional convention (*see* Appendix B)
- through initiative (*see* Appendix B)
- through the General Assembly (*see* Appendix B)

annexation, 545
Anti-Saloon League, 40, 66–67
anti-monopoly. *See* monopoly
appellate jurisdiction
- of court of appeals, 305–6
- of Supreme Court, 298, 299–301

Appendix A, 579
Appendix B, 581
appointment power. *See* advice and consent
- of General Assembly, 27–28, 40, 88, 286
- of governor, 21–22, 24, 59, 71, 77–78, 227, 248–49, 271, 281, 284, 286, 355–56, 435, 436–37
- restriction on General Assembly's power, 40, 191–92, 212, 227, 248–49, 284

apportionment, 447–70, 553–66
- Article XI, 447–70
- Article XIX, 553–66
- background, 448–49, 454–55
- congressional redistricting, 553–66
- house districts, 460
- method of apportionment, 454–55, 459
- Ohio Redistricting Commission, 447, 451–54, 462, 463, 464, 553, 554–55, 558–60, 565
- Ohio Supreme Court jurisdiction, 453–54, 468, 469, 470, 565, 566
- population, 459–60
- senate districts, 461
- severability, 469
- state redistricting, 447–70
- *See also* Hanna Amendment

appropriations, 48, 191–92, 238, 243. *See also* line item veto; onesubject rule; referendum
Arizona Constitution, 362–63
Arkansas Constitution, 362–63
Arms, right to bear, 81, 120, 127–28
Article I (Bill of Rights), 105–90
Article II (Legislative), 191–270
Article III (Executive), 271–87
Article IV (Judicial), 289–316
Article V (Elective Franchise), 317–29
Article VI (Education), 331–51
Article VII (Public Institutions), 353–56
Article VIII (Public Debt and Public Works), 357–434

Article IX (Militia), 435–37
Article X (County and Township Organizations), 439–46
Article XI (Apportionment), 447–70
Article XII (Finance and Taxation), 471–85
Article XIII (Corporations), 487–94
Article XIV (Jurisprudence), 495–98
Article XV (Miscellaneous), 499–516
Article XVI (Amendments), 517–26
Article XVII (Elections), 527–29
Article XVIII (Municipal Corporations), 357–434
Article XIX (Congressional Redistricting), 553–66
articles of compact, 11–12, 14–15, 87
Articles of Confederation, 3–4, 11–12, 23, 126
assemble, right to. *See* rights: to assemble
assessment, on property for taxation, 68, 473, 476, 492–93, 549. *See also* property taxation: uniformity rule (taxation)
Attorney discipline, 302
Attorney General, 43, 194, 197, 199, 202, 203, 220–21, 244, 272–73, 293, 325–26, 425, 509
  ban on reduction of compensation, 285
  opinions, 51, 219, 423–24, 445–46, 548
  standing to sue, 273
  term, 71, 274–75, 528
  vacancy, 282, 284
Atwater, Caleb, 9, 16, 21, 30, 54
auditor of state, 21, 43, 227, 272, 334, 425, 448, 452–53
  ban on reduction of compensation, 285
  term, 274–75, 282
  vacancy, 284

bail, right to. *See* rights: to bail
Baker, Newton D., 55–56, 65
Baldwin, Michael, 16
ballot
  Australian, 49, 323
  "bedsheet," 328
  definition of, 324–26
  language, 218
  name of candidates on ballot, 324–26
  nonpartisan ballot, 52–53, 55, 89 (*see also* nonpartisan judicial ballot)
  requirements, 325–26
  secret, 324
  voting machines, 51, 61, 62, 324–15, 325–26, 328 (*see also* Ohio ballot board)
banks and financial institutions, 4, 10, 25, 34, 40, 490
Bebb, Governor William, 31
Bigelow, Herbert S., 51–52, 54–55, 59, 60, 68–69, 531, 540
bills. *See also* one-subject rule; line-item veto; veto
  amending and reviving clauses, 239–40
  how bills become laws, 235–37
  overriding veto, 241
  repeal by implication, 239
  signature requirements, 239–41
  three-reading requirement, 236–37
  when take effect, 201 (*see also* one-subject rule)
bingo. *See* gambling: bingo and charitable bingo
"Black Laws," 18–19, 36–37
Blaine Amendment, 339
bonds. *See also* public debt
  for capital improvements and infrastructure, 94–97, 253, 260, 264
  for coal research, 430–31
  for economic development, 421–22, 427–29
  for education, 376–79, 380–81, 397–99, 433
  for environmental conservation, 399–402
  general obligation bonds, 70–71, 74, 358, 433
  for higher education, 380–81, 397–99
  for highways, 370–71, 379–80
  for housing, 422, 428–29, 430, 432
  limitations on debt, 357, 365, 420–8
  for municipal public utilities, 550
  for parks, recreation, and natural resources, 376–79, 380–81, 391–94
  for public buildings, 94–97, 374–76, 389–91, 394–97
  for public uitilities, 550
  revenue bonds, 337, 358, 361, 363–64, 370, 384–85, 411, 420, 421, 427, 428–29
  for Third Frontier programs, 83, 407–8
  for veterans (*see* veterans: compensation for)
  See also internal Improvements
British (Britain). *See* Great Britain
Bryan, William Jennings, 53–54, 57

California Constitution, 162, 163
campaigns for conventions
for 1802 constitutional convention, 15, 16
for 1850-51 constitutional convention, 31–32, 38–39
for 1873-74 constitutional convention, 45–47
for 1912 constitutional convention, 51–53, 60–61
canals. *See* internal improvements
capital punishment, 38, 61, 139–41. *See also* death penalty appeals
"case or controversy" requirement, 290–91, 293, 295–96. *See also* mootness; political question; public-rights actions; ripeness; standing
casino control commission, 513
Celebrezze, Jr., Chief Justice Frank D., 78–79
Celeste, Governor Richard, 74, 280
Celoron de Bienville, 5–6
census, 25–26, 41, 71–72, 454, 458, 460, 461, 464, 556, 557
certified questions from federal courts. *See* Supreme Court: certified questions
charitable bingo. *See* gambling: bingo and charitable bingo
charter schools. *See* education: charter schools
charters
corporate, 25, 34, 43, 124–25, 168, 487–89
county, 73, 73n.304, 75, 77–78, 78n.314, 211, 214, 215, 439, 441–43, 444–46, 528, 529
municipal, 50, 75, 211, 213, 215–16, 295, 493, 528, 529, 532, 534, 545–48
Chase, Salmon P., 22, 507
Chief Justice of the Ohio Supreme Court. *See also* justices of Ohio Supreme Court
election of, 56, 57, 90–91, 289–90, 300
power to disqualify judges, 309
superintendence over courts, 72, 308
term, 310, 311
Chillicothe, 5, 13–14, 15, 16, 499–500
"Chillicothe faction," 13–14, 16
Cincinnati, 13–14, 15, 29, 32–33, 45, 47, 51–52, 59, 136, 335, 343, 511, 533
circumvention conventions, 30, 31
cities and villages. *See* municipal corporations
civil (civilian) power, 127, 435
civil service, 39–40, 184–85, 499, 515, 538. *See also* employees; labor; workers' compensation
claims against the state. *See* sovereign immunity
Cleveland, 52, 55–56, 65, 339–40, 344, 345, 424, 443, 510, 511, 533
Colorado Constitution, 362–63
Columbus, 32–33, 45, 53–54, 83, 139–40, 499–500, 511
commission on civil procedure, 72, 496
common law, 7–8, 11–12, 22, 23, 37–38, 46, 129–30, 131, 136–37, 143, 144, 156, 164, 174, 183, 184, 186–87, 255, 258–59, 263, 264, 272–73, 291–92, 297, 301
common pleas court. *See* Court of Common Pleas
compelling state interest, 119, 134–35, 180
competence to vote, 327
Confederation Congress, 3n.2, 6–7, 8, 10, 12, 331, 333
Congress, U.S., 7, 9, 10–11, 13–15, 17, 19–20, 66–67, 76, 126, 133, 162, 184, 272, 323, 328–29, 332–34, 339, 436
congressional redistricting, 553–66
connecticut, 6–7, 16
Connecticut Constitution, 6–7, 162
Connecticut Western Reserve. *See* Western Reserve
conservation of natural resources, 75–76, 265–66, 358, 378, 381, 393, 401, 411
Constitution, U.S., 3n.2, 11–12, 23, 26, 36–37, 45–46, 66–68, 71, 73, 81–82, 87, 94, 95, 96, 97, 99, 106, 107–8, 110–11, 113, 116, 118, 124, 126, 127, 129–31, 133, 134, 136–37, 138, 139, 143, 144–45, 147, 149, 151, 157, 160, 165, 166, 167–68, 169, 171–72, 174, 183, 184, 185, 188, 193, 203, 206, 227, 228, 231, 232, 234, 243, 244, 248, 250, 251, 276, 277, 279, 290–92, 293, 308–9, 317, 320–21, 327, 328–29, 458, 472, 479, 501, 512–13, 516, 554, 563

Constitutional Conventions
1802 Constitutional Convention, 16–20
1851-52 Constitutional Convention, 3–4, 25–26, 28, 32–38
1873-74 Constitutional Convention, 4, 44–47, 48, 49, 54, 66, 106, 292, 300, 320, 339
1912 Constitutional Conventeial, 53–62 (*see also* run-up to 1912 convention)
twenty-year rule, 45, 47, 52, 62, 73, 74, 86, 517, 524, 525–26
Constitutional Modernization Commission, 82–83, 86–88, 192, 199, 200–1, 314, 327, 339, 353, 358, 518
Constitutional Revision Commission, 16, 72–74, 206, 218, 226, 228, 230–31, 233, 235, 236, 269, 273, 282–83, 313–14, 315–16, 317, 326, 327, 336, 347–48, 354, 361, 474, 478, 479, 492, 494, 521, 527, 528, 529
constitutional courts, 289, 305
Continental Congress, 3n.2, 8
continuity of government, 219–20
contracts
obligation of, 11–12, 251–52, 294, 489
right to contract, 50n.242, 77, 78, 107, 113, 175–76, 179, 180, 256, 257–58, 266
conventions. *See* constitutional conventions
corporate charters
inviolability of, 34, 125
legislature's power to amend or repeal, 43, 209–10, 250, 489
prohibition against special acts, 124, 487–88
corporations
Article XIII, 487–94
association with banking powers, 487–94
corporate powers, 487–88
creation of, 488–89
dues, 490–91
municipal corporations, 492–93
prohibition against joint ventures with state or political subdivisions, 40–41, 423–24
prohibition against special acts, 124, 487–88
rights of way, 491–92 (*see also* eminent domain)
taxation, 491 (*see also* corporate charters; municipal corporations)
counsel, right to. *See* rights: to counsel
counties
boards of election, 212, 213, 214, 223–24, 302
charters, 439–43
creation of, 252–53
home rule, 68, 211, 313, 439–4, 442–10
number of, 25–26, 439–40
organization and government, 440–41
powers of, 442–43 (*see generally* counties and townships [Article X])
reservation of initiative and referendum, 443
counties and Townships (Article X), 439
county clerk, 226–27, 313
county commissioners, 268, 316, 440, 443, 445–46
county sheriff. *See* sheriff, county
court of Appeals. *See also* Appellate Jurisdiction of court of appeals
districts, 303
number, 290, 304
organization and jurisdiction, 302–4
Court of Claims, 183–84, 298, 311
court of common pleas
jurisdiction, 306–7
number, 290
organization, 305–6
courts. *See* court of appeals; court of common pleas; courts of conciliation; district courts; Ohio Supreme Court; Probate Courts; *see also* Constitutional courts; judicial branch; judicial power; statutory courts
courts, district, 41–43, 297
abolished, 48, 303
courts, circuit, 56–57, 289–90, 303
abolition of, 57
courts of conciliation, 74, 83–84, 86–87, 314, 315–16
credit of state
prohibition against credit to private entities, 25, 357, 360, 408, 421–22, 423–24, 427–29, 431, 432
crime victims rights. *See* rights: victims
cruel and unusual punishment. *See* rights: to be free from cruel and unusual punishment
currency, 25, 87, 491, 493–94
Cutler, Ephraim, 16, 17, 18

Cutler, Manasseh, 7, 17

damage caps, 94n.359, 95–96, 130, 186–87. *See also* tort reform
death penalty. *See* capital punishment
death penalty appeals, 302, 304
Debs, Eugene, 53–54
debt. *See* Public Debt
Declaration of Independence, 6, 35, 113, 114, 116, 123–24
defamation, 163 – –64
Delaware Declaration of Rights, 173
delegates
  to 1802 constitutional convention, 16–17
  to 1850-51 constitutional convention, 32–33
  to 1873-74 constitutional convention, 16
  to 1912 constitutional convention, 53–54
delegation of legislative authority, 194–95, 214, 247–48
  to counties, 440–41
  legislative submission, 247–48
  to private corporations, 492
Democrats (Democratic Party), 7, 21–22, 31, 34, 44–45, 48, 52, 53–54, 300, 322, 555. *See also* Jacksonian Democrats
DeRolph litigation. *See* education: *DeRolph* litigation
Dillon's Rule, 56, 532, 534, 540, 543
Direct Legislation League, 51–52, 53, 54
discrimination
  gender, 118 (*see also* elective franchise: removal of race and gender restrictions)
  racial, 118 (*see also* elective franchise: removal of race and gender restrictions)
  religious, 133–34
  See also equal protection
divorce, 194, 253, 254
double jeopardy. *See* rights: against double jeopardy
due course of law, 174, 176, 178, 181–82. *See also* juveniles, rights of
  Law of the land. 174–75
due process. *See also* due course of law
  procedural due process, 174, 177–78
  substantive due process, 107, 174, 179–80, 182, 256, 257–58, 263–64. See also *Lochner*; reputational interests

education. *See also* higher education
  Article VI, 331–51
  board of education, 334, 344–46
  charter schools, 340, 343–44, 345
  DeRolph litigation: 80, 336–39
  encouragement of, 136, 331
  ministerial lands, 333–34
  religious schools, 339–40
  rural schools, 346
  sale of lands for, 332–33
  school vouchers, 134, 238, 338–40
  segregation, 340–41
  state board of education, 346, 349
  Superintendent of Public Superintendent of Public Instruction, 346–47
  "thorough and efficient system of common schools," 334–36
Eighteenth Amendment, 66–67, 193, 514–15
Eighth Amendment, 138, 139, 140, 141–42, 143
elections
  Article XVII, 527–29
  ballot requirement (*see* ballot)
  for constitutional conventions, 30, 31–32, 44–45, 51–53 (*see also* Appendix A)
  contested, 14, 243
  for initiative and referendum (*see* initiative)
  joint election of governor and lieutenant governor, 275–76
  judicial, 21, 41–42, 90, 289, 310–11
  of legislators, 224–25
  primary elections, 68–69, 89–90, 249, 327–28
  returns, 275–76
  terms of office in case of vacancies, 528–29
  time for holding, 527–28
  See also ballot; campaigns; term limits
elective franchise
  Article V, 317–29
  felons, 326
  idiots and insane persons, 87, 327
  non-citizens, 22, 319
  removal of race and gender restrictions, 45–46, 320
  removal of tax and work requirement, 22, 472–73
  voter qualifications, 317–21 (*see also* African Americans; voting rights; women's suffrage)
  voter registration, 74, 77, 219, 321–23

eligibility of term-limited office holders, 329
eligibility of office holders, 500
embezzlement, of public funds, 227–28
eminent domain, 85, 97, 185–86, 492
public use, 97, 543, 548–49
employees
  public, 541–42
  welfare of, 256–59 (*see also* civil service; labor; workers' compensation)
employment
  accommodation of religious practice, 96, 134–35 (*see also* employees; labor; right to contract)
Enabling acts, 11, 14–15, 17, 20, 22, 103–4, 318, 319. *See also* admission into the union
England (English), 118, 126, 129, 154, 164–65, 166, 170, 171, 234, 333–34. *See also* Great Britain
environment and natural resources. *See* bonds: for environmental conservation
equal protection
  equal protection and benefit (Ohio), 95–96, 97–98, 98n.364, 106, 107, 110, 115, 116–24, 176, 178, 182, 246–47, 302, 323, 337
  equal protedtion (Fourteenth Amendment), 71, 97–98, 176, 178, 291, 302, 311, 326, 327, 336, 341, 448, 460, 472, 507, 512, 516
equal protection and benefit. *See* equal protection
Establishment Clause
  First Amendment, 133–34, 334, 340
  Ohio's, 133–34
ex post facto laws, 250, 251
exclusionary rule, good-faith exception, 169
executive branch, 20–22, 43
  Article III, 271–87
  departments, 271–73
  governor and other specific offices, 271–73
  power, 276 (*see also* executive officers)
executive officers
  ban on reduction of compensation, 285
  terms, 274–75
  term limits, 274–75
expert witness testimony, 58, 268
Fallen Timbers, Battle of, 9
Federalists, 4, 9, 12–17
"field" code, 308, 495–96
Fifteenth Amendment, 45–46, 67–68, 194–95, 320
Fifth Amendment, 97, 113, 144–45, 151–54, 174, 175, 179, 185
finance
  state's obligation to raise sufficient revenues, 479 (*see also* taxes and taxation)
fines. *See* rights: to be free from excessive fines
First Amendment, 90, 91–92, 126–27, 133, 134–35, 162–64, 171–72, 179, 203, 215, 300–1, 334, 339, 340
forfeiture for crime, 165
Fourteenth Amendment, 71, 97–98, 106, 108, 109, 113, 116, 120–21, 123, 140, 143, 144, 160, 175, 177–81, 215, 302, 311, 323, 448, 472, 516, 542, 543
Fourth Amendment. *See* search and seizure
Frame of Government of the Colony of Pennsylvania, 1682, 171
France (French), 5–6
Free Soil Party (Free-Soilers), 31
freedom. *See* rights
French-Canadian, 5–6
fuel tax, 480–81
Fundamental Laws of West New Jersey, 171
fundamental rights, 9, 11–12, 81, 114–15, 119–20, 180, 189–90, 335–36, 337, 516
funds
  bar on use of school fund for religious schools, 339–40
  for religious and educational purposes, 332–34
  for schools, 334–39
  tuition trust fund, 349–51 (*see also* sinking fund)

Galbreath, C. B., 33
gambling
  bingo and charitable bingo, 74, 501, 508, 509–10, 511
  casino gaming, 499, 510–12, 513–14
  lotteries (*see* lottery)
  sports gambling, 512–14
  video lottery terminals (VLTs), 205, 291, 512

General Assembly
adjournment, 234–35, 242
annual and biennial sessions, 41n.207, 230
how bills become laws, 235–37
journal, 231
organization of the General Assembly 229–30
power of appointment in cases of vacancies, 248–49
powers of each house, 228–29
prohibition on granting divorces and exercising judicial power, 253–54
regular and special sessions, 230–31 (*see also* appropriations; bills; House of Representatives; legislators; plenary power of the General Assembly; senate)
gerrymandering, 24–25, 30, 41, 447, 448, 452, 553–54, 555
Giles, William B., 14–15
government powers, generally
county, 439–40, 442–43
municipal, 534–41
powers of the branches of state government, 191, 271, 289–90
townships, 441
Governor, 16, 21–22
ban on reduction of compensation, 285
commander-in-chief, 278–79, 435
disability, 287
duty to communicate condition of the state (annual message), 277
duty to serve as commissioner of sinking fund, 425
election of, 275–76
ineligibility for office, 281–82
line-item veto (*see* line-item veto)
power to appoint militia officers, 435, 436–37
power to appoint trustees of state institutions, 355
power to call forth the militia, 435, 437
power to call special sessions of the General Assembly, 230–31
power to fill vacancies, 284
power to limit and adjourn sessions of the General Assembly, 278
reprieve, commutation, and pardon power, 279–80
signature required, 240
term, 274–75
term limits, 274–75
vacancies, 282–84
veto power (*see* veto: governor's:)
under the Northwest Ordinance (*see* veto under the Northwest Ordinance)
grand jury, 144–45, 172
grants and commissions, 281
Great Britain; 5, 6, 7
Great Lakes Water Compact, 187–89
great seal, 280–81

habeas corpus, 11–12, 41, 105, 136–37, 138, 301
Hanna Amendment, 448, 454, 455
hereditary privileges, prohibition against, 184
higher education, funding for. *See* bonds: for higher education
guaranteed loans, 348–49
tuition credit program, 349–51
highway funding. *See* bonds: for highways; *see also* taxes and taxation: motor vehicle use and fuel
home rule. *See* counties; municipal corporations; home rule
homelessness, proposed amendment to address, 38
homestead exemptions, 74, 75–76, 475–76
House of Representatives. *See* General Assembly
human life amendment, proposed, 38
Huntington, Samuel, 16, 26–28

impeachment, 27, 244–45, 267, 268, 279, 282, 283, 313. *See also* Pease, Judge Calvin; removal of state officers; Tod, Judge George
implied rights of action, 296–97
in pari materia, 110, 114–15, 125, 175, 246, 544, 545
inalienable rights, 97, 113–15
Indian Boundary Line of 1768, 8
Indiana Constitution, 3n.1, 175
Indians. *See* Native Americans
indictment, 144–45, 150, 155, 314
Industrial Commission, 68

initiative. *See also* referendum
constitutional initiative, 196–97
in counties, 443
effective dates and conflicting enactments, 201, 210
history of initiative, 54–55
limitations on constitutional initiative, 208–9
limitations on statutory initiative, 208
majority vote requirement, 222–23
monopolies, special procedures, 209–10
in municipalities, 211–16
pre-election judicial review, 212–15
self-executomg provisions and facilitating legislation, 220–21
signature and other requirements, 196–97, 216–20
statutory initiative, 198–201
See also one amendment; separate vote requirement; Ohio Ballot Board
institutions for "deaf, dumb, blind and insane," 353–55
intermediate scrutiny, 119
internal improvements, 25, 32, 40–41, 357, 360, 362, 391, 420, 427, 479, 482
intoxication beverages. *See* liquor
involuntary servitude. *See* African Americans: slavery

Jackson, Andrew, 34–35, 58n.273
Jacksonian democracy, 4, 35
Jacksonian Democrats, 30, 40, 116, 124–25
Jefferson, Thomas, 4, 10, 12, 14–15, 20, 21
Jeffersonian Republicans, 19–20, 191
Jeffersonians, 17, 19–20, 191, 271
JobsOhio, 291, 292, 301, 306–7, 422, 512
Johnson, Hiram, 53–54, 59
Johnson, Mayor Tom L., 51–52, 56, 65
judges
compensation, 311
disqualification, 309
election of (*see* elections: judicial)
mandatory retirement, 83–84, 311, 314, 315–16
number of, 56, 290, 304, 305
removal of, 267–68, 300–1 (*see also* impeachment)
service in more than one court, 316
temporary assignments, 305, 307
terms, 310–11
vacancies, 312
judicial branch. *See* Article IV, 289–316
judges. *See* judicial power; *specific courts*
judicial recall. *See* recall of judicial decisions
judicial power, 41, 193–94, 253–54, 268, 269, 290, 297
judicial review, 26–29, 49–50, 76–77, 112–13, 161, 206, 210, 212, 215, 229, 245, 268, 280, 297, 466, 521
judicial selection. *See* elections: judicial
jury trial, right to. *See* rights; right to jury trial
justice administered without delay. *See* rights: to justice administered without delay
justices of the peace, 21–22, 26–28, 56, 57, 297, 310
abolition of as constitutional officers, 289–90, 302–3, 311
Justices of Ohio Supreme Court. *See also* chief justice of the Ohio Supreme Court
burden of circuit-riding, 25–26
election (*see* elections: Judicial)
number, 56
retirement (*see* judges: manatory retirement)
term (*see* judges: terms)
juveniles, rights of, 181–82
justiciability. *See* mootness; political question; public-rights actions; ripeness; standing

Kentucky, 16, 132–33
Kentucky Constitution, 23, 24, 105, 154, 166, 174–75
King, Rufus, 45
Knight, George, 342, 346, 532–33, 539, 545

La Salle, 5–6
labor
eight-hour work day, 50, 58, 114, 266
See also civil service; employees; prison labor; workers' compensation
labor unions, 51, 60, 77
Lake Erie Bill of Rights, 213, 542
Land Ordinance of 1785, 7, 332
land titles and registration, 269. *See also* Torrens land registration

law of the land. *See* due course of law: law of the land
League of Women Voters, 91, 554
legislative branch. *See* Article II; General Assembly; House of Representatives; legislative power; legislators; senate
legislative power. *See* General Assembly; plenary power of the general Assembly
Legislative Service Commission, 236, 306–7
legislative submission. *See* delegation of legislative authority
legislators
  compensation, 227
  election and terms, 225
  ineligibility for office, 227–28
  privileges, 233–34
  residence, 226
  right to protest, 231–32
  term limits, 225, 328–29
  vacancies, 232–33
legislature. *See* General Assembly
Length of Ohio Constitution (word count), 5, 39–40, 45, 86
libel, 23, 129, 162, 163–64
licensing (of liquor). *See l*iquor
liens
  mechanics' and builders'; 50, 58, 114, 117–18, 254–55
lieutenant governor
  ban on reduction of compensation, 285
  duties, 273–74
  election of, 43, 272
  joint election with governor, 273, 276, 277
  term, 71, 274
  vacancies, 281–84
  limitations on legislative power. *See* appropriations; bonds: limitations on debt; one-subject rule; retroactive laws; three considerations; uniformity rule (laws)
Linde, Hans A., 79, 108–9, 175
line item veto, 48, 195, 214
liquor, 37–39, 44, 46, 48, 52–53, 56, 60–61, 65–67, 77, 188–89, 193, 208, 428–29, 507, 514–15, 540
Liu, Goodwin, 99
Lochner, 175–76, 179
lock-stepping approach (constitutional interpretation), 98, 107–8, 109–10, 112, 120
Locofocos, 34
logrolling, 227, 237, 238, 522
Longworth Act, 47–48, 49, 241
lottery, 74–75, 205, 291, 433, 499, 507–10, 511–13
Lottery Commission. *See* Ohio Lottery Commission

Magna Carta, 9, 129, 172, 174, 182
Marietta, 7–8, 13, 16
Marijuana, proposed amendments on, 84, 85, 208–9, 210
marriage. *See* same-sex marriage ban
Marsy's Law. *See* rights: victims
Maryland, 16
Maryland Declaration of Rights, 125–26, 173
Massachusetts, 209, 334
Massachusetts Body of Liberties, 154
Massachusetts Constitution, 6–7, 20n.91
Massachusetts Declaration of Rights, 125–26
Massie, Nathaniel, 13–14, 15–17
Medary, Samuel. *See* the new constitution
medical malpractice, 79–80, 173–74, 176. *See also* tort reform
Medill, William, 32–33
merit selection. *See* elections: judicial
Michigan, 11, 511, 513–14
military, subordinate to civil power, 127, 435
militia, 10, 21, 23–24, 36–37, 45–46, 67–68, 127, 271, 274, 278–79, 435–37. *See also* Article IX
minimum wage amendment; 84, 85, 87, 179, 256–58, 259–61. *See also* municipal minimum wage
ministerial lands. *See* education: ministerial lands
Miranda warnings, 152–53
Modern Courts Amendment, 290, 293–94, 298, 300–2, 303, 304, 305, 306–7, 309, 310, 311, 312, 496
monopoly, 208–9, 511, 512–13
Monroe, James, 10
mootness, 290–91, 295–96
Moyer, Chief Justice Thomas J., 92, 93, 94–95, 156

municipal corporations
appropriation of property for public use, 548–49
charters (*see* charters: municipal)
classification, 56, 531–32, 533 (*see also* uniformity rule [taxation])
creation and organization, 533–34
debt and credit, 423–24, 550
elections, 551–52
home rule, 50, 55–56, 59, 77–78, 87, 96, 128, 185, 213–14, 256–57, 262, 294, 298, 320, 342, 439, 493, 531–52
limitations on municipal power, 541–42
municipal initiative and referendum, 211–16
municipal minimum wage, 261–62, 541–42
municipal sovereign immunity, 184
plenary power of municipalities, 534, 543
powers, 534–42, 545–46 (*see also* Dillon's Rule)
public utilities, 532, 542–45 (*see also* bonds: for public uitilities)
residency requirements, 256–57
special legislation, 24–25, 56, 246, 488–89, 492–93
taxation and finance, 541, 550–51
municipalities. *See* municipal corporations

national guard, 436
Native Americans
Cuyuga, 8n.27
Delaware, 5, 9
Erie, 5
Iroquois, 5, 6–7, 8, 8n.27
Miami, 5, 6, 9
Oneida, 8n.27
Onondaga, 8n.27
Seneca, 8n.27
Shawnee, 5, 9
Tuscarora, 8n.27
Wyandot, 5
natural law, 113, 114
Nebraska Constitution, 361
New Constitution, The, 31–32. *See also* Medary
New Hampshire, 108
New Hampshire Constitution, 30, 154
New Jersey Constitution, 318. *See also* Fundamental Laws of West New Jersey
New Jersey Supreme Court, 163
New Judicial Federalism, 80–82, 95–100, 107
New York, 263, 290, 495–96
New York Constitution, 162, 174, 279
Nineteenth Amendment, 67–68, 320
nonpartisan ballot. *See* ballot: nonpartisan
nonpartisan judicial ballot, 89–90, 319–20, 321
North Carolina, 173
North Carolina Declaration of Rights, 173
Northwest Ordinance of 1787
admission to the union, 13–15, 103–4
fundamental rights (*see* articles of compact; *see also* fundamental rights)
governance under the Northwest Ordinance, 12–13
Ohio's first constitution, 9
three-stage process for statehood, 10–11
notaries, 21–22, 61, 226
nuisance, 44, 99, 493–94

oath
of office, 28, 29, 33, 514
of witnesses, 135–36
O'Connor, Chief Justice Maureen, 92, 93, 122, 538–39
Ohio Ballot Board, 197, 199, 208, 209–10, 216, 218, 221–22, 519–196, 522
Ohio Bond Commission, 70–71, 360, 361, 433
Ohio Company, The, 6, 7, 17, 333
Ohio Constitutional Modernization Commission (OCMC). *See* Constitutional Modernization Commission
Ohio Constitutional Revision Commission. *See* Constitutional Revision Commission
"Ohio country," 5, 6
Ohio Lottery Commission, 509, 512, 513
Ohio Redistricting Commission. *See* apportionment: Ohio Redistricting Commission
Ohio State Board of Commerce, 52, 53, 60
Ohio Supreme Court
certified questions, 203–4, 293–94
exclusive jurisdiction, 210, 223–24, 287, 301, 468, 469, 520–21, 566
intracircuit conflicts, 304–5

organization and jurisdiction of, 290–91, 298–301 (*see also* appellate jurisdiction of Ohio Supreme Court)
original jurisdiction, 41, 205, 218, 292, 301, 302, 422, 443, 468, 470, 520–21, 566
primary arbiter of constitution, 79–80, 99–100, 122, 298
rulemaking power, 308–9
superintendence over courts, 72, 308
Supreme Court "in Bank," 300, 468, 469, 520–21, 566
(*see also* Supreme Court Commission)
One-percent limitation on property tax, 68, 474–76
one amendment, separate vote requirement, 209–10, 221–22, 228, 522
one-subject rule, 79–80, 87, 96, 134, 173, 237–39, 522
open-subject, municipal initiatives, 215–16, 445–46
open courts. *See* rights: to open courts
Ordinance of 1784, 10
Ordinance of 1787. *See* Northwest Ordinance
Oregon, 296
Oregon Constitution, 173, 362–63. *See also* Linde, Justice Hans A.
OSBC. *See* Ohio State Board of Commerce

pardon power, of governor, 21–22, 164–65, 271, 279–80
parks. *See* bonds: for parks
parole, 141–42, 160, 164–65, 167, 326
parole officers, 111, 153
patronage, 24–25, 41, 249
Pease, Judge Calvin, 26–28, 244
penitentiary, 38, 86–87, 139–40, 353, 355
Pennsylvania, 5, 7–8, 12, 13, 16, 23, 24, 511, 513–14
Pennsylvania Constitution, 24, 105, 113, 116, 125–26, 133, 154, 162, 166, 170, 174–75
Pennsylvania Declaration of Rights, 125–26
pensions, 50, 58, 68–69, 114, 117–18, 231
personal property, 25, 47, 165, 186, 473, 475, 482–83. *See also* private property
petition. *See* initiative
petition, right of, 125–27
plenary power of the General Assembly, 21, 40–41, 193, 256, 258, 260–61, 266, 335, 354, 355, 508. *See also* municipal corporations: home rule; municipal corporations: plenary power of municipalities
"Plunder" Law, 25
police power, 23, 25, 41, 44, 176, 188–89, 226–27, 256, 534–35, 536, 539–40
political question, 245, 296, 448–49
poll tax, prohibition against, 23, 68–69, 471–73
poor, laws protecting the, 23, 43, 106, 331–32, 334
practice of law, determination, 115, 130, 302
preamble, 20–21
preservation of the freedom to choose health care. *See* rights: to choose health care
president of the senate, 21, 233, 273–74, 282, 283–84
presumption of constitutionality, 112–13
pre-election judicial review, 125, 212, 214, 223, 521
primacy approach (constitutional interpretation), 108, 109
primaries. *See* elections: primary
prison labor, 73, 269, 354
prisons. *See* penitentiary
priv, 58, 90, 97, 144, 149, 151–53
private property, 97, 106, 107, 175–76, 180, 185–86, 187–88, 492, 549. *See also* eminent domain
privilege against self-incrimination. *See* righs: to privilege against self-incrimination
probable cause, 166
probate courts, 22, 41, 42, 89, 123, 175, 290, 297, 298, 306
Progressives, 4–5, 51–52, 53–56, 58, 60, 61, 62, 65, 77, 89, 110–11, 191–92, 328, 475, 531
prohibition, 66–67. *See also* liquor
property taxation
classification, 47–48, 52, 60, 208, 473–77 (*see also* assessmenton property for taxation; uniformity rule [taxation])
tax exemption, 476
ten-mill limit (*see* one-percent limitation on property tax)
See also taxes; homestead exemptions

public debt. *See also* Article VIII
of counties, 423–24
debt limit, 362–63, 364
emergency exception to debt limit, 364–65
and the initiative, 531
limitation on direct obligations, 433–34
prohibition on assumption of debt, 422–23
prohibition on debt for internal improvements, 481–82 (*see also* internal improvements)
prohibition on private ventures, 420–22
requirement to raise sufficient revenues, 479
restrictions on municipalities and other political subdivisions, 423–24
See also bonds: sinking fund
public health or safety, 176, 180, 543, 544
public institutions
Article VII, 353–56
directors, 355–56
for "insane, blind, and deaf and dumb," 353–55
vacancies in office, 356 (*see also* penitentiary)
public-rights actions, 292–93
public schools. *See* education
public use. *See* eminent domain
public utilities. *See* municipal corporations: public utilities
Putnam, Rufus, 16

quartering of soldiers, 165–66

Ranney, Rufus P. 33, 116, 124–25
real estate taxes. *See* property taxation
reapportionment. *See* apportionment
recall, of judicial decisions, 58
redistricting, congressional. *See* apportionment
redress, for wrongs. *See* rights: to remedy
referendum, 191–93, 196, 200, 201–4
in counties, 443
inapplicable to appropriations, 54–55, 204, 205, 206
inapplicable to emergency laws, 204–7
limitations on, 204–24
in municipalities, 211
requirements, 201–4 (*see also* initiative)
remedy, right to. *See* rights: to remedy
removal of state officers, 58, 244, 267–68. *See also* impeachment
representatives. *See* legislators; House of Representatives; speaker of the house
republican form of government, 10
Republicans (Republican party), 4, 17, 18–20, 23, 27–28, 44–45, 48, 52, 53–54, 112–16, 300
reputational interests, 178–79
residency. *See* municipal corporations: residency requirements
retroactive laws, prohibition against, 249–52, 489
revenue, state, 479
revenue bonds. *See* bonds; public debt
Revolutionary War, 6–7, 8, 12, 164–65, 166
Rhodes, Governor James A., 74, 75, 320–21, 322
rights
against double jeopardy, 97, 107, 154–58, 161, 177
to alter or abolish government, 30, 115, 123–24
to assemble, 106, 125–27
to bail, 11–12, 76, 105, 106, 136–37, 161
to bear arms, 81, 120, 127–28
to choose health care, 189–90
to compulsory process, 146, 149
to confront witnesses (*see* witnesses)
of conscience, 134–35, 331
to contract, 50n.242, 77, 78, 107, 113–15, 175–76, 179, 180, 256, 257–58, 266
to counsel, 3n.3, 145–46, 181
to be free from cruel and unusual punishment, 26–27, 80, 128–31, 181–82
to be free from excessive fines, 11–12, 105, 138, 139, 143
to be free from imprisonment for debt, 43, 106, 169–70
of free press, 162–63
of free speech, 162, 164, 171–72
to grand jury indictment, 144–45
to an impartial jury, 149, 150–51
to instruct legislators, 126
to jury trial, 26–27, 80, 128–31, 181–82
to justice administered without delay, 182–83
to open courts, 79, 95–96, 150–51, 163, 171–72

to privacy, 114, 158, 167–68, 324
to privilege against self-incrimination, 58, 90, 97, 144, 149, 151–53
of religious freedom, 7–8, 11–12, 96, 106, 133–36
to remedy, 106, 172–74
to a speedy, public trial, 149, 151, 160–61
unenumerated, 188–89
victims (Marsy's Law), 76, 84, 158–61
See also forfeiture for crime
ripeness, 294
Roosevelt, Theodore, 53–54, 58, 59, 61
Royal Proclamation of 1763, 6
run-up to 1912 convention, 51–53

same-sex marriage ban on, 84, 85, 87, 261, 515–16
schools. *See* education
Scottish-Irish, 7–8
seal. *See* great seal
search and seizure, 81–82, 97–98, 107, 166–69
exclusionary rule, 78, 166–67, 168, 169
seat of government, 499–500
Second Amendment, 127–28
secretary of state, 21, 43, 59–60, 71, 196–97, 199, 203, 204, 205, 206, 218, 223–24, 227, 241, 272, 274–75, 276, 282, 284, 346–47, 425, 448, 452–53, 466, 514, 519, 528, 548, 554–55, 558–59
ban on reduction of compensation, 285
term, 71, 274–75
vacancy, 284
Senate. *See* General Assembly; *see also* advice and consent
Senators. *See* General Assembly; legislators; president of the senate
separation of powers, 23, 42n.209, 80, 95–96, 131, 193–94, 195–96, 212, 214, 241, 253–54, 277, 338
Seventeenth Amendment, 87, 227, 248–49, 328
Seventh Amendment, 129, 131–32
Sheriff, county, 128, 267, 443
Short Ballot Movement, 59–60
single subject rule. *See* one-subject rule
single tax, 54–55, 208
sinking fund, 40–41, 86–87, 357, 361, 365, 424–26
Sixth Amendment, 129–30, 143, 144–45, 146, 147–48, 149
slavery and involuntary solitude. *See* African Americans: slavery; Northwest Ordinance
South Carolina Constitution, 22
sovereign immunity, 78–79, 170, 171, 174, 183–84, 298. *See also* municipalities: municipal sovereign immunity
speaker of the house, 21, 212, 233, 282, 283–84, 452–53, 497, 554–55
special privileges or immunities, 34, 40, 43, 106, 115, 116, 124–25, 133, 203
stare decisis, 93–95, 112
state constitutional interpretation. *See* lock-stepping; primacy; state-specific factors
state debt. *See* public debt
state institutions. *See* public institutions
state remedies for violations of federal law, 296. *See also* implied rights of action
state-specific factors (constitutional interpretation), 97, 98–99, 107–8, 110–11, 123, 182
"statewide concern," doctrine of, 262, 537–39, 542
statutes of limitation, 119, 150, 173, 176, 250, 261
statutes of repose, 95–96, 173–74
statutory courts, 298
St. Clair, Arthur, 9, 12–14, 15, 17, 21, 271
Steubenville, 16
Stony Point, Battle of, 9
style, of process, 314
succession to office of governor, 282–84
suffrage. *See* African Americans: voting rights; elective franchise; women's suffrage
superintendent of public works, 358, 426
supermajority requirement
for calling conventions, 523–24
for constitutional amendments, 43–44, 45, 47–48, 49, 60, 62–63, 519
elimination of, 62–63
for holding statutes unconstitutional, 77, 289–90, 300–1
Supreme Court. *See* Ohio Supreme Court; U.S. Supreme Court
Supreme Court Commission, 315–16
surplus utility productsa, sale of, 543, 544–45

Sutton, Jeffrey S., 99n.366, 108, 121, 122, 169, 336
"sweeping resolution" (1810), 27–28, 310, 313

tables
of amendments proposed and adopted by decade since 1912, 65*t*
of amendments proposed by the General Assembly and by Initiative, 1913–2021, 64*t*
of amendments to the 1851 Constitution, 63*t*
of number of approved amendments by articles (1913 to 2021), 70*t*
of proposed constitutional amendments and votes, 581
of votes on holding constitutional conventions, 579
Taft, Governor Bob, 83
Taft, Pres. William Howard, 53–54, 58, 59
takings. *See* eminent domain
taxes and taxation
corporate, 491
estate and inheritance, 50, 120–21, 471, 478, 482–83
income, 74, 478, 482
motor vehicle use and fuel tax, 371, 376, 379–80, 381, 391, 397, 399, 408, 411, 417, 419, 480–81
prohibition on wholesale tax on food (and soft drinks), 484–85
sales, 68, 76, 479, 484
See generally Article XII; property taxation
Tennessee Constitution, 23–24, 116, 133, 143, 151, 154, 170
Tennessee Declaration of Rights, 23–24, 125–26
Tenth Amendment, 512–13
term limits, 76, 85, 87, 225, 328–29
Third Frontier bonds, 83, 407
Thirteenth Amendment, 133
three-considerations requirement. *See* bills: three-readings requirement
Tiffin, Edward, 13–14, 16–17, 18–19, 318,
Tod, Judge George, 26–27, 244
Torrens land registration, 22–23, 59, 268–69. *See also* land title and registration
tort reform, 79–80, 94, 95–96, 121, 131, 177, 181
townships, 10, 15, 16, 22, 48, 85, 184–85, 226, 318–19, 328, 331–32, 343, 344, 423, 458–59. *See generally* Article X, county and township organizations
traffic cameras, 536, 537
transportation, prohibition against for crime, 164–65
treasurer, state, 13–14, 43, 59–60, 227, 272
ban on reduction of compensation, 285
term, 71, 274–75, 276, 528
vacancy, 284
Treaty of Greenville, 9
Treaty of Paris of 1763, 6
Treaty of Paris of 1783, 8
trial, public, 149, 150–51, 171
trial by jury, 11–12, 94n.359, 95–96, 97, 105, 128–32, 136–37, 181–82, 183
Truman, Harry, 67–68
Twelfth Amendment, 13
Twenty-first Amendment, 514–15
Twenty-sixth Amendment, 321

unions. *See* labor unions
University and colleges. *See* higher education
U.S. Constitution. *See* Constitution, U.S.
U.S. Supreme Court, 26, 66–67, 71, 73, 74, 76, 77, 78, 80, 82, 91–92, 96–97, 99, 107–8, 109, 110–42, 144–46, 147, 148, 149–53, 154, 155, 156, 159, 162–64, 167, 168–69, 171–72, 176, 177–81, 186, 189, 193, 219, 248, 255, 277, 290–91, 293, 294, 295, 298, 308–9, 311, 321, 323, 326, 328–29, 334, 336, 338, 340, 341, 376, 448, 455, 460, 468, 472, 489, 512–13, 516, 554
uniformity rule (laws), 124, 191–92, 246–47
uniformity rule (taxation), 40, 47–48, 52, 60, 74–75, 208, 266, 473–76, 477, 478, 482–83

veterans, 6, 7, 390
compensation for, 68, 74, 83, 357, 358–59, 365, 366–69, 371–74, 385–89, 411–17, 428, 482, 484

veto
governor's, 4, 21–22, 23–25, 32–33, 43, 45–46, 48, 49, 54–55, 63, 191–92, 194, 195–96, 199–200, 227, 240–42, 271, 272–74, 519, 558–59
legislative, 202, 309
override, 43, 48, 60–61, 198, 200, 213–14
under the Northwest Ordinance, 10–11, 96 (*see also* line item veto)
victims rights. *See* rights: victims
Virginia, 6–8, 14, 16, 18–19, 23
Virginia Constitution, 23
Virginia Declaration of Rights, 116
Virginia Military District, 35–36
voting machines. *See* ballot: voting machines
voting rights. *See* African Americans: voting rights; elective franchise; women's suffrage
vouchers, school. *See* education: school vouchers

Washington, George, 9, 12
Wayne, Maj. Gen. "Mad" Anthony, 9
welfare
economic, 427, 428
general or public, 185–266, 424
West Virginia, 505–6, 511, 513–14
West Virginia Constitution, 363
West Virginia Supreme Court, 335–36
Western Reserve, 7, 35–36, 37
Whigs, 30, 31, 32–33, 34, 38–39, 124, 125
Wisconsin Constitution, 3n.1
witnesses, 106, 135–36, 149. *See also* privilege against self-incrimination
right to confront, 146–49 (*see also* expert witness testimony)
women's suffrage, 37, 38, 44, 45–46, 51–52, 59, 61–62, 65, 67–68, 141, 318, 320, 501
workers' Compensation, 51, 58, 75, 96, 119, 258, 262–65, 520. *See also* civil service; employees; labor
Worthington, James, 35
Worthington, Thomas, 13–17, 20, 25–26, 27–28, 35
writs of assistance, 166
wrongful death, 58, 106, 186–87

Zanesville, 16, 499–500
zoning, 127, 186

Printed in the USA/Agawam, MA
September 2, 2022

798017.001